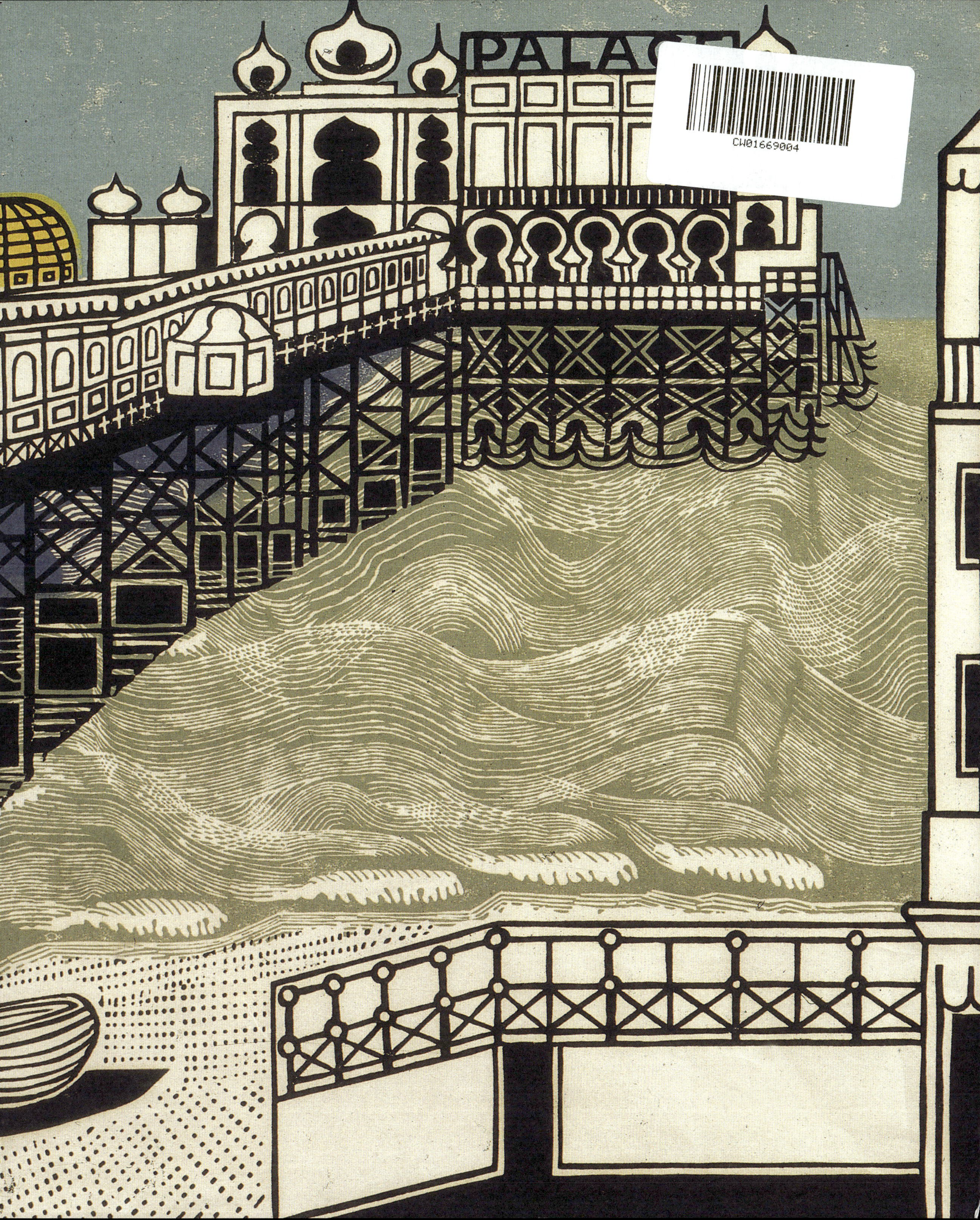
PALAC

Edward Bawden & His Circle

THE INWARD LAUGH

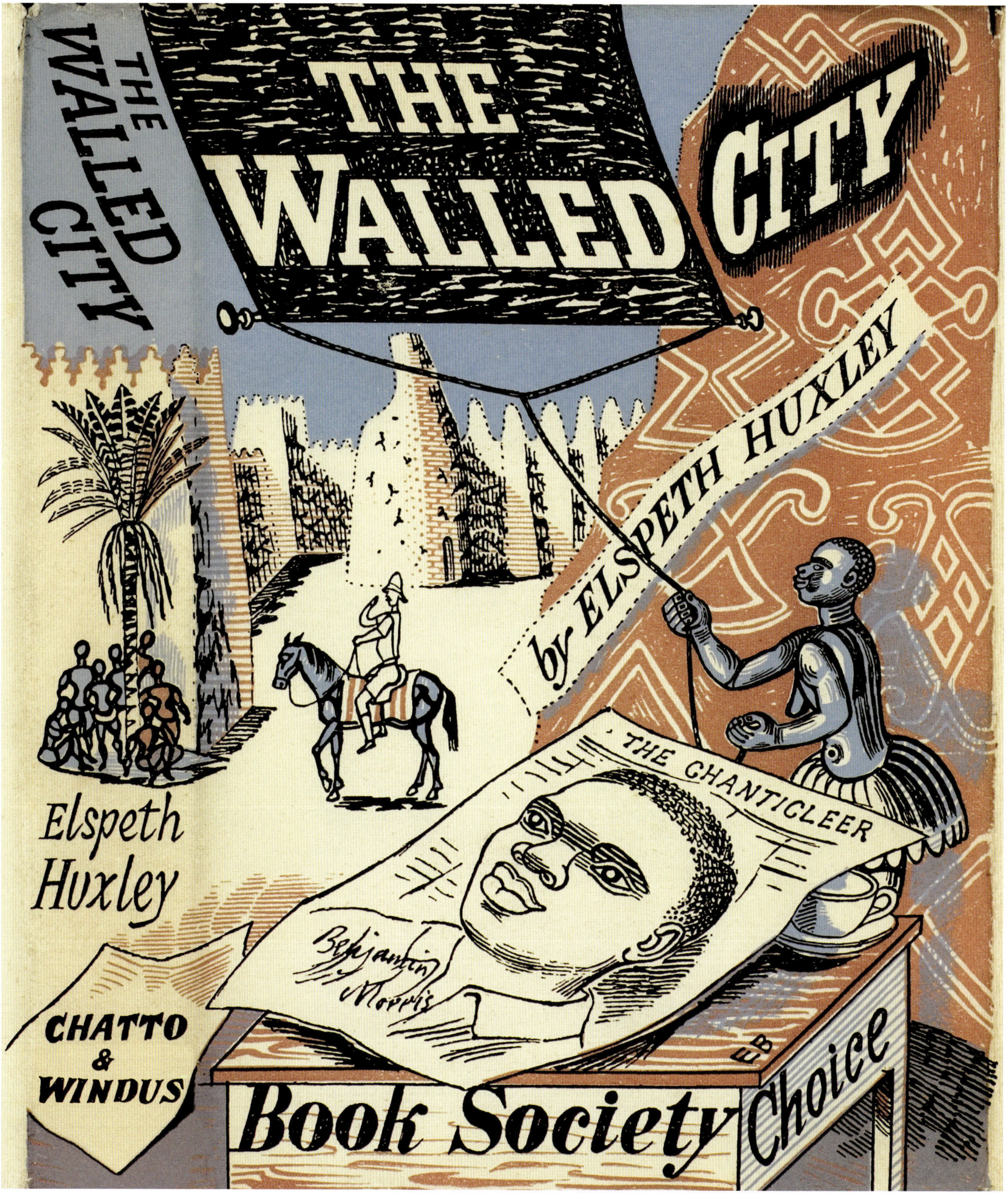
THE WALLED CITY
Elspeth Huxley
CHATTO & WINDUS
THE WALLED CITY
by ELSPETH HUXLEY
THE CHANTICLEER
Benjamin Morris
EB
Book Society Choice

Edward Bawden & His Circle

THE INWARD LAUGH

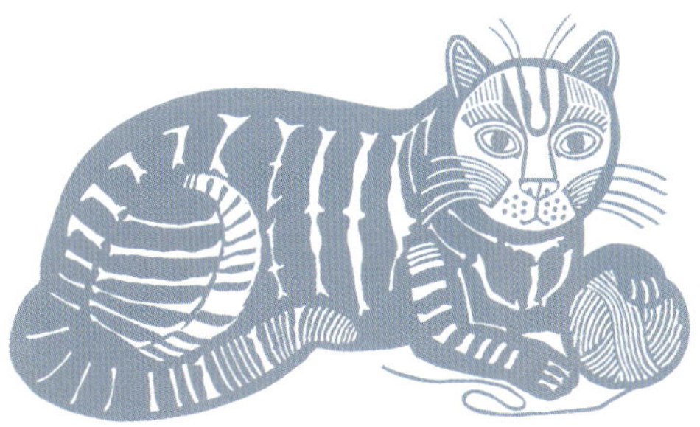

Malcolm Yorke

Antique Collectors' Club

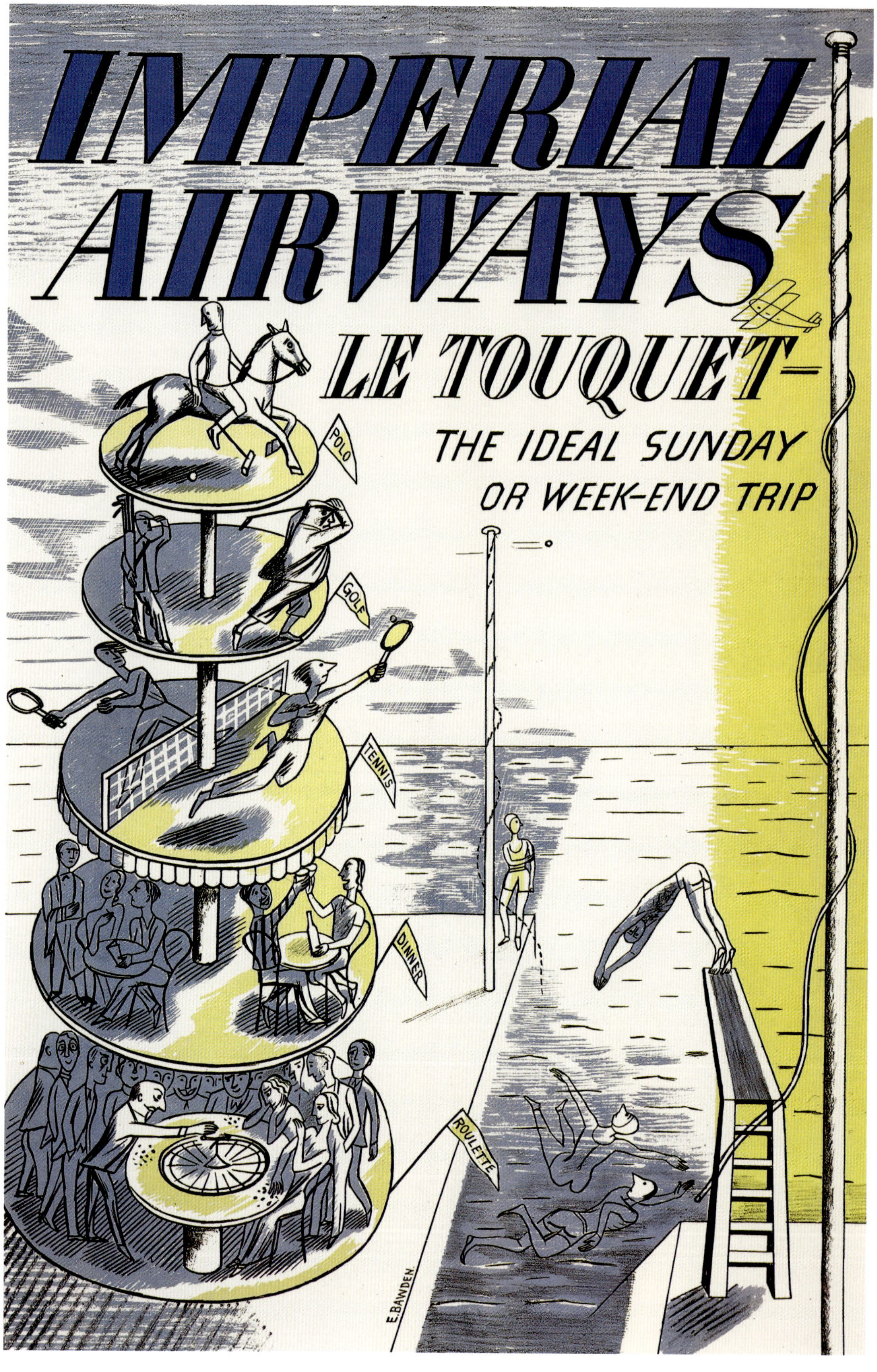

Imperial Airways poster, 1935; 495 x 316mm. Colour lithograph printed at the Curwen Press.
(Reproduced by permission of Cambridge University Library)

CONTENTS

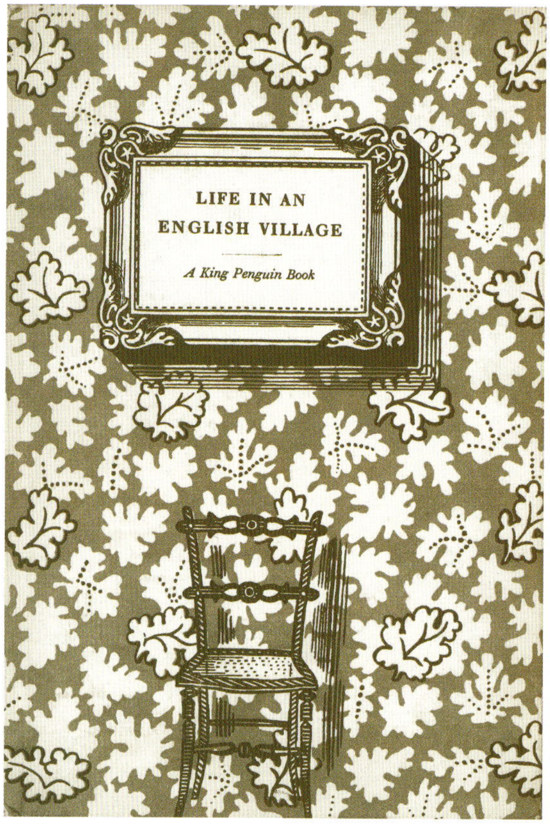

Bawden designed cover for King Penguin Book, *Life in an English Village*, 1949.

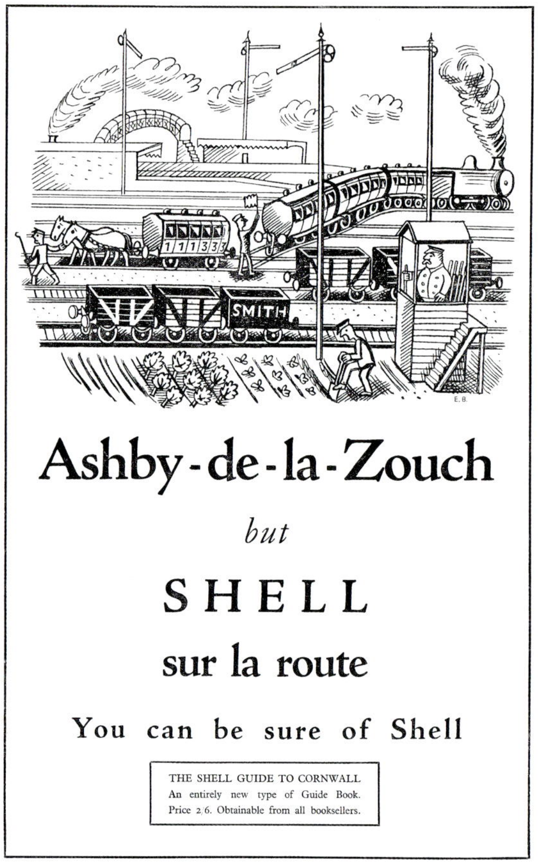

Ashby-de-la-Zouch Shell advertisement drawn by Bawden.

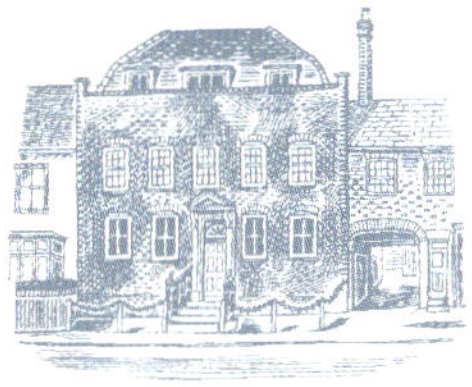

FOREWORD

I was exposed to Edward Bawden's drawings pretty early on. My father worked in the Shell studio before the war, and admired Bawden's work; and at some point he had brought home a solid and durable book called *Well on the Road*, with a linocut cover and filled with the pen drawings Bawden had made for Shell ads, linked in the book by the story of a journey taking in all the oddly-named places like Coton-in-the-Clay and Chorlton-cum-Hardy that he had drawn. My favourite, of railway sidings with trains shunting and a fat moustache signalman in his box, was Ashby-de-la-Zouch. I must have pored over these lovely sardonic pen-and-ink drawings well before I could read. Later, as a schoolboy, I enjoyed his lithographed Penguin Picture Book *The Arabs*; we also had Eric Ravilious' *High Street* and Robert Harling's small book of his wood engravings. And later still, when I was at art school at St Albans, my father gave me the Bawden volume in *Penguin Modern Painters* and his King Penguin *Life in an English Village*.

So when in 1951 I first met Bawden I was already something of a disciple. By then I was a first-year student at the Royal College of Art, and he was at work on a panel of his enormous mural for the Lion and Unicorn Pavilion of the Festival of Britain. He was tall, slim, with a courteous manner and a penetrating eye; he was wearing a sort of boiler suit of dark blue denim. I resolved then and there to change from graphics to the illustration school as soon as I could, in order to be taught by him.

We got on together, and several times he invited me to stay with his family at Brick House in Great Bardfield. I cycled the twenty-odd miles from Hertford past rural Stansted, without any planes, and pretty Thaxted. Knowing Bawden's vaguely Puritanical style I had half-expected the Brick House atmosphere might be a bit austere, but it wasn't. The house, shown above, which had been a wedding present from his father, was warm and comfortable. It was full of Bawden's pictures, and in some rooms he had stencilled wall decorations. He let me work at the large wooden desk in his attic studio and use his remarkable library of reference books. There was good food and plenty of wine – Bawden had recently done some drawings for Gilbey's, the London wine-shipper and had been paid in kind.

His wife Charlotte, a Quaker, was warm, sociable and welcoming; she had been a potter, and she gave me a Swedish plate decorated with a beautiful engraving of a jungle; I've still got it on the dresser today, next to a Ravilious plate. She talked a little about Ravilious but Bawden never did. Their two children Richard and Joanna, three or four years younger than me, were friendly and fun and we went for long walks in the Essex fields and woods. Once, perhaps hoping to impress Joanna, I accepted Richard's dare to jump over a small stream, only slightly wider than it looked; I didn't quite make it across. We also biked to nearby Braintree to visit the white weather-boarded factory of Warners, the silk weavers, where Bawden's friend and neighbour Marianne Straub had her design office.

I also met some of his other neighbours. It seemed pretty clear to me that Bawden was indeed the central figure or doyen of the group of artists then living at Bardfield. We walked across the road to John Aldridge's house to look at his oil paintings and rather Bawdenesque wallpapers. Other friends were Walter Hoyle, George

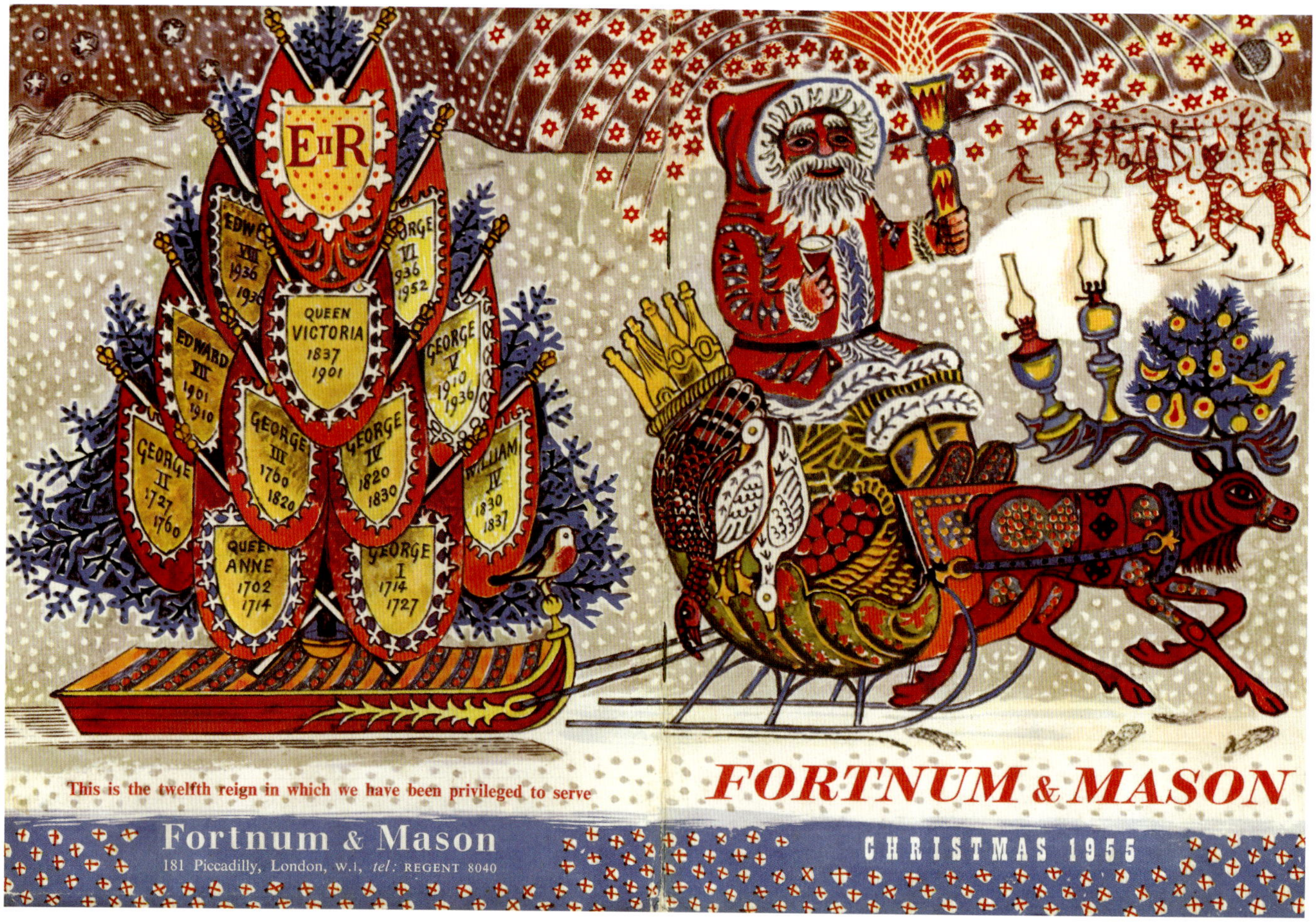

Fortnum & Mason 1955 Catalogue, front and back cover design.

Chapman, and Michael and Duffy Rothenstein. With Sheila Robinson and Bernard Cheese, who I knew already from the RCA, we explored some barns used by a junk dealer as a warehouse for second-hand treasures: straw dollies, pictures made of seashells, Staffordshire figures, astonishingly cheap chests of drawers, garden chairs and wrought-iron bedsteads – none of these things yet the clichés they were to become. One afternoon I went with Bawden to another nearby farmyard so that he could draw me pushing a farm implement as one of his illustrations for *How Animals Move*.

One of these Bardfield visits was just after Christmas. Despite the acid aphorisms about wives and children quoted in this book, life with the Bawdens looked idyllic enough. There can't have been a television. In the evenings everyone played consequences, or heads, bodies and legs, and we all looked through the scrapbooks into which Bawden squirreled away his as yet unused ideas. One evening after a heavy snowfall Charlotte drove us to Thaxted for someone's party in a house whose windows looked out onto white streets even more picturesque than Bardfield's, with half-timbered houses like a Victorian Christmas card.

Sometimes Bawden would disappear for a morning's painting. He had never learned to drive, so Charlotte would drive him in her Morris Minor to any subject too far away for cycling; he would draw there for two or three hours until Charlotte came back in the car to pick him up again. He was quite hardy: if it was cold or even snowy he could apparently work outside for two hours at a stretch as long as he had one of the large boiled sweets then called gob-stoppers to keep him going.

At the College, Bawden turned out to be a good teacher, both by example and by precept: generally supportive, accessible and encouraging to anyone who was trying hard, but also exacting and critical where it was useful, and irritated by pretentiousness and laziness. His quizzical mien kept some at a distance (whereas his friend and fellow tutor John Nash was well-disposed to everyone, especially the girls, of whom Bawden seemed a bit wary). He had a keen eye for everyone's quirks and oddities; but he was also self critical and self-mocking, maybe in order to pre-empt other people's criticism by getting any impending mockery in first himself. He was also a tease; one never quite knew if he was being serious. He approved of candle-grease used as a resist, but once, when I was diligently making some hopefully trendy textures on a watercolour with a razor blade, he told me I was too young to be scratching. He said that stretching watercolour paper, something he never did, was cruel. Later on, when someone told him I'd just bought a tiny dinghy and then my first car, his comment was 'What next? A plane?' But he probably meant it when he said that the approach of spring made him gloomy because it reduced the enticingly varied colours of the winter countryside to a tedious sea of green. He claimed not to enjoy teaching, saying it was a waste of time, undertaken only because he needed the cash. But I doubt if this was what he really thought, for he came up from Bardfield unfailingly once a week on the Jennings' bus to the College, where he was both liked and respected by his students and his colleagues. When I stayed on at the RCA for an extra two years as a junior tutor, I remember him enjoying the company (which was anyway extremely interesting) and conviviality of the Senior Common Room, though he might disappear after lunch to draw a building or to fit in a meeting at the Tate Gallery, of which he was a trustee. I was once surprised by his temerity in defying Robin Darwin, the intimidating and somewhat bullying Rector, who was trying without success to prise out of him a bit of insider gossip about some Tate Gallery spat. More significant was his stamina during the exhausting entrance exams, particularly his tirelessness late in the afternoon: when everyone else was flagging, he went on energetically lugging around and reconsidering the more borderline candidates' unwieldy portfolios. He was also fierce in his determination (and sound judgement) in sticking up for those students – John Norris Wood a notable example – whose work he particularly admired. And he followed the careers of his ex-students with interest.

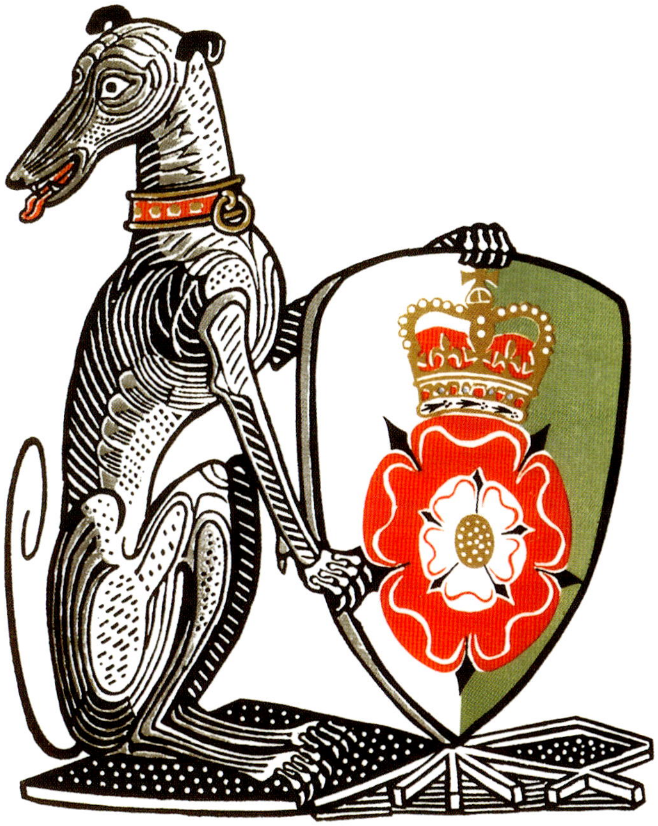

Linocut lithographed and coloured of the White Greyhound of Richmond from *The Queen's Beasts*, 1954, 240 x 192 mm.

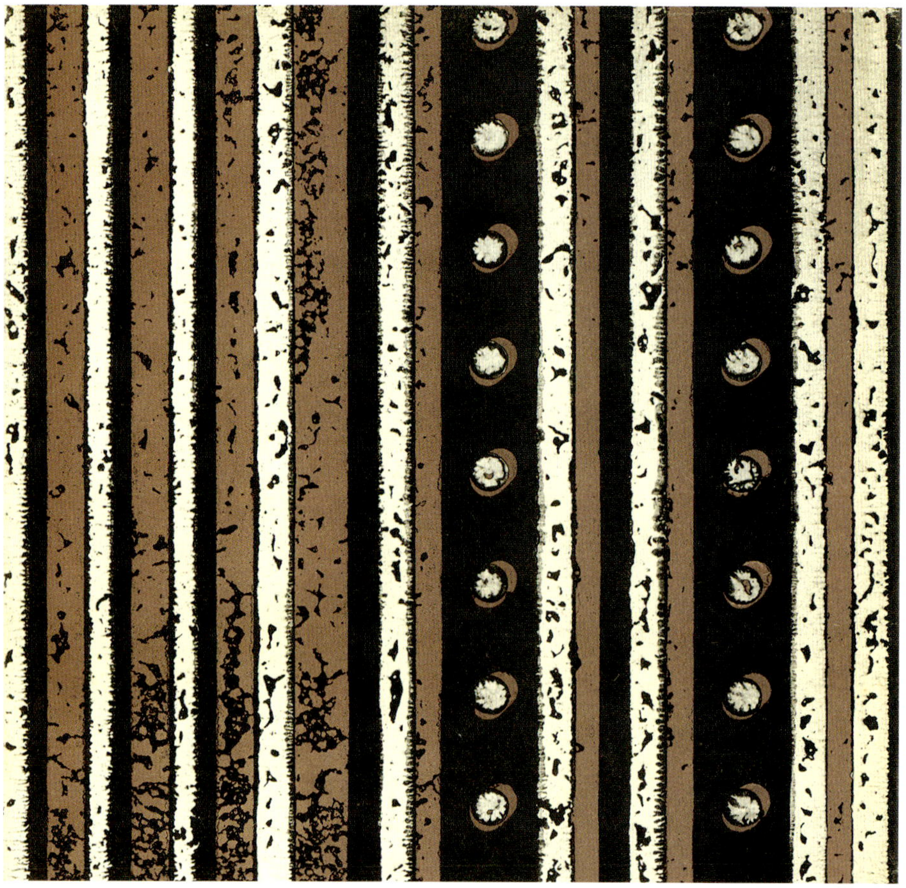

Doric wallpaper design as used on the jacket of *Edward Bawden* by Douglas Percy Bliss, 1979.

Bawden's work had quite a high profile at the time: his book on Portugal was being published by the RCA's Lion and Unicorn Press, his lithograph of *The Dolls at Home* was up in every Lyons teashop. His linocut Underground poster of the City was in the Tube stations; his murals were on Orient liners: his splendid black-and-white striped wallpaper Doric hung in the RCA's Senior Common Room. Bawden once asked me to help him by carefully drawing out a complicated geometric repeat pattern for a later wallpaper, which took me so long that he never asked me again. He did however hand over to me one or two early jobs that he didn't feel like doing himself, but which at the time helped to keep me afloat.

After I'd finally left the RCA we went on for many years exchanging Christmas cards, many of his being line drawings of Bardfield, and he wrote occasional letters in his careful, legible and beautiful hand. He was well read and he wrote expressively and humorously.

In his work, he was energetic and very determined, always seeming essentially secure and confident in what he wanted to do. But without ever showing it, he must surely have been prey to any artist's doubts about whatever he was currently working on: much later on, in the seventies, when I happened to meet him at the Curwen Studio, when he was surprisingly self-critical about a beautiful print for *Rasselas* which he was proofing there.

Apart from my father, Bawden was the only person I actually knew whose whole attitude to work influenced me permanently. Once I realised that I was also adopting some of his more easily imitated graphic mannerisms, I did my best to grow out of the most obvious of them. But I've always remained unshakeably impressed by his outlook; his independence, made possible by his readiness to take on any kind of job; his unique range, from commercial illustrations for ads to linocuts, posters, copper-engravings, wallpapers; and his ability to tackle any subject with a consistently detailed but observant eye. And I love the clear, precise line of his drawings, the inventiveness and scope of his landscape watercolours whose subjects extend from Essex to the Middle East, North Africa, Canada, Italy; and the relish for the formal qualities of structure, repetition and pattern in his designs.

His paintings too usually have a strong design element and a feeling for pattern, as do the wallpapers and the big linocuts – *Brighton Pier, Liverpool Street*, and *Lindsell Church* – with their strong black and whites. I enjoy his use of unconventional, even barely respectable materials, like cobbler's heel-ball for its intense blacks, and indeed lino itself. And I admire his often unrealistic perspectives, unconstrained by the customary conventions, using bold and often mechanically ruled lines which still manage to sit well with the freehand of his precisely drawn and sardonic figures.

Bawden's most characteristic qualities, both artistic and personal, shine out from every page of this admirable book. As a person, he was fuelled by persistence, energy and tirelessness; as an artist, the clear-headed and rational command of structure and organisation that constitute design underlie almost all his work. Often this sense of structure is quite obvious, as in the murals and linocuts, which essentially depend on it, works in which observation of reality is secondary to its transmutation

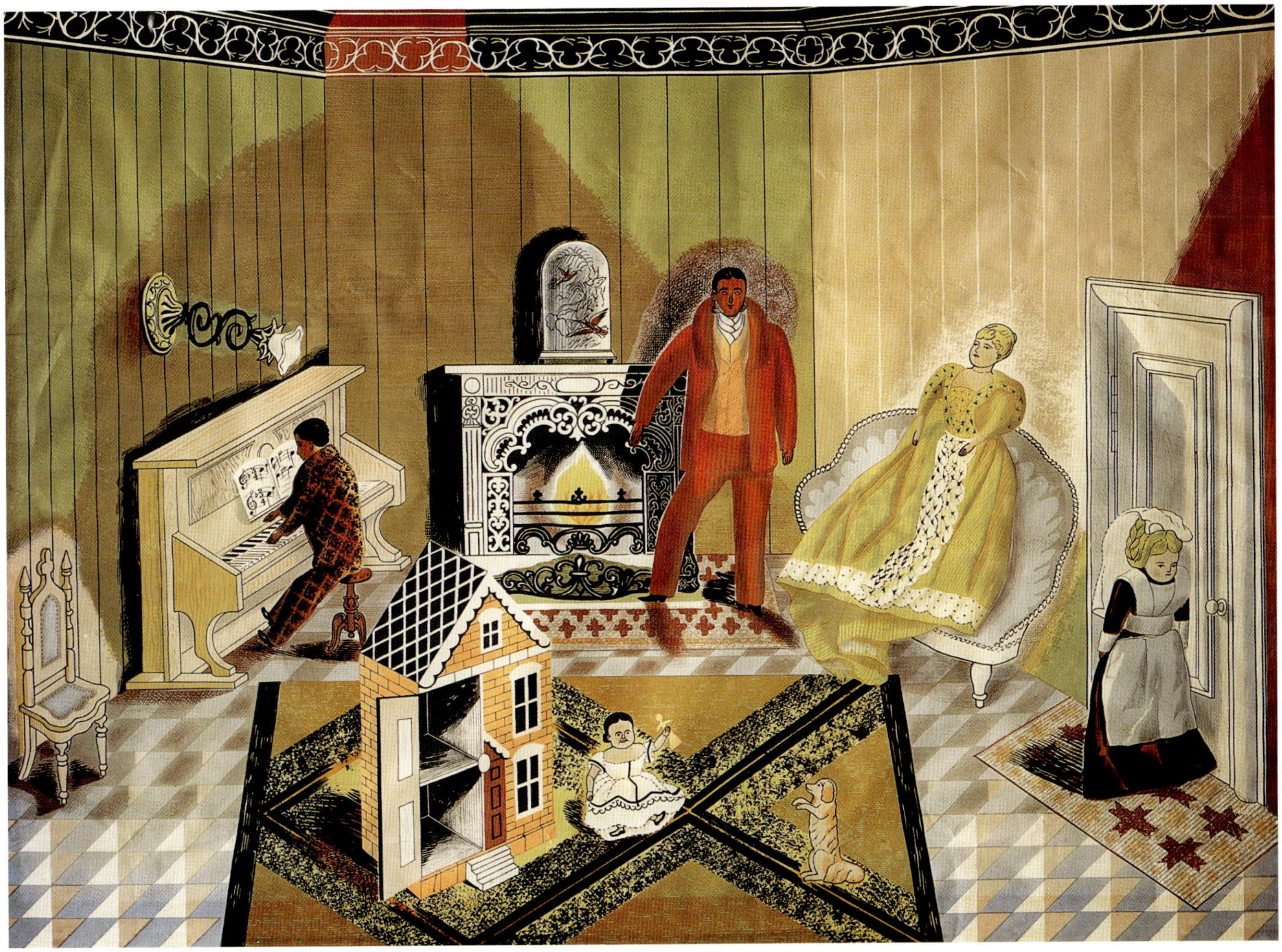

Colour lithograph *The Dolls at Home*, 1947, one of the Lyons lithographs.

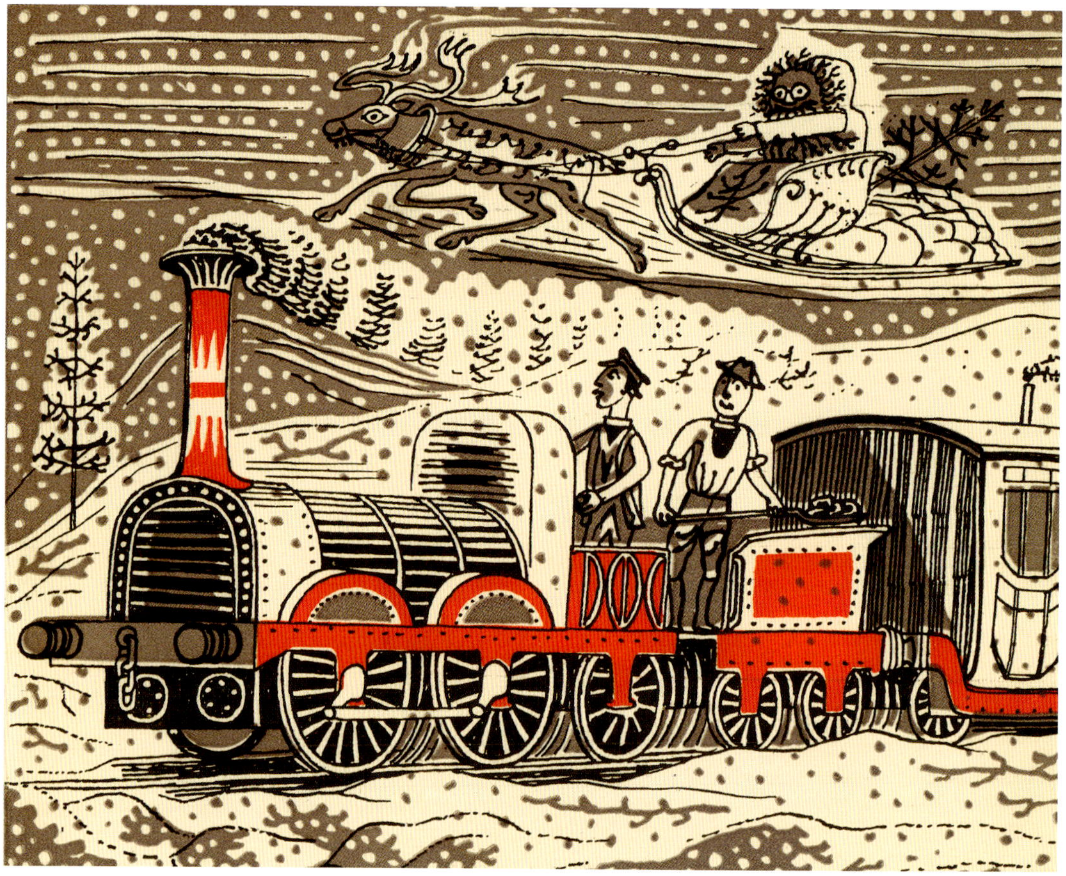

Titfield Thunderbolt Christmas card drawn and sent out by Bawden in 1953.

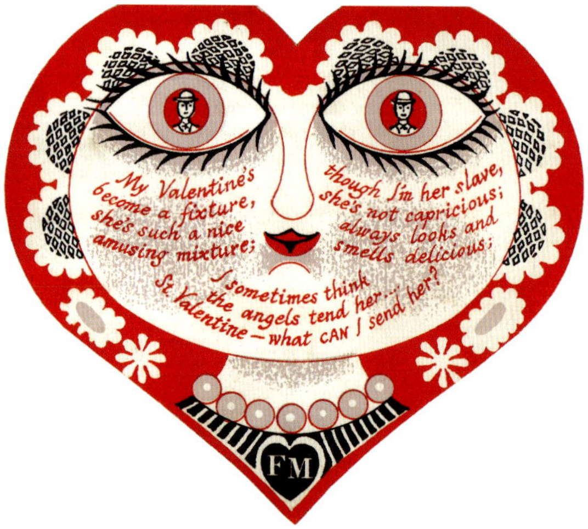

Back cover of Fortnum & Mason Valentine mail order catalogue *c*.1956.

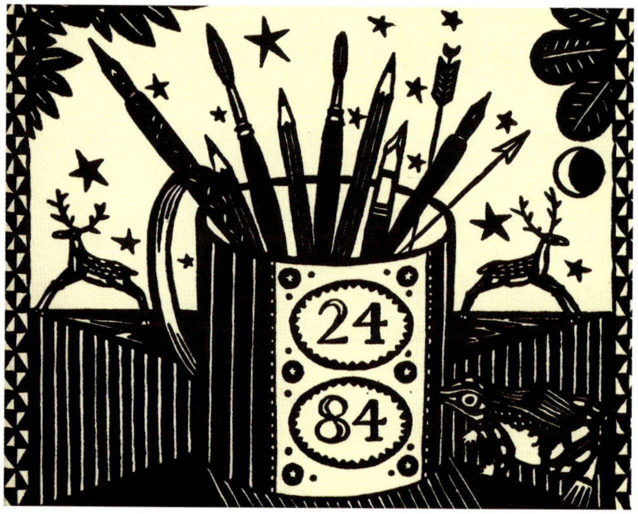

Bawden cover for 1984 exhibition catalogue *The Artist as Illustrator 1924–1984*.

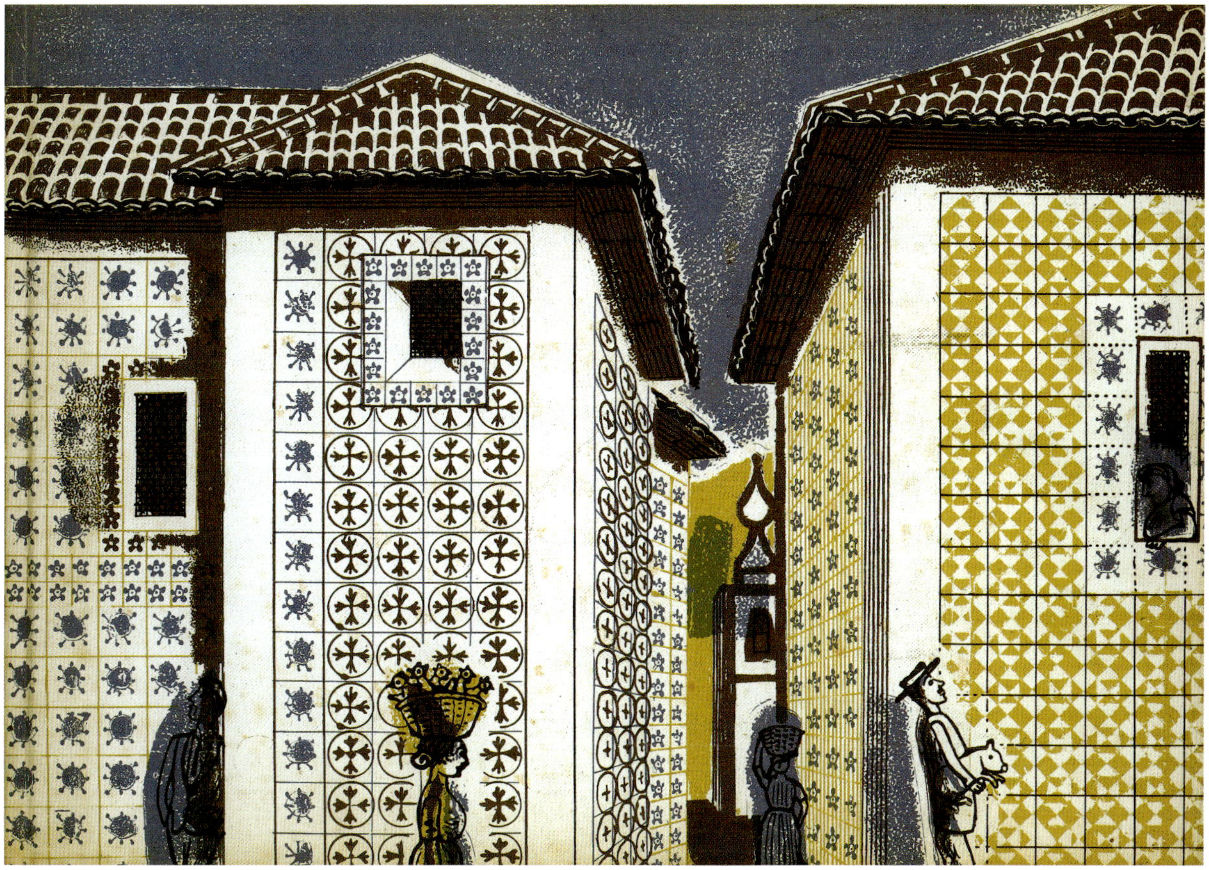

Front cover for *English as She is Spoke* published by Lion and Unicorn Press 1960 in a limited edition of 200 copies.

into a characteristic step towards semi-abstraction. Sometimes however, as in his watercolours, one can more easily overlook the structure and organisation; yet they're almost always there. Only occasionally does he dispense with them altogether, as in his unexpectedly naturalistic portraits of uniformed soldiers in Asmara or the Lebanon. And I particularly like the fresh and almost instantaneous observation, of people into whose company he was thrown at Dunkirk, or of fellow-internees after his ship was torpedoed off Dakar, where his vivid shorthand drawings show what unconscious attitudes exhausted or despairing people slump into. In such drawings, he can have had no time to formalise anything, tidy it up, get it right; yet one senses instantly that this was what real life looked like.

Bawden was an artist of a high order. Yet he never became a national treasure or icon, a household word, in the way his contemporary Moore or his hero Hockney did. Looking afresh now, as this book allows one to do, at the whole sweeping output of his long and productive life, two things are most striking. The first is his intense individuality, doggedly independent of the reverently or credulously accepted artistic fashions of the time. The second is the intelligence and independence of mind that enabled him to leave behind, and to communicate to a still-growing following, a substantial, vivid, coherent and honest record of his whole life's experience – of time not only well, but intelligibly, spent.

David Gentleman, London 2007

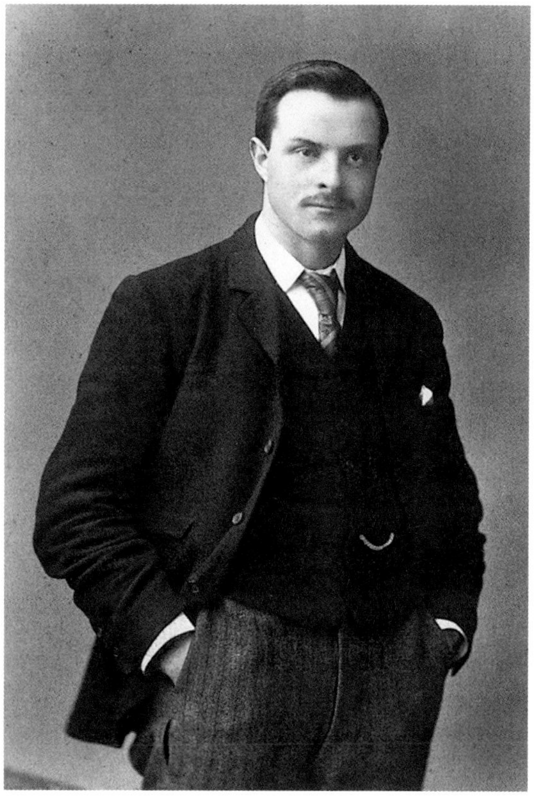

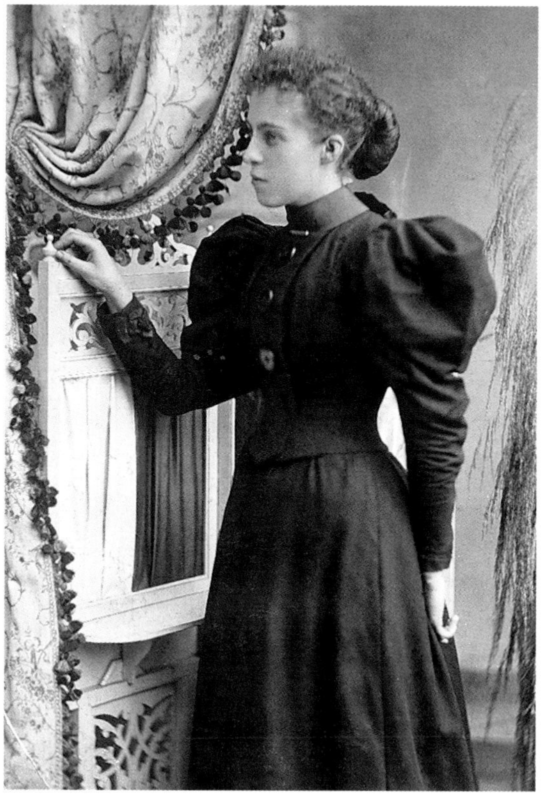

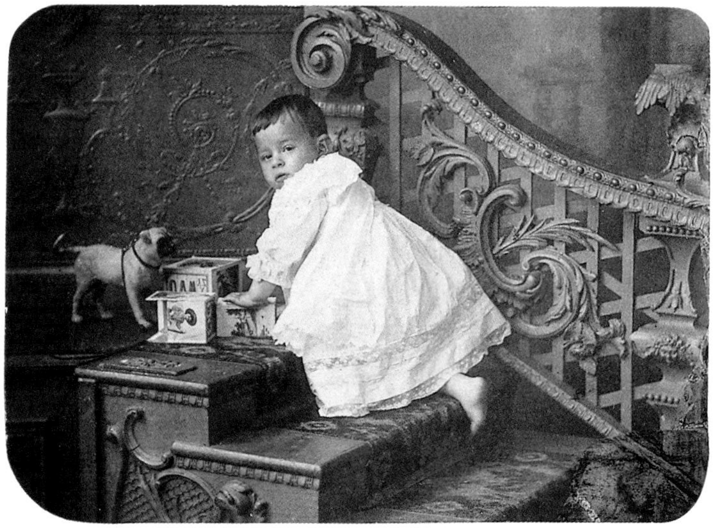

Bawden's father, Edward (1871-1952), his mother Eleanor (née Game, 1877-1941), and Edward at a year old.

1. THE EARLY YEARS

Edward Bawden was born on the 10th of March 1903 in Braintree, Essex, the only child of Edward Bawden (1871-1952) an ironmonger of Cornish stock, and his wife Eleanor (née Game, 1877-1941), the daughter of a Suffolk gamekeeper. The parents were strict Methodists, puritanical and hard-working. Bawden Senior had moved from Liskeard to Bury St Edmunds, where he met his wife, then after marriage in 1902 transferred to Braintree in order to manage Crittall and Winterton's ironmongery shop. Later he bought the shop and continued to work there until he retired.

Apart from these few verifiable facts everything else we know about his childhood comes from Bawden himself. He recalled how conscious his parents were about their hard-won lower-middle class status: 'How diffcult it was to talk to someone who was a little higher or lower than your father's class. It was excruciating. I would go out of my way at school to avoid board school boys: I went to high school and had a badge in my cap, a sort of elitist thing. Nor was I allowed to play with the boys across the road whose parents were working class. It takes a long time to get over a father who was teetotal and these rigid class differences.'[1] In consequence he was a solitary, self-suffcient child: 'I spent most of my time wandering around with a butterfly net and drawing', or studying pond life 'as befitted a brat with a microscope', which led to a life-long fascination with creepy-crawlies. Eleanor had been a haberdasher's assistant before marriage and she continued to sew, embroider, knit and work with materials, sometimes assisted by her son who felt emotionally nearer to her than to his father. Later he suggested that if his biography was ever written the chapter on his early life should be titled 'The Sissy Years'.

The only thing to do with Braintree itself was to bomb it, he declared as an adult. If he found no stimulus in the town there was even less in Braintree High School, where he was sent at the age of seven. By his own admission he was badly behaved, rebellious and unpopular. Even the art lessons bored him, but in his own time at home he copied Louis Wain's mad drawings of cats and illustrations from the *Girls' Own Paper*, which he preferred to the Boys' version which came through the letter box: 'I loved copying. I built up a sort of compost heap which has served me very well ever since – because by copying one remembers things.'

Many solitary children find companionship amongst books and once he had outgrown Beatrix Potter and the usual boys' adventure stories Bawden remembered reading Malory's *Morte d'Arthur* in order to understand better the illustrations of Burne-Jones ('I thought I was bringing myself up to date'). As an old man he would illustrate this classic himself and deliberately choose to depict all the gory episodes that Burne-Jones had squeamishly avoided.

Eventually, after being given between four and six hundred lines a week to write as punishment, the school was glad to see the back of him and he was transferred to the fee-paying co-educational Friends' School at Saffron Walden. There were no time-wasting punishments at this enlightened Quaker establishment, even when he pushed another pupil down a manhole ('which he richly deserved'). During a swimming lesson he is supposed to have strained his heart (though there were never any signs of this after his school days), which excused him from any more of 'those dreadful sports in which one throws stupid balls about'. He recalled that he lay in bed for several weeks enjoying a French book: 'the text didn't interest me in the least, but every page had an illustration'. It was soon clear he had little academic ability and was a show-off: 'I did unkind caricatures of the staff; also wore a silk handkerchief for a tie and would have sported a beard if I could have grown it – for I was a budding juvenile exhibitionist. The Headmaster – who had a taste for pictorial recording – scotched the trouble that was brewing by persuading my parents when I was fifteen to allow me to be sent for one day a week to Cambridge Municipal Art School. This weekly jaunt diverted my attention from working for mischievous ends. And so that saved my life. I've been a good boy ever since.'

His parents, seeing the way his talents were veering, asked the daughter of a local Congregational minister to give him some sketching lessons. 'In her opinion I showed a facility for design but no ability as a draughtsman. Teachers have given the same opinion many times since; whenever in my life the road has forked there has always been on duty a cop holding up an unattractive reproduction of something by Michelangelo or Alfred Stevens to indicate that the classy main road was not for the likes of me.' [2]

When he left school in 1919 it was an easy transition to full-time attendance at the Cambridge Art School because 'if you're no good at anything art is a very easy option'. His father had hoped he would work in the family business but, said Bawden, 'I had no interest in nails and screws', so his disappointed father gave in – though he insisted that Edward took lodgings with a strict Chapel-attending family to safeguard his morals in the big city. Cambridge Art School was then one of those numerous provincial institutions whose students were expected to go

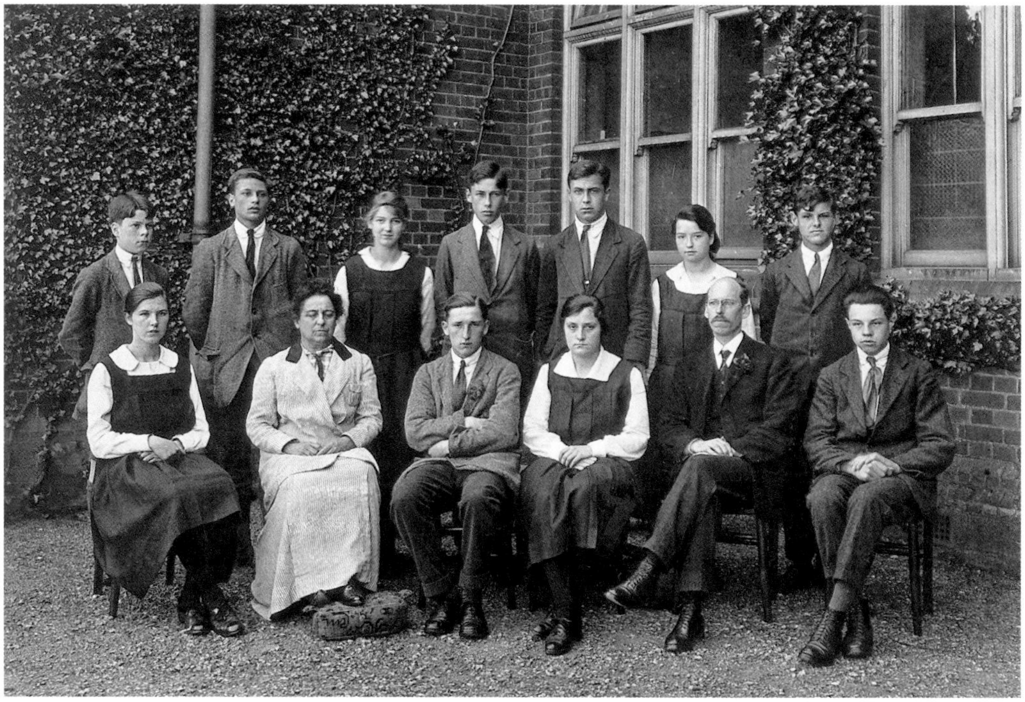

Bawden sitting right, in a school photograph at Saffron Walden.

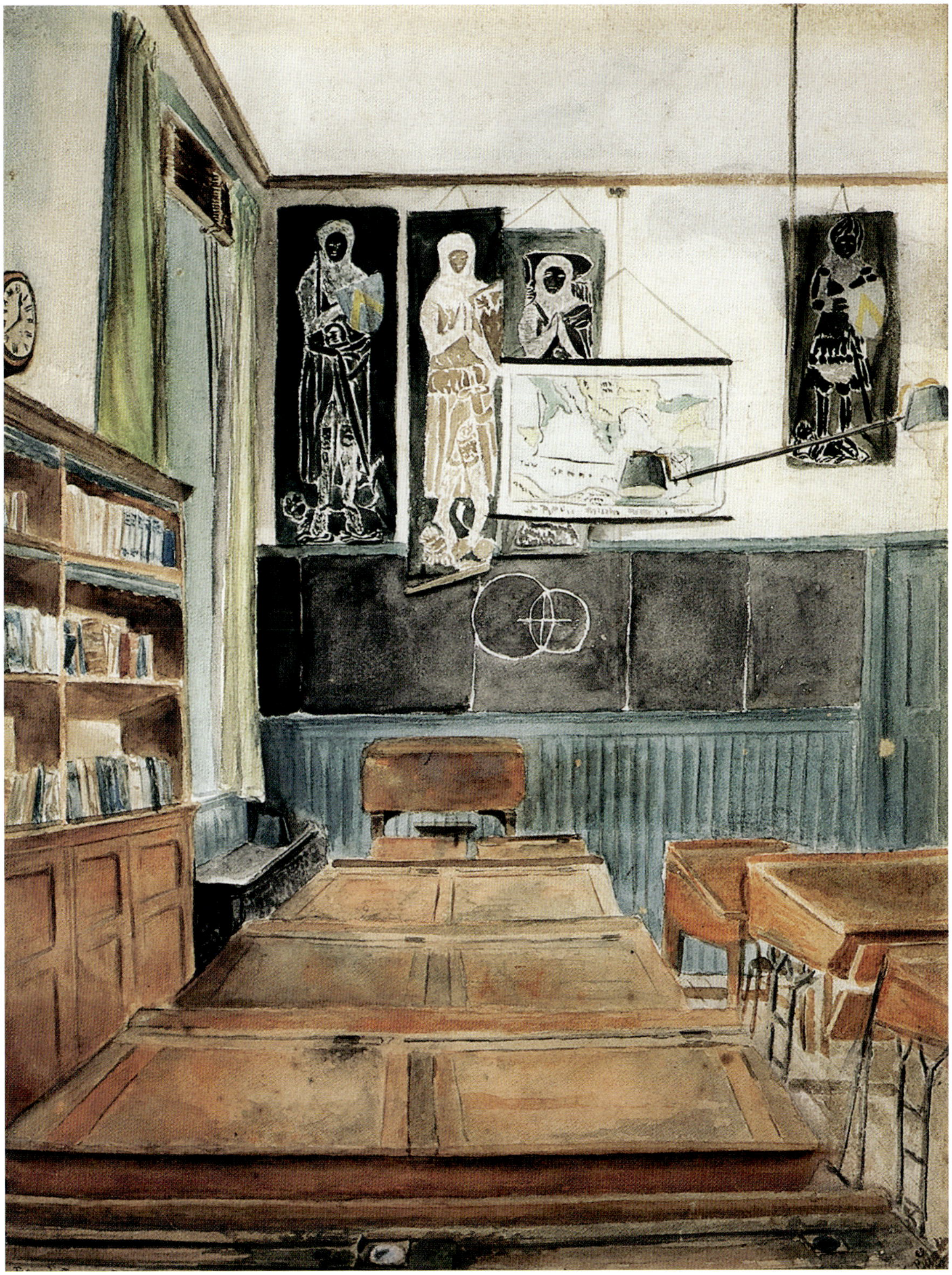

Bawden's Saffron Walden schoolroom *c.*1918, painted by him in watercolour,
345 x 250 mm (Fry Art Gallery).

on to school teaching or into the applied arts of industry or design. He recalled that there were only about a dozen full-time students, which was perhaps not so surprising immediately after the most brutal war in history. He had a work room to himself and the freedom to make his own syllabus. Bawden chose to concentrate on calligraphy under a disciple of the great letterman Edward Johnston: 'It wasn't that I had a special feeling for calligraphy, but anything new thrilled me.' However, compulsory drawing from the antique did not, nor did pottery decoration, though 'I expressed my horrid little nature in designing large elaborately enamelled plates'.

Outside of college hours he was also finding his own exemplars amongst the unfashionable Victorians, the first being Aubrey Beardsley whose work he discovered in *The Studio* magazine, though the teenager's admiration was not entirely for his drawing skills: 'In those days Beardsley was under a cloud; I was taken aside by one of the teachers and warned of the danger – what danger, I don't know! Beardsley was a wonderful boy. No one has produced such pornography. And pornography to be good has to be elegant. He is a great master, I think. I would rank him with Blake.'[3]

Dicky Doyle's teeming, grotesque and detailed illustrations were another source of pleasure and inspiration; he kept books by Doyle on his bookshelves all his life and later drew a *Homage to Dicky Doyle* for the Curwen Press. Bawden confessed later that as a young man he wanted to be 'an important chap like William Morris and do lots of things covering the whole field of design as he did. He is still very much a hero', which indicates that he must have had an early knowledge of that polymath designer of wallpapers, furniture, textiles and books. Many commentators on Bawden's later work have pointed out the parallels with another Victorian artist, Edward Lear, and obviously he would have found Lear's humour and line congenial, but apparently he did not discover Lear until after college when his own style was already maturing. Of the pre-war convulsions in the Paris art world he seems to have known nothing, which is not surprising since few of those pictures were then on display in Britain, and none of them in East Anglia. Only in the London coteries and art college staff-rooms were Cubism and Post-Impressionism topics of conversation, and Roger Fry's and Clive Bell's ideas on 'significant form' thought significant.

It was now time for Bawden to go to the capital and encounter more challenges than Cambridge could offer.

---

1. Berthoud, R., 'Why Bawden Approves of Change', *Illustrated London News*, May 1983, p.20.
2. Harling, R., 'Edward Bawden', *Art and Technics*, 1950, p.12.
3. Spalding, F., 'Edward Bawden', *Arts Review*, 26th September 1980, p.417.

2. THE ROYAL COLLEGE

In 1922 Bawden won a £60 per annum scholarship to the Royal College of Art (RCA) in London. This institution had been founded in 1837 as a post graduate college, that is, one which took students only after they had completed a course at their local art schools. Bawden had taken the entrance examinations in calligraphy and illumination and was therefore assigned to the Department of Industrial Design (it had dropped the word 'Decorative' from its title in 1920 as being too frivolous). At Cambridge, he claimed, he'd been 'cock of the walk' and was now shocked to find he looked like a provincial 'ignoramus', a country mouse amongst town mice, and had been thrown in amongst the most talented intake the RCA had ever seen: Henry Moore, Barbara Hepworth, Edward Burra, Barnett Freedman, Percy Horton, Vivian Pitchforth, John Tunnard, Phyllis Dodd, Raymond Coxon, James Betts, Enid Marx, Peggy Angus and Helen Binyon were there, whilst overlapping or treading on their heels came Cecil Collins, Albert Houthuesen, Morris Kestelman, Charles Tunnicliffe and Ceri Richards. This was indeed a remarkable generation because in addition to the Royal College cohort, John Piper, Graham Sutherland, Tom Hennell, Eileen Agar, John Aldridge, Edward Ardizzone, John Banting, Richard Eurich, William Gaunt, Anthony Gross, Stanley Hayter, Gertrude Hermes, Tristram Hillier, Blair Hughes-Stanton, Edward le Bas, Robert Medley, Kenneth Martin, Oliver Messel, Roland Penrose, Mary Potter, Fred Uhlman and Rex Whistler were all born during the first five years of the twentieth century. So was Kenneth Clark, the most influential pundit and arts administrator of his generation who, when the war came, was able to ensure that many of his generation became War Artists. These would be the stars, supporting cast, and

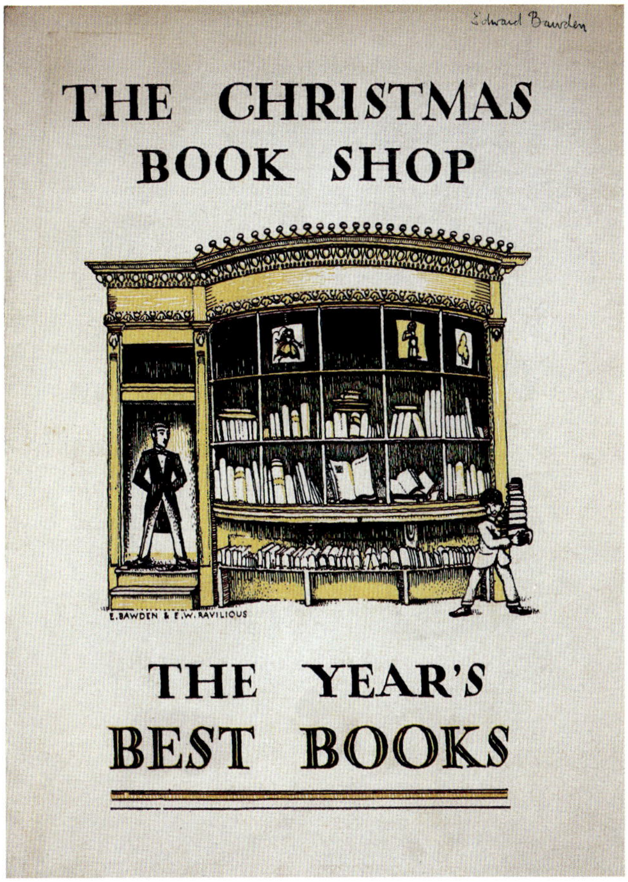

The Christmas Book Shop, Edward Bawden and Eric Ravilious, an advertising insert for *The Studio*, 1924; from Bawden's personal scrapbook, 290 x 210 mm.

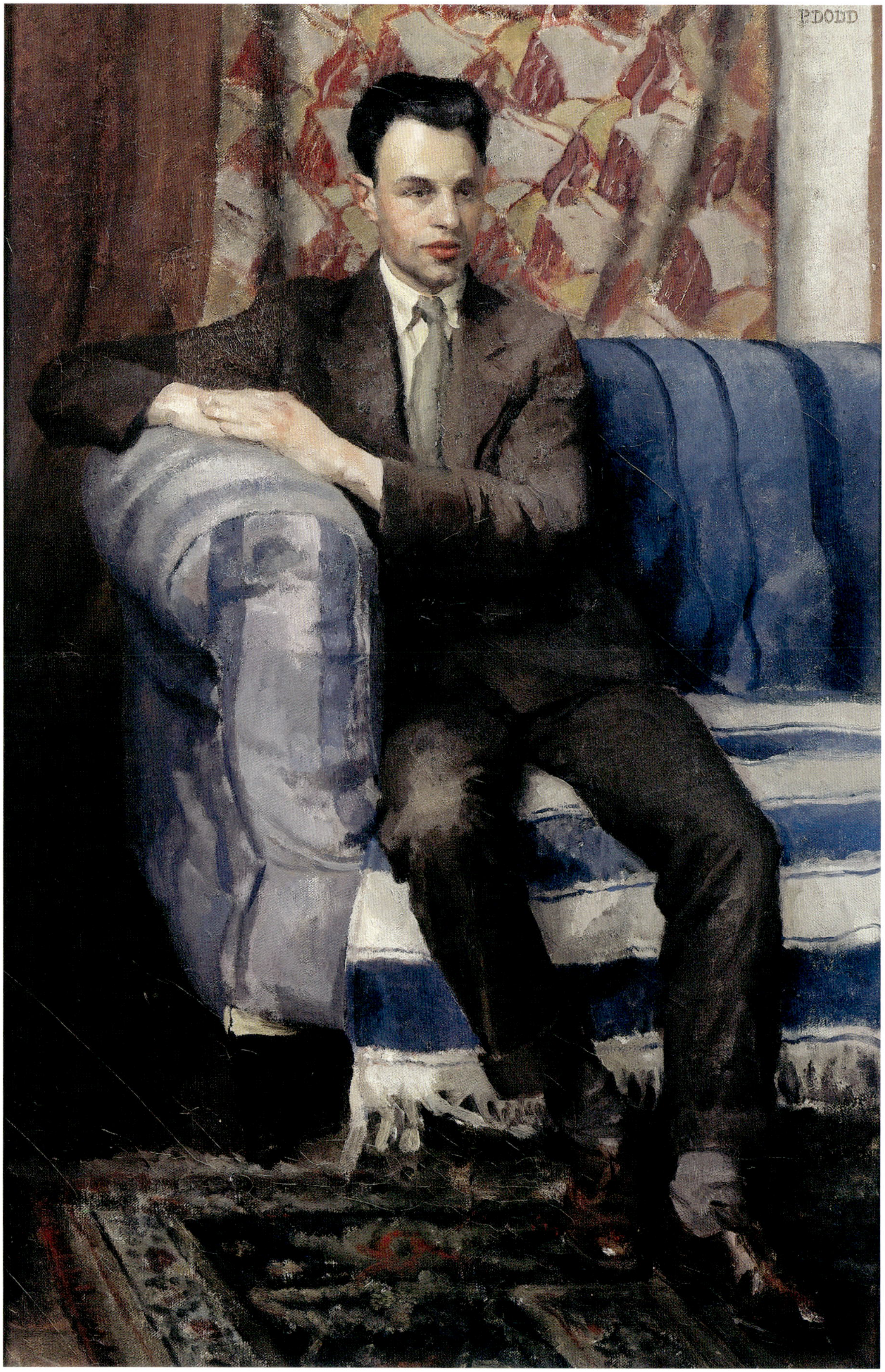
P DODD

spear-carriers who were going to dominate the stage of British art during the next fifty years.

In his long life Bawden would cross the paths of most of these people, but in the 1920s Bawden's inseparable friends were two men who started college on the same day that he did: Eric Ravilious (1903-1942) and Douglas Percy Bliss (1900-1984). Both left interesting accounts of their new friend which show that he retained a liking for his own company and seemed shy of entering any gathering of strangers – so bashful was Bawden that he couldn't bring himself to enter shops or ride on buses which meant he had to walk everywhere. Now that he was amongst his peers there seems to have been a change in his personality from that of the cocky extroverted schoolboy to something much more insecure, although he retained a self-assurance about his work and showed Bliss his portfolio of drawings with a certain arrogance. As he tramped London alone he kept a sardonic eye and a sketch book open for human absurdities, architectural oddities, posters, lettering, junk shops and window displays. He was irritating to his two new friends in his industriousness, and in the tidy, methodical and single-minded way he worked. But away from work they found he had a mordant, sometimes malicious, humour – he sent Bliss a dead mouse in a loaf, and another student, who had just fathered a child, received a contraceptive.

Bliss observed: 'girls scared him and he hated all hale and hearty fellows. He stood a little outside life. He saw it like a foreigner at a cricket match, marvelling at its madness.' [1] Bawden later admitted he was inhibited as a student by his strait-laced upbringing and so became a solitary, 'avoiding my own kind', especially women, 'the Great Untouchables', from whom he flinched. Several people who knew him have suggested there was an ambivalence about Bawden's sexuality at this period.

He neither smoked nor drank, read no newspapers, saw no film or theatre, attended no parties, couldn't dance, played no sport, had no political views and was making do on six pounds a month and a diet of 'buns, chocolate and coffee dashes'. After college hours he would mutter: 'got some hack work to do', and walk back alone to draw and sleep in a bed-sitter in Parsons Green or South Kensington where his work-table was set out meticulously, all his instruments aligned, clean and tidy like surgeons' scalpels and his pencils 'sharpened like daggers', according to Bliss. This prissiness and his taciturnity, even downright rudeness, and lack of interest in other people annoyed both Bliss and Ravilious and they began to wonder why they put up with him. Bliss reluctantly concluded: 'Bawden was unique and we were lucky to have him'.

The RCA's curriculum at that time was conventional but not onerous and left the students very much to their own devices. The School of Design in Bawden's day was first led by Professor Robert Anning Bell (1863-1933), a Master of the Art Workers' Guild and an all-rounder in watercolours, pottery design, stained glass, sculpture, mosaic, crafts and Beardsley-influenced Shakespearian illustration, and next by the shy but popular Professor Ernest Tristram (1882-1952), painter and expert on the copying and restoration of medieval wall painting. Tristram, Bawden claimed, gave him more inspiration than any other teacher and he kept in touch with him throughout his career. Anning Bell had been a pupil of Walter Crane, formerly and briefly Principal at the RCA, and Tristram had studied under William Lethaby, his predecessor as Professor of Design at the college. This meant that both men provided immediate links back to William Morris and all he stood for in terms of breaking down the barriers of class and creativity between makers and designers, and between Fine and Applied Arts. For all these people specialisation represented stultification.

Left: Phyllis Dodd, *Edward Bawden*, 1929, oil, 71 x 47.5 cm.

The new Principal, William Rothenstein (1872-1945), who had taken up his post in 1920, declared himself in the same tradition: 'The separation between craftsmen and artists is already too wide. Each has lessons of value to learn from the other. The craftsman's education has tended towards a somewhat doctrinaire pedantry of pseudo-medieval character, while the painter's training has been based too exclusively on the study of the single human model . . . nor is it desirable to limit, early in a young aspirant's career, his future activities.' [2] Such ideals Bawden absorbed early and lived by all his life, forever willing to approach the design problems of a menu card, a garden bench, a teacup, a watercolour landscape, or a sixty foot mural with equal enthusiasm. More immediately he sought out extra-curricular classes in bookbinding and line engraving in the evenings, and wasted a frustrating amount of time attempting to set up a printing press with Bliss in order to make poetry broadsheets.

This willingness to tackle any medium and any design task was not necessarily admired by the staff and students in the other faculties who had in mind a kind of hierarchy of purity with Fine Art at the pinnacle. It rankled with Bawden that he was made to feel that the Design School: 'was the habitat of the lowest of the low. The Royal College of Art in the early twenties was smaller than the smallest provincial school today: it was divided into four schools, Painting, Sculpture, Engraving, Design and accordingly the first three ranked as Fine Art and the last as Applied Art. This distinction, absurd though it is, is still maintained today by the dealers for commercial reasons, but then it was as real as being a child of acknowledged parentage or being an orphan, the offspring of a gentleman and a whore. As a designer I felt it keenly.' [3] The painting students sneered: 'Designers do bad drawings and mount them beautifully. We do good drawings and don't bother with mounts.'

Farmyard near Braintree, 1923, watercolour; from Bawden's personal scrapbook, 200 x 290 mm.

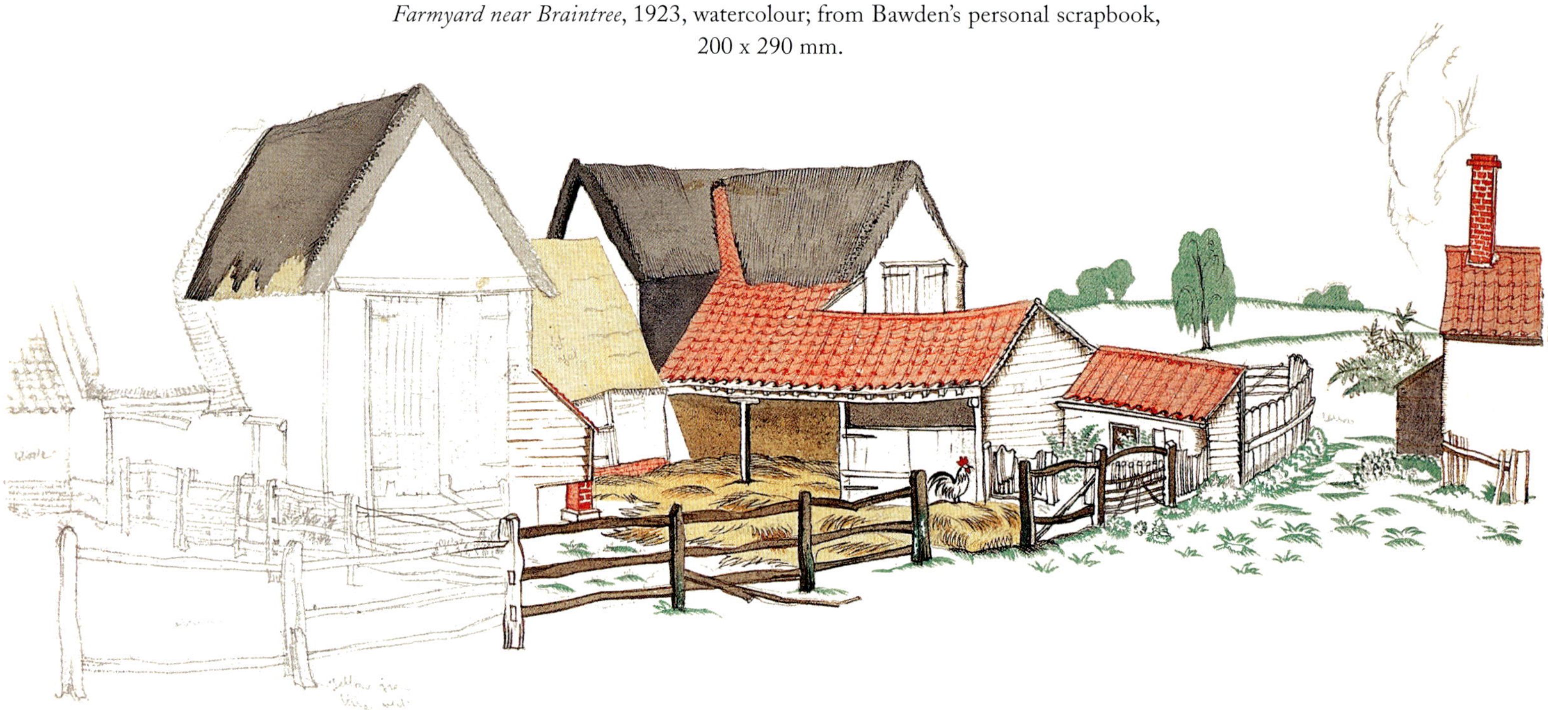

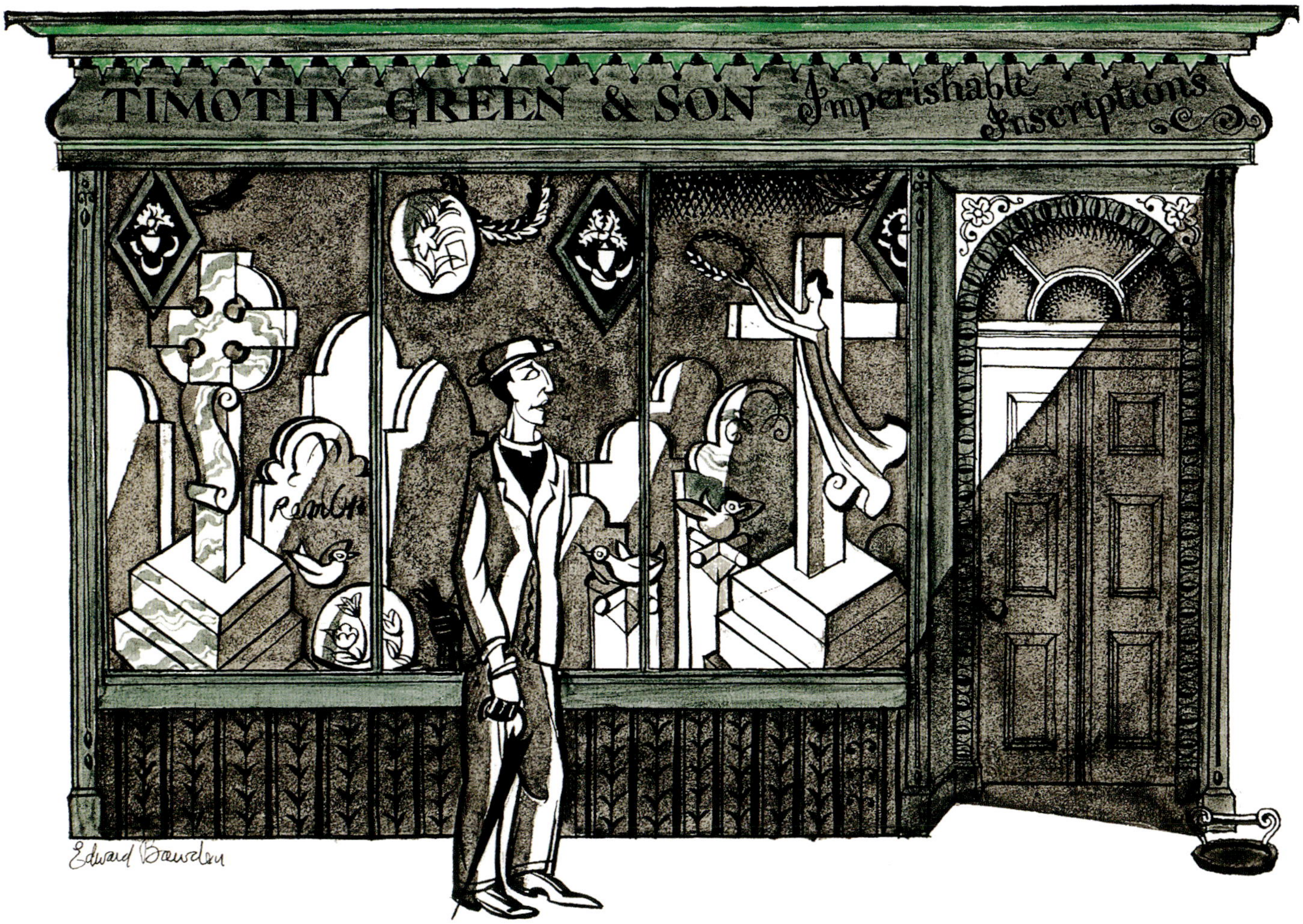

Shop front design *Timothy Green & Son, Imperishable Inscriptions*, *c.*1925, given to Eric Ravilious, 125 x 165 mm.

However, there was one area of art that Bawden did shy away from and that was life-drawing which, by this date, had become an integral and compulsory part of the design course as well as those in Fine Arts. 'I had no antipathy to the figure, only incompetence', he admitted later. At the first session Rothenstein, who also doubled as Professor of Painting, looked over Bawden's drawing of a nude model and said, 'Well, we must start a class for beginners'. Bawden's figure drawing would never conform to either Rothenstein's ideal of the suave outlines of Ingres, or to that of their other teacher, the sculptor Leon Underwood who demanded solidly rounded form modelled by chiaroscuro. The handful of nudes by Bawden which have survived from this period are painstakingly rendered, but as lifeless as dummies. Nor did he want to compete with the painting students by using oils: their subtlety of tone, glazings, scumbles, impastos, the whole business of 'painterly' paintings which attracted attention to their brush marks and surface didn't interest him: he was already committed to line, and anyway he hated the smell of turpentine. Oil paint was prose, and watercolour poetry, he claimed, though watercolour painting was not on the RCA's curriculum. Just one Bawden oil painting, a beach scene, is known.

The time saved by avoiding the more academic

By the Sea, 1929-30, oil on panel, 635 x 864 mm (Fine Art Society).

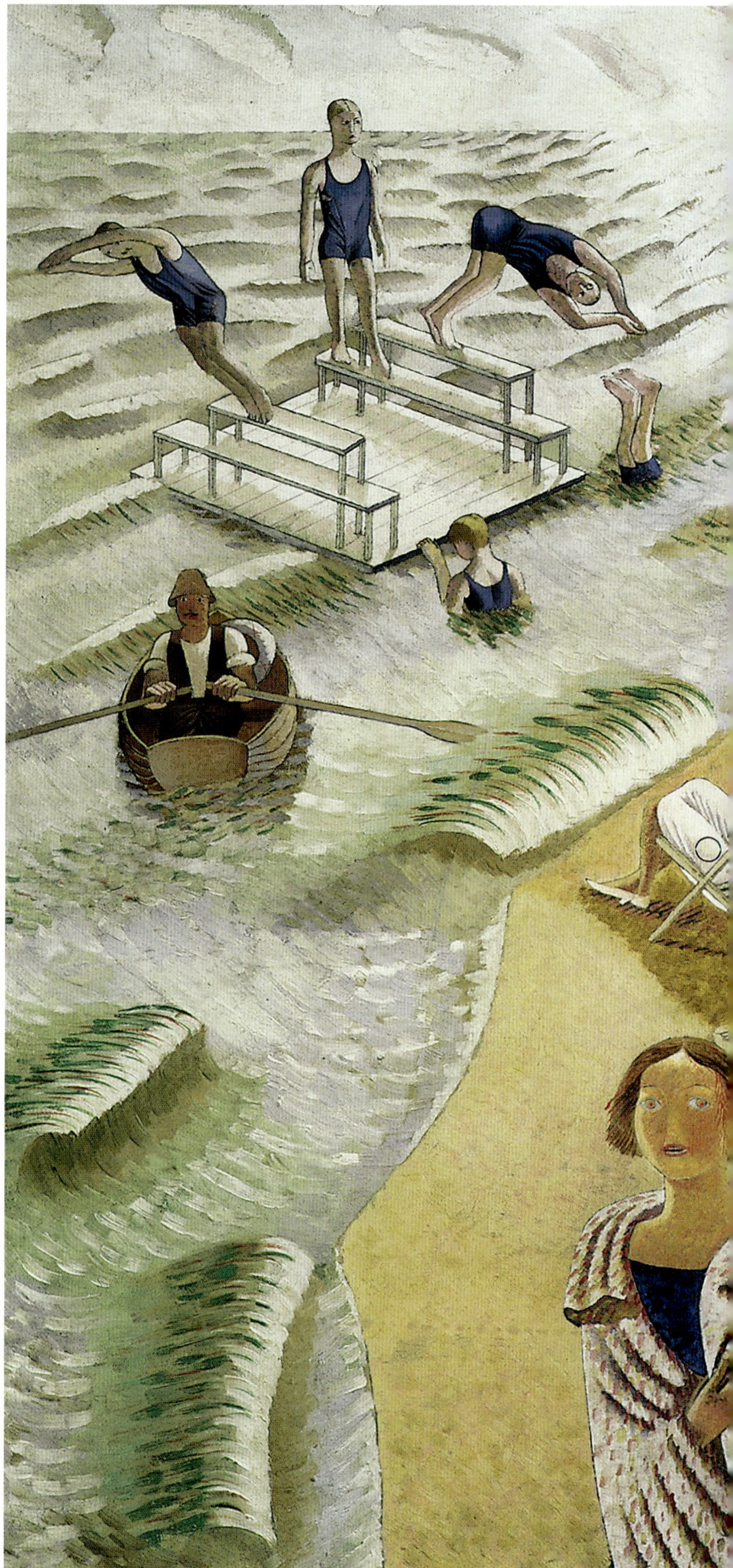

disciplines he spent elsewhere, haunting the Victoria and Albert Museum, which was literally next door to the college and permanently open to its students, and copying from its displays of textiles, Persian miniatures, French tapestries, Gothic carvings, heraldry, and medieval manuscripts – all decorative arts in which there was a high degree of formalisation and pattern-making. The Tate Gallery and British Museum provided other intellectual fodder for this omnivorous mind: 'For relaxation I had no use . . . . My life became increasingly like that of a museum attendant,' Bawden remembered.

On one occasion in 1926 the Victoria and Albert Museum held an exhibition of Samuel Palmer's idyllic landscapes and Bawden, Bliss and Ravilious were inspired enough by this to go on a pilgrimage to Palmer's 'Valley of Vision' at Shoreham. They also admired traditional English watercolours, Bawden and Ravilious in particular noting how John Sell Cotman simplified foliage and organised silhouettes, and how several of the others such as Towne, Rowlandson and Blake made pictures which were virtually tinted line drawings. Thomas Bewick and Joseph Crawhall were other enthusiasms, Bawden sending an undated letter to Ravilious in the holidays saying that he'd just bought the latter illustrator's *Old Tayles Newlye Related* and was colouring it in, and 'I bought another Legrand book – very good and Boutet de Monvel and 5 comic annuals and a German printing magazine and several books of plays. Slowly I'm cultivating an appreciation of Elizabethan plays: Ben Jonson gives me great pleasure and I've reread *The Knight of the Burning Pestle*.' He also reports that 'Sterne is one of the greatest novelists'. Whilst other students might have been agog for the latest news from Paris where Cubism was still alive and Surrealism was struggling to be born, Bawden was plunging backwards through art and literary history. However, he did have one curious attempt at printmaking that presaged Yves Klein's 'Anthropometries' of 1960, where the artist took prints from naked models he had brushed with blue paint. Bawden inked himself all over and attempted to take a body print on a roll of ceiling

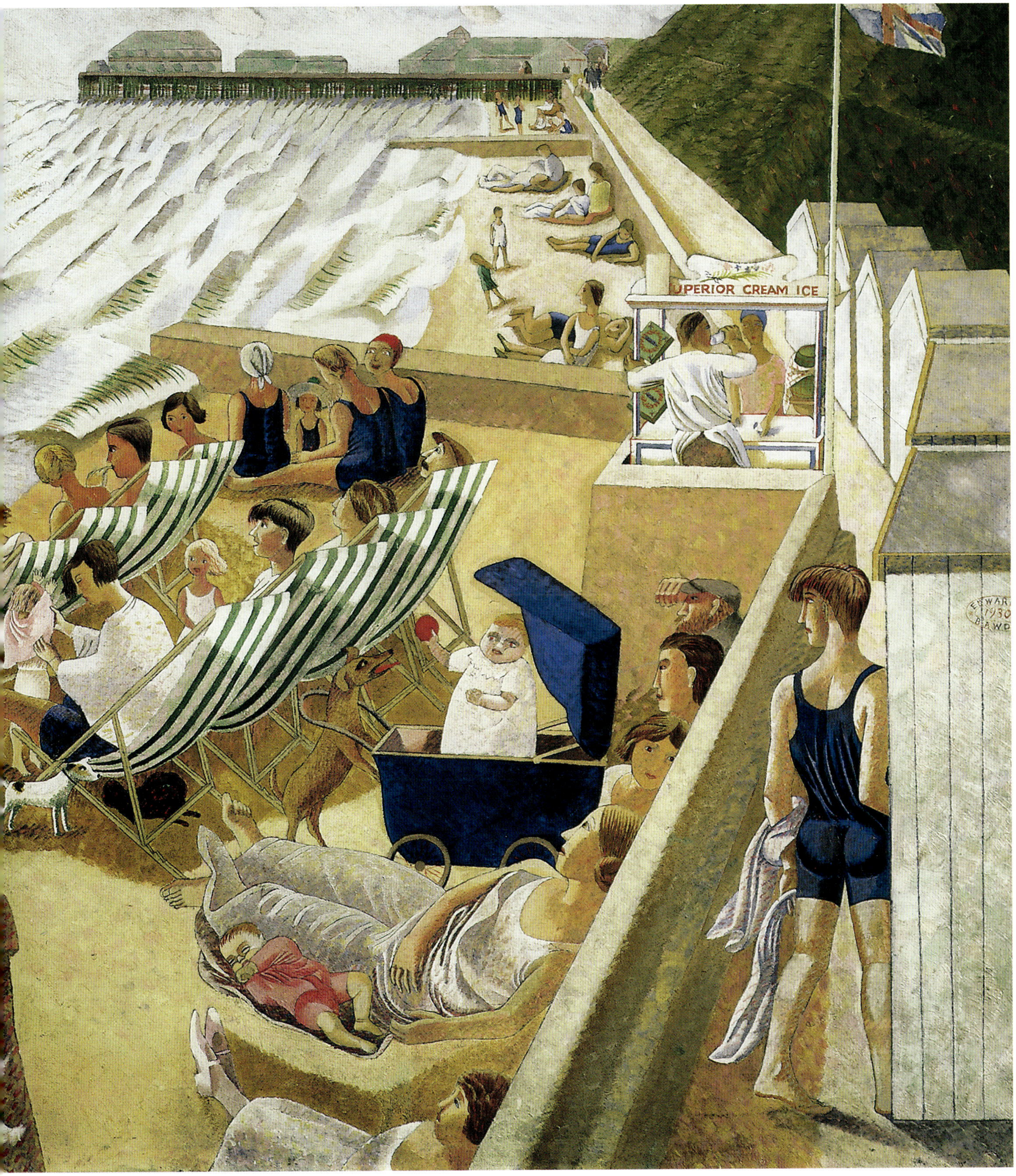
UPERIOR CREAM ICE

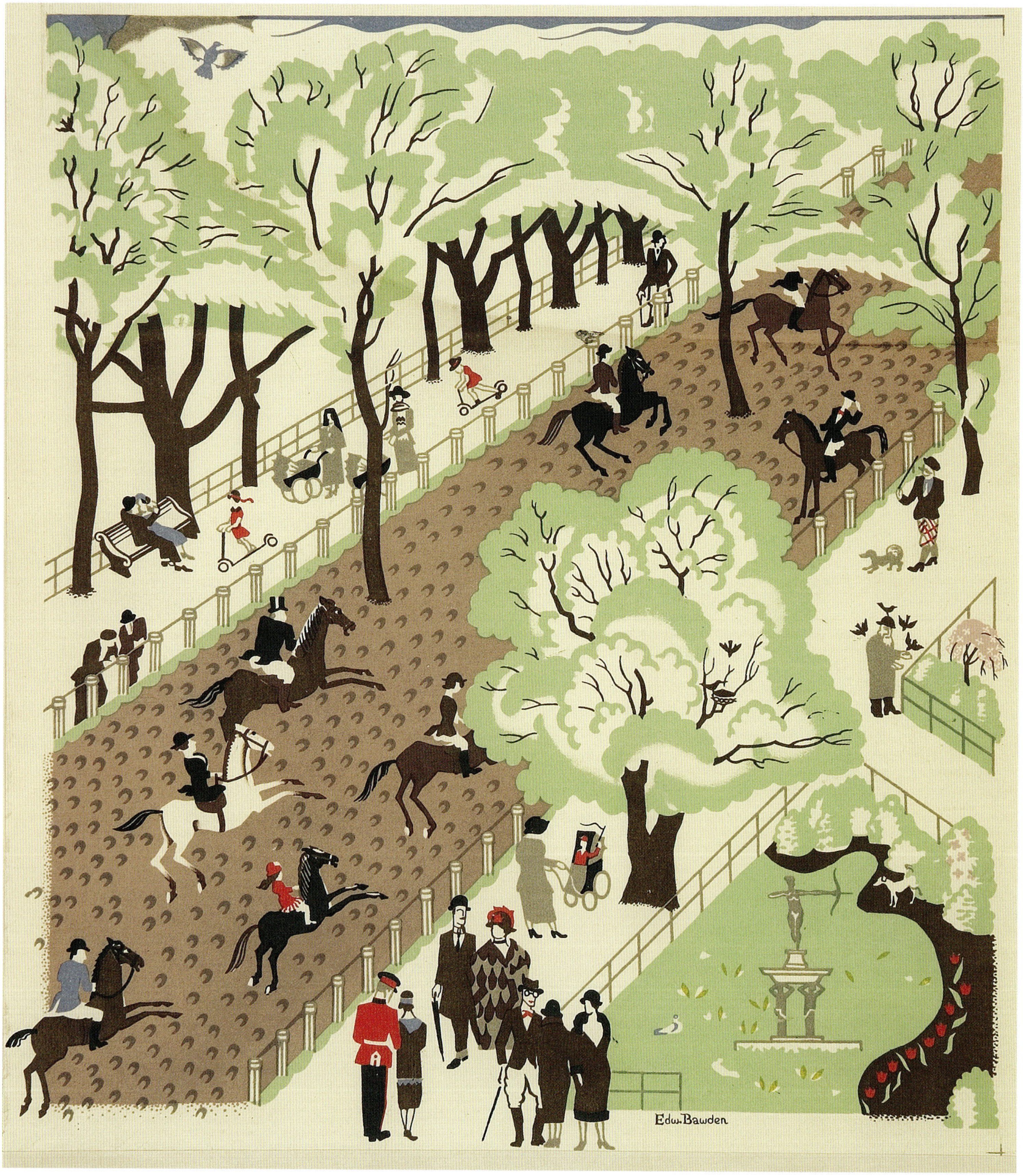
Edw. Bawden

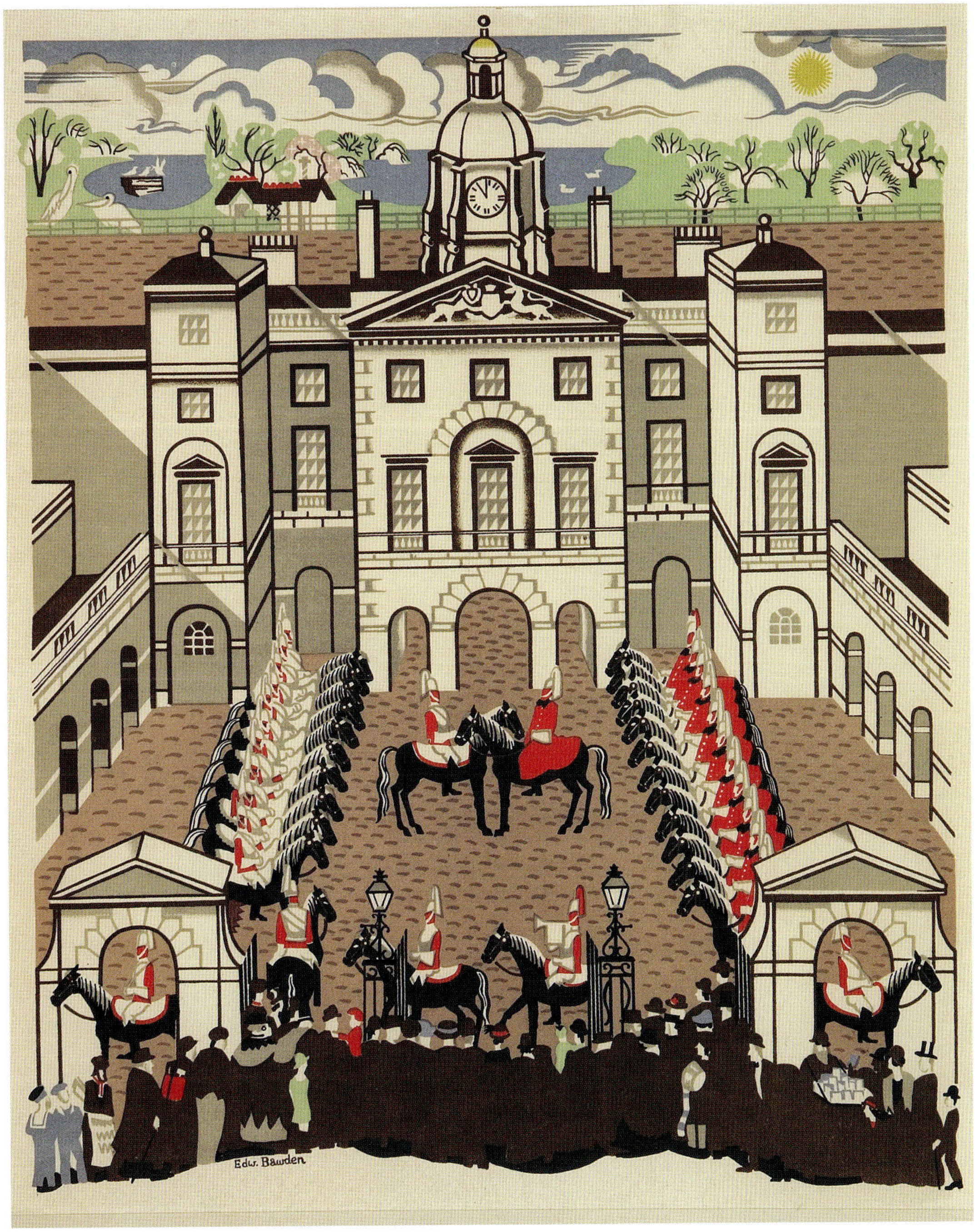

Lithographed images in seven colours printed at the Curwen Press, used for poster designs for London Underground, 1925.

Left: *Hyde Park: The Stage of London Life* (which bears the additional verse: Every Day / Like a Play / See Rotten Row's / Free Horse Shows), 638 x 558 mm.
Above: *Changing the Guard: London's Daily Military Tattoos* (672 x 543 mm).
(Manchester Metropolitan University Library.)

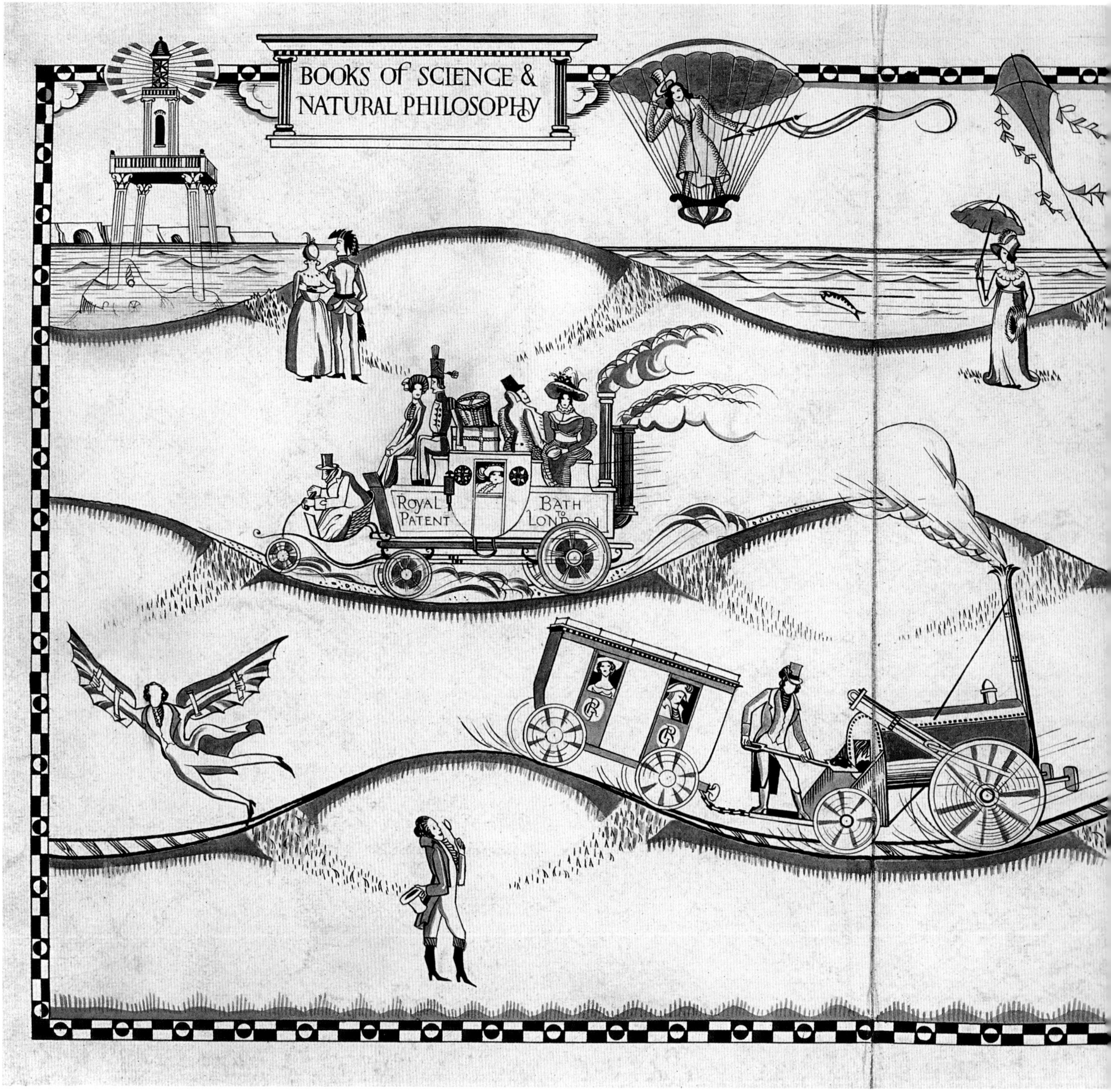

paper. He later recalled that his backside printed best but what he really needed was somebody to trample on him to get the correct pressure. Cleaning off the paint with turps also presented its own problems and he did not repeat the experiment. Bawden's relentless work rate brought him some commercial success even while he was a student. He admired and began to collect the London Underground posters of the American artist, McKnight Kauffer (1890-1954), who was first influenced by the German, Ludwig Holwein, and later employed a vigorous but accessible

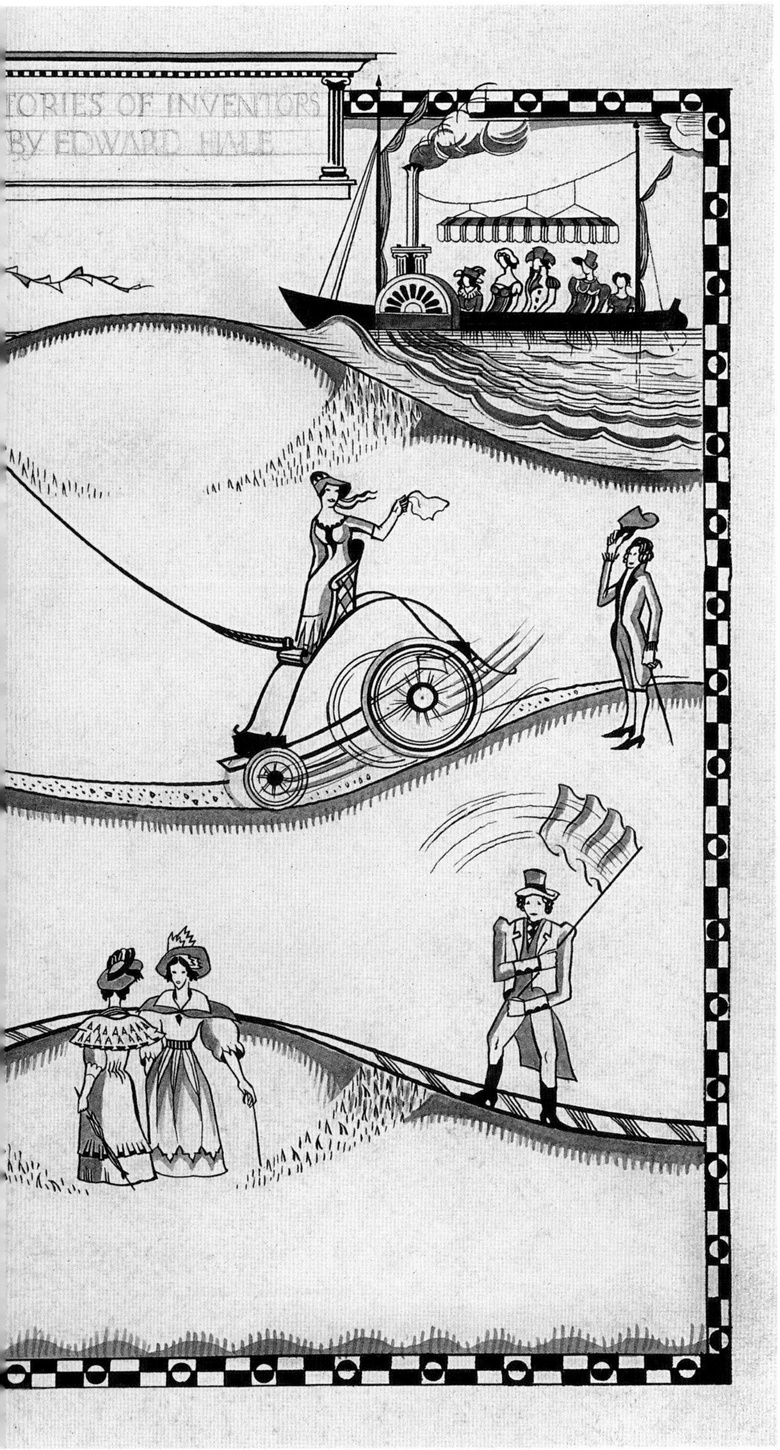

Books of Science & Natural Philosophy, and Stories of Invention, *c.*1925, unfinished design from Bawden's personal scrapbook, 340 x 560 mm.

Vorticist style in his designs, all clean lines and flat colours expressing speed and modernity. One hundred and fifty of these had been commissioned by the enlightened Frank Pick of London Underground, who was responsible for all aspects of its design from the stations to its time-tables, and soon Bawden was designing for Pick himself, having been introduced by Paul Nash. This meant his posters, among them *The Stage of London Life, Seeing the Dahlias in Hyde Park* and *Changing the Guard* appeared all over London in 'the poor man's art gallery' during 1925.

Another artist hero for Bawden and the other students at this time was Claud Lovat Fraser (1890-1921), an illustrator of clarity and imagination, then much talked about for his stage designs, early death and the posthumous book on his work by John Drinkwater and Albert Rutherston (younger brother of William Rothenstein and another artist whose graphic work Bawden admired). Fraser had been badly gassed at Loos and was a friend of another war survivor, Paul Nash. Fraser was 'greater than Veronese', Bawden assured Bliss, but instead of adopting Fraser's characteristic reed pen which gave a tough wood-cut effect to his drawings for books, Bawden used a thin brush for linear work in black and white. It was in book illustration that he opted to take his Diploma examinations in 1925. He passed, but is nowhere to be seen on his group's graduation photograph, being too camera-shy to appear.

Bawden thought Eric Ravilious 'a bit of a layabout' and recalled, 'we were very close friends, but I think we were rivalling each other. He was much cleverer, but never gave the appearance of working. I think I rather showed off that I was being busy.' Apart from taking the same course they shared very similar backgrounds. Ravilious' grandfather was a marine who retired from the sea to be a coachman in Tonbridge. Eric's father, Frank, was one of his thirteen children and, after marriage to Emily, who was in service, he ran an upholstery business in Acton, which failed. The family then moved to Eastbourne where he set up in the antique trade and it was there that Eric, the last of his four children, was born. Ravilious never took friends home because his father was so embarrassingly devout, being quick to show the 'God is Love' motto written round the lining of his hat and eager to thrust devotional pamphlets into the hands of visitors.

Eric attended the local grammar school and then Eastbourne School of Art for three years before winning an identical scholarship to Bawden's. His entry subject to the School of Design was book illustration.

At college Ravilious impressed the others with his good manners, bookishness and successes with the prettiest female students. He was known as 'Rav' or 'The Boy'. Bliss thought 'he was a real charmer. Gay, elegant, sensitive, amusing, he could dance and he could whistle. Bawden and I liked him enormously.' [4] He also enjoyed billiards, football, tennis, cricket, followed boxing and enjoyed his beer. Whilst he was never a solitary like the socially inept Bawden, nevertheless friends felt that behind his insouciance there was an emotional reticence and withdrawal which prevented any binding intimacy.

Bliss was the eldest and most intellectual of the three, and also the most exotic, having been born in Karachi where his father was a successful pharmacist who sent him home at the age of six to be raised and educated at Watson's College, Edinburgh. He was darkly handsome and had a Scottish accent, which later faded. His Latin and French were good and later he could read Dante in the original. After brief service in the Highland Light Infantry at the end of the First World War he went to Edinburgh University in 1919 for three years to take a degree in English with subsidiary History and Art History, so that he lacked the four year grounding in a provincial art school that the other two had acquired. Nevertheless, he was the only one of the three to be accepted into the prestigious Painting School, even though he too was full of William Morris' craft ideals and would have preferred to be studying Design with his two friends. He was also the most literary and in future years would support his friends in his reviews of their exhibitions, and by a biography of Bawden which would help establish him as one of the great characters of British art, as well as one of its outstanding practitioners. In turn Bawden thought Bliss 'combined an intense interest in books and a corrosive wit. In satisfying his own curiosity he opened for me many vistas full of strange surprises, so I must still feel grateful to him for that, and for helping to rub off a little ridiculous provincialism.' [5]

Bawden himself was no slouch in devouring books if we are to believe Bliss' memories of finding Bawden at the breakfast table each morning 'his social temperature near freezing' but bent over a book: 'I remember he went steadily through *Anna Karenina*, Fergusson on Architecture and Jackson's *History of Wood Engraving*. He read to learn, unlike Ravilious who read for fun and whose favourite book was *Huckleberry Finn*. Once or twice I found EB deep in an article on ironmongery and hardware . . . which he would recommend to me . . . as "good sensible stuff." ' [6]

Then in September 1924 the friends were fortunate to be given a part-time tutor for a year who would set all three in the right direction. At this time Paul Nash represented English modernity, having returned from the trenches of the Ypres Salient with a landscape style stripped of all its pre-war echoes of Samuel Palmer and the Pre-Raphaelites and stark enough to convey his rage at the obscenities he had seen. He now saw himself as 'a war artist without a war', turning away, like fellow war veterans Wyndham Lewis, David Bomberg and William Roberts, from the destructive machine towards a more humane subject matter. The three friends had seen his paintings and were thrilled by them, particularly the pale, cool, dry palette used in his watercolours. After demobilisation Nash's travels had helped him see art in a modern European context and he now strove to make his own landscape painting embody meanings beyond mere topographical appearances. From 1919 he had also taken up wood-engraving and helped the revival of that exacting medium.

At the RCA Nash was given a cubby-hole and students could drop in with work to show, and the three friends did, as Bawden still remembered when he had himself been teaching many years: 'the fact that he did not make the usual remarks common to teachers which have an air of being profound and yet are evasive, but instead tried only to give his own reaction plainly and clearly, gave a good deal of personal value to his teaching. But though his

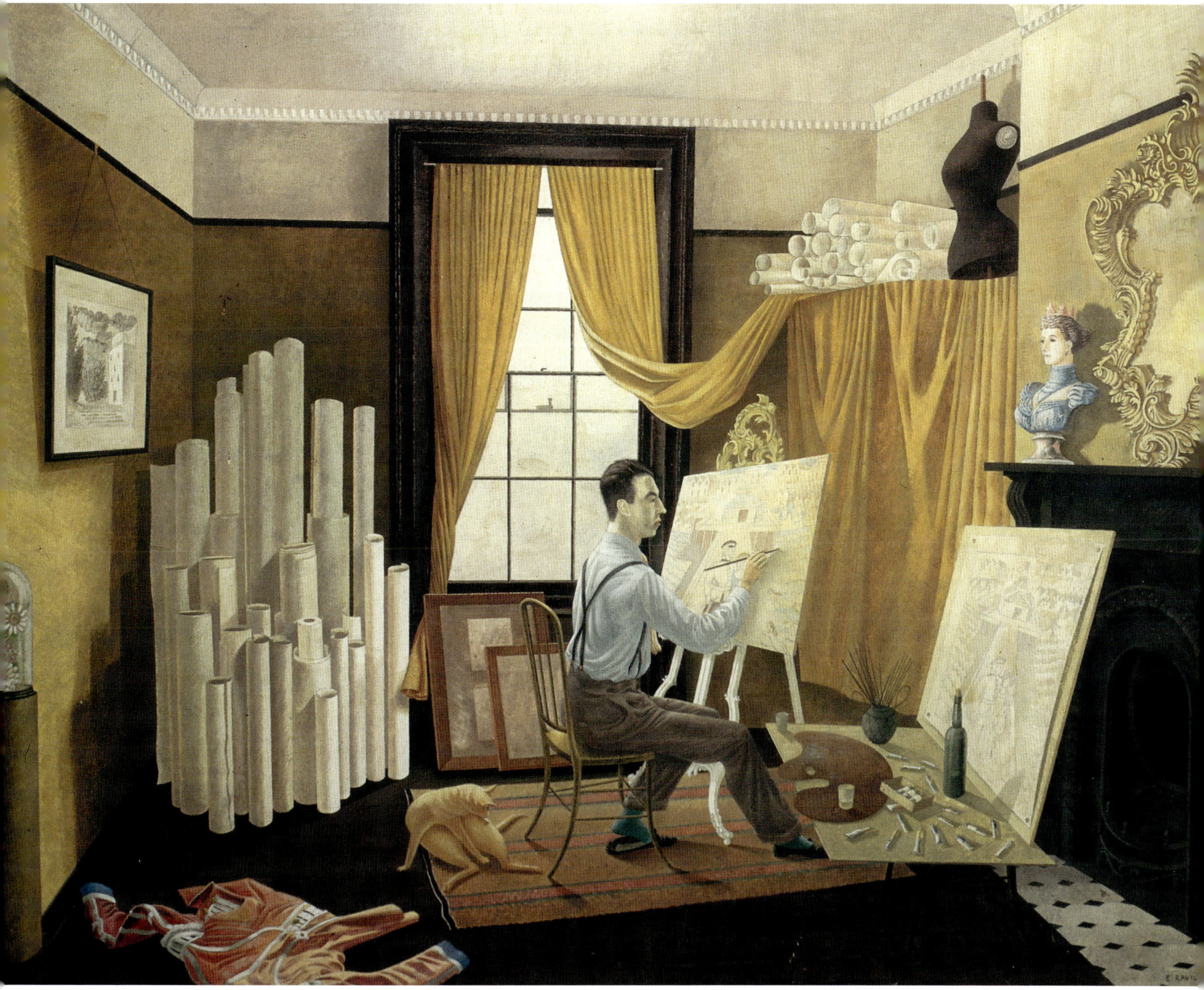

Eric Ravilious, *Edward Bawden working in his studio*, 1927, tempera on board, 76 x 92 cm (Royal College of Art). The rolls of paper are Bawden's preparatory designs for the Morley College mural.

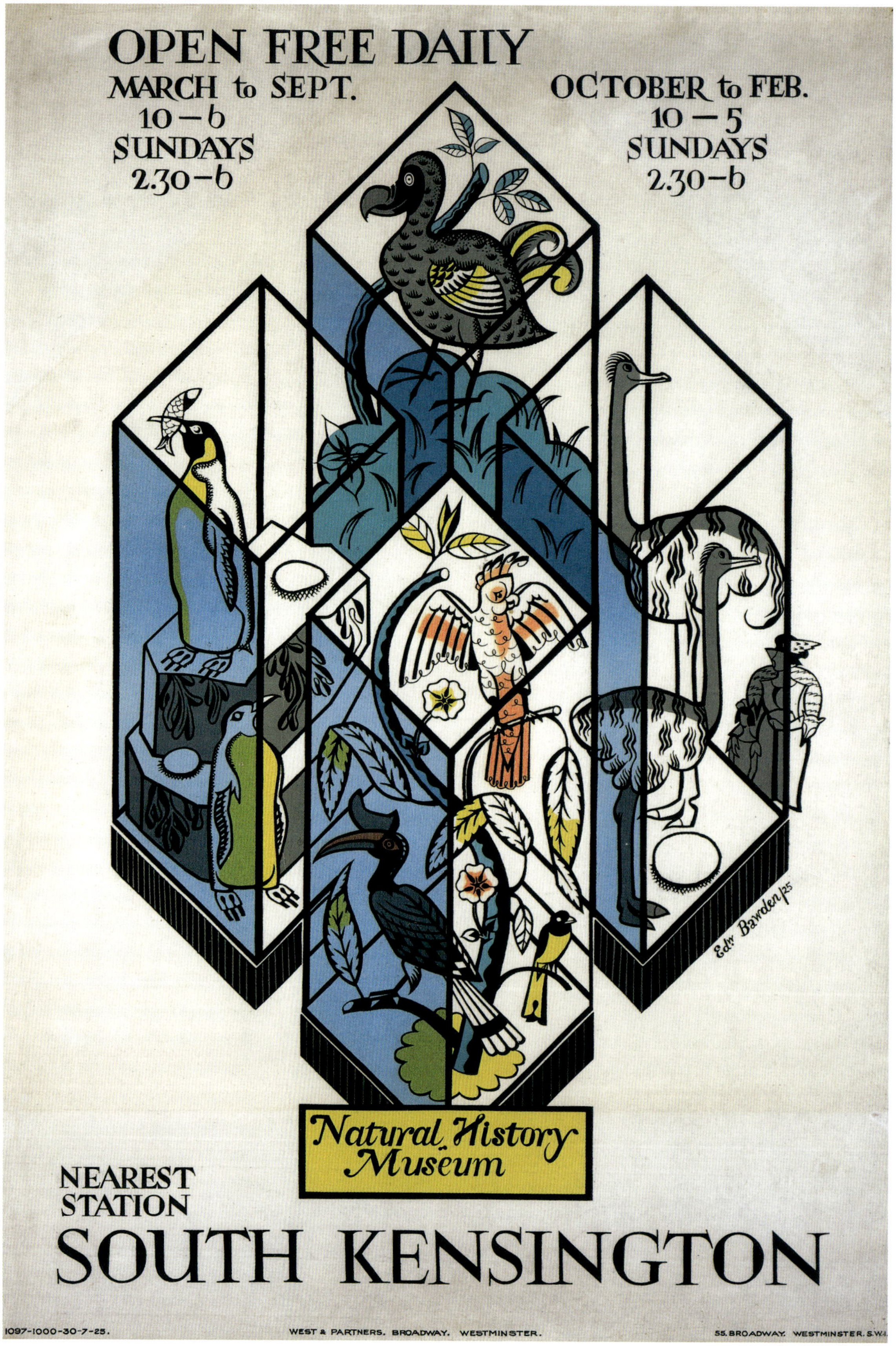
OPEN FREE DAILY
MARCH to SEPT.
10 – 6
SUNDAYS
2.30 – 6
OCTOBER to FEB.
10 – 5
SUNDAYS
2.30 – 6
Edw Bawden '25
Natural History Museum
NEAREST STATION
SOUTH KENSINGTON
1097-1000-30-7-25.
WEST & PARTNERS. BROADWAY. WESTMINSTER.
55. BROADWAY. WESTMINSTER. S.W.1.

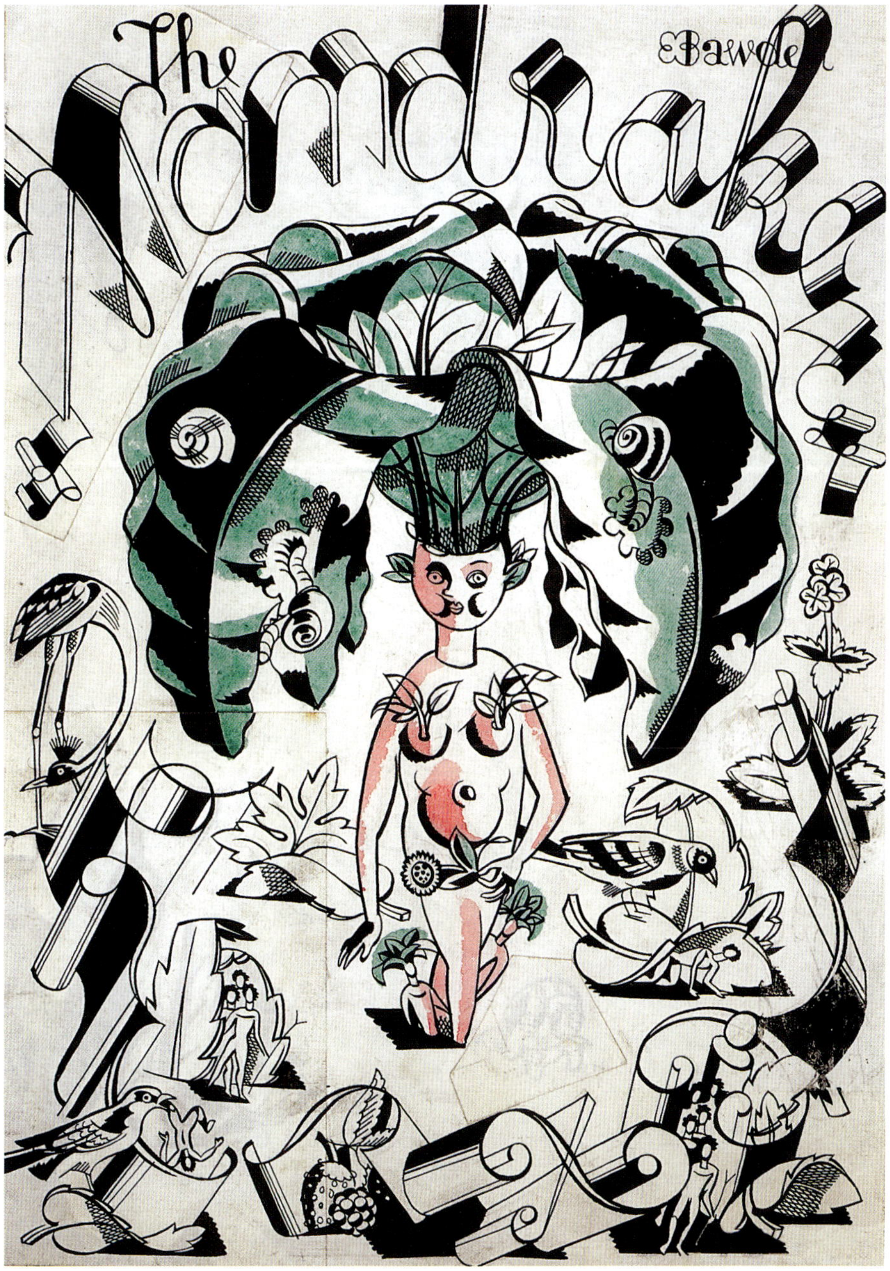

Cover designed by Bawden for the Royal College of Art students' magazine *The Mandrake*, 1926, from his personal scrapbook, 26 x 18 cm.

London Underground poster, *Natural History Museum, South Kensington*, 1925; printed by West and Partners, Westminster, 75 x 50 cm.

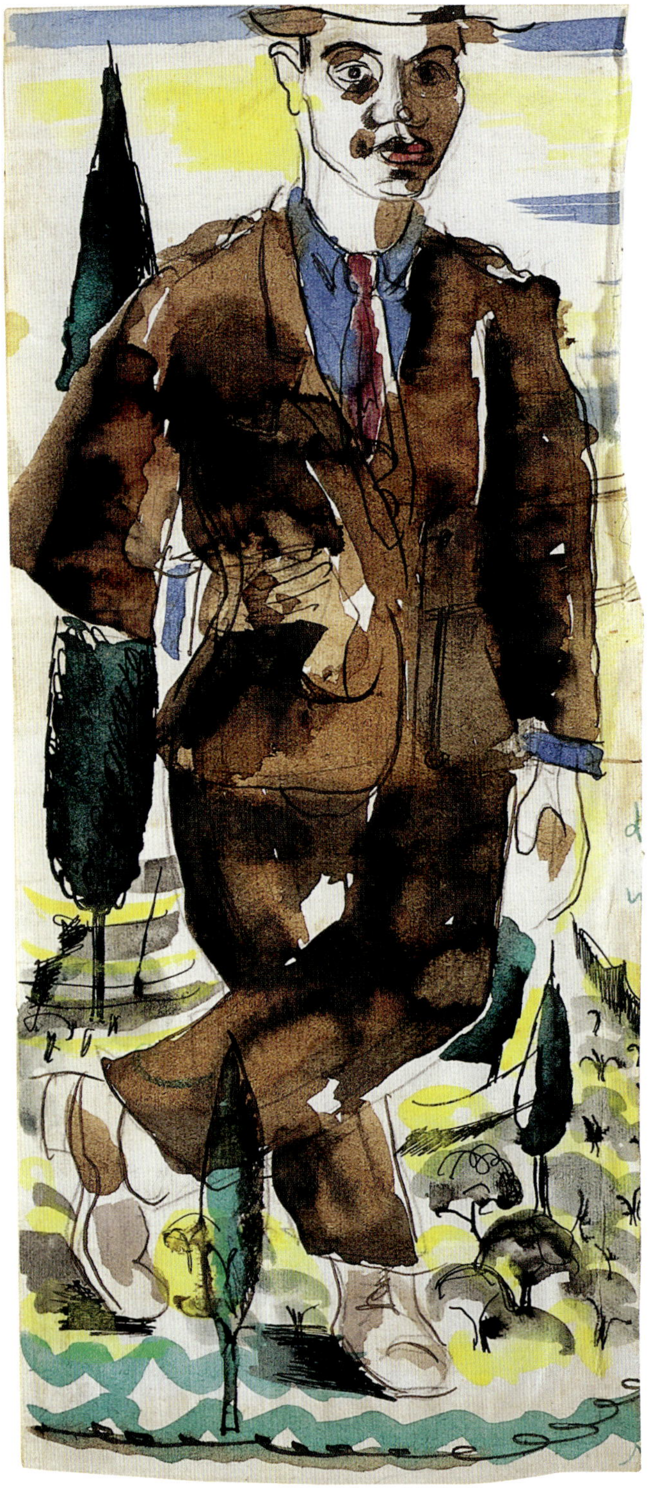

Sketch from Bawden's letters to Ravilious while on his Italian tour, 1926. 'Look at the figure on the opposite side of the page & ask yourself whether it is not a fine & noble Pose? & the landscape gay & varied under the blue & lemon sky? or whether a smile of happiness (unutterable happiness) does not play over the young fellow's face as the winds from Fiesole blow through his hair & caress his cheeks.' 215 x 90mm.

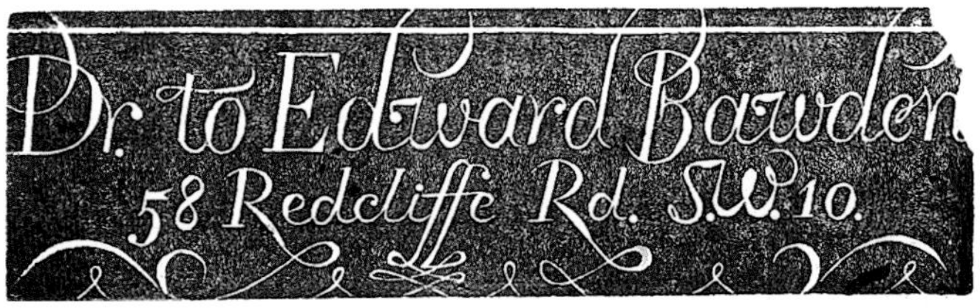

Wood-engraved bill-heading 'Dr. to Edward Bawden, 58 Redcliffe Road, SW10', from Bawden's personal scrapbook, probably by Eric Ravilious or Douglas Percy Bliss, 20 x 70 mm.

teaching was personal it was always related to what he conceived was individual to each student; in other words he did not hand out propaganda for his own point of view but endeavoured to bring out instead whatever – slight though it might be – seemed unique in the student.' [7] Bawden later admitted 'I fell flat on my face for Paul Nash'. Others in their social group such as Enid Marx and Edward Burra from the Painting School and Cecilia Dunbar Kilburn from Sculpture also, figuratively, sat at Nash's feet and absorbed his creed that artists, craftsmen and architects should cross boundaries – he set an example for them by designing a black-glass bathroom, china, guidebooks and even a chocolate box for Cadbury's.

Ravilious and Bliss also admired Nash as a tutor and under his guidance took up wood-engraving. The medium was enjoying something of a boom with the private presses at this time with Eric Gill, Gwen Raverat, Robert Gibbings, Iain Macnab, John Nash, David Jones and others all illustrating fine books. The attraction for publishers was that engraved wood-blocks were 'type high' and so printed with the same printing presses used for metal type. Paul Nash helped Ravilious join the Society of Wood Engravers in 1925 and subsequently Ravilious received commissions from Robert Gibbings at his Golden Cockerel Press. Bliss too had some success with his wood-engravings and whilst still in college had been commissioned to select and illustrate *Scottish Border Ballads* for Oxford University Press (1925) and *The History of Rasselas* by Dr Johnson for J.M.Dent (1926). The two friends sat each side of the fire in their digs sharing scorpers and spitstickers and cutting their end-grain boxwood blocks.

Bliss took wood-engraving as his specialism for his Diploma, but Ravilious, tiring perhaps of small scale wood-pecking, opted for mural painting even though he had to rush three years' work into two because his Eastbourne grant had run out. In spite of his off-hand disdain for traditional Renaissance techniques as taught by Tristram he achieved distinctions and won a travelling scholarship to Italy in 1924, where he spent most of his time in Florence with other students from the Royal College, including Henry Moore with whom he got drunk. He complained Italy was either too hot or too cold, or he was too constipated, or all the old religious paintings of the High Renaissance didn't seem to relate to his own concerns as a student of design, though he loved the so-called Primitives Duccio and Cimabue. The only Italian he learned in three months was to ask for the lavatory. If, as D.H.Lawrence claimed, an Englishman is constitutionally either a Mediterranean or a Nordic, Ravilious was definitely a Viking. Like Bawden, who won the scholarship a year after him, he failed to notice that Italy was taking a Fascist turn.

Before leaving the RCA the three friends combined to take over the student magazine. The 1924 edition had an editorial by Bliss saying 'This magazine is put together in

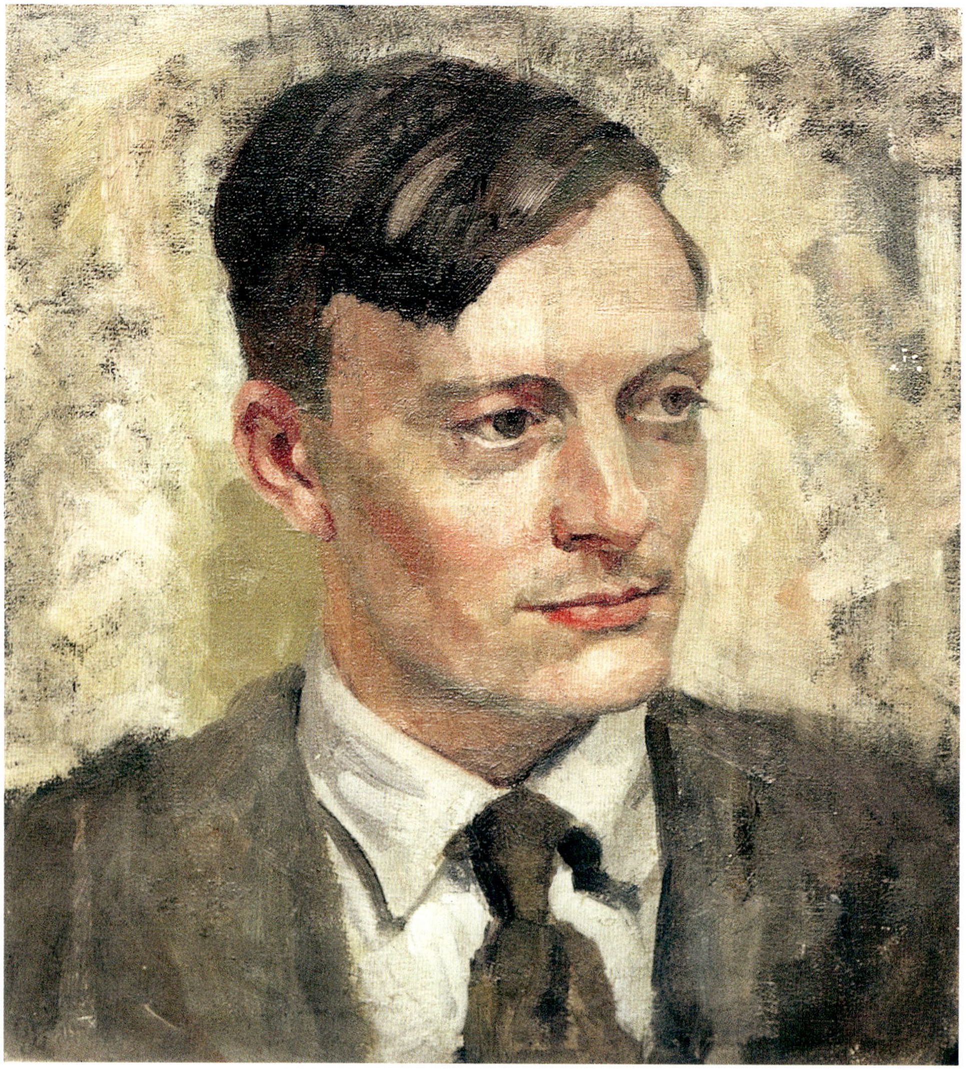

Phyllis Dodd, *Portrait of Eric Ravilious*, 1929, oil on canvas, 35 x 29 cm.
Opposite: Phyllis Dodd, *Bliss*, 1926-27, oil, 76 x 51 cm.

the Valley of the Shadow of Diploma' and it goes on to pull the legs of their professors: Tristram is 'an expert in malodorous media – eager to instruct in all the temperas, skim milk, egg size, calf's foot, sardine tail etc.' and Rothenstein, 'The Holbein of today . . . portraits in oil and sanguine – has head hunted for a generation – few celebrities have eluded him.' By the following year the three had taken it over entirely, changed the dull cover for a Ravilious design of flower and bee, used stencils to apply colour (they had been looking at French publications) and given it the title *Gallimaufry*. Bawden mocked a South African student's tales of big-game hunting with a drawing of a flattened orange lion, the bullet holes arrowed and a swarm of insects (*Microgaster Baudenius*) devouring it. There were also wood-engravings by Bliss and Enid Marx amongst other student contributions.

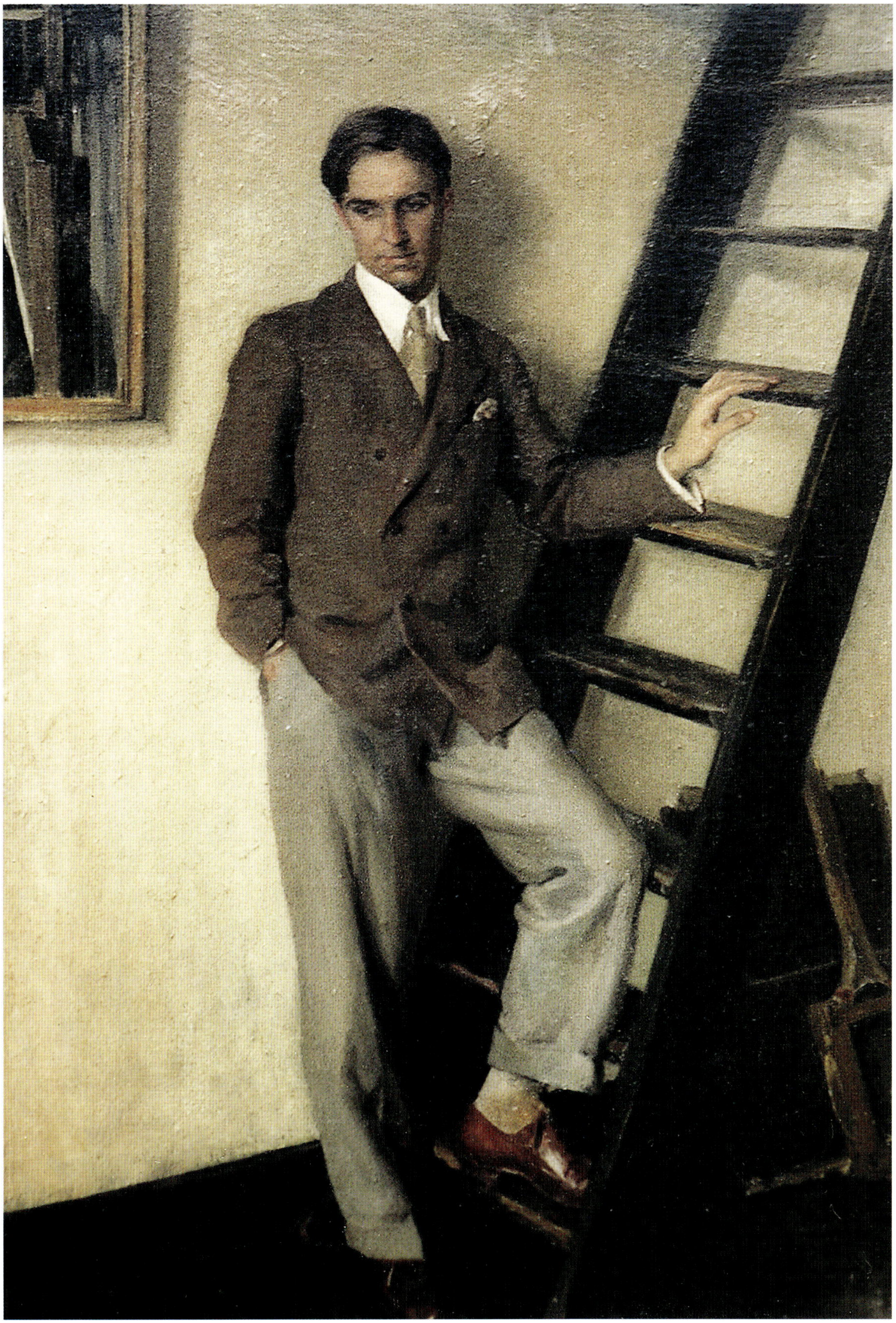

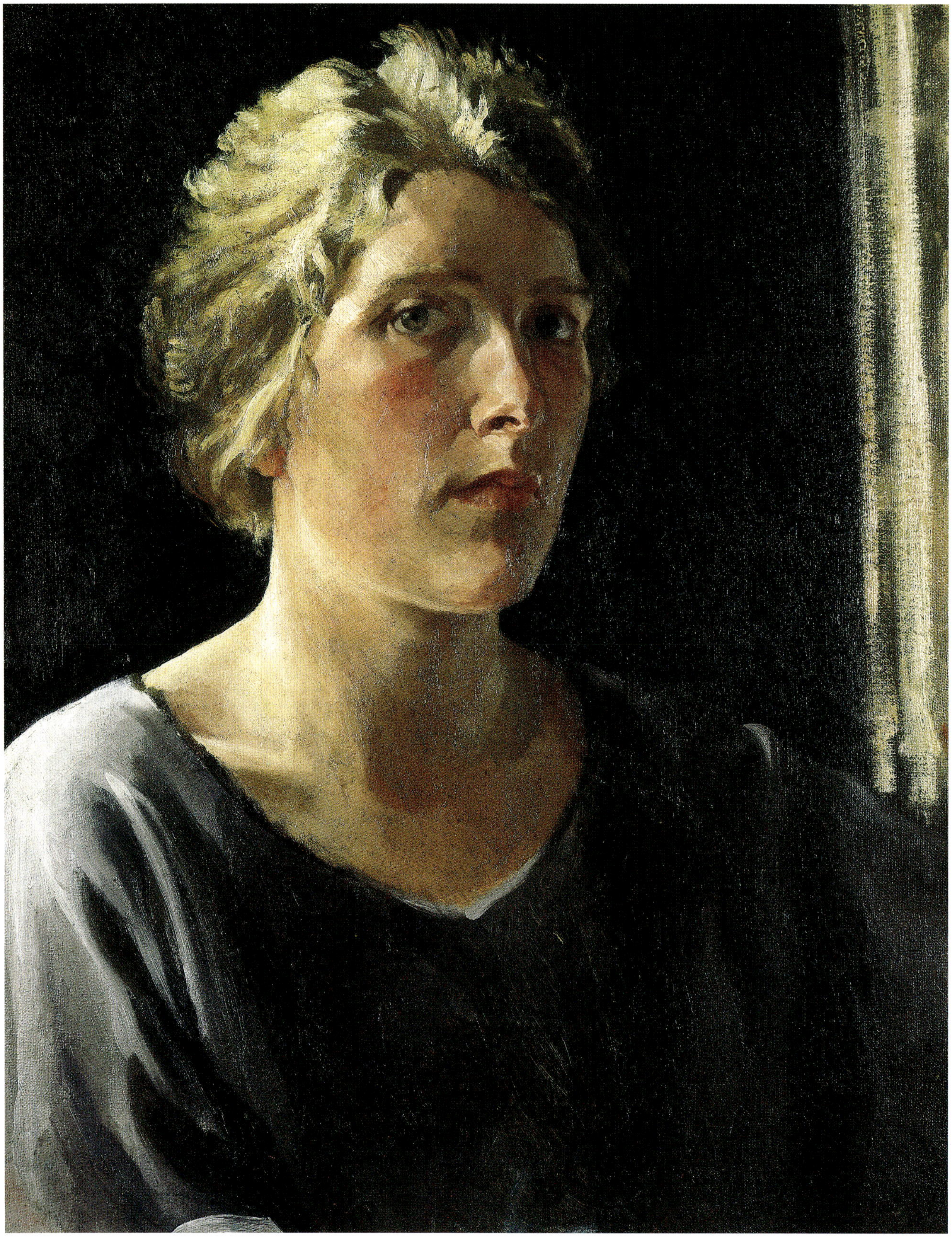

Phyllis Dodd, *Self portrait*, *c.*1922, oil on canvas, 610 x 510 mm.

Gallimaufry then transmogrified into *Mandrake* and had a hand-coloured cover by Bawden.

On his return from Italy Ravilious shared an attic studio with Bliss in Earls Court and when Bawden returned from his scholarship tour in 1925 the three friends took lodgings in Redcliffe Road, where Lovat Fraser once had a studio. Also nearby were fellow ex-RCA students such as Henry Moore, Cecilia Dunbar Kilburn (the only one with a private income), and the beautiful Phyllis Dodd. Phyllis had come from Cheshire via Liverpool Art College to the Painting School in 1921 and was soon one of Rothenstein's star students to whom he could confidently pass on some of his distinguished sitters. Bliss volunteered to sit for her as a ruse to get her attention; soon they became a pair and he introduced her to his two friends. In 1929 she painted a likeness of Bawden sitting stiffly in his best suit and then she made portraits of Ravilious and later still his wife. Her 1927 portrait simply titled *Bliss* was exhibited at the Royal Academy that year and in April of the next, she and Douglas Percy Bliss were married and settled in a flat in Lambeth.

In 1930 Ravilious also made a tempera portrait of Bawden. He shows Bawden at work in his tidy bed-sitter with some telling props around him: a cat, rolled up drawings, a bottle of wine and a Victorian bust painted blue, dried flowers under a glass dome and an ornate mirror on the mantelpiece. He is working with tiny brushes on a picture of a girl and a soldier in a garden and has a red army uniform for reference. Later Bawden got his revenge by drawing 'The Boy' working at his drawing board with a cat on his chair, but with his features entirely obscured by a huge vase of flowers in the foreground.

Ravilious wrote to Cecilia Dunbar Kilburn: 'Aren't Bliss and Bawden going it just at the present; publishers fall to them, Bliss says, at the rate of four a week. Bawden is overdoing it now I think, he will kill himself. When I told him this he told me of some idea he had of joining a club, a very quiet club it would have to be of course: incredible notion. Do you know anyone he could marry? Perhaps God will create a wife (from a rib) for such a diligent servant as Edward. He is quite as particular a case as Adam.' (6th November 1927). There was only one possible candidate, a fellow student called Charlotte Epton, known to them all as 'Eppie'. She had played tennis with Ravilious, who introduced them to each other, and later she took pity on Bawden sitting by himself in the canteen and talked to him. She was a year ahead in the Design School and a friend of Moore, but her first love was ceramics and she went from college to work in the newly-opened pottery of Bernard Leach in St Ives. Charlotte was extrovert, willing to take charge and chatter in ways Bawden never could and these opposites seemed to attract, though before things could get serious Bawden had to take up his Italian travel scholarship.

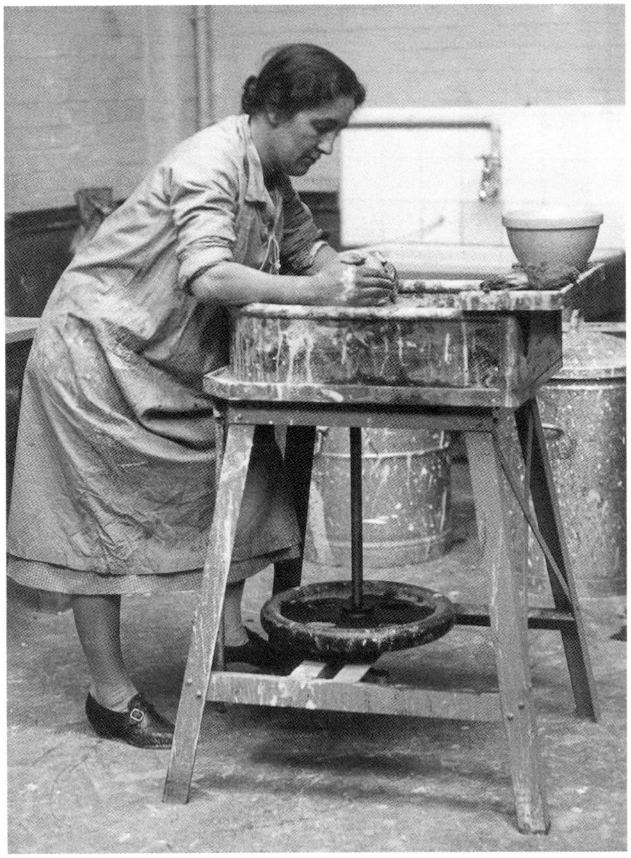

Charlotte Epton at Bernard Leach's pottery, St Ives, late 1920s.

It was his first time abroad and he wrote 'It gave me the

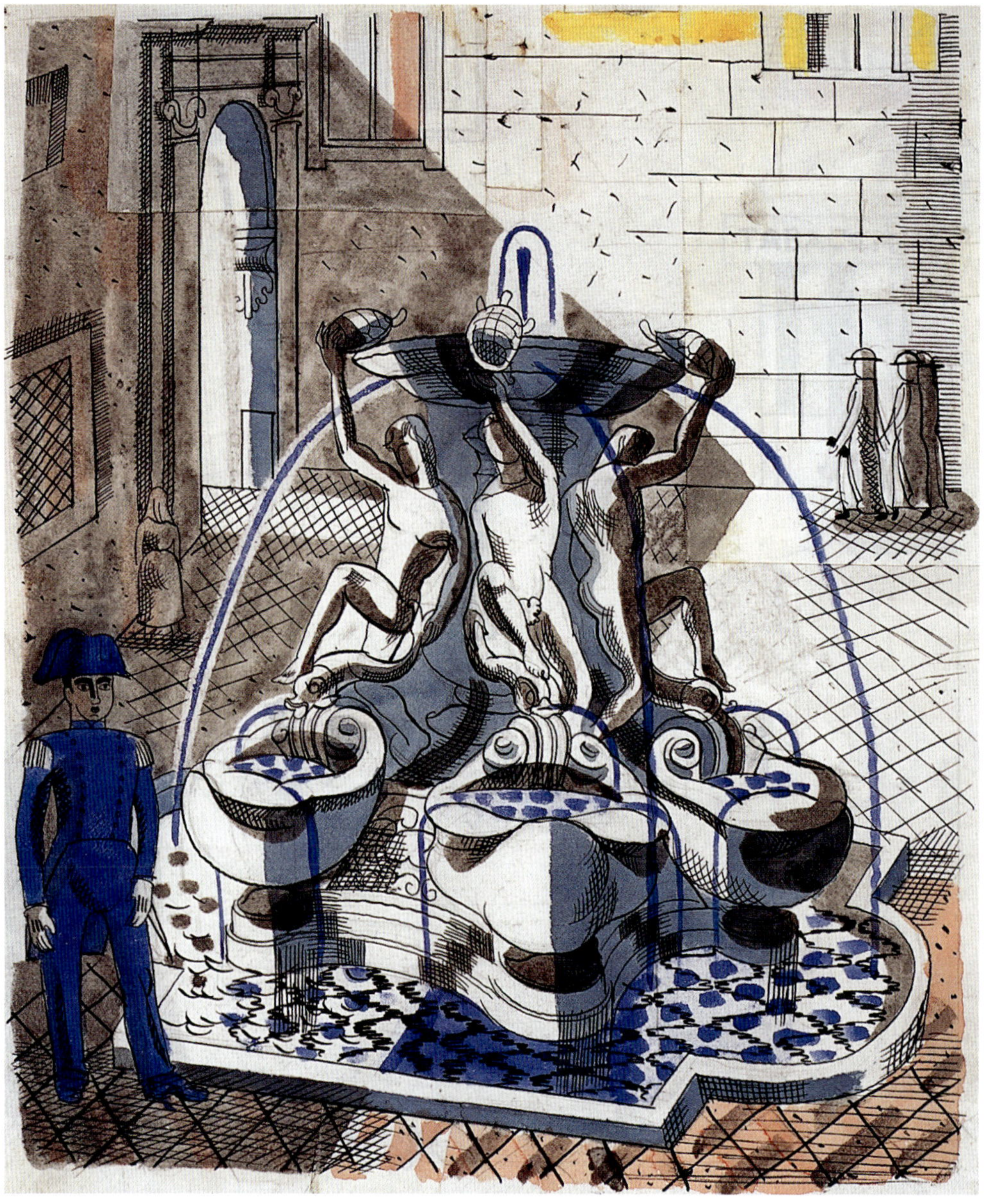

Italian fountain, watercolour from Bawden's personal scrapbook, 1926, 23 x 19 cm.

biggest shock of my life'; this haunter of museums found the whole country like one big museum. He didn't seem to do much drawing but he certainly did a lot of solitary wandering and looking in Rome, Venice, Padua, Florence, Ravenna, San Gimigniano, Naples and Pompeii. The 'lustful staring' of the sun got him down and, as he wrote to Percy Horton, 'it was a relief when he closeted himself behind a cloud and pulled the chain'. In Florence he encountered a painter from the RCA, Lionel Ellis, who also had his new wife and a dog along with him. They joined up to sketch but the couple were too hearty for Bawden, as he complained in a letter to Bliss (whom he always addressed by his surname) 'I hate to have smoke blown through a hole in my door, or thistles put into my bed for scorpions, or, worst of all, to be involved in an indecent struggle, to be tickled by Mrs Ellis and to have to bear the dreadful agony in silent writhing. Also Ellis will persist in calling me Eddie or Edward or Ted or Teddie – just as the wind blows. These are familiarities I never allow you or Ravilious to use.' [8] Years later Walter Hoyle, who frequently collaborated with Bawden and knew him for forty years admitted he never dared address him informally: 'it would be as strange as calling William Blake Bill'. [9]

Nevertheless, Italy appealed to Bawden in a way it never had to Ravilious. The Primitives, Simone Martini and Duccio ('quite as great as Giotto'), he found stunning and he must have noted the hard-edged little clouds of Piero della Francesca because similar ones appeared in his own work in later years. The early painters showed him that one did not have to model by light and shade, or conform to academic one-point perspective and that colour could be applied bright and flat. 'Baroque painting leaves me cold, though not Baroque sculpture', he told Ravilious. 'The great fountains and statues by Bernini, the wonderful church facades of Borromini, gave me an eyeful that has not staled with time. If pressed for an opinion I should plump for the Baroque as the most deliriously beautiful style ever invented. That visit to Italy was the most shattering experience I have ever had. I returned home with less complacency and in the next few years strained hard to set a higher standard in my own work. The visual sense had been shaken up thoroughly: it took time to regain a personal focus and when at last it was achieved, my scale of values had changed. For one thing I looked upon contemporary work with a shrewder eye.' [10]

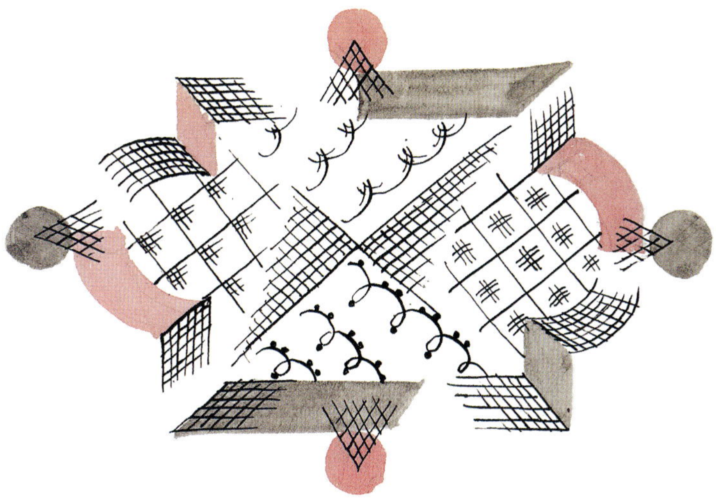

Design from Bawden's scrapbook, probably 1925-30.

1. Bliss, D. P., *Edward Bawden*, Pendomer Press, 1979, p.28.
2. Frayling, C., *Royal College of Art: 150 Years of Art and Design*, Barrie and Jenkins, 1987, p.90.
3. Huxley, P., *Exhibition Road: Painters at the Royal College of Art*, Phaidon, 1988, p.20.
4. Bliss, D. P., ibid, p.19.
5. Harling, R., 'Edward Bawden', *Art and Technics*, 1950, p.14.
6. Bliss, D. P., ibid, p.24.
7. Gilmore, P., *Artists at Curwen*, Tate Gallery, 1977, p.45.
8. Bliss, D. P., ibid, p.33.
9. Hoyle, W., *To Sicily with Edward Bawden*, Previous Parrott Press, 1998, p.57.
10. Harling, R., ibid, p.17.

3. A PRESS AND A MURAL

Once college was over Bawden felt: 'Now I have passed the Caterpillar and Chrysalis and can come out into the sunshine. Now I can flutter my fancy from flower to flower.' He wrote to Bliss: 'Lord, how I long to work – to reveal Inspiration, to satisfy Restlessness, to delight in Industry, and above all to keep the foul fiend Ennui at bay.' From their bed-sits in Redcliffe Road, West Kensington ('The manure beds of genius' Bawden called them) the three friends began the quest for work.

In spring 1927 Paul Nash, always helpful to younger artists, had suggested to Bliss and Ravilious that they were ready to try the Bond Street Galleries. Ravilious was well received at the Redfern while the St George's Gallery's director liked Bliss' wood-engravings but asked if he would be interested in recruiting two other artists for an exhibition of watercolours in September-October of that year. Under this sudden pressure to produce a score or more works each, Bliss went off to paint in the Hebrides whilst Ravilious went first to Sussex before joining Bawden at his Braintree family home from where they both cycled around looking for suitable sites to paint where the self-conscious Bawden couldn't be disturbed by spectators, or seen by anyone who knew him. At this time he was using small sheets of unsuitable lettering paper, drawing in a sharp hard pencil and tinting the drawing with washes which the paper could not absorb. These early works appear naïve and he knew it, lamenting to Ravilious: 'Nature is always in a muddle and 'abhors a straight line' so what can I do but fail?' But slowly, by studying the looser but still 'starved' brushwork of Paul

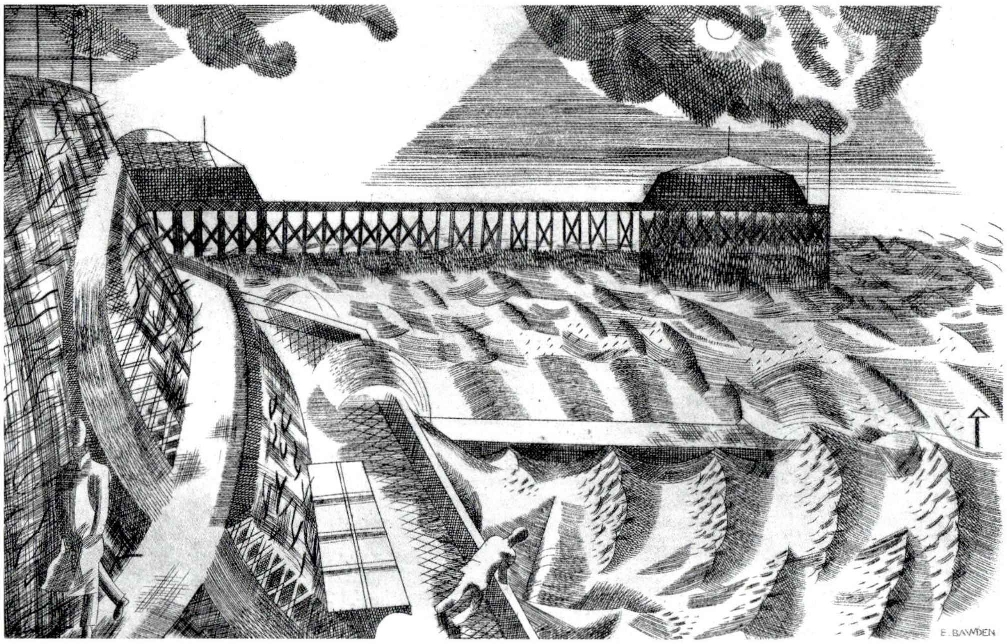

The Pier, 1927, copper engraving, 107 x 167 mm.

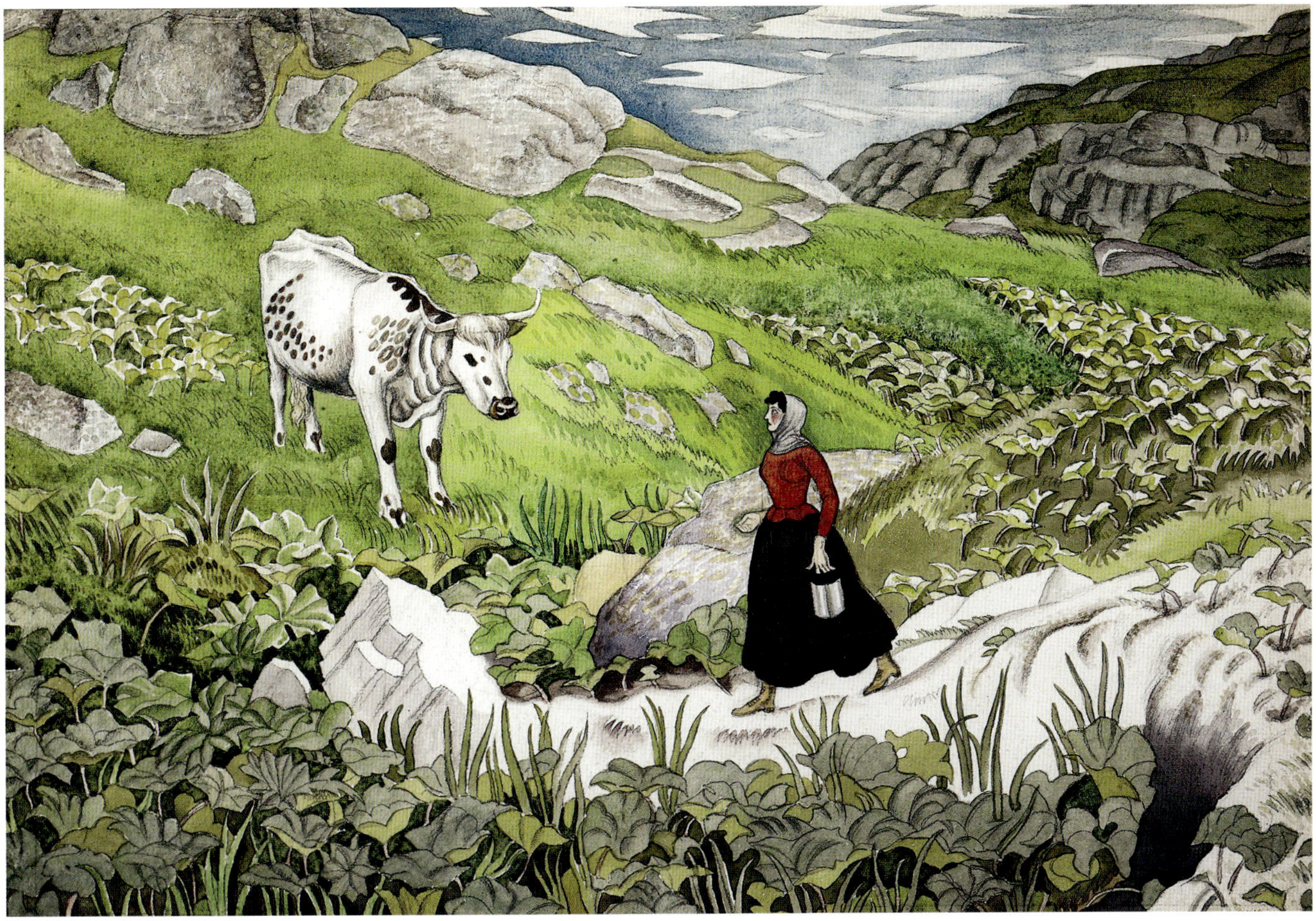

Douglas Percy Bliss, *Red Milkmaid*, 1927, watercolour, 350 x 510 mm.

Nash and seeing Ravilious' more adventurous approach his works would get bigger and bolder.

Bawden showed twenty-nine works in the St George's Gallery including, apart from his watercolours and six line-engravings, three illustrations of imaginary architecture, each priced at twenty guineas, twice the price of any work by his friends. All three drawings are brilliantly inventive, but to take just the one based on a reading of Francis Bacon, we can see an aerial view of a square garden in false perspective in which people are working, flirting, walking, playing and going about the seventeenth century occupations that Bawden must have researched in the Victoria and Albert Museum. The colours are flat, outlines clear, and the drawing stylised in a mock-medieval manner. Of course when the exhibition opened the critics ignored these startling works, but spotted how much all three artists owed to their ex-tutor Paul Nash and patronised their 'mild and mannered modernity'. *The Times* critic could only commend it to those readers 'not repelled by a certain cool detachment in the treatment of landscape'.

At the time Bawden's incursion into copper plate line-engravings of Redcliffe Road, Brighton Beach, Clacton, and Kew Gardens also drew little attention and they weren't editioned, even though Bliss in his spare time rôle as art critic later tried to alert the public to their merits: 'Recently he has taken up line-engraving for which the clear and intellectual character of his line was manifestly

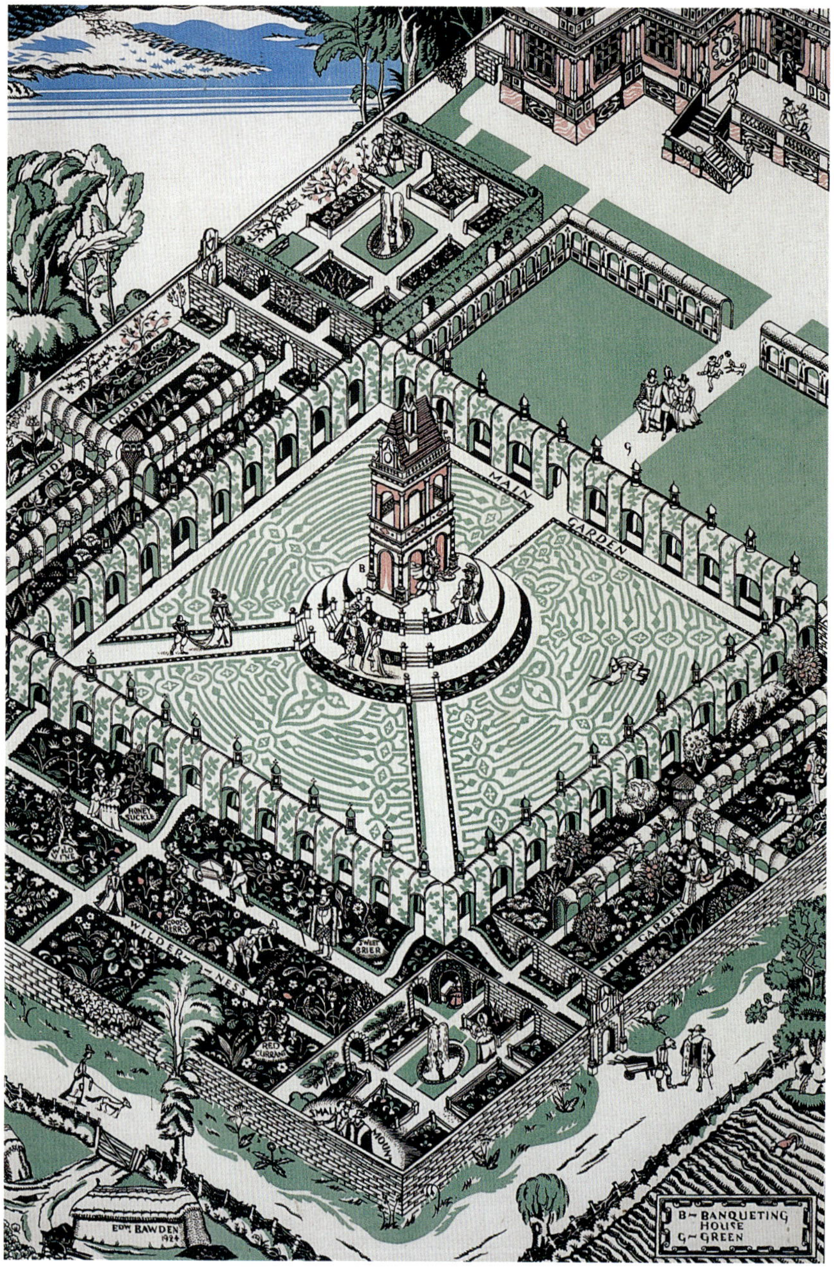

Francis Bacon's Garden, 1924, coloured drawing editioned as a print by the Curwen Press from a series of three unpublished book illustrations of 'Imaginary Architecture'.

adapted. He employs pure graver-work for his effects, and never relieves the austerity of his style by 'mixing' graver lines with etched or drypoint lines, as so many popular etchers now do. His work is technically akin to that of Laboureur in that he is economical on line, but is less sweet and witty in style, harder, more caustic at bottom than that of the Frenchman.'[1] Jean Emile Laboureur (1877-1943) was indeed somebody Bawden was enthusiastic about, having seen reproductions of his prints in such magazines as *Artwork*. These early plates were rediscovered in 1970 by Bawden's son Richard and new impressions taken then, and later, right up to the 1980s. More recently an oil painting of a similar beach scene from this period has surfaced.

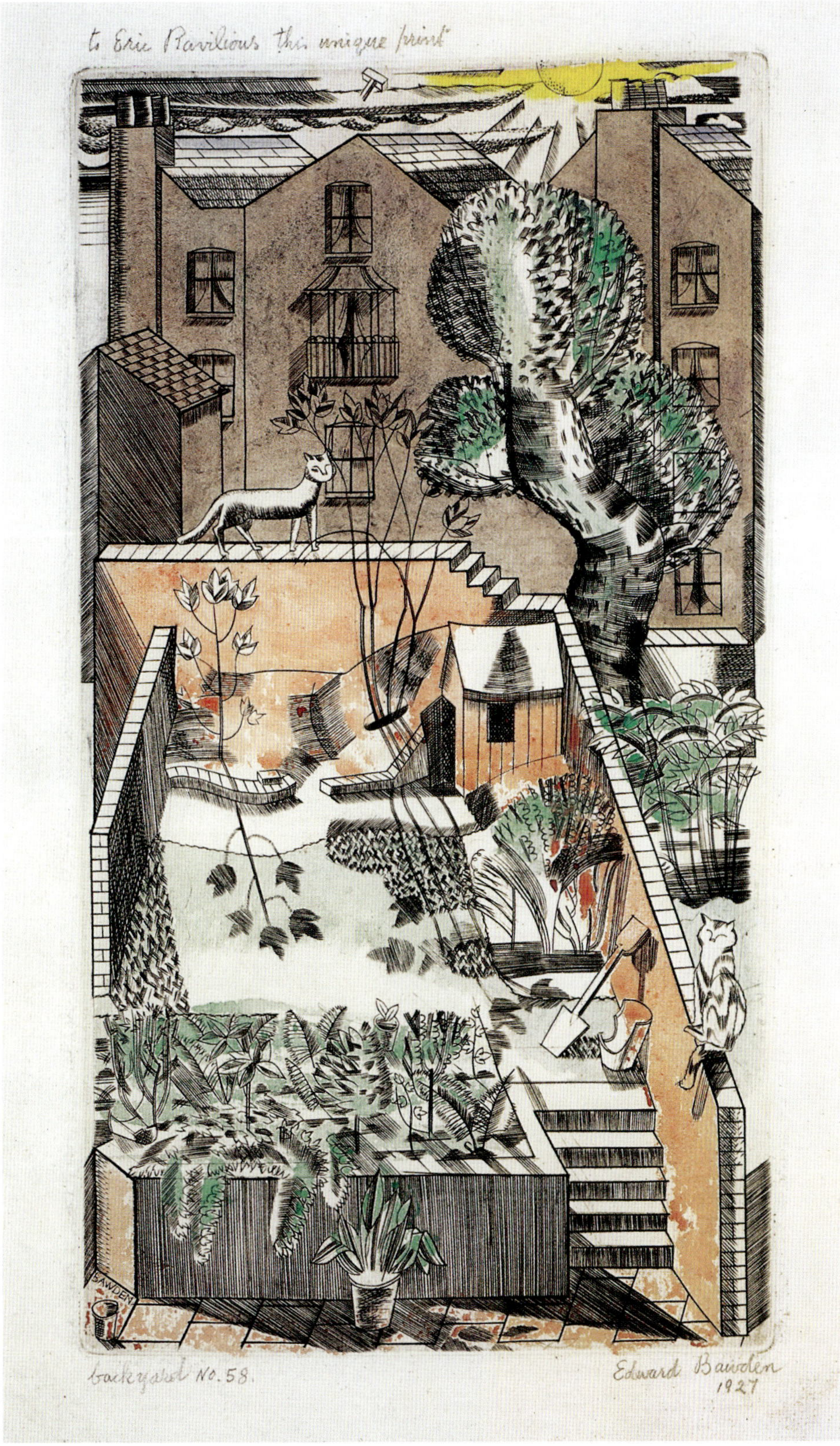

Copper engraving by Bawden, hand-coloured and inscribed 'To Eric Ravilious, this unique print. Back yard No 58. EB 1927'. 195 x 103 mm. This is the rear of the house in Redcliffe Road where the friends had lodgings.

In 1928 Bliss published something much more substantial than his occasional reviews: this was *A History of Wood-Engraving* published by J.M.Dent. It is still a readable, thoroughly researched and important book. He had begun work on it whilst still at college and it has some of the student's impudence about it in the way he takes his elders and betters to task. So, Eric Gill has no sense of humour and 'a cold, stark Neo-Byzantine style'; Gwen Raverat is 'lacking in real imaginative intensity'; and surprisingly, he prefers John Nash's engravings to those of Paul. 'John Nash's work is gentler and more reticent than that of his brother, and not tortured with the same dæmonic urge. He is more sensitive, more whimsical, more interested in natural objects for their own sakes.' Paul's work he finds too austere, formally preoccupied and lacking in humanity. He is also disrespectful to Derain and Dufy, but he is loyal to his friends: he reproduces Ravilious' *Church under a Hill* and we are told: 'he has already done some personal and felicitous work. His designs are exceptionally graceful and his engraving very neat.' Bliss even slips in a reference to someone who had never done a wood-engraving: 'Linoleum is often used, but seldom successfully, except in the wallpaper designs of Edward Bawden.'

The ever-generous Paul Nash took no offence and encouraged the trio in their contacts with the Curwen Press. Another RCA tutor, Harold Stabler, had initiated an introduction for Bawden to one of its directors, book designer and typographer Oliver Simon (1895-1956), who was only eight years older than Bawden himself, but he had seen more of the world having grown up in Lancashire, Yorkshire, Germany and Argentina (where his cotton

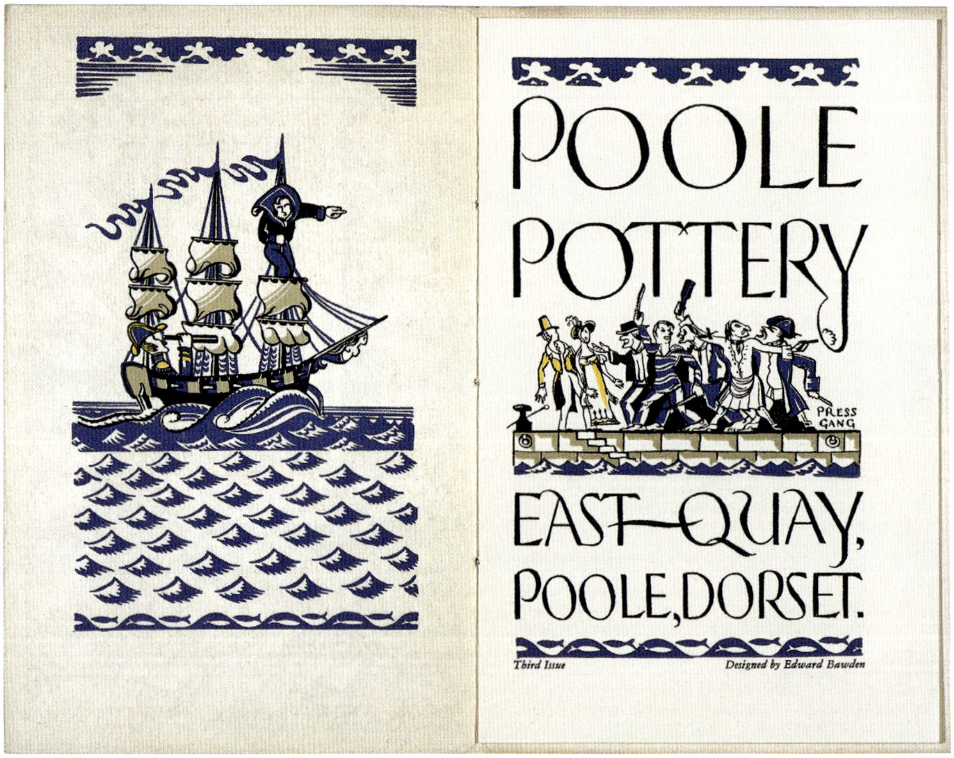

Title page from *Pottery Making at Poole,* 1925, one of Bawden's first commissions, 198 x 158 mm.
(Reproduced by permission of Cambridge University Library).
Right: Tile panel *c.*1930, adapted by Margaret Holder from the town plan in Bawden's *Pottery Making at Poole*, 1925 (Christie's Images).

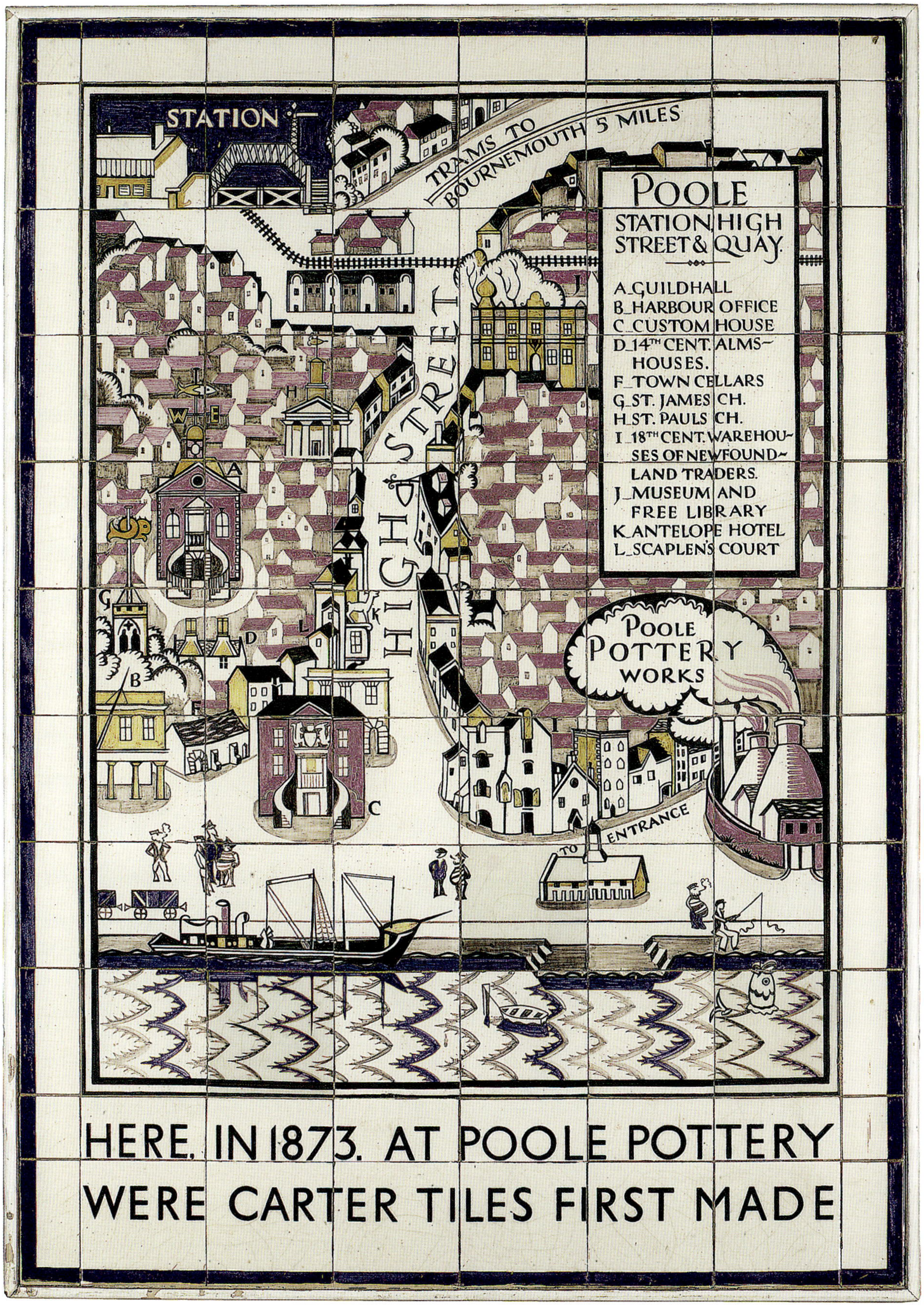
STATION
TRAMS TO BOURNEMOUTH 5 MILES
POOLE
STATION, HIGH STREET & QUAY.
A_GUILDHALL
B_HARBOUR OFFICE
C_CUSTOM HOUSE
D_14TH CENT. ALMS-HOUSES.
F_TOWN CELLARS
G_ST. JAMES CH.
H_ST. PAULS CH.
I_18TH CENT. WAREHOUSES OF NEWFOUNDLAND TRADERS.
J_MUSEUM AND FREE LIBRARY
K_ANTELOPE HOTEL
L_SCAPLEN'S COURT
HIGH STREET
POOLE POTTERY WORKS
TO ENTRANCE
HERE, IN 1873, AT POOLE POTTERY
WERE CARTER TILES FIRST MADE

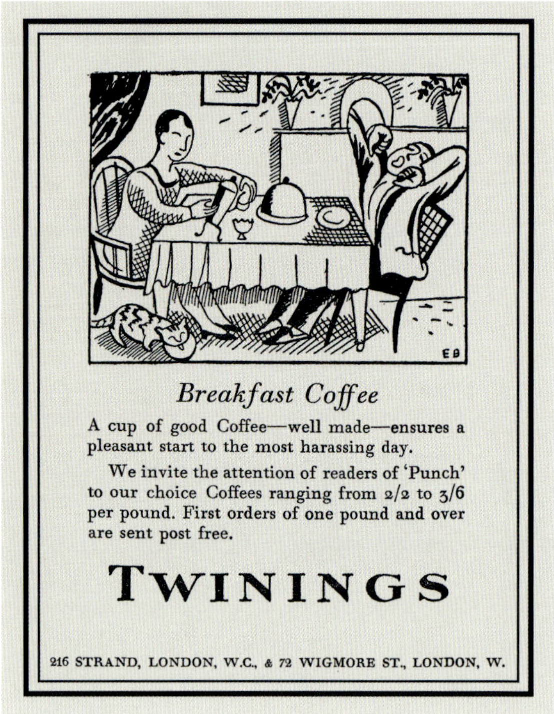

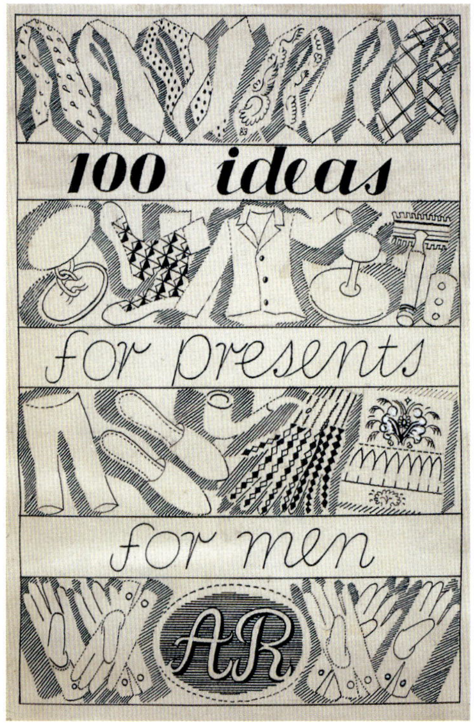

Above left: Advertisement for Twinings' Coffee, *c.*1928, 130 x 95 mm.
Above right: Design for Austin Reed, outfitters, *c.*1930, found in Eric Ravilious' scrapbook; by either Eric or Bawden, 163 x 108 mm.

merchant father had business connections) followed by service in World War One at Gallipoli, Egypt, and Palestine. As a youth he'd been inspired by William Morris' Kelmscott Press books, but by 1920 when he joined forces with the master printer and lithographer Harold Curwen in his family printing firm (founded 1863), Simon had rejected Morris' overly decorated and near-illegible style and dedicated himself to making the Curwen Press a home of clear elegant typography and modern illustration, no matter whether the job was a fine edition novel or a boot polish label. In recruiting artists to help him it was no handicap that his mother was sister to William Rothenstein and Albert Rutherston.

However, the door to this idealistic firm was almost closed on Bawden because of his crippling diffidence. Simon described his first meeting with the man who was to become their most frequent contributor: 'The year before he left the Royal College of Art in 1925, he visited me one day at Great Russell Street armed with an introduction. He laid his portfolio of drawings before me on my table and I examined them with great interest. When I had finished I looked up, prepared to make some appreciative comments, only to find that Bawden had already picked up his portfolio and was silently withdrawing, backwards from the room. Infected by his shyness, I opened the door for him and, still without a word, the visit was over. In spite of this inauspicious start, he accepted an invitation to do a drawing in colour which pleased our client and, from that time onwards, many commissions followed, not only for books but for a variety of jobbing work, advertisement settings and business printing.' [2]

The press was at Plaistow in East London and Bawden was soon a regular visitor: 'I went down to the press one day a week as a student, which I thought was thrilling and Harold Curwen, who looked a bit like a scoutmaster, loved explaining how things were done. So I got in among the litho sweats – the men who worked on the litho stones. I did a lot of little tiddley jobs for Curwen. He'd say, "Oh come down and we'll do a jam label" – but he'd spend the time explaining how this or that was done.' There Bawden

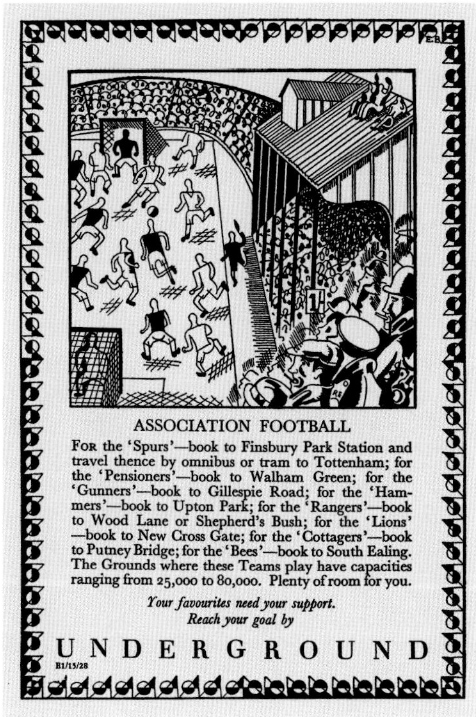

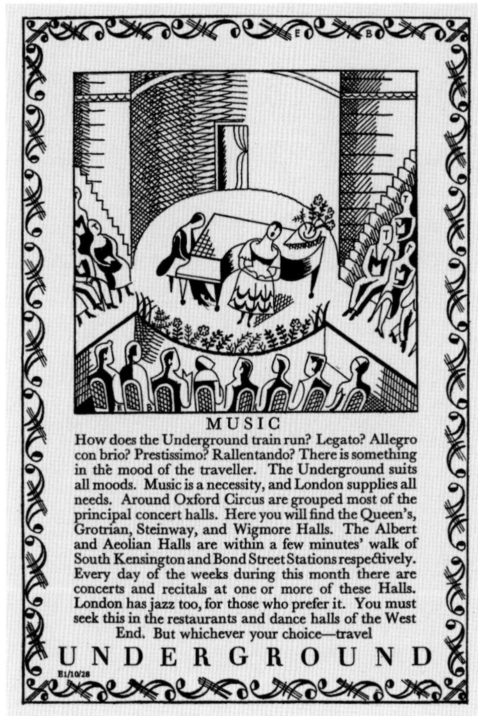

Two advertisements for London Underground, 1928, 20 x 13 cm.

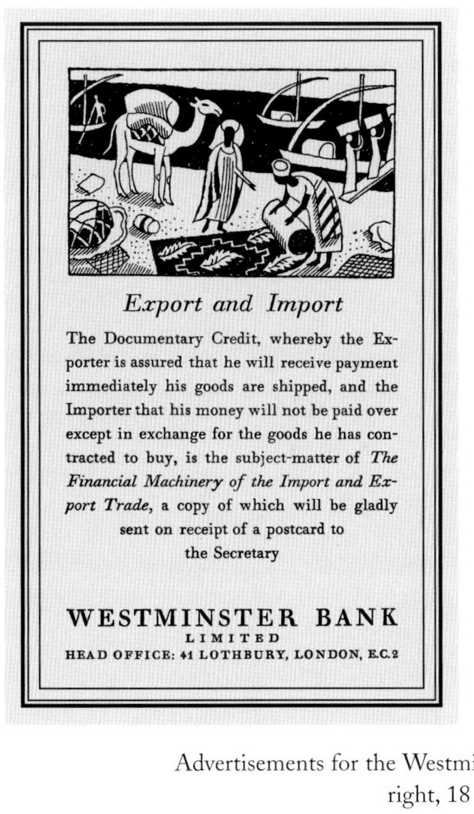

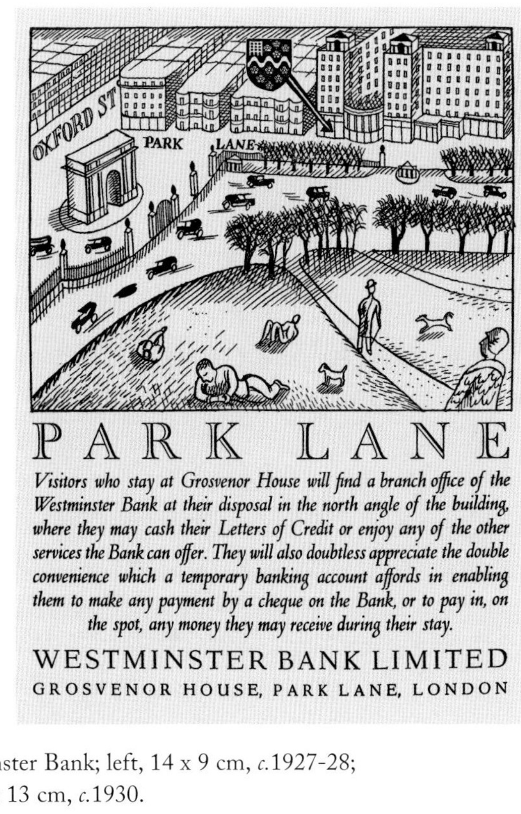

Advertisements for the Westminster Bank; left, 14 x 9 cm, *c.*1927-28; right, 18 x 13 cm, *c.*1930.

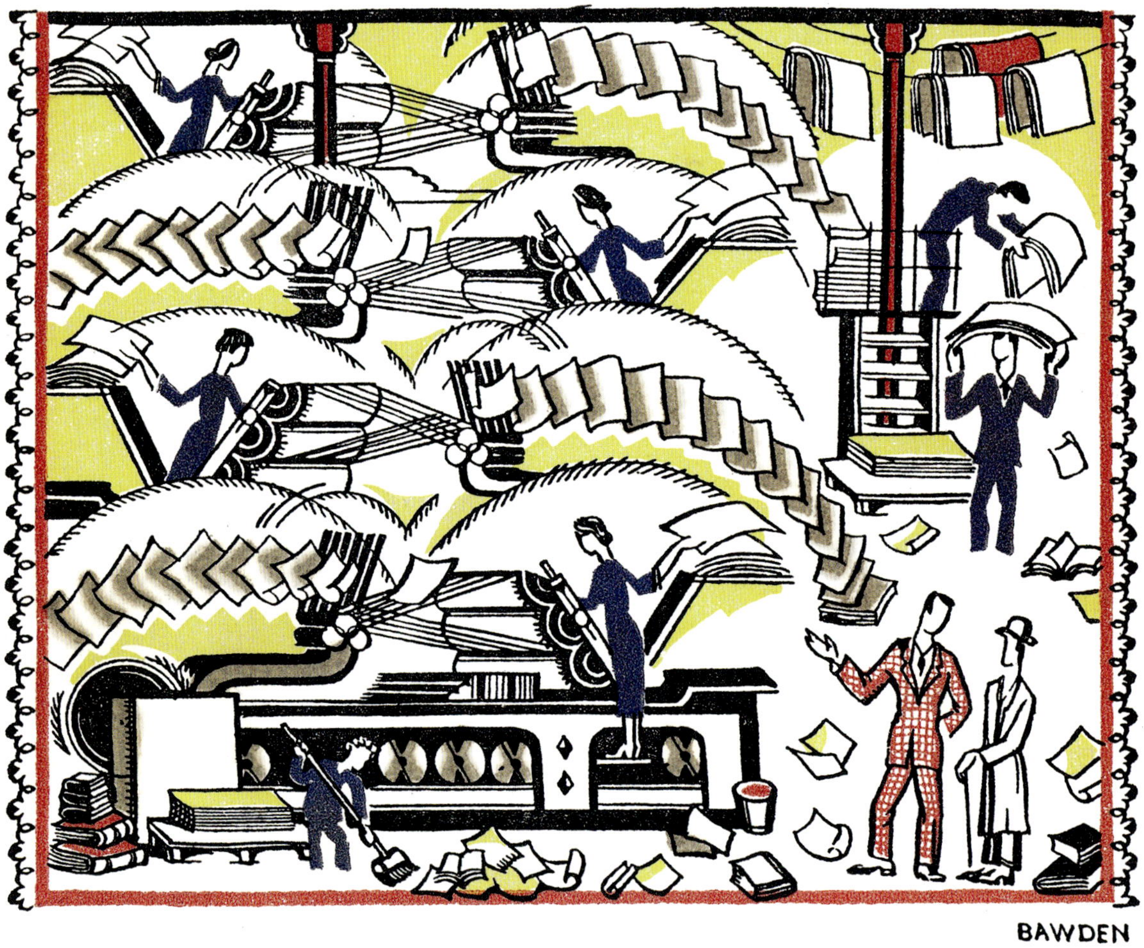

Illustrated portion of a Curwen Press calendar for 1925, showing the operation of the Press, 155 mm wide; one of Bawden's earliest commissions. (Reproduced by permission of Cambridge University Library).

observed how separations were made for each colour area in lithography, or how pen and ink was reproduced by line-block, and he learned to adjust his style accordingly. Later he would realise that this was 'the last great period of printing, when movable type was used, and interesting papers and the Monotype Corporation was bringing out new type faces based on old models. Nowadays it's all done by photolitho and the paper has to be shiny and looks like that terrible woman's dress material that doesn't crease.'[3] Towards the end of his career he sadly observed the breakdown of this centuries-old personal collaboration between artist and printer as photographic and mechanical processes took over. One such early commission, done while he was still a student, was an illustrated leaflet *Pottery Making at Poole* including an aerial view in line and three colours full of jokey incident and architectural detail, which Douglas Percy Bliss thought 'a delightful little job perfectly fitted for the purpose, and perhaps for the first time exhibiting to the public the playfulness of a style which was soon to become known and imitated in every art school and commercial studio in the land.'[4] It is clearly related to his imaginary architecture drawings and for a twenty-two year old it was astonishingly confident. For time-consuming but small tasks like this Bawden was paid between two and five guineas.

Bawden was not confining himself to works on paper. On 22nd December 1926 he wrote one of his droll letters to Bliss, who was home in Edinburgh for Christmas: 'Of Bawden I have seen far too much. He is I imagine one of the worst bores in Redcliffe Road and belongs to that

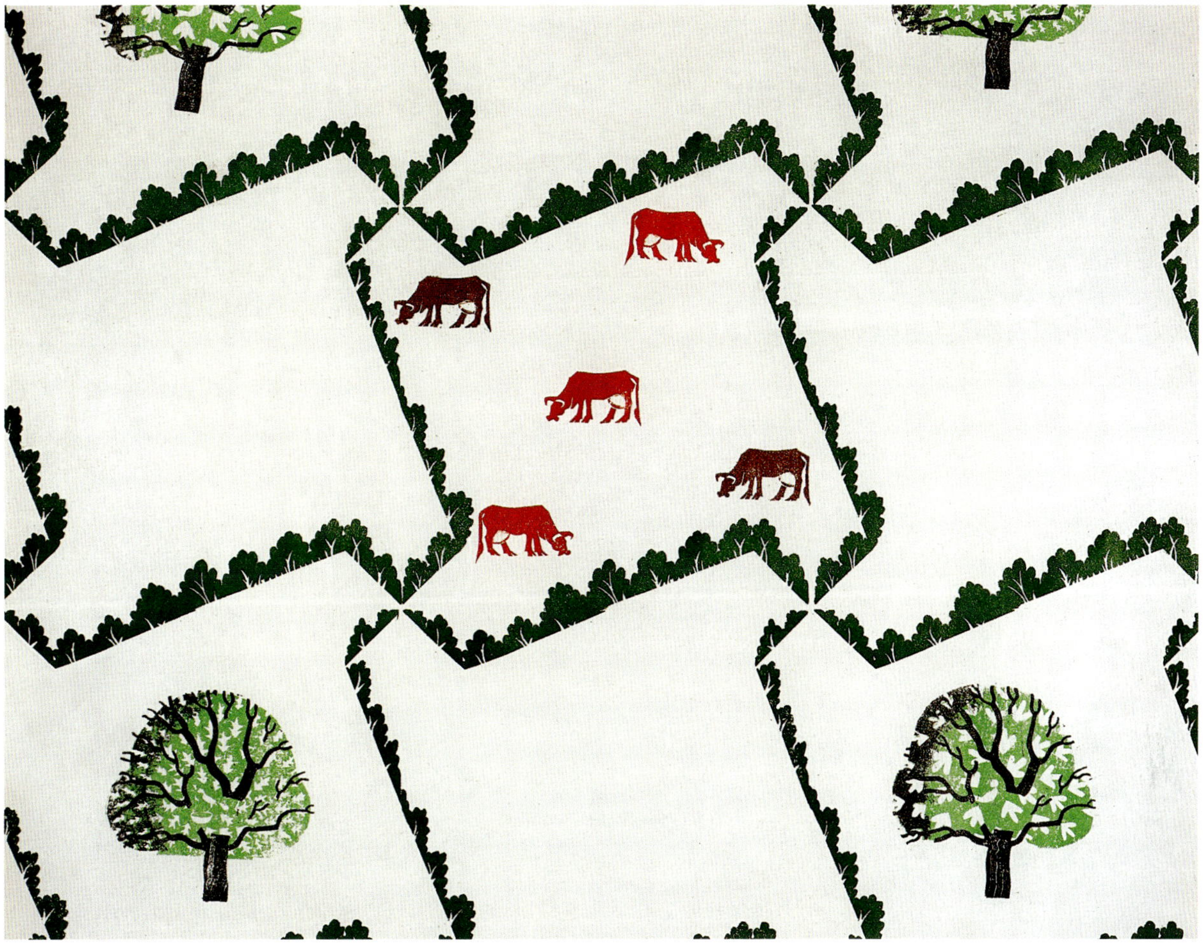

Wallpaper designed by Bawden: *Tree and Cow*, 1927 (Fry Art Gallery).

vicious section of those who move continually round themselves. From his prattle I gather that he has been the success at Brook Street during the present exhibition of Applied Art and that the Underground have commissioned him to make a series of Press drawings on the lines of those he did for the Westminster Bank. Curwen is in the business as well for the typography and printing. Bawden tells me that some designs for painted furniture which he did for someone or other have been accepted with no end of cheering. Of course you can't believe the fellow much, he is so dashed immodest and conceited. Anyway the lady seems to have told him they were charming and just the thing she wanted, and would he go along to Heals' and help to choose the stuff etc, etc. Did you ever hear the likes of it?'[5]

Oliver Simon helped to continue the theoretical and practical education of young graphic artists like Bawden, Bliss and Ravilious by founding, with Stanley Morison (another significant figure in the revival of type and book design) *The Fleuron* magazine in 1923. The three were also readers (in the RCA library or browsing in Zwemmer's bookshop in Tottenham Court Road) of *Signature, Imprint, Typography*, *The Woodcut*, and *Studio* magazines. Later, in the thirties, Simon produced the Curwen Press *News-Letter* for the trade and employed Bawden to do the covers. Because of their growing reputations Bawden and Ravilious were invited to become members of the Double Crown Club, a collective of typographers, artists, printers and publishers dedicated to improving specialist book production and to having

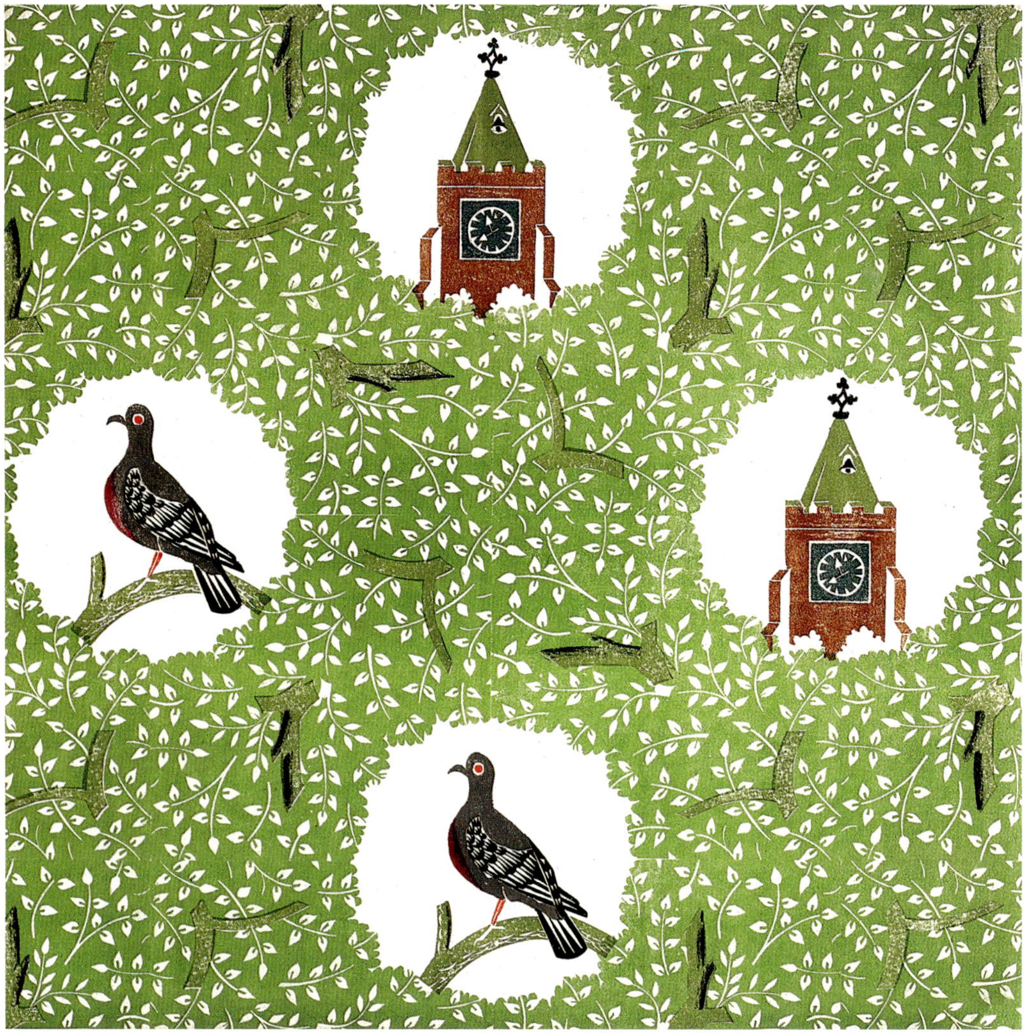

Wallpaper designed by Bawden: *Woodpigeon* (also known as *Church and Dove,* or *Pigeon and Clocktower*), 1927 (Fry Art Gallery).

splendidly boozy eight-course dinners. Bawden designed two witty menu cards for them but soon resigned on the grounds that he had a lamentable ignorance of fine wines. In 1935 Ravilious also designed a menu and even played for the Club at cricket against a Great Bardfield village eleven. Bliss fared less well with Simon, which he claimed was because he had protested about the late payment of his own and Bawden's fees.

Ever on the lookout for new technical challenges, Bawden turned his hand to linocutting. Linoleum, a mixture of cork and linseed oil on a canvas backing, had been used as a cheap floor covering since the 1860s and the German Expressionists had seen its possibilities for black and white relief prints earlier in the twentieth century. Apart from a few examples nothing much was made of it in England until Claude Flight (1881-1955) began to exploit it in the 1920s, using one block per colour to build up prints expressing dynamism and speed in the Italian Futurist manner. Flight saw the medium as democratic because it was cheap, required no specialist tools or press, had no inhibiting Fine

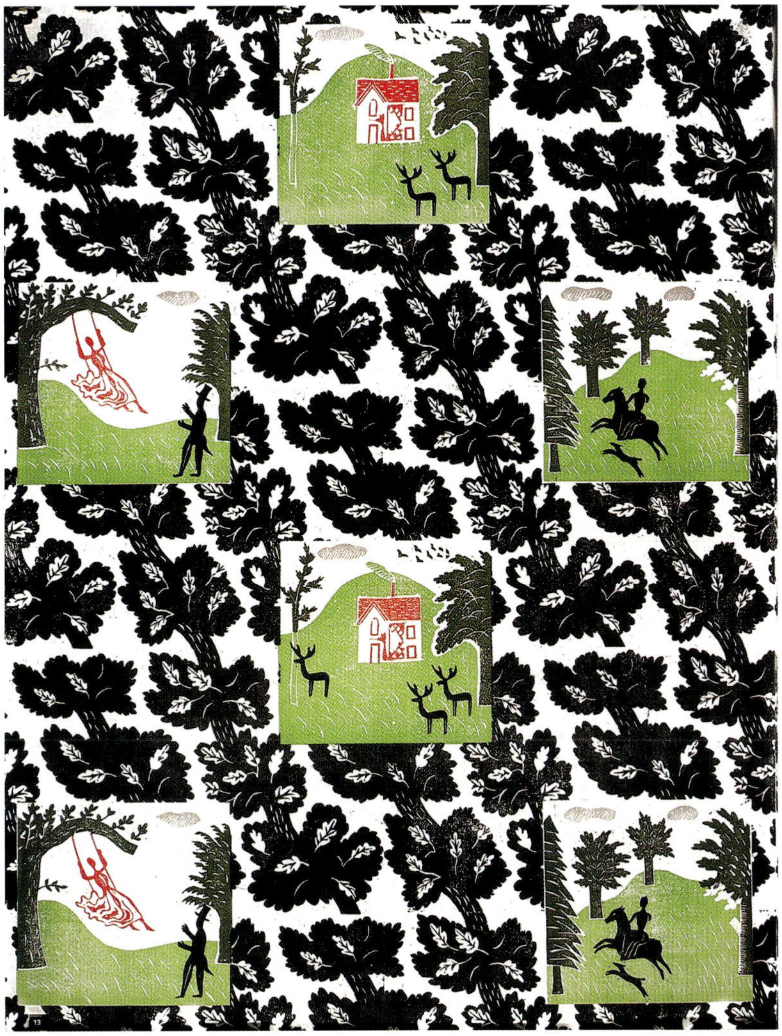

Bawden's wallpaper design *Knole Park*, 1929 (Fry Art Gallery).

Art tradition behind it, and its lack of nuance in colour and line prevented complicated detail and prettification.

From 1926 Bawden tried using repeated linocuts for wallpaper design in this era before plain walls became fashionable, one of his first efforts being several red cows surrounded by a green hedge. He had no modernist pretensions in this, having been inspired by seeing William Morris' 'Daisy' pattern at the Wembley exhibition of 1923, and Claude Flight would have found his designs both frivolous and pretty. In his bedsitter ('being unsociable I had to occupy myself somehow in the evenings') he cut lino blocks with a penknife, stippled them with oil paint and pressed them with his feet onto lining paper on the floor, using repeated prints to make nine patterns in all, the most elaborate being *Pigeon and Clocktower* in seven colours. *Knole Park* had heavy foliage squares alternating with genteel pastimes in five colours and *Sahara* had a pattern of sand dunes and a tiny four-camel caravan, which would turn out to be curiously prophetic of how the artist would spend the war years.

As he persisted he found better ways to do things: so after drawing the design in a soft pencil on thin paper it could be laid face down on a whitened sheet of lino and the design transferred by rubbing with a spoon. Cutting with a Japanese knife then began from the middle towards the edges, the knife becoming a drawing instrument as the hand became more skilled. Compared to cutting end-grain boxwood for wood-engraving, warmed lino sliced like butter. The cut lino was then inked on its raised surface and placed, face down, on a sheet of paper on a drawing board and printed by standing on it.

Curwen then transformed these amateurish lino prints into lithographs for mass production. Nash introduced Bawden to Elspeth Little and her 'Modern Textiles' shop in Beauchamp Place for a sales outlet, but his royalties over six years and sales of 507 sheets came to a miserly £2. 0s. 10d. In 1933 Curwen lithographed five more of his lino wallpaper designs, this time of abstracted stripy patterns which were popular, though at £5 on account for each they were not going to make Bawden rich.

Oliver Simon asked his friend Paul Nash for vignettes, covers, and patterned papers which were always in demand for use as wrappers or endpapers. Nash, Bawden, Ravilious, Enid Marx (another Nash protégé from the RCA) and Albert Rutherston all designed patterned papers for machine reproduction by Curwen, and other artists employed for tasks large or small at various dates were Lovat Fraser, Nash's brother John, Barnett Freedman, McKnight Kauffer, Edward Ardizzone, Graham Sutherland, and many more. Bawden was now mixing with his peers at Curwen and rapidly earning respect within the trade.

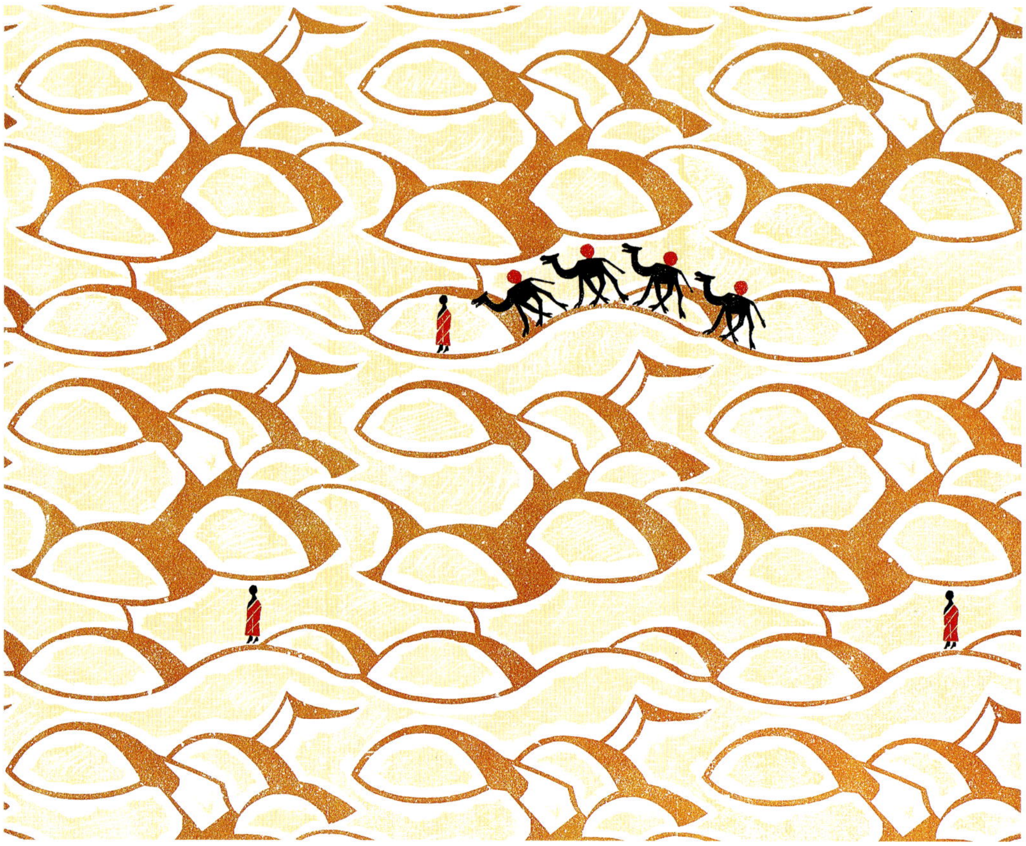

Bawden's wallpaper design *Sahara*, 1928 (Fry Art Gallery).

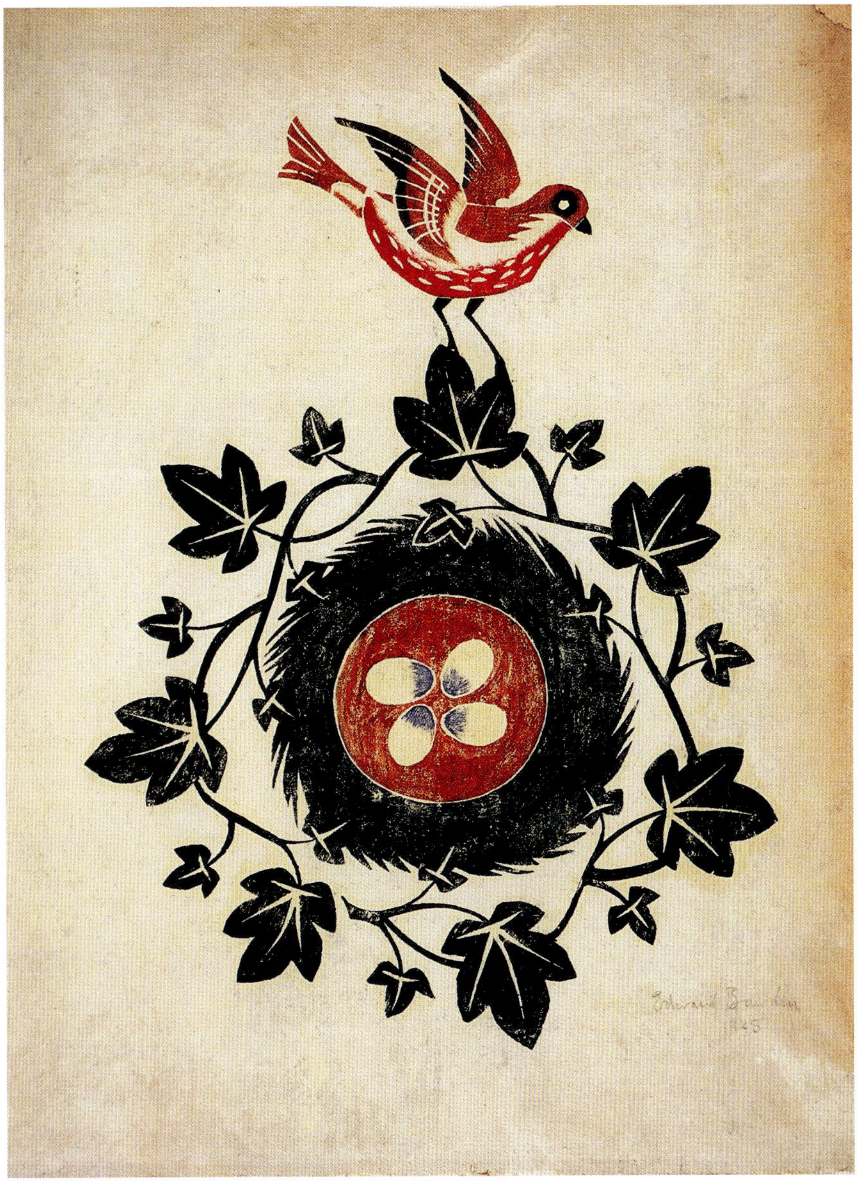

Bird's Nest pattern, 1925, 320 x 235 mm.

Then, in 1928, Bawden and Ravilious were offered a joint commission which established their reputations with a wider public. It happened because William Rothenstein went along to the opening ceremony for the Rex Whistler mural in the restaurant of the Tate Gallery. Whistler had trained under Professor Tonks at the rival and the then more prestigious Slade School, and Rothenstein wanted the same kind of publicity for his own RCA graduates. This was not just pique: Rothenstein sincerely believed that all students should be involved in making accessible public art and he helped organise murals for St Stephen's Hall, India House, County Hall, and employment bureaux in the docklands. Rothenstein persuaded Lord Duveen to fund three newly graduated RCA students, Bawden, Ravilious, and Charles Mahoney ('we were the bright boys' said Bawden), as he had done Whistler. They

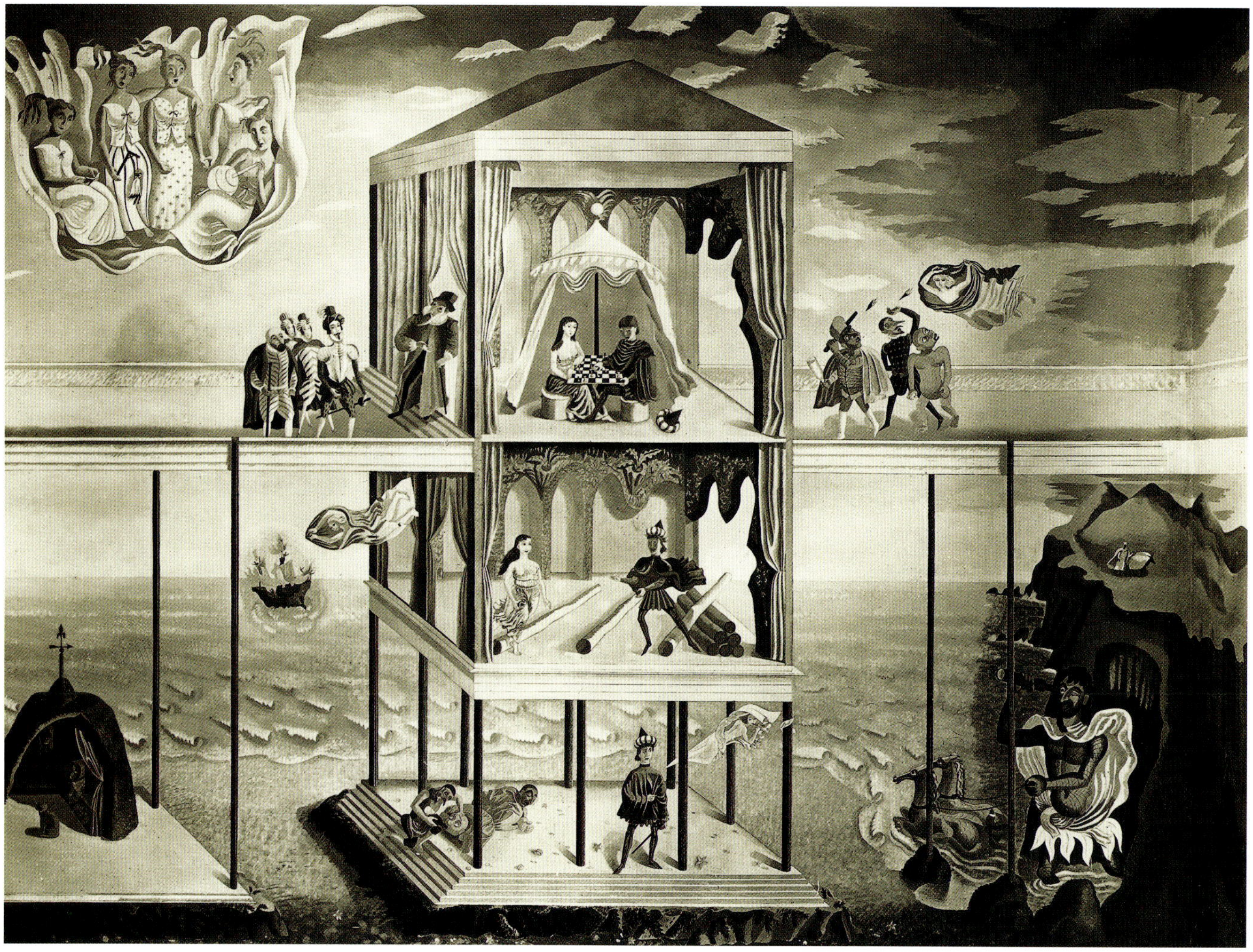

Part of Bawden's finished work at Morley College.

were to provide murals for the refectory and stage of Morley Working Men's College on Westminster Bridge Road, Lambeth. There would be no fee but materials were free (on the advice of Tristram they used oils mixed with beeswax and thinned with turpentine) and each received a pound a day for the whole of the two years the project lasted. Ravilious took two walls badly interrupted by doors and Bawden had one continuous wall of the refectory and, since there was no English mural tradition to draw upon, they recalled what they had seen on their Italian scholarship tours and what they knew of medieval works. Their first suggested subject was to be 'London', but Rothenstein didn't like their preliminary sketches and instead set them loose on 'Fantasy,' with the hint that drama might be an appropriate theme since the college had links with the Old Vic Theatre.

Neither Bawden nor Ravilious had previously seen figure painting as a primary concern, but now they had to overcome that and people the walls with scores of characters in fantastic costumes and active poses. Bawden wrote: 'The impact of early Florentine and Sienese work was terrific. I'd been a bit further south to Pompeii, and the structure of the murals – little pillars with platforms and boxes and so on – was derived from what I'd seen

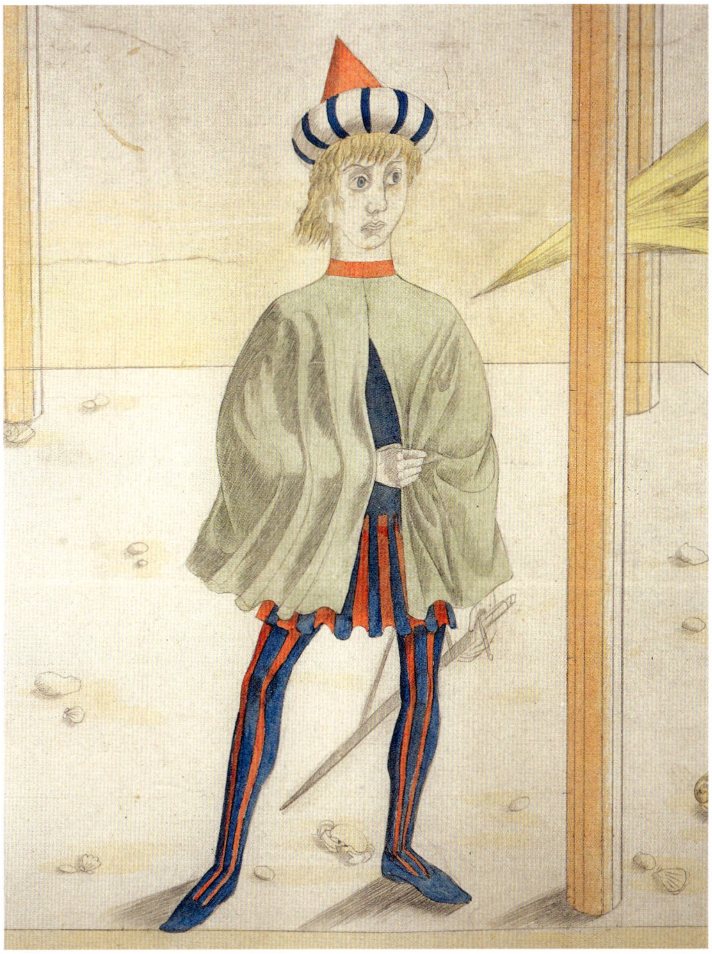

Preliminary designs by Bawden for the Morley College Murals, *c.*1928. These were placed in his garden well for safekeeping at the onset of war.

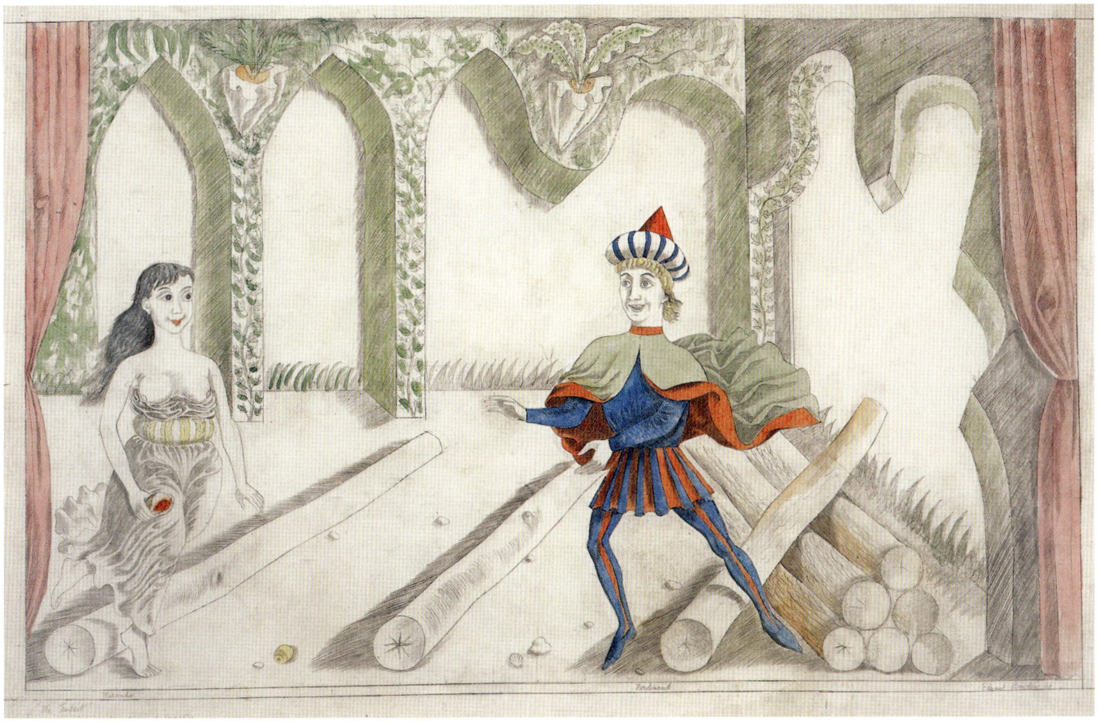

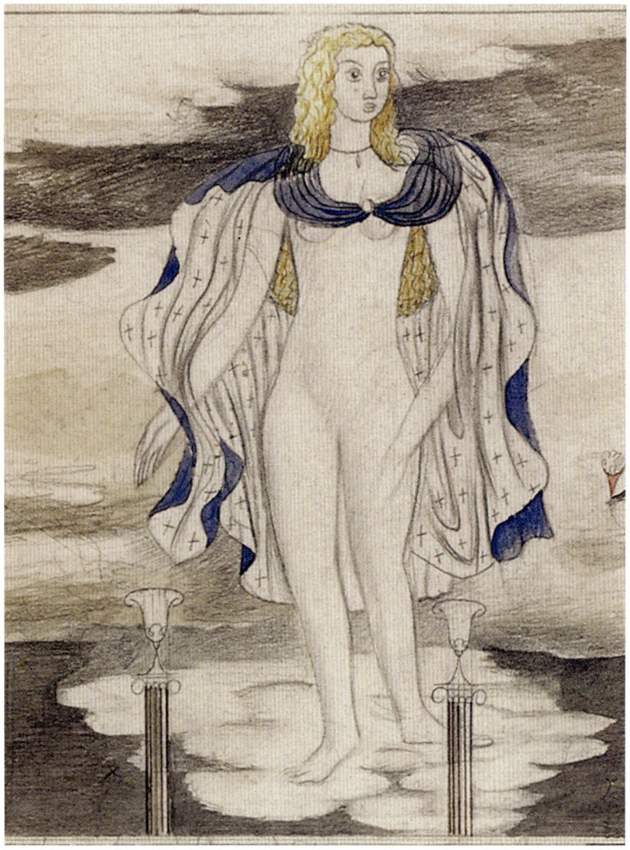

Ravilious' Venus, from one of his preliminary designs.
Opposite: London Underground poster. Printed April-May 1930 by Waterlow & Sons, 100 x 63 cm.

there.' The subject matter drew on both men's reading, probably with some input from Bliss: 'Elizabethan plays, Shakespeare, Olympian Gods and Goddesses, Punch and Judy, Miracle Plays and a doll's house – Gosh! What a riot it was', Bawden recalled. Mythological figures floated through the air, Elizabethans postured against a river backdrop whilst others were in modern dress, playing the piano or carrying a bucket of coal. Fortunately diners in the refectory were provided with a written key to all the characters. Since Ravilious had had some mural training at college he did the cartoons and Bawden confessed to Bliss: 'I think the Boy's drawings are wonderful and I don't know how a clumsy clodhopper like myself is going to do anything like 'em'. In the event their styles blended perfectly and are almost indistinguishable.

Bawden was particularly impressed by Ravilious' naked Venus, as he told Bliss: 'Venus is a fine upstanding lady of three-and-twenty, with long but thick and serviceable legs. Her thighs and torso are beyond reproach and are all a lover could desire. Her little twiddly breasts are high up in the Empire style . . . behind her blows out a blue cloak conveniently arranged so as to expose her nudity. I confess I received a slight shock upon meeting this beauty's stare, but it will be nothing to what honest work-a-day folk will experience.' Friends thought that some of the female figures, including the Venus, bore a distinct resemblance to Tirzah Garwood, one of Ravilious' young students at Eastbourne College of Art, where from 1926 he had been teaching wood-engraving part-time. Not one of Bawden's own Three Graces which he 'painted deliberately to resemble a type of Jewish beauty' was a match for Venus.

Bawden came to think of it as 'a young man's folly', but once the mural had been unveiled by Prime Minister Stanley Baldwin in 1930 it received widespread praise as 'amusing', then a term of approval, and even Rex Whistler found it 'quite enchanting'. Bliss, who was by now supplementing his income as London Art Critic for *The Scotsman*, wrote a review of it, concluding 'The decoration is not free in parts from freakishness and even affectation and its irrelevancies may seem to a few hardly justifiable, but there is no question that a more highly spiced and daintily dished entertainment has seldom been afforded upon any walls, far less those of a college for working men and women.'[6] Poor Charles Mahoney's contribution in another room was largely overshadowed, but he later returned to the RCA as a specialist teacher of mural painting. Today we know the work only from photographs as the whole mural was lost (along with fifty-seven people) when the college was bombed in 1940. In 1958 Bawden replaced it with another mural based on the *Canterbury Tales*.

In their breaks from painting the mural Ravilious and Bawden would call in to see Bliss and Phyllis in nearby Lambeth. Bliss was now illustrating with wood-

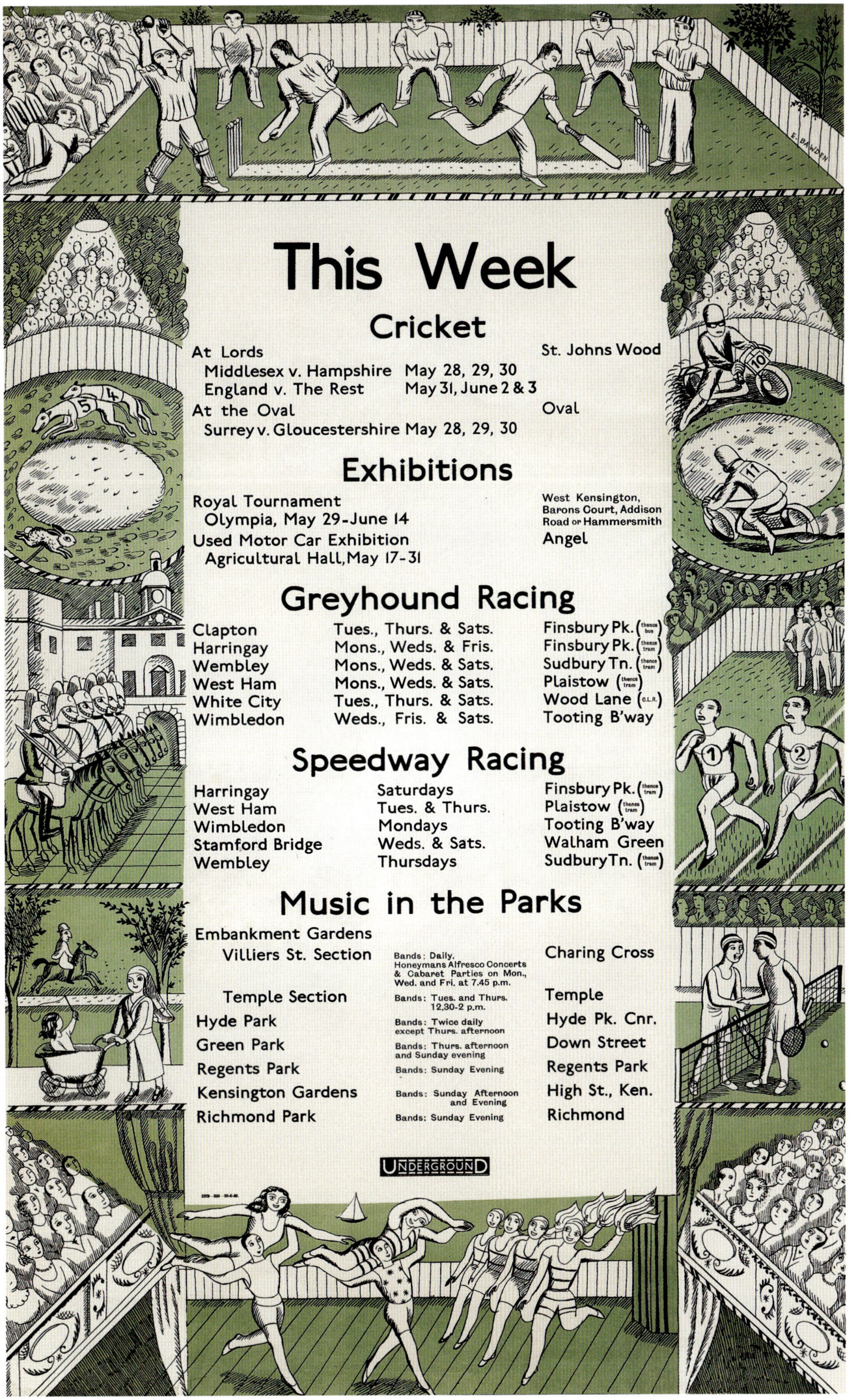

E. BAWDEN
This Week
Cricket
At Lords
St. Johns Wood
Middlesex v. Hampshire May 28, 29, 30
England v. The Rest May 31, June 2 & 3
At the Oval
Oval
Surrey v. Gloucestershire May 28, 29, 30
Exhibitions
Royal Tournament
Olympia, May 29-June 14
West Kensington, Barons Court, Addison Road or Hammersmith
Used Motor Car Exhibition
Agricultural Hall, May 17-31
Angel
Greyhound Racing
Clapton Tues., Thurs. & Sats. Finsbury Pk. (thence bus)
Harringay Mons., Weds. & Fris. Finsbury Pk. (thence tram)
Wembley Mons., Weds. & Sats. Sudbury Tn. (thence tram)
West Ham Mons., Weds. & Sats. Plaistow (thence tram)
White City Tues., Thurs. & Sats. Wood Lane (C.L.R.)
Wimbledon Weds., Fris. & Sats. Tooting B'way
Speedway Racing
Harringay Saturdays Finsbury Pk. (thence tram)
West Ham Tues. & Thurs. Plaistow (thence tram)
Wimbledon Mondays Tooting B'way
Stamford Bridge Weds. & Sats. Walham Green
Wembley Thursdays Sudbury Tn. (thence tram)
Music in the Parks
Embankment Gardens
Villiers St. Section
Bands: Daily. Honeymans Alfresco Concerts & Cabaret Parties on Mon., Wed. and Fri. at 7.45 p.m.
Charing Cross
Temple Section
Bands: Tues. and Thurs. 12.30-2 p.m.
Temple
Hyde Park
Bands: Twice daily except Thurs. afternoon
Hyde Pk. Cnr.
Green Park
Bands: Thurs. afternoon and Sunday evening
Down Street
Regents Park
Bands: Sunday Evening
Regents Park
Kensington Gardens
Bands: Sunday Afternoon and Evening
High St., Ken.
Richmond Park
Bands: Sunday Evening
Richmond
UNDERGROUND

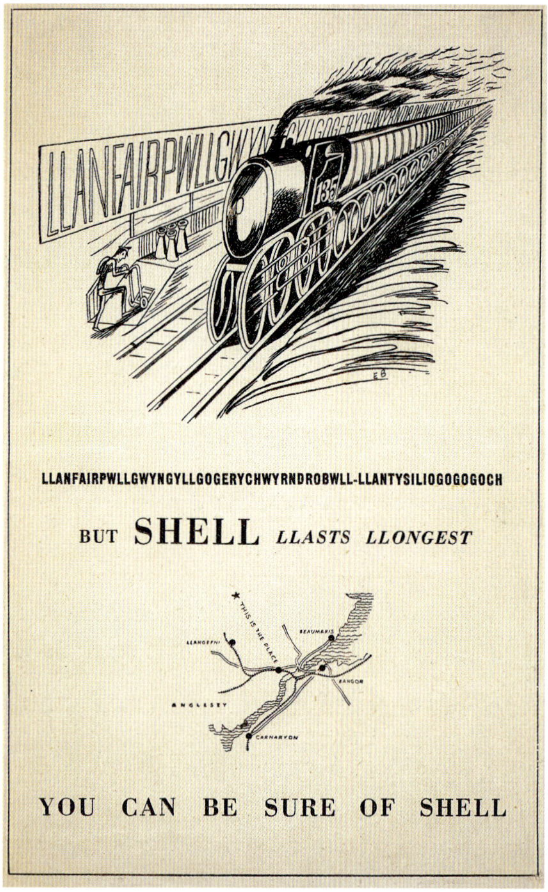

Advertisement for Shell, *c.*1932, 30 x 17 cm.

Original pen and ink design for Shell, dated 1936, 165 mm wide. *Thames Reaches but Shell goes furthest.*

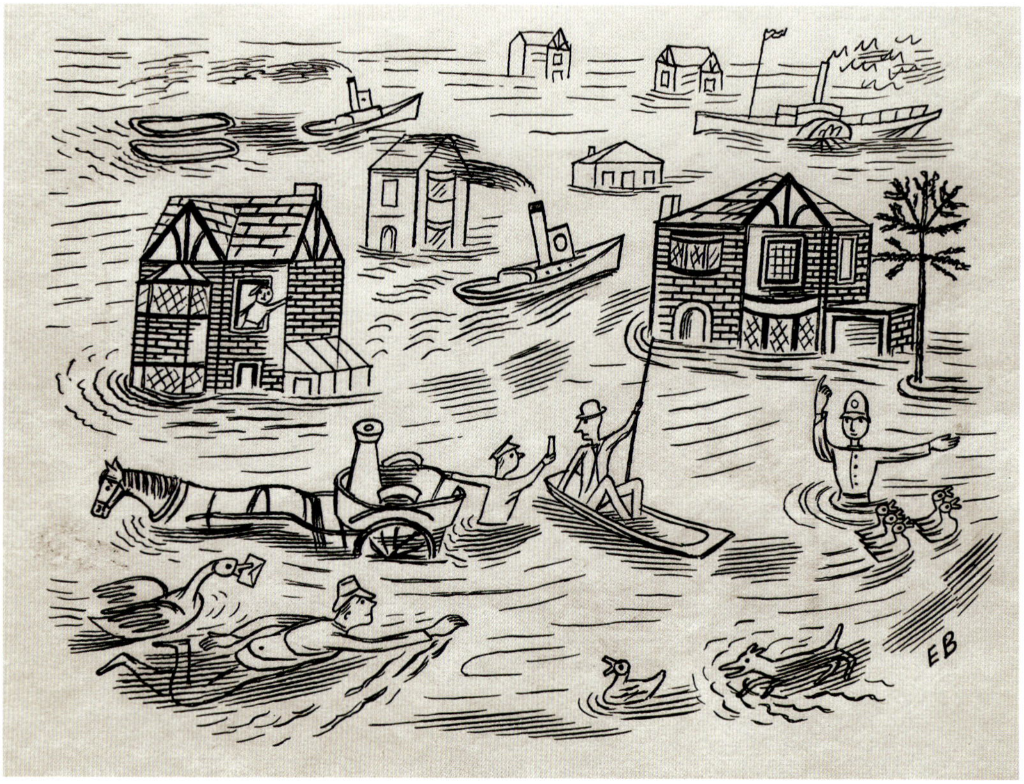

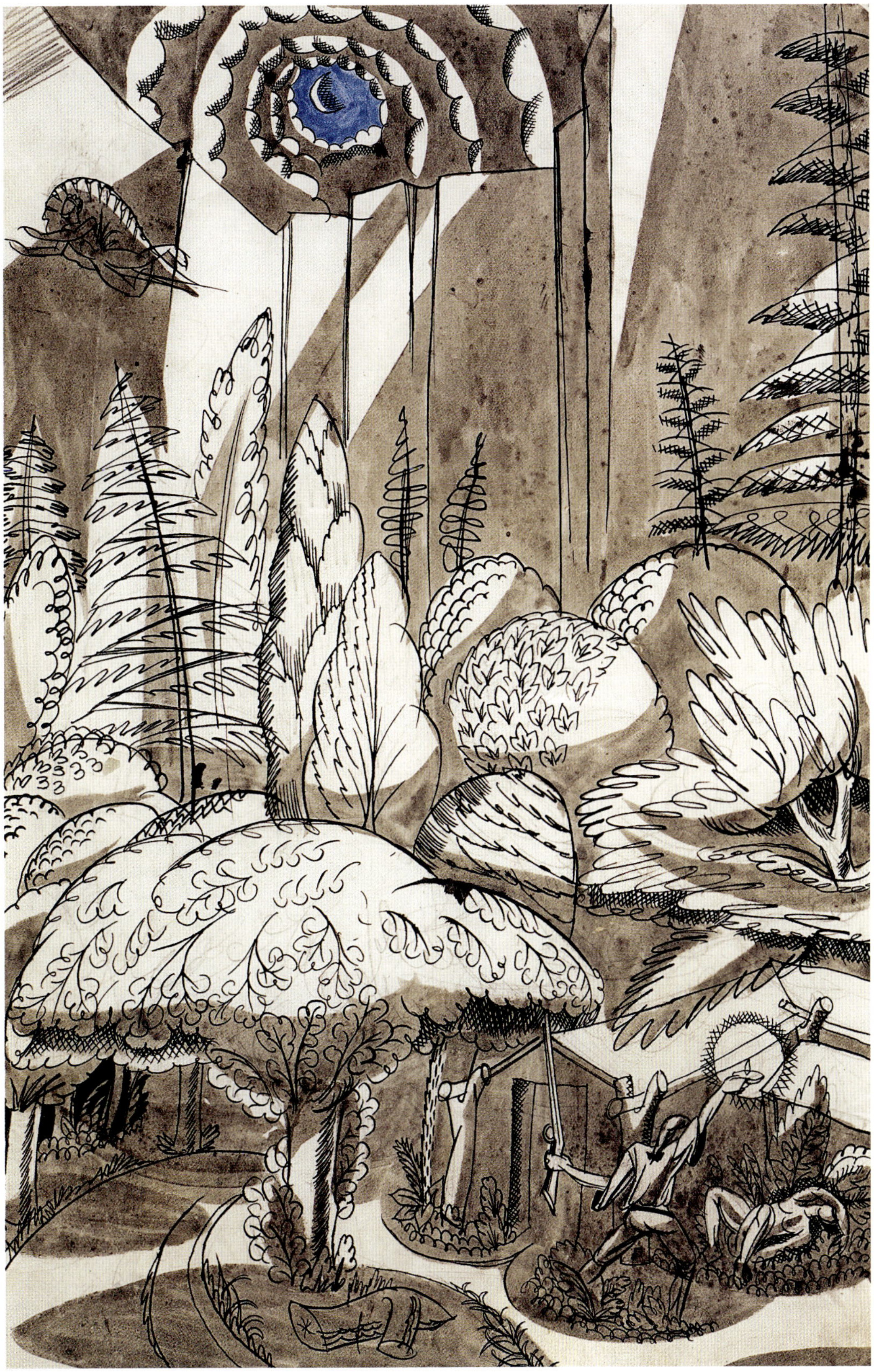

Preliminary sketch for Peter Wilkins: 'Mr Wilkins meets his future wife', 1928,
325 x 205 mm.

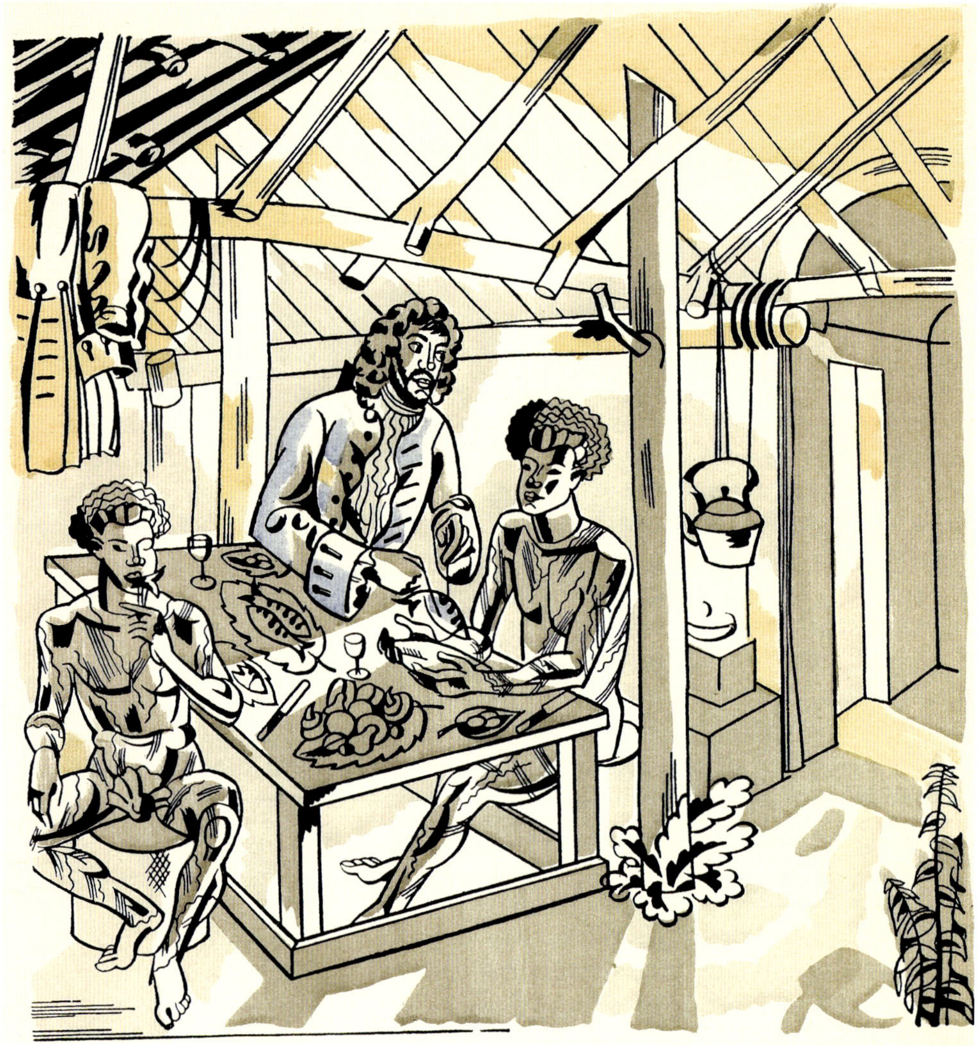

Illustration from Bawden's first illustrated book, *The Life and Adventures of Peter Wilkins*, 1928: 'Quangrollart and Rosig have supper with Wilkins', 208 x 223 mm (Manchester Metropolitan University Library). Opposite: preliminary sketch for the same illustration.

engravings *The History of Rasselas* by Dr Johnson for J.M.Dent, and soon after *The Spanish Lady* and *Two Other Stories from Cervantes*, in line and stencilled colour, was printed by Curwen for Oxford University Press. He generously puffed the work of Ravilious in *Artwork* magazine, defending his 'clean, graceful and highly stylised watercolours' against the charge of facility. 'Ravilious,' he claims, 'has no delusions about his ability. He has always felt what it was in him to do and sets himself tasks no greater than his power of accomplishment. He has always known that the light, the elegant, the graceful were his province; that the grand, the sublime, the woodenly serious most emphatically were not his province. His sense of humour adds charm to his creations and keeps him from the pitfalls of the pompous and altisonant.'[7] Perhaps because he was busy and newly married he had neglected Bawden, because at Christmas 1928 Bawden wrote one of his macabre letters to Bliss in an envelope decorated with skulls: 'Shall we carry the corpse of our friendship and lay it to rest? The fee is moderate. At present it lies in the mortuary where it has lain these many months. A trance or death?' It must have been a trance because the friendship revived.

The posters Bawden had designed for Frank Pick whilst still a student were seen only on the London Underground, but the 1932 Shell Mex campaign for Jack Beddington (1893-1959), the dynamic publicity manager for the petroleum company, was conducted in the national press and made Bawden's style widely known. Each of the thirty petrol advertisements Bawden designed had a stereotyped caricature of a town and beneath in a suitable typeface the campaign slogan. So under pottery kilns and barges was *Stoke-on-Trent but Shell on the Road*, and under a busy railway junction *Ashby-de-la-Zouch but Shell sur la route*. Others read *Stonehenge Wilts but Shell goes on for ever*; *Chorlton-cum-Hardy, Winter Shell comes Monday*; *Gerrard's Cross but Shell's pleasing*; *Wormwood Scrubs but Shell sweeps the board*. This very English kind of punning daftness was matched by Bawden's little beetle-like men swarming over his toy-town landscapes. He himself did not own a car and never learned to drive, but he certainly helped the Shell company target the road haulage and transport companies and those affluent and middle income groups who, by 1937, were registering 300,000 new cars each year.

It was in Beddington's office that Bawden first ran into the poet John Betjeman with whom he shared a quirky humour, a taste for Victoriana and that love of English church architecture which made Betjeman such an ideal editor of the Shell Guides to the English counties. Betjeman had also coined many of the Shell slogans Bawden illustrated.[8] On their first encounter Bawden said Betjeman 'danced about and was very amusing. He showed us how people prayed in the High Church and the Broad Church and the Low Church.' One suspects that this was a Betjeman party-piece.

The break into book illustration could not be long delayed and in 1928 Bawden decorated *The Life and Adventures of Peter Wilkins* by Robert Paltock, published by J.M.Dent and printed by Curwen with sixteen pictures, twenty-five head and tail pieces, endpapers and

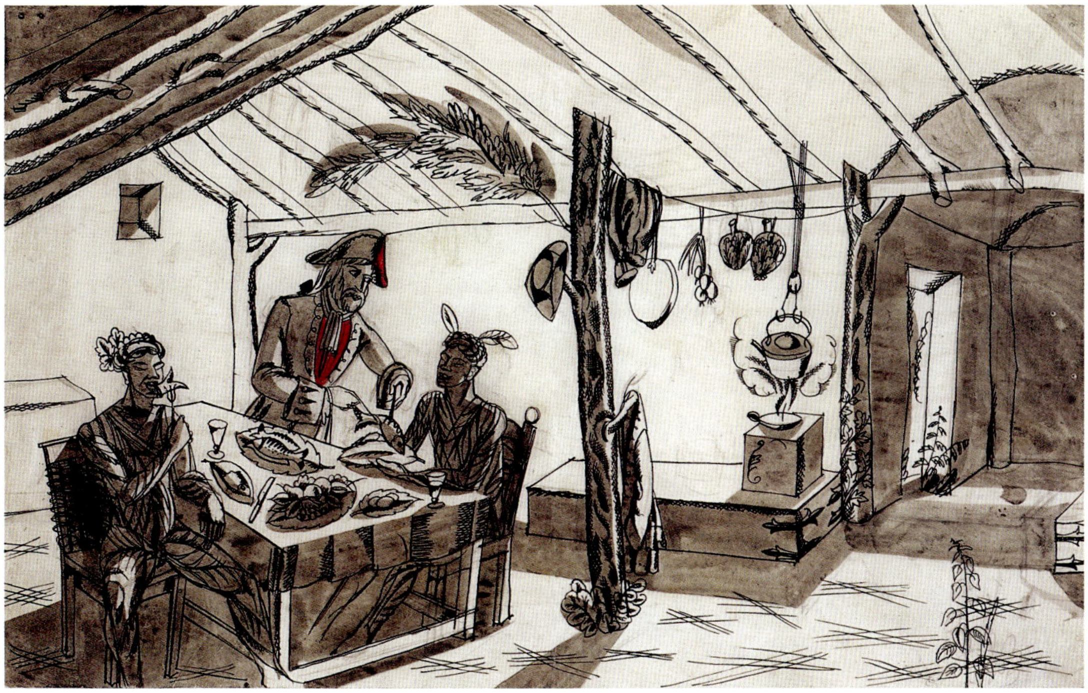

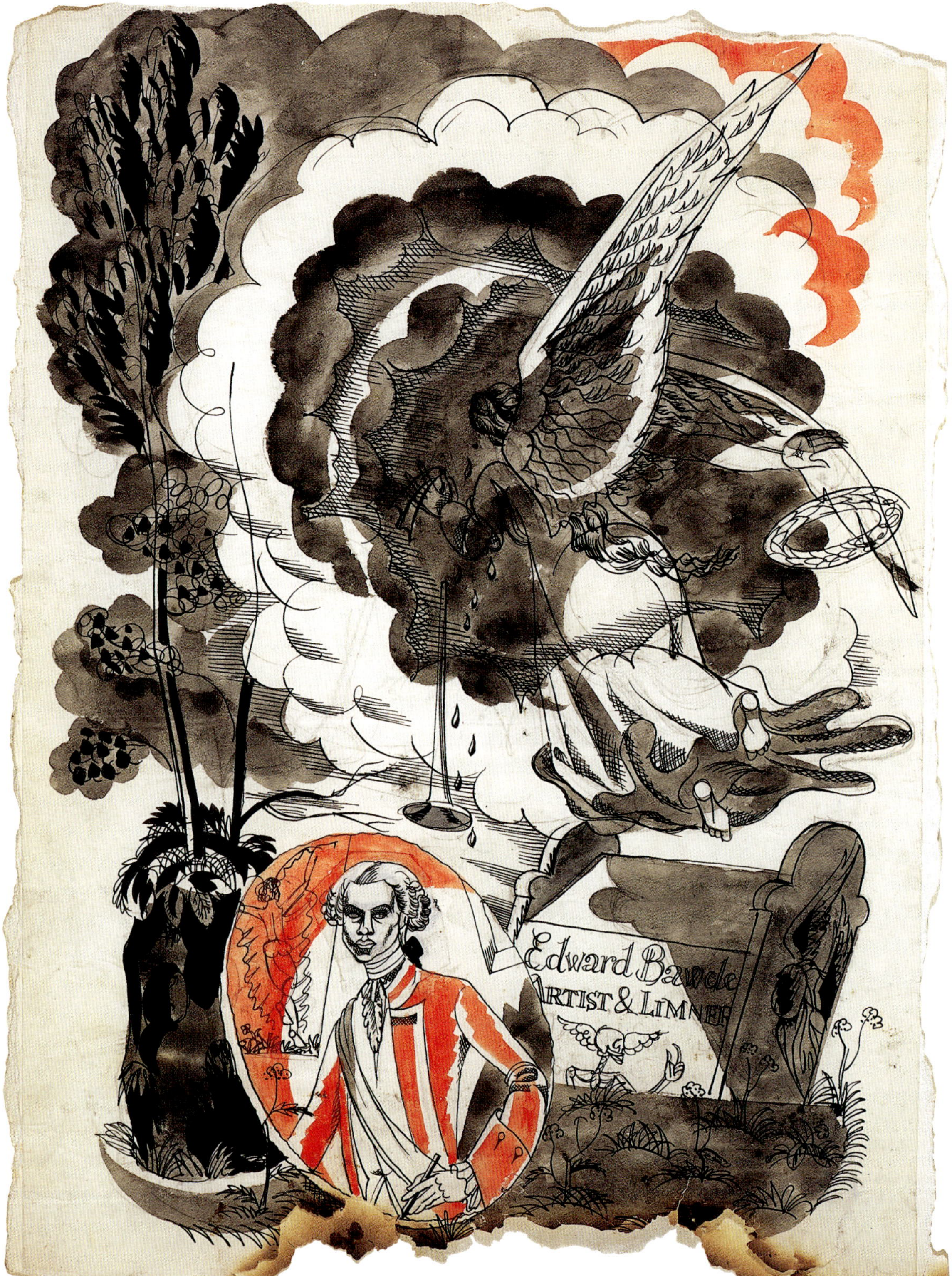

Illustration, possibly a rejected design for *Peter Wilkins*, evidently saved from the fire and included in Eric Ravilious' scrapbook. The figure may be a mocking self-portrait. *c.*1928; 300 x 205 mm.

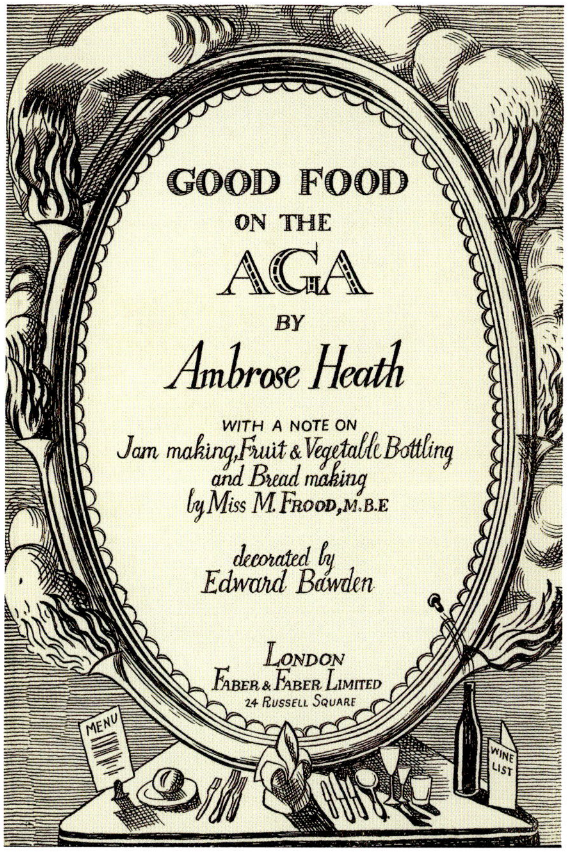

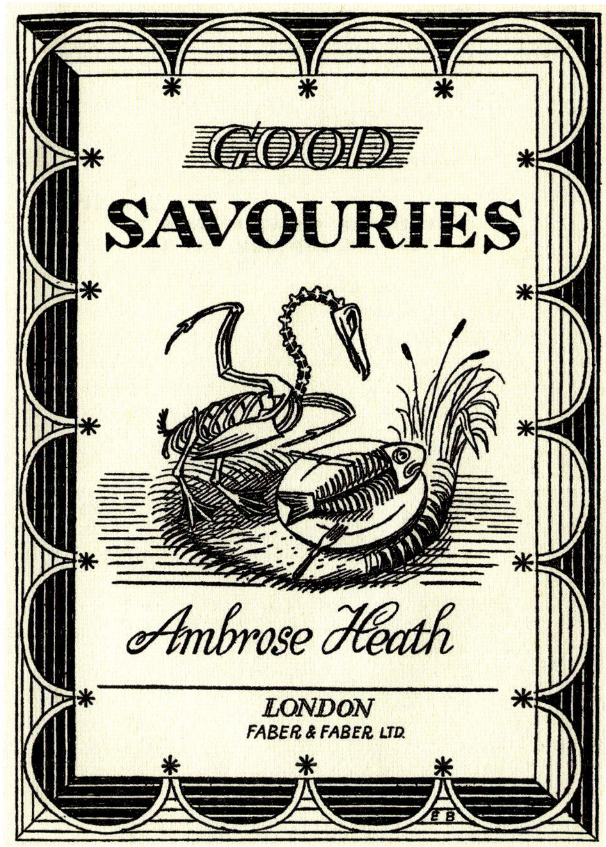

Title page designs for *Good Food on the Aga*, 1932, and *Good Savouries*, 1934, 202 x 135 mm (Manchester Metropolitan University Library and private collection).

dust jacket, the colours being stencilled by hand through holes cut in transparent plastic sheets. This was a rare technique in England, though common enough in France and Bawden is known to have owned copies of stencilled and hand-coloured books by Guy Arnoux. It is a curious story with elements of *Gulliver's Travels* and *Robinson Crusoe*, but without the misanthropic satire of the former or the verisimilitude of the latter. It purports to be the story of a seventeenth century Cornishman, Peter Wilkins, the sole survivor of a shipwreck who becomes lost in a strange underground country where the inhabitants can fly. He marries one, the beautiful Youwarkee, has children, persuades the people to wear clothes, sorts out a rebellion, converts the populace to Christianity and finally attempts to return to England. He falls from the sky and is supposedly rescued by the author, Robert Paltock (1697-1767) who presents his story to us. The original edition of 1751 was much admired by Coleridge, Shelley, Lamb and Scott.

Bawden's illustrations for Dent are masterly, modern in composition but with an antiquarian flavour in detail. They build upon his imaginary architecture drawings in their aerial views and formulaic figures and are both satisfactory as stylised accounts of the fantastic events but also as near abstract designs touched with flat patches of non-realistic colour. I suspect he had also been looking closely at the work of the French illustrator Edouard-Leon-Louis Edy-Legrand (1892-1970), especially his

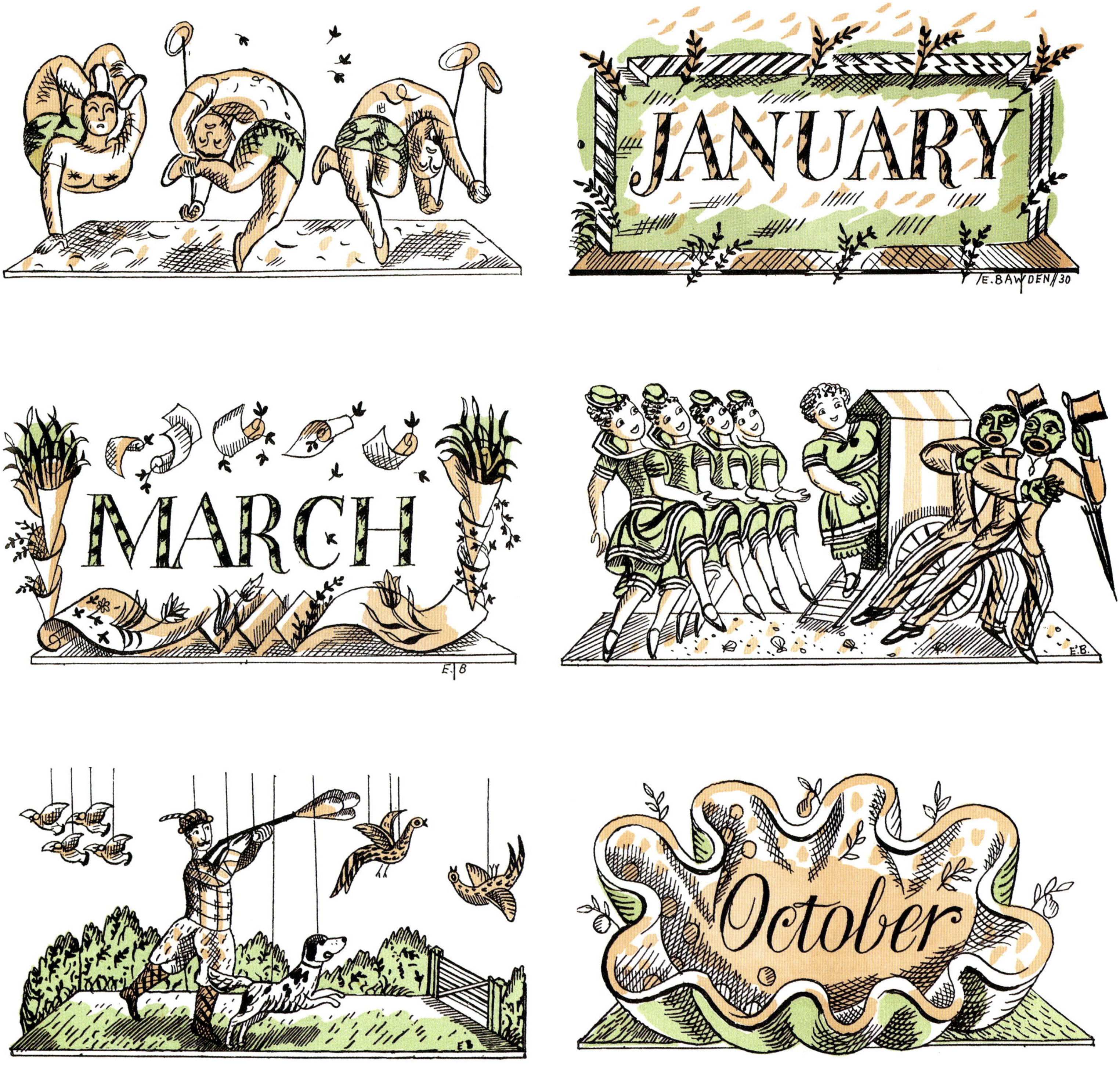

Calendar illustrations for
Review of Revues, 1930.

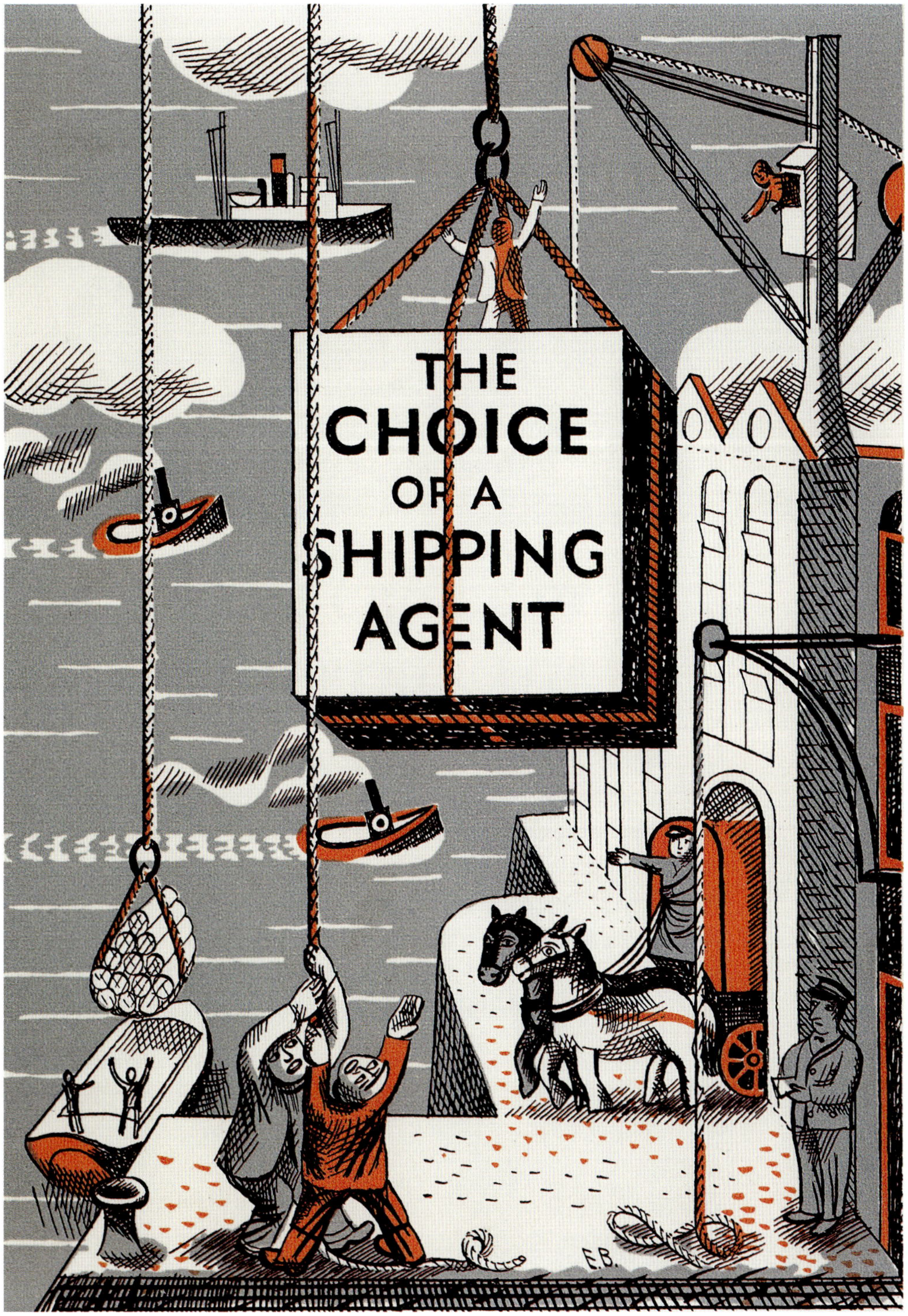

The Choice of a Shipping Agent, title page design for a booklet issued by Thomas Meadows & Co, *c.*1930; printed at the Curwen Press. (Reproduced by permission of Cambridge University Library). 200 x 137 mm, (also printed in larger format, 280 x 200 mm).

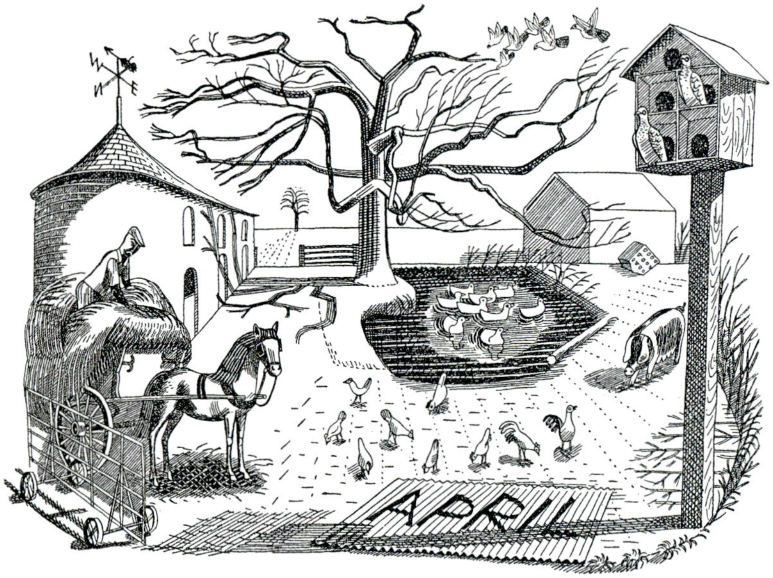

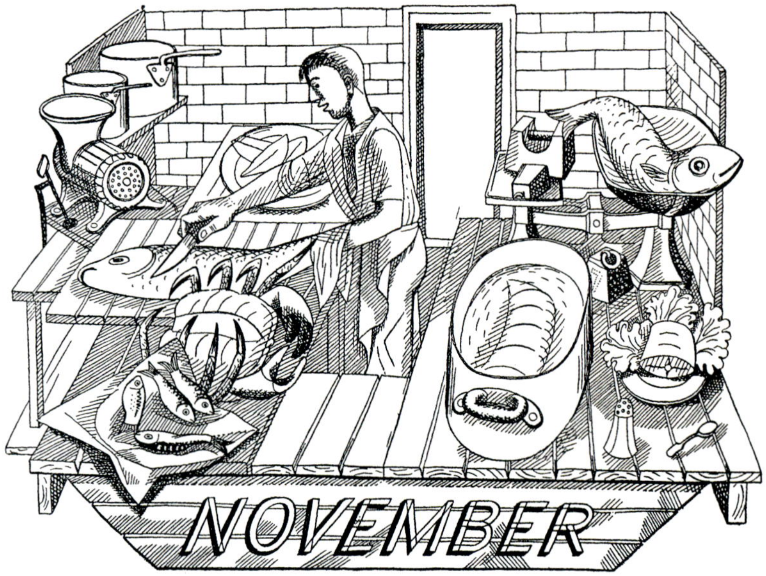

Two chapter headings from the *Good Food* books, 90 x 116 mm
(Manchester Metropolitan University Library).

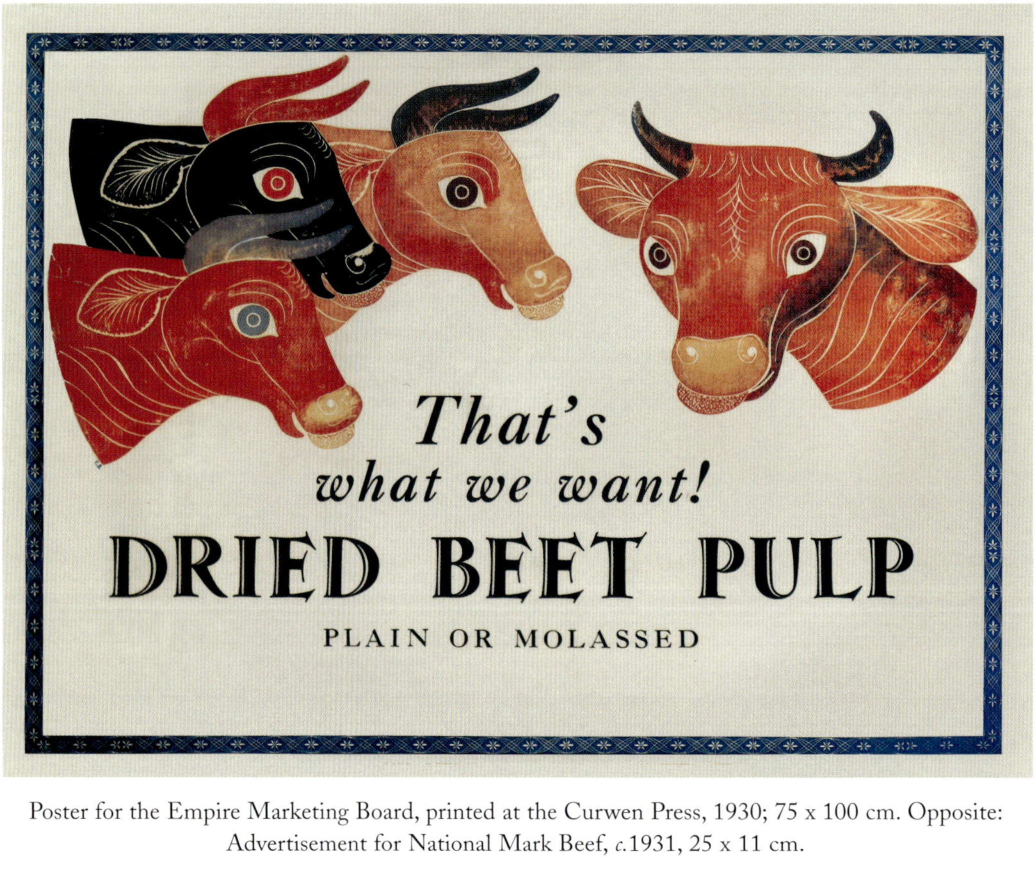

Poster for the Empire Marketing Board, printed at the Curwen Press, 1930; 75 x 100 cm. Opposite: Advertisement for National Mark Beef, *c.*1931, 25 x 11 cm.

Macao et Cosmage (1919) and *L'Isle Rose*, a copy of which he bought in 1925. Whatever its precedents, this is a wonderfully assured start to his prolific career as an illustrator and deserves to be better known.

Although Bawden himself always resented the separation of his paintings and his illustrations in people's estimation of him, it is obvious that the two make different creative demands. Paintings start from nature, illustrations from words. Sitting alone in a field with a box of watercolours and a sheet of paper is very different from receiving a book through the post and a commission for sixteen line drawings and twelve vignettes to accompany a text set in Perpetua. Bawden trained himself to subordinate his own ideas to the author's and also to collaborate with the demands of the printer and book designer. He assembled a reference library for costume and architecture and a rich visual bank of stance and gesture to draw upon dating back to those solitary student wanderings around London, and if both of these failed he would go out and research what he needed for costume or architectural detail. He despised cameras and never owned one. As a watercolourist he had little use for a sketchbook since he always worked on the spot, but there are numerous surviving sketchbooks of research for his book illustrations. This did not mean aiming at literalism because there was no point in re-telling the author's story in pictures: the ideal being to create a parallel to the text which would be suggestive, reinforce the atmosphere and still leave the reader scope for his own imaginative interaction with the story. His first commission, the Paltock, set enormous problems and few of his previous observations had prepared him for the depiction of a subterranean fantasy land where people had wings, but he handled double-spread crowd scenes and aerial views of landscapes and towns with enormous panache.

Other commissions came his way during this period from the Westminster Bank, Fortnum and Mason, the Empire Marketing Board, Twinings' Tea, a peep show for a Scarborough hotel, and miscellaneous calendars, diaries, invitation cards, menus, pictorial maps, dust jackets,

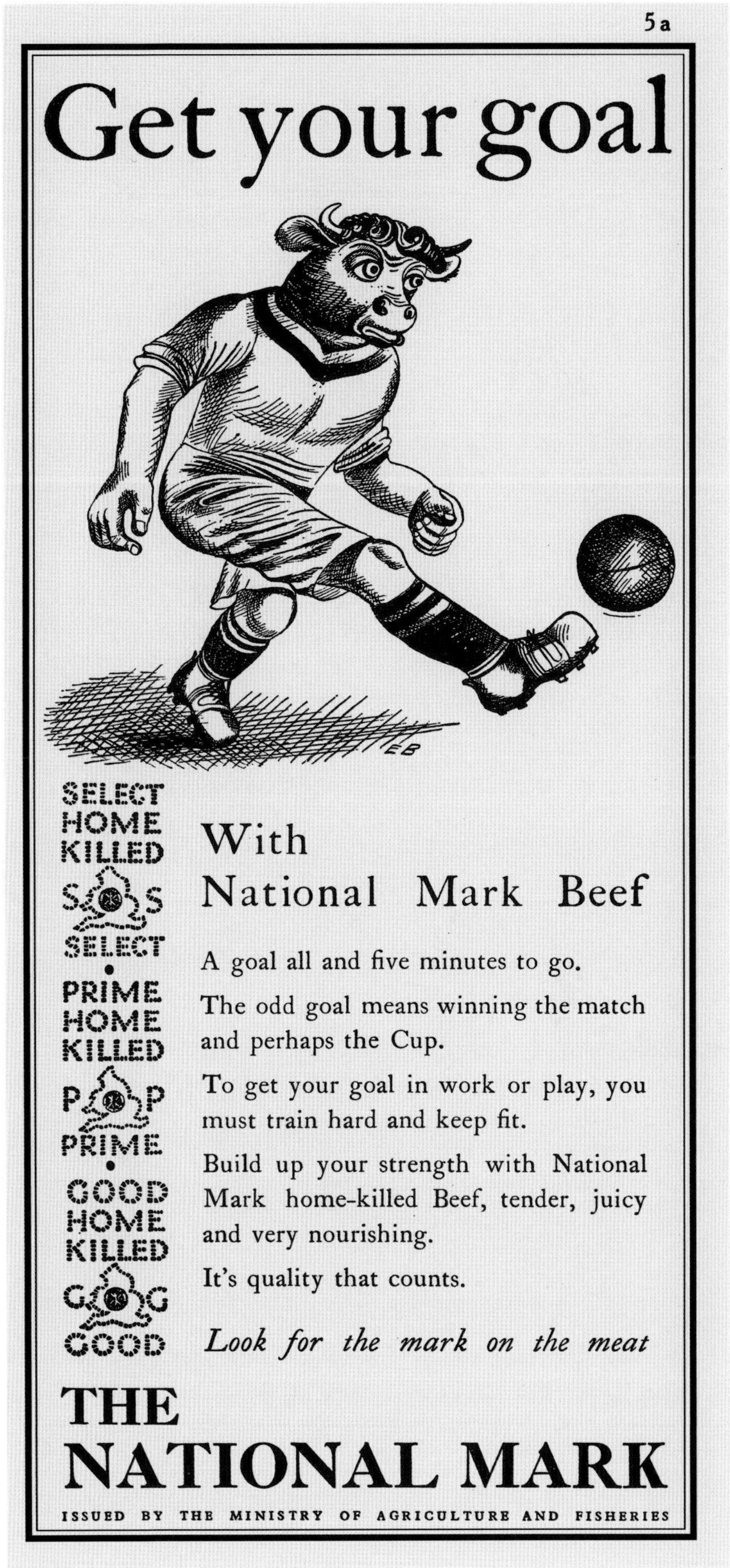

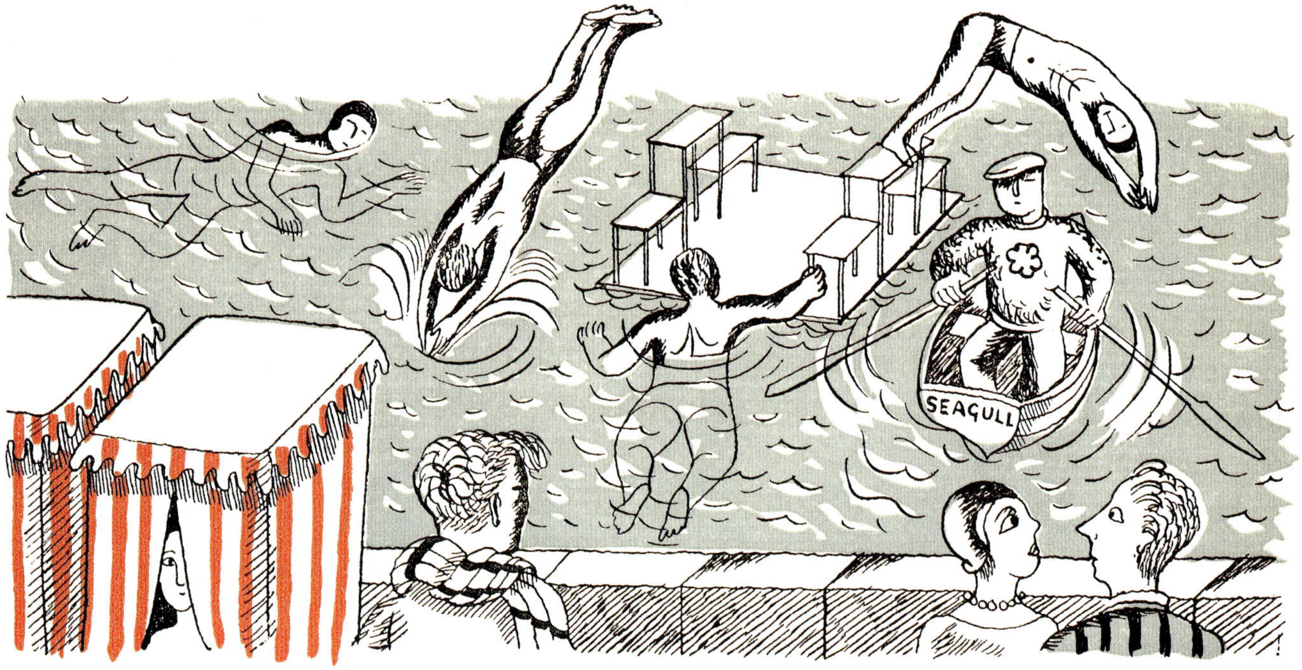

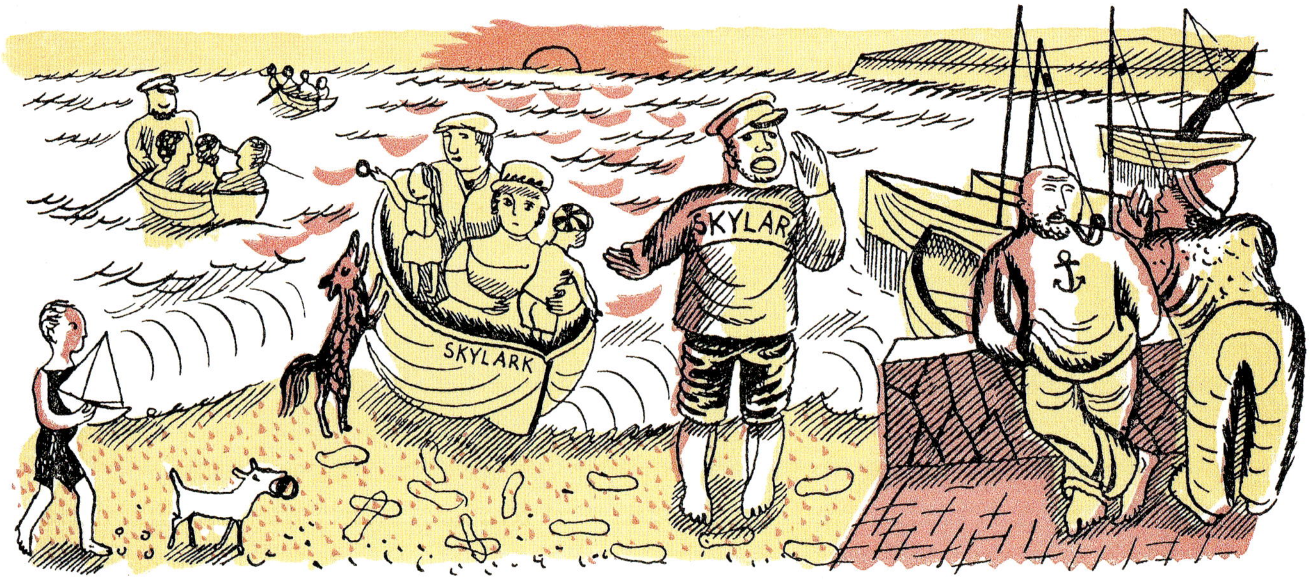

Illustrations from *East Coasting*, 1930, each about 7 x 15 cm, with original title page design (opposite), painted and amended by Bawden, dedicated 'To Eric Ravilious, & Tirzah his wife. August – something – 1930'; 250 x 150 mm (Manchester Metropolitan University Library and private collection).

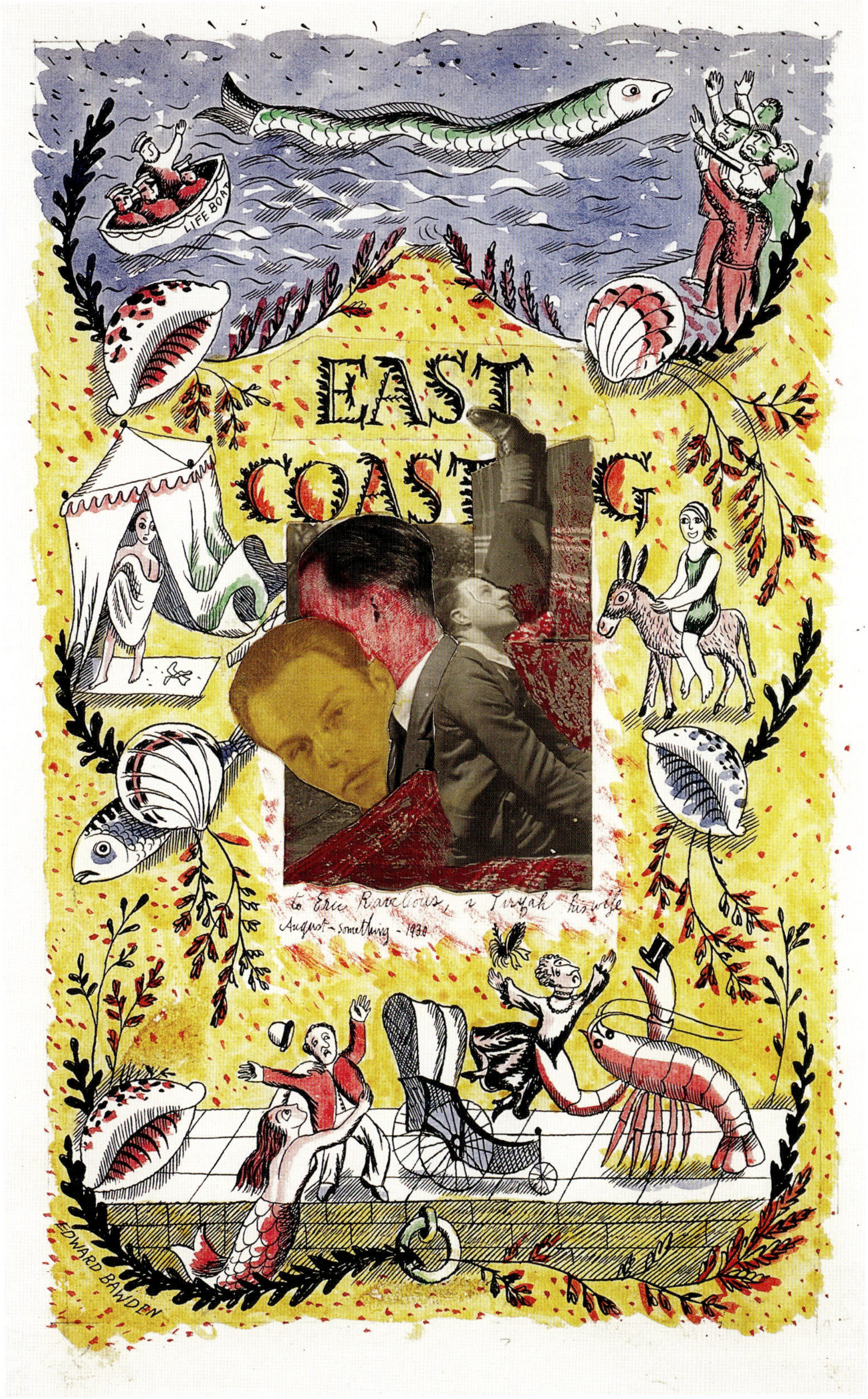
LIFE BOAT
EAST
COASTING
to Eric Ravilious, & Tirzah his wife
August – something – 1930
EDWARD BAWDEN

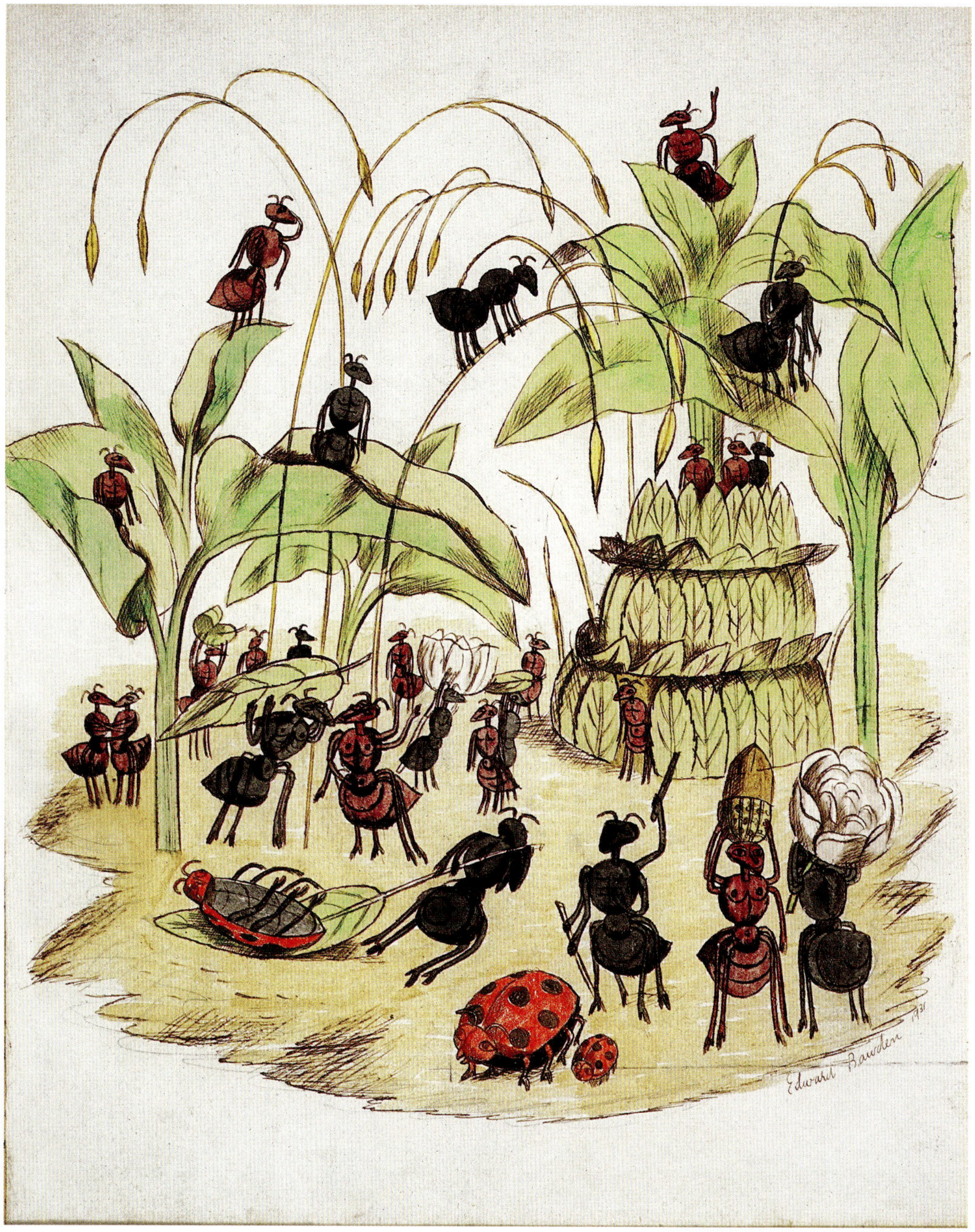

Above: Watercolour design 28 x 22 cm by Bawden from Ravilious' scrapbook, 1931.
Bawden enjoyed drawing the antics of anthropomorphised insects, which recur throughout his work.
Right: *Homage to Dicky Doyle*, 1931; Douglas Percy Bliss wrote that it was 'specially done to show the use of colour applied by stencilling' at the Curwen Press; 17 x 22 cm (Fine Art Society).

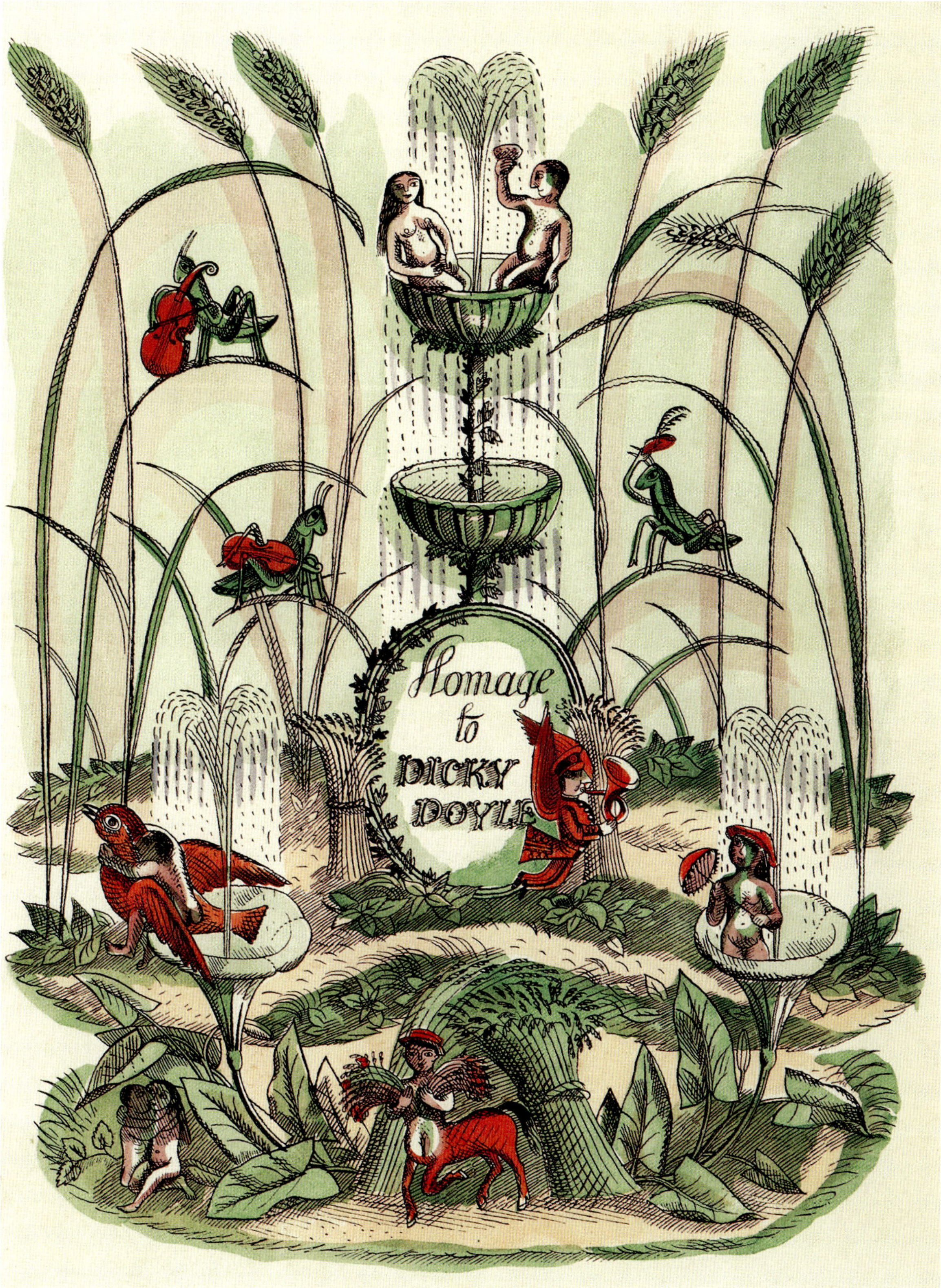
Homage
to
DICKY
DOYLE

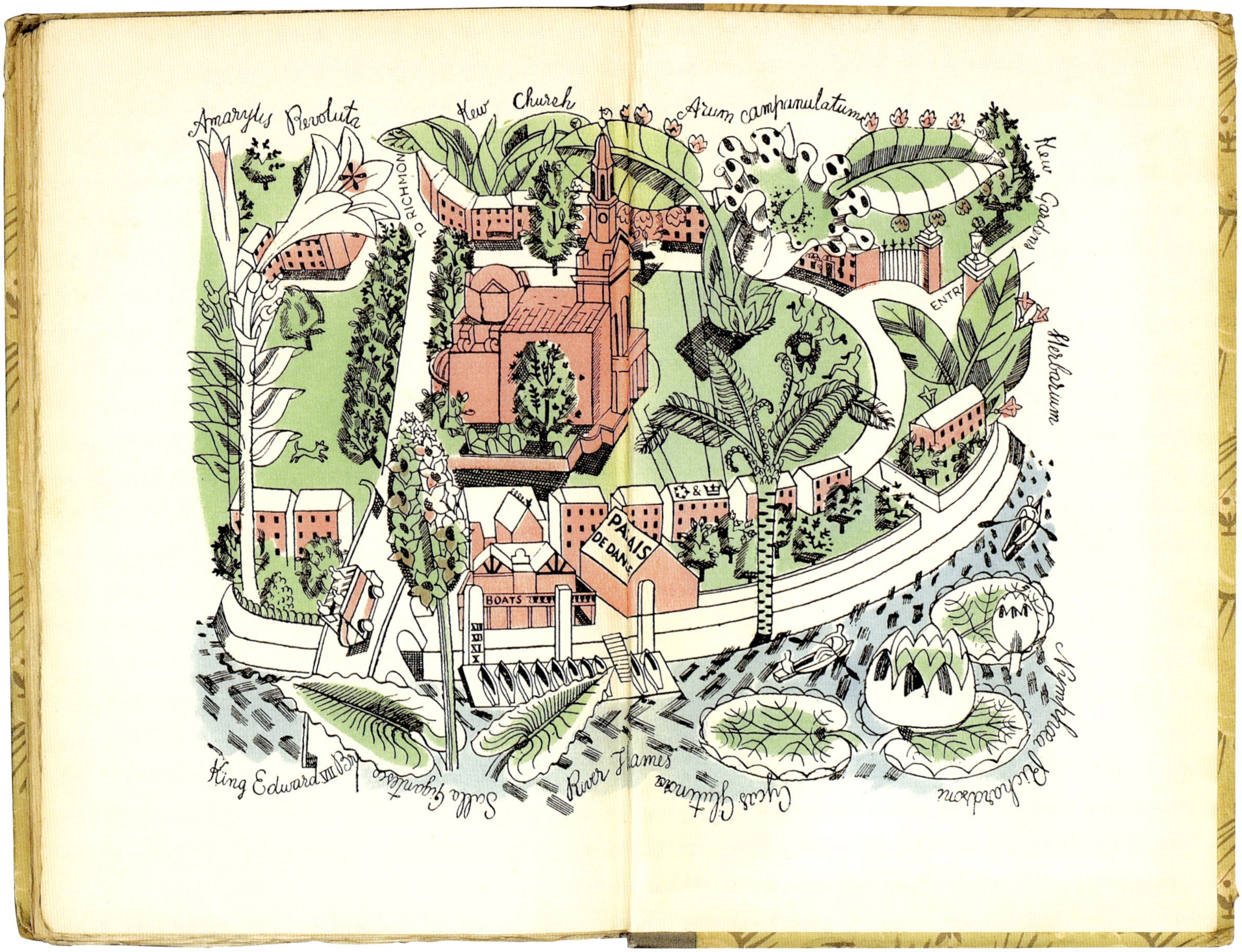

Illustration (opposite) and endpaper for *Adam and Evelyn at Kew*, 1930,
173 x 116 and 172 x 225 mm; (Manchester Metropolitan University Library).

patterned papers, wine lists and typographical ornaments; some of them follow these pages. A steady job for Bawden during the thirties was decorating the *Good Food* guides by Ambrose Heath, published by Faber and Faber. There were ten of these with a dozen line-drawn illustrations inside, and a witty linocut cover, each with superbly inventive margins, different lettering styles and a central illustration – for example, *Good Soups* has a bird picking the peas from a pod and *Good Savouries* has a skeleton fowl contemplating a skeleton fish on a plate, and elsewhere you might see flies on the crumbs, or find mice on the cheese. It's doubtful if any modern client would accept Bawden's lack of reverence for the product. Ravilious too illustrated an Ambrose Heath cook-book and it is interesting to compare the two now

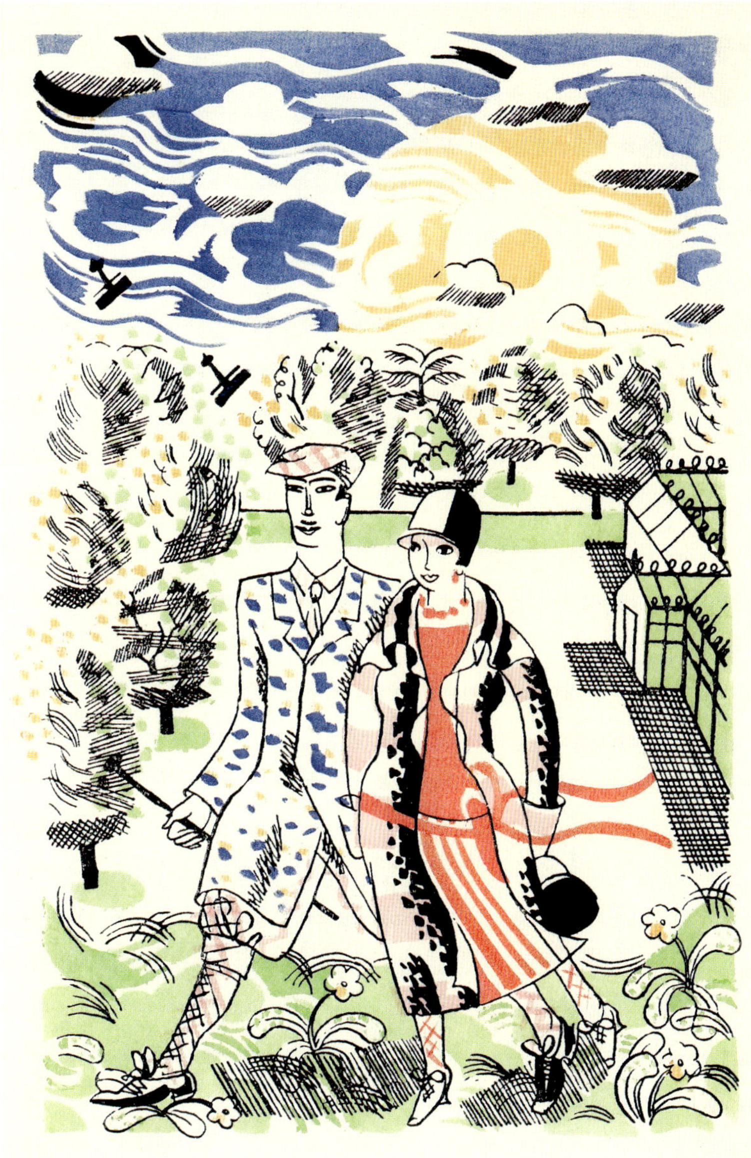

diverging styles. Bawden would tackle any design job that came along, including chair and bathroom design, but claimed he never made more than £400 from his commercial work in any single year before the war. Of course that mattered little when you were a bachelor of frugal tastes, but that was soon to change.

1. Bliss, D. P., *Artwork*, No. 15, Autumn 1928
2. Simon, O., *Printer and Playground*, Faber and Faber, 1956, p.80.
3. Hillier, B., 'Bawden Comes of Age', *The Telegraph Sunday Magazine*, October 1979.
4. Bliss, D. P., *Edward Bawden*, The Pendomer Press, 1979, p.40.
5. Bliss, D. P., ibid, p.39.
6. Bliss, D. P., ibid, p.37.
7. Bliss, D. P., *Artwork*, No. 15, Autumn 1928.
8. Hillier, B., *John Betjeman: New Fame, New Love*, John Murray, 2002, p.76.

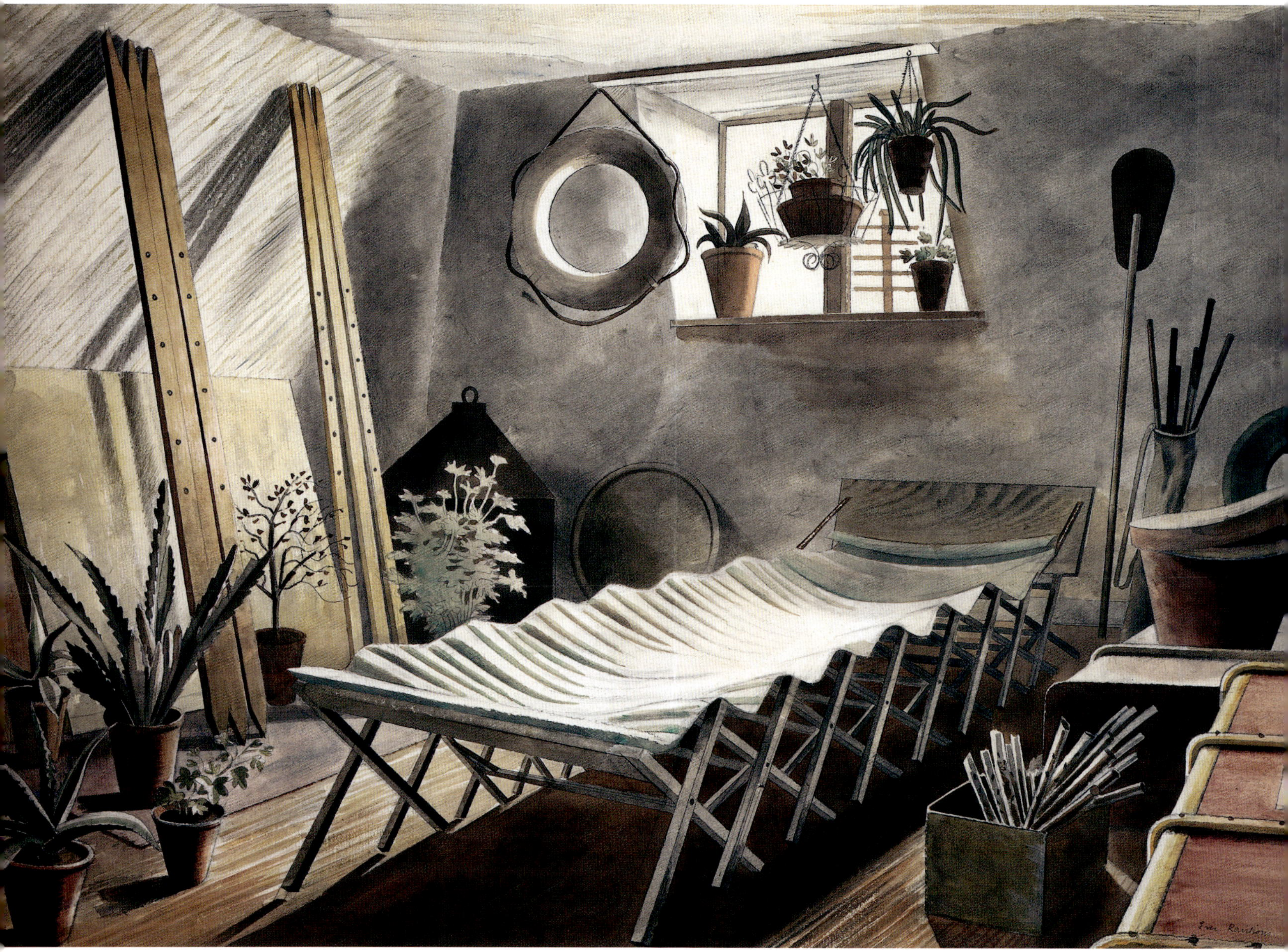

Eric Ravilious, *The Attic Bedroom, Brick House, Great Bardfield*, *c.*1932-34, watercolour, 445 x 625 mm (Fry Art Gallery).

4. BRICK HOUSE

The friends now needed a steady source of income which would also allow them the freedom to paint – the art form in which all three were most ambitious. Teaching was the obvious solution. Bawden and Ravilious were employed for two days each week back at the RCA while Bliss taught at Hornsey and, from 1932, at Blackheath Art School, near where he then lived. Sometimes, though, they tired of teaching and meeting commission deadlines and they would pack watercolours, escape by train or bus, hire bicycles and have a weekend touring and painting in Essex. On one such trip in 1925 Bawden and Ravilious found the village of Great Bardfield and took lodgings with a retired ship's-stewardess at Brick House, next to the village police station. Brick House, a former fur factory and carriage-maker's, was a squarely symmetrical Queen Anne structure of three storeys with a field of almost an acre at the rear, all of it far too large for its single resident. The owner agreed to let half of it as a weekend retreat to the two friends: two rooms upstairs, two down and a shared kitchen for seven shillings and six pence per week.

After Redcliffe Road this was an idyllic retreat: the roads of north-west Essex were still almost free of cars and the countryside unexplored by previous painters, except for the grand old English Impressionist Sir George Clausen (1852-1944), a friend of Monet's, who lived nearby at Duton Hill and who went into the RCA as a Visitor. The settlement at Great Bardfield is supposed to have existed before the Romans came and it was certainly mentioned in the Domesday Book. A flower, the Bardfield

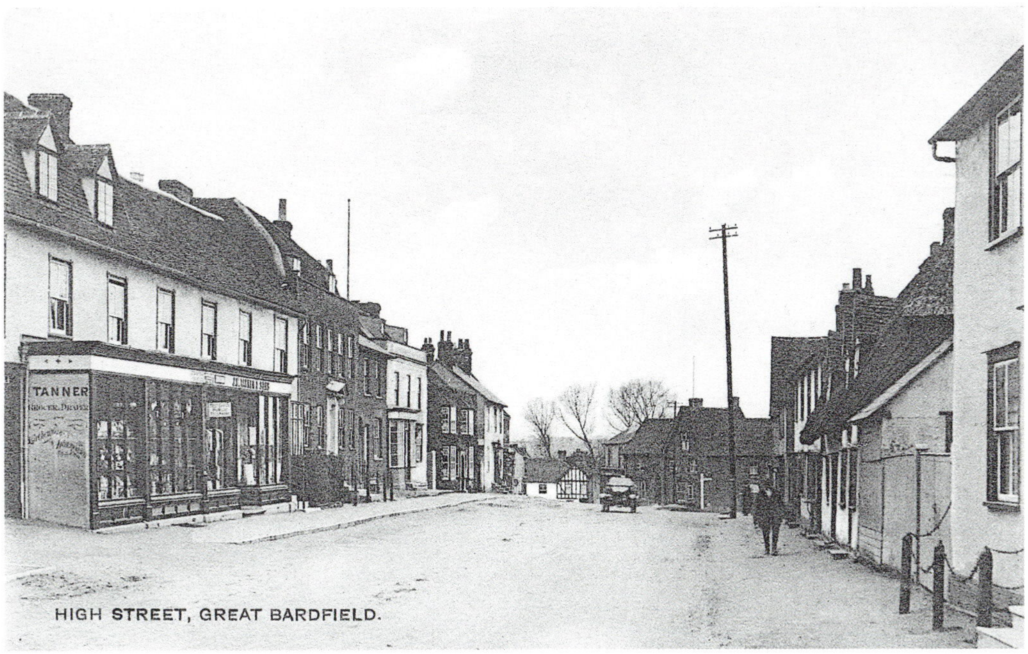

Great Bardfield High Street in 1932, postcard. Brick House is beyond the shop on the left.

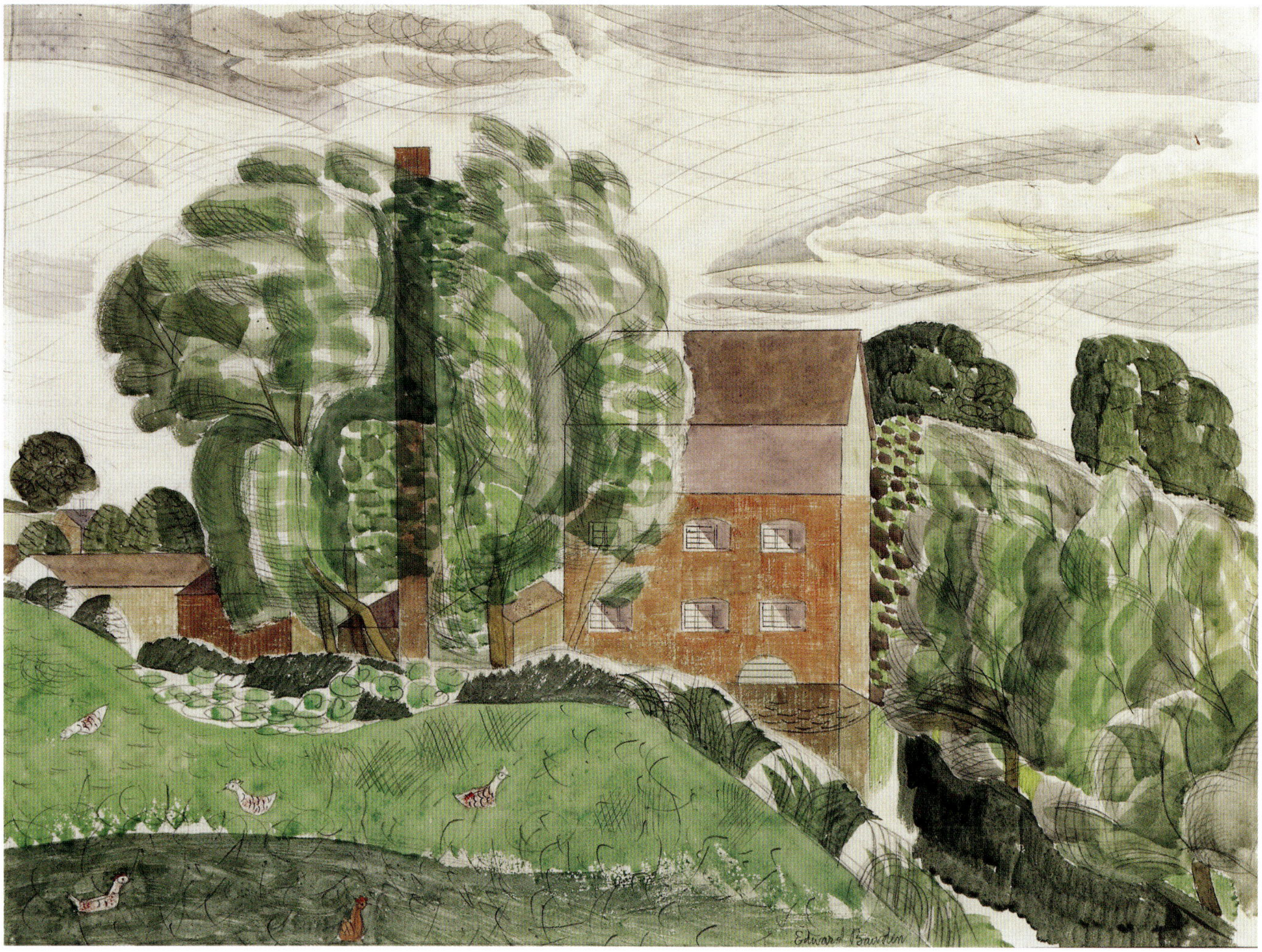

Bullford Mill, near Cressing, Essex, 1927, watercolour,
306 x 405 mm (Fry Art Gallery).

Oxlip (*primula elatior*) had been named after it. The population when Bawden arrived was around seven hundred, mostly dwelling in thatched and pargetted cottages along its High Street. There was a Town Hall, three pubs, a water mill, windmill, disused lock-up, chapel, alms houses, primary school, and shops supplying most local needs. The High Street divided at its east end around a triangle of land on which there was a Friends' Meeting House (built 1848), the right fork leading to the school and St Mary's Church (partly Norman), and the left, northerly, one led past more cottages to the river Pant and open country. There were even two village idiots.

Most villagers still earned a living from the land, but agriculture was in decline during these years and the number of land workers fell sharply right up to the 1939 war leaving houses empty and cheap to rent or buy. Amenities townsfolk took for granted had not reached most villages and Bawden recalled: 'There was no water, no electricity, no drains. Very exciting. If you're young! We pumped our water from a contaminated well, we had a lavatory outside with three holes showing how important the house was, and oil lamps indoors. It was lovely. It was almost like camping.'

During one of their visits to Brick House another artist took lodgings with their landlady. Bawden describes Thomas Hennell thus: 'One morning in 1931 when Eric

Ravilious and I came down to the kitchen in Brick House to wash ourselves we found a stranger, stripped to the waist, pumping water over his head and making quite a splash in the large slate sink. He was tall, thin with black beady eyes rather close set, dark slightly curly hair, and as he greeted us his voice had a deep booming parsonic ring, echoed even more loudly when he laughed. Outside leaning against the doorpost was a heavy, khaki-coloured Army bike and on it, tied to the bar between saddle and steering wheel, a large and perfect specimen of a corn dollie, of the sort called the Lord's table. Tom greeted us in the most friendly manner. Our identity was divulged in a matter of seconds and friendship established immediately.'[1] Hennell was cycling round Essex researching his first book, *Change on the Farm* (1934).

Bawden and Ravilious regarded Hennell (1903-1945) as a near genius, but he was not a relaxing man to be with as Bawden explained in a letter to a friend: 'Tom was a very intense, solitary man, profoundly serious. I don't believe he possessed a natural facility, either as draughtsman or painter. He acquired skill painfully, by infinite persistence, but he was determined, dedicated.' Compared to Bawden's and Ravilious' carefully composed and skilfully crafted works Hennell's watercolours of country scenes and activities look untidy, unpremeditated and unfinished though some of them were worked up from field sketches back in his studio.

Hennell came from an austere background and had grown up in Kent where his father was a vicar. After boarding school in Broadstairs he attended the

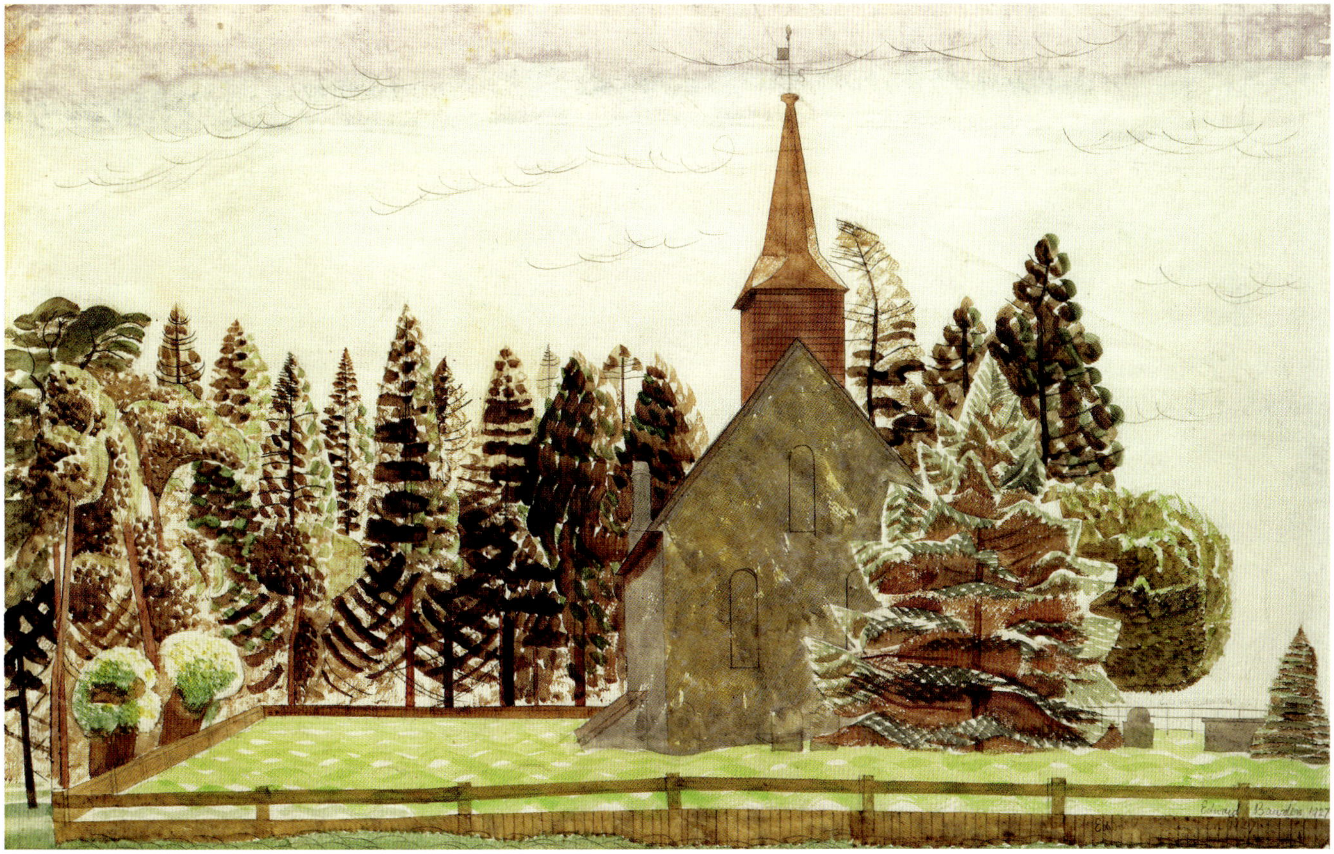

Faulkbourne Church, Essex, 1927, watercolour, 292 x 378 mm (Fine Art Society).

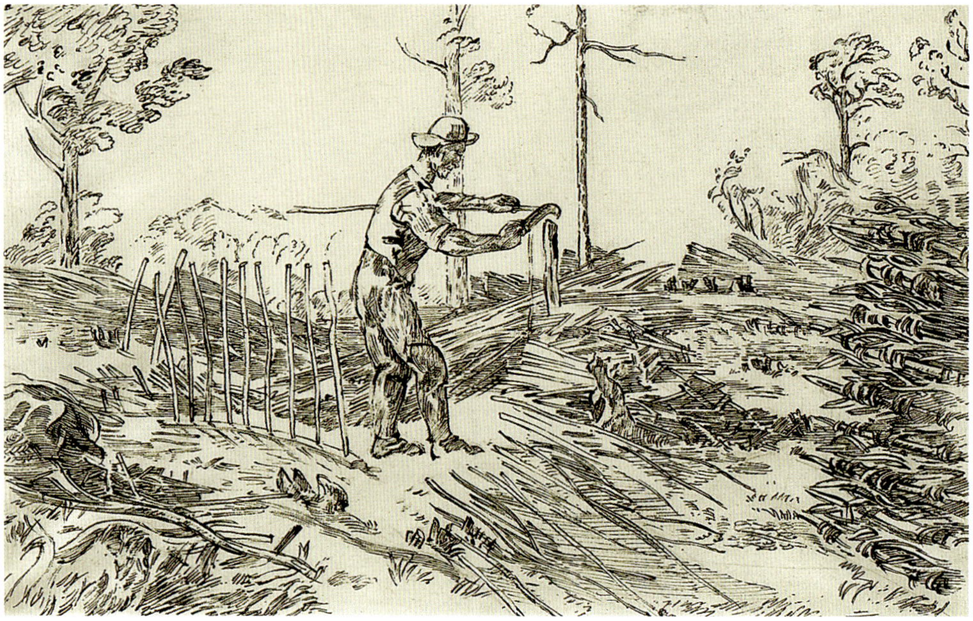

Thomas Hennell, *Hurdle Making*, *c.*1941, pen and ink, 290 x 470 mm.

unglamorous Regent Street Polytechnic to study art at the same time Bawden was at the RCA, and then went for teacher training at London Day Training College where, unfortunately, he fell violently in love with Marion Richardson (1892-1946), an influential teacher of children's art. When his passion was not reciprocated he had a mental breakdown and between 1932 and 1935 became an inpatient at Aylesbury, Maudsley and Claybury mental hospitals. After recovery from his schizophrenia he returned to Brick House and described his hallucinations to Bawden who recalled: 'these he had seen in detail with an almost microscopic intensity, including, may I add, two evil figures he recognised – Eric and myself. I urged him strongly to write it all down, and that advice he took.' The result was Hennell's book *The Witnesses* (1938). His two friends admired Hennell's self-imposed task of recording in prose, poetry and watercolours the vanishing crafts of rural England such as chair making, pottery, basketry, thatching, cooperage, hedging, cider making and so on – all subjects of interest to Bawden and Ravilious too now they had a country outpost of their own.

This fascination with all things rural was widespread from the 1920s onwards and such artists as Fred Griggs, Robin Tanner, Paul Drury and Graham Sutherland had been inspired by Samuel Palmer to depict a romantic, melancholy and nostalgic view of pastoral life. Hennell's findings were therefore welcomed when they were published in *Change in the Farm* (1934) and *British Craftsmen* (1943) and the posthumously-published *The Countryman at Work* (1947). He had been encouraged in his art by Sutherland who lived at Trottiscliffe, near Hennell's cottage at Ridley in Kent, and Paul Nash was another supporter and influence. When his *Poems by Thomas Hennell* were published in a small edition of fifty by Oxford University Press in 1936 Ravilious supplied the wood-engraved decorations for them.

In 1932 Douglas Percy Bliss and his wife moved to a large house in Blackheath where their first daughter Prudence was born, followed five years later by a second, Rosalind. He was elected a member of the Society of Wood Engravers in 1934 and in the same year illustrated *The Devil in Scotland* with thirty-nine vigorous little

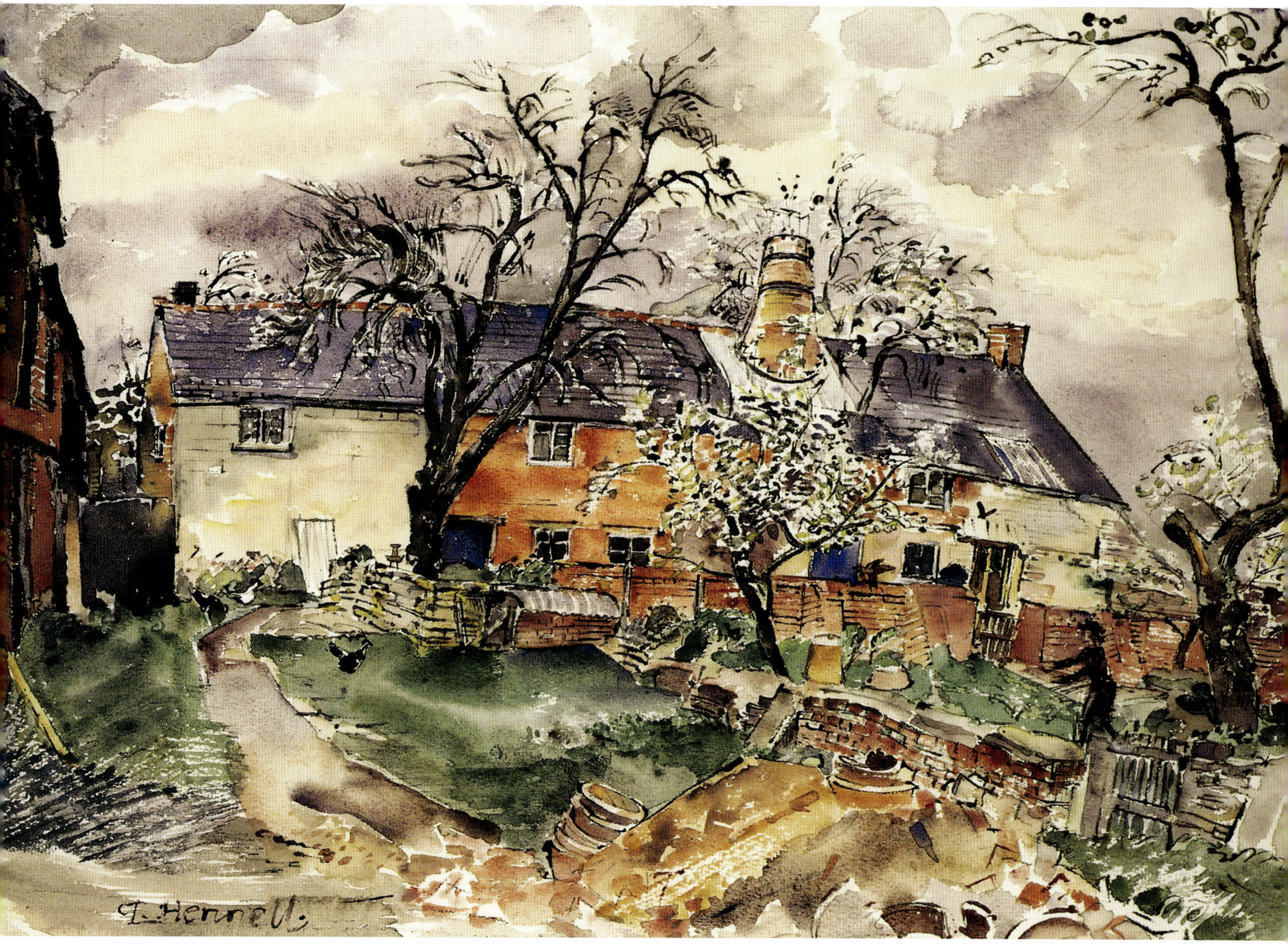

Thomas Hennell, *Winchcombe Pottery*, *c.*1940, 457 x 578 mm, watercolour (Victoria & Albert Museum).

wood-engravings of witches, lightning flashes and various Celtic shenanigans.

Ravilious was also busy wood-engraving and commuting to teach the skill part-time at Eastbourne College of Art, staying overnight with his parents there, and lodging with the Blisses when back in London at the weekends, or going to stay at Brick House with Bawden. In his class was an eighteen year old student of wood-engraving called Tirzah Garwood who was eager to break out from her middle-class background, even if it meant offending her Lieutenant Colonel father and her genteel family by marrying an artist from a humbler Eastbourne background than their own. The Garwoods did not conceal their prejudices from Ravilious. Tirzah described her tutor and soon-to-be suitor in her diary: 'a smart double-breasted suit, shy and diffident manners, not

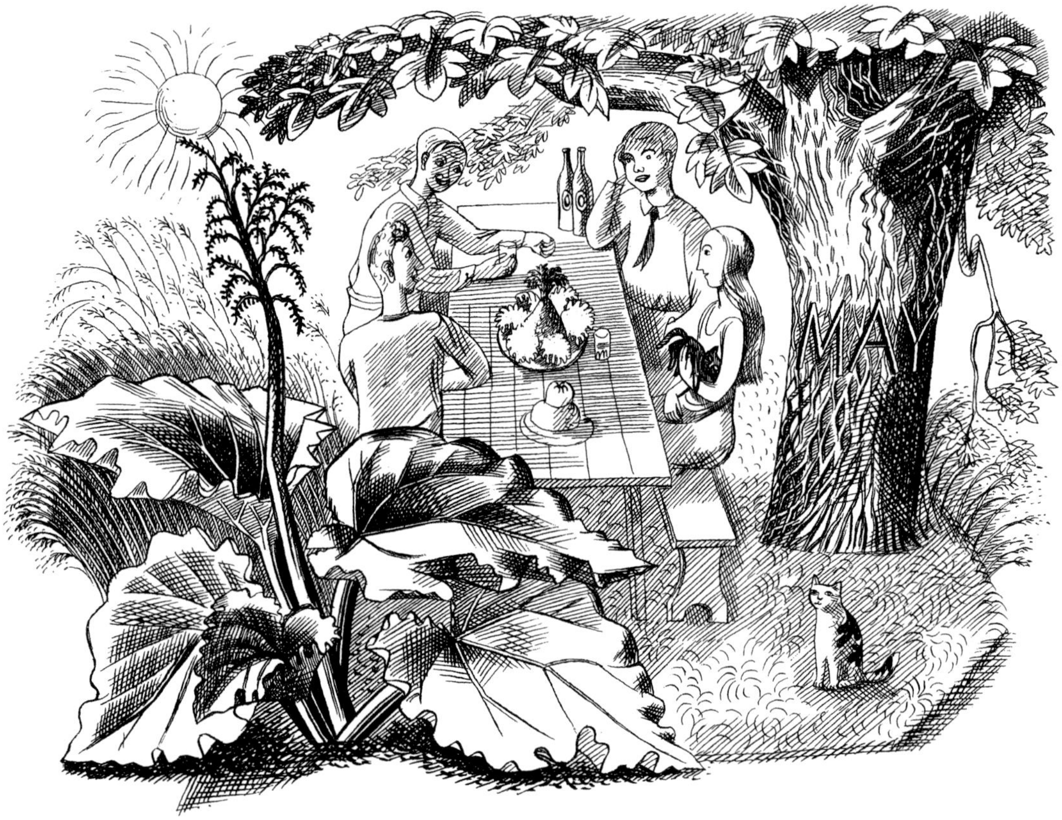

Brick House Garden Party, 1931, pen and ink, printed in *Good Food*, 1932. Thomas Hennell is seated near left, next to Ravilious, with Edward far right, seated next to Tirzah, 90 x 115 mm.
Opposite: Duffy Rothenstein (later Ayers), *Portrait of Tirzah Garwood*, oil, *c.*1949.

unlike those of a curate . . . he was tall and thin, with a head which jutted out at the back, his eyes were large, light brown or hazel, with long girlish lashes which gave him an appealing look, so that motherly women often offered him cups of tea. This look was only superficial; he wasn't really at all effeminate nor did he need sympathy, though it was true he was inordinately fond of tea.' They were married in July 1930, with Bawden as an awkward best man and with Bliss and William Rothenstein in support.

The couple briefly set up home in Earls Court and then moved to a ground floor flat in Hammersmith overlooking the Thames, which inspired Ravilious to paint the training ship *Stork* which was moored opposite his window. They also had a good view of the annual Boat Race and became known for their race day parties. From there he began to commute to teach at the Ruskin School of Art in Oxford, though he passed this post on to Enid Marx when his commissions started to make a profit and he could finally stop teaching in 1937.

Ravilious had illustrated *Desert, a Legend* by Martin Armstrong (Cape, 1926) and *The Atrocities of the Pirates* by Aaron Smith (Golden Cockerel Press, 1929), but he won most acclaim for his wood-engravings for the Golden Cockerel Press' *Twelfth Night* of 1932 which developed his Morley College mural liking for scaffolds, fences, trellises, arbours and buildings without solid walls, and for delicately engraved texturing with tickings, dots and

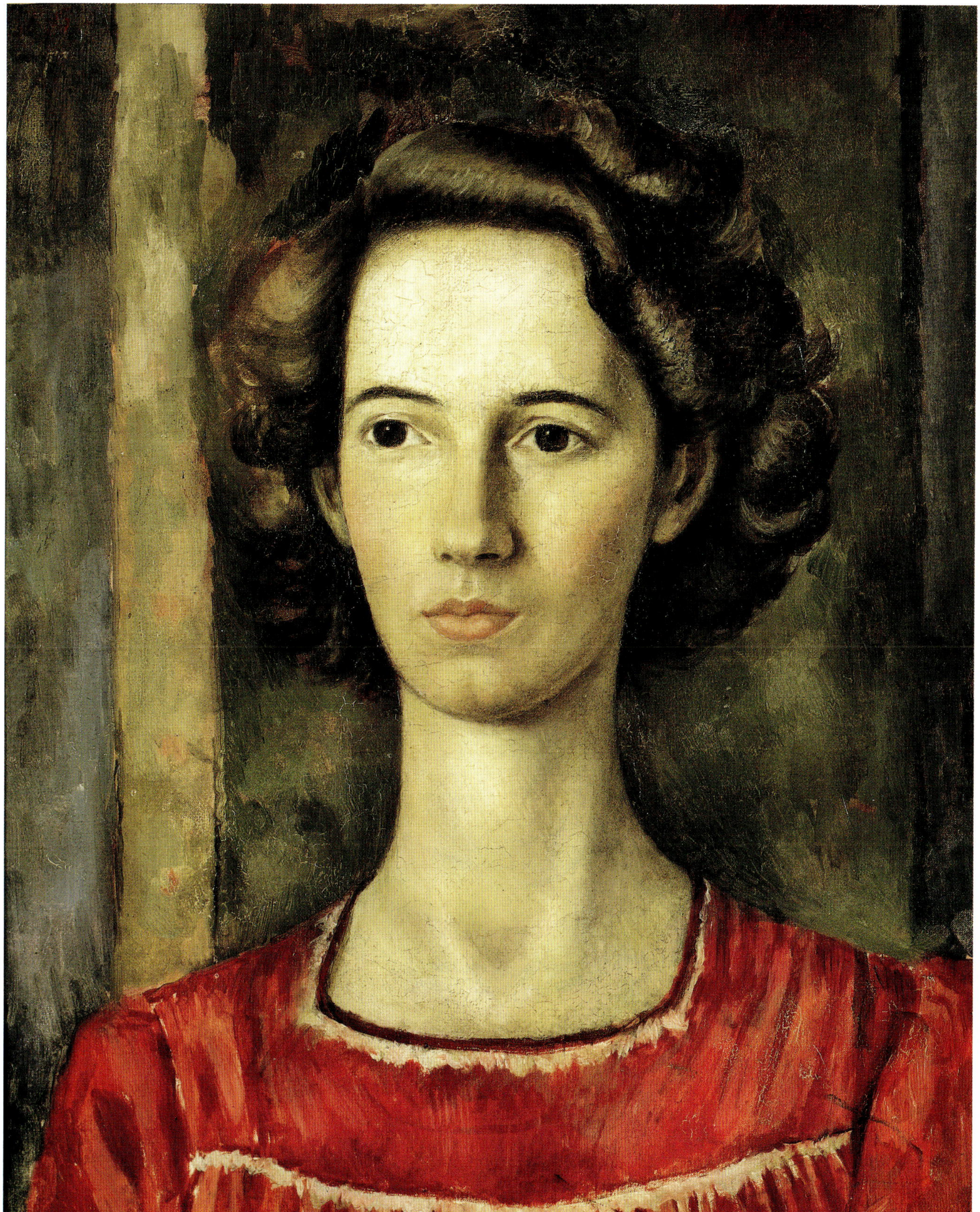

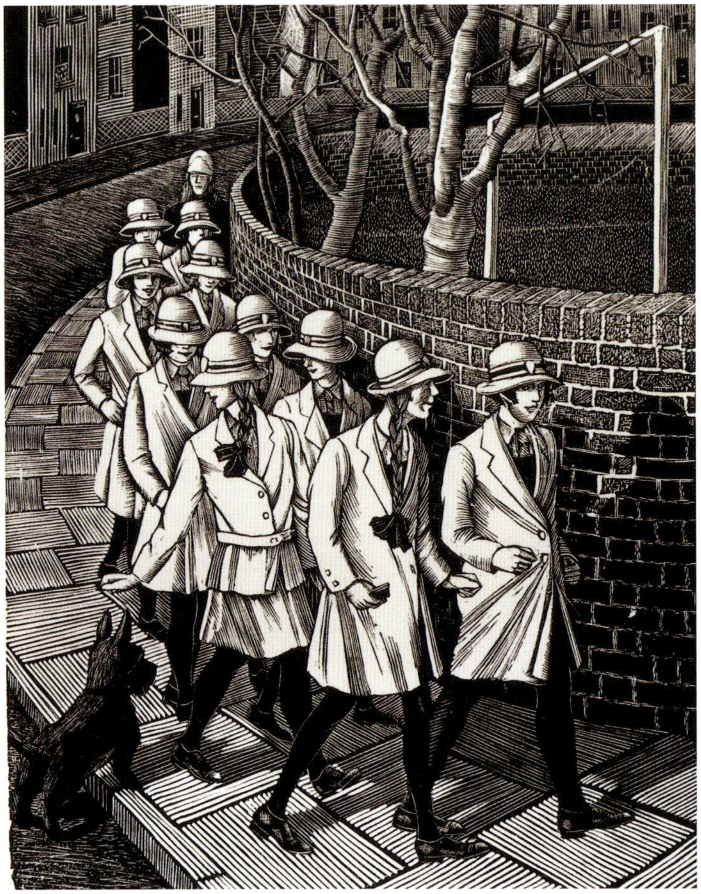

Tirzah Garwood, *The Crocodile*, 1929, wood engraving, 165 x 125 mm (Fry Art Gallery).

Marbled paper made by Tirzah, and Charlotte Bawden.

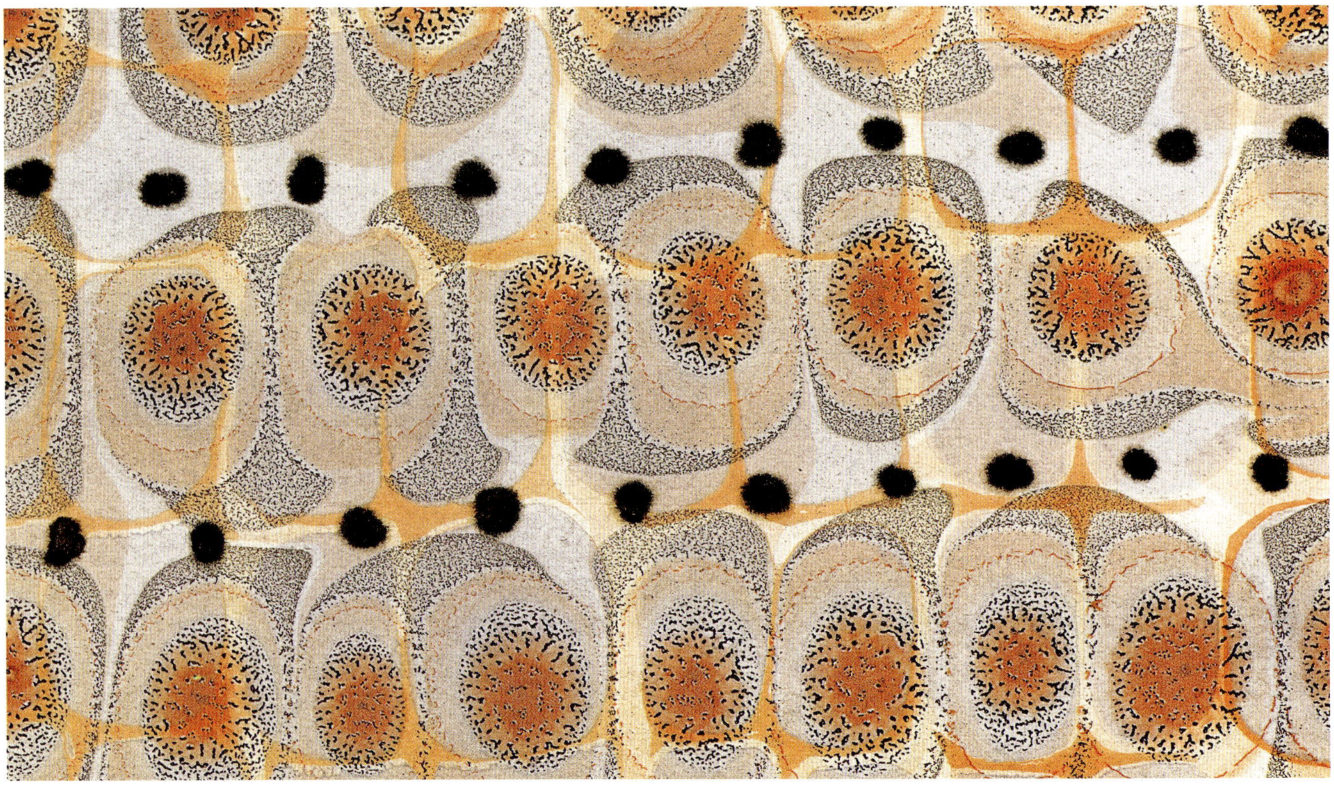

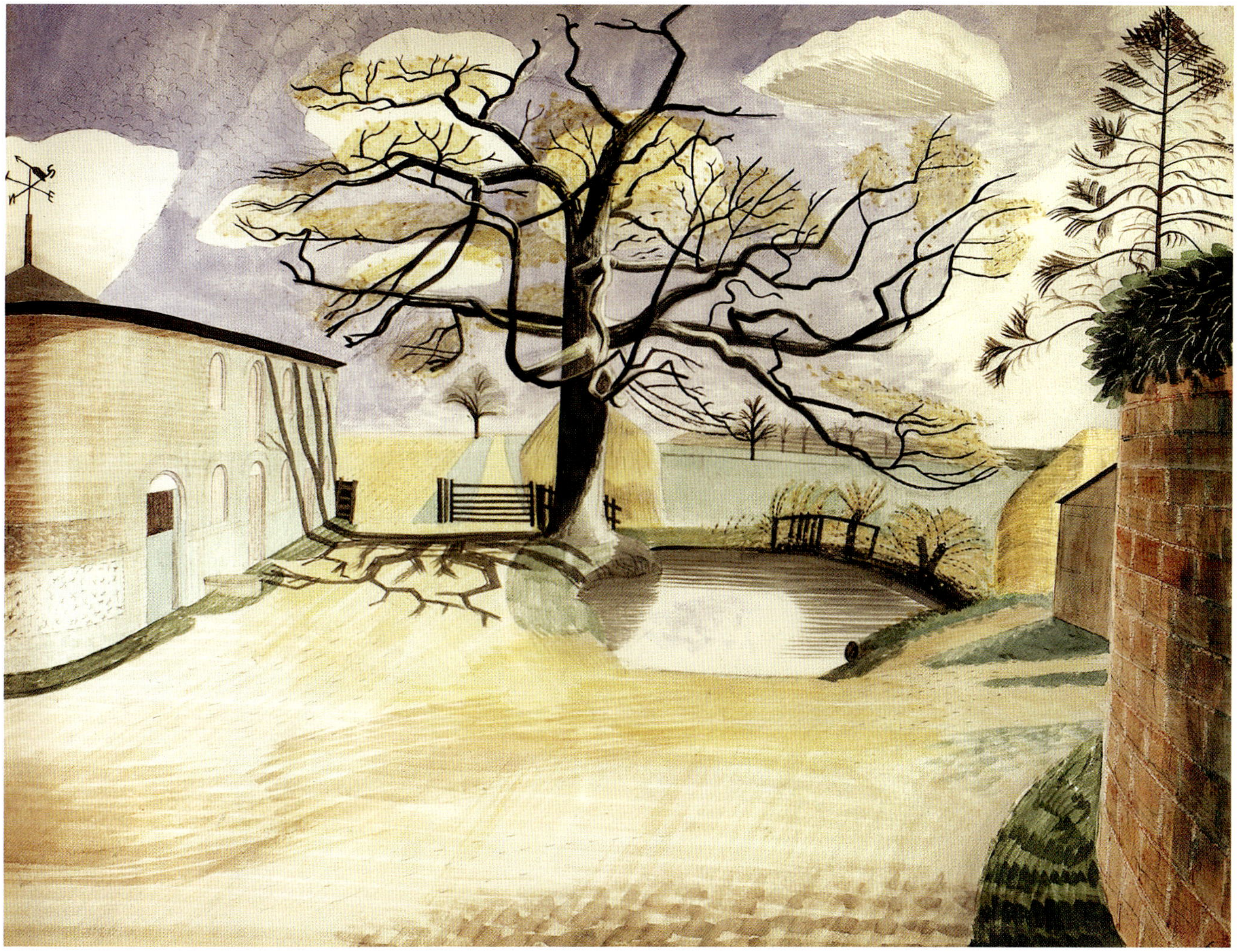

The Pond, Great Bardfield (Turning while your bones last), 1933, watercolour, approx. 450 x 570 mm (Scarborough Art Gallery).

cross-hatchings, all giving a range of greys and silvers. The elaborately costumed figures are still rather stiff and expressionless and subordinate to their intricate settings. Tirzah helped with the immense labour of cutting all these blocks. Unfortunately the British economy had taken a downturn and sales were so slow, even at three guineas each, that the Golden Cockerel Press had to be sold by Robert Gibbings soon after. However, for *The Tragedy of the Rich Jew of Malta* published the next year, Ravilious switched publishers to the Golden Hours Press and for *The Natural History of Selborne* (1938) worked with the Nonesuch Press.

In 1932, four years after Bliss and two years after Ravilious had married, Bawden became the husband of Charlotte Epton, painter, potter, and former RCA student who came from a Lincolnshire family of farmers and solicitors. Bawden's father bought the whole of Brick House for them as a wedding present for £500. Since it was so large and neither couple had any children as yet, the Bawdens persuaded the Raviliouses to leave London and join them. The two painters now worked side by side each day, as Tirzah remembered: 'the garden and country round Bardfield inspired them both and they competed with one another in conditions of various hardships, such as ghastly weather, or working with the sun bang in their eyes. They painted several pictures very early in the morning from the roof of their house, and on one occasion had to come down, nearly overpowered by the smell of kippers cooking for breakfast. Bawden thought you ought to finish the painting on the spot, but Eric might do half his at home. They always worked very hard and got up very early in the morning.' [2]

The two men were very different in character but Bliss surmised: 'Eric admired Edward's dour creativeness, his sheer professionalism, and Edward believed in elegance and fastidious taste with which Eric was endowed. They worked together in perfect amity. They stimulated each other. It was a rare friendship and partnership.' [3]

Meanwhile the two wives collaborated on making marbled papers, a craft Charlotte was keen to revive: the papers were then printed by the Curwen Press and sold in London shops. Bawden was cruelly dismissive of this as 'amusing themselves on the kitchen table'. Charlotte's own painting and pottery making seem to have been severely scaled down, without resentment, early in the marriage, but Tirzah had begun to acquire a reputation as a wood-engraver with the Golden Cockerel and Kynoch Presses and with other works appearing in *Radio Times*, *The Listener* and *The Studio*. Unlike her husband she drew inspiration from modern urban life – a crocodile of schoolgirls, a bored woman in her bedroom, a dog show, or card players, for example. She had also worked alongside Eric on his fireworks murals for a Morecambe hotel in 1933, though these quickly deteriorated on the damp walls. Unfortunately, once isolated from the London publishing and gallery networks her wood-engraving commissions seemed to dry up and soon household chores began to bore her. Charlotte was more domesticated, a splendid cook and popular hostess, especially at their Christmas parties when the whole house was decorated with original art. Another of her new skills was driving and she acquired a Morris car in which she and Tirzah went off to junk shops and auctions for antiques, their artistic impulses now being channelled into home-making. Charlotte was as sturdy, gay, gregarious and extrovert as her husband was austere, moody, introspective and retiring. One of her skills was flower arranging, using blooms from the now burgeoning garden – Bawden having discovered a talent for horticulture, though he was oddly prejudiced against rhododendrons, and dahlias which he thought vulgar and banished them to the vegetable garden.

A couple, the Bransons, friends from the RCA, visited Brick House and Mary Branson recalled how Tirzah and 'Eppie' 'set off with baskets early to collect food. When we came back from painting the boys played ping-pong – very fast. The table, full size, took up the middle of the living room. After a time Eppie came in with delicious hot-pots, and we sat around with soup bowls on the ping-pong table and on our knees. What delicious flavours! One afternoon the Boy insisted in going to the bottom of the garden where there was a stream. He insisted on bathing with not a stitch on – not so odd when one remembers that we all lived in life classes male and female.' [4] Constable Baker, the local policeman and Charlotte's driving instructor who lived next door, was too embarrassed to stop their summer frolics in the River Pant.

One way in which the two couples and Charlotte's former colleague at Cheltenham Ladies' College and then an English don from Girton College called Gwyneth Lloyd Thomas (1899-1978), passed the lamp-lit evenings was to invent characters and spin plots for them. Bawden recalled sitting round the table and the stories becoming surreal and occasionally rude. 'It was great fun, but one does easily slide down the slope to indecency, at least what seemed indecent in those days. Today it would be quite normal.' Several of the episodes seemed to be coming together into a story which Hennell, the most experienced writer amongst them, drew together and Bawden

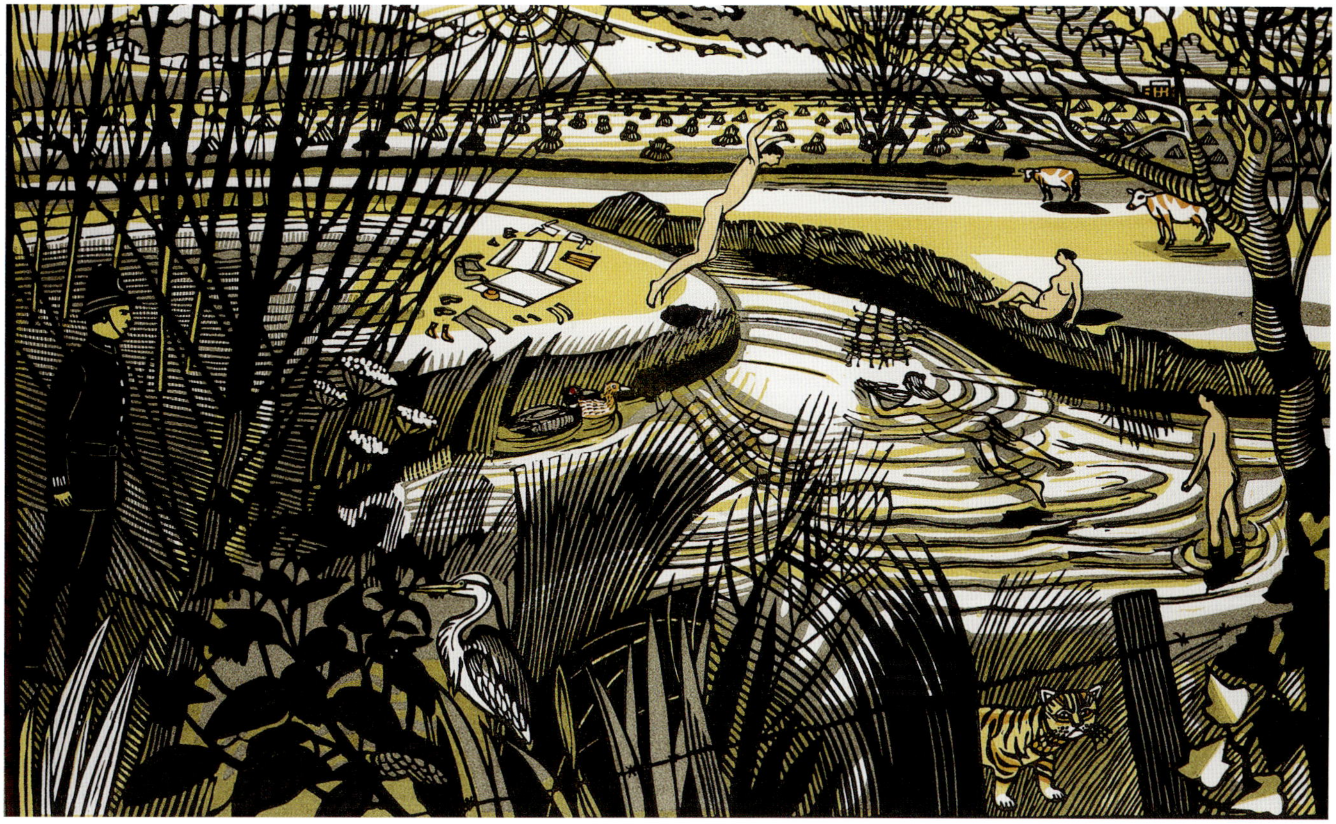

Richard Bawden, *A Splash in the Pant*, 1992, linocut, 420 x 660 mm; '. . . it occurred to me that the four of them: Edward, Charlotte, Eric and Tirzah splashing around naked in the Pant would make a jolly print, particularly as my mother had told me several times how Sergeant Baker had seen them and was too embarrassed to apprehend them.'

illustrated. They gave it the title *Lady Filmy Fern*, or *The Voyage of the Window Box*, submitted it to one publisher and when it was rejected put it aside.

It is a bizarre and innocent little story. The glamorous Lady Filmy Fern has retired from Society and its pressures to live under a bell-jar at the bottom of a cliff, her only neighbour being a deferential carpenter, Mr Virgin Cork. However, their privacy is disturbed by an intrusive paparazzo called the Welsh Polypod, a giant spider with a camera. They flee in a floating window box pursued by the villainous spider as far as India and beyond, but after various alarms it ends satisfactorily for all three characters. Bawden's ink drawings are free-flowing and bizarre enough to be called surreal – the final image, for example, of the spider in the bell-jar on the sea bed holding up an oil lamp to read his book 'Of Fishes' in order to identify the sea monsters swimming all round him. An interviewer asked Bawden if it was written with children in mind: 'Well, that's what we all pretended to ourselves. It would have got across easier in the '30s, but today there are child psychologists and the first question that's asked is "What age is it for?"' It seems a reasonable question given the range of social and geographical knowledge embedded in the text, but there were no children around the house at that time on whom to try it out.[5]

Later Bawden was asked if he would like to illustrate a real children's book and replied: 'I don't think a children's novel would suit me at all: I am handicapped by having no interest whatever in drawing children – fantasia is another matter, but little tots bore me stiff.' [6] According to Bawden, fantasia or fantasy is usually confined to the male imagination because women are such incorrigible realists:

'I mean we [men] don't have our feet on the ground, unless we have a love affair and then our feet are put on the ground. I think fantasy is a serious matter. It's a means of reconciling opposites which can't rationally be combined.'

In 1940 when a German invasion looked likely Bawden wrapped up the text and drawings of *Lady Filmy Fern*, along with his Morley mural designs and engraved copper plates and hid them all down a well in his Brick House garden, intending to retrieve them 'after the Germans had retreated', but then he forgot all about them. The men were happy enough painting together at home or on trips to the south coast, but eventually the strain of two women taking turns to cook began to show and the couples are said to have parted because of the too frequent appearance of the Queen of Puddings, the only one Tirzah could make. The wives were also thinking of space for children. The friendships remained intact but in 1934 the Raviliouses moved ten miles away to Bank House in Castle Hedingham, a former shop with a big bow window which illuminated Ravilious' immaculate studio. It was another pretty Essex village, but there were no fellow artists in it and Ravilious had to cycle to Brick House if he wanted to talk about work. There the first of their three children, John, was born in 1935, and in the same year Charlotte gave birth to a daughter, Joanna.

Before he left Brick House Ravilious had developed a distinctive watercolour style and at his first one-man show in 1933 at the Zwemmer Gallery its main characteristics were on display. He avoided the medium's temptations to use a fully loaded brush, washes bleeding into each other, accidental felicities of runs, granulations and splatters or any bravura effects which drew attention away from the subject matter. Wood-engraving had taught him to value clear boundaries, crisp focus over every square inch, variety in mark-making, sound design and precise drawing with no fudging. He was fond of sponging, scratching, stippling, cross-hatching, wax resists or parallel strokes to achieve textures on furrows, or skies, or grass, but always he stopped short of overworking the surface and allowed plenty of white paper to show through. The resulting tableaux are like stage sets, uncluttered, coolly and evenly lit, immaculate and empty, awaiting the entry of a human actor to bring their drama to life. On the rare occasions figures do appear they are faceless and seen at a distance.

If the means were reticent, so were the subjects: there was nothing here of the Sublime or the Picturesque, only wire fences, lace curtains, flower pots, lighthouses, tea in the garden, deckchairs, paddle-steamers, harrows, empty country lanes, or, coming indoors, sparsely-furnished cottage bedrooms, greenhouses, a glimpse of a chalk horse on the Downs from a railway carriage, flowers on a pine table, and the views from his windows at Castle Hedingham. He also had a taste for the melancholy dereliction of old buses and cars, abandoned farm machinery, rusted tractors and redundant steam engines.

He was a severe critic of his own work and destroyed many failures so that it was not until his third one-man show at Tooth's Gallery in 1939 that he felt he was getting anywhere. Of one painting he said: 'I so want the thing not to look washed out as they so often do.' But temperamentally he knew he was a painter of restraint, editing away superfluous detail, yet painstakingly recording every plant-pot in a greenhouse, the ropes on a ship's rigging or every stave in a fence until the ordinary became portentous.

By the time war became inevitable in 1939 Ravilious was a father twice over, but all was not well at Bank House and from 1934 his affections had been divided. At the RCA a member of their group had been Helen Binyon (1904-1979), one of the twin daughters of the poet Laurence Binyon, best known perhaps for his lines on the fallen in the 1914 war:

They shall not grow old, as we that are left grow old:
Age shall not weary them, nor the years condemn.
At the going down of the sun and in the morning
We shall remember them.

Binyon was also Keeper of Prints at the British Museum

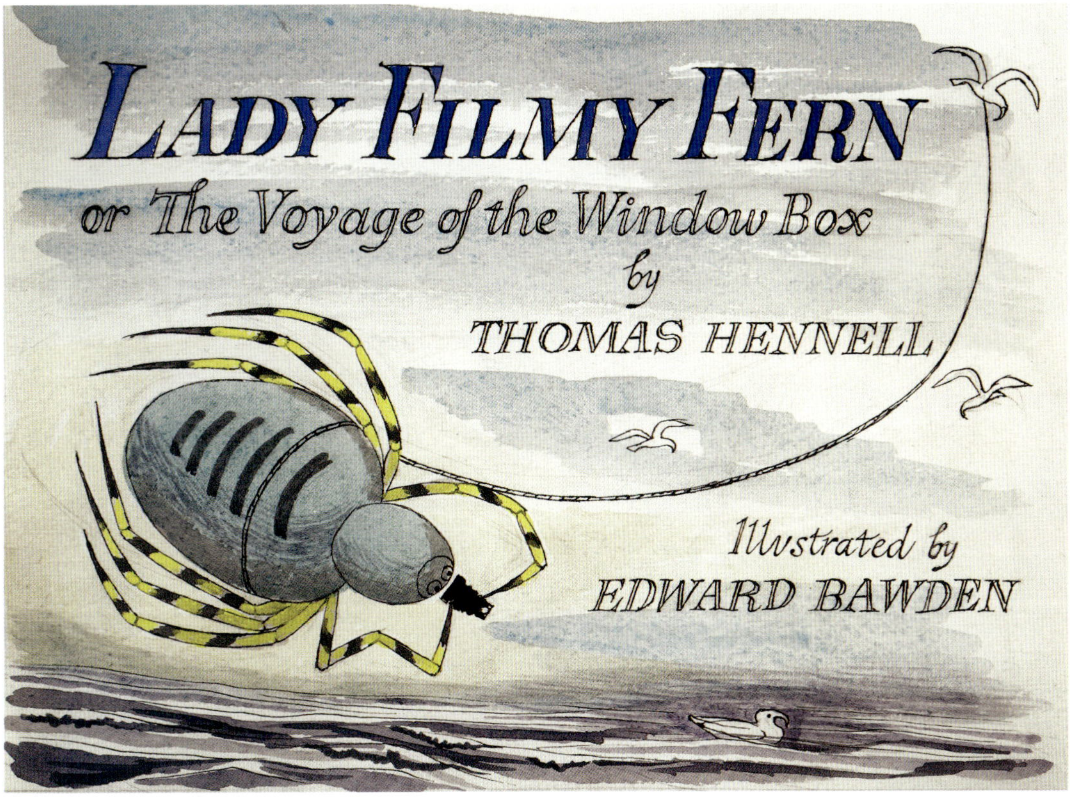

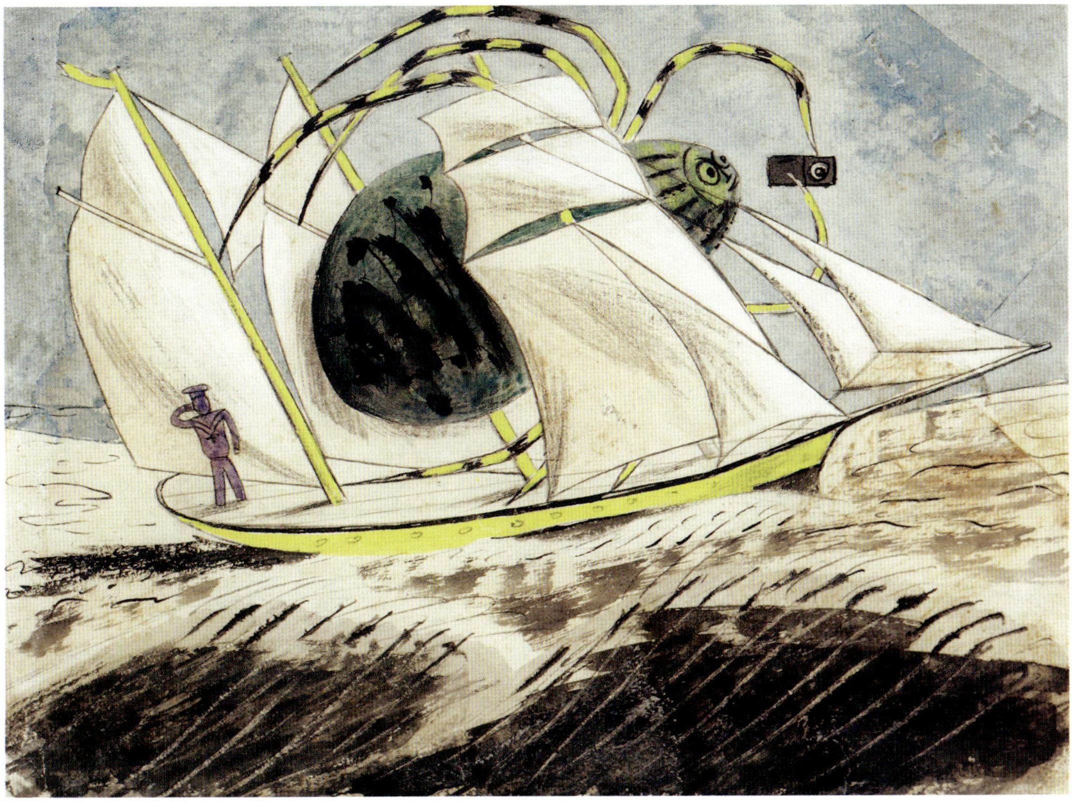

Two of Bawden's original illustrations from *Lady Filmy Fern*, *c.*1933, pen and ink and gouache; written by Tom Hennell in the early 1930s, and first published in 1980. (Fine Art Society).

and the author of two influential books on English watercolours and landscape painting. As a visiting lecturer at the RCA he had talked to them all about Chinese painting and shown them the works of Cotman and Towne. Helen Binyon moved in grander circles than her contemporaries and was presented at court whilst still a student. From college she went on to Paris and America, spending a year in each. Like Ravilious, Binyon was encouraged by Nash to take up wood-engraving, her best-known illustrations being for *Pride and Prejudice* (Penguin Books, 1938) and she and her twin sister also became expert puppeteers.

The collection of letters from Ravilious to Binyon written between the years 1934 and 1942, now in the East Sussex Record Office at Lewes, chart the passionate rise and sharp cooling off of their affair. At first their

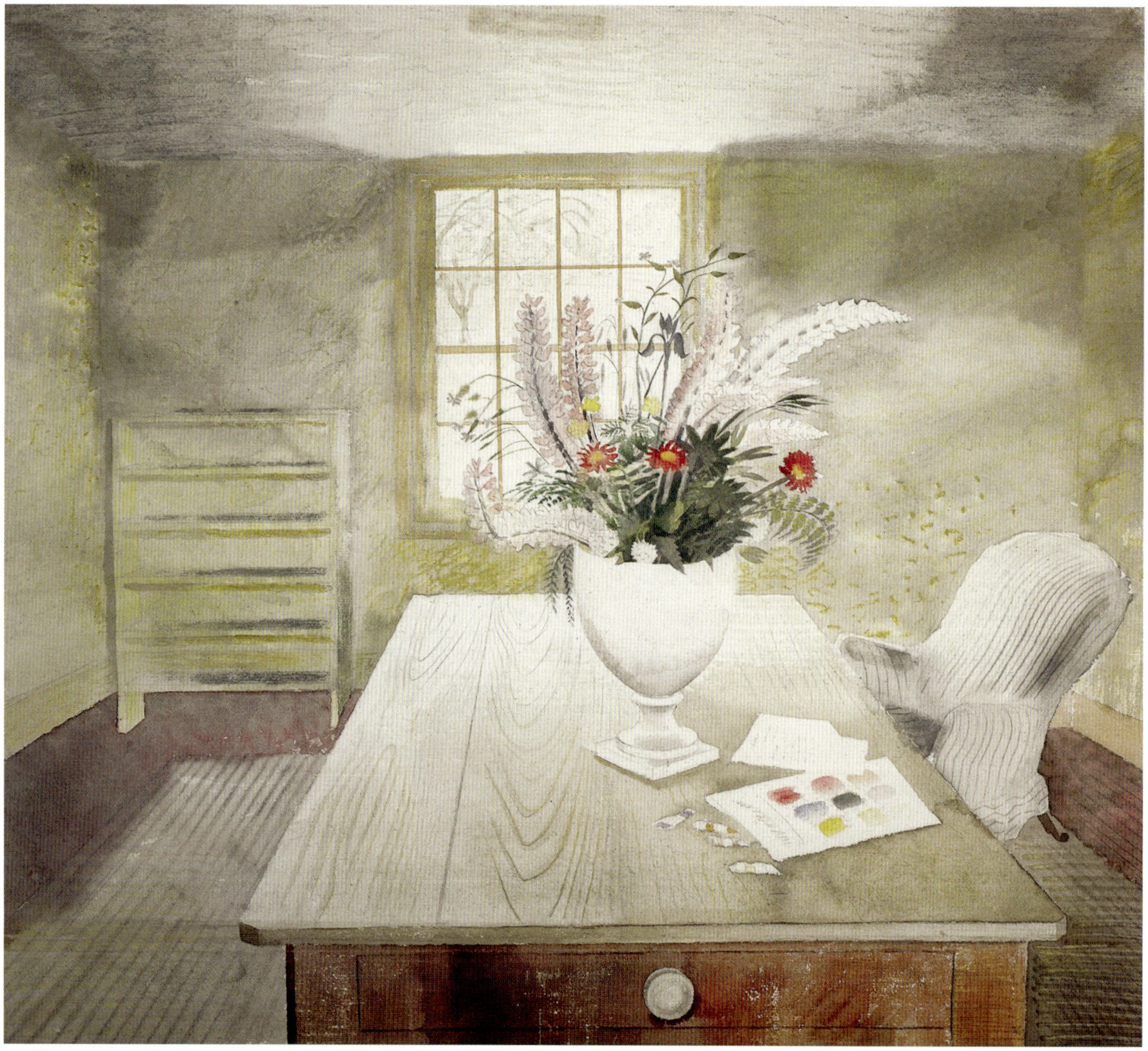

Eric Ravilious: *Garden Flowers on a Cottage Table*, 1941, watercolour, 514 x 559 mm.

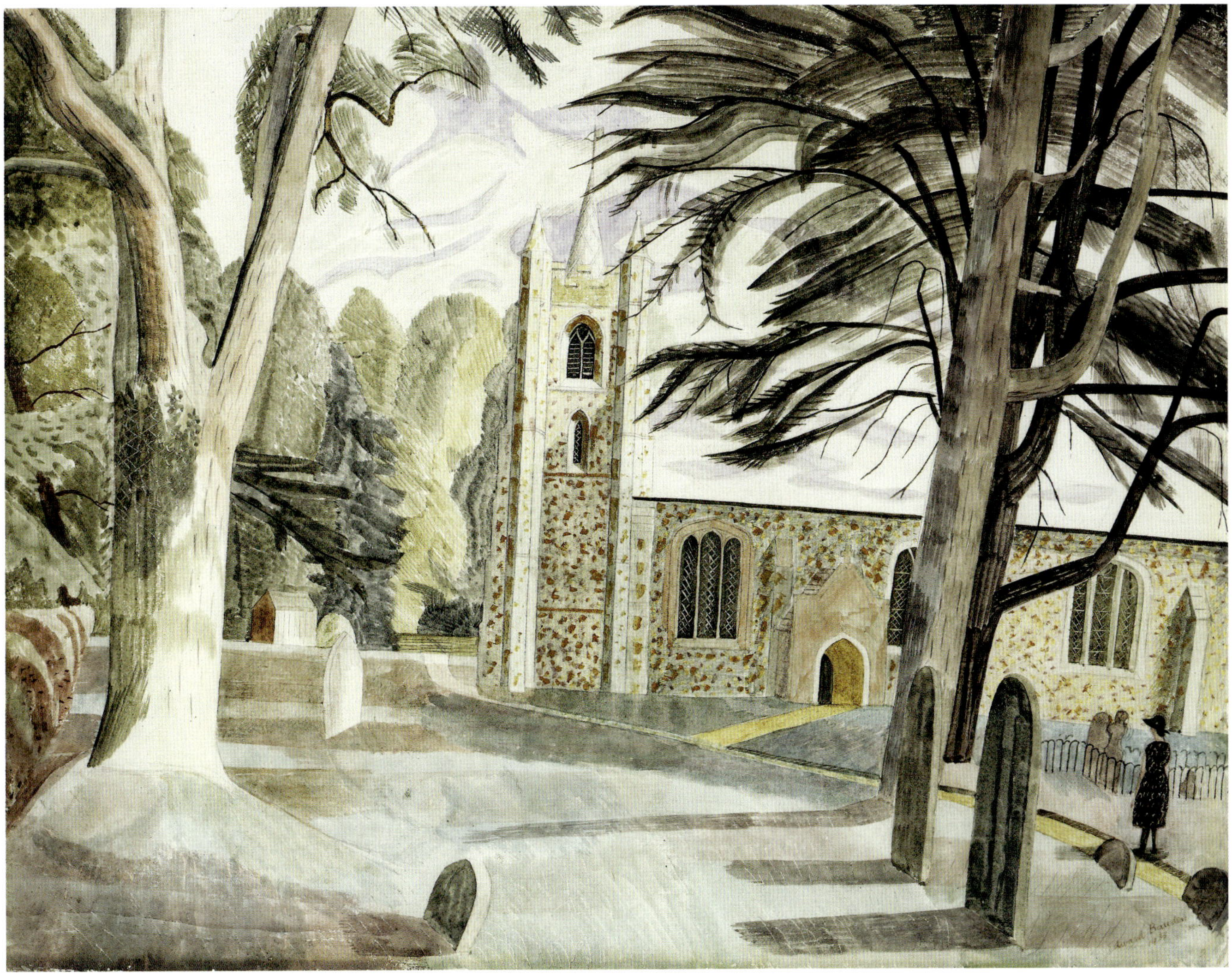

Christ! I have been a many times to Church (Little Sampford Church), 1933, watercolour, 460 x 580 mm (Victoria & Albert Museum).

assignations were in London when Ravilious went up to teach, but then they began to meet at a primitive cottage called Furlongs situated on the South Downs near Glynde. This was owned by Peggy Angus (1904-1993), known to her RCA contemporaries as 'Red' Angus because of her socialist views. Angus shared this retreat with James (Jim) Maude Richards (1907-1992), editor of *The Architectural Review* who in 1936 became her husband. To this cottage came the Bawdens, the Raviliouses, Pipers, Hortons and Oliver Simon for weekend parties. Few of these friends suspected the affair at first but eventually Ravilious felt he had to tell his two closest friends and reported to Binyon: 'Charlotte didn't seem to mind but Edward does very much. He would, I knew though is almost certain to recover later.' Tirzah knew too but, as her daughter Anne wrote later, 'Tirzah accepted the affair with good hearted resignation, possessing a strongly-reasoned approach to such episodes in their lives'.[7] Tirzah wrote to Binyon: 'Dear Helen, I'm awfully sorry about this wretched mess, it must have been awful for you. Eric is sure he wants to live with you more than he does with me and I don't mind his doing so because as you know I'm not in love with him myself. I definitely am in love with John Aldridge now though it is

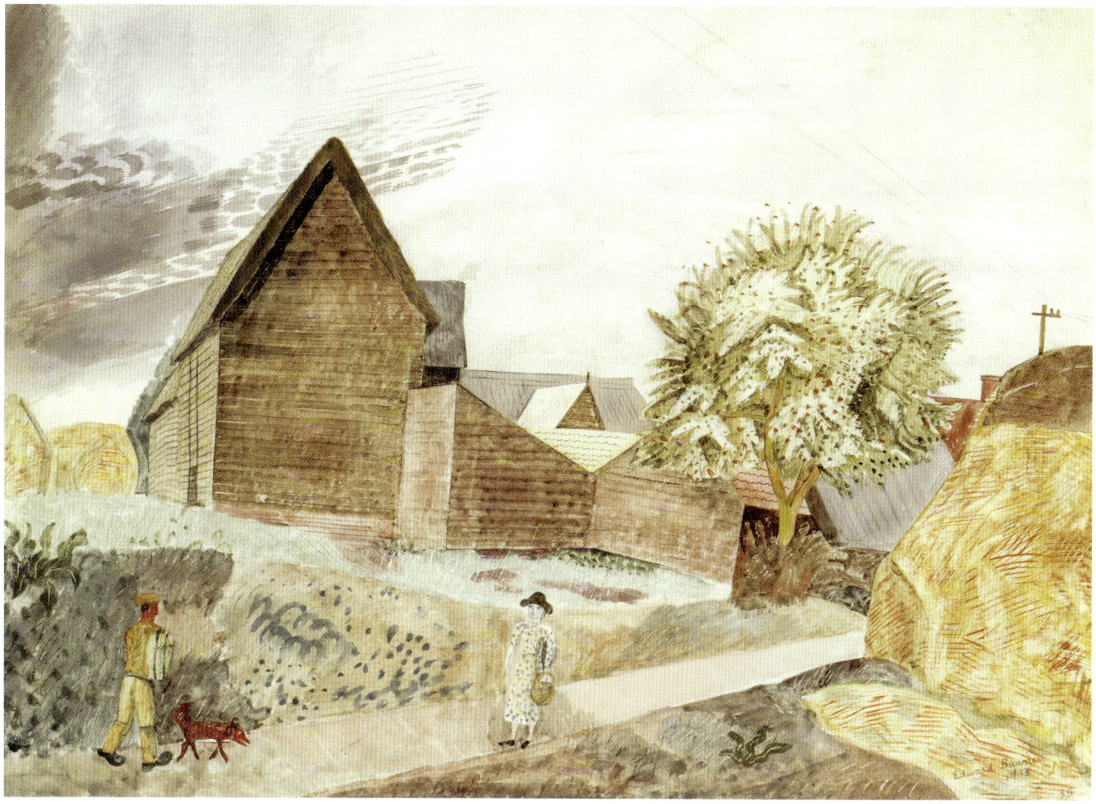

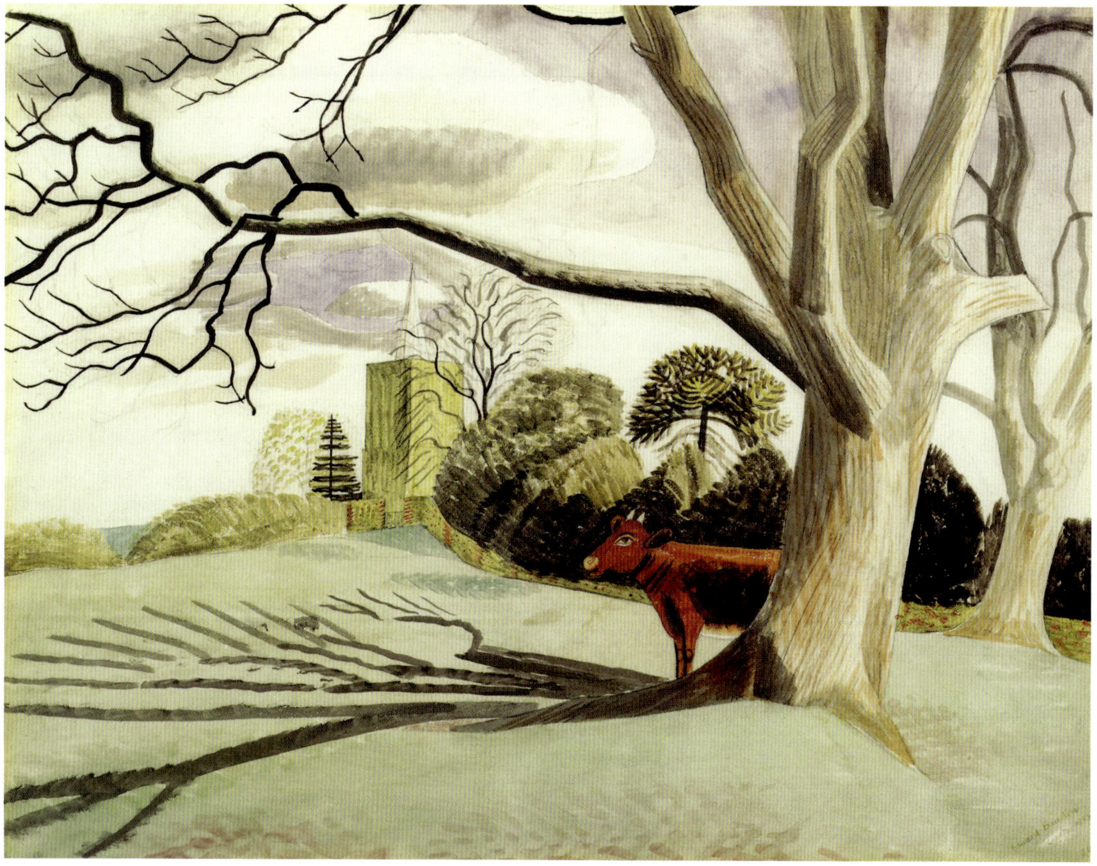

extremely unlikely that anything will happen about it as he is living with a neurotic woman who never leaves his side and he thinks he's fairly happy that way and doesn't want to change.' (26th April 1936). John Aldridge was a Great Bardfield artist we have yet to meet.

Surprisingly Ravilious and Binyon did not go ahead and live together, because soon after this letter was written Binyon seduced John Nash at one of Angus' parties and became his mistress, and later still attracted the advances of Jim Richards.[8] After Ravilious' and Tirzah's deaths Binyon wrote her *Eric Ravilious: Memoir of an Artist*, published four years after she died, still unmarried, in 1979 and this became his standard biography.

Ravilious continued to live with Tirzah and his children but frequently returned to the cottage because he found the treeless swellings of the Downs and big skies inspiring and a

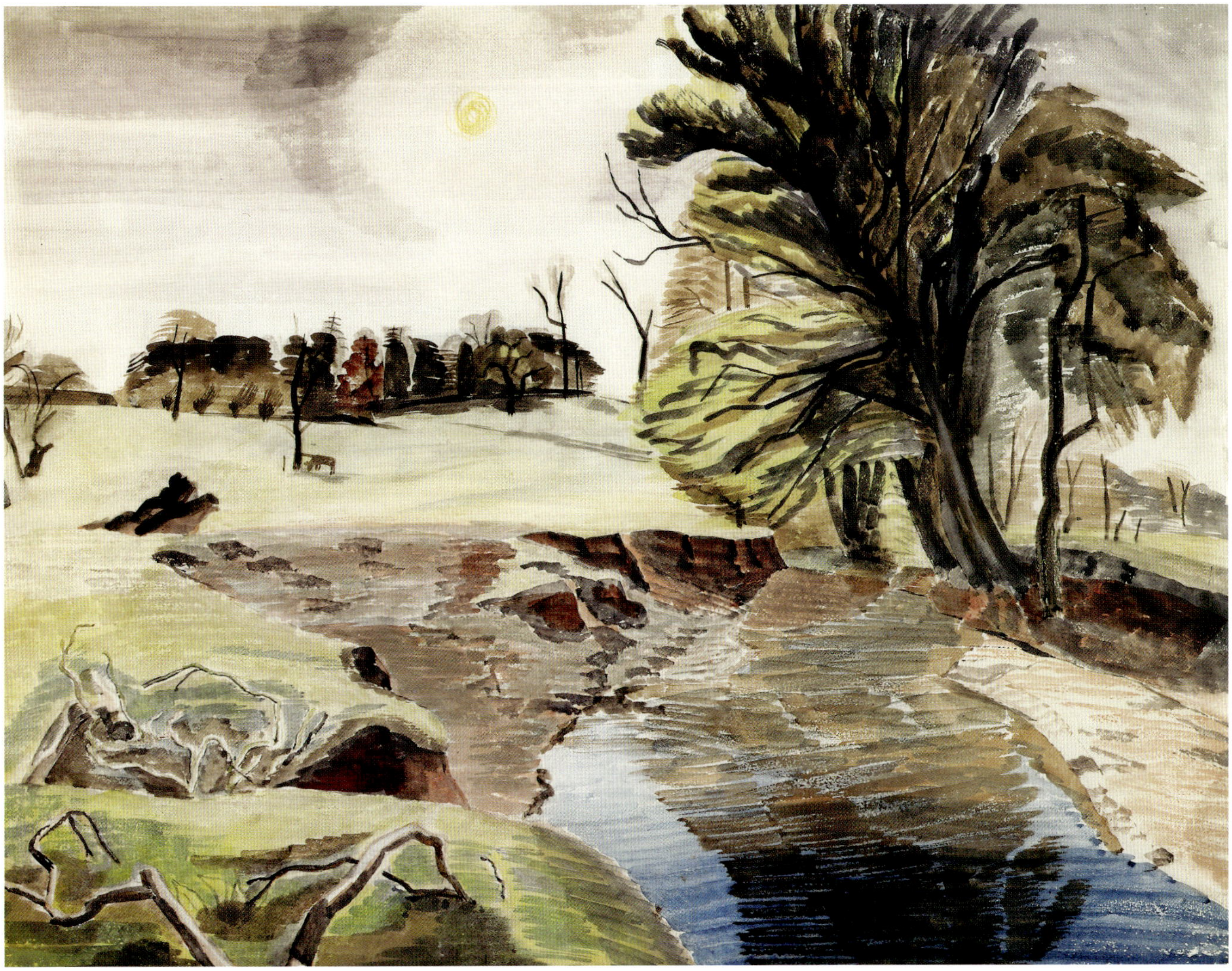

Above: *Beslyns*, watercolour, 1938, 445 x 570 mm (Fine Art Society).
Opposite top: *Now with religious awe the farewell light Blends with the solemn colouring of the night, 1933*, watercolour, 412 x 560 mm (© Queen's Printer and Controller of HMSO, 2005. UK Government Art Collection).
Opposite bottom: *The Red Cow, 1933*, watercolour, approx. 450 x 570 mm (Fine Art Society).

welcome change from the florid greenery of Castle Hedingham. Soon he was painting more Sussex than Essex pictures and exploring wind pumps, greenhouses, eerily white cement works and the garden and interior of the flint-covered cottage itself. He also made a series of paintings of the prehistoric figures and horses cut into the chalk hillsides.

Like his friendly rival, Bawden too had an exhibition at the Zwemmer Gallery in October 1933, – one month before Ravilious. To show at the Zwemmer Gallery was an accolade – after all, Dali and Picasso had been amongst those who had preceded them. The Dutchman, Anton Zwemmer, had opened the gallery in 1929 at 26 Litchfield Street, just round the corner from his specialist art bookshop in Charing Cross Road. Artists flocked to Zwemmer to see the new art and to browse, unmolested, through the Skira volumes and continental art magazines. Kenneth Clark, Herbert Read and Anthony Blunt all claimed to have completed their education amongst its shelves. As one might expect, Bawden's latest watercolours were all views of rural Essex and they sold well in spite of

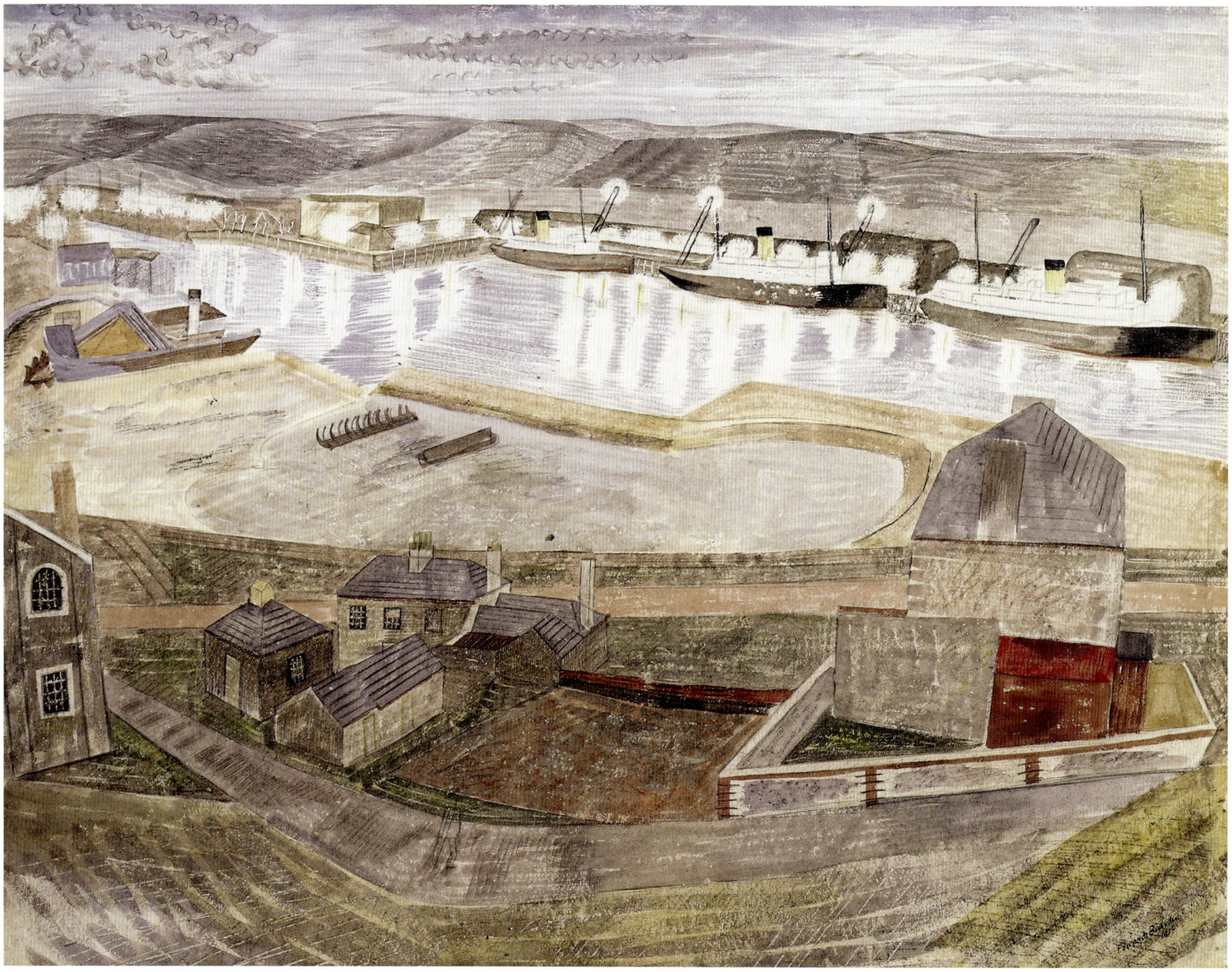

10 September: 8.30 pm (Newhaven), 1935, watercolour, 460 x 560 mm (Peyton Skipwith).

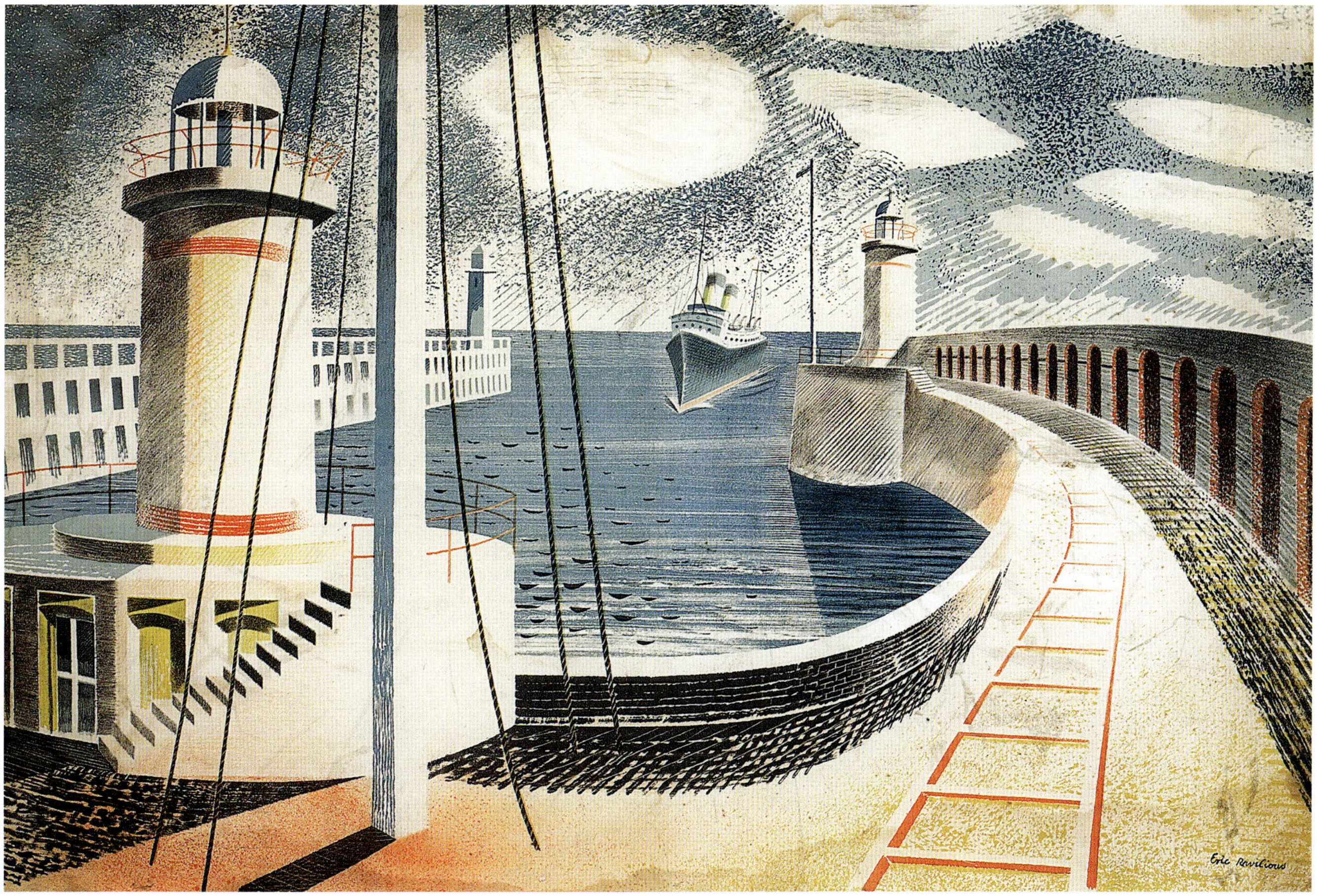

Eric Ravilious, *Newhaven Harbour, Homage to Seurat*, 1937, lithograph, 520 x 760 mm.

having no titles to identify the places. Instead they had fragments of George Herbert's verse suggested by Gwyneth Lloyd Thomas, which Bliss realised was another aspect of Bawden's offbeat sense of humour. The critics were kind: *The Times* one wrote on the 7th of October: '*All point, all edge, all sharpness*', applied to a drawing of a village square, 'is really an apt description of the flavour of the whole series – a surprising flavour, like that of watercress'. Bliss reviewing the show in *The Scotsman* two days later seems sometimes to be pulling his friend's leg ('He has always sought for the cleverest way of expressing a thing, and has often found it') and at others to be offering genuine insights: 'he looks around his Essex landscape wide-eyed and eagerly, but he sees it all as no one else would. He sees it without depth and atmosphere, preternaturally bright and clean and colourful; and, as though he were regarding them in a distorting mirror, he makes all objects diminutive and droll. The men and cows are jointed dolls; the trees and barns and churches "properties" in a first class puppet show.' Technically there were 'clever and original tricks in plenty: he sets off transparent passages with passages opaque with body-colour, and he deftly splashes ink and scratches out lights with the point of his knife'. Later Bawden claimed he never had another success like this one – everything sold and there was a profit of £150.

In 1937 Bawden had another successful exhibition in the same gallery and in 1938 one at the prestigious Leicester Galleries. This time he attached the time, date and place to each landscape instead of a conventional title, an indication that he was out to capture the specific conditions under which he had viewed the scene. Eric Newton, the foremost critic of the time, was impressed that Bawden had broken all the text-book rules for watercolours: 'the result is that they are neither slick nor charming nor fresh. They are dry and worried and patchy. But they are immensely serious.' They were interpretations, not likenesses, for 'Bawden's landscapes make no attempt to deceive the eye. Nature in his work is sternly conventionalised, not thoughtlessly imitated, but Bawden's conventions are alive. Each one is invented (with a fertile invention too) to fit the thing he has to say. That is a rarer thing than one might suppose. To divine the pattern that will express the texture and "feel" of a tree or a railing or a snowstorm demands constant awareness. It is the lazy artist who contents himself with stylising nature and forcing her to fit into a set of ready-made patterns.' [9]

Like Ravilious, Bawden concentrated on the commonplace aspect of country life ('trite Essex' one reviewer sneered). Betjeman had a similar feel for the unspectacular charms of the county:

> Like streams the little by-roads run
> Through oats and barley round a hill
> To where blue willows catch the sun
> By some white weather-boarded mill.
>
> The deepest Essex few explore
> Where steepest thatch is sunk in flowers
> And out of elm and sycamore
> Rise flinty fifteenth-century towers. from *Essex*

Later Bawden told a friend he had no interest in painting the picturesque – 'it's like painting bluebell woods'. He deplored the uniform greenness of England and, like Ravilious, favoured muted colours such as sepias, browns, blues, greys, and ochres applied by a dryish brush over a clear scaffolding of drawing. As with his design work, nothing was left to chance. Outdoor paintings usually gain in spontaneity because they are painted under pressures of time, weather, fading light, wind, nosy spectators, midges and so on, but they lose in coherence when compared to works completed at leisure indoors. Paradoxically Bawden was able to work in a field and still make compositions of the utmost deliberation.

Both Ravilious and Bawden had learned a good deal from Paul Nash, and indeed from each other and this was noticed. Norbert Lynton commented: 'What joins them is the sense of craft as well as their strong roots in the English scene. But where Bawden is muscular and summary, Ravilious is delicate and precise, bulldog versus greyhound.' [10] Ravilious, after being caught in a storm, described it as 'like one of those extravagant and formless pictures of Turner's' and one can see that both men would give a shudder of distaste if either adjective were applied to their own work; they could never be accused of painting 'tinted steam' as Turner was. Some people have found this emotional coolness not to their taste and think their paintings to be bloodless and overly refined. Frances Spalding, for example, wrote: 'Bawden's and Ravilious' watercolours with their bleak winter light are often severely beautiful but they retain a clinical distance: the scene excludes not only the viewer but also the artist. The attempt to extract permanence from impermanent conditions results in a predominantly mental grasp of landscape.' [11]

In 1936 the Bawdens had a second child, Richard (Tom Hennell was his godfather) and the financial pressures increased. The Curwen Press were again helpful, as Oliver Simon recalled: 'the circumstances were propitious for besides ourselves several more of our clients were persuaded to use his [Bawden's] unique and highly original talents. His range and mastery of techniques, in addition to his paintings in watercolours, were by now remarkable. He had taken the measure of the difficult art

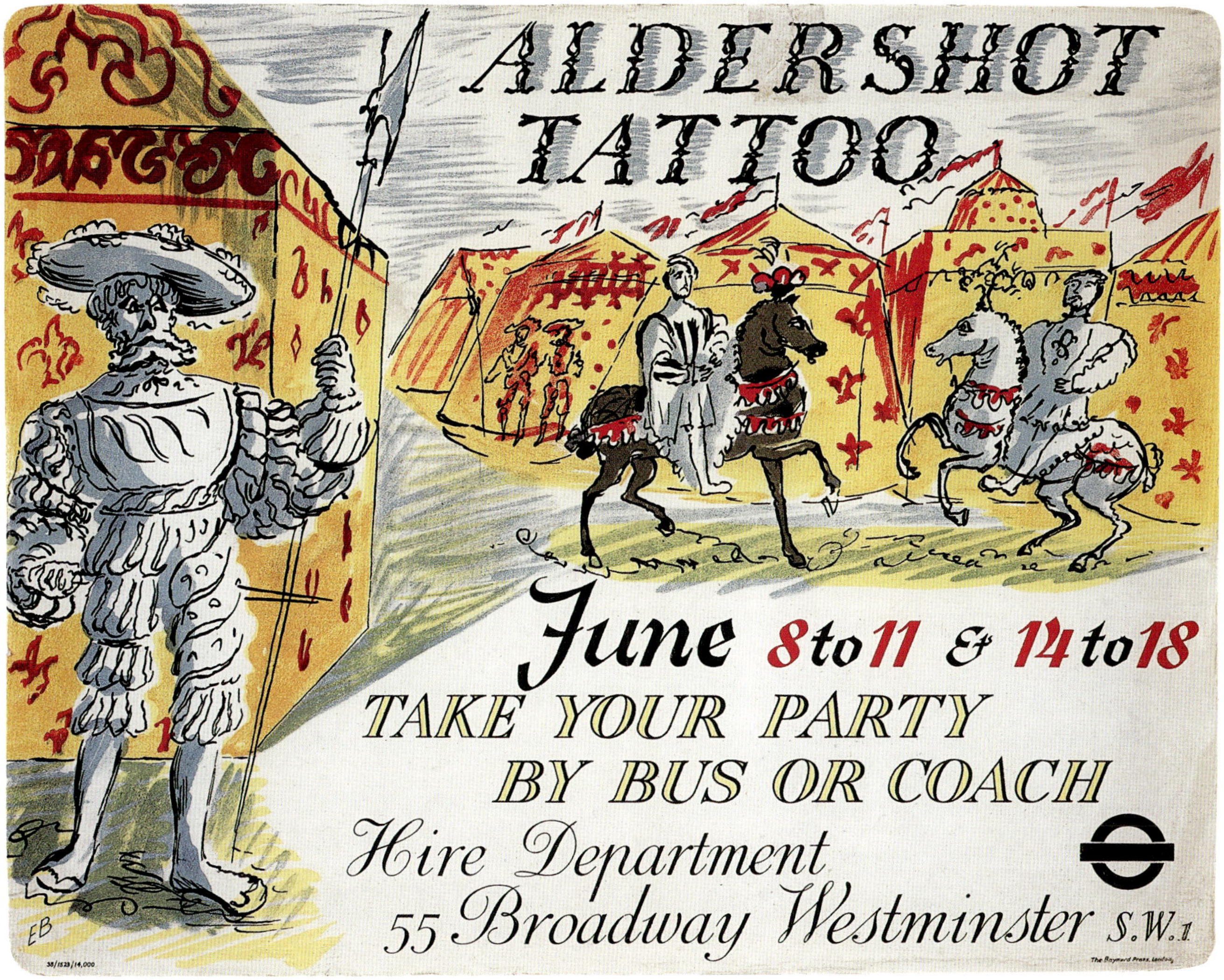

Small London Underground poster for Aldershot Tattoo, 1938, printed at the Baynard Press; 25 x 32 cm.

of engraving his compositions direct on copper; he exploited the coloured lino-block to the best advantage for his designs. His wallpapers were subtle, fresh and beautiful; vignettes and borders poured from his fertile imagination, and he had become the leading exponent of the art of linoleum cut and his work in this genre stood in splendid isolation. He cut the various separated pieces of linoleum for each colour; transfers were then made from each piece (there might be two or three dozen pieces for a poster) on to lithographic plates for printing, which was executed in close cooperation with Harold Curwen, for posters, book jackets and so on. He firmly refused to be on the telephone in his house, but the numerous letters he wrote always contained an element of sardonic humour whatever the occasion.' [12]

Simon, now a close friend, visited Brick House often: 'The Bawdens were an excellent foil for each other. Edward taciturn, but likely to burst out at any moment, at war with the peccadilloes of business; Charlotte warm-hearted and brimful of laughter. Although the Bawdens were vegetarians, the meals were highly imaginative and by no means teetotal. In Charlotte's hands vegetarianism became a pleasure. The meals were inevitably the background to moments of vigorous sparring between

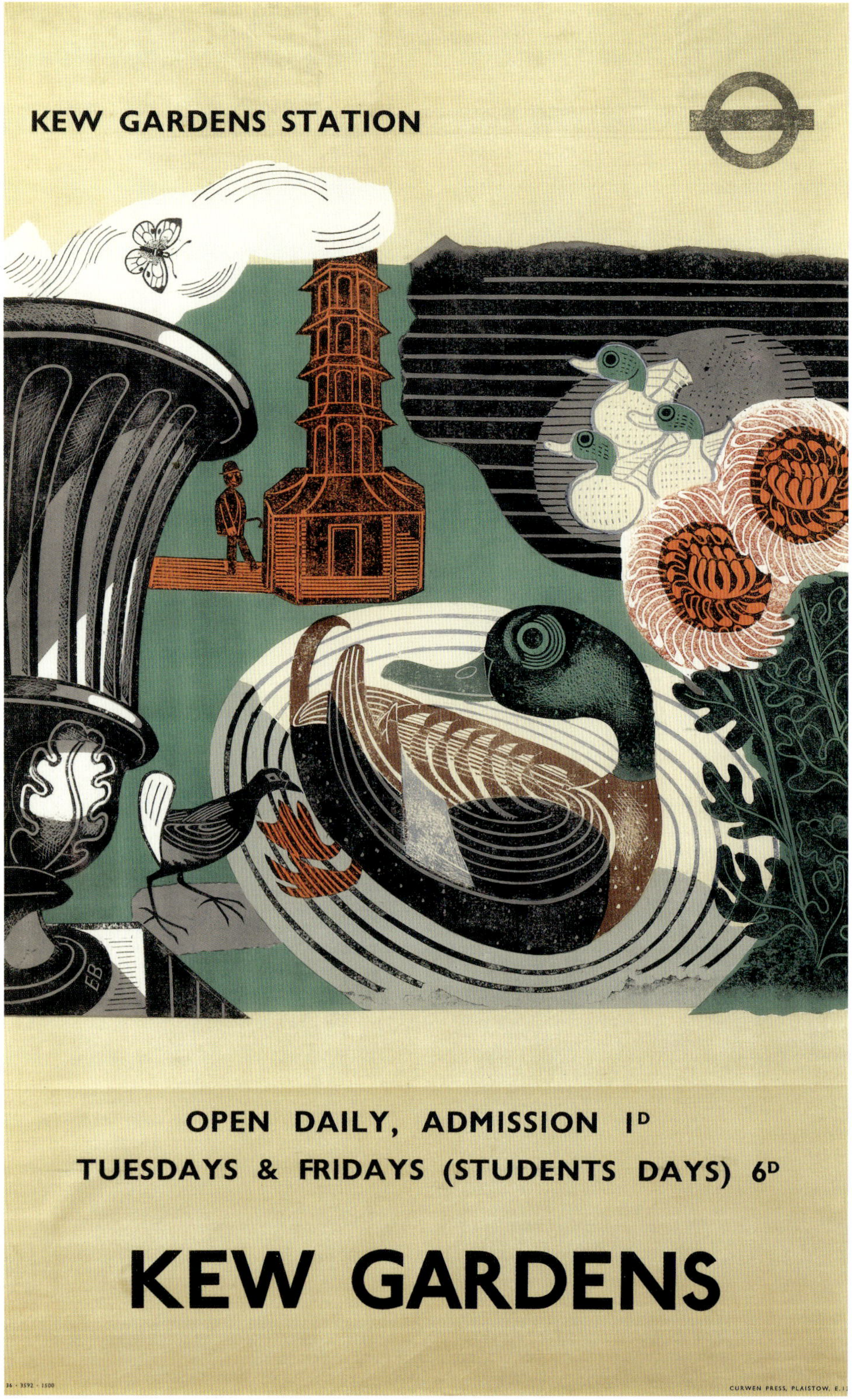

Kew Gardens poster for London Underground, 1936,
printed at the Curwen Press (Fine Art Society).

Opposite: London Underground poster, 1936, printed at the Curwen Press for the London Passenger Transport Board, 100 x 63 cm.

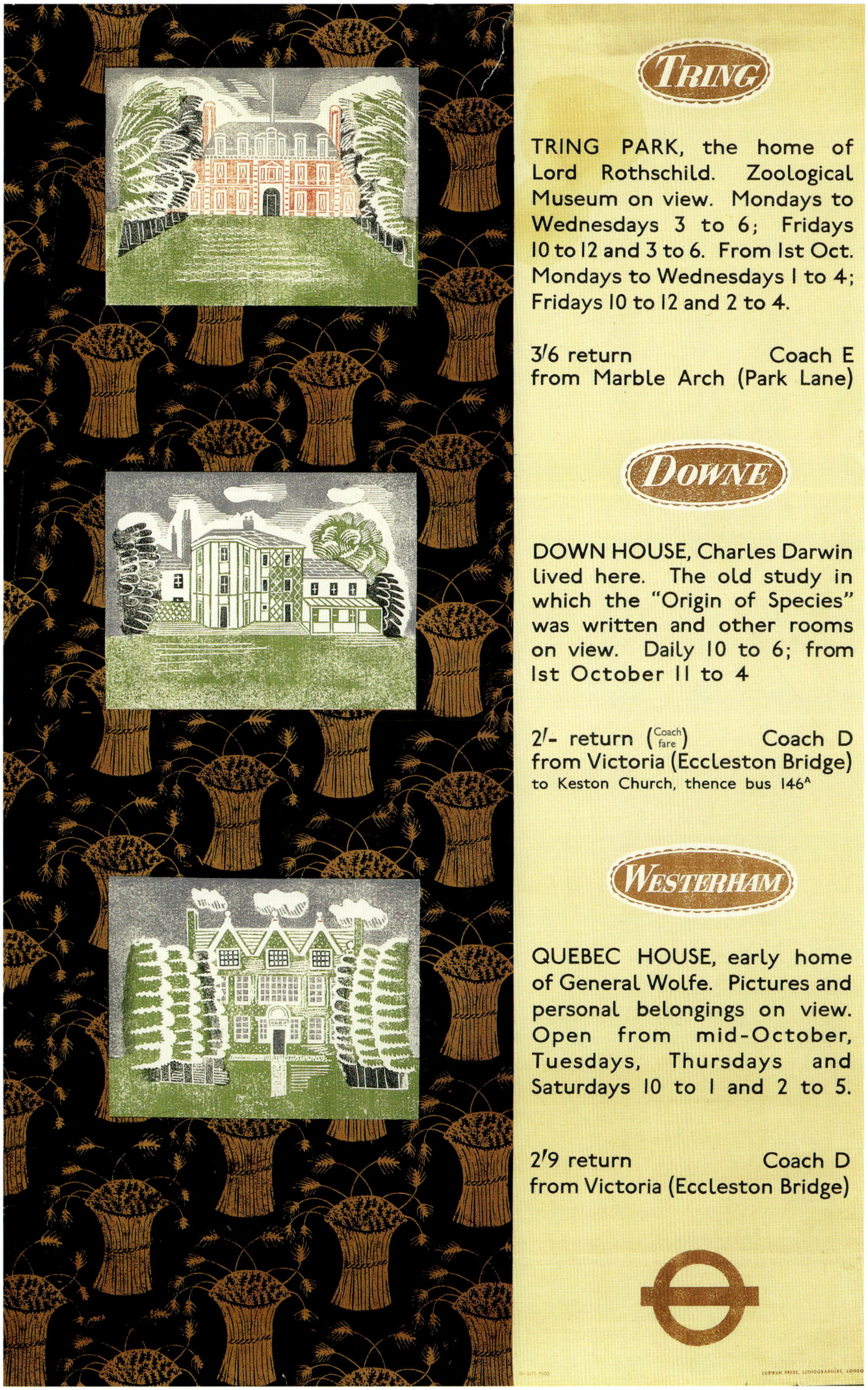
TRING
TRING PARK, the home of Lord Rothschild. Zoological Museum on view. Mondays to Wednesdays 3 to 6; Fridays 10 to 12 and 3 to 6. From 1st Oct. Mondays to Wednesdays 1 to 4; Fridays 10 to 12 and 2 to 4.
3/6 return Coach E
from Marble Arch (Park Lane)
DOWNE
DOWN HOUSE, Charles Darwin lived here. The old study in which the "Origin of Species" was written and other rooms on view. Daily 10 to 6; from 1st October 11 to 4
2/- return (Coach fare) Coach D
from Victoria (Eccleston Bridge)
to Keston Church, thence bus 146A
WESTERHAM
QUEBEC HOUSE, early home of General Wolfe. Pictures and personal belongings on view. Open from mid-October, Tuesdays, Thursdays and Saturdays 10 to 1 and 2 to 5.
2/9 return Coach D
from Victoria (Eccleston Bridge)

Edward and me.' He also introduced the Bawdens and Raviliouses to the dandy, epicure, bibliophile and biographer A. J. Symons who lived a mile away at Finchingfield and who owned a wonderful library and a collection of musical boxes.

For the five years between 1935 and 1940 Oliver Simon edited a magazine of graphic art and typography, *Signature*, and in its first edition was an article by Paul Nash praising and contrasting the nervy, energetic drawing style of Graham Sutherland with Bawden's more precise, controlled and cautious line. Simon reproduced in the magazine works by both Ravilious and Bawden as well as Piper, Nash, Sutherland, Freedman and Ardizzone alongside such foreign stars as Miro, Dufy and Picasso without any suggestion that the Europeans were superior. For the two decades before his death in 1934, Roger Fry and his Bloomsbury followers had persuaded English artists and collectors that all good art originated in Paris, but now there was a new confidence in the land and a feeling we could hold our own with these continentals in painting and design.

Ravilious, for one, felt able to give up teaching and to move into two new areas: lithography and ceramics. The Director at the Zwemmer Gallery, Robert Wellington, and John Piper decided to commission ten artists to make 'Contemporary Prints' which could be reproduced cheaply enough for schools to buy them, so bringing modern English art to the next generation. The Nash brothers

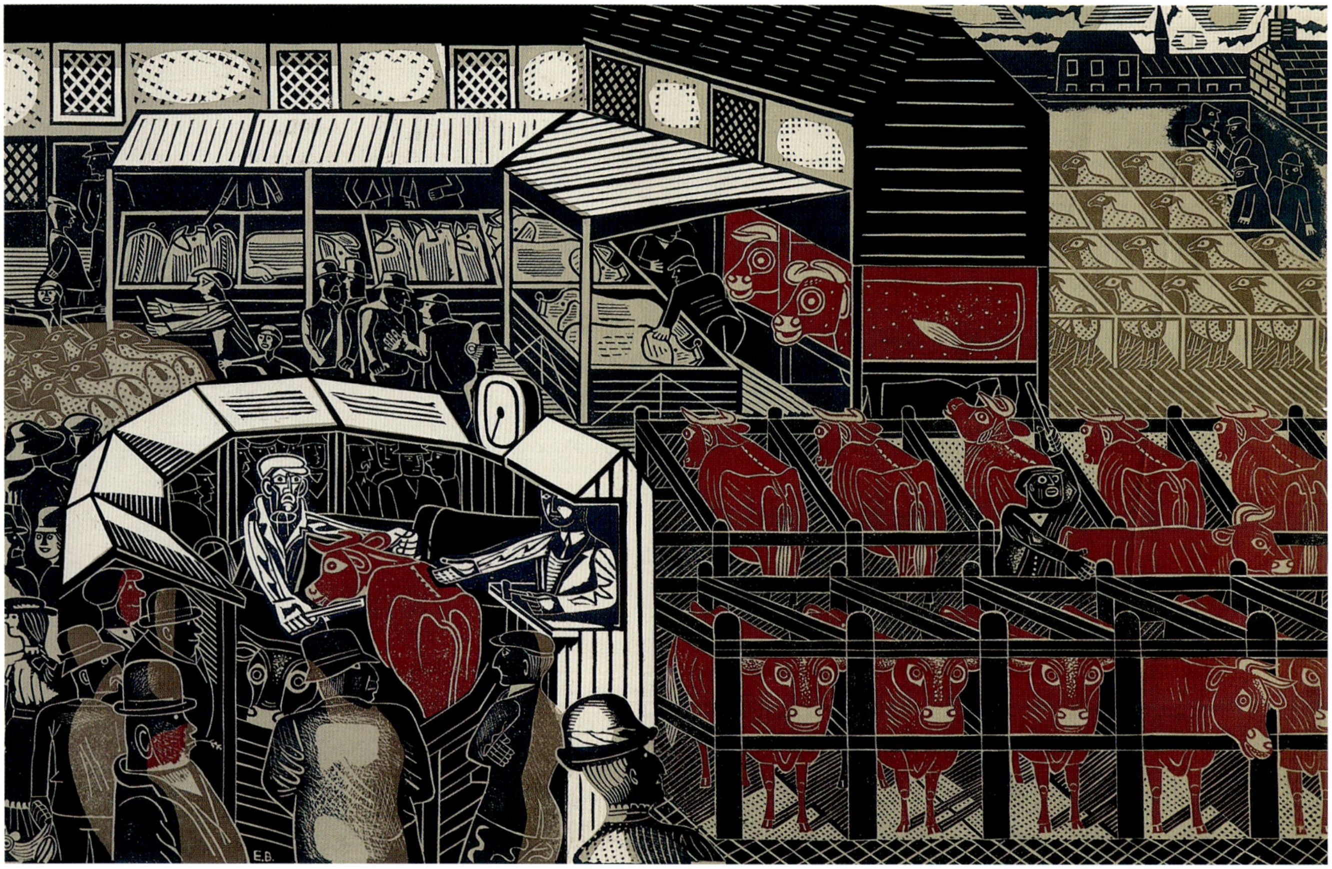

Cattle Market, Braintree, Essex, 1937, lithograph after linocut, 507 x 760 mm (Trustees of Cecil Higgins Art Gallery, Bedford).

were included of course, as were Sutherland, Freedman, Bawden and Ravilious. Bawden made a bright lithograph after a linocut called Cattle Market, Braintree, Essex, showing the cows, pigs and sheep in their pens. Ravilious' contribution was Newhaven Harbour: *Homage to Seurat* (1937) developed from studies made on a week-long painting expedition to the port with Bawden in August 1935. This lithograph shows in four luminous colours a ship gliding into the spotless and deserted harbour and evokes Seurat's calm and glinting depictions of ports across the Channel. Having enjoyed his work with Harold Curwen and his technicians Ravilious was keen to do more, especially as wood-engraving was being replaced by lithography as the favourite means of reproduction.

In 1938 he collaborated with Jim Richards and Harold Curwen on *High Street*, making twenty-four lithos of shops that took his fancy, selling, for example, bread, fireworks, funerals, furs and feathers, cakes, model ships and railways, fire appliances, theatrical props, cheese, clerical outfits, oysters and submarine engineering equipment. Ravilious worked up his on-the-spot sketches directly onto zinc plates at Curwen's press in Plaistow, each illustration being printed in four colours with a separate plate for each, though there seem to be many more because of the superimpositions. The result is a charming record of emporia swept away by post-war chain stores and supermarkets and the volume is now an expensive rarity.

Then came another challenge. A friend who had been a student at the Royal College of Art with Bawden and Ravilious, Cecilia Alice Dunbar Kilburn (1903-1984), joined with the college's Registrar, Athole Hay, in setting up a shop, Dunbar Hay, in Albermarle Street which would be true to the Design School's ideals. Ravilious engraved the trade card, designed mahogany and boxwood carver and dining chairs with two tables, and soon they were selling his ceramic designs, embroidery patterns and carpets. They also sold Charlotte and Tirzah's marbled papers. Kilburn introduced Ravilious to Tom Wedgwood and yet another RCA alumnus, Victor Skellern, who had become Head of Design at the Wedgwood Pottery in Stoke-on-Trent. They invited Ravilious to make images which could be applied by skilled tradesmen to standard earthenware or china shapes by a transfer process or lithography. His first was an Edward VIII coronation mug of 1936 with a firework motif. After the Abdication, Bawden pulled his leg: 'As a supporter of the monarchy – & ipso facto of the present vicious capitalist system – I

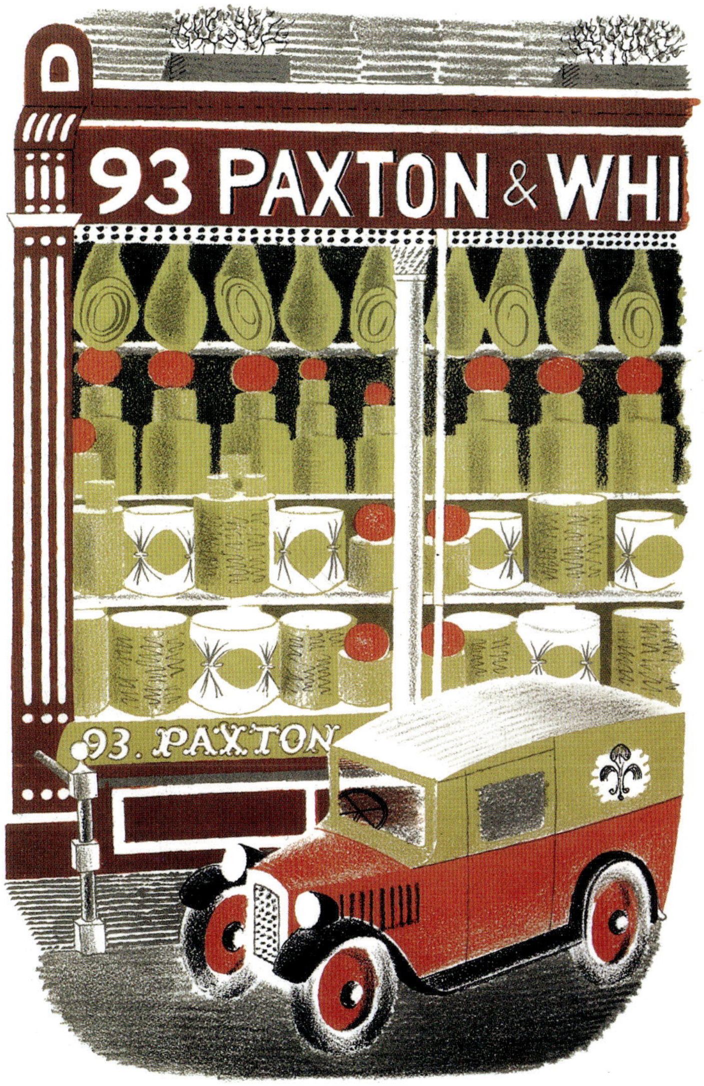

'Paxton and Whitfield, Cheesemongers', lithograph; one of Ravilious' illustrations to *High Street*, written by J. M. Richards, 1938 (Fry Art Gallery).

suppose you will provide the same form of persuasive publicity for Geo. 6.' (13th January 1937). Indeed the mug was adapted for George's accession. In between he decorated plates, an Alphabet mug for children, bowls and full tea-sets using favourite motifs from his paintings and wood-engravings such as sheaves of corn, tea-tables, boats, trains, scenes from Boat Race day (1938) and the Garden (1938). He also designed the Four Continents bowl (1939) and a London underground plate of 1939 which were not made, and his final design was for the Barlaston Mug which celebrated Wedgwood's new factory opening in 1939. All relied on silhouettes, witty, delicate lines and subdued colours such as silver grey and lemon yellow – precisely the techniques he had developed in watercolour. Of course all this came to an end with the war, but when peace arrived some of Ravilious' designs would be produced posthumously, and Bawden too would be asked to design for Wedgwood.

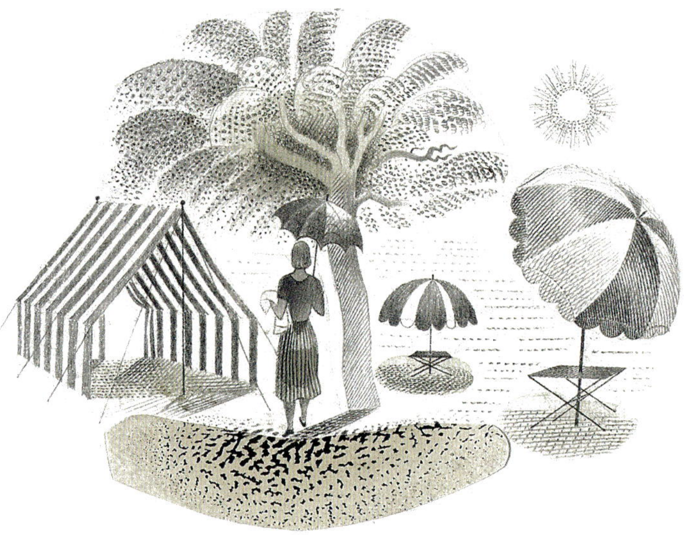

Eric Ravilious: design for Wedgwood's *Garden* series, 1938,
115 x 145 mm.

1. Fine Art Society catalogue for Thomas Hennell exhibition, November-December 1988.
2. Binyon, H., *Eric Ravilious: Memoir of an Artist*, Lutterworth Press, 1983, p.59.
3. Bliss, D. P., *Edward Bawden*, The Pendomer Press, 1979, p.72.
4. Bliss, D. P., ibid, p.71.
5. Spalding, F. 'Edward Bawden', *Arts Review*, 26th September 1980, p.417.
6. Harling, R., 'Edward Bawden', *Art and Technics*, 1950, p.37.
7. Ullmann, A. (ed.), *Ravilious at War*, Fleece Press, 2002, p.12.
8. The letters between John Nash, Christine Nash & Helen Binyon are in the Tate Britain Gallery Archives.
9. Quoted by Howes, J., in *Edward Bawden: A Retrospective Survey*, Combined Arts, 1988, p.117.
10. Lynton, N., *The Sussex Scene: Artists in Sussex in the Twentieth Century*, Hove Art Gallery and Towner Art Gallery, Eastbourne, 1993, p.42.
11. Spalding, F., *British Art Since 1900*, Thames and Hudson, 1986, p.71.
12. Simon, O., *Printer and Playground*, Faber and Faber, 1956, p.120.

5. ADVANCED GARDENERS

Apart from his days spent commuting from Great Bardfield to London and back during term time Bawden was content to stay and work in his rural backwater. He painted his own environs, or places he could walk or cycle to, or to which he could persuade Charlotte to drive him. Longer excursions were rare, though he did go painting to Newhaven in 1936, Bath in 1937 and to Geneva in 1939. When not doing watercolours or making designs for Curwen or the Monotype Corporation he was gardening in his one-acre plot behind the house, or reading about gardening: herbals, pomology, old-fashioned roses, poisonous plants, the more obscure the lore the better he liked it. He shared this horticultural enthusiasm with several close artist friends.

Perhaps the most assiduous, successful and erudite local gardener was John Aldridge (1905-1983) who came cycling into Great Bardfield in 1933. He was the son of a Royal Horse Artillery officer based in Woolwich, from where he was sent to Uppingham public school before going on to Corpus Christi, Oxford, where he read Greats. There, according to his friend John Betjeman, he was an 'aesthete' in Neville Coghill's circle: 'In this exotic group of pleasure lovers and drivers of bull-nosed Morrises, the tall self-effacing fair-haired figure of John Aldridge was outstanding but not out of place. He was outstanding because even with the distractions of those days he wanted to be an artist, and used his rooms in Corpus as his studio. What sort of painter he wanted to be he could not be quite sure . . . . In those days John Aldridge had two qualities remarkable in an Oxford aesthete. He was good at games and he got a degree.' [1] He was also interested in opera and rugby and had the future actress Margaret Rawlings as his girlfriend. After graduating in 1928 he first lived in Chiswick with the poet Norman Cameron and then began extensive European travels in order to teach himself to paint in oils, the medium he was to use for the rest of his life. He also expanded his social circle in London to include poets such as Ruthven Todd, John Betjeman, and Robert Graves for whom he designed the covers of *I Claudius* and painted a fine portrait, now in the National Portrait Gallery. For Laura Riding, the formidable poet who lived with Graves, he drew torture, bondage, skeletons and devils to illustrate her volume *Life of the Dead* (1933), with Riding standing over him telling him what to draw. Not surprisingly he seemed to have little enthusiasm for illustration after this. He married and in 1933 settled with his wife Lucie (née Cecilia Lucie Leeds Brown) in Great Bardfield in a magnificent half-timbered Elizabethan dwelling called Place House. This became a showcase of advanced good taste with Lucie's hand-made rugs on the floors and with Ben Nicholson, Frances Hodgkins and six Alfred Wallis paintings on the walls. The house had its own disused chapel and a large garden watered by a stream. The development of this garden Aldridge considered 'a process which combines selection, precision and an understanding of the nature and possibilities of the material in a way which is analogous to that of painting.'

For a self-taught painter he had achieved notice remarkably quickly with an invitation in 1931 from Ben Nicholson to exhibit with the progressive Seven and Five Society. A solo exhibition followed at the prestigious Leicester Galleries in 1933 and representation at the Venice Biennale in 1934. But, because he had private

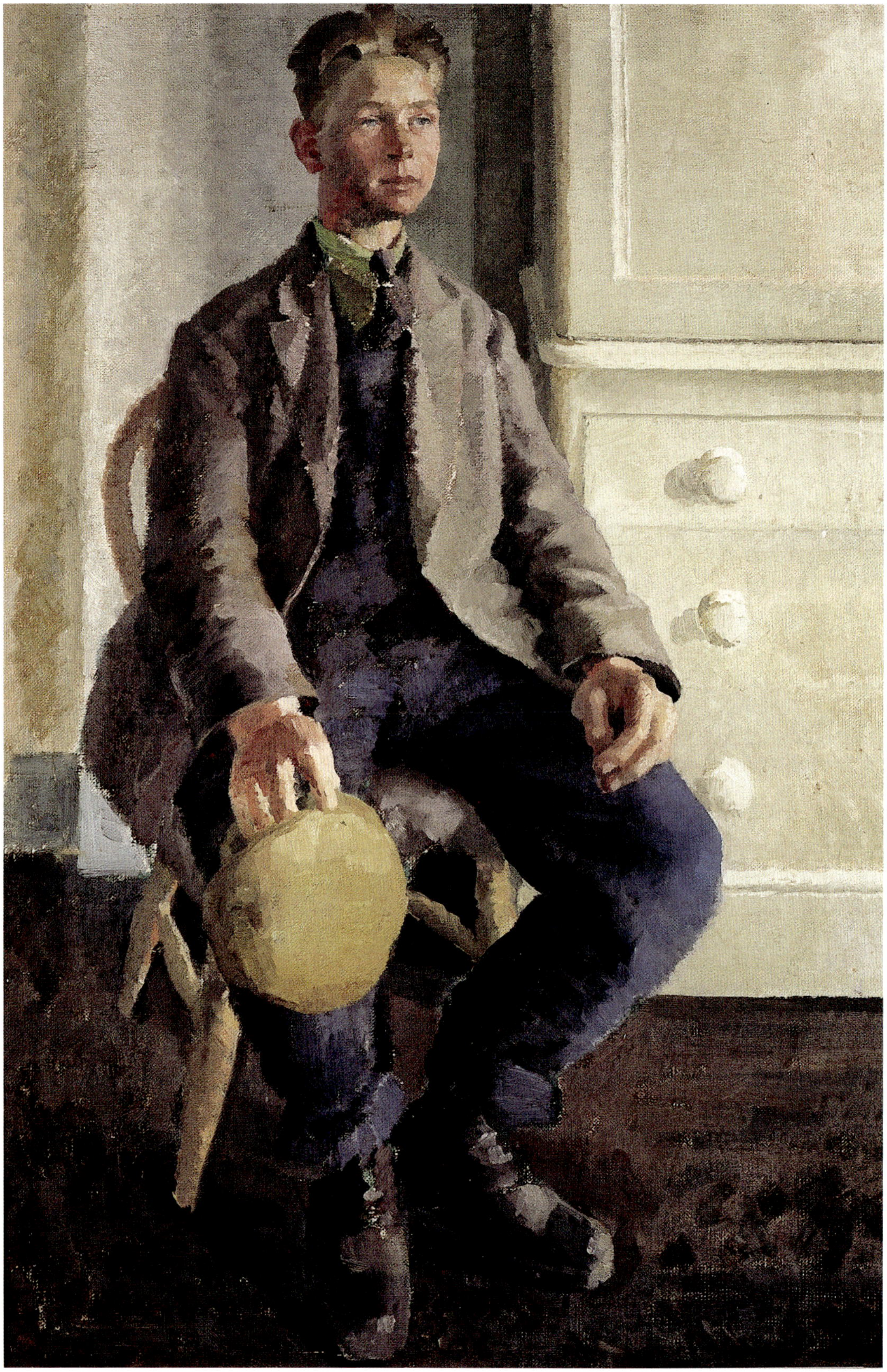

Charlotte Bawden, *Eric Townsend the Gardener's boy*, 1932, oil, 760 x 490 mm (Fry Art Gallery).

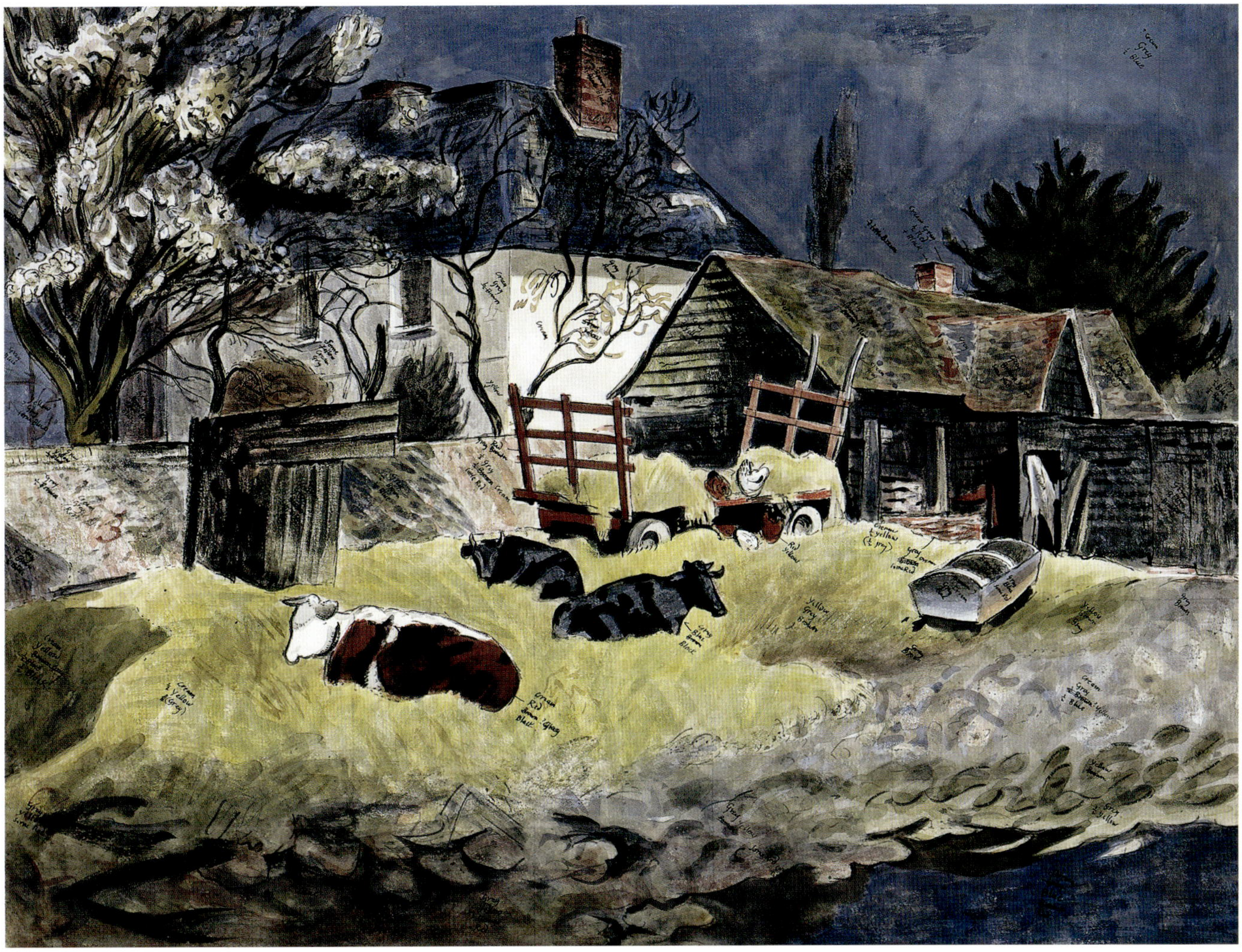

John Aldridge, *Essex Farmyard*, 1948, watercolour, 450 x 560 mm (Fry Art Gallery).

means and felt no pressure to show or sell his work or to take notice of any passing fad, he had only himself to please – which was a freedom no other Bardfield artist ever enjoyed. And what pleased him best was the Essex countryside, its farm buildings and his own back yard which he portrayed realistically but in strong dark colours with dramatic light effects.

Betjeman wrote: 'His painting is consistent, impervious to fashion and cheerfully representational. He belongs to an English tradition of local pastoral artists. He likes painting upturned earth, ploughed fields and mild landscapes. He is also the gardener's artist. You can see that he is happy in every part of his garden at Great Bardfield, looking at the vegetables as well as the flowers; the winter as well as the summer; the potting shed as well as the park; and fields of roots as well as meadows. When he goes to a Spanish island on holidays where Robert Graves lives, he delights in the cultivation of the dry Mediterranean coast, the gnarled olive trees and terraced strips and broken stones. He paints with a calm gratitude to the earth for what it yields, and his pictures grow on one like home.'

Aldridge and Bawden were soon close friends: both loved cats and both were rather shy men, happiest painting or gardening. Soon they were swapping cuttings and seeds, and in 1938-39 they collaborated on making around fifteen wallpaper designs. Bawden had tried this as early as 1927 when the Curwen Press had printed nine of his patterns, but they failed to sell. Bawden invited

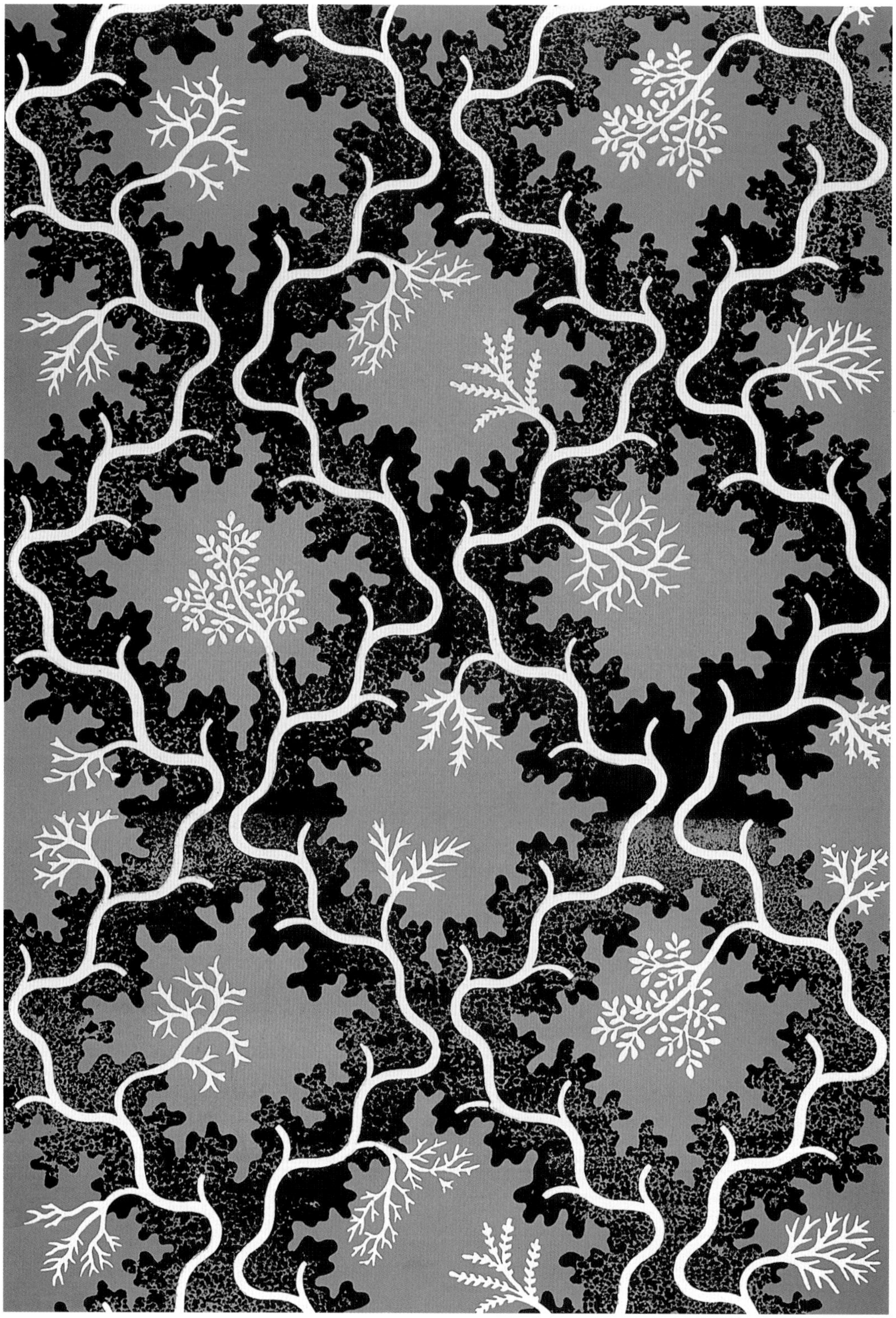

John Aldridge, *Moss*, 1938-39,
design from the 'Bardfield Wallpapers' series (Fry Art Gallery).

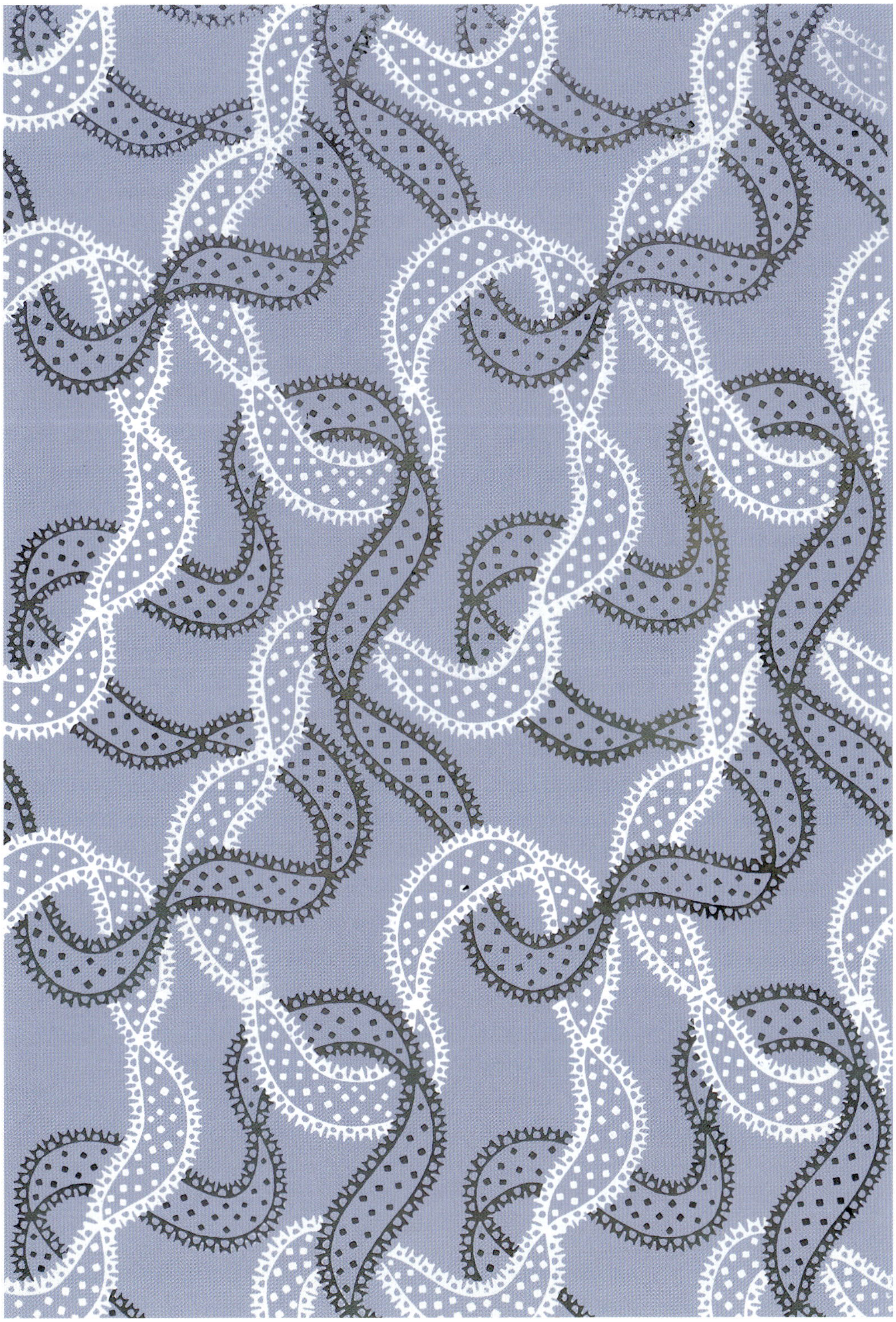

John Aldridge, *Ribbon and Lace*, 1938-39,
design from the 'Bardfield Wallpapers' series (Fry Art Gallery).

Aldridge to join him in trying again in a joint enterprise to be called Bardfield Wallpapers. Bawden explained: 'John Aldridge and I, who lived in the same village, decided that we would try to print our own designs by the roll from our own blocks. A few lengths were produced and these amateurish efforts were seen by a director of Coles who was passing through Braintree and happened to look in at the art exhibition in the Institute. From then onwards we cut full-size wallpaper blocks faced with lino and passed on the blocks to Coles who printed and sold the designs.' Unfortunately the war came along and wiped out the whole enterprise.

Another gardener of distinction was John Nash (1893-1977). Like Aldridge he too was self-taught as a painter, his brother Paul having advised him against attendance at the Slade where he himself had been so disappointed. Both Nashes had served in the trenches during World War One and between them, working side by side, had produced four of the most memorable images to come out of that sorry conflict: Paul's *Menin Road* and *We Are Creating A New World*, and John's *Over the Top* and *Oppy Wood*. Bawden and Ravilious had known and admired John's work before he began teaching alongside them at the Royal College of Art from 1934 to 1940, commuting in from Buckinghamshire. In 1937 Nash and Ravilious stayed at each other's houses to paint and a year later they went together to draw in Bristol docks, Nash producing watercolours very similar to the more talented younger man's. By that date Helen Binyon had transferred her attentions from Ravilious to Nash (who had a very open marriage with Christine Kühlenthal, a Slade-trained painter whose eyesight failed and ruined her career), whilst as already seen, Tirzah had formed an unrequited passion for John Aldridge, though none of these events seemed to diminish their interweaving friendships.

Like his friends John Nash had a designer's eye, as he declared: 'in looking at landscape its abstract features appeal pretty quickly. Although representational I am primarily interested in the structure underneath, though I hope not obviously. In fact such changes as I make are based more on selection than specific alteration . . . . I am extremely interested in "close-ups", in half a haystack as much as in a wide sweep of landscape.' [2] It would not be until 1944 that he and Christine moved nearer to Great Bardfield, to Wormingford in Essex, and after the war, began to share frequent painting expeditions with Bawden.

Yet another artist-gardener, this time with an international reputation as an expert on irises, was Cedric Morris (1889-1982). He had moved to Benton End near Hadleigh, Suffolk, and in 1937 established the East Anglian School of Painting. His own landscapes and flower paintings were bold, colourful and, considering his contacts with Parisian art and the progressives in the Seven and Five Society, rather awkward and unsophisticated in appearance. He and his partner Lette Haines soon became part of the plant-swapping network and close friends with Bawden and Aldridge.

For a few years in the 1930s Ravilious had taught part-time at the Ruskin School in Oxford where William Rothenstein's brother, Albert Rutherston, was Principal. There between 1930 and 1934 he taught a painting student, Kenneth Rowntree (1915-1997), who in 1939 married an architectural historian, Diana Buckley, and desperately needed a cheap house outside London. Tirzah Ravilious found them Town House to rent in Great Bardfield and they moved in with their new baby, later shifting up the road to a house called Simpkins. There Rowntree settled down to painting the local landscape in a neat, solidly traditional and attractive way, but with an underlying interest in shapes for their own sake which would eventually lead him to experimentation with abstraction.

Bawden, Ravilious, Aldridge, John Nash, Morris and Rowntree were of a similar turn of mind: they saw themselves as working within the English pastoral tradition, celebrating the rural landscape and still finding fresh things to say about it using conventional media. This set them aside from the inbred squabbling art world in London, though they were aware of its factions from reviews, exhibitions and the common-room chat in the London colleges where they taught. At Great Bardfield

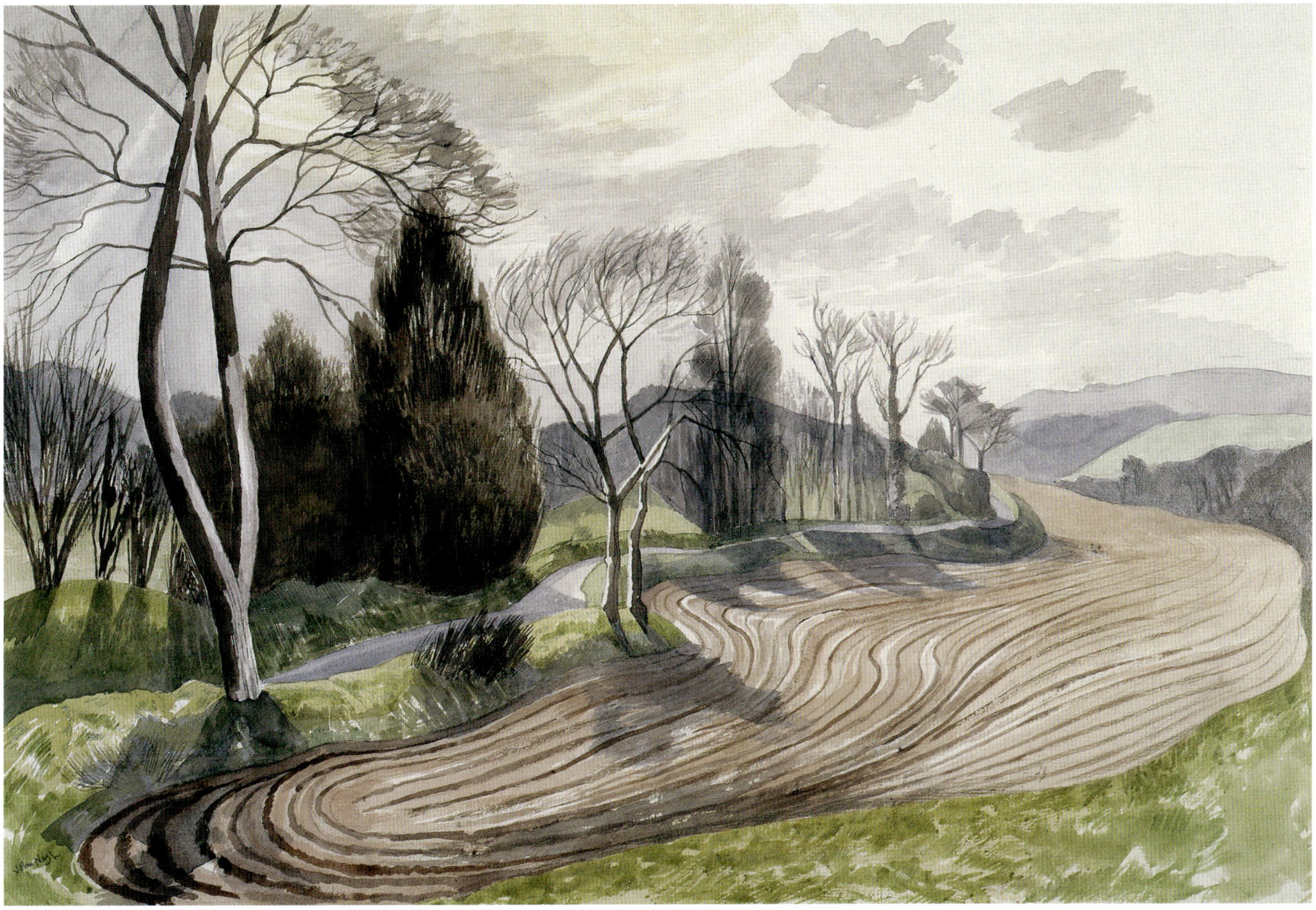

John Nash, *Landscape near Hadleigh*, date not known but probably *c.*1945, watercolour, 368 x 520 mm (Harlow Council Collection).

they were avid gardeners but not avant-garde-ners.

It took a lot of energy to be modern in the 1930s. There were arguments and groupings both artistic and political, many of them spurred on by refugees from the gathering storm in Germany. It was, of course, nothing new for English artists to band together, hammer out a doctrine, quarrel, and disperse: for example, after the Pre-Raphaelites came the New English Art Club, Camden Town Group, Allied Artists' Association, London Group, Vorticists, and the Seven and Five Society which has already been mentioned several times. This last Society was founded in 1919 by a group of largely second-rank artists and architects who in their first joint catalogue made a battle-weary plea not to have to be bothered by all the pre-war innovations: 'The SEVEN AND FIVE are grateful to the pioneers, but feel that there has been of late too much pioneering along too many lines in altogether too much of a hurry, and themselves desire the pursuit of their own calling rather than the confusion of conflict. The object of the SEVEN AND FIVE is merely to express what they feel in terms that shall be intelligible, and not to demonstrate a theory nor to attack a tradition.'[3] Their timidity was all they had in common but this left them vulnerable to more forceful infiltrators. Ivon Hitchens, an early though not founding member, introduced Ben Nicholson who by 1926 had become chairman and introduced several associates, including Henry Moore, who wanted to connect directly to European Modernism and bypass the Bloomsbury version of Post-Impressionism then still widely seen by the public as the *dernier cri*. The society also took on other, less radical, recruits who were painting lyrical English landscapes with a modernist flavour such as Winifred Nicholson, Cedric Morris, David Jones, Frances Hodgkins, John Aldridge and, from 1932 to 1934 Edward Bawden himself. It was untypical of him to join anything so structured and polemical but he exhibited with them three times at the Leicester Galleries.

Ben Nicholson soon redrafted the constitution so that every member had to be re-elected each year by a straight majority vote and thus any opposition could be more easily purged. Then in 1934 Nicholson manipulated things further so that only non-representational works could be shown under the society's aegis. John Aldridge, Cedric Morris, Christopher Wood, Frances Hodgkins and Percy Jowett (who would succeed Rothenstein at the RCA) fell by the wayside and Bawden, who is supposed to have smudged his voting paper and thus shown himself indecisive, was pushed out. Nicholson's doctrinal zeal for non-figurative painting left him with ten members and a broken society, and to his dying day the mention of Nicholson brought a snort of derision from Bawden.

Temperamentally Bawden would have been more in sympathy with the new UNIT ONE, announced by Paul Nash in the letter columns of *The Times* on 2nd June 1933. Nash thought English art had 'one crippling

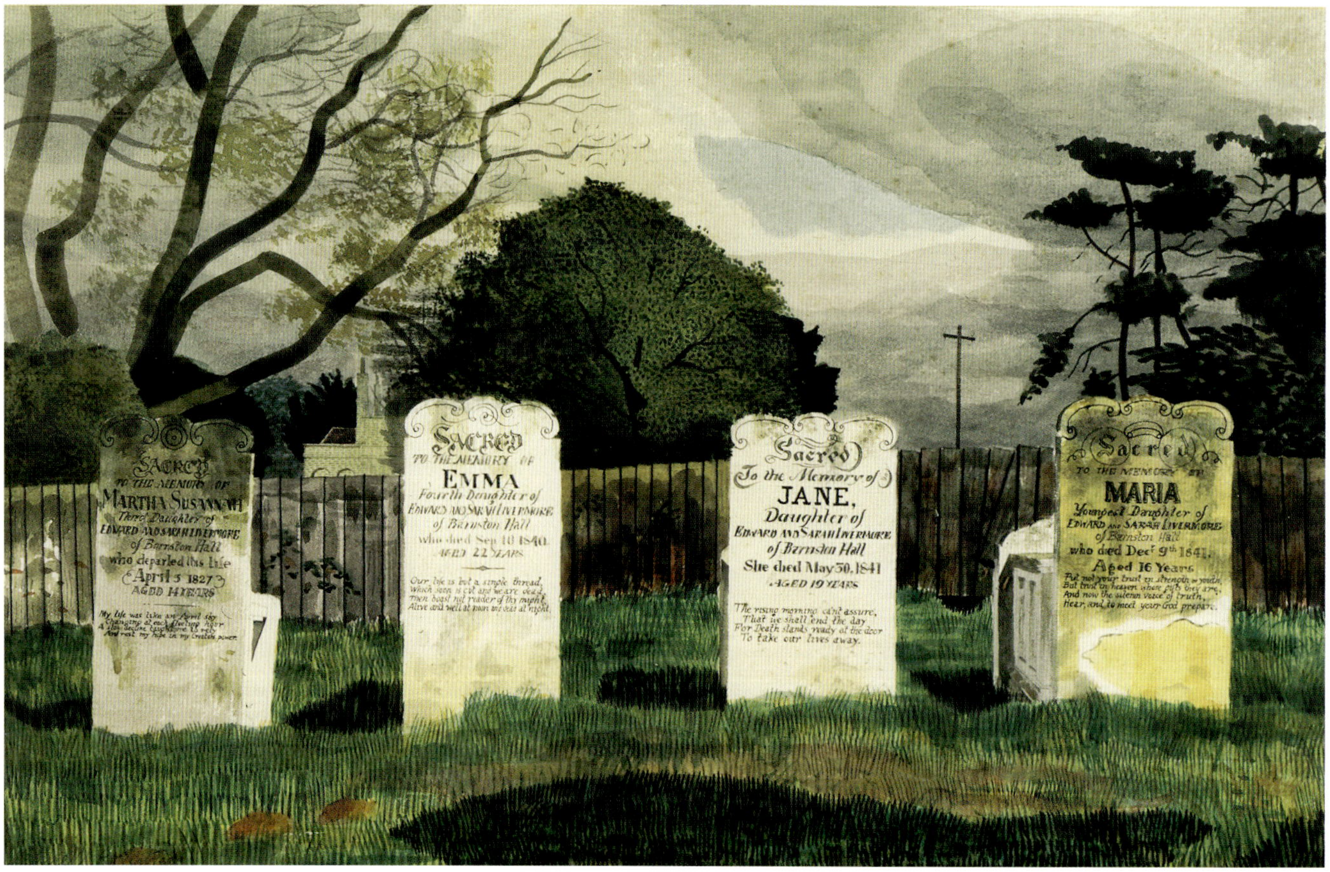

Kenneth Rowntree, *The Livermore Gravestones, Barnston, near Dunmow, Essex*, *c.*1941, watercolour, 319 x 480 mm (Victoria & Albert Museum).

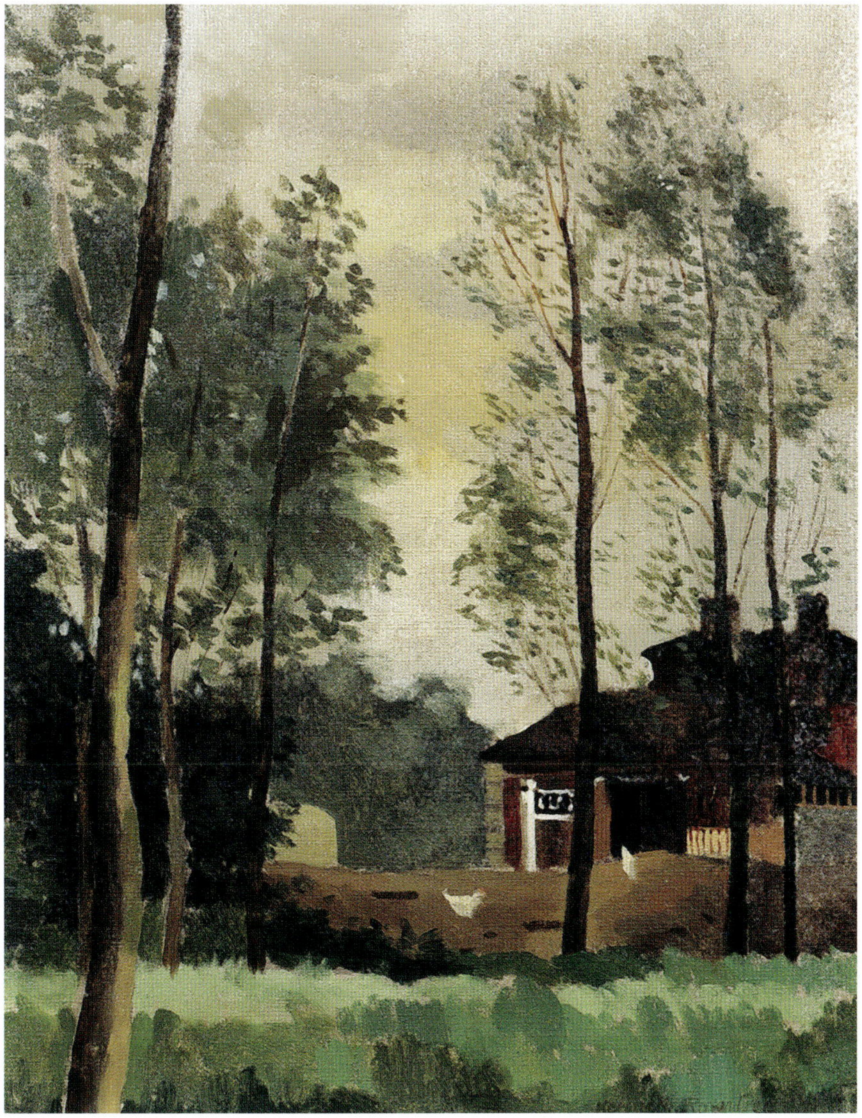

Kenneth Rowntree, *Station Willows*, *c.*1941, oil on canvas, 860 x 460 mm (Fry Art Gallery).

weakness – the lack of structural purpose' and 'this immunity from the responsibility of design has become a tradition . . . . Nature we do not deny, but art, we are inclined to feel, should control.' Both Bawden and Ravilious would have cheered that statement, but might have smiled at Nash's intent to pursue 'design . . . considered as a structural pursuit: imagination explored apart from literature or metaphysics.' This was a bit much coming from Nash who had written his own awful poems to accompany some of his early images and would soon be basing his 'metaphysical landscapes' on a reading of Fraser's *Golden Bough*. Nash's eleven recruits were an odd assortment, doomed to quarrel (Nicholson was amongst them and still pushing for abstraction), and by 1935, after one exhibition at the Mayor Gallery, Unit One was as dead as the Seven and Five. Herbert Read had been its theoretical spokesman but his enthusiasm quickly shifted to the latest continental movement – Surrealism.

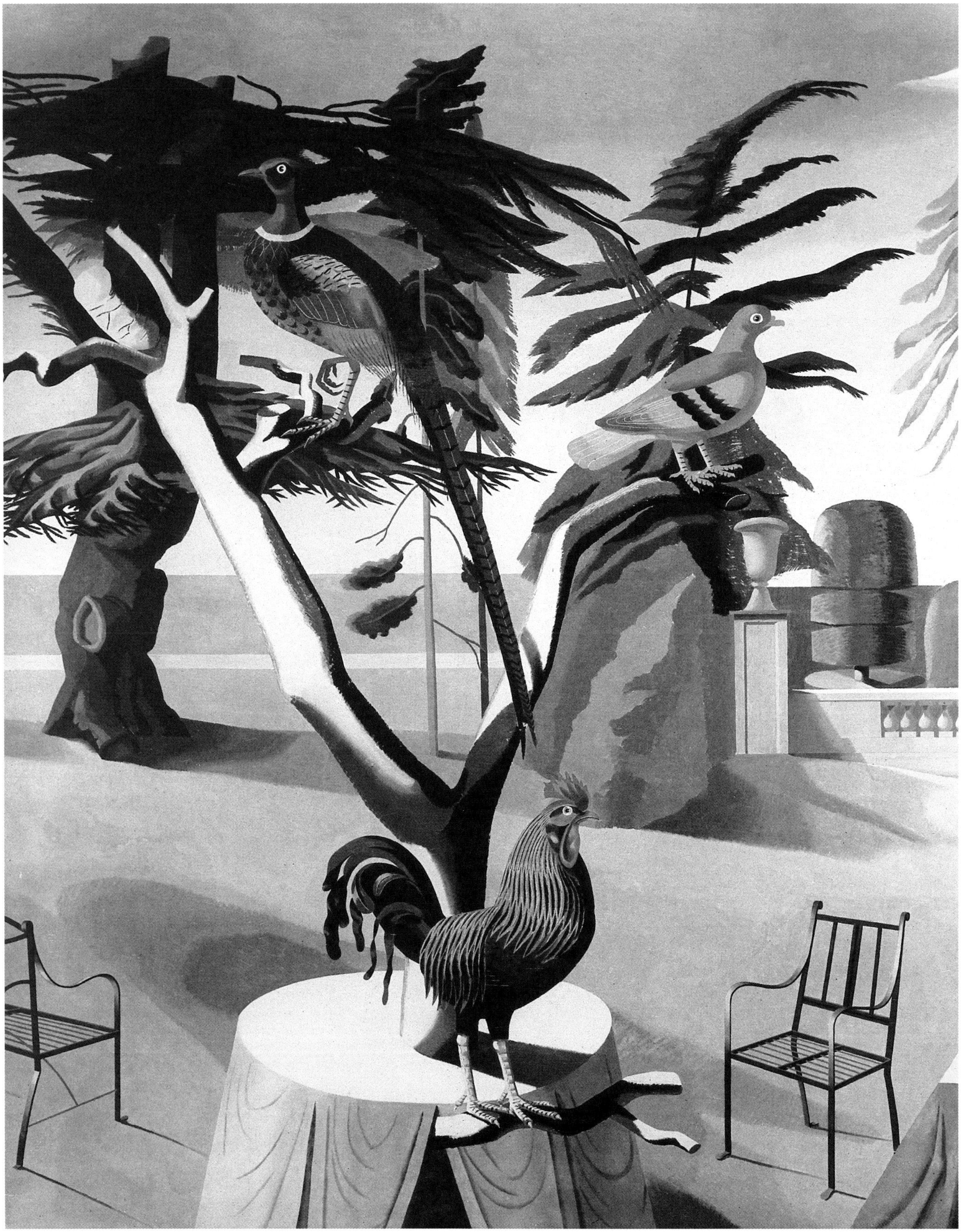

The International Surrealist Exhibition of 1936 was held in London with Read writing the catalogue (printed by Curwen) in which he claimed William Blake and Lewis Carroll were proto-surrealists. The press were predictably agog at the Surrealists' publicity stunts and their intentions to smash all preconceptions about art and break down habitual ways of seeing by overthrowing logic and depth-charging the unconscious with unexpected conjunctions of objects in art and random words in literature. Our English surrealists took the London Gallery as their headquarters until its closure in 1940, but they were never at ease with the Europeans' Communist posturings and resented the bullying ways of André Breton, the movement's leader. Paul Nash was the only major artist who seemed to derive any lasting benefit from the freedoms it offered with his discovery of *objets trouvés*, his monster trees, his placing of giant geometric 'equivalents' in the landscape and the freedom it gave him in the late Equinox and Solstice landscapes to play with archetypal symbols.

Predictably this exhibition did not cause many ripples in Great Bardfield, though it might have confirmed the taste for odd juxtapositions or strange encounters between objects that Bawden and Ravilious had long exploited in their watercolours of old buses or abandoned farm equipment – though neither would resort to Nash's anthropomorphism.

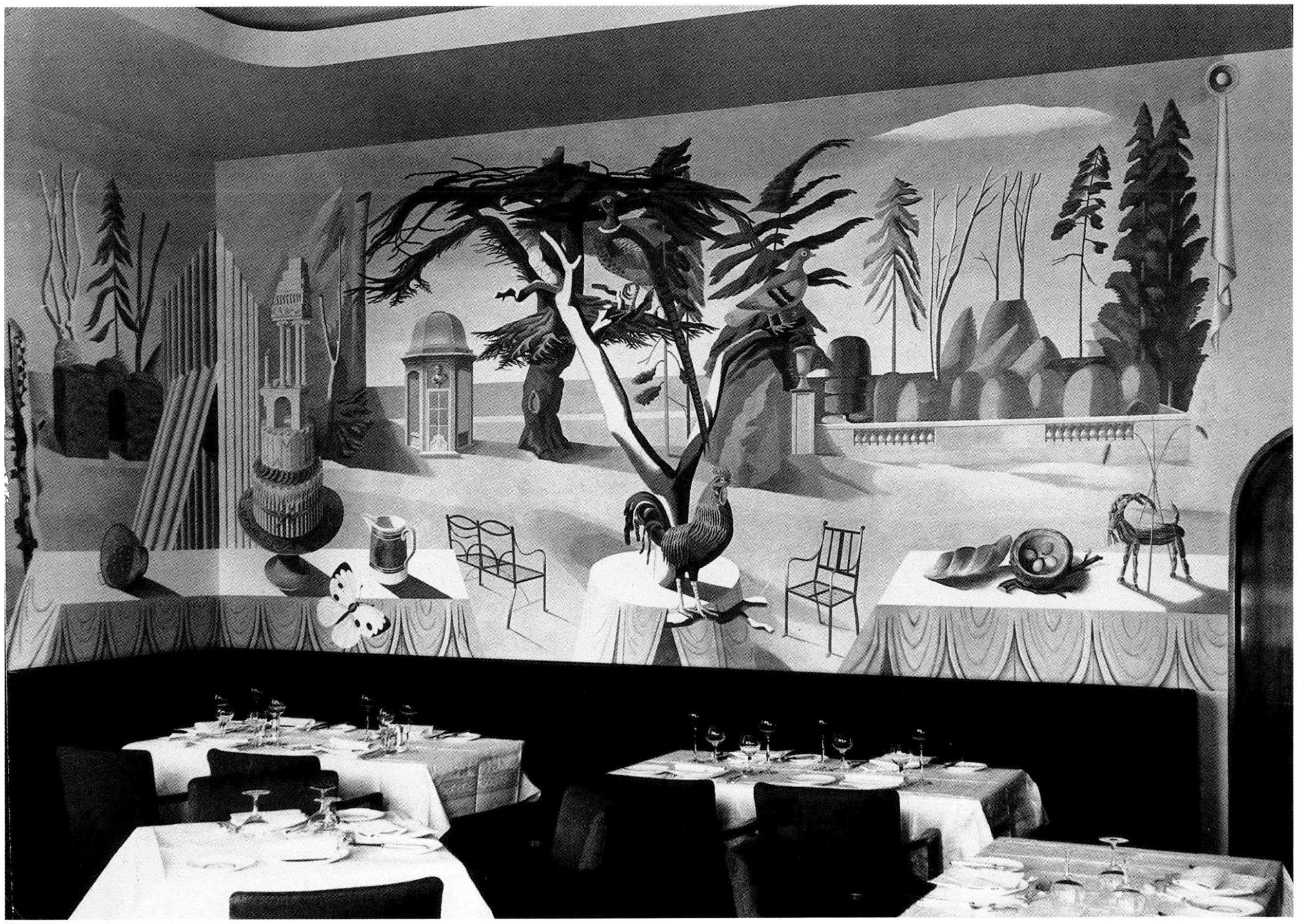

Bawden's mural for the International Building Society Club Dining Room, Park Lane, London, 1937-38 and *left* a detail (Trustees of Cecil Higgins Art Gallery, Bedford).

The chief opposition to Surrealism's insistence on dwelling in dream worlds and playing games with bizarre objects came from a sturdy socially-aware Realist group led by the founders of the Euston Road School: Coldstream, Pasmore, Rogers and Bell. They were heirs to Sickert and the Camden Town Group's interest in working-class lives, and they expressed it by a carefully measured, drably coloured fidelity to appearances in the belief that dour realism was the only way for art to make contact with a wider audience. This was to continue through the war years and re-emerge post-war when Coldstream passed on its tenets at Camberwell, before he became an influential Professor at the Slade from 1949 to 1975. This attempt, and others by the Marxist Artists' International Association to raise the population's social conscience with its slogan of 'conservative in art but radical in politics' also had no visible effect on the art of Bawden and Ravilious who, despite sincere left-wing sympathies, had ignored in their optimistic images the Spanish Civil War, the Depression, the rise of Fascism, Marxism, widespread labour unrest, unemployment and urban and rural poverty. It might be claimed that in having such a selective vision the two friends were escapists: they and Aldridge, Hennell, Rowntree, John Nash, Gilbert and Stanley Spencer, Cedric Morris, Robin Tanner, David Jones, Winifred Nicholson, John Piper, Graham Sutherland and others were perhaps projecting their nostalgia onto the rural landscape, usually showing it unpeopled, or depicting redundant farming methods, all as unreal as those lush idylls of Samuel Palmer to which some of them consciously harked back. All this was soon to change and they would be cast out of their Eden by the war.

Before the lamps went out for a second time in Europe Ravilious managed a quick trip to Normandy in March 1939 and returned in time for the birth of his second son James. Then in the August of 1939, just before war was declared, Bawden, Tom Hennell, and Muriel Rose, a good friend who ran the Little Gallery near Sloane Square, went off to Geneva to see paintings on loan from the Prado before going on to the International Exhibition at Zurich. They arrived in Zurich on September 1st and found the whole place closed and in a panic because of the crisis. They scuttled home in packed railway carriages just in time.

When the war came Bawden was the father of two young children: Joanna aged four and Richard, three. He was not an enthusiastic parent, as he later told a shocked interviewer: 'It wasn't my choice to have children, though I'm grateful now. I had a baize door put up which they couldn't open. I still don't like small children. They're wet smelly things and make an awful lot of noise. No, I can't see any merit in them. Can you?' To add to his irritation when the German bombing began the Government evacuated children from vulnerable city centres and billeted them on families in the country. Great Bardfield received many from London's East End and villagers were shocked by their head lice and table manners. The Bawdens did not take in children but accepted two adult refugees from the Spanish Civil War, Davide and Ricardo, as Bawden explained to Ravilious: 'During the last few weeks we have given over our attics to two Spanish refugees – a Colonel and a Major in the Republican army, in ordinary life a medical student walking the hospital and a barber from Seville. The Latin mind is refreshing by contrast with the Teutonic – it's delightful having vivacious and polite people in the house and what good cooks they are.' (18th December 1938). With Robert Graves' help he set them up in a barber's shop in the village: 'who would not snatch the chance of painting a barber's pole – I mean among painters and odd-job men like ourselves!' The Raviliouses did their bit by taking in a German refugee, Tirzah canvassed for the Labour Party, and Eric gave works to the Artists' International Association for their fund-raising exhibitions.

Not only did Bawden now lack the right tranquil atmosphere for his work, he had very little work to do. The private presses were closing down; Frank Pick had retired from London Underground so that no more posters were being commissioned; demands for murals, prints and gallery paintings were in abeyance and publishers were suffering paper rationing and therefore

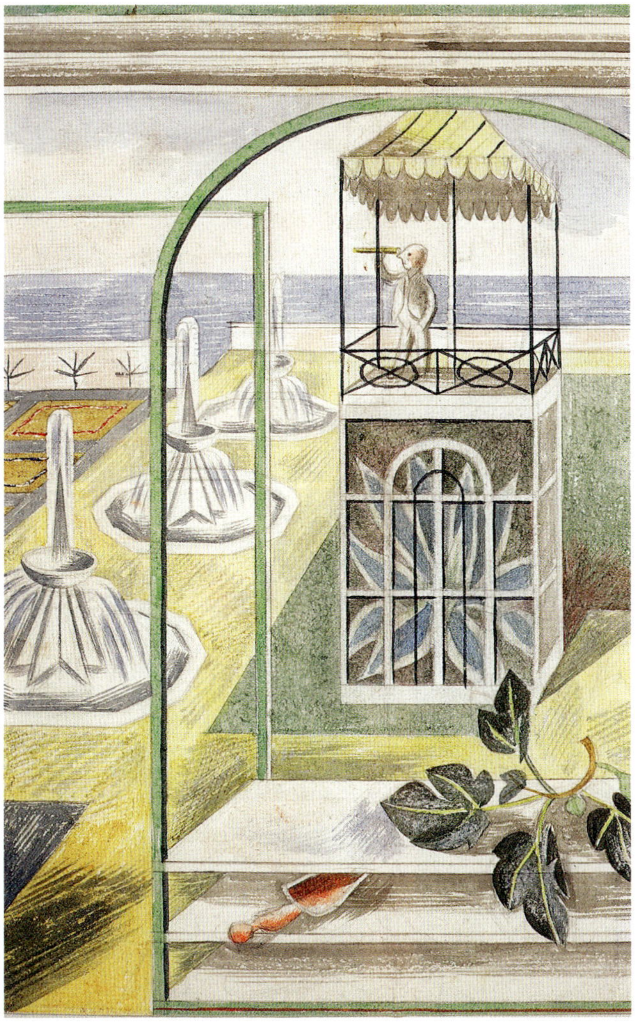

Mural design, date not known though possibly *c.*1936-40.

cutting back on illustrations. Then the RCA evacuated to Ambleside in the Lake District with Percy Horton and Charles Mahoney in charge, so even teaching was no longer an option. The only way that Bawden could escape his domestic frustrations, continue painting full-time, and be paid for it, was to become an official war artist.

Bawden's former Principal, William Rothenstein, now knighted and retired from the RCA but still campaigning for his ex-students, said: 'the Empire is concentrating all its moral forces against the powers of evil: in this the arts have their part to play.' Paul Nash had tried to ensure artists' continuing employment by setting up an Arts Bureau in Oxford; while the Pilgrim Trust commissioned a few painters to record the architecture and landscapes threatened by wartime bombing and development, and others worked for the newly formed Council for the Encouragement of Music and Arts (CEMA) which would eventually transmogrify into the Arts Council. In addition Lord Esher, Paul Nash and John Betjeman were intriguing behind the scenes to ensure that our best musicians, writers and artists were spared front-line action. Aldridge, Bawden and Ravilious were on their list but, as Ravilious wrote to John Nash: 'Why artists should be so privileged as to expect other people to fight for them I don't know.' (27th October 1939).[4] A man with influence in all these enterprises was Kenneth Clark, aged thirty-six at the outbreak of war, who had wielded enormous influence in art politics on both sides of the Atlantic ever since he had been made Director of the National Gallery at the astonishingly early age of twenty-nine. His avowed intention in forming a War Artists' Advisory Committee (WAAC) was 'simply to keep artists at work on any pretext, and, as far as possible, to prevent them being killed.' He persuaded the Ministry of Information and the three Forces to co-operate, and after their first committee meeting on 23rd November 1939 the WAAC began recruiting. Two thousand artists applied and three hundred were employed: some of these were given specific commissions, others were on short contracts, and a lucky few were salaried. Bawden was one of the first four to receive a salary.

1. Betjeman, J., catalogue to the 1971 Aldridge exhibition at the Upper Grosvenor Galleries.
2. Rothenstein, J., *John Nash*, Macdonald and Co., 1983, p.119.
3. Quoted in Harrison, C., *English Art and Modernism 1900-1939*, Allen Lane, 1981, p.164.
4. Esher, L., 'The Plot to Save the Artists', *Times Literary Supplement*, 2nd January 1987, pp.12-13.

6. BAWDEN'S WAR, PART ONE

The coming of war shook all the artists out of their comfortable routines. After a brief spell in a hilltop Observer Post looking out for enemy aircraft over Castle Hedingham, Eric Ravilious began a six-month contract with the Admiralty in February 1940. Douglas Percy Bliss was less fortunate. First his home in Blackheath was bombed and looters stole all his wood-engraved blocks, and then he was convinced that because he had offended Kenneth Clark in a discussion over the attribution of some old masters he was not offered work with the War Artists Advisory Committee. Instead he served in the Royal Air Force Volunteer Reserve in the Department of Concealment and Decoy where one of his jobs was to light up desolate Scottish hillsides in the hope that the Luftwaffe would be deceived into dropping bombs on them instead of on Edinburgh or Glasgow. Thomas Hennell had not yet fully recovered from his mental problems but, appropriately, he was told by the WAAC to depict the harvesting of the record wheat crop of 1941, though he would be asked to do much more dangerous tasks later. Percy Horton was a Conscientious Objector in this war as he had been in the first and went with the RCA to the Lake District as a tutor, together with Charles Mahoney. Both Nash brothers were made War Artists for a second time.

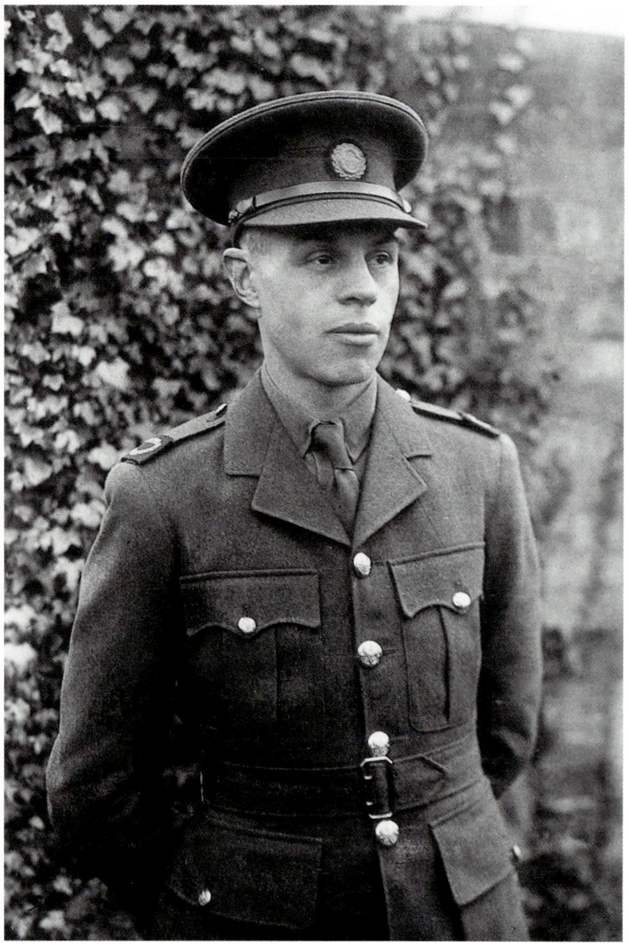

Bawden as official war artist.

Charlotte had by now abandoned her artistic ambitions, but she was anxious to teach again and obtained a post in Cheltenham where she had taught before her marriage. At the Grammar School she taught art, supervised the catering, and fitted in two nights of fire watching each week. In a letter Bawden expressed his approval 'because you will feel occupied and not just a mother hen cackling at Fate and shielding your chicks'. Joanna and Richard, together with the Ravilious boys were soon sent away to a boarding school in the Cotswolds, and Brick House was closed. Later in the war it would be used, and abused, by the Home Guard and Americans from a nearby airbase.

On 3rd March 1940 Bawden wrote to his sick mother

that he had just been taken on at a salary of £650 a year: 'appointment can be terminated at one month's notice either side: uniform that of a special correspondent: all work belongs to the Crown: transport 1st class on boat-trains, channel boats, and in France, 3rd class in England: rations and accommodation provided: travel allowance – given in France – when temporarily absent from duty: hospital treatment free (?): death – "in accordance with the regulations applicable to civilians". ' Bawden thought he had a good deal.

During the next five years he wrote around ninety letters to Charlotte telling of his adventures abroad together with a few to his father (his mother having died in early 1941) and more official ones to the Secretaries of the WAAC, E.M.O'Rourke Dickey and E.C.Gregory. In 1980 he donated these to the Imperial War Museum, each helpfully annotated for future researchers with comments such as: 'boring', 'moderately interesting', 'good first paragraph' and so on. They are written in beautiful script, without grammar or spelling mistakes, and are full of detailed observations of people, customs, plants, animals, insects, landscapes and wry accounts of the pleasures and frustrations of his journeys. However, they are not as spontaneous as they appear since numerous drafts are scattered amongst his family papers and he clearly had posterity in mind. They offer a clear insight into both man and artist and enable us to tell the story of Bawden's war mostly in his own words.[1] When asked if he kept Charlotte's letters to him, he said he had not since they were mostly about nappies and babies. All minors were babies to Bawden, and his letters show few signs of missing his own two offspring condemned so early to a remote boarding school.

Besides Bawden the three other salaried War Artists to be appointed initially were Barnett Freedman (1901-58), Edward Ardizzone (1900-79), and Reginald Eves (1876-1941). Eves had been a protégé of Sargent and studied under Tonks at the Slade. He was also a Royal Academician and society portrait painter who could command more than his year's salary as a War Artist for just one peacetime canvas. He was installed in a first class hotel in Arras where the British HQ was situated, to make portraits of the British Generals in oils.

The other three were best known as illustrators and were obviously trusted to communicate clearly what they saw in line and watercolour, with no abstract or surreal nonsense or pretensions to 'Fine' art. Barnett Freedman was the eldest of five children of Polish-Jewish immigrants to London's East End. He had spent four years of his youth in bed with a weak heart and so was more or less self-taught. After lettering work with a gravestone designer he attended evening classes in art until William Rothenstein got him a scholarship to the RCA where he became a good friend to Bawden, Bliss and Ravilious. Freedman was a charming rebel and much admired by the other students who nicknamed him 'Soc', short for Socrates. After leaving college he worked for the same patrons as Bawden – the Curwen Press, Shell-Mex, London Transport, and the Post Office, as well as teaching at Ruskin College and back at the RCA. On the basis of his illustrations to *War and Peace* (1938) he was acknowledged as a master of lithography. When Ravilious heard that Freedman and Bawden were appointed he wrote to Bawden on the 9th of February 1940 'very good luck to you and Barnett on the Western Front, and may you have a smooth Channel crossing', and added enviously 'Oh how sick I shall be'.

Edward Ardizzone was regarded with suspicion by the army because of his surname and the fact that he had been born in Haiphong to a Franco-Italian father and Scottish mother before the family moved to London in 1905. He worked as a clerk and took evening classes under the painter Bernard Meninsky at Westminster School of Art, but only after seven years of this felt bold enough to take up illustration full time, especially of children's books and drawings for *Radio Times*. Like Freedman and Bawden he worked for the Curwen Press and was a member of the Double Crown Club.

Bawden and Ardizzone crossed to France together on 31st March 1940 and Bawden found him an 'excellent travelling companion', in spite of his crippling lumbago,

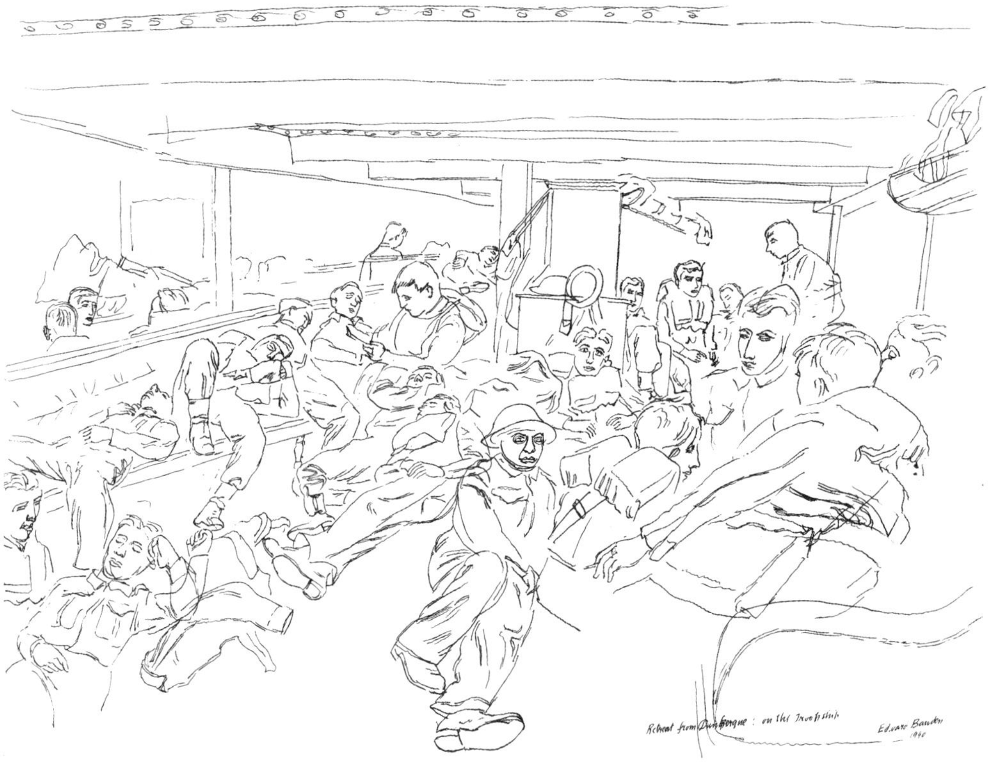

The Troopship – on the way Home from Dunkirk, 1940, ink on paper, 444 x 561 mm (Imperial War Museum, LD 189).

which meant Bawden had to lift him into bed and hold his chamber pot. The two artists shared a batman and enjoyed the local wine and food and the ministrations of their landlady, who cured Bawden's stomach-ache with a heated brick. Bawden found the 2nd Northamptons, to whom he was attached, 'nice simple fellows most of them who tear about wagging their tails, fetching sticks and retrieving balls, behaving like well-trained dogs who have plenty of bark and no bite'. (24th April 1940).

There was no fighting as yet in this 'Phoney War' and the army didn't know what to do with these badgeless, unarmed, rankless, arty parasites who expected to be fed, housed and transported, so they despatched Bawden and Ardizzone to draw the building of those pill-boxes on the Belgian border which later proved so useless. Then with equally idle journalists and photographers they were taken to see WW1 memorials and trenches. Ardizzone next attached himself to a Highland battery and recorded everyday work and play, while Freedman was sent to sketch the construction of a runway and Bawden to draw a post office. These three were the first to try out the role of War Artist in the field in WW2 but they found it difficult to get past the red tape and suspicion – Bawden was briefly arrested for making a drawing of a gun and Freedman always feared he was about to be shot as a Fifth Columnist.

On May 10th 1940 when the Germans invaded Belgium and Luxembourg the three became a profound nuisance to the army as the disorderly retreat by the British Expeditionary Force began. Ardizzone and Freedman were in Boulogne during the night the GHQ was bombed and Ardizzone calmly made sketch notes of the dead and injured being dragged from the building. Freedman played

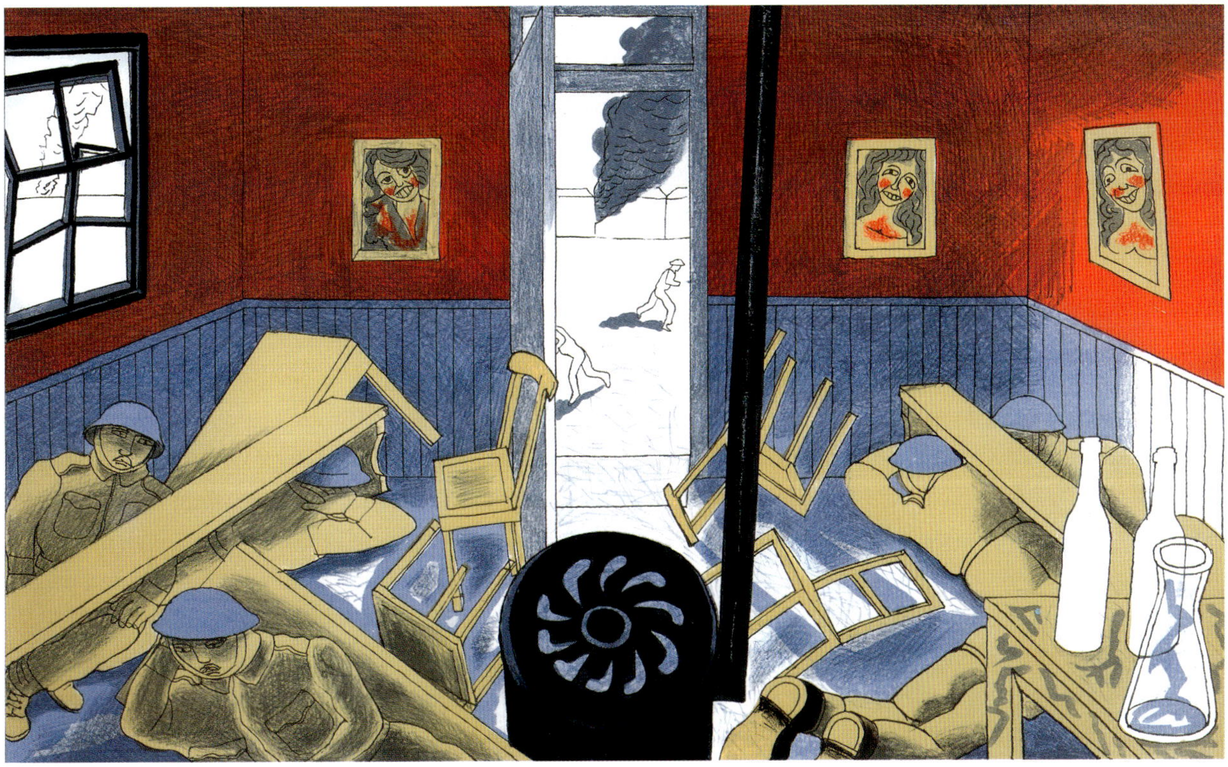

Edward Bawden, 'Dunkirk' – colour lithograph, 1986.
From a watercolour of 1940 now in the Imperial War Museum. 363 x 562 mm. (Fry Art Gallery).

Handel and Bach on the HQ piano as the bombs fell, and when ordered onto a boat suddenly remembered his best work was still in a hotel room and promptly got off again to fetch it. Freedman's last meal in France consisted of 'three bottles of champagne and a tin of bully beef taken sitting by himself on the railway lines at the quayside'.[2] He then found a boat and followed Ardizzone to safety.

Meanwhile, up the coast, Bawden marched into Dunkirk with the retreating troops through lines of jeering French. The generals had already left by then, as Bawden noted: 'Well, the rats go first'. Later he said: 'By temperament I am a pacifist. War horrifies me; it horrified me then . . . . I hated the big bangs. No one knew what was happening, and I was just tossed about like a bad penny. Nobody wanted a war artist. Every day I got shoved off to a new unit.' At Dunkirk he didn't head for the beach and the rescue boats but to the docks where he holed up for two days making notes of chaotic smoke-filled scenes as thousands of troops tried to get away under constant strafing and shellfire. Eventually a boat came near enough to scramble aboard and he found it full of exhausted men 'lying in heaps everywhere, some only half dressed. I did a drawing of that. I couldn't put any colour on it but I drew it in line.' Once home he slept for forty-eight hours and then worked up his hasty but vivid sketches into rather understated images of these dramatic events, the figures stiff and unindividualised.

Bawden told how he'd abandoned everything except his drawings: 'Like a soldier I had to keep my only weapon', and 'I didn't feel it was time for me to buzz off yet . . . most of the time I remember lying down under privet bushes in a small park, or dodging around. I remember feeling curiously calm probably because I react rather slowly, my flashpoint is a high one.'[3] What really irked him was that he was later given £16 compensation for the loss of his army gear but nothing for the loss of his precious art satchel and his paints.

He wrote to John Rothenstein: 'The man who is drawing in the field must accept what he sees, self-conscious arrangement is hardly possible, the scene is always changing & masses of men are moving about & not posing to be drawn. In fact it was a rough life: I simply had to draw reasonably well, whether in a cookhouse or in a repair depot for tanks or a court martial. I think it was the most valuable experience I have ever had to be pitched straight into what was happening in France & to remain – moving about from day to day – until the evacuation of Dunkirk took place.'[4] The meticulous craftsman with all his pens laid out parallel on his desk in the secluded attic studio was already learning to loosen up and extemporise a little.

Following his return to Aldershot Bawden was reunited with Charlotte, but now he had seen action he was soon restless to be off again. After the fall of France Bawden managed to escape 'Fortress Britain' once he made it clear that he had little interest in drawing home defence preparations. On 7th July 1940 he sailed on the Union Castle Line for Cairo via the Cape to join Middle East Command, seeing on the way three burning torpedoed cargo boats with no survivors, and noting sardonically as they approached the Tropic: 'Casual flirtations become exclusive; cliques are formed. Shirts and shorts, bare arms and knees are de rigeur. The bath water runs less hot, then runs cold.' When Italy came into the war in June 1940 her forces began to push out of Italian territories (Eritrea, Ethiopia, Italian Somaliland) and into British ones (Sudan, Kenya, British Somaliland); between September 1940 and August 1941 Bawden followed the Allied campaign south and east to push the Italians back and out of Africa.

He flew north from Durban in a seaplane, skimming low over the elephants and giraffes and landing on each of the five nights to re-fuel. On arrival in Cairo he contributed

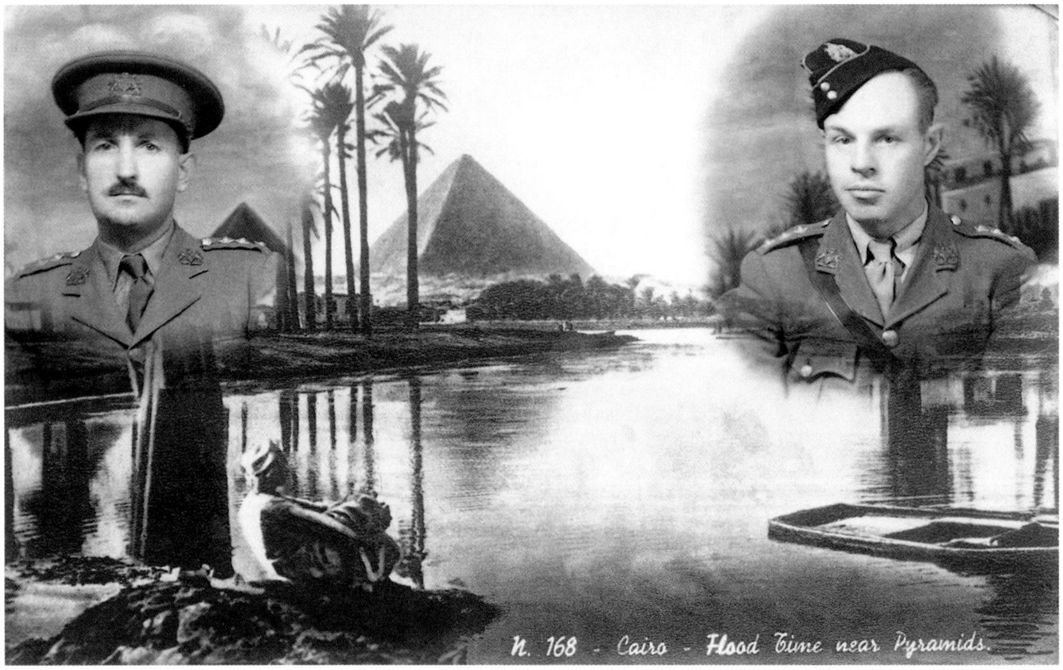

Anthony Gross and Edward Bawden on a Cairo postcard, 1942.

some rather unsophisticated cartoons to a forces' journal Parade showing the experiences of 'Freddie', who is seen leaving his country mansion and saying: 'goodbye to blood sports – to huntin' fishin' and shootin'. Goodbye to Mum, Dad and the dogs.' Our hero is then seen lounging on shipboard, in officers' clubs and ordering his servants around. The artist wrote to Charlotte on 29th August 1940: 'Freddie, I may explain is my hero, myself, and his adventures mine.' Bawden was obviously enjoying a higher status and standard of living in Cairo than he was used to in Great Bardfield, but the authorities soon spotted this and sent him off to Khartoum by train and paddle steamer to draw native troops. Because it was Ramadan and they were fasting 'after they'd been posing for about an hour they began to wilt'. Close-up figures in their settings were a new challenge to someone who had shirked student life classes, and so was the climate: he complained to Charlotte about how he showered sweat on his drawings and letters: 'you cannot sit with your back to a tebaldi tree and write with a block supported on your knee when there are white ants moving underneath, black ticks climbing the legs and all het up to break an interminable fast; and flies skilfully searching for sores and abrasions.'[5] Some of the insects must have been mosquitoes because the next few weeks he spent in a hospital where no white man had ever been with malignant tertium malaria, and then convalesced in the District Commissioner's house by the Blue Nile. While there he was given three stars on his shoulder straps and told Charlotte she could now hold her own with Mrs Captain Ravilious.

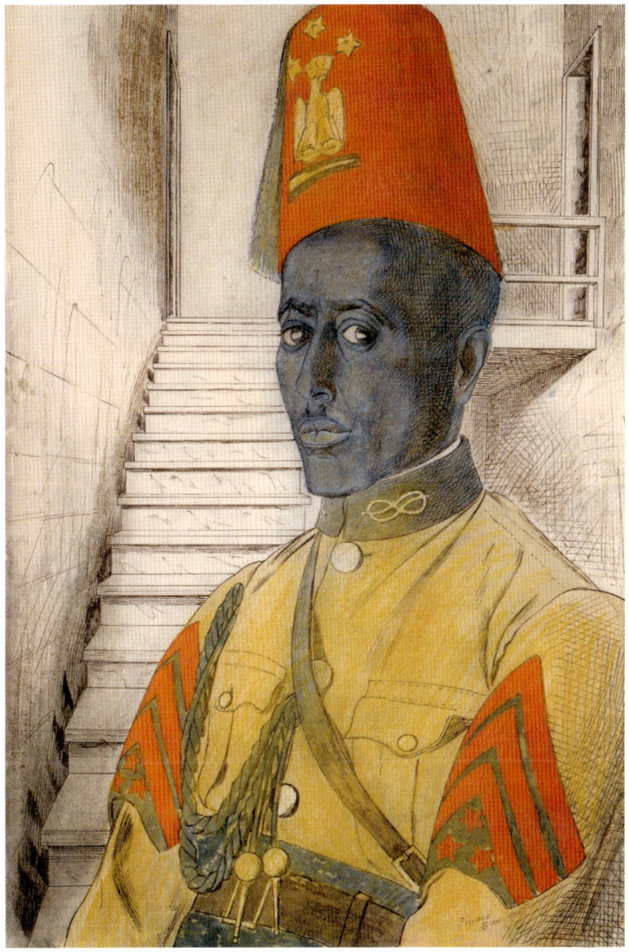

Scium Basci Tesfalidet Ghidai: Polizia Africana Italiana, Asmara. A Sergeant in the Police Force formed by the Italians, chalk, ink and watercolour, 501 x 336 mm (Imperial War Museum, LD 1791).

In late April 1941 an English contingent of ten from the 1st Battalion of the Essex Regiment with camels and Sudanese and Ethiopian soldiers set off for Ethiopia, taking Bawden along on the two month trek and driving the Italians before them. They were led by Colonel Athill on a white horse, and two separate columns on the same expedition were led by Orde Wingate and Laurens van der Post. During the 300 mile journey Bawden climbed a mountain, explored a jungle ('it resembles the barer parts of Epping Forest') and while travelling with some Sudanese troops who set up his tea table he was shown obeisance by four Galla girls who knelt at his feet: 'They were nude except for a chic hair sporran between the thighs, a gold fillet round the braided hair, and numerous bright bead necklaces and tummy rings. It was done with simple natural dignity; the white man was moved and showed his teeth amiably, but the boys spoiled the scene by laughing. Around me stood a silent crowd of completely nude boys and young men, some with spears or the queer throwing stick or boomerang, just looking on and staring.' (11th April 1941).

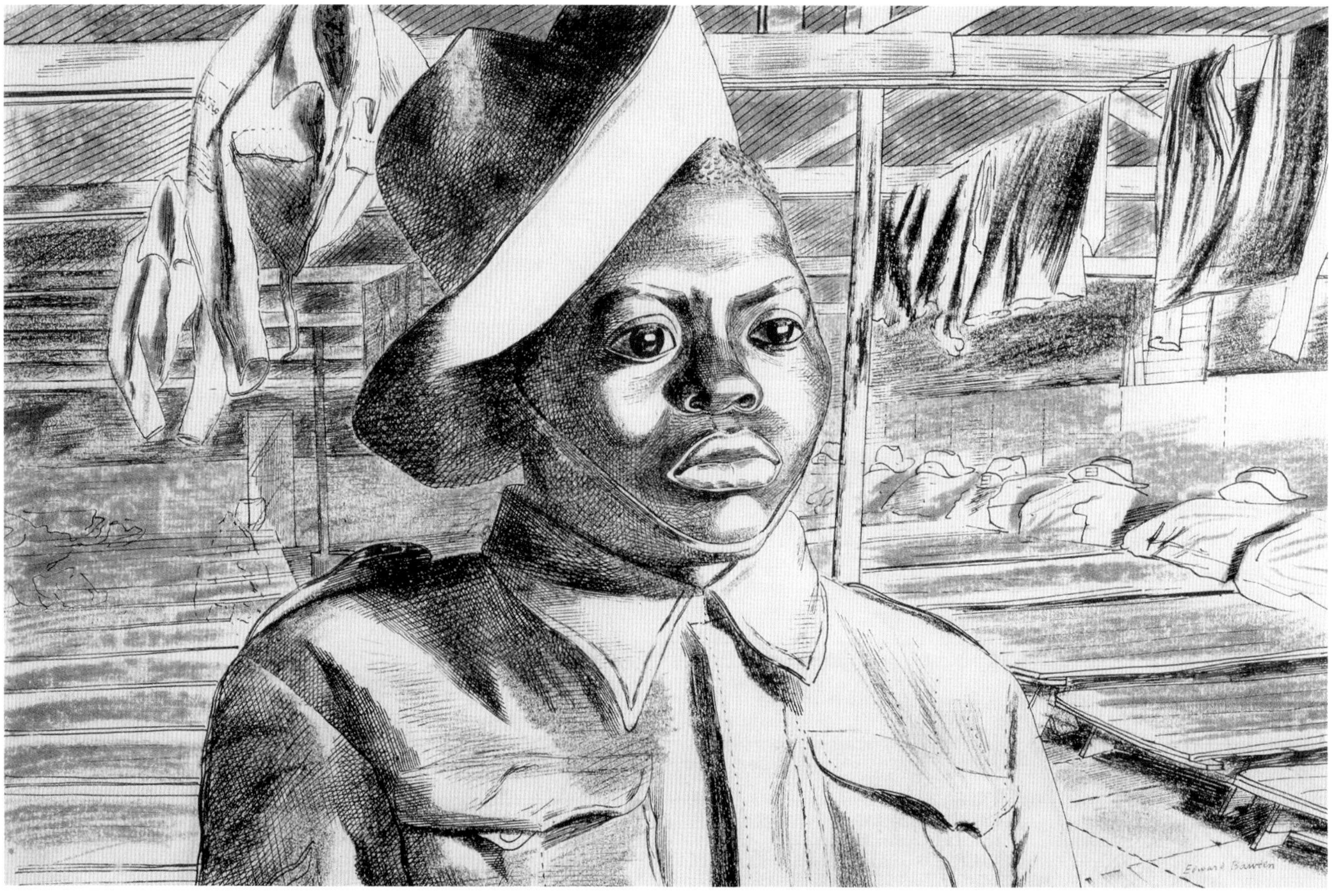

Corporal Harry Brown, 1975th Bechuana Company, 64 Group, AAPC, near Jdeide, Lebanon, 1942, watercolour on paper, 355 x 552 mm (Imperial War Museum, LD2185).

He gave them an empty tobacco tin as a present. Another aesthetic experience was examining a dead camel: 'It was covered with maggots, there was no room for another maggot. It was simply like a cloak all over. But what was so nice it shimmered and quivered too in a most curious way all over. Fascinating sight.' Further on he found two human skeletons but, to his regret, had no time to draw them.

In the desert he collected flower seeds, ('the crassulaceae and euphorbiaceae grow luxuriantly between the rocks' he informed Ravilious), no doubt with a mental picture of where they might be made to bloom in his lush acre of garden at Brick House, and perhaps of trade with his floricultural-artist friends such as John Aldridge, John Nash and Cedric Morris.

Sometimes, however, boredom and home-sickness got him down: 'Do not think that I despise a green thicket peopled by Ludovic's chicks, or would not be cheered by a cedar shaded lawn and table spread with tea and cakes and strawberries and cream. In my present mood I would give all the pomegranates, mangoes, paw-paws, melons, figs, sweet lemons, dates, for one large, sour, hard, green English cooking apple.' (13th November 1941).

By now some of his pictures had returned to England and been put on show in London. Ravilious saw them and wrote to Binyon: 'Have you seen . . . Edward's superb drawings of Africa. My goodness he has done well.' (20th July 1941). Thomas Hennell had seen them too and enthused to Tirzah: 'I have intended to write to Edward for a long time. His drawings from the East are a great achievement, and will give delight to posterity. I doubt if anyone has more perfect taste, in the true sense, apart from his technical perfection.' (17th August 1941).

Whilst enduring rain, icy wind and sandstorms he wrote at length to Ravilious: 'I believe I have already said enough to convince you that a certain part of Essex is by comparison a landscape painter's paradise – it is – make no error about it. If my aide de camp Mohammed Ahmed came to Essex I expect he would see little except for a blur of green. We know what to look for – a rabbit flick, the scurry of a stoat, primroses in ditches or dogroses in hedgerows are caught in the corner of an eye but Mohammed would not see that.' Not that those Essex days were all dog-roses, as he wrote to Charlotte: 'Don't I wish we were back in Bardfield! I don't dare think of those days; the last few years weren't pleasant, too much worry, too many distractions, a horrible feeling of instability: the future will be different I'm hoping'. (16th February 1942).

If the landscape was a disappointment at this stage of his travels the people were not for he informs Ravilious: 'The Sudan is populated by black men and white ants: black men and women of surpassing beauty of form and colour such as the life classes of Europe have never seen; and having that nutty aromatic body odour which is one of the most agreeable of all smells, though not all Europeans will agree with my opinion – indeed, I have not found one who does; they prefer their own acrid stink caused by taking exercise like a dog, e.g. running after balls. Consequently after exercise there must be a bath, and medical opinion confirms the fact that hot water has a sterilising effect. Raise a ram's balls – this is an experiment anyone can try – one degree in temperature and that ram is sterile when turned among ewes. With hot baths there is necessarily a drop in the birth rate: remember that.' (21st February 1942).

He was getting a taste for adventure but, given his puritanical upbringing, felt guilty about how much fun he was having. He wrote in October 1941 to Dickey: 'it often seems to me unfair that I should enjoy the privilege of remaining an Official War Artist in the Middle East when there are so many competent painters at home . . . . If you decide to withdraw my appointment in order that I could join the Forces as an ordinary soldier . . . . I should consider it fair treatment . . . . I must admit I thoroughly enjoy the life, the trekking and camping or a long march gives immense pleasure and I am pretty well furnished with equipment to undertake that sort of thing – if need be alone.'

When they arrived in Addis Ababa ('charming, splendid Italian food') he lived in a deserted royal palace and painted one of his finest watercolours of it, drew portraits of Ethiopian soldiers, suffered another bout of malaria and was nursed by his batman Mohammed and Italian nuns ('very pleasant indeed'). The portraits raised a technical problem: 'When the model is the colour of a grape it is difficult to disassociate form and colour, more especially in the region of the cheek & cheek bone, a rounded expanse of fat with no geographical features & impossible to map with accuracy.' Nevertheless, these are impressive portraits, anatomically credible, solid individuals and they demonstrate that Bawden had now overcome some of those weaknesses that Rothenstein had disparaged so publicly in the RCA life-room. 'I like drawing black chaps . . . . I think they're simply beautiful' he concluded. Surprisingly, having solved this problem of drawing likenesses he rarely used this skill after the war, perhaps because as a reserved man he disliked the enforced intimacy of the portrait sitting. At least with the African and Indian troops he would not feel obliged to conduct small talk.

After three months in Addis he trekked on to Asmara in Eritrea, then Khartoum again where he painted Haile Selassie (known to the English as 'Tiger Tim') in silence, both sides using only 'courteous gestures'. He wrote to his father 'I was impressed by the nobility of his features, the dignity of his manner, and the regal gestures which mark him as the greatest personality in the war on this front.' Then across the Western Desert to Siwa Oasis, and along the coast to Benghazi where he drew ships sunk in the harbour, but soon he had to retreat via Tobruck, Bardia and Mersa Matruh as Rommel's army began pushing east.

He wrote to O'Rourke Dickey on 27th July 1942 that he had been invited by a local sheik to accompany his caravan across the desert to Yemen but had reluctantly refused because he didn't trust the WAAC to retrieve him if it went wrong and 'I should have returned a polygamous Muslim with a smattering of Arabic and a liking for a whole boiled sheep for lunch and dinner, and few – very few – drawings'. The Islamic way of life had its appeal for a man, as he wrote to Ravilious: 'Give me a bad Moslem to a lent-ridden Christian. I don't care if they have 3 wives, or if divorce is easy, they do have the sense to make them wear the most frightful frumpy dirty clothes and that wonderful mercy the yash-mak, or veil, which hides what ought never to be seen. To put a ring on the nose and silver anklets on the feet keeps the women orthodox and one's savings safe.' (21st February 1942).

He wrote home: 'In the last 30 days I have covered between 2000 and 2500 miles across desert and semi-desert country, sleeping in the open, in the truck, in ruined houses and under canvas; doing a stretch of five days without spare water for washing or shaving and even for cleaning teeth; living on bully and hard biscuits for three weeks, and baked turkey, roast pork and Chianti for one; making my bed, washing dirty linen, packing and unpacking nearly every day – and trying to paint.'

That sort of physical privation he could endure cheerfully, but the sensibilities acquired in his strait-laced home and Quaker school were offended by the coarser behaviours of the British Tommy in a troop camp, 'where our ridiculous sense of humour and too frequent use of a common expletive are needed in order to put up with conditions which with a little care and thought could easily be improved. Natives without exception have better manners.'[6] Even amongst the officers whom Bawden regarded as more his class equals he found none with similar intellectual interests. In various letters he mentions enjoying Macaulay's essays, Herodotus, Wordsworth, T. S. Eliot, W. H. Davies, Gibbon, Jane Austen and Evelyn Waugh: he carried Milton's poems with him and despised P. G. Wodehouse (who had been a Ravilious favourite). 'I know it sounds priggish; but books are not picked up and dropped. They are taken about, read carefully, criticised and talked of, and handed on'. On a later occasion he was given an English driver whose boredom, sloppiness, racism, dirtiness and lack of work ethic drove Bawden to fury, as he told Charlotte: 'This London pastry-cook sitting on his arse all day, doing bugger-all, and complaining of being "browned off" has been a slight drag on my own efforts. I can't blame him; I feel sorry that an elementary education gives a man no resources of his own – only a pathetic dependence upon newspapers, wireless noise, cinemas, and trash reading. It is very unsatisfactory and deplorable when combined with a snooty feeling of colour superiority.' (1st November 1943).

He endured yet more malaria and a flash flood through his tent on the way, but he was back in Cairo by February and pleased to meet a fellow artist, Anthony Gross (1905-1984) who became a friend in spite of their different temperaments. 'He is an awfully nice fellow to meet', Bawden reported and he respected Gross as an artist: 'Fresh observations and quiet humour – unpretentious and good; the school of Ardizzone and Topolski – the sound tradition of English draughtsmanship and illustration which harks back to Rowlandson and Bunbury, don't you agree?' (16th February 1942). Actually Gross, who was of Hungarian-Jewish-Irish-Anglo-Italian descent and had a French wife, had trained all over Europe and had more in common with such French artists as Dufy than he did with the English School. The two lonely men could have a moan together about how theirs was the worst of wartime jobs – rootless, lonely, never settled long enough to make friends and nobody was interested in what they were doing. They gossiped about Rothenstein, and Bawden diffidently showed Gross his new portraits: 'you would not conceive how exciting it is after nearly twenty months to talk openly about painters and painting, or what it has been like working without that stimulus: I tell you that I look at any postcard reproduction of a painting as I would look at green fields.' Together they visited Coptic churches and Bawden enthused to Charlotte: 'Oh the complexity and the flamboyance of the decoration, counter-change and interlacing, inlay and veneer, fret and carving, the strong bright red and blue and profusion of gilt.'

By March 1942 he was on the move again with an Indian mule company near Tripoli, then to Beirut where he fished in the harbour with Gross and Mohammed. They then went their separate ways, Gross eventually surpassing even Bawden in producing 421 drawings and watercolours for WAAC during his travels through Iran, Iraq, Egypt, Syria, Malaysia, India, Burma, France and Germany.

In the Lebanon in March Bawden tried to paint a word picture for his wife of the scene outside his tent: 'The hillside was terraced with olive groves. The reddish soil of other hillsides was spotted and the profiles softened by the light, warm terre verte of the olive trees. Between one terrace and another was a rocky bank bright with wild flowers, a strip garden where the stately asphodel grew, the crimson and purple anemone opening in the morning, and sheets of pink and rosy red cyclamen, scillas, orchids, arums and that little brownish purple mullein, *Verbascum Phoenicium*, I have grown at home. Milk thistles, soapworts, daisies, buttercups and a beautiful small, clear blue Iris. Over the hills, no great distance away stretched the mountains with snow-capped peaks which sparkled in the sunlight, and there where the winter sports take place are the famous cedars – a hundred of them, and an hotel.' (17th March 1942).

Bawden made a short side trip to visit the Mustafiq Marsh Arabs hidden up palm-shaded creeks off the Tigris river: 'No one has – so far as I know – attempted to penetrate this wild region with a paint brush' and he vowed to return. At last he was told he would be replaced by Ardizzone, which he accepted 'sedately' but wrote to the WAAC: 'It is good that someone else should do some work literally with the sweat of his brow & return later a more emaciated and healthier man. I am glad your choice has fallen on one who can willingly spare some fat in the service of his country . . . but why do you wish to recall me when to the present moment I have not had the opportunity to contract dysentery, bilhartzia or hookworm!'[7] He went south via the Suez Canal to join his return ship at Cape Town.

On 1st September 1942 Bawden sailed for home on the *Laconia*, a 20,000 ton twenty-year-old former liner built on the Tyne and then adapted as a troop carrier. It had sailed from Suez via Aden, Mombasa, Durban and Cape Town picking up a total of 2,732 people. There were 286 British service-men (some wounded), 1,800 Italian Prisoners of War captured in Libya, 103 Poles whose job it was to guard the Italians, 80 civilians including women and children, and 463 officers and crew under Captain Rudolph Sharp. The Italians were locked in the hold but allowed on deck twice a day for exercise and showers while the other passengers amused themselves with lectures, dances and the bars. They were badly overloaded for an unescorted journey expected to take a month and, ominously, there were only 32 lifeboats and 40 rafts on board.

What Bawden could not know was that on the second day of the voyage the closest and dearest friend he was ever to have, Eric Ravilious, was killed in Iceland, lost at sea.

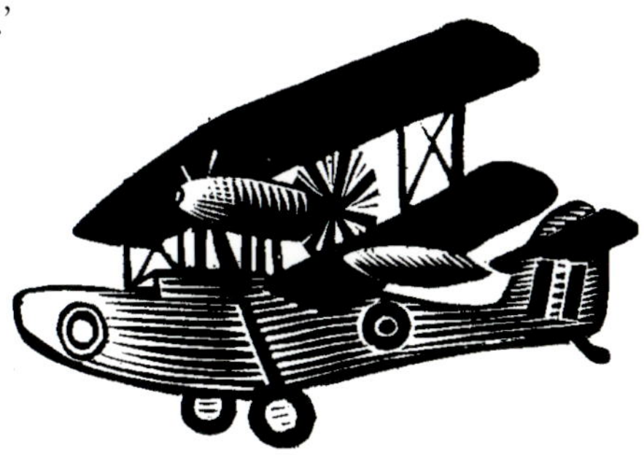

Engraving by Ravilious for the Admiralty's *Weekly Intelligence Report*, early 1942 (not used).

1. In 1989 Ruari McLean published a selection of these in *Edward Bawden: War Artist* (Scolar Press in association with the Imperial War Museum).
2. Ardizzone, E., *Baggage to the Enemy*, John Murray, 1941, p.121.
3. Harries, M. and S., *The War Artists*, Michael Joseph, 1983, p.170.
4. Rothenstein, J., *Modern English Painters*, Vol 11, Macdonald, 1984, p.310.
5. Bliss, D. P., *Edward Bawden*, Pendomer Press, 1979, p.84.
6. Harries, M. and S., ibid, p.228.
7. Harries, M. and S., ibid, p.229.

7. BAWDEN'S WAR, PART TWO

The *Laconia* was nearing the Equator in temperatures of 110 degrees Fahrenheit when, at 8pm on the evening of 12th September, 1942, it was hit twice below water level by torpedoes from the German U-boat U156 under the command of Werner Hartenstein. Many of the Italians in the hold were killed instantly while the others forced their way out and began to fight for the lifeboats, many of which were unlaunchable because the ship was listing sharply to starboard. Bawden with typical sang froid resigned himself to death by drowning: 'so I thought I'd

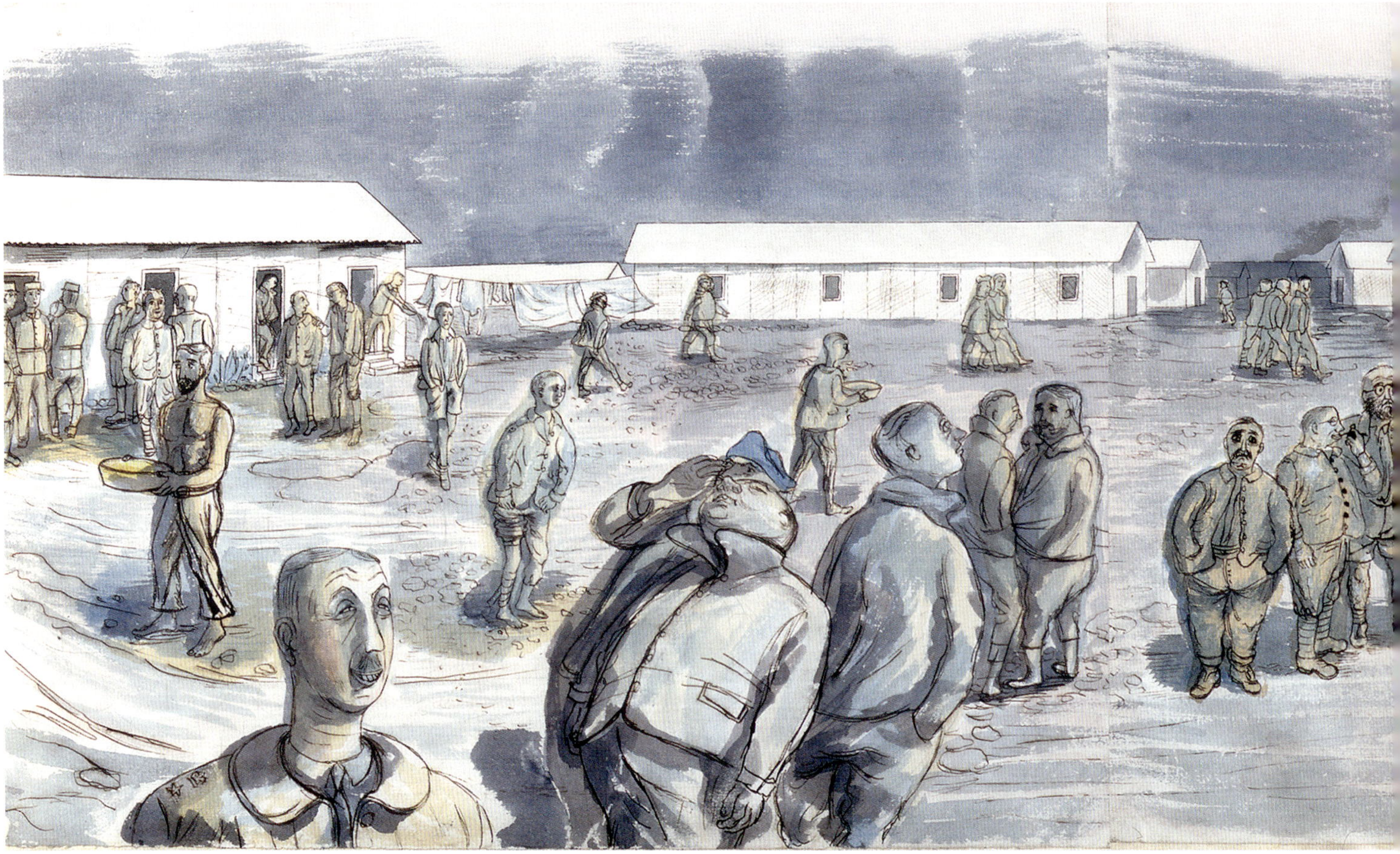

Mediouna Internment Camp, Casablanca, 8th November 1942: The bombardment of Casablanca harbour. Interned British subjects awaiting release, 1942. Watercolour on paper, 504 x 1170 mm (Imperial War Museum, LD2888).

wander round a bit and have a look. I went down to my cabin – I'd bought my wife a watch and thought I might as well go down with the watch as not.' Then, 'on returning from my cabin I saw ropes hanging down on the side where life-boats had been lowered and standing by one of these I was joined by a major: 'After you, Sir' I said. He descended – there was a splash. Sliding down the next ropes I found myself being gripped and guided into a boat. A few minutes later all the boats pulled away to a safe distance and there we sat waiting, still and silent and tense for the sound of the ship's final end. I did not see it disappear because I had my arm round a little girl who had become separated from her mother and brother, but, luckily, they were later discovered on another boat.'[1] He was fortunate to survive, but he had lost his precious drawings, a collection of exotic hats and his beloved sketching umbrella.

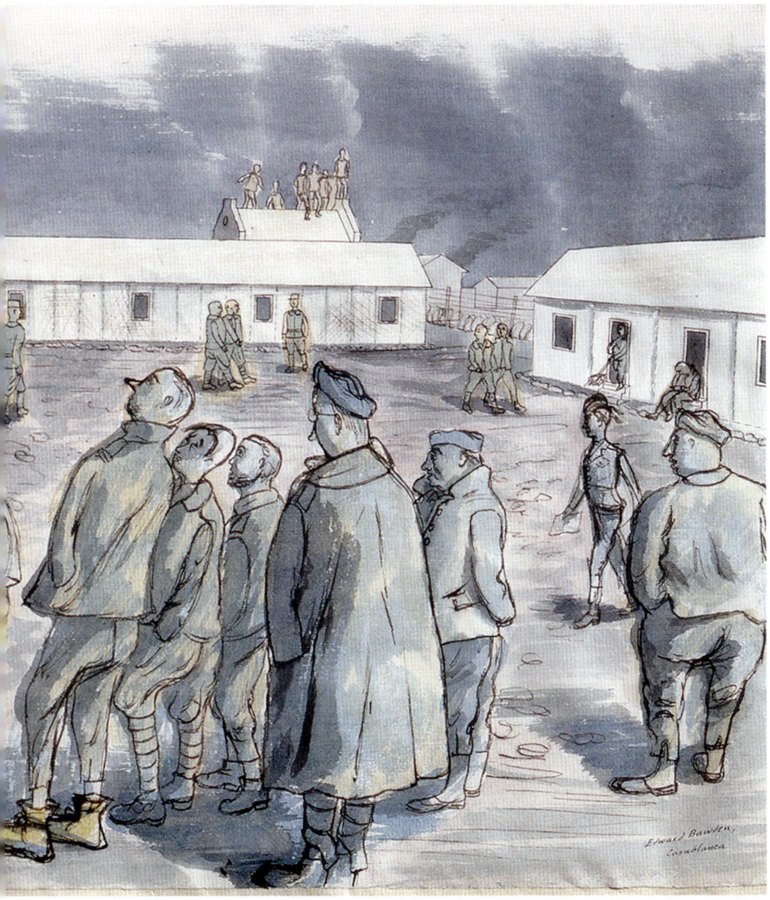

The *Laconia* took nearly ninety minutes to sink, bows first, and Captain Sharp deliberately stayed on the bridge and went down with her. Many of the passengers were now swimming in the water; some were attacked by barracudas in the gathering dark and other swallowed oil after the ship's boilers exploded. The submarine surfaced and from the survivors' cries its crew realised that many of those in the water were Italians, and therefore German allies, and so began to take them on board. Hartenstein signalled Admiral Donitz in Paris to send more submarines to help and thus avoid political embarrassment with Mussolini. After long delay two eventually arrived. He also broadcast openly in English to any ships in the vicinity to come and help survivors with the promise that he would not attack them, but none came.

Only eighteen lifeboats had been launched and there were up to ninety people in some of them. They had pemican, Horlicks tablets and biscuits but little water and the next day's blinding sun caused sunburn and a raging thirst. 'There was quite a lot to watch', Bawden recalled: 'Lots of people were drowned, especially Italian prisoners. We saw them floating about in the water a day or two afterwards and the sharks were nuzzling round the boats.' For five days he drifted: 'our boat would have been terrible but for the fact that we picked up a young Air Force officer who made himself felt and established order. We then counted up how much food we had, and so on. If it hadn't been for him, I think the merchant seamen would have thrown us soldiers out as we were in such a small minority.' Each day every individual in Bawden's boat was issued with two biscuits and one cup of water, hardly adequate in the blazing Equatorial heat.

The Germans were in a dilemma: they humanely gave food and medicine, transferred people from boat to boat and took women and children on board the submarines,

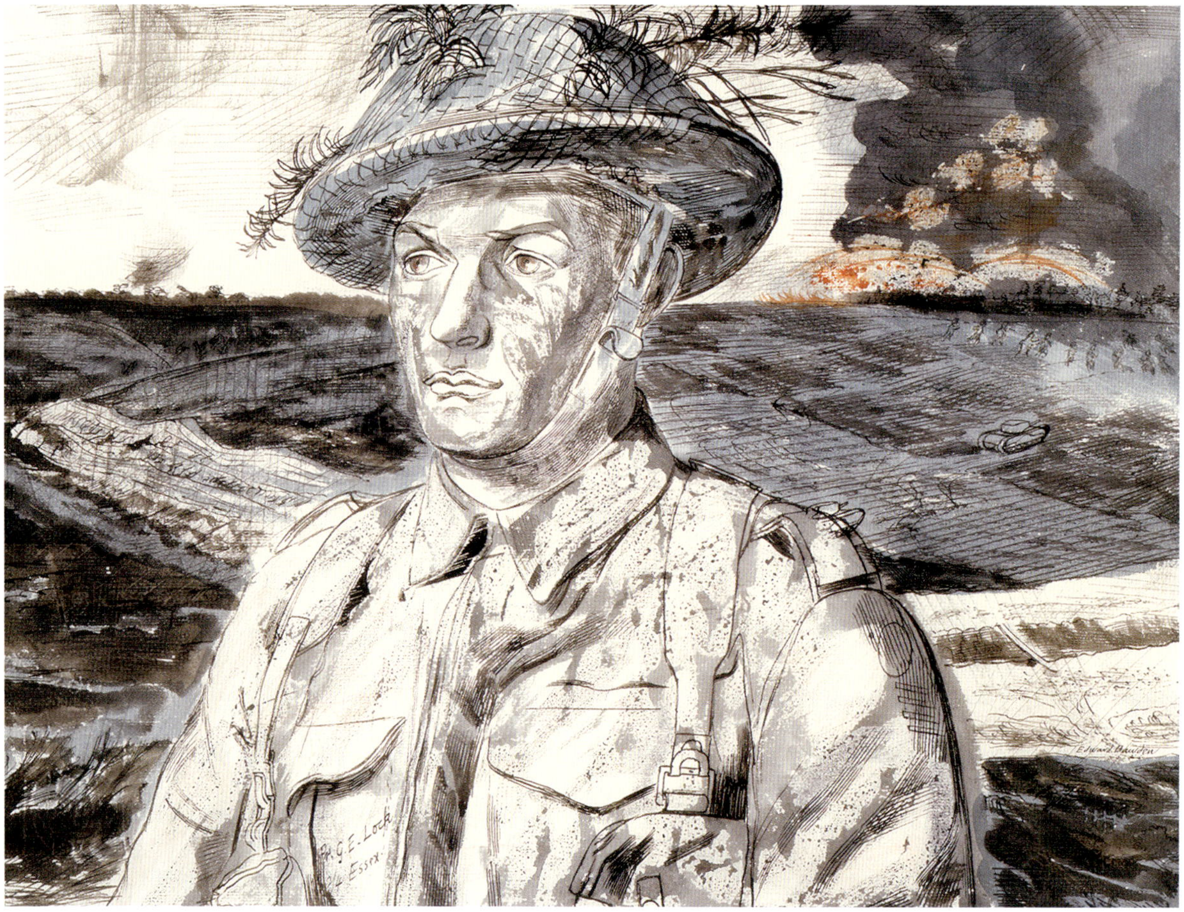

Exercise Kruschen (Dunwich Common): A Demonstration of the Ronson Flame-thrower, 1943, watercolour on paper, 393 x 514 mm (Imperial War Museum, LD2893).

but they were on the surface and exposed to attack from the air now that their position had been broadcast. They flew the Red Cross flag and took the lifeboats in tow, but an American B-24 Liberator aircraft came from Ascension Island and dropped five bombs on the little fleet, damaging one submarine and sinking a lifeboat full of passengers. The alarmed Germans were then forced to put the survivors back in the sea or boats and leave the scene.

Eventually the Italian ship *Cappellini* arrived on the 16th and the Vichy French *Gloire* on the 17th under orders from Paris. In all 1,041 survivors were hauled onto the *Gloire* by ropes with loops on them which took nearly the whole day and Bawden was one of these. Pails of coffee and brandy awaited them on deck, but no friendliness. They were on board a week, British forrard, Italians aft, men and officers separated, as they sailed back to Casablanca via Dakar and somehow Bawden managed to draw the packed British survivors. Several of the rescued died on reaching shore. The British were then taken by cattle trucks to the internment camp at Mediouna and the 450 Italians sent back to fight in the desert where the battle of El Alamein was about to begin on October 23rd.

After Bawden's hardships in the desert the camp was bearable, apart from the vile latrines: 'life in the camp for the next two and a half months was uneventful, we walked about the compound aimlessly, taking exercise and talking to each other. For warmth French Foreign Legion uniforms were issued, our food was beans washed down with coffee substitute. We slept in small wooden huts and because I woke early by habit and also possessed a watch

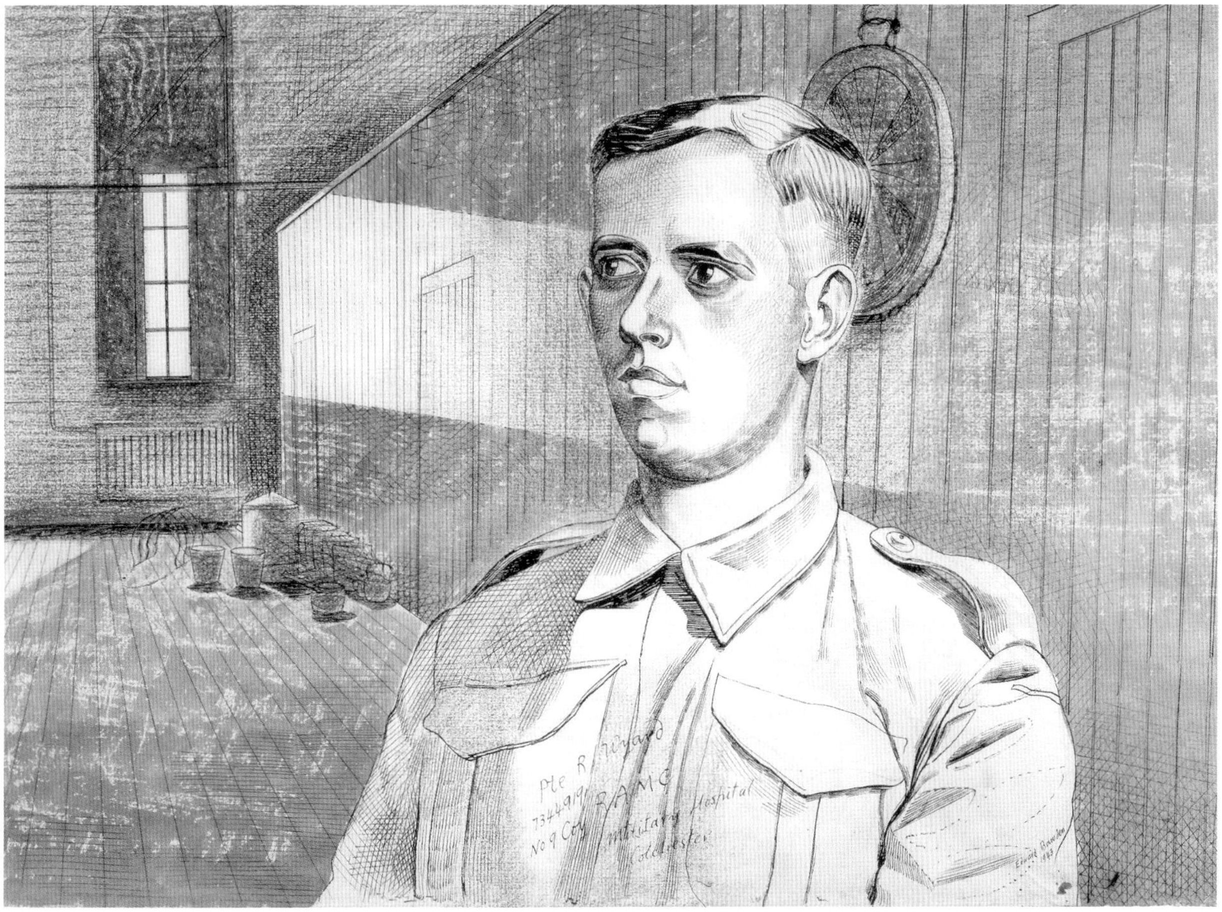

Private R. Wyard, RAMC, 1943, watercolour on paper, 393 x 514mm (Imperial War Museum, LD3043).

I was given the job of rousing everybody for breakfast.' From somewhere he scrounged paper and pencil and drew the camp and the men queuing up for their weekly baths. He said of the tragedy: 'a most unfamiliar experience . . . all the best people died and the worst got saved'. This experience left him with a lifelong dislike of the French, so that in future he would pass through France on his way to Italy, but he would never stay there.

When the Allies, under Eisenhower, invaded French North Africa in early November the prisoners were released by American troops and shipped to Norfolk in Virginia. Bawden was kitted out with a GI uniform but without badges 'so I came back to England wearing a mixture of uniforms'. After a brief stay in New York he crossed the submarine-menaced Atlantic aboard the SS *Westerland* and produced a Christmas magazine for the passengers on the office duplicator with sketches of his companions and an American eagle and British lion tucking into a turkey on the cover. He was back in England by the end of 1942.

The *Laconia* incident had further consequences. Because the submarines had been bombed by the Americans whilst on the surface, Admiral Donitz gave the order that in future all U-boats were to ignore survivors in the sea. When he was on trial for war crimes in Nuremberg after the war he was sent to Spandau for ten years for issuing this brutal directive.[2]

After a reunion with Charlotte in Cheltenham, Bawden was given a short leave, then sent to the Suffolk coast to draw anti-invasion tactics being practised. From there he wrote to the widowed Tirzah: 'I was really looking forward to seeing Eric again. There was no one whose opinion I valued more highly than his, no one I know or have known seems to possess what he had, an almost flawless taste, that and our long friendship which commenced on the first day each of us entered South Kensington produced I think by habit and intimacy an understanding of each other that went deeper than with anyone else ... on my part I relied very greatly on Eric's opinion and advice, that I took the former seriously and more often than not acted upon the latter . . . . But my dear Tirzah, it is so much more than all that – I simply can't tell you, or anyone else, or even myself what it is, or how much it is I miss by losing Eric – I find myself in tears at the moment – and hope the servant does not come in to clear the tea things for a while.' (17th March 1943).

His next assignment was at Colchester Military Hospital where he attended and drew a post-mortem on a decaying corpse. As the body was opened he 'recognised several objects familiar to the kitchen' and was amused by the Pathologist saying to the nurse 'Sister do you grow tomatoes?' He disengaged a hand from the towel to point to a bucket of bloody mess. 'You're very practical, Major' I said. 'Yes, I hate to see good stuff wasted.' (May 1943). Then he was sent to watch Poles learning to parachute in Scotland, though none of these subjects inspired him. To rise above mere recording he set himself technical problems to solve, so at Aldeburgh in Suffolk he made a five-sheet panorama in watercolour over eight feet in length which took him ten days, adding extra sheets on either side as he worked. It included 150 figures and a 'purple-black plum' for a sun – 'It is the third or fourth blue sun I have painted, a preposterous colour to have chosen, but yellow which 999 in a 1000 might have picked would have made the whole drawing look unreal. It is amusing that one can juggle with what might seem to give no scope for juggling, and intellectually satisfying to reflect that only by such a flagrant distortion can a truthful

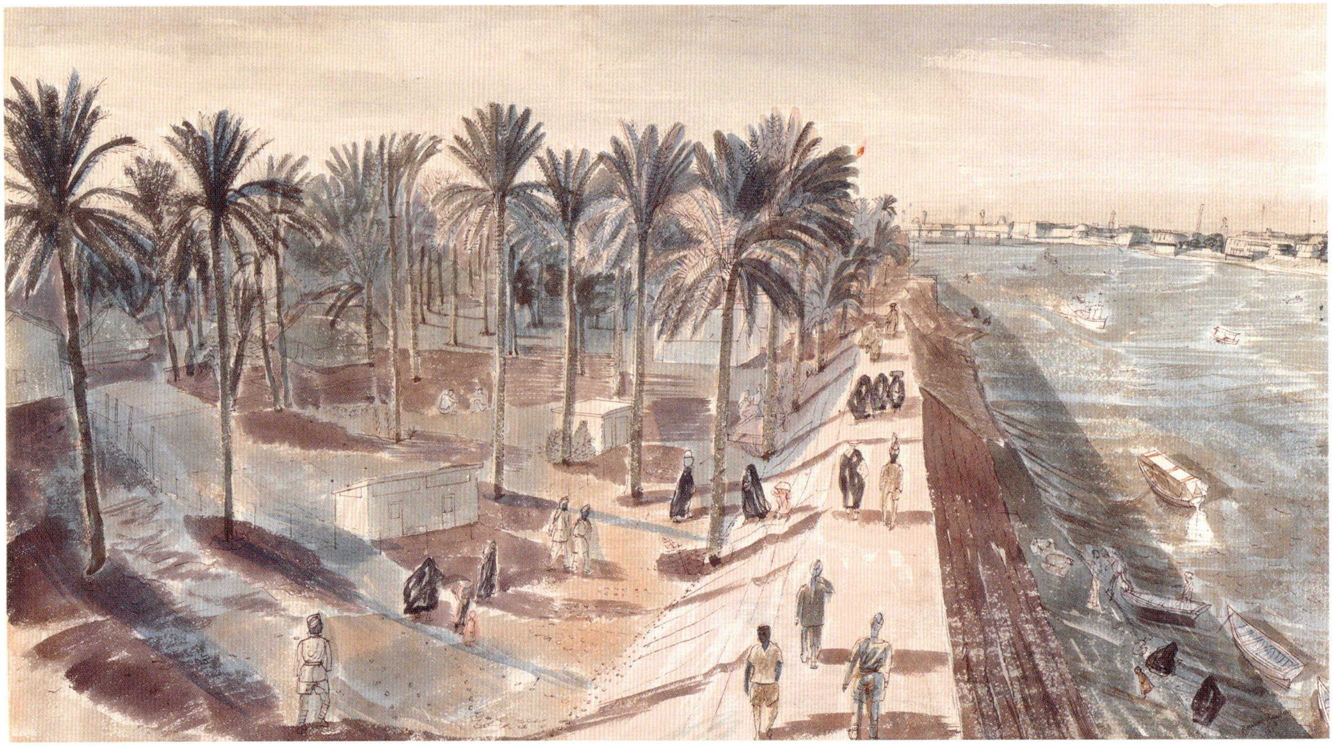

Baghdad: A View of the River Tigris and of the Camp of the Hygiene Section, an Indian Unit, 1943, watercolour on paper, 431 x 774 mm (Imperial War Museum, LD4114).

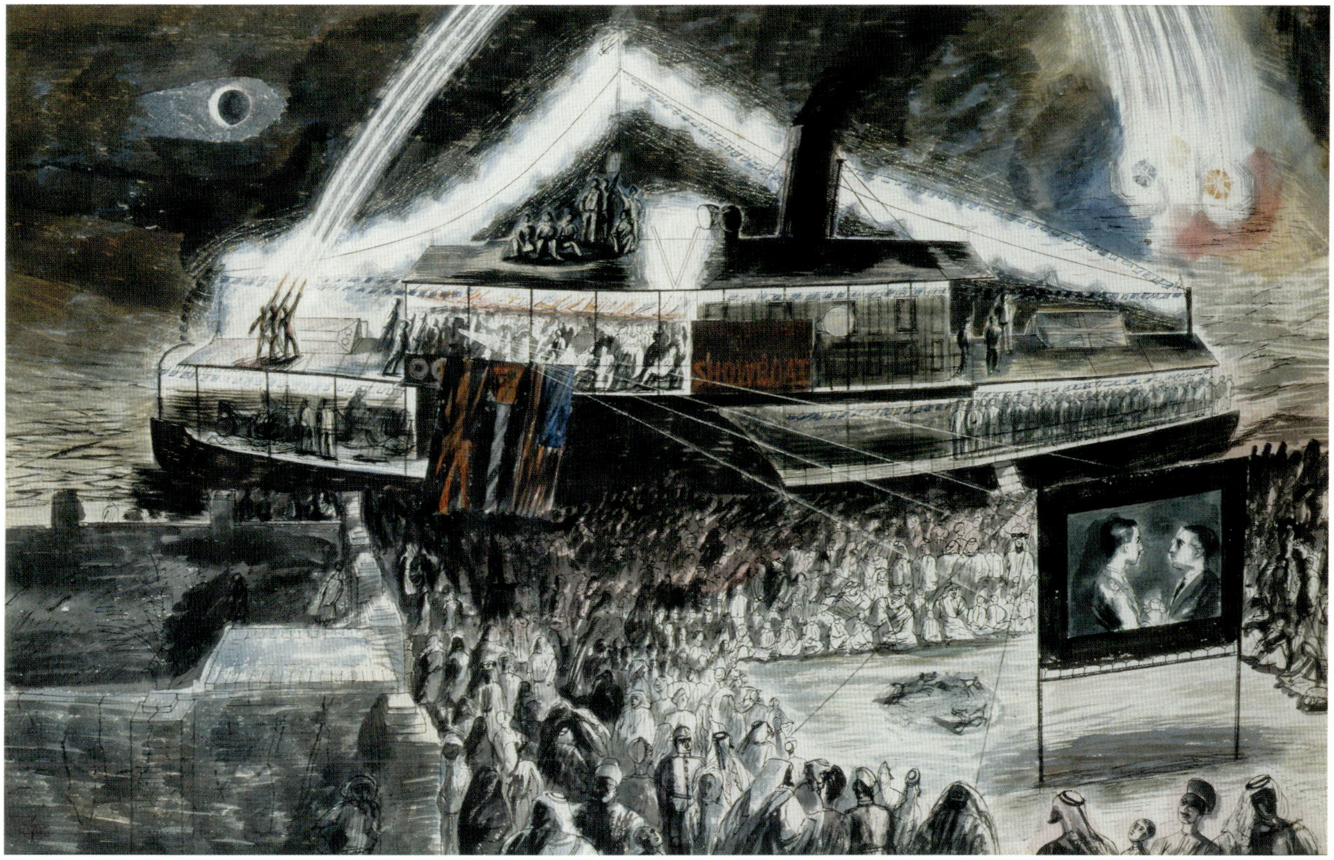

The Showboat at Baghdad, 1944, watercolour, 660 x 1005 mm
(© Queen's Printer and Controller of HMSO, 2005. UK Government Art Collection).

effect be represented.' (14th April 1943). Drawing crowds and panoramas always appealed to him.

After his break in England Bawden was back in Cairo by September 1943, but now working for the Ministry of Information rather than the War Office which meant he dressed all in white instead of khaki. Someone observed he wore this uniform sardonically, as if it were a stage costume. From there he was sent by slow train to Baghdad, which crippled him with haemorrhoids ('like being impaled on an iron spike'), and found himself amongst more artists than he had in Great Bardfield. A 'modernist' Pole had been there before him and taught all the local artists to paint shadows purple and dab primary colours on in dots like pointillists. Consequently when Bawden put on an exhibition of his recent work the Iraqis thought him hopelessly old fashioned and the English thought him insufficiently advanced, romantic or amusing. He, however, felt he was making progress, relying less on line filled in with colour as he had before the war: 'I cannot altogether dispense with pen but colour takes the place of black ink, naturally too colour predominates over line – so that I am justified in describing them as paintings & not tinted drawings: also the colour helps to give a sensation of solidity . . . an effect I couldn't achieve while using ingenious cross hatchings and heel ball. I think I'm on the track of something which at least for me is new.' Faced with a 'sensationally baroque' landscape of red rocks he had to shed those dry-brush mannerisms and genteel colours he had acquired painting alongside Ravilious in the green Essex fields.

In Baghdad he ran into another War Artist, Feliks Topolski, and they showed each other their works in progress: Topolski 'was fulsome in praise of some of them. I did my best to knock back as many compliments as I received, but failed to equal anything so asinine as the comparison with Gauguin (Iraq as my South Sea Island!)' (16th February 1944). Later he sarcastically observed that Topolski had been in Cairo ten minutes and thought that made him a War Artist.

Back in Cairo he met up with Alec Waugh the novelist and he could also talk over times past with an old friend, *The Times* architectural correspondent, Jim Richards, who had collaborated with Ravilious on the *High Street* book of 1938. This contact was important because Richards would write the first book on Bawden after the war[3] and in 1972 edit the definitive volume of Ravilious' engravings.

Next Bawden sailed to Jedda and set off into Saudi Arabia on an international non-military expedition to kill locusts, though they saw disappointingly few locusts to poison. He had malaria again and then found he couldn't catch up with his drawing because the Arabs, children, camels and sheep were all too inquisitive. The enforced leisure of Bedouin life was irritating to a workaholic like Bawden as he wrote to Gregory: 'A day wasted in Arabia may be no more than an hour of laziness in London, the time passes slowly from the hour before dawn to the hour after sunset punctuated by the passing of the coffee cup and the hours for prayer: coffee and prayer are the diversions for the rest, like Mr Eliot's Gumbie Cat one just sits and sits and sits and sits until the European arse is sore. Sometimes, sitting uncomfortably cross-legged I saw in an inner mirage a Tottenham Court Road armchair . . . .' (5th May 1944). Yet he managed some very impressive watercolours of the 'grim, desolate and

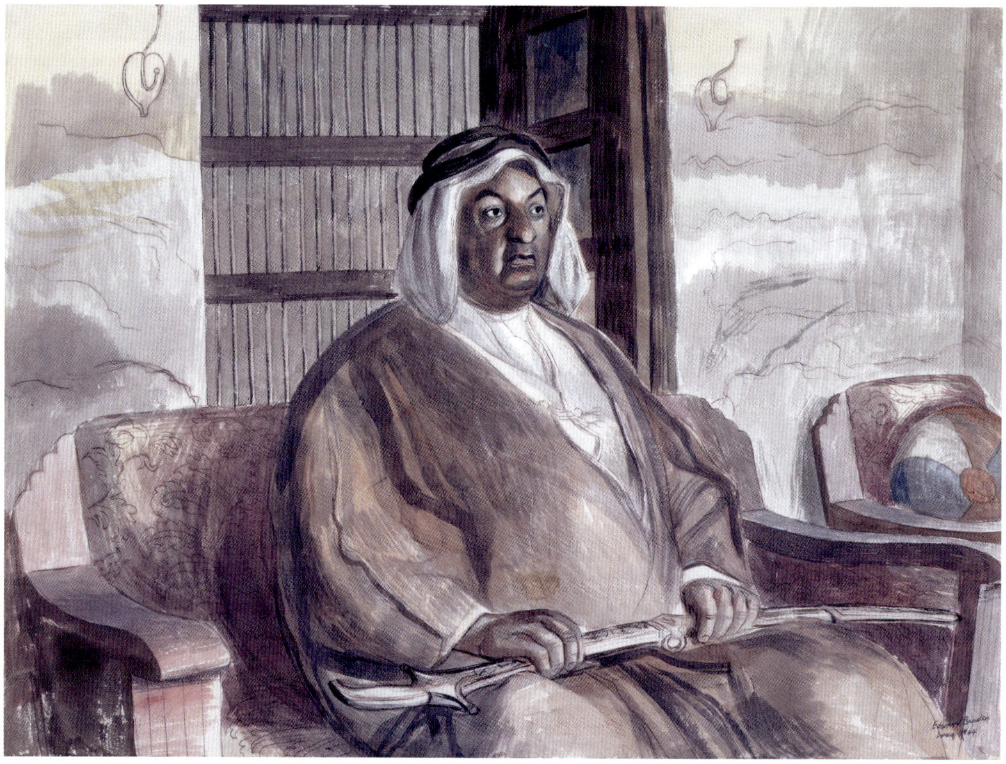

Shaikh Haji Khaiyun al-Ubaid, Paramount Shaikh of the 'Ubudah Tribe, 1944, watercolour on paper, 393 x 508 mm (Imperial War Museum, LD4563).

forbidding' landscapes round Hail in the middle of the country where 'the volcanic reds and blacks, austerely rich by juxtaposition, had the dim fiery glow of a Russian ikon'. In Hail camel market he drew while two policemen held back the curious crowds with whips.

On Easter Sunday 1944 he wrote that he had 'crossed this goddam desert from the Red Sea coast to the Persian Gulf', and was tired of living on tinned food and biscuits, enduring sandstorms and Arab salesmen hustling them, even when the Europeans were sitting on the toilet. If the Native and English company wasn't to his liking the wildlife was – he was inquisitive about architecture, local dress, flowers, birds and insects – even cockroaches: 'The largest cockroaches I have ever seen walked by night, great fellows four inches long with thread-like antennae. There is something splendid in a cockroach of these dimensions. Naturally I never killed them, I hate the crunchy sound of a beetle flattened under foot, and their numbers would not have been reduced by making a mess on the floor. I suppose they do a job of work about as useful as my own.' (4th April 1943).

By mid-July he was back in Baghdad, sleepless as the jackals and pi-dogs howled through the night and up to work from 5am to 7am before the heat and swirling dust made it impossible. On these treks Bawden had for company his man-servant Mohammed but made few new friends, though an exception was the journalist Richard Wyndham ('a good travel mate') with whom he made a four week trip in June to revisit the Marsh Arabs of the Euphrates and to draw the portraits of the Sheiks in their reed houses. He never met Arab women, 'except on one occasion I was allowed to draw some women soldiers, fierce old things with guns, but veiled. Not much to hide I must say.' None of his Arab sitters ever showed any

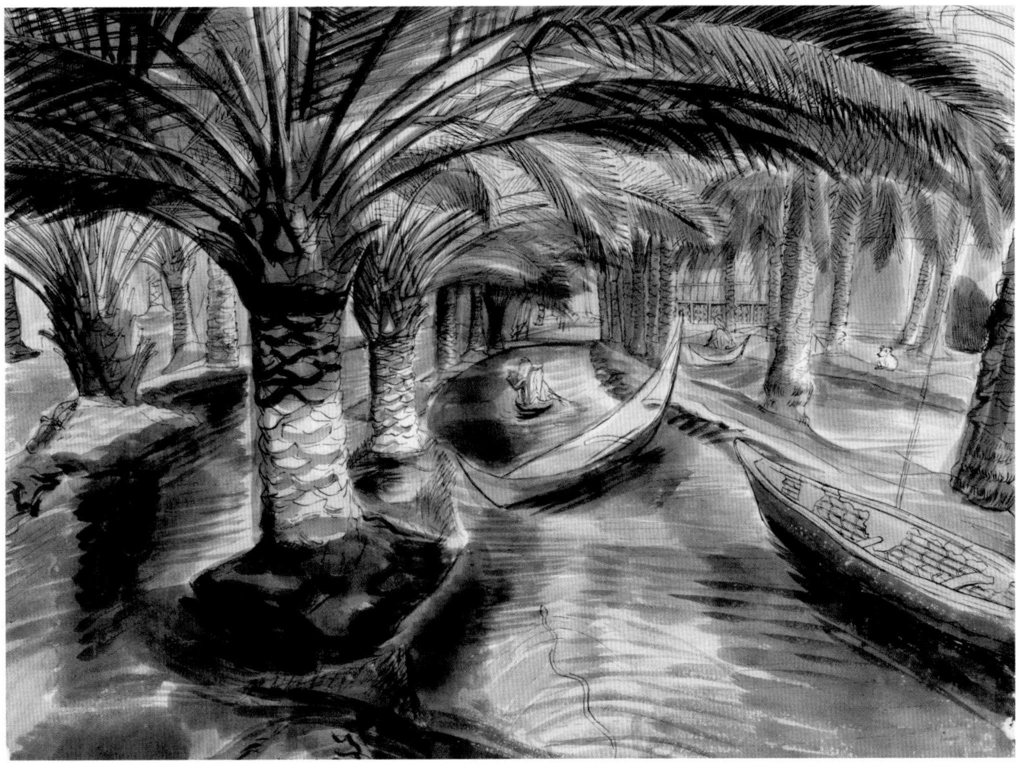

A creek scene with the local means of river conveyance, 1944, watercolour, 390 x 515 mm (© Queen's Printer and Controller of HMSO, 2005. UK Government Art Collection).

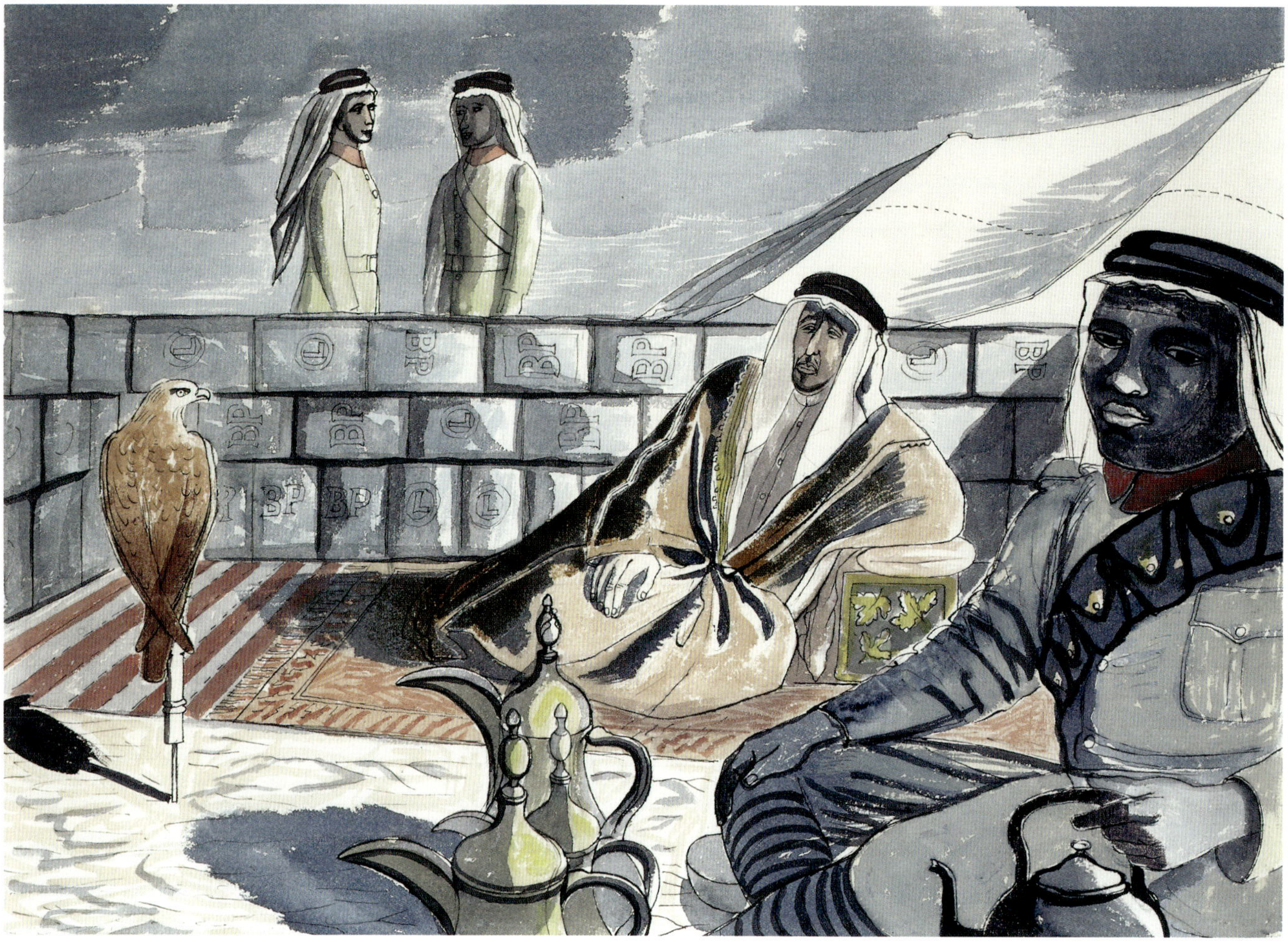

*Mohammed Bin Abdullah El'Atshan, King Ibn Saud's representative at Rumaliya, c.*1966, copy of a painting done in 1943, made at the request of a British Petroleum executive when Bawden painted the mural at the British Petroleum restaurant. The petrol cans were given the BP logo at the executive's suggestion; watercolour, size not known (Fine Art Society).

interest in the finished drawings, though they dressed up and posed stoically without moving.

One other new friend was John Morgan (1919-1987), Welfare Officer with the 6th Indian Division who seemed to be on Bawden's wavelength sufficiently for them to meet after the war. Bawden was unusually forward: 'I should like to see you again – you're one of the very few with whom I should like to keep in touch – but don't ask why! Why does one choose one's friends?' (18th July 1944). In his diary entry for the 6th August 1944 Morgan writes: 'Bawden has been in and out doing some studies of the Pai-y-yak pass; I find his conversation pleasant because I know him and his ways of thought, but other officers in the mess don't get on with him at all. He doesn't open out with strangers and replies almost brusquely, saying that he's quite happy listening to other people talking. I should think that a most depressing pastime in our mess.' Many of the officers and administrators Bawden met along the way were trying to maintain Home Counties standards in this hostile world and were not pleased when he appeared at dinner in a lounge suit from which 'wartime moths had removed the flies'.

The Pai-y-yak Pass was a snaking mountainous route into Persia by which goods could be sent to our Russian allies and Bawden drew a remarkable double sheet panorama of this happening. Another unique work was of an open-air cinema show on the moonlit banks of the Tigris drawn by Bawden as he accompanied the paddle steamer on its round of the riverside villages. A film on sheep-breeding topped the bill.

News came that his next mission would be to China, ('I am as wildly excited as it is proper to be at the age of forty') and he told Gregory at the WAAC 'I shall feel a little sad leaving Irak [sic] as I like the country and the people: I like shoddy, drab old Baghdad, the mud walls and flimsy balconies, the narrow stinking lanes in the bazaars, the picturesque river front, and the great muddy river itself floating garbage to the sea, I like the men in their sweeping abbas who take life with a leisurely dignity, and the women who get on with it as drawers of water and hewers of wood – and, on those infrequent wet days smacking their feet about in the cold, wet mud – not that a woman minds a little discomfort if she is wearing a pretty pair of heavy, silver anklets! I shall miss sand and palm trees, turtles, terrapins and watersnakes, lizards and geckos.' (17th September 1944). However, the China posting was cancelled and he was sent north instead.

Bawden spent November 1944 in Rome, which had been liberated on the 5th of June. There he met William Coldstream, co-founder of the realist Euston Road School, who felt guilty that his plodding scrupulous way of making pictures was not suited to war reportage – his portraits in oil, for example, often took more than thirty long sittings while Bawden had to make do with just one

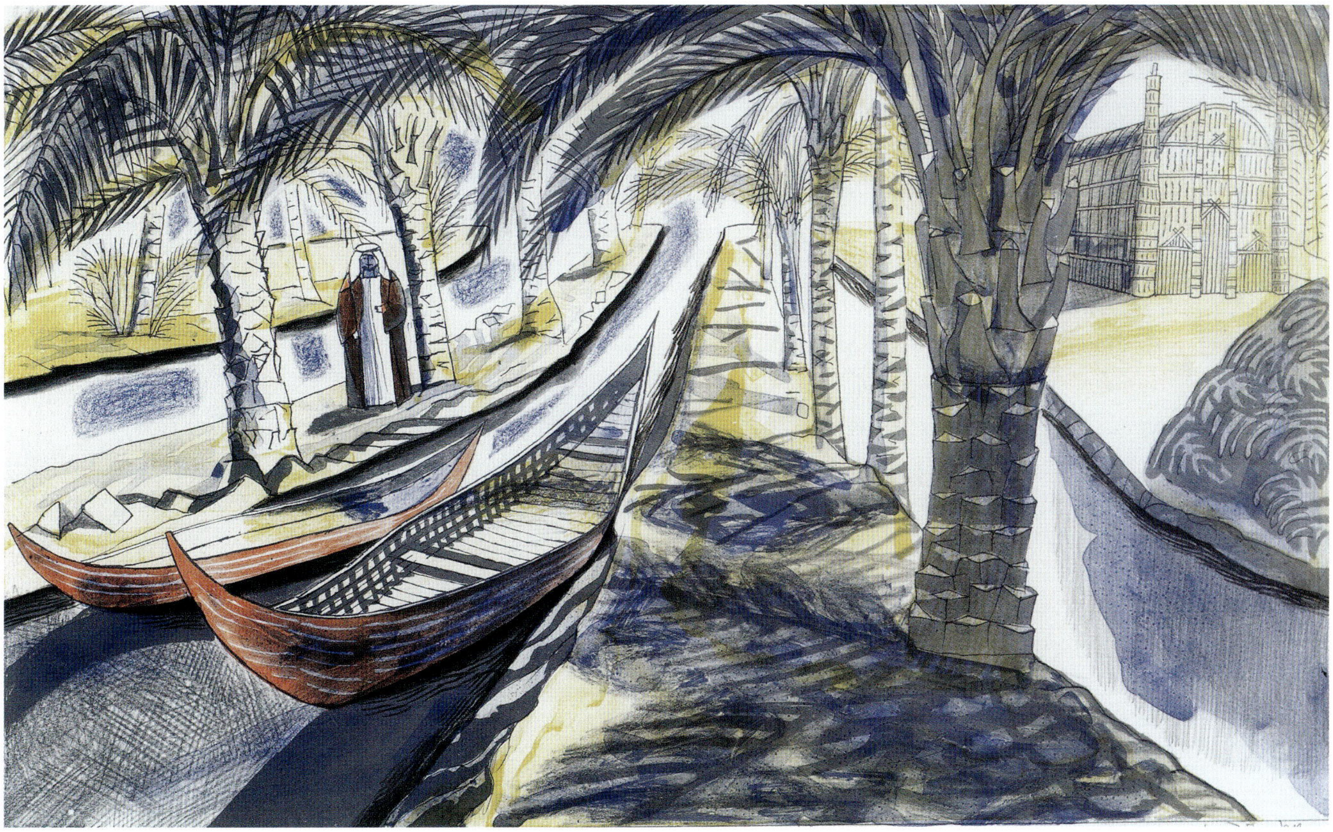

Among the Marsh Arabs, 1986, lithograph, 363 x 563 mm (Fry Art Gallery).

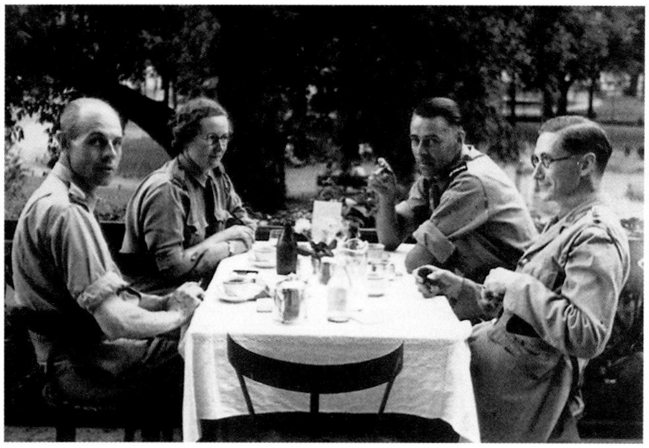

Bawden, left, in Rome, 1944 with John Aldridge, right, and two others, unidentified.

hour for his watercolours. He was also glad to be reunited with Ardizzone who had briefly replaced Bawden in North Africa, before crossing to Sicily where, unarmed, he and a photographer friend had between them accidentally captured the town of Taormina, plus a colonel and four hundred Italian troops.[4] On the way Ardizzone had seen some horrors but his genial draughtsmanship, full of little curves and theatrical lighting originally developed for children's books and humorous works, never changed even when he was drawing corpses and burial parties.

Over dinner the three discussed art and the watercolours of Beatrix Potter, then Coldstream did an amusing mime of Topolski drawing in his wild and whirling manner and 'a wicked imitation of a prayer meeting led by Herbert Read with Ben [Nicholson] and Barbara [Hepworth] praying with Salvation Army gusto, confessing their sins of Representation and asking the good Lord to make them abstract and advanced.' (2nd December 1944). Having been cast out of the Seven and Five Society by Nicholson for just such sins Bawden enjoyed the performance.

Bawden never wasted time when there were churches and galleries to be seen so he took the others sight-seeing to San Clemente and the Sistine Chapel and reported home: 'Guiding Ted is like persuading a large bluebottle to take a certain course across a window pane, but Coldstream comes very quietly at heel . . . . He is appreciative of almost everything but Ted sometimes jibs, he gives a wild stare, pulls himself up with a start, stares again in a defiant manner and declares that he doesn't really like it . . . . Both of them are delightfully amusing companions.'

As winter came on Bawden drew shivering Basuto troops camped near Ravenna. In Rimini he was depressed by the poverty and hopelessness of the defeated Italians, but a children's Christmas party given by the British officers cheered him up and he thought it the best Christmas he'd had in six years.

His blood must have been thinned by his time in the Middle East because Bawden complained constantly of the winter chill in Italy. He explained to the WAAC: 'All the drawings you will receive have been done with cold fingers. Sometimes, as I may have told you, I pee'd into my enamelled mug & then cupped my hands around it to try & receive back some of the heat I had lost. To work under uncomfortably cold conditions does not I fear confer any merit on the work itself, nor excuse any deficiencies, though if the former could be claimed then Thomas Hennell deserves the pot, as he tells me that on one occasion he painted an especially lovely sky in Iceland with his own water.'

In January Bawden drew the Italian partisans, sketching them as they stood around talking, then combining his sketches into one composition: 'the finished painting is the most successful I have yet done of that type of subject: I also like the method of working, for me it is new and enjoyable.' (13th January 1945). It was also Ardizzone's method, working from memory and notes. From the roof of a building in Ravenna's main square Bawden painted a vertiginous view of the presentation of the Medaglio d'Oro to the partisan leader Bulow standing beneath the statue of Garibaldi – another of his tour-de-force crowd scenes. 1945 he began in Rome, then went on to Florence, revisiting places he'd seen on his student scholarship.

After trips with Ardizzone to Ravenna and with Coldstream to Rimini, Bawden was sent on an expedition to Greece but only managed three imperial-sized

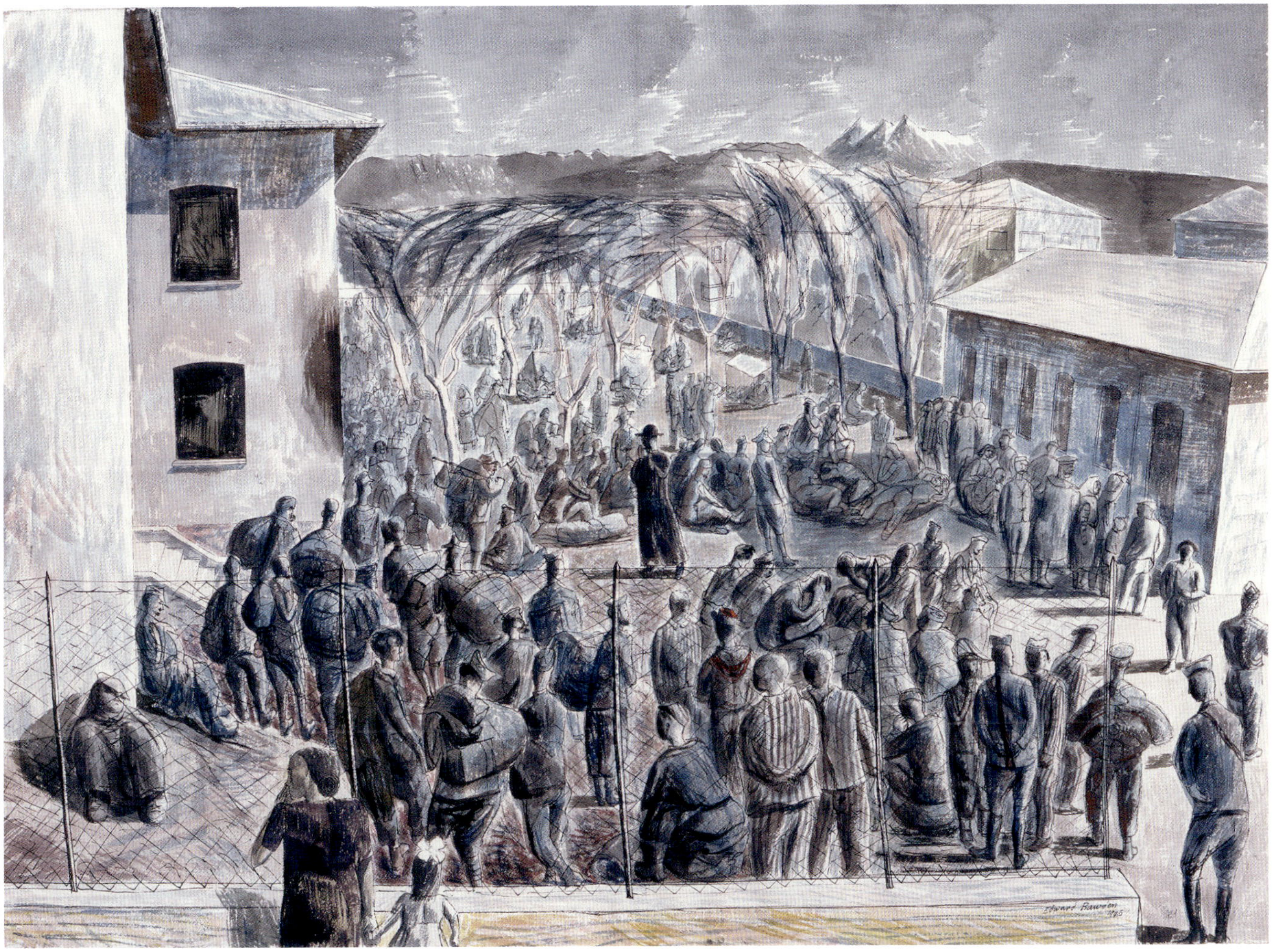

Refugees at Udine, 1945, watercolour on paper, 552 x 762 mm (Imperial War Museum, LD5210).

drawings in ten days because the travel was so strenuous. Osbert Lancaster the cartoonist showed him round and he met the Greek artist Ghika. He was back in Italy as Berlin fell and soon after saw Italian slave-workers returning from the concentration camps in their striped uniforms, 18,000 in one night, and went to draw them: 'Thousands come crowding into a refugee centre, a hungry, ragged, dirty, stinking crew of men and women who have been trudging for days along the white dusty roads . . . the camp into which they are banged is as malodorous as a lavatory pan. It stinks.' (14th May 1945). But even this he could hold at arm's length and draw dispassionately: nothing he saw in his time as a War Artist politicised him or made him as enraged as Nash had been after his experiences in the trenches of WW1. In Jim Richards' book on Bawden published in 1946 he commented: 'His work is not impulsive. Instead, all his pictures, however moving or significant in the end, are the product of study. Their vitality is intensified, not by a strong emotional urgency, but by being passed, as it were, through the tempering process of an exacting technique.' Bawden himself called it 'keeping a clean eye'.

In May he joined Coldstream in Udine where their beds were teeming with bugs and they had to sleep on the floor.

Then in quick succession he was in Florence, Rome, Naples and back to Rome. Carel Weight, Bawden's former student and Ardizzone's replacement, together with Coldstream, went on a trek round Roman churches led by Bawden and the men were soon exhausted with his relentless energy and bookshop searches for novels by the prolific nineteenth century writer Margaret Oliphant.[5] He also met his Great Bardfield neighbour and pre-war wallpaper collaborator John Aldridge, working his way north after being in North Africa as a Photographic Interpreter in the Intelligence Corps. In spite of Viscount Esher's request that he be spared military service Aldridge had never been appointed an official war artist, so had to paint where and when he could, though he managed enough works for there to be an exhibition of his African and Italian war paintings held after his death.[6]

A few days before the war in Europe ended Bawden wrote from Rome to his wife about money matters and his hopes for the future. Perhaps, he suggested, they could get a tent and a baker's van and go off painting together 'among magnificent scenery and under blue skies' (though she would do the driving and he the painting). But then he remembered something: 'there's the question of the children's education – depressing I feel because it's a long and senseless routine, deadening in its effects on most children. Parental influence is also bad for children if they have to suffer too much of Dad and Mum's pet prejudices. I wish children would go off and live together in caves until they're grown up and fit to return to the company of other grown ups: I would send them off willingly with a bow and some arrows and a copy of Lord Chesterfield's Letters. Also getting children civilised is an expensive business – just at the age when they ought to be tearing up hills and exploring a tough countryside they must sit at desks doing geography from books! Dear, dear! I'm not being helpful in the least – but I do hate the system.' (2nd May 1945). Bawden's professed socialism was no match for the class consciousness he had inherited from his father, so he could entertain no thought of sending the children to the free local schools and they received their entire education at fee-paying boarding schools well away from home.

By July 1945 Bawden was back in England, though with Charlotte in Cheltenham rather than Great Bardfield. On the first day home he rose before breakfast to sort out a work space: 'a job that took the greater part of the day, but, now the shelves are in order and there is nothing to vex my return to married life', he told John Morgan. Only one bomb had fallen on Great Bardfield during the war and it had damaged Brick House which now needed extensive repairs and modernisation. He had written to Charlotte from the Middle East: 'Once I get home I'll never travel again – except for a holiday with you' – though this was not a promise he kept.

Charlotte must have found him profoundly changed. In many ways the war had been the making of Bawden as a man and an artist. In 1940 he was a rather grumpy introvert, comfortable with life in a pretty village in an unremarkable county, meeting only like-minded artists in neighbouring houses or on his commutes to teach at his old college. The man who had once shirked all exercise and was too shy to enter shops or board a bus had now found reserves of courage and physical endurance and had held his own with desert Arabs and professional soldiers. In his pre-war art he had been content to depict the small-scale felicities of rural England and to provide graphics for other men's projects in a style that was beginning to come a little too easily. 'The war made me mature. Before that experience I would regard myself as being immature, taking refuge in fantasy to evade reality', he confessed. Suddenly he'd been forced to emulate the feats of Charles Doughty whose *Travels in Arabia Deserta* he'd read as a boy: he'd seen extraordinary cities and landforms, and he'd had to rub along with men of all classes and races in the most trying circumstances. 'It was a drawing lesson as well as a Cook's tour,' he admitted, and when he had forgotten the shipwreck, malaria, stomach troubles, fleas, scorpions, ants, and meals of gazelle liver and sheep's eyes offered by people who had never heard of a vegetarian, he said: 'it was thrilling. I was in heaven. It was a wonderful

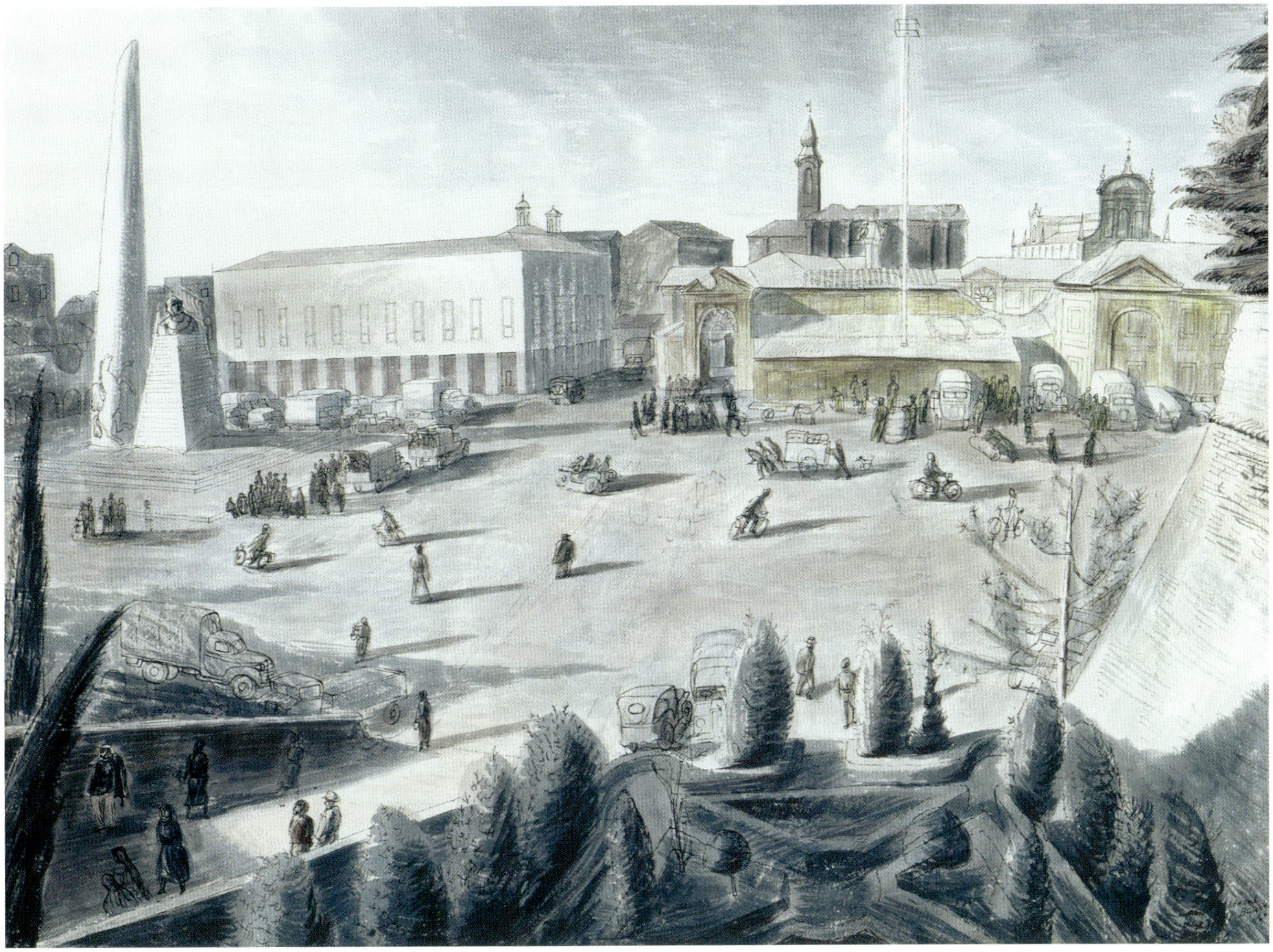

Lugo, a few days after its liberation, 1945, watercolour, 583 x 793 mm
(© Queen's Printer and Controller of HMSO, 2005. UK Government Art Collection).

opportunity, and very educational. I just had to draw people, and it developed my watercolour technique.' The watercolours which survived his adventures confirm that the encounter with the figure was a breakthrough. He told one reporter: 'If it hadn't been for the war – ' he holds up a matchbox – 'I'd have gone on drawing figures no bigger than THAT. But when you sit at a court-martial and you have to draw someone as close as you are – it's a challenge', and to another he said: 'at first I kept my distance when drawing people. Then I became less fearful, and towards the end, in Italy with the partisans I was feeling not so much an observer as a participant.' Before the war his figures had been mostly cartoon homunculi swarming round fantastical architectural settings, but his portraits of Indian or Ethiopian soldiers were close-up and realistic, although never profound studies of their interior lives. Moreover they were not always just single figures, he had learned to do group portraits of Arab families sitting in their tents. He was pleased and proud of this breakthrough, but once home he seems to have dropped this skill: I can find no trace of a portrait or of large scale or group figures from life in his long post-war career, apart perhaps from those small ones in *Life in an English Village* of 1949. He is the only artist I know of who never drew a living member of his own family.

His compulsive neatness had also been modified by having to use simple equipment in difficult conditions and at speed with each sitter expecting a likeness to appear within the hour. 'It sets up tensions, and it's necessary to be in a state of tension when you're drawing. That's why I prefer bad weather to good, wind, clouds, everything changing. It stimulates you. There's nothing worse than pleasant circumstances bothered only by flies. You tend to go to sleep.'[7]

Nearly forty years later, in 1983, the Imperial War Museum, to which the WAAC had sent most of his war work, held an exhibition of it and he viewed it with some pride. 'Interesting to me as a reminder of places that I was thrilled to visit – such is one's romantic nature – and now as an old wodger interesting because I can trace a development in the work from stiff simple drawings to late ones that are rather dashing, more accomplished, the medium used more flexibly and fearlessly.'

After a month at home in England Bawden wrote to his friend John Morgan: 'To be plucked out of Persia and put on a draughty hill near Cheltenham is not exciting, the changeover from sweating to shivering is much too sudden to be appreciated. Despite incessant rain and forbidding fertility, ragged clouds tearing over stone walls and the blackish green vegetation of high summer there are compensations which, reasonably considered probably outweigh the physical discomforts; it is pleasant to sit in a room surrounded by the nice things one has collected together on no other principle than that of personal taste, to sit before a warm fire watching the flames; it is delightful to be near friends; and comforting to find one's own family accepting the returned prodigal; rather as though no break had occurred, even with some enthusiasm which might be imputed perhaps to the natural exuberance of children.' (Undated).[8]

The presence of lively children home for the holidays evidently still bothered him because when Morgan was back in England in July, Bawden invited him for a weekend stay: 'My wife and I live in a fairly commodious flat but I must warn you that we have children, Joanna and Richard aged 10 and 9 respectively. Other people's children are not much fun, and an unmarried person might wonder why imps and mischief should arise in wedlock to break up the happy home . . . as I say there is enough room in the flat provided that you are strong enough to stand the strain of infantile high spirits.' (26th July 1945).

On the very last day of the same year he sat in his studio avoiding the New Year celebrations and confessed in a letter to Morgan: 'No one is more frightened of parties than I am, or more sincerely cordial than when leaving a party upon a trumped-up excuse hours before anyone else dreams of leaving. During the course of any jollifications I am sad, grim, bitter and silent; I look often towards the clock and get more exasperated as the hours go by.' He later suggested he would like to throw a gloom party serving only charcoal biscuits and water. One celebration he could not avoid in the coming year was the award of the CBE – both he and Barnett Freedman were awarded this for their services as War Artists. 'It cheered me up a little', he conceded.

Like many returning servicemen it would take him time to readjust to family life. He had also to meet those artists who had moved into Great Bardfield while he was away and to catch up on the fate of those friends who had been scattered across the globe, some of them, such as Hennell and Ravilious, never to return.

---

1. McLean, R., *Edward Bawden: War Artist*, Scolar Press, 1989, p.15.
2. For a full account see Leonce Peillard's *U-Boats to the Rescue: The Laconia Incident*, Jonathan Cape, 1963.
3. Richards, J. M., *Edward Bawden*, Penguin Modern Painters, 1946.
4. Ardizzone, E., *Diary of a War Artist*, Bodley Head, 1975, p.44.
5. See *Tribute to Edward Bawden*, Fine Art Society catalogue, July 1992.
6. 'An Artist's War, North Africa and Italy 1943-45' held at Abbott and Holder, London, May 2001.
7. Berthoud, R., *Illustrated London News*, May 1983.
8. Morgan's widow gave his Bawden letters and relevant entries from his war diaries to the Fry Public Art Gallery in Saffron Walden.

8. OTHER ARTISTS' WAR WORK

Bawden had written to his wife from the desert on 26th May 1942 'I am afraid I shall be a prize bore whenever I return. A solitary life for 2 years has no doubt wrought a change – I have adapted myself to new interests and lost temporarily the old ones. The people I want to see can almost be counted on one hand.' Fortunately, Charlotte was still one of these favoured few, though her main role was to take over where Mohammed had left off. Bawden had described his man-servant to Gregory: 'It is immensely helpful to have a publicity agent who can keep models amused, give me tips on correct behaviour, clean shoes, wash shirts and boil chickens.' (17th January 1944). Henceforth Charlotte would manage not only her husband's life but much of the village's too; Bawden's only domestic duties, he told a friend, were to be 'coalman, fireman, scullion and hoover boy'. Charlotte, meanwhile, became a governor of several local schools, a member of Essex Education Committee, and a significant force in the Woman's Institute, helping to found its Denman College, and then teaching art history and pottery there. Later in the 1950s she studied law and became a Justice of the Peace. Bawden was happy to let her so long as he could get back to work because, 'my upbringing from the lower middle class gutter has unfitted me for the carefree life of a bedouin' (5th April 1944 to Gregory). However, there was something he could never get back to and that was his friendly competition with Eric Ravilious.

In September 1939 Ravilious had joined the Royal Observer Corps, which meant spending nights playing darts in a hilltop shed near Castle Hedingham; then on Christmas Eve he received an offer of six months' attachment to the Royal Marines with a £325 fee for all the works he produced in this time. He was delighted and secretly relieved to pass the severest winter since 1894 in cosy navy quarters rather than in the frozen family home. He was made an Honorary Captain and sent around Britain painting coastal defences and then to Arctic Norway in HMS *Highlander*, where he saw the *Ark Royal* aircraft carrier in action at Scapa Flow. Before he left he made his will: 'I give and bequeath all that I have to my wife, with the exception of the painting of the Redcliffe Rd interior which I leave to Edward Bawden of Brick House Great Bardfield'. (12th May 1940).

Back home while painting more south coast defences he heard from the Principal of Morley College that their mural had been destroyed by bombs. In 1941 he took time off from his duties depicting the interiors of submarines to move his family (with newly born daughter Anne) from Castle Hedingham to Ironbridge Farm at Shalfont in the Pant valley near Braintree. He resumed work in Dover and then in Rosyth where he stayed with John Nash and his wife. Nash had resigned as a War Artist and was then working in Military Intelligence. Both men had long abandoned their affairs with Binyon, though they both continued to write to her. She was now being pursued by Jim Richards, Peggy Angus' husband. For his next six month engagement Ravilious was transferred to the RAF because the Chief of the Nore, Sir Reginald Aylmer Ranfurly Plunkett-Ernle-Erle-Drax had taken a dislike to his naval pictures. Spring 1942 brought more aeroplane pictures and at the end of August he was sent to the Anglo-American airbase of Kaldadarnes in Iceland, virgin territory to artists though not to poets. William Morris had visited its 'mountain wastes voiceless as death' and in

1936 Auden and MacNeice followed. On September 2nd Ravilious joined the three man crew of a plane belonging to 269 Squadron which set out on an air-sea rescue mission, but it failed to return and after four days' search it was presumed to have crashed in the ocean. On September 8th a solitary wheel was washed ashore. Ravilious was aged thirty-nine. Christine Nash's reaction was typical of many to this tragedy: 'It is an utter waste of a good artist and a charming personality. All one's hopes of an after war life in East Anglia were centred round the pleasure of living somewhere near Eric and Tirzah and the games we could play. He was the liveliest mind, always jumping to the ridiculous and the fantastic.' [1]

Ravilious' career as a War Artist was a brief but remarkable one. Some of the coastal pictures were a continuation of his earlier themes, though now coiled wire and concrete blocks littered his favourite beaches and warships occupied the harbours. His depiction of a pigeon loft and a sick-room bed also built on pre-war preoccupations and a ship's screw on a rail carriage relates to the incongruously abandoned machinery he had been so fond of in Essex and Sussex. As a civilian he had been excited by fire-works after the Boat Race, Guy Fawkes night and the Coronation and now he enjoyed depicting star shells, gun flashes and search lights. However, planes were something new, especially the Walrus: 'I do very much enjoy drawing these queer flying machines and hope to produce a set of aircraft paintings', he wrote, 'I hope Paul Nash hasn't already painted Walruses – what I like about them is that they are comic things with strong personalities like a duck, and designed to go slow. You put your head out of the window and it's no more windy than a train.' (13th January 1941). Nash, though sick, was indeed working on a series of anthropomorphised planes 'watching', 'sunning', 'at play' or sitting for their portraits in their 'nests', and wrote to Ravilious for help in depicting a Sunderland plane encountering an enemy U-boat.[2] Nash had never seen a submarine but Ravilious was busy with lithographs showing the crews in training and working aboard these craft which he admired because the apparatus had the 'intricacy of a Swiss watch' and they 'didn't roll when submerged'. His original plan was to publish them through the Curwen Press but it was bombed and at his own expense he had to enlist an Ipswich firm, Cowells, to make a limited edition of fifty sets of ten prints costing £100 per set. Like Bawden he was forced by his war work to cope with figures but, unlike his friend, he failed to individualise them and the sailors' faces are either blank or bland, the stress being on them as uniform members of a team rather than as idiosyncratic characters.[3]

While Bawden sweated in the desert Ravilious spent his war in chilly climes which ideally suited his coolly clinical vision and fondness for the blue end of the spectrum. Round the wintry coast of Britain and in the fjords of Norway his liking for snowfall, night skies, wide vistas and northern seas all combine to give us some of the most memorable images of the war at sea, though he shuns the depiction of close-up action. His watercolour technique had reached such a level of accomplishment it is difficult to see in what direction he could have developed it further, had he lived. He now drops out of our story, though his name will forever be twinned with Bawden's in the history of British twentieth century art.

Letters in the Imperial War Museum show what a struggle his widow had to get any recognition that she deserved a war pension, the bureaucrats' stance being that since his rank in the Royal Marines was honorary and he wasn't fighting the enemy she had no entitlement. Tirzah had just undergone a mastectomy and then the termination of a pregnancy she could probably not have survived, the pipes were frozen, she had three sickly children aged seven, three and one year and had to maintain Ravilious' eighty-five year old father. They had just about coped when Ravilious was alive and earning £350 per annum from his War Artist fees, plus shares which yielded £11, but now she was hard-pressed. Her mother and Charlotte Bawden rallied to help and John Nash bought Ravilious' greenhouse and set it up in his own garden. Tirzah wrote from Shalford to Binyon, now

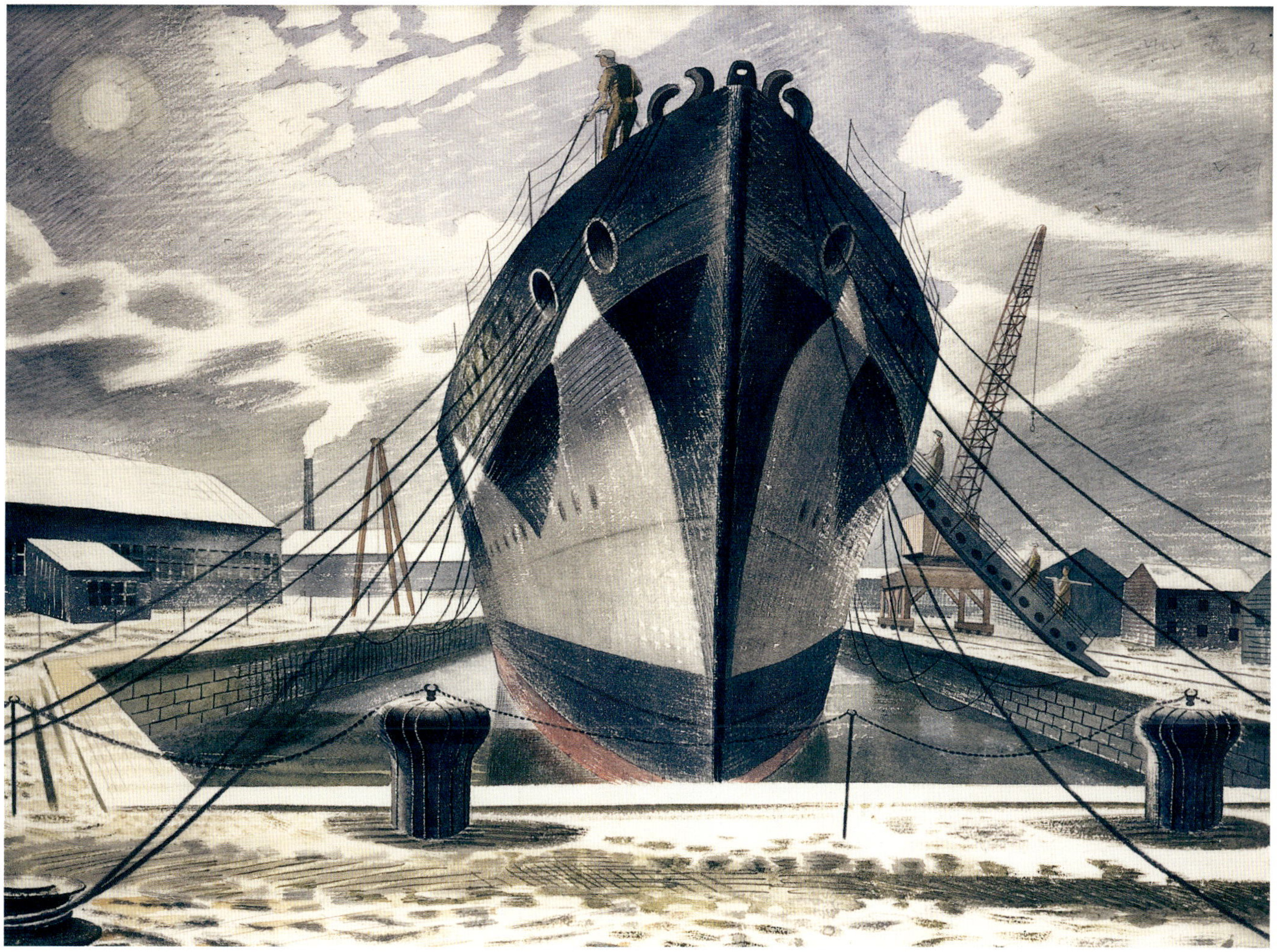

Eric Ravilious, *A Warship in Dock*, 1940, watercolour, 431 x 577 mm
(Trustees of the Imperial War Museum). Probably painted in Chatham Dockyard.

a WAAF in Bath, giving her details of Eric's death and thanking her for her offer to help with school fees. 'When you have more time one day please remember you may share any of these children', and she signed off, 'If ever you feel like coming here I would love to have you'. (12th October 1942). She battled through and in March 1946 she married again, this time not to an artist but to a BBC man, Henry Swanzy, and they left Essex for Hampstead. In spite of the return of her cancer she began to create again, this time making models in paper of Essex buildings. She died in March 1951 near Colchester, just short of her 43rd birthday and her children were happily raised by Swanzy's brother John.

When Ravilious' position as Official War Artist in Iceland became vacant his friend Tom Hennell applied for it and went out as replacement in July 1943. Following this spell in Iceland with the navy he was sent to serve in France during June 1944 where he impressed Ardizzone with 'his shy manner and moral courage', and by November had moved into Holland and Belgium. After the Allied victory in Europe he was transferred to the Air Ministry, then sent to the Far East in May 1945 to a base

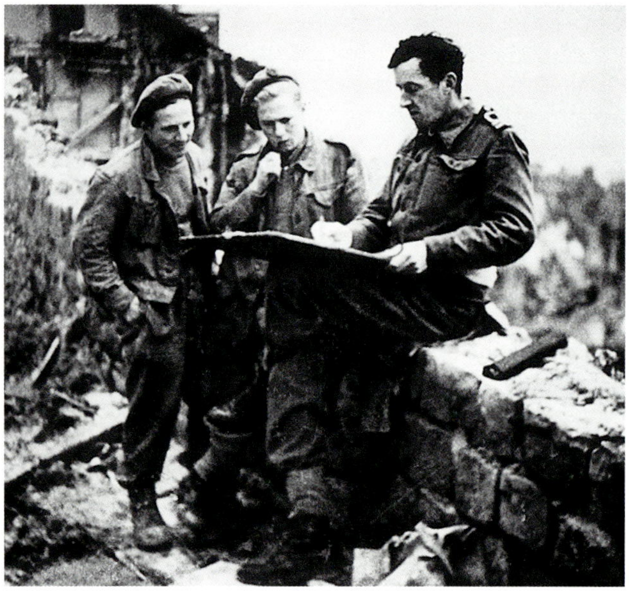

Thomas Hennell, war artist, at work in the ruins of Caen, 13 July 1944.

in Rangoon, Burma, and from there to Ceylon via India. He was present when Japan surrendered on 14th August 1945 and then went on by aircraft carrier to Malaysia and Djakarta. Then, in late 1945, he died in mysterious circumstances, possibly torn to pieces by a Javanese mob who, thinking he was Dutch, set on him whilst he was sketching in the grounds of the house where he was billeted in Surabaya. He thus became the third War Artist to be killed, the others being Ravilious and Albert Richards (a former RCA student) who died near the river Maas. Rex Whistler, although never a War Artist, was also killed.

The other member of the pre-war trio, Douglas Percy Bliss, was forced by the bombing of his Blackheath house to evacuate his wife and two daughters to a cottage in Derbyshire where in the coming decades the garden would give him a great deal of pleasure, both to cultivate and to record in paint. In 1946 Bliss was offered the Directorship of Glasgow School of Art and the family moved there, though they retained their cottage. From then onwards his connections to Bawden would be through jokey letters, occasional visits to Great Bardfield and the network of external examining which kept Art College tutors criss-crossing the country every summer. By 1952 he had become tired of wood-engraving and began to concentrate on sunny, optimistic oil paintings of Derbyshire farmlands and gardens in a soundly traditional style. His wife Phyllis, perhaps the better painter of the two, continued her portrait painting.

It must have been a relief for Aldridge, John Nash and Bawden to return to gardening in rural Essex after their war adventures. Here by patience and slow planning they could bring beauty out of the dark: a solitary, contemplative occupation where part of the world is under your hand to be selected, discarded, pruned, re-arranged as one's imagination dictates and yet at the end it will have a life of its own with a few surprises in store. The parallels with painting are obvious.

John Aldridge came back from his war adventures to work as a painting tutor under William Coldstream, who had been appointed Professor of Painting at the Slade in 1949. He also illustrated Henry Warren's book *Adam was a Ploughman* (Eyre and Spottiswood, 1947) which was dedicated to the memory of Tom Hennell and concerned with fast-vanishing country crafts and characters. Aldridge's pen and ink drawings are skilfully literal depictions of the Essex countryside, very near in their verisimilitude to Bawden's *Life in an English Village*, published two years later. From now on he took no flights of experimental fantasy or liberties with appearances but settled down to painting local and Majorcan landscapes for submission to the Royal Academy each summer. He became an ARA in 1954 and a full RA in 1963.

Paul Nash, having made in *Totes Meer* the definitive image for World War Two died in 1946, but his brother John survived his second stint as a war artist (though with little to show for it compared to his first) and returned to teach alongside Bawden again at the RCA. After his demobilisation in 1944 he and his devoted and tolerant wife Christine moved to Bottengoms Farmhouse near Wormingford, about sixteen miles east of Great Bardfield, where he remained for the rest of his life. In spite of his pre-war success he had tired of wood-engraving and turned to painting, and gardening his two acres, calling himself an 'artist-plantsman'. He taught botanical drawing, made watercolours and worked up his unsentimental, straightforward, soundly-structured landscapes in oils from detailed notes made on the spot. Winter was his favourite season since the snow hid the overpowering green of the English countryside. Nash was a party animal, dressy, fussy, a womaniser, hypochondriac, and a great grumbler who was nannied by his wife who drove him everywhere and who selected the sites for him to paint. In spite of their temperamental differences he and Bawden were great friends and undertook painting expeditions together to the Gower Peninsula, Haverfordwest, Cornwall (De Lank Quarry), Dunwich in

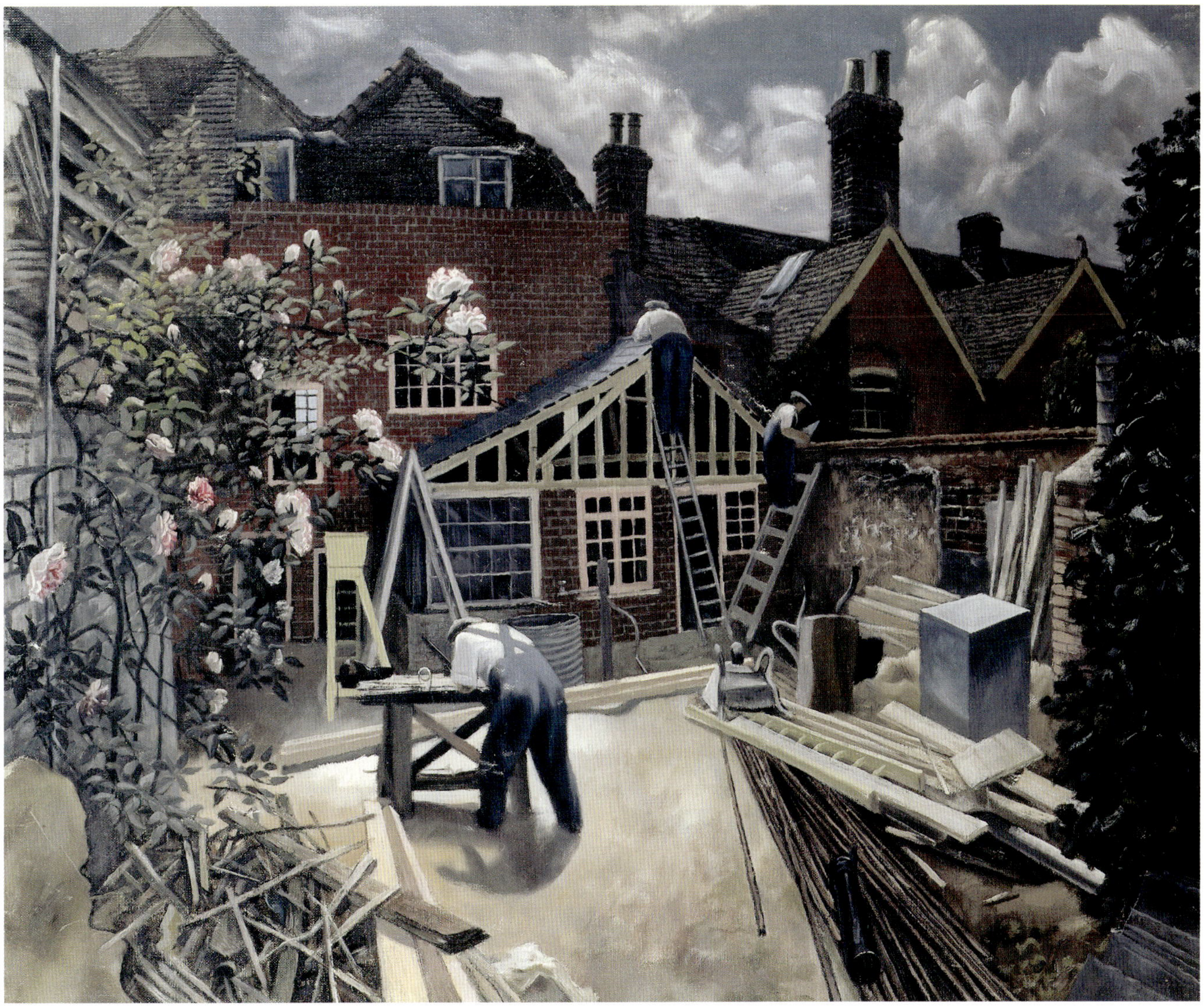

John Aldridge, *Builders at Work, Brick House, Great Bardfield*, 1946, oil (Fry Art Gallery).
The only wartime bomb to fall on Great Bardfield had damaged Brick House.

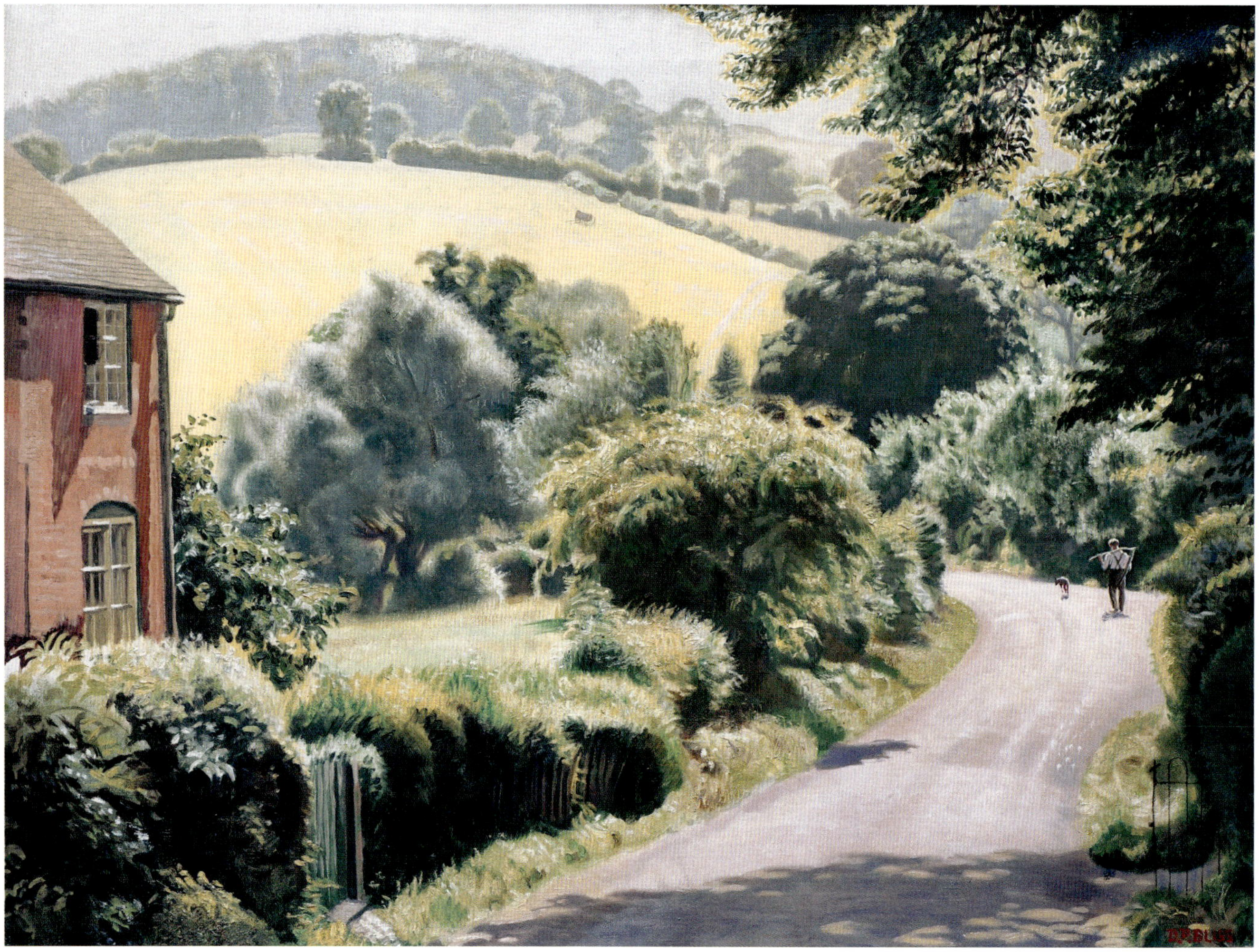

Douglas Percy Bliss, *High Noon, Windley Lane*, 1951, oil on canvas, 760 x 1010 mm (Chelmsford Museums. Photograph Paul Starr).

Suffolk, and Ironbridge in Shropshire. On this last trip they took along Carel Weight, then Tutor in Painting at the RCA, and later Professor. Nash wrote: 'The Ironbridge is very handsome but a teaser to draw with three upright supports and five curved spans to every three so that a sideways view is very complicated . . . we dodge between showers and somehow I've done three drawings and a bit – but Carel has done an oil painting every day it seems while Edward keeps his work secretly in his rooms and does not divulge progress. Carel and I play bar billiards every night, but Bawden will not join these simple diversions.'[4]

While these artists had been overseas there had been a home-grown movement they might have heard little about unless they read of it in *Penguin New Writing* or *Horizon*. As fighting submerged the Continent, and England became isolated, an inward and backward-looking style emerged, that of Neo-Romanticism, its chief protagonists being John Piper and Graham Sutherland. This had its pre-war roots in the fashion for Samuel

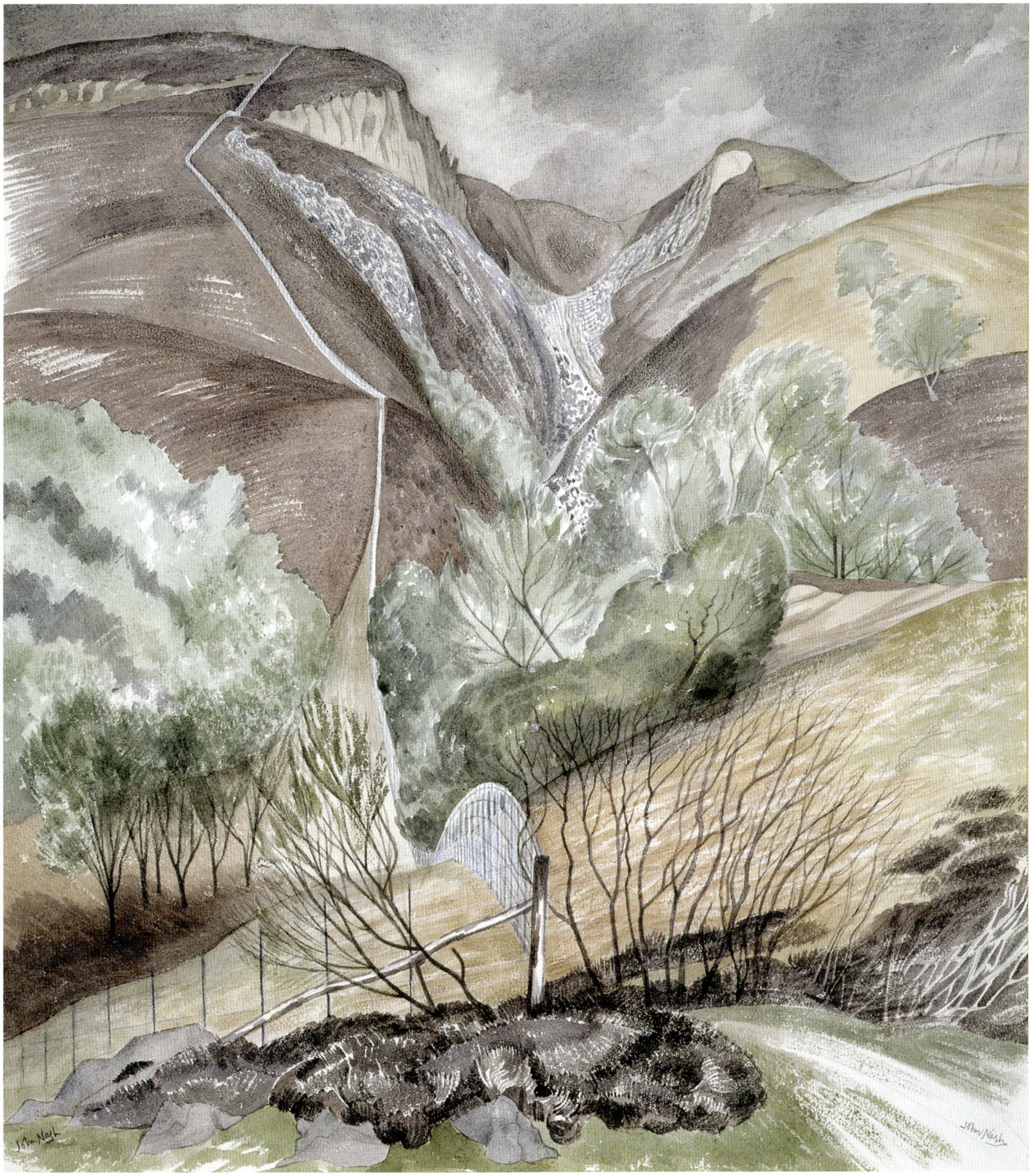

John Nash, *Deer Fence*, date not known, watercolour, 502 x 438 mm (Harlow Council Collection).

Palmer but when his harvest moon turned into a bomber's moon the landscape took on a new threat. Thorn trees writhed and extended twiggy fingers, shadows became hard-edged and threats lurked round the corners of lanes. A style originally developed to cope with pleasing decay in picturesque buildings soon lent itself to scenes of devastation, bombed cathedrals, ruined houses, mines, quarries, steelworks, but all devoid of figures. Younger painters who were exempt from war service for various reasons, such as Minton, Vaughan, Ayrton, Craxton and Colquhoun took up the mannerisms of Neo-Romanticism enthusiastically and after the war used them in book illustrations as well as paintings. When Bawden had shown his watercolours in Baghdad he was irritated to have them described as 'Romantic' because, he wrote: 'Romantic is any representation of a chance encounter in the slums by moonlight' – evidently a barbed reference to Minton's pale waifs drooping around the bomb-sites.

Two artists who had remained at home and been exposed to Neo-Romanticism were Michael Rothenstein (1908-1993) and Kenneth Rowntree (1915-1997), and both had settled in Great Bardfield to escape the London bombs. Rothenstein was the more gifted of the two incomers and an uncomfortably big fish for the returning Bawden to find in his small Bardfield pond. Michael was the younger son of Sir William Rothenstein, brother to John Rothenstein (Director of the Tate Gallery from 1938), nephew to Albert Rutherston, (the Ruskin Master of Drawing) and cousin to Oliver Simon. Given this lineage he was always destined to be an artist but after a precocious start he was struck at the age of eighteen by a debilitating disease, possibly myxoedema or thyroid

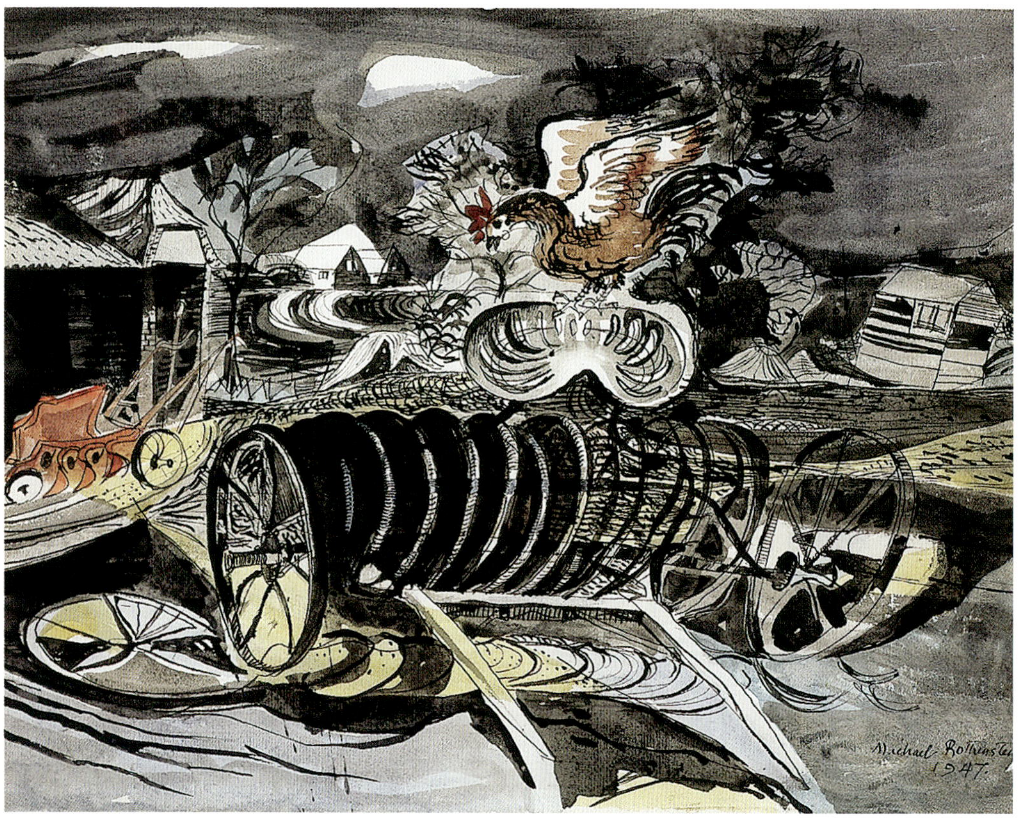

Michael Rothenstein, *Farm Scene*, 1947, watercolour, 370 x 460 mm.

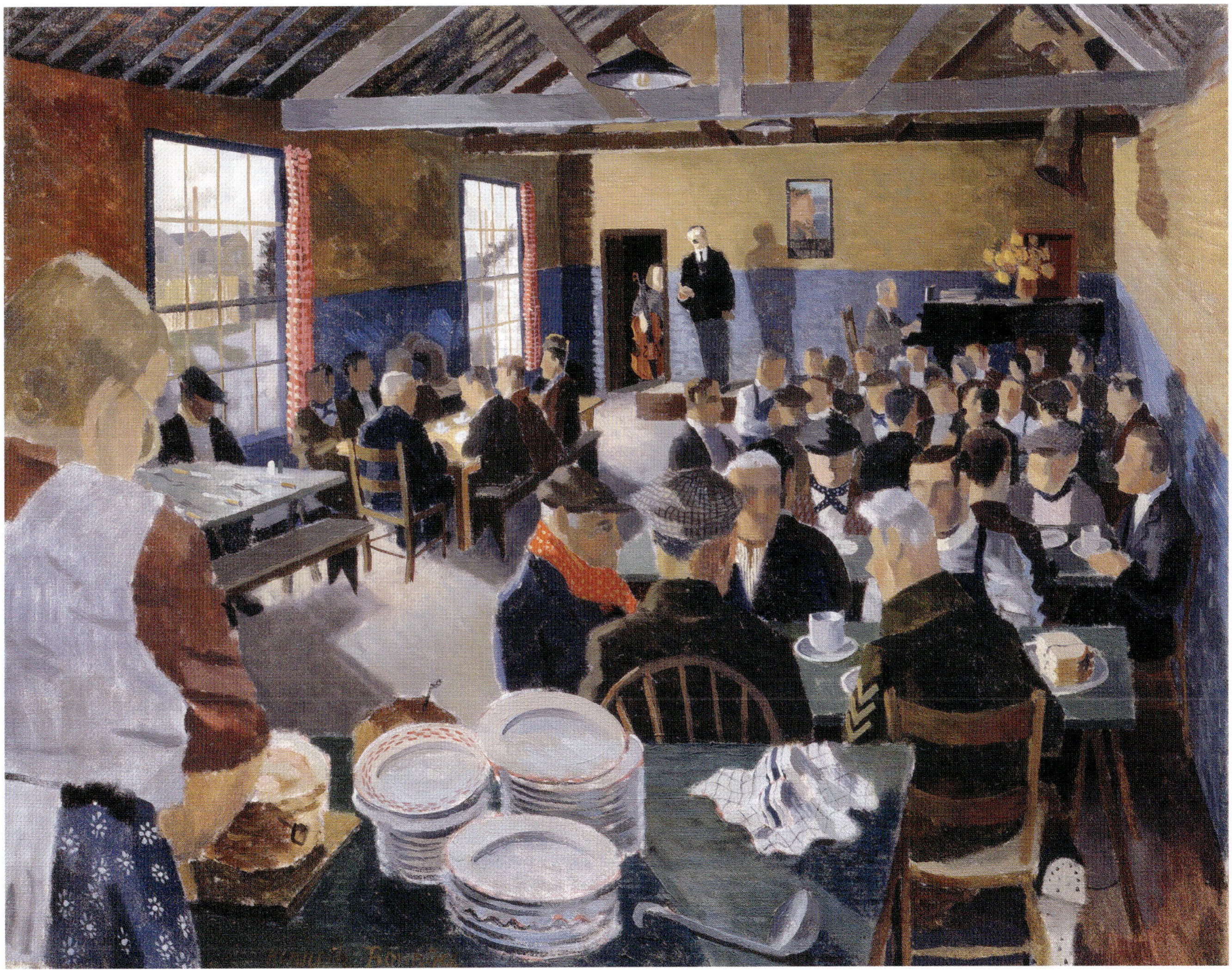

Kenneth Rowntree, *CEMA Canteen Concert, Isle of Dogs, London E14*, 1941, oil on canvas, 609 x 762 mm (Imperial War Museum).

deficiency, which prevented him painting for several years. When he recovered he worked feverishly to make up for lost time and it was in this state of mind that he and his glamorous young wife Duffy moved to Great Bardfield in 1941. Duffy (formerly Elizabeth Fitzgerald), had trained at the Central School of Art in London and her strength was in portraiture, examples of which she later frequently showed at the Royal Academy. At first the couple rented the lath and plaster chapel in John Aldridge's garden for twenty shillings a week, before moving exactly opposite the Bawdens into Ethel House.

Rothenstein was unfit to serve as a soldier and spent part of the war years working for the Recording Britain scheme. This was set up in 1939 in the expectation that there would be widespread destruction of historic buildings and landscapes by both developers and German bombing. The Pilgrim Trust granted £6,000 to pay the ninety-seven artists who took part and to purchase the 1,549 works they produced. Rothenstein's paintings at this time were influenced by the prevalent Neo-Romanticism.

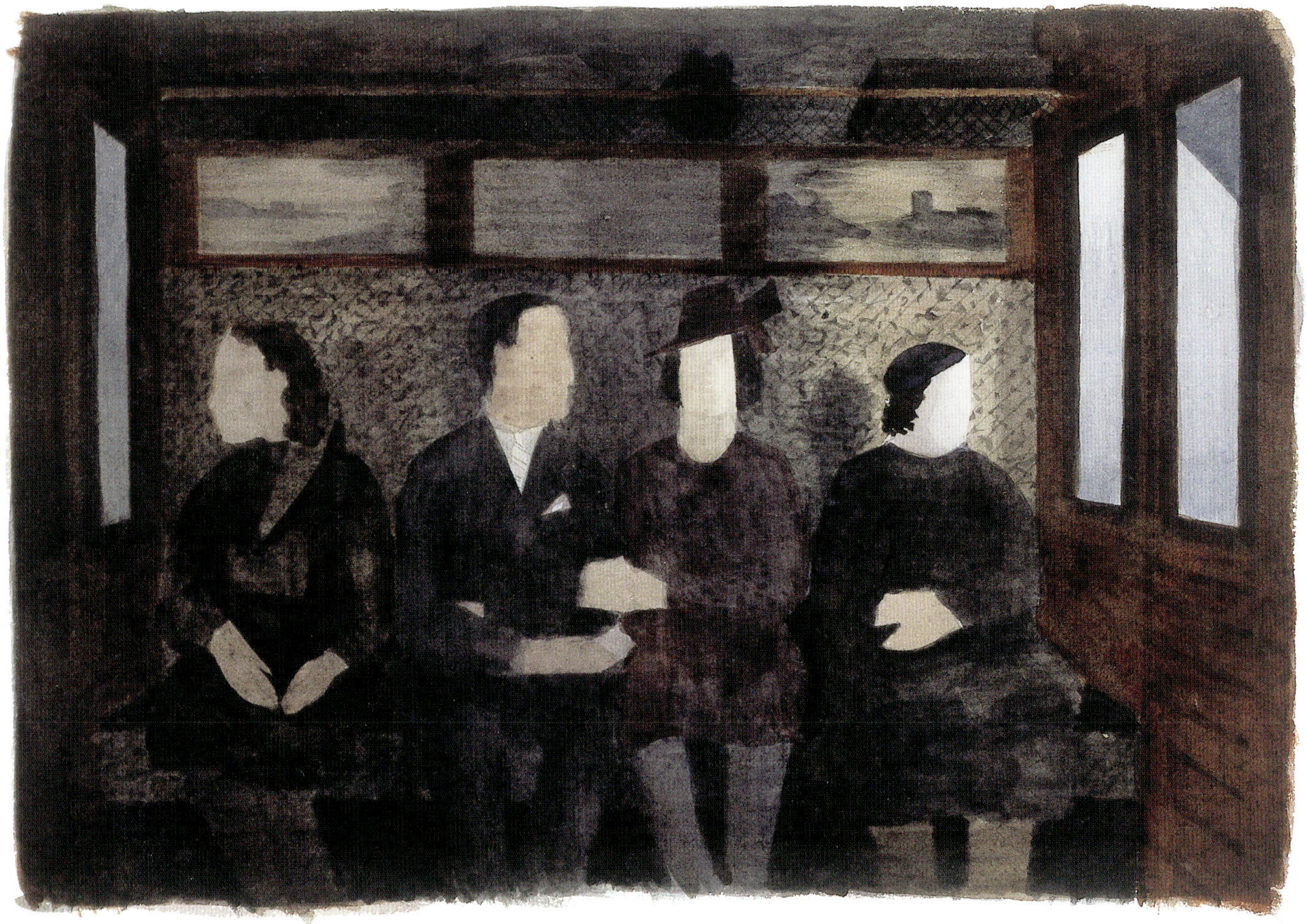

Kenneth Rowntree, *The Railway Carriage, Blackout*, *c.*1942, watercolour, 302 x 427 mm (Fry Art Gallery).

He took the Essex countryside, its workers, houses, churches, signposts and farm machinery as his themes and developed his obsession with cockerels which appeared in his work at all periods. But, given his background, it was not surprising that he was soon impatient with the prevailing English rural naturalism of the Bardfield artists and anxious to respond to modern movements on the continent. Bawden taught him linocutting and encouraged him to buy an old Albion Press for £5, which he later supplemented with an etching press. Later still he built a print studio on the side of his house and began monoprint, relief and intaglio print-making of an experimental kind unseen in England before.

Duffy was quickly involved with the Dr Barnardo's Home at Little Bardfield which the village artists helped to decorate at Christmas and for which they painted eggs for Easter egg hunts. She also began teaching at Denman College after Charlotte took pity on their relative poverty and found her work. At first the Rothensteins had no electricity, only an oil stove to cook on and lived 'on tick' at Hitchcock's shop opposite. Soon they had two children and Duffy found little time for her portrait painting, though she did one of the matron of Dr Barnardo's and another of her close friend Tirzah Ravilious (see page 83) before Tirzah moved away from the village. Like the other artists' wives she soon found her main role was in supporting her husband's career and taking his works round the galleries.

Rothenstein became close friends with the other artist who had settled in Great Bardfield during the war years – Kenneth Rowntree. Once Rothenstein's career as an experimental printer was under way he taught Rowntree etching and allowed him to use his press. Rowntree had been raised as a Quaker in Scarborough and it was his beliefs which made him a Conscientious Objector and non-combatant during the war. He had attended the Ruskin Art School under Albert Rutherston and had been taught there by Ravilious and Barnett Freedman. Rowntree dropped out of a later course at the Slade but began to establish a London reputation during the 1930s. In 1939 he married Diana, an architect, and in 1942 Tirzah Ravilious found them a house to rent in Great Bardfield until they could take over Simpkin's Cottage and move in with their newly born son Adam. Then, like most of the village houses, it had few facilities but John Nash gave them a rogue cat to make it seem more homely. Today Diana remembers Robert Graves arriving to stay with Aldridge, Sir William Rothenstein driving up in his Rolls Royce to visit his son, Charlotte Bawden's pre-eminence amongst the wives, the occasional bitchiness of village life, and the German Prisoners of War working the land round about.

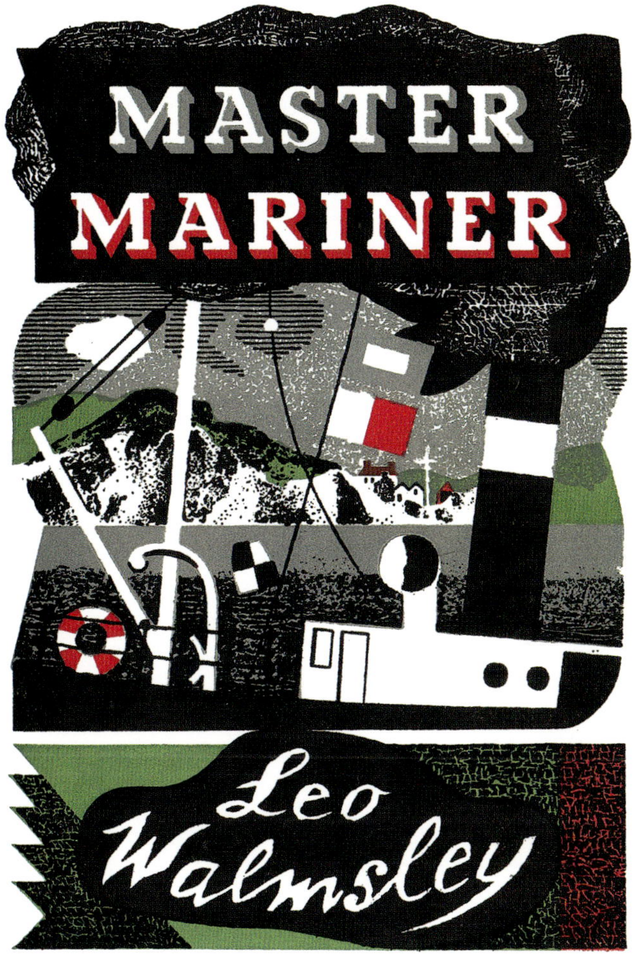

Kenneth Rowntree, dustwrapper design for Collins, 1948, 205 x 175 mm.

His pacifist beliefs did not prevent Rowntree from working for the Recording Britain scheme, which just kept them going and later he made a lithograph for the School Prints scheme. At this period he painted realistic, decorative and sometimes rather naïve pictures of buildings, village life and landscapes in Essex, Yorkshire, Derbyshire and Wales and in these it is possible to detect the influence of Ravilious and Bawden. In 1946 he was offered his first one-man show at the Leicester Galleries and in 1948 produced an illustrated King Penguin book *A Prospect of Wales*, followed by one in The Vision of England series called *The Isle of Wight*. Also in 1948 he was offered a contract as Mural Tutor at the RCA and the family moved from the village to live in Putney.

1. Eric Ravilious' Curwen and Dent Stock Blocks and Devices, Garton and Company, 1993, p.35.
2. Binyon, H., Eric Ravilious: *Memoir of an Artist*, Lutterworth Press, 1983, p.128.
3. See *Ravilious at War* (edited by Anne Ullmann), Fleece Press, 2002, where all his war pictures and most of his letters are reproduced.
4. Rothenstein, J., *John Nash*, Macdonald and Company, 1983, p.84.

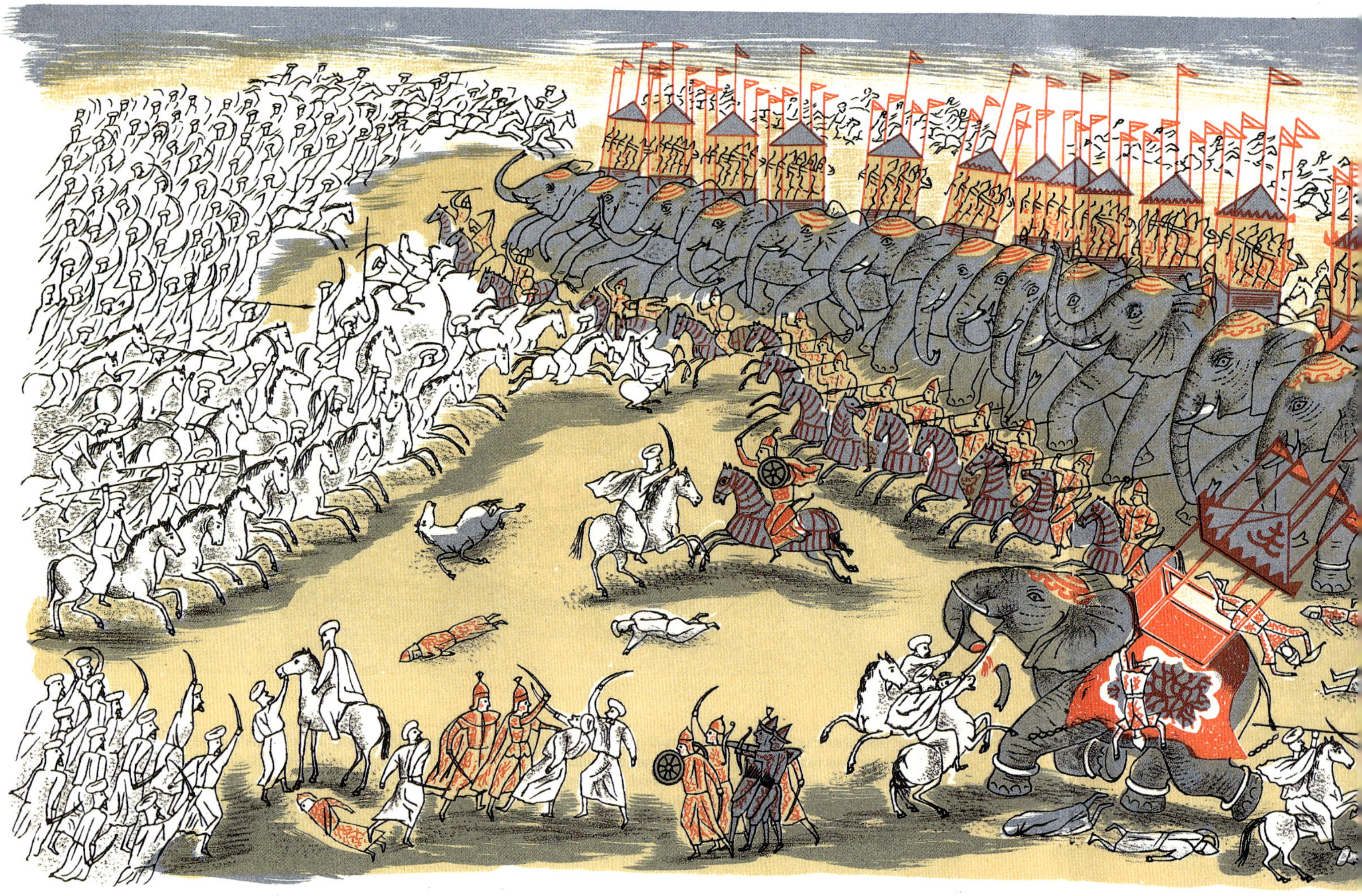

9. TEACHING AND A FESTIVAL

As an old man Bawden claimed that when he returned from the war, 'I found myself forgotten. Another generation of artists had come up. The only people who remembered me were the income tax. There was a new generation but I went on doing what I'd done before, except the pattern had changed – I worked for publishers rather than posters and murals for architects.' [1]

As a statement this is almost completely untrue: he was better known than before the war, few young rivals had yet emerged and work of all kinds continued to come his way. In 1947, a year after receiving his CBE, he was made an Associate of the Royal Academy (the first such honour awarded to a draughtsman rather than to a painter or sculptor), even though he had never shown a work within those august walls, and by 1951 he was a Trustee of the Tate Gallery at the invitation of John Rothenstein. These were art

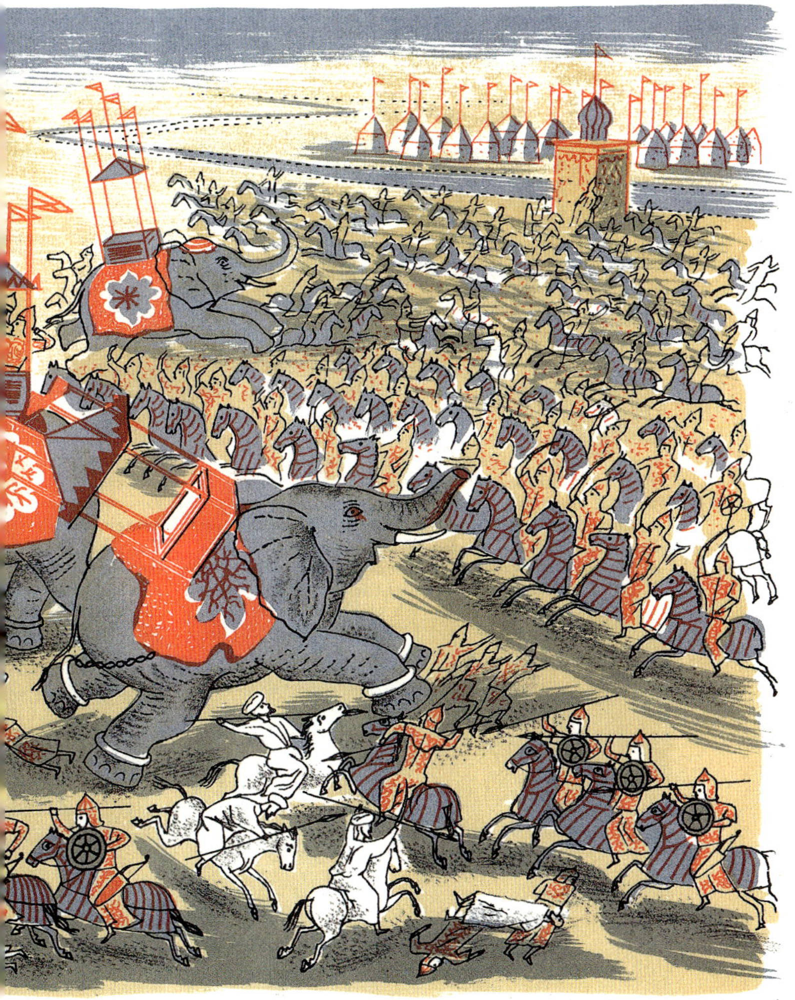

The Battle of Qadisiya, one of two double-page lithographic spreads for *The Arabs*, by R. B. Serjeant, 1949, 188 x 455 mm.

world honours, but then a book devoted entirely to his work brought him to the attention of the wider public in 1946.

Kenneth Clark continued his paternalistic care of British artists after the war by suggesting there should be a series of inexpensive Penguin paperbacks, generously illustrated in colour and black and white, to bring certain individuals to the notice of a general audience: Henry Moore, Duncan Grant, Paul Nash, Matthew Smith, John Piper, Stanley Spencer, Ben Nicholson, Frances Hodgkins and Edward Bawden were all honoured. Jim Richards, whom Bawden had met at Furlongs before the war and had encountered again in Cairo, was chosen to write the text to accompany the pictures. Richards points out that Bawden had a pre-war career of barely a dozen years and was known to the public only for witty advertisements and regional watercolours. The war works, therefore, may surprise the readers, though there is a continuity in the artist's approach: '. . . he is different from other painters because he was trained as a designer. This does not only mean that organisation and a strong sense of rhythm are present in his work; it means that his whole emotional approach is different – in fact it means that there is no effort to interpret emotion immediately in paint, in the way the painter brought up in the ivory tower of self-expression aims at doing. His work is not impulsive. Instead, all his pictures, however moving and significant in the end, are the product of study. Their vitality is intensified, not by a strong emotional urgency, but by being passed, as it were, through the tempering process of an exacting technique.' It was this 'detached regard' which enabled Bawden to rise to the challenge when plucked from rural Essex and dropped into the Arabian desert. Considering the drab post-war conditions under which it was produced this little book does Bawden proud.

One way Bawden could continue to use his unique experiences of the Middle East was to illustrate another inexpensive Penguin production, *The Arabs* by R. B. Serjeant (1949). These cheap and popular Picture Puffin books had begun in 1940 and had a format of thirty two pages with alternating colour and black and white. Bawden's eleven colour plates were printed at the Curwen Press by autolithography, though by now Harold Curwen had suffered a breakdown and had retired to run

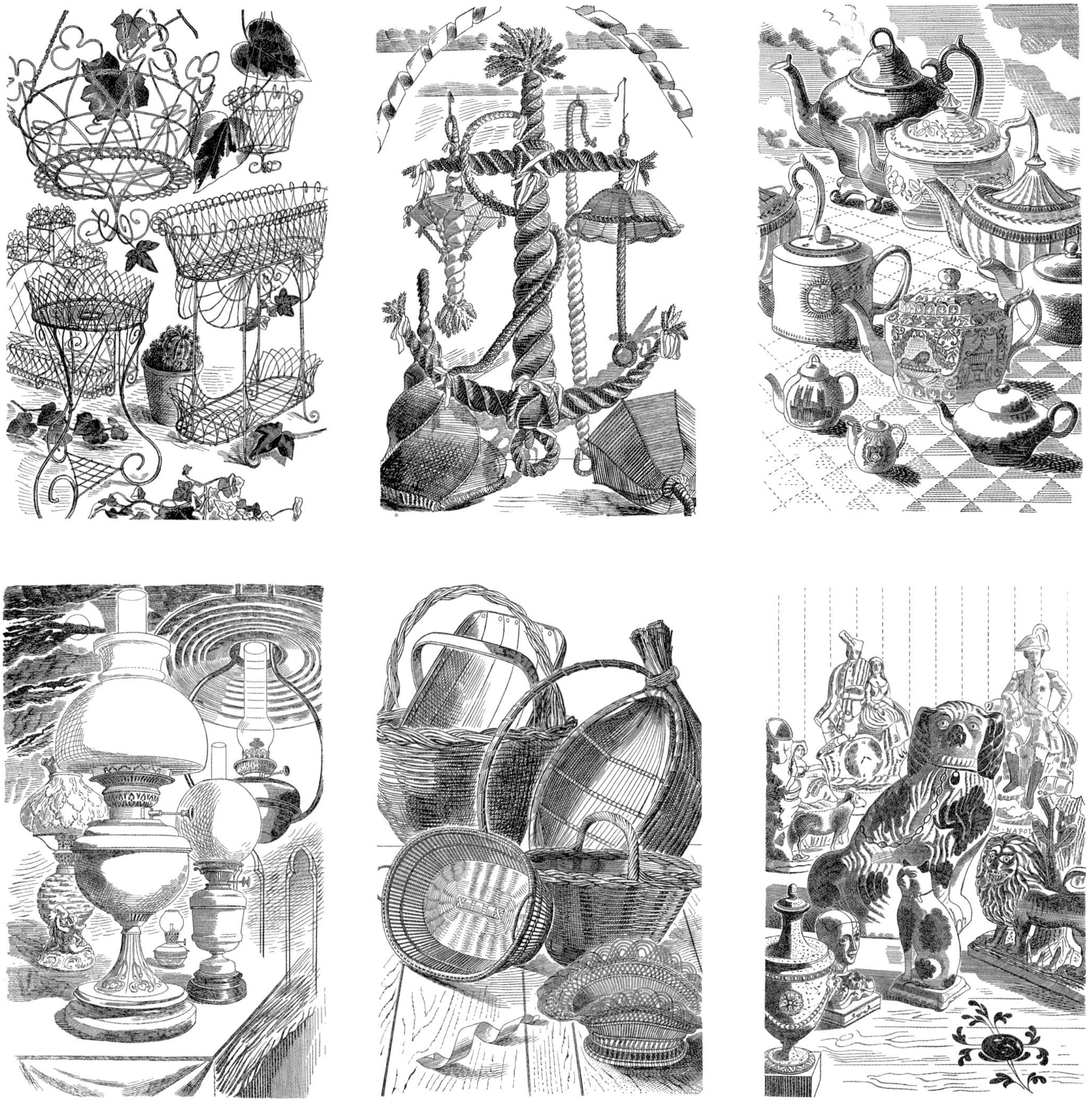

Six still-life illustrations for *Life in an English Village*, 1949, of oil lamps, Staffordshire pottery, wire plant-holders, corn dollies, teapots and baskets printed from line-block.

a grocer's shop but Bawden still tracked him down and sought his advice. The two double-page spreads using four colours show the Kaaba at Mecca with its circulating pilgrims, and the battle of Qadisiya where the blue elephants of Rustrum charge from the right of the page into the wedge of white cavalry on the left. Both are

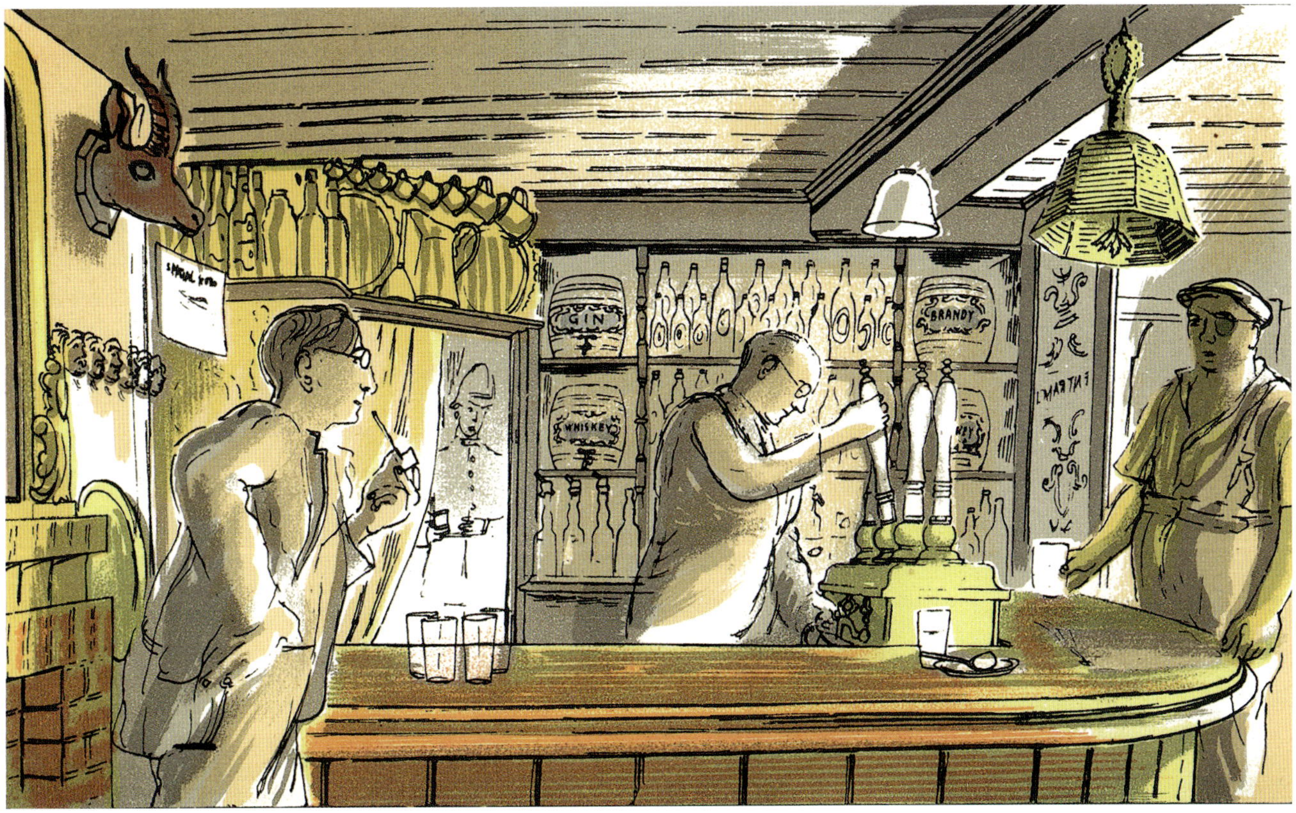

Lithographic illustration 'The Bell' for *Life in an English Village*, 1949.
Based on the Great Bardfield public house.

examples of Bawden's mastery of the high viewpoint and panoramic sweep combined with tiny details and the deliberate contrast of realistic drawing and abstract colour. Bawden said the battle itself had lasted three days but it took him slightly longer to draw it.

The next commission was less exotic, in fact it meant he didn't even have to stir from Great Bardfield. This was Bawden's own idea which he submitted to King Penguin publishers: *Life in an English Village* (1949) with a text by Noel Carrington (1894-1989) in a series edited by Nikolaus Pevsner, the great expert on the Englishness of the English and their architecture. There are sixteen autolithos in four rather unattractive colours over sharply literal pen drawings done on the spot, and six wonderfully skilful pen and ink still-lifes of oil lamps, Staffordshire pottery, wire plant-holders, corn dollies, teapots and baskets printed from line-blocks.

Noel Carrington, the brother of the artist Dora Carrington and publisher of the Country Life books wrote an essay which is a vigorous demolition of the myth of 'Merrie England' and which shows how the village labourer has had to endure cruel injustices from squires, big farmers and tithing parsons, together with brutal land enclosures, workhouses, transportations, class prejudices and the townee's sentimentality. His hope is that the post-war English village is about to be revived with a new social structure, allotments, schools, clean water, electricity, buses, shops, and such unifying organisations as the Women's Institute and Young Farmers. Even the drift of the urban middle class into village housing should have its part to play in the democratisation of village life.

This was a period of rationing and austerity but the returning servicemen had overturned the old order and installed a Labour government under Attlee, and already things were changing for the better in education and health care. Bawden must have shared Carrington's optimism since he had recently supplied five drawings of happy labourers for the Saffron Walden Labour Party's leaflet *Food for Thought*, or 'Five points for men and women who believe in GREAT Britain and in British fairness', all printed by the Curwen Press which boasted of being fully unionised.

In *Life in an English Village* Bawden, using his new-found skill in capturing likenesses, introduces us to the Great Bardfielders: Mr Cartwright the lonely bachelor vicar writing his sermon; Mrs Buttle the Bawdens' charlady making tea; another of their helpers, Daisy Letch, in the butcher's; friends Mr and Mrs Ives and her sister sitting glumly on Sunday evening; Mr Davies the carpenter who made Bawden's picture frames, and Mr Suckling the cross-legged tailor in his shop window situated exactly opposite Brick House. We peer into the church, chapel, school, clinic, agricultural machine repair shop, cabinet maker's, baker's, saddler's, and the market gardener's greenhouse. Inside *The Bell* pub the village policeman has a swift half behind a curtain and sharp-featured John Aldridge props up the bar opposite old one-eyed Fred Mizen the corn-dolly maker who was also Bawden's and Aldridge's jobbing gardener. While the men were away at war Mizen had stolen 40 pounds of jam from Charlotte and bullied Lucie Aldridge. There's certainly no Merrie England sentimentality here, just sharp reportage of the singularities of a specific but unremarkable place – though it is never named in the book. Bliss thought he

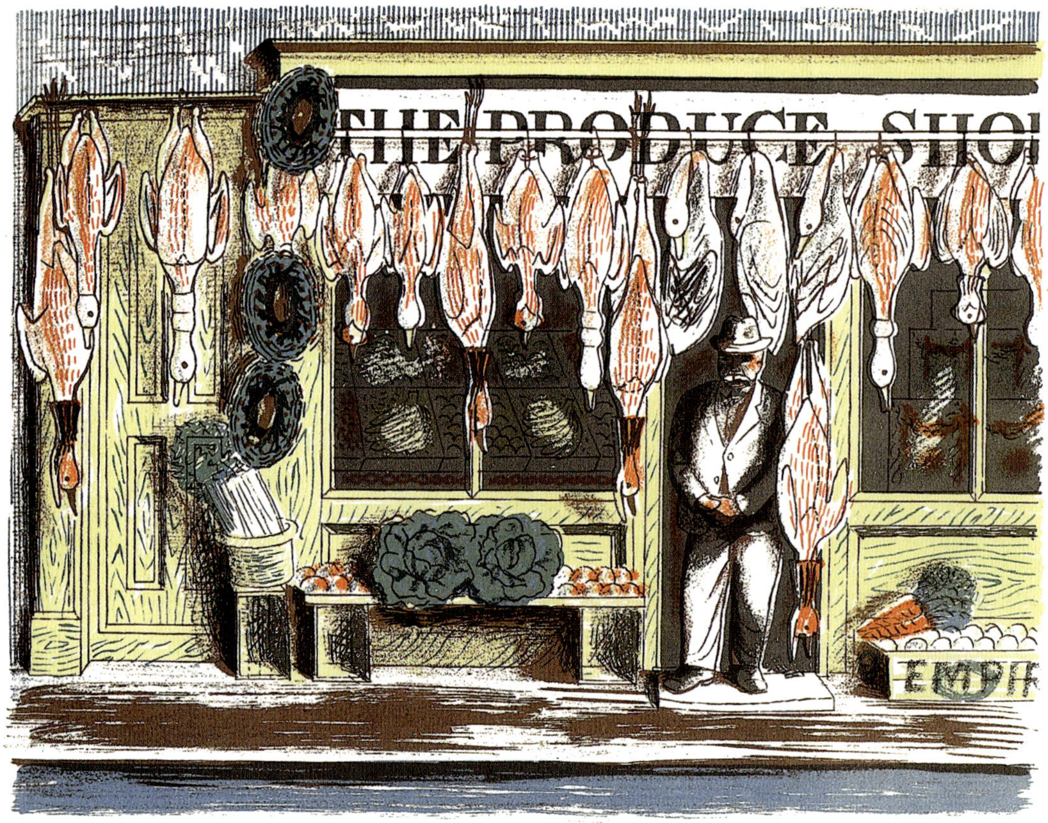

'The Produce Shop', from *Edward Bawden's England* by Denis Saurat, in *Alphabet & Image 2*, September 1946; 120 x 152 mm. Based on the Great Bardfield shop.

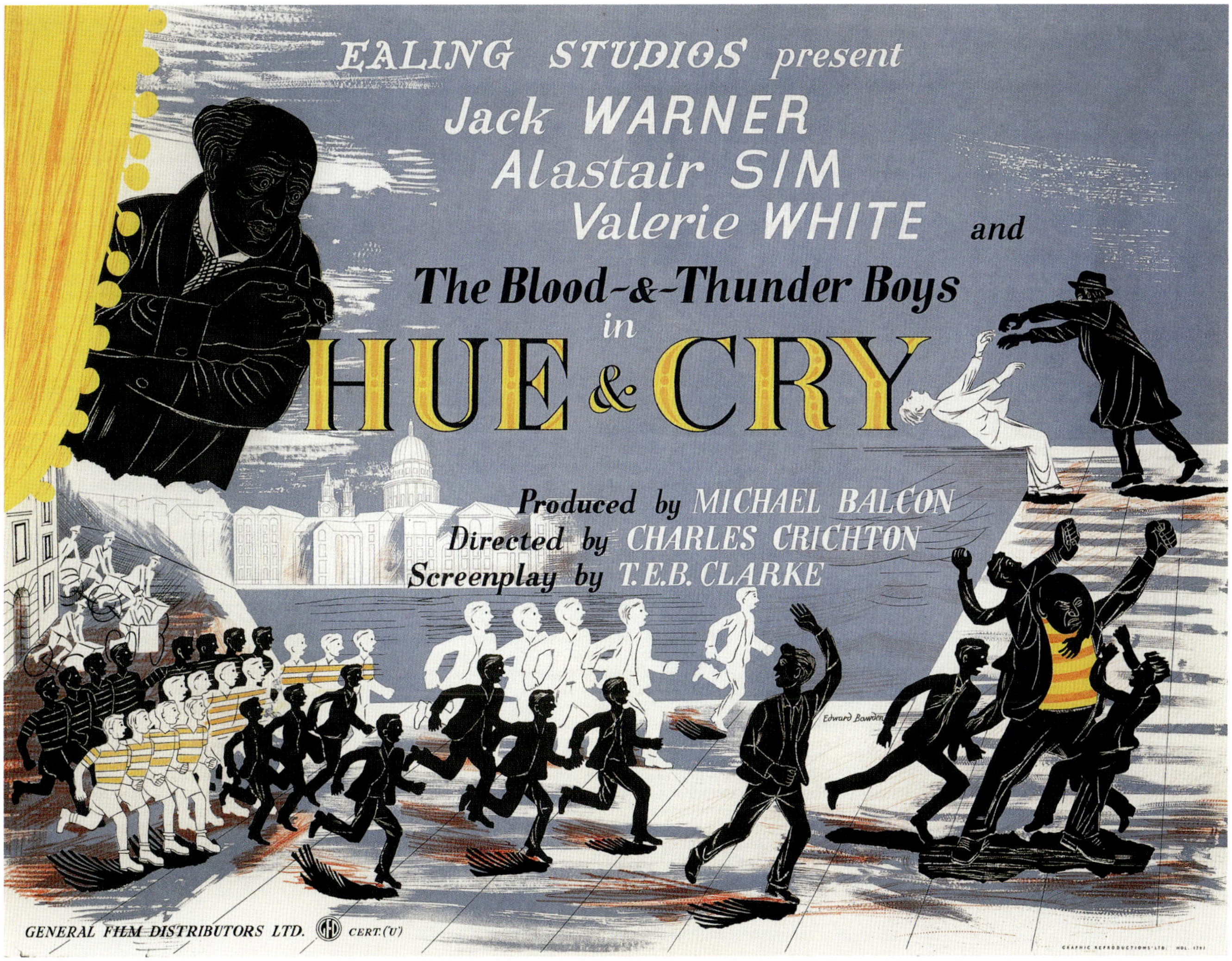

Poster design for the film *Hue & Cry*, 1947; 56 x 71 cm, printed by Graphic Reproductions Ltd.

had taken the task of graphic reporter too seriously: 'he had not let his fancy roam'. Perhaps he had in mind a comparison with Ravilious' *High Street*, which is indeed a more attractive and imaginative volume.

One of the post-war improvements in Great Bardfield was that Mr Jennings, the local garage owner, now ran a bus service. Those catching his bus to shop in Braintree or even in London might have seen another piece of Bawden's work on the advertising hoardings. In 1947 Ealing Studios asked him for a colour-litho poster for the film *Hue and Cry* showing, among others, Alastair Sim. Bawden did his best: 'I was given a completely free hand. Perhaps I ought to have been given more guidance. I worked completely in the dark – never saw a film being shot, never saw the finished film before I designed the poster.' He certainly crammed so much information into it that it would have very little impact when seen from a distance.

Other work was flooding in for book jackets, theatre programmes, Christmas cards, more cookery books, vignettes, holiday brochures, printers' devices, and some

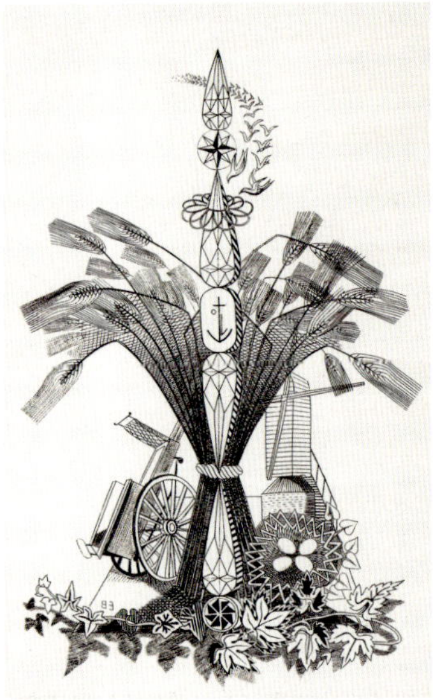

Corn Dolly, menu blank for the Orient Line, 1949, copper engraving, 192 x 119 mm (Trustees of Cecil Higgins Art Gallery, Bedford).

exquisitely fine copper-engraved menu decorations for the Orient Line ships SS *Oronsay* and SS *Orcades*.

Bawden also did twelve press advertisements in the architectural press for the Zinc Development Association – not a glamorous assignment one would have thought, but he made the newly-planned post-war docks, houses, farms and so on an exercise in detail and texture. Perhaps with this in mind the Royal Society of Arts made him a life-long Royal Designer for Industry in 1949. So busy was he in these years that he had little time for watercolour painting so he wrote to the Royal Watercolour Society on 24th July 1946 to resign: 'My talent – such as it is – is most uncertain; I have done no watercolour drawings for the last year, I have felt no desire to do so. I cannot tell when that desire will again be felt and being felt will be obeyed.' [2]

When Bawden arrived home from the war he had said: 'what I would like to do would be to paint, to do advertising work, books and wallpapers: what I don't want to do is waste time teaching.' But money was scarce, colleges were desperate for tutors as they were being asked to expand and take in the returning servicemen as well as a new generation of students, and so Bawden was recruited to the Department of Graphic Design at the RCA on a part-time basis of one day each week. 'It gave marginal security' he claimed, in a life where he was 'always working hard and always hard up'.

The college had returned from exile in the Lake District to Exhibition Road and from 1948 Robin Darwin was Principal with Government instructions to train more designers for industry and put less stress on easel painting. Darwin also weeded out staff: Kenneth Rowntree and Charles Mahoney were amongst those who soon departed and Percy Horton left to run the Ruskin School. 'Dear Ruskin', wrote Bawden, 'I understand that Mr Horton is now firmly in the saddle at your school, riding the old horse hard and taking all jumps in his usual robust style.' (11th November 1949).

Into the staffroom came John Minton and Keith Vaughan, two of the most talented of the war-time Neo-Romantics. Carel Weight remembered a staff meeting in which Darwin asked them all to put in claims for new equipment: 'Edward electrified everybody by asking for a supply of candles – 'candle light is excellent for drawing.' [3] It should be remembered that Brick House did not have electricity for some years after the Bawdens moved in so candles and oil lamps were part of his studio equipment. So, not only was he back at the RCA but eventually he ended up teaching at Goldsmiths, Wimbledon and later commuting to Leicester and Glasgow as teacher and examiner, though by then he had no financial need to do any of these.

As a teacher he was uncomfortable with groups, but inspiring when working one to one with students who were on his wavelength and adopted his work ethic. Some found him 'waspish', but others discovered that he could be intimidated and if one took a step towards him he instinctively took a step back because he hated to be touched and in this way could be made to retreat around the whole studio. One, John Ward, found him 'In character a sort of Clement Attlee, a deeply conservative radical who ruthlessly grasped the guts of a subject and set it out tersely, beautifully and uniquely. His place in British Art is as secure as that of Thomas Bewick.' [4] Another recalled that he had a showcase outside the Design Studio at the RCA and 'here

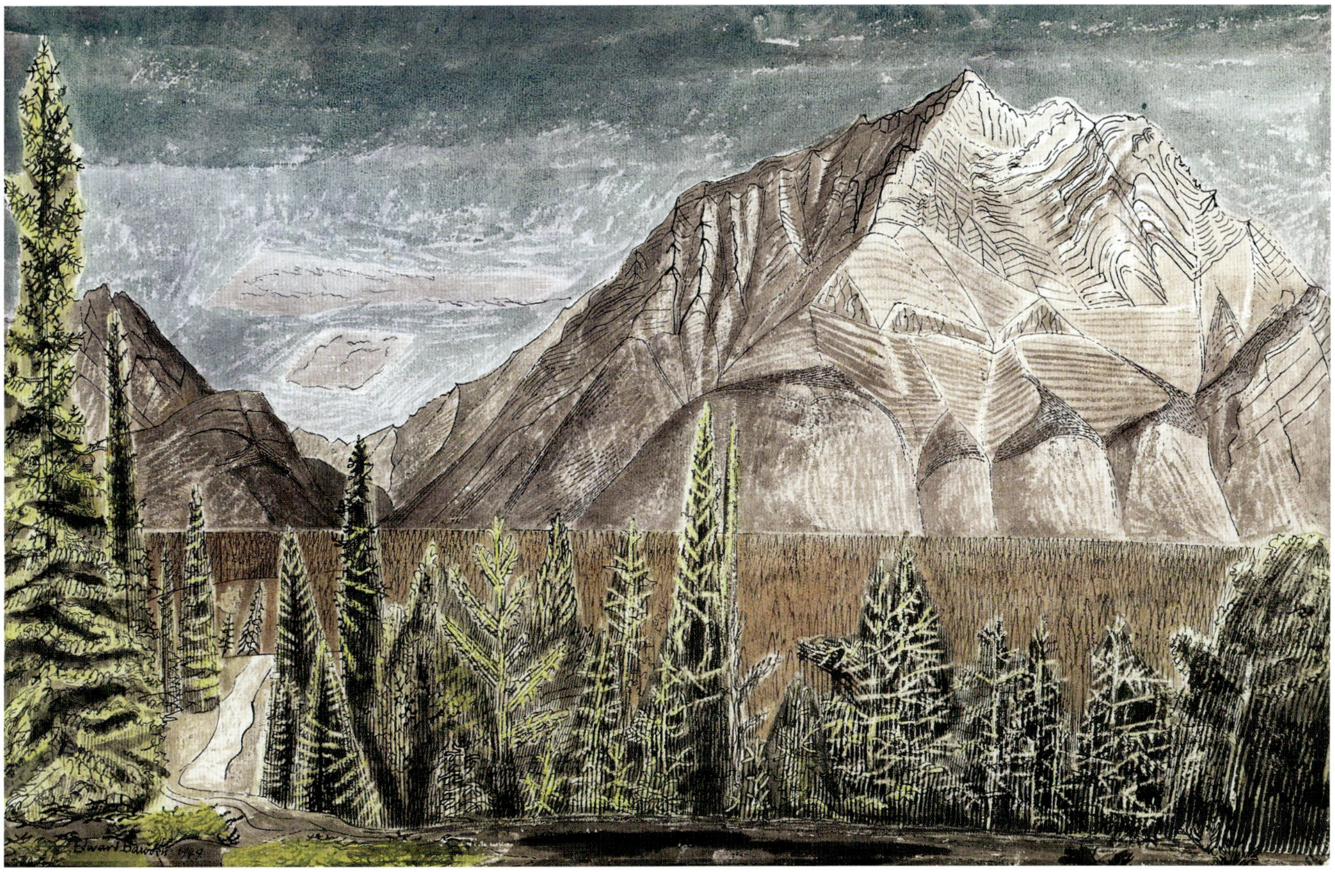

Cascade Mountain, Canadian Rockies, 1949, watercolour, 405 x 610 mm (Fine Art Society).

we were invited to enjoy the designs of sardine tins . . . there were diploma tea packets, spaghetti wrappings and sheep drenches, horse pills and a peep-hole to view sugar mice at play. He revelled in the small change of Art.' [5]

One student who did get on with Bawden so well that he became a collaborator and friend was Walter Hoyle (1922-2000). He had first been to Beckenham School of Art and then to the RCA during 1940-42 before being conscripted into the army. He returned in 1947 and at his Diploma show so impressed an American visitor that he was offered seven months' work in the Byzantine Institute in Istanbul. After his return for his final year Bawden popped into his studio and invited him out to lunch together with Kenneth Rowntree and John Nash, during which the old friends Bawden and Nash bantered like professional comedians. Hoyle was kept on the hop by Bawden's tutorial style: 'He was difficult. He could be very critical, he was rather naughty, he could say things which seemed rather bitter on occasion. On the other hand he could be helpful, he could rejoice in any success that you had, he was not at all secretive, he was very willing to pass on any of his secrets – his painting or printing techniques for example, he could be very generous.' [6]

After returning from another spell in Turkey, Hoyle was invited to visit Brick House but so convoluted were the train and bus connections that it took him nine hours to get there from London. He was welcomed by Charlotte: 'She was sort of middle-class and middle-aged, she never seemed young and she never seemed to be old. She was rather like – have you seen the actress Margaret

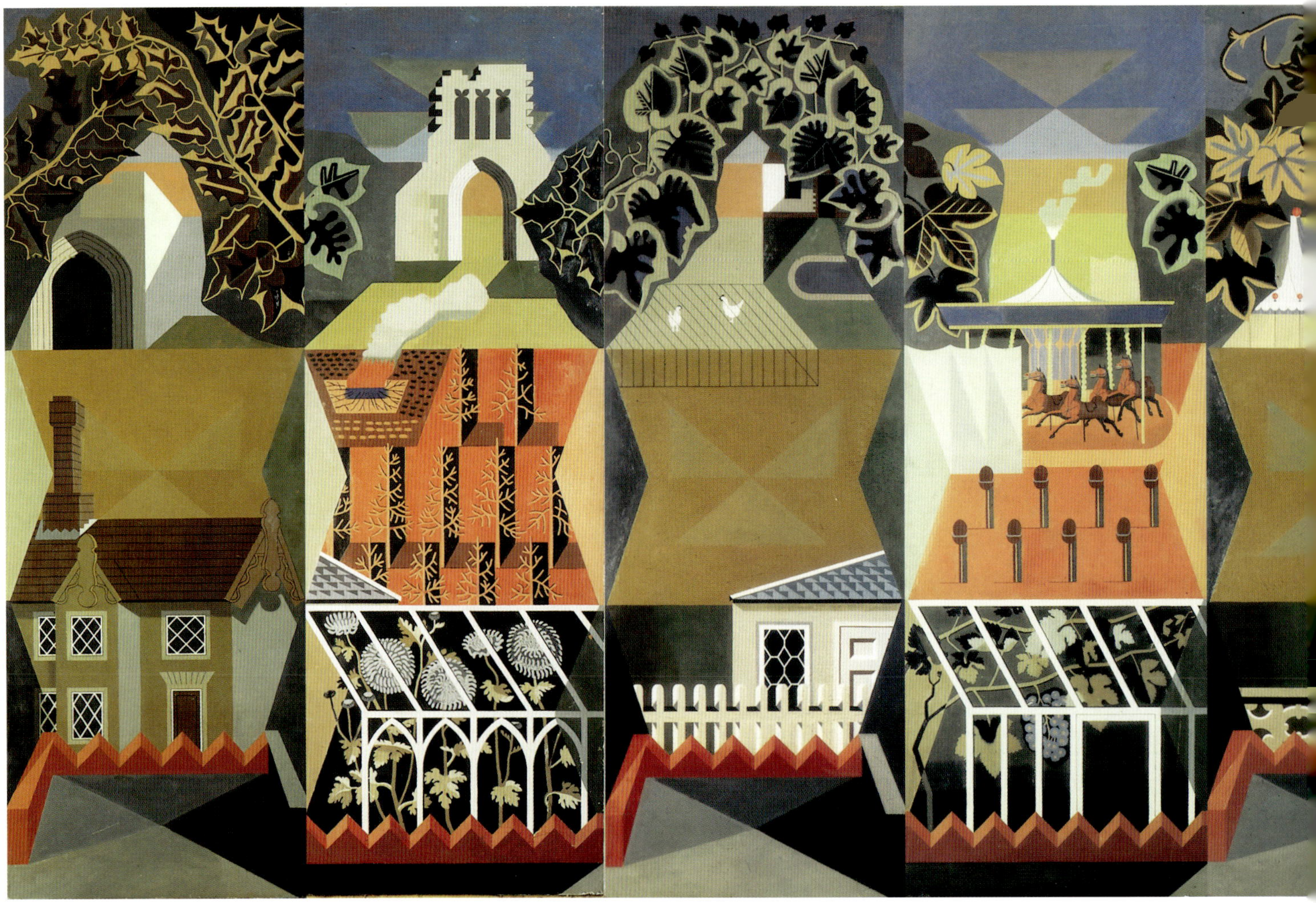

The nine-panel mural *English Garden Delights*, each about 2 metres high, made for SS *Orcades* in 1947 (Fine Art Society).

Rutherford? Edward wasn't really a devoted husband or father.' In spite of his travel problems, Hoyle must have been impressed because he later accepted Bawden's suggestion that he move into Great Bardfield permanently.

In 1949 Bawden accepted an invitation to be a Visiting Instructor in Banff, Canada. From there he wrote to John Nash that he was fed up with mosquitoes and trees: 'in my opinion nothing will ever open up this country for painting better than some forest fires on a vast scale'. Surprisingly he almost enjoyed it when the students slapped him on the back and called him Ed and made fun of his English hat and jacket. In self-defence he bought jeans and a denim jacket and so became one of the first to wear this outfit on the London art scene. He completed several watercolours in and around Alberta which came in handy for an exhibition at the Leicester Galleries on his return, and when he was asked to do a Canadian mural for the lounge of the liner *The Empress of France*, he created a sixty-four feet long mural by printing lino-cuts onto panels with the assistance of Walter Hoyle. The subjects

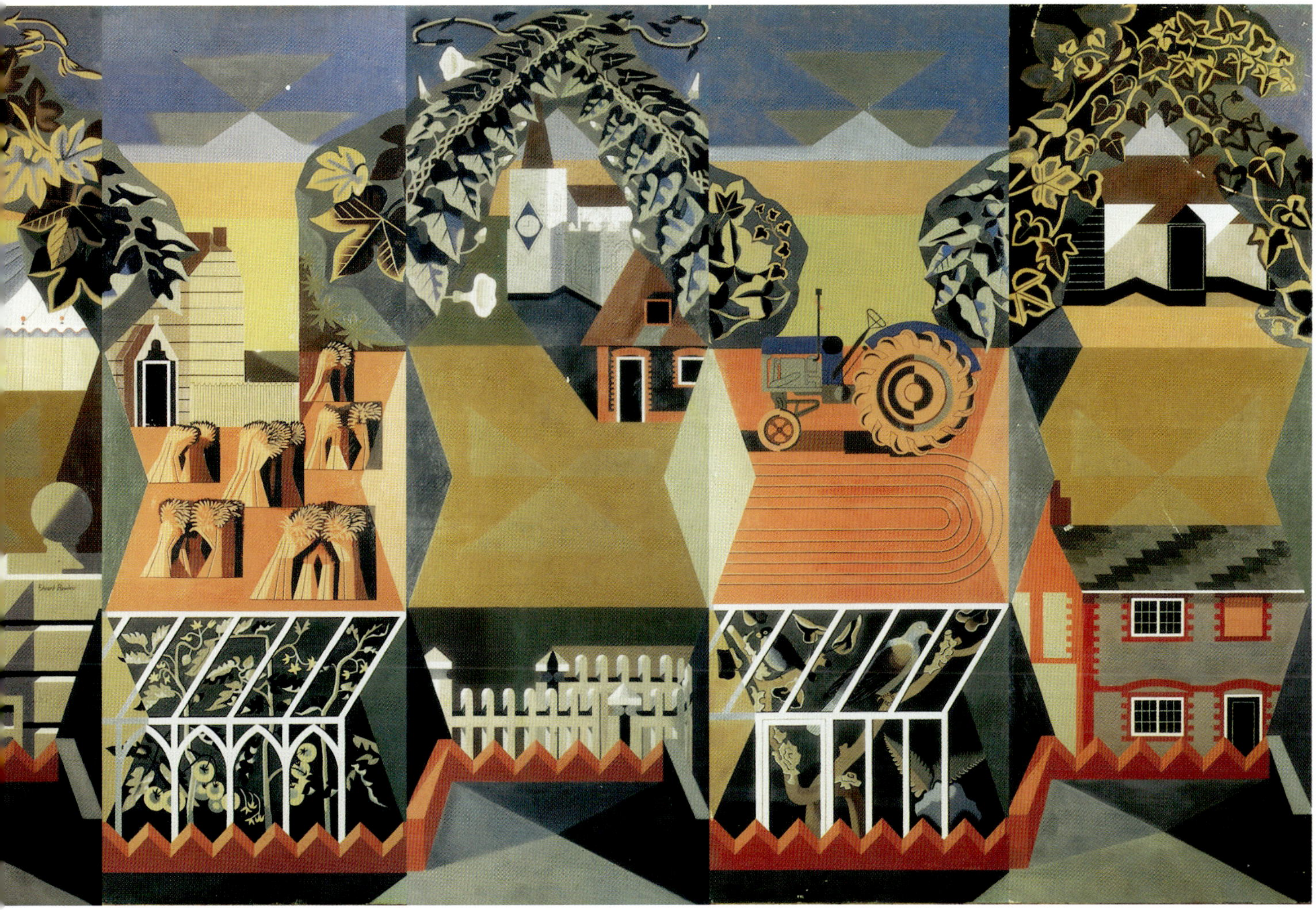

were the Canadian seasons, mountains, lakes, forests and involved historical figures on horseback or on board ships. Coniferous forest covered much of the surface, this being achieved by multiple printings from a few large, medium and small lino blocks of fir trees. It was a daring but efficient solution, though the original is now lost and we can only judge its impact from photographs.

Bawden made something of a specialism of ship's murals at this time, though with the subsequent rise of air travel most of these elegant ships were broken up and his works destroyed. Colin Anderson, director of the Orient Shipping Line was a friend of Kenneth Clark who introduced him to John Piper, Ceri Richards, McKnight Kauffer, Kenneth Rowntree, Edward Bawden and others with the suggestion they could make posters and wall decorations for his cruise ships.

For the SS *Orcades* Bawden depicted a theme near to his heart of English Garden Delights, foliage cascading down from the arched tops of nine vertical panels. There were no people in the finished version and little attempt to

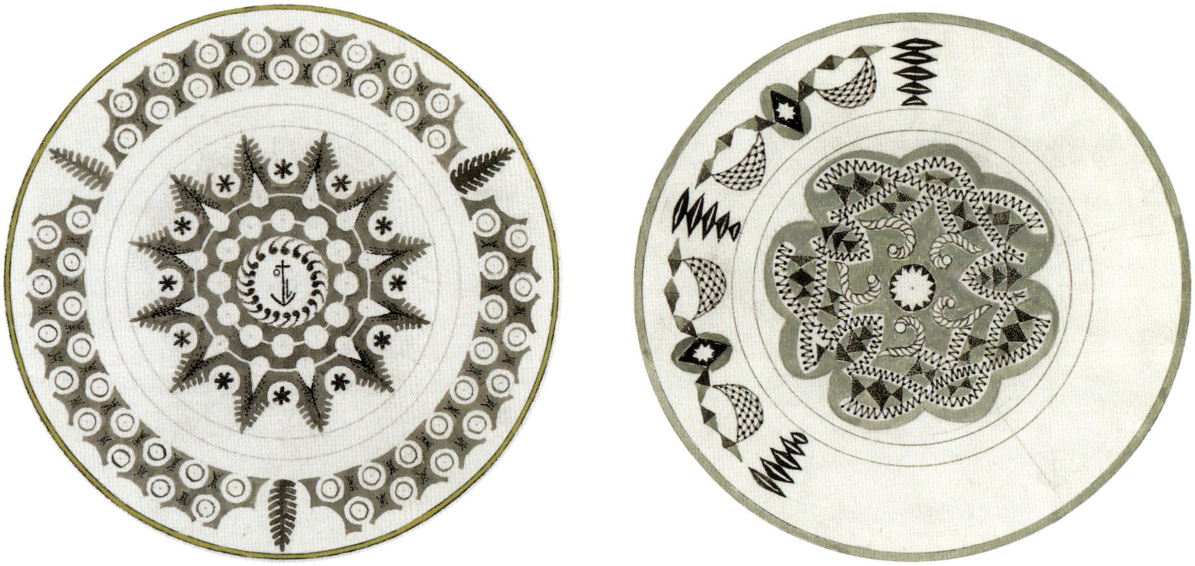

Two designs for Wedgwood plates to be used on the Orient Line, *c.*1952 (Fine Art Society).

convey deep recession. The ship was launched in 1947, at a cost of £3,418,000 and broken up in 1973. Bawden received £600 for his efforts. For the SS *Oronsay* in 1951 his subject was the English Pub and this time there were eleven vertical panels, each 70 x 18 inches (176 x 46 cm), full of Tourist Board details of stately homes, parsonages, race courses, steam trains, harvest festivals, churches, stations and thatched cottages with the heraldic pub signs of the Cock, Rose and Crown, and so on, hung like medallions between them. This time there was a single figure, an ice-cream seller on his 'Stop Me and Buy One' bike. Again Bawden needed assistance with this and called upon two former students, Walter Hoyle and Sheila Robinson to work in the lofty studio newly built onto the back of Brick House.

Not only did Bawden provide the ship's mural but he designed the menus, the curtain fabric and a whole bone-china dinner service called 'Heartsease' decorated with English flowers and a petal motif in mauve and grey. This challenge to his versatility had come from Wedgwood Pottery who invited him to design crockery for them, as they had invited Ravilious before the war. Bawden made experimental designs for dinner plates and then in 1952 and 1953 whole dinner services, made by Wedgwood for the Orient Line and New Zealand Shipping Line. Later he told his friend Peyton Skipwith, 'my experiences with Wedgwood were very unhappy. The present managing director, then a salesman, had an unerring eye for mediocrity.'

By 1950 Bawden admitted he 'was getting middle aged and browned off about it'. He was also well enough respected to deserve having a another book written about him. This was *Edward Bawden*, published by London Art and Technics and written by Robert Harling, editor of *House and Garden* who had used some of Bawden's illustrations in the magazine. The author tells us that Bawden currently leads a blameless life in Great Bardfield and 'works hours no self-respecting trade-unionist would consider, and no shop steward would condone for a moment'. The artist's 'workroom' (never 'studio') is a low white attic on two levels from which he can see both the village street and the farmlands beyond. All is order, no bohemian clutter here, only 'a scarlet tunic quickens the dry sobriety of the room, a nineteenth century print, and one wall is hung with wallpaper blocks, the first experimental blocks cut by Bawden, which he printed before cutting full size blocks for the printer'.

The denizen of this graphics laboratory is 'a slim, almost spare man, above the middle height, quick moving, giving always an impression of considerable nervous energy, seeming always wishful to be away, back to the work he has unwillingly left'. There are hints he is not always an easy man to be around: 'His manner is of a shy, modest man, wary of the social scene. His eyes are watchful and usually sceptical in some degree of the world and its residents. He talks but rarely and then briefly. He asks questions, often innocently phrased, not so innocently intended. He does not suffer fools gladly, usually not at all. He is, most of his friends would agree, a man of moods, one of them an obviously pleasurable melancholia and another a mood of mocking humour. In such moods he is apt to intimidate all but the most hardened and impervious of his friends and enemies. He is more than usually sceptical. His humour is bitter. Only a response in kind has any effect, and then he is apt to smile and leave his own depression, as if willingly.' We are told his conversation 'is frequently enlivened by astringent observations apt to be taken over-seriously by the over-sensitive. The innocent tongue partners the innocent eye, but a far-from-innocent mind guides both.'

Harling spares a thought for Charlotte: 'to a woman of less characterful ebullience these moods of gloom which afflict the artist might prove oppressive: as it happens they are cunningly diverted and then disarmed.' Bawden told

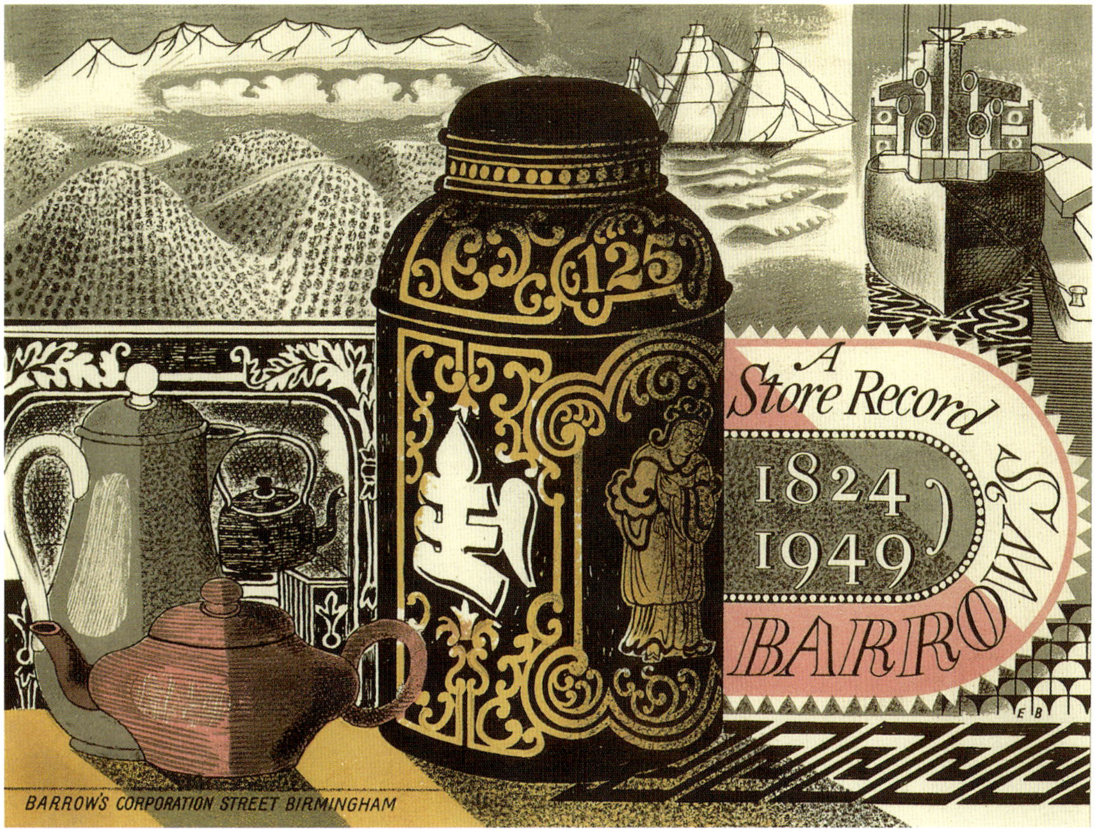

Lithographed cover design for an advertising booklet for Barrow's Store, Birmingham, 1949, printed in at least two sizes.

John Nash that sometimes it was a relief when Charlotte was away and he could escape her 'buzz' of energy. Harling didn't say so but we know that some of the younger artists' wives were a little intimidated by Charlotte's 'characterful ebullience', even bossiness, and occasionally, when provoked, by her use of colourful language. They also joked, behind her back, that she had three children, the most dependent being Edward.

Around this time Bawden pricked his finger on a rose thorn in his garden and it turned septic. Harling recalls 'his interest in the medical examinations which preceded the removal of the top joint of that finger was an education in detachment, that rare gift of stepping outside oneself and looking on. A visitor to the hospital asked him whether he thought the operation would make much difference to his drawing. No, he said, he was already beginning to write quite legibly with the pen between his two middle fingers and could think of no reason why he should be prevented from drawing as before. The patient claimed: "Twelve days in Ward 7 has been a grand experience: I'll try to go back in the autumn for a few days in Sister's care and have another inch of the finger pruned back. I shall put the middle finger on to some art work tomorrow!"'

There was plenty of art work awaiting his attention. His book illustrations were now much in demand and he gave an account of how he set about them which is worth quoting at length.

'As I aspire to draw with an easy naturalness I collect all sorts of nibs, writing and also drawing kinds. For making preliminary notes or sketches I use writing materials, a nib of the J-family comfortably worn down by letter writing and a bottle of black writing ink. With homely materials I seem better able to catch a 'conversational' fluency, as though the lines were appearing on the paper without pre-meditation. I work rapidly, drawing without the intervention of pencil lines and without much care whether the ink blots or sketches overlap, but exerting myself to avoid corrections by drawing accurately and clearly – and always in line only, without shading or any attempt at it. Sketches, however mean they may be, are indispensable. I generally make sketches of an object from several points of view with, if need be, separate scribbles of details. If, for instance I am standing on a London street corner, I try not to forget familiar objects, a letter box or a bollard, or to miss counting the number of buttons worn by the policeman.

Finished drawings are done indoors. As a background to working I would like to have a well-ordered library, or my present makeshift of a few shelves of books. I like to work on a polished mahogany table and to give its surface a lick of beeswax on the completion of every job. I need silence. On the drawing board I keep a T-square and set-square, within reach a diminishing glass and, with luck, nearby a cup of coffee. The sketches or notes are often put aside for several days until I feel I have an idea of what I want to do. Working blindly from sketches leads to a reliance upon them, and stimulates an anxiety about verisimilitude – anyhow, the finished drawing will be sketch-bound and likely to be dull.

I begin the finished drawing by a good deal of random scribbling with an H-grade pencil, drawing the main construction of the design which may be either of a geometrical or architectural character, and fixing with precision anything about which I may feel nervous. The real drawing must be done with a pen and not with a pen following a pencil line, so areas in the design are left to be drawn directly in ink. I begin drawing in pen whatever has caused most fuss and bother to draw in pencil, working painfully at first, then with more confidence, until the pen becomes master – until it is moving no longer by jerks, or scratching hesitantly, but putting down the ink with certainty. If a drawing is to become a casualty I like it to show signs of doing so at an early stage, and I do not hesitate to scrap the result at once in favour of another beginning.

My manner of drawing for reproduction has been influenced by an amateur skill in line-engraving and a spectator's interest in Victorian facsimile wood-engraving. In line-engraving tone is created by a field of closely-laid straight or curved parallel lines and much depends not only upon the spacing of these lines but on the angle to them of subsequent parallel lines to make cross-hatching.[7]

It is interesting to note that he stresses both the amount of detailed research and drafting he does and his nervousness during the execution of the work, neither of which could be guessed at from the perfection and seeming inevitability of the final results. However, one can see from the surviving roughs that he frequently cuts out mistakes and glues on patches of reworked details, or uses poster white to correct small areas. When ready the reproduction copyright to the drawings would be granted to the publishers, but the originals retained in his files for later sale. Somehow he combined both an eccentrically unworldly imagination and a shrewd professionalism.

By 1950 it was becoming clear that the Labour government could not deliver the reborn Britain as quickly as everyone hoped they would. People were still exhausted by the after-effects of war and there were new anxieties to cope with about the Atom-bomb, the division of Europe, the start of the Cold War and the real war in Korea. *Horizon Magazine*, which had helped keep culture alive all through the war was closed down by its editor

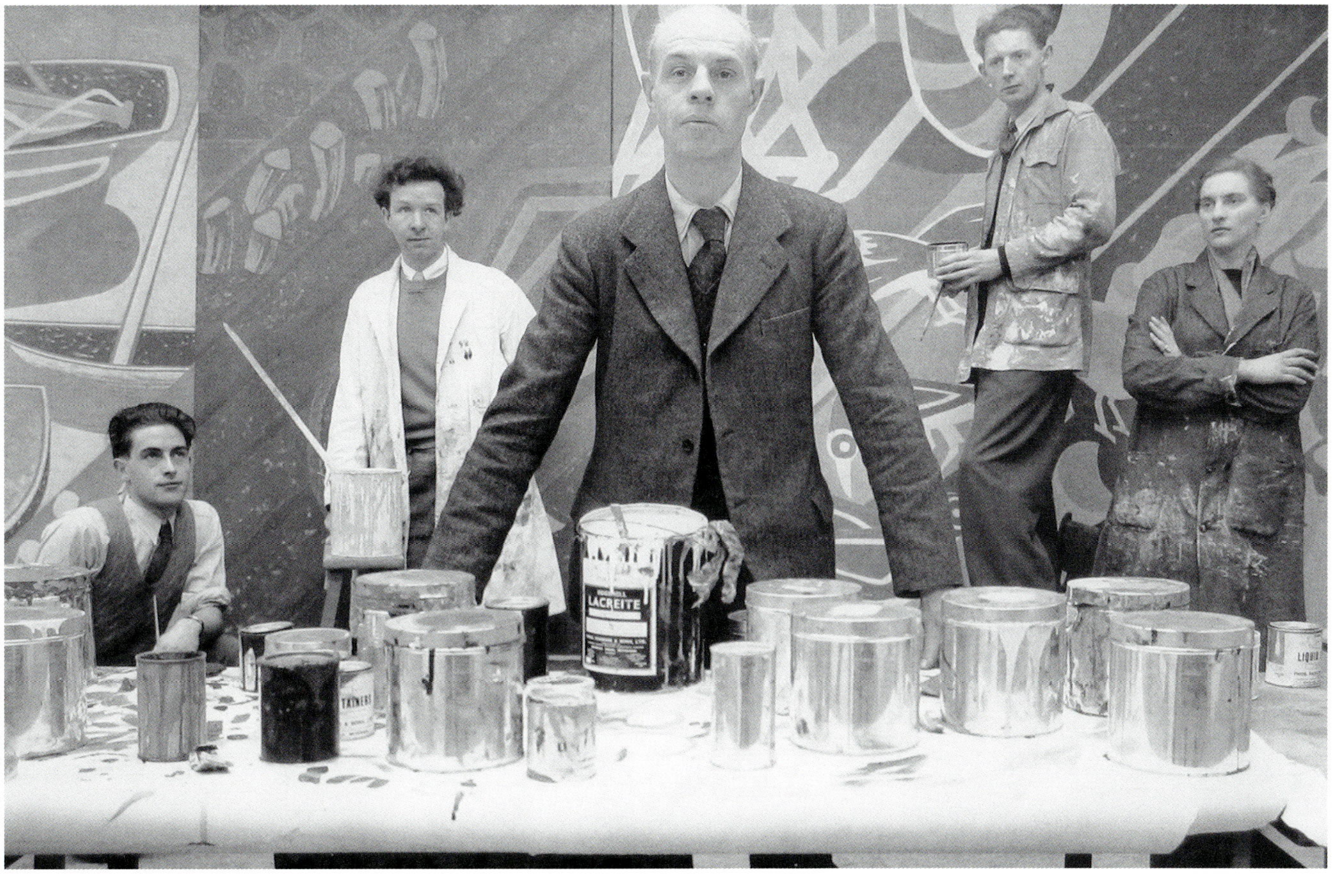

'Edward Bawden with four of his assistants at work on his display addressing The Character of the British people', by Norman Parkinson, 1951; the assistants are Roy Sharp, Walter Hoyle, William Fenton and Sheila Robinson (Norman Parkinson Ltd / Fiona Cowan).

Cyril Connolly in 1950 with the words 'from now on an artist will be judged only by the resonance of his solitude and the quality of his despair'. To dispel such gloom the Government decided to throw a party in 1951 to demonstrate to the world the recovery of the United Kingdom from the effects of the war in the moral, cultural, spiritual and material fields and to show the nation's unique contributions to civilisation. In spite of the usual moaners, political point scoring, and a serious shortage of building materials after all the bombing, the Festival of Britain went ahead with its main focus being situated on the south bank of the Thames.

Twenty architects were recruited to make a conglomerate of buildings which deliberately lacked an overall style – though after the event it was clear that one had emerged which set the tone for 'modernism' in design for some years to come. One writer saw it as 'Braced legs, indoor plants, colour-rinse concrete, lily-of-the-valley splays of light bulbs, casework, aluminium lattices, Cotswold-type walling with picture windows, flying staircases, blond wood, the thorn, the spike, the molecule: all these became the Festival Style.' [8] The style never achieved grandeur but it was linear, bright and clean and it spread to airports, the new towns and trendy houses, though not to the dwellings of the Great Bardfield artists – the exception being the home of Michael Rothenstein. The Festival designers and architects were told to balance a variety of themes such as tradition and the future, technology and culture, the rural and the industrial, and the stolidity and eccentricity of the British character.

Hugh Casson was made Director of Architecture. He had also recently been appointed by Robin Darwin to be Head of Interior Design at the RCA and naturally he pushed for RCA staff to be employed. Accordingly, Robert Yorke Goodden (1909-2002), who was Professor of Silversmithing as well as being an architect, was asked to provide a building and interior design for the Lion and Unicorn Pavilion, immediately south of the Festival Hall and hard up against Hungerford Bridge. He and colleague R. D. Russell designed a type of barn with two glass walls and upswept eaves. A viewing gallery ran the whole length and there were side-shows on the English language, miniature stage sets, Law, Christianity, the Constitution, and British Eccentricity which consisted of an egg roundabout, a smoke-grinder and a life-size white plaster figure of Lewis Carroll's White Knight on a horse. Behind these on the west wall was a long mural by Kenneth Rowntree with scenes from British history to show Freedom of Worship, Democratic Freedom and Freedom under the Law. There were also displays of crafts on glass tables which unfortunately cracked just as the show was about to open. Then came a screen illustrating British Landscape with paintings by Constable, Gainsborough, Turner and, to show how modern we were, Paul Nash. The whole took its name from large straw effigies of the Lion and the Unicorn made by Fred Mizen from Great Bardfield. Poet Laurie Lee wrote all the captions.

Competing with all this clutter and standing in front of the end wall was Bawden's free-standing painted screen consisting of twelve large vertical panels showing 'The British Character and Tradition' as shown in rural life. For this he had set himself some formidable design problems: each panel would be complete in itself but also linked to the ones on either side, they would alternate light and dark so giving a zig-zag effect, and there would be visual puns so, for example, upward furrows being ploughed on one panel become downward runners in a corrugated roof in the next one. The images are relentlessly jolly: Old World pubs, churches, chapels, country houses, cottages, stations, birds, beasts, milk-men, ploughmen with tractors, horses and hounds, gardeners and miners and healthy rustics at work and play, each image conventionalised and firmly enclosed in a line. At the bottom of each panel was a table with still-lifes of country products on it, a wire fence and finally what seem to be five bricks. At the top is the gentle arc of a hill. It is a triumph of decorative ingenuity. To help him paint it he employed former students Walter Hoyle, Sheila Robinson, Roy Sharp and William Fenton, and his daughter Joanna was roped in to assist for two weeks.

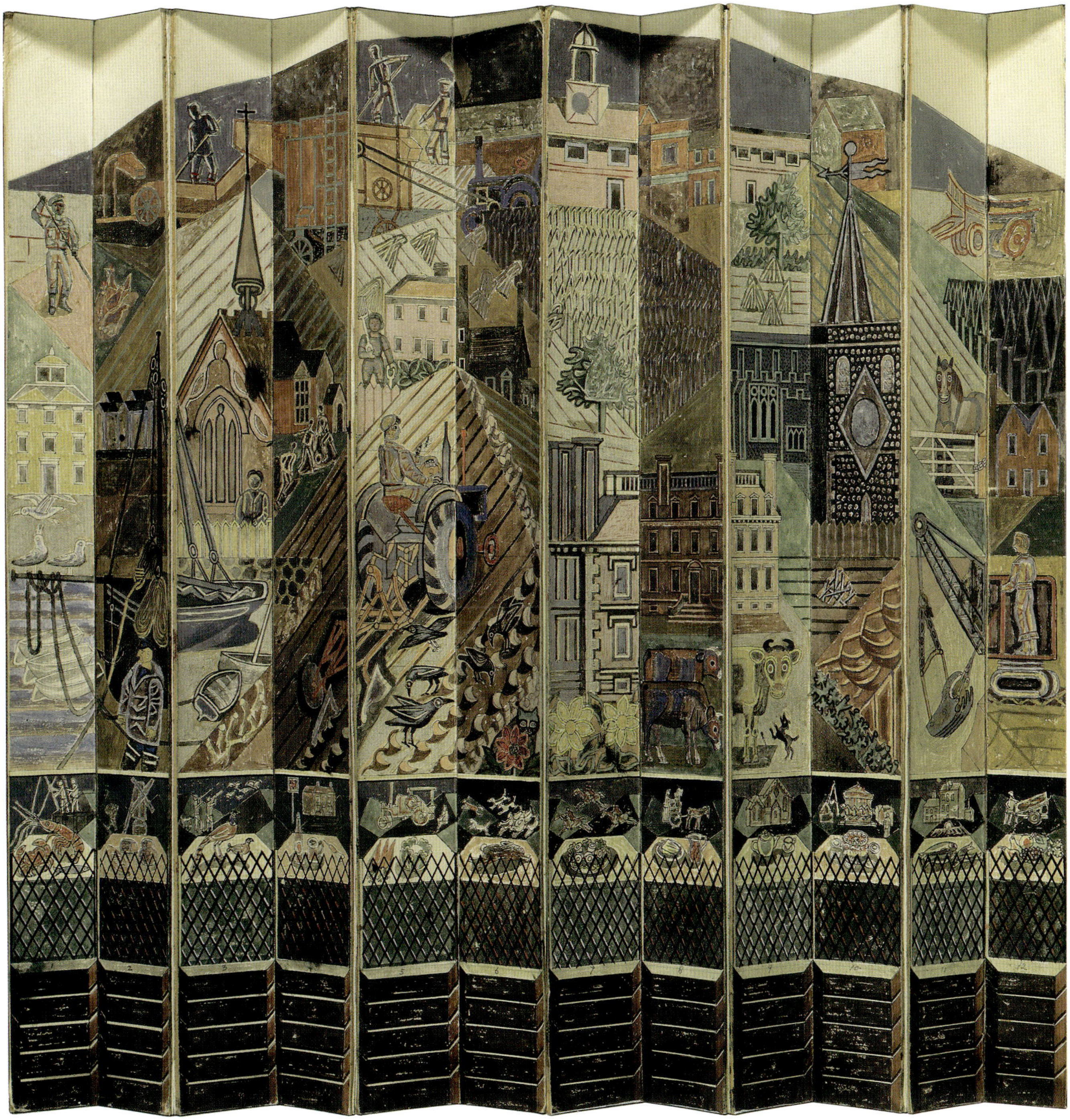

Screen for the Festival of Britain, 1951; it consisted of twelve panels (36 by 45 feet) depicting *The British Character and Tradition*, and was shown in the Royal College of Art's Lion and Unicorn Pavilion. After the exhibition the mural was stored in a Ministry of Works building and has since vanished.
This is a watercolour study for the mural, 517 x 484 mm (Trustees of Cecil Higgins Art Gallery, Bedford).

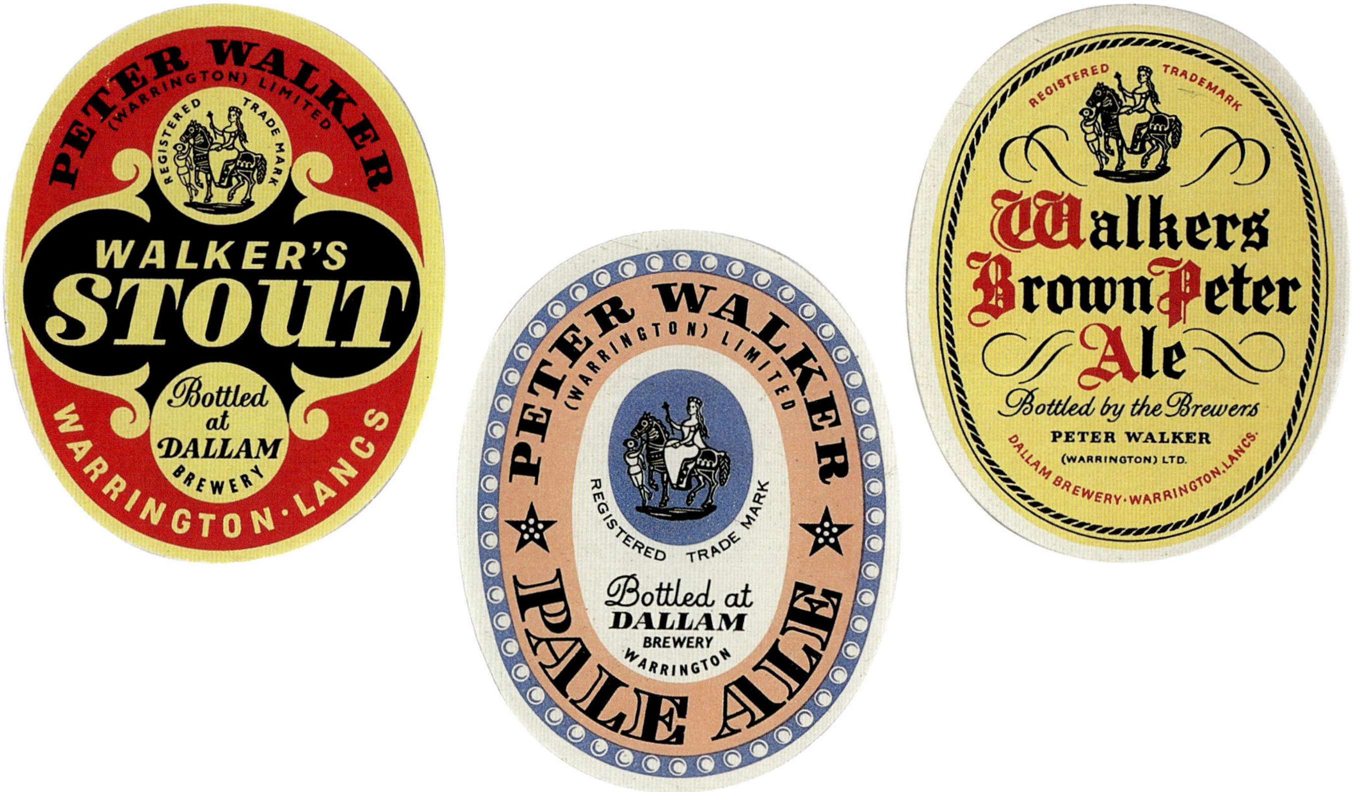

Bottle labels designed by Bawden and John Brinkley for Peter Walker's Brewery, Warrington, 1952, each 85 x 65 mm.

Bawden had planned it in such detail that they had very little to do except fill in the colours on the easy bits.

When it was finished he wrote to Joanna: 'A workman was asked what he thought of it and replied: "If a kid of mine did that I'd kick him out of the house at once." Another workman looking at one of my paintings remarked: "Threw away a better thing of my own last week." Typical Fred Mizen humour as you can see.' (12th March 1951). Every would-be revolutionary likes to comfort himself with the belief he is not understood by the masses, but in this case the work was bland enough to shock no one.

The Festival was a big success, eight million people passing through the South Bank between May and September. Soon after it closed the Labour party lost the General Election of autumn 1951 and Churchill was back as Prime Minister. With the exception of the Festival Hall this first large scale building project of the post-war years was demolished, and somehow in the process Bawden's screen was dismantled and lost, leaving only photographs behind.

1. Anglia Television, 'Edward Bawden', film broadcast November 1983.
2. French, S., and Smith, G., *The Business of Watercolour: A Guide to the Archives of the Royal Watercolour Society*, Ashgate, 1997, p.84.
3. Weight, C., contribution to the catalogue of the Bawden exhibition at the Fine Art Society, February to March 1978.
4. Howell, S., 'Diary', *World of Interiors*, July 1992, p.108.
5. Ward, J., contribution to catalogue 'Tribute to Edward Bawden', Fine Art Society, 7-31st July 1992, p.21.
6. Hoyle, W., 'Born Romantic', *Line*, No. 1, APU, Department of Arts and Design, Cambridge, 2000, pp.32-38.
7. Harling, R., 'Edward Bawden', *Art and Technics*, 1950, p.33.
8. Feaver, W., 'Festival Star', *A Tonic for the Nation: The Festival of Britain 1951*, ed. Banham, M., and Hillier, B., Thames and Hudson, 1976, p.54.

10. THE GREAT BARDFIELD ARTISTS

The Festival of Britain was a nation-wide celebration and many communities organised their own events. For example, Thaxted, Finchingfield and Great Bardfield pooled resources, and the artists' contribution to the jollifications was to hold an open week. Bawden, Rothenstein and Aldridge opened their studios so that the villagers and others from further afield could come inside their houses and see them working and making prints.

The Great Bardfield artists were not directly involved in the everyday working life of the village – none of them owned arable land or kept cattle or had much contact with the locals, though they did employ them as nannies, charladies and gardeners. Bawden went to the Quaker Meeting House across the road (he claimed to enjoy the silence but deplored the 'vulgar protestations' which broke it) but never spent time in the pubs or the church and his children were not sent to the village school, apart from a brief period before the war when Joanna attended. However he did attempt to build bridges by running a free Sunday afternoon class for any locals who wished to come along and learn printmaking or watercolour painting. One beneficiary of this was the teenager John Norris Wood who went on to be a student of Bawden's at the RCA and eventually a well-known wildlife artist.

The villagers took up the invitation to visit on the open days with enthusiasm and poked around the kitchens and other rooms besides the studios to see how these strange people lived. In Brick House they discovered the walls were covered with Bawden's own wallpapers, and in the dining room he had hand-blocked maroon stripes on the walls and painted the cupboard doors with crossed truncheons one day when Charlotte was safely out of the way. Modern ceramics, Staffordshire pottery, copper jelly moulds, folk art and Victoriana were arranged on every flat surface, with contemporary pictures on every wall and books on every shelf. Those expecting to find either bohemian slumminess or avant-garde chic would be disappointed.

Bawden wrote to his son (7th July 1951) 'when a school arrives or a party of W. I. people I nearly get pushed out of the house by the crush of bosoms. The last person to sign the book came from Madrid and others from Falkland Islands, Denmark, France, Malaya and Canada.' It was evidently a success in terms of sales and the first murmurs about a 'Bardfield School' of painters began around this time.

After the Festival of Britain mural was finished and the open day over there came a lull and Bawden suggested to Walter Hoyle they might go on a painting holiday together, not to France which he disliked, but to Sicily. Bawden reluctantly agreed that Charlotte could join them after the three weeks of painting were over, but predicted she would hate it. Hoyle has left a handwritten account of their time together which offers insights into Bawden both as companion and artist. Hoyle was obviously very much under Bawden's influence at this stage and never quite managed to shake this off later: not only his graphic and watercolour styles echo Bawden's but even his handwriting is very similar in its calligraphic manner.[1]

Sicily was then primitive, firmly in the Mafia's grip and with acute contrasts in poverty and wealth. It offered extreme terrains, diverse architecture, turbulent history and a mixture of pagan and Catholic customs – in its way almost as exotic as Ethiopia. The two men soon retreated

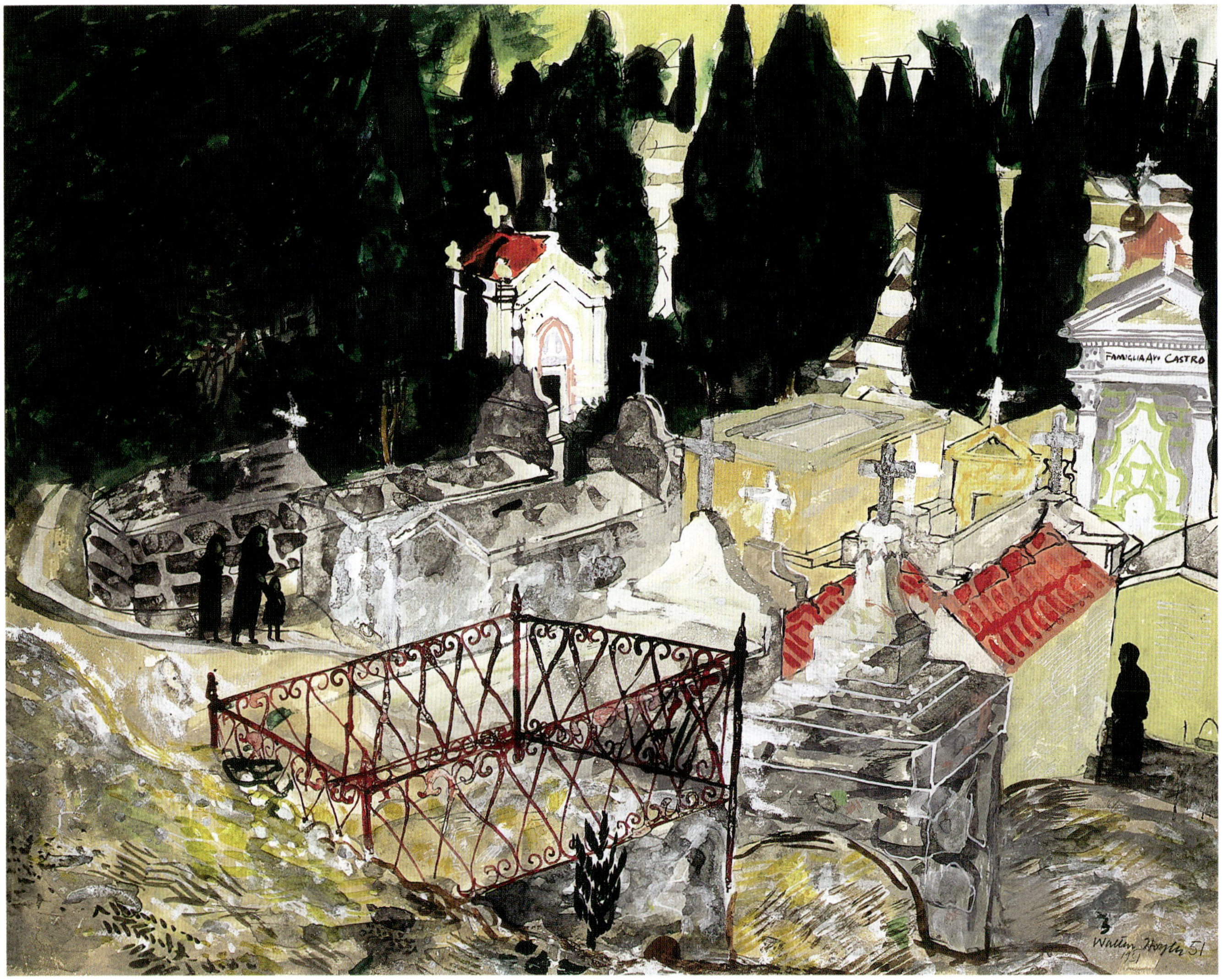

Walter Hoyle, *Cemetery in Enna, Sicily*, 1951, watercolour, 475 x 590 mm (Fry Art Gallery).

from baking Palermo inland to Enna where it was cooler, being 3000 feet higher, but also more basic in its facilities. Hoyle found his companion taciturn company in this isolated place: Bawden rose at five, finished the previous day's painting on site before breakfast, roused Hoyle from his bed, painted all morning, had lunch, a siesta, did more painting before dinner, read a book and was in bed by nine. He was also very competitive, painting eight works to every five of Hoyle's, though he was willing to pass on what he called his 'tricks' or discoveries to the younger man. One of these 'tricks' was to apply to the paper heel ball, a brown or black wax which cobblers use to colour and waterproof new leather, and others use for brass-rubbing. Watercolours will not soak through this wax-resist layer, and dry on its surface in speckled droplets which suggest textures, of weathered stones for example. Bawden explained this weird practice: 'Henry Moore and Sutherland used candle grease at this time, but I preferred using heel ball, which was I think my own invention. Once the heel ball is ironed on through a piece of blotting paper, it cannot be taken off. I feel that this is typical of my work for I do not use a wide range of colours, only four or five and the mixtures that could be made by applying one colour glaze over another.' [2]

Bawden obviously enjoyed the freedom to experiment which watercolour gave him since he had no client to please. Hoyle noted: 'Edward also developed a personal colour sense in which he used infinite variations of the complementary colours, blue and yellow. He was also devoted to greys – Davy's grey, Payne's grey, Charcoal grey, Neutral tint – and his work was recognisable not only by style, but by colour.' [3] Bawden later said of himself as a watercolourist, 'I had no sense of tone values'. Hoyle observed the master's technique: he made a careful pencil drawing, simplifying the scene by a selection of its essentials, then using large sable brushes he applied washes one on top of another to create a third, rather like a lithograph, and sometimes he floated white on top of a dark colour. He then pulled the whole together by re-asserting the line. It usually took him two or three sessions to complete a work.

Conversation was hard work, Bawden having learned in the desert 'it is polite to be silent among Arabs if you have nothing to say', but Hoyle did raise the name of Ravilious and detected Bawden's affection for his old friend, 'but also that he considered him a rival. Edward could be

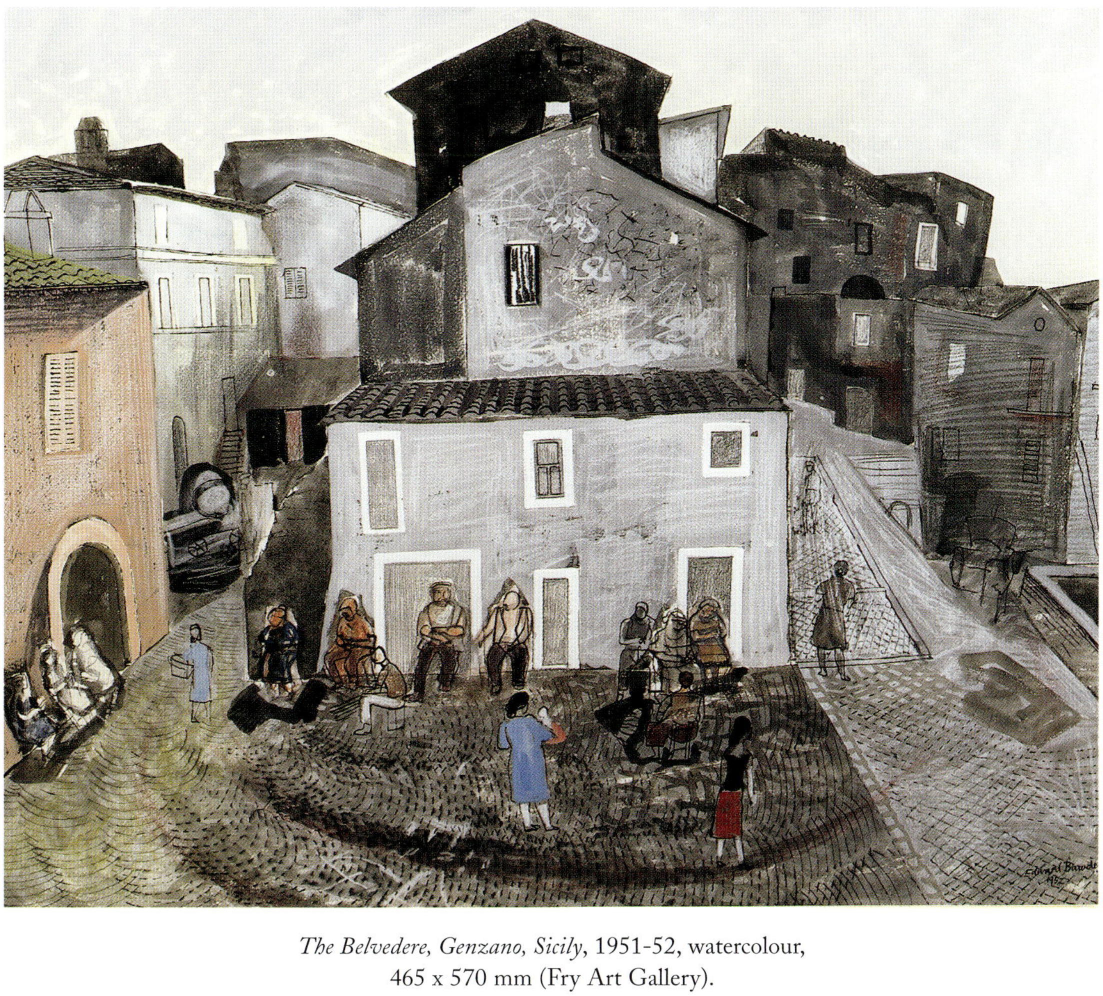

The Belvedere, Genzano, Sicily, 1951-52, watercolour, 465 x 570 mm (Fry Art Gallery).

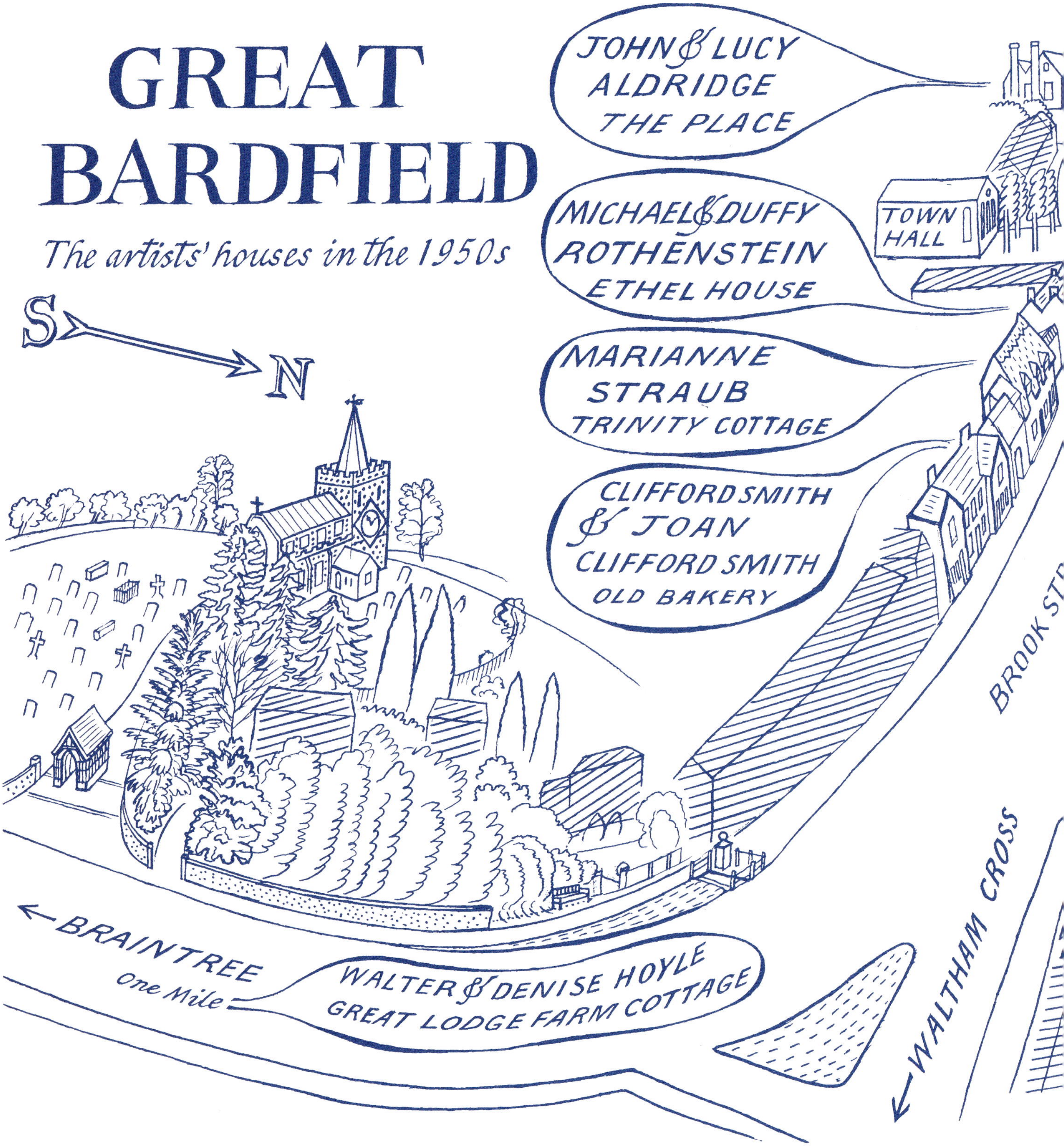
GREAT BARDFIELD
The artists' houses in the 1950s
S
N
JOHN & LUCY ALDRIDGE THE PLACE
TOWN HALL
MICHAEL & DUFFY ROTHENSTEIN ETHEL HOUSE
MARIANNE STRAUB TRINITY COTTAGE
CLIFFORD SMITH & JOAN CLIFFORD SMITH OLD BAKERY
BROOK ST
← BRAINTREE One Mile
WALTER & DENISE HOYLE GREAT LODGE FARM COTTAGE
← WALTHAM CROSS

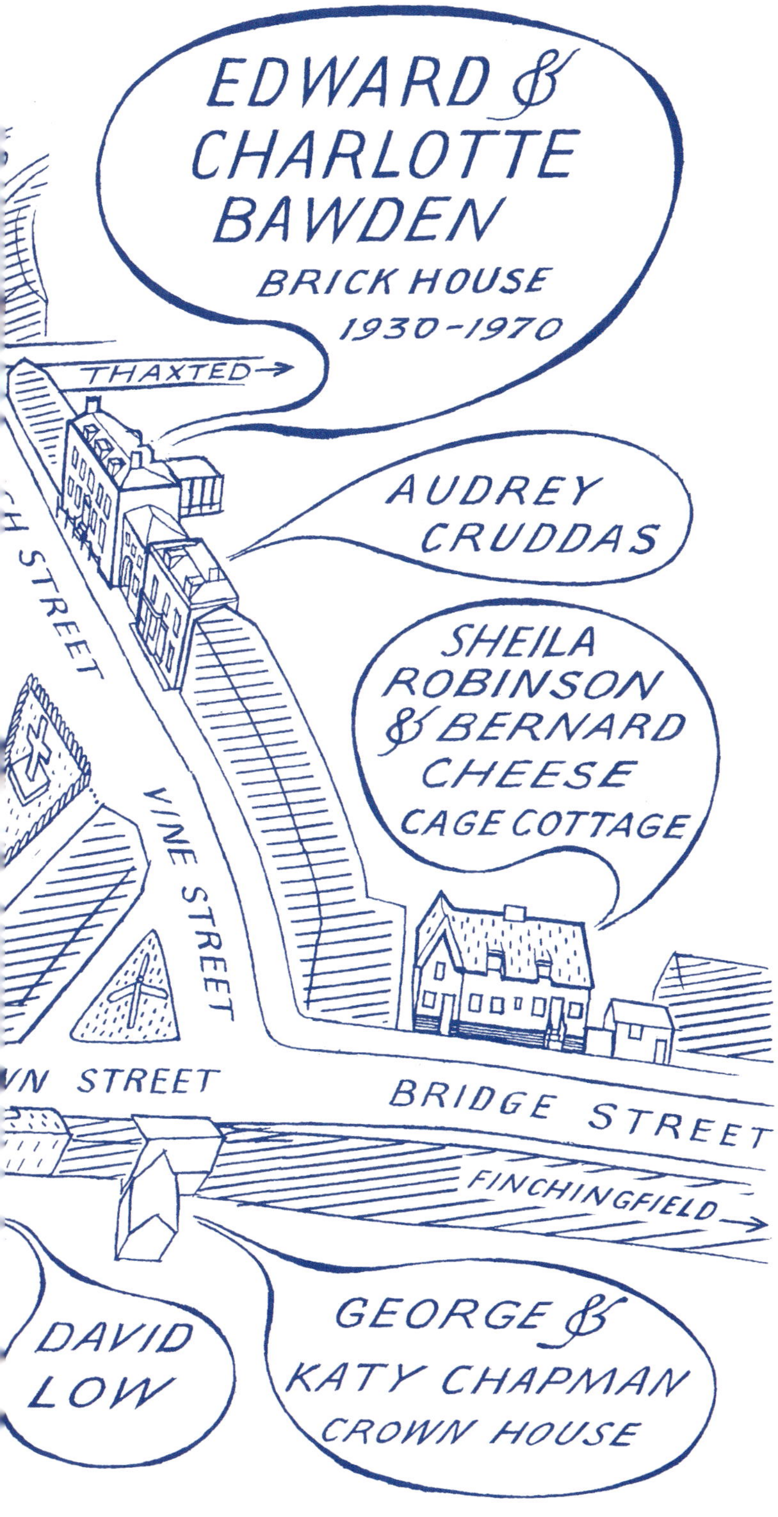

Great Bardfield map drawn by Richard Bawden. (2005).

jealous of a contemporary, especially one as talented as himself'. He was preoccupied with work to the exclusion of almost everything else, including people: 'he could be intimidating, also unkind and rude, but he could also be sympathetic, generous and supportive. This mixture of positive and opposite qualities could make one nervous.'

The two men enjoyed themselves painting, especially in the graveyard, and staying in the seedy Hotel Paradiso until Charlotte arrived when, as Bawden had predicted, she hated the food, the plumbing, the town and having to share a double bed with her husband. On the boat back to Italy Bawden had neglected to book her a berth and she had to sleep all night on deck under showers of soot from the funnel, and then on the mainland suffer the indignities of bed bugs and stomach upsets, all of which Bawden somehow avoided.

On their return to England Bawden helped Hoyle move into a near-derelict farm cottage previously used for raising chickens situated near Great Bardfield on Great Lodge Farm. Hoyle slowly refurbished it, had water and electricity brought in and learned to drive a car. Bawden indulged his own peculiar humour and exploited Hoyle's ignorance by giving him poisonous plants for his garden and giant hog-weeds which quickly grew twelve feet tall and nearly blocked the doorway, but he showed a sweeter side of his nature in the gift to his former student of a rare nineteenth century flower manual. So Hoyle became another valuable recruit to the growing community of artists in the village and he found an immediate rapport with another talented artist who had settled just before him: George Chapman.

Chapman (1908-1993), was a Londoner who was profoundly deaf and dyslexic from early childhood. He was educated in Scotland and Devon and from 1924 to 1928 attended Gravesend School of Art to train as a commercial designer; then from 1928 to 1930 he worked two days a week for Jack Beddington, the man responsible for the Shell-Mex posters which Bawden had helped make famous. Chapman occasionally did graphic work for London Transport and whilst working in London he

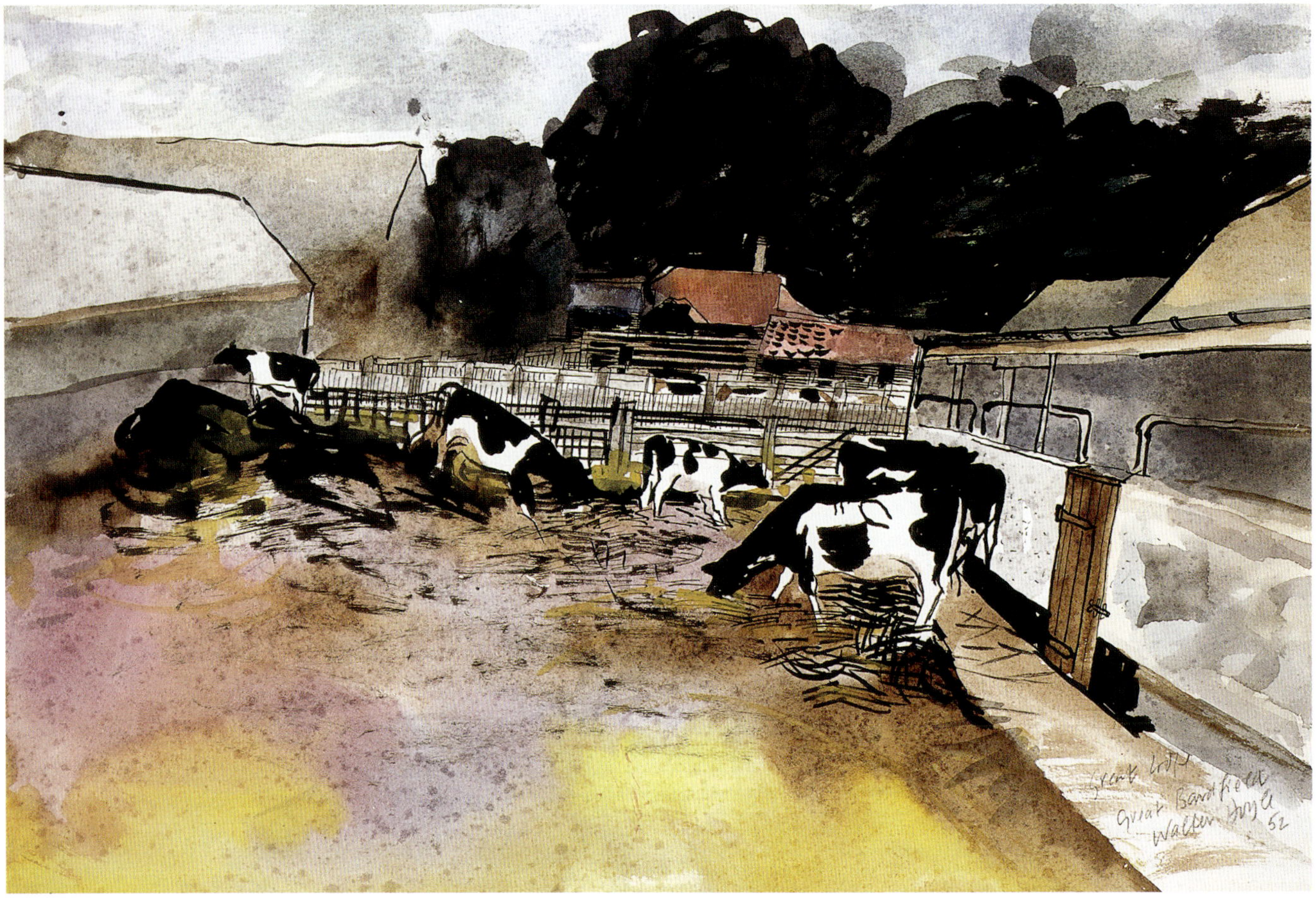

Walter Hoyle, *Great Lodge Farm, Great Bardfield*, 1953, watercolour and gouache, 386 x 540 mm (Fry Art Gallery).

came to know Sutherland, John Nash, Piper, Freedman and Betjeman.

Inspired by these contacts he saved enough money to pay his way through a Fine Art course at the Slade, but after one year was persuaded by Barnett Freedman to transfer to the RCA to study painting under himself and Gilbert Spencer. Chapman, having been a trained graphic designer, told Freedman that he made a distinction between commercial art and the kind of things he was now painting at the RCA. 'What do you mean by commercial art? There is only good art and bad art' roared Freedman, true to the college ethos in which he and Bawden were trained.

Chapman married May Codlin, a designer, in 1938 and a son was born in the year war broke out, but his deafness meant he could serve neither as a soldier nor a war artist and he became Assistant Head at Worcester School of Art. In 1943 his wife left him and their son, but in 1947 he married Kate Ablett, eighteen years his junior who had been trained at Norwich School of Art. She was glamorous and lively, with a talent for painted and collaged still-lifes. He continued to work in advertising in London and even set up his own firm with a partner, though his heart was still set on painting full-time. In 1948 he moved to the cheap but picturesquely derelict Vine Cottage in Great Bardfield which had a big garden and room for a studio. Fortunately Chapman loved doing up ruined properties and accepted the challenge; mean-

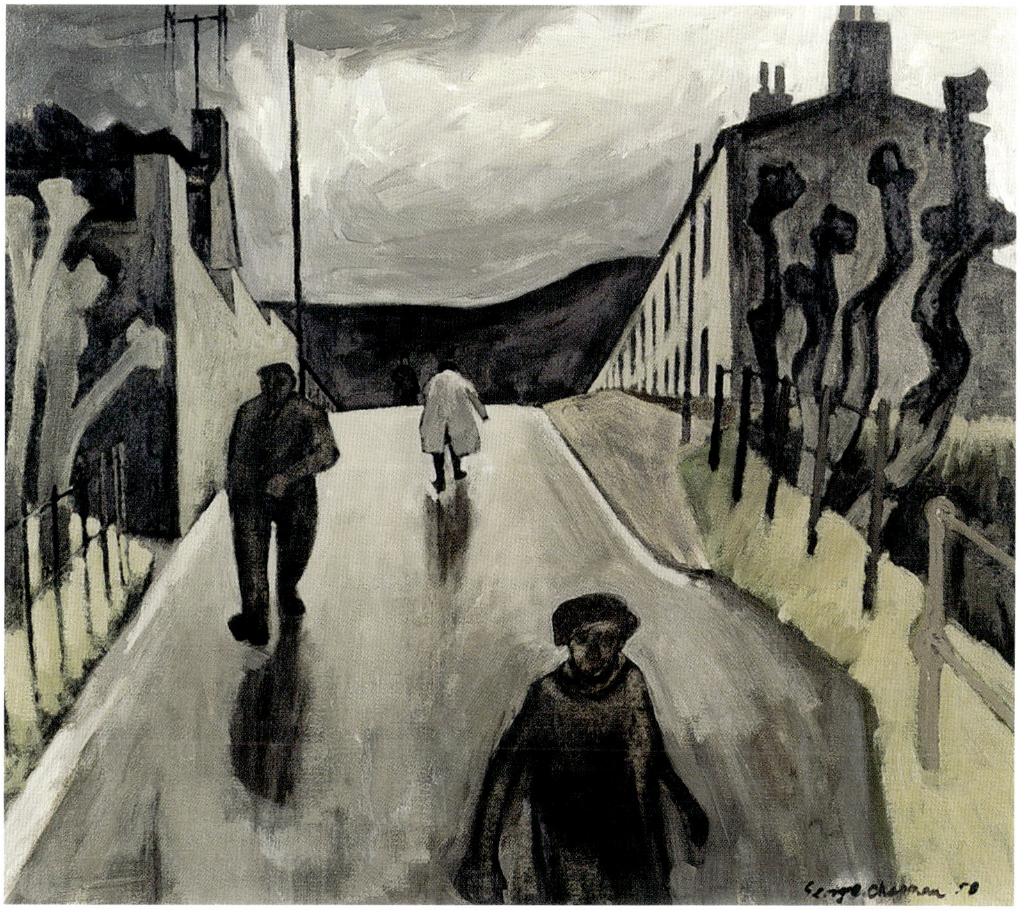

George Chapman, *A Steep Road*, 1958, oil on canvas, 555 x 615 mm (Fry Art Gallery).

while the couple lived in a caravan until it was ready. Soon after the Chapmans arrived Bawden cycled over and invited them to tea and through him they met the Rothensteins and Aldridges and quickly became part of the artistic grouping in the village. 'I have never regretted it', he wrote, 'as I have found tremendous help from the three artists who were already in the village before me'.

As a painter Chapman took some time to find his own language, swerving between Rouault and Soutine-like expressionism and Euston Road realism. He also had a period when he painted agricultural machinery in a simplified, heavily outlined manner reminiscent of Robert Colquhoun and Robert MacBryde, two wildly bohemian painters who had moved into nearby Tilty Mill in 1950. Then in 1952 Chapman made his first etchings under Michael Rothenstein's guidance, the earliest ones being nudes of his pregnant wife Kate – which was certainly not a subject any Great Bardfield artist had tried before. From the start his etchings were heavily worked and aquatinted and many of them were drawn on the spot, the plate being held on a board hanging from his shoulders. One day he set off in his Italian Lancia tourer on his first visit to Wales and made many sketches and notes of the Pennant area near Cardigan, working them up into oil paintings and etchings back in Essex.

Soon Chapman sold his share of the advertising agency and commuted from the village to teach part-time at the London College of Printing and Graphic Arts, the

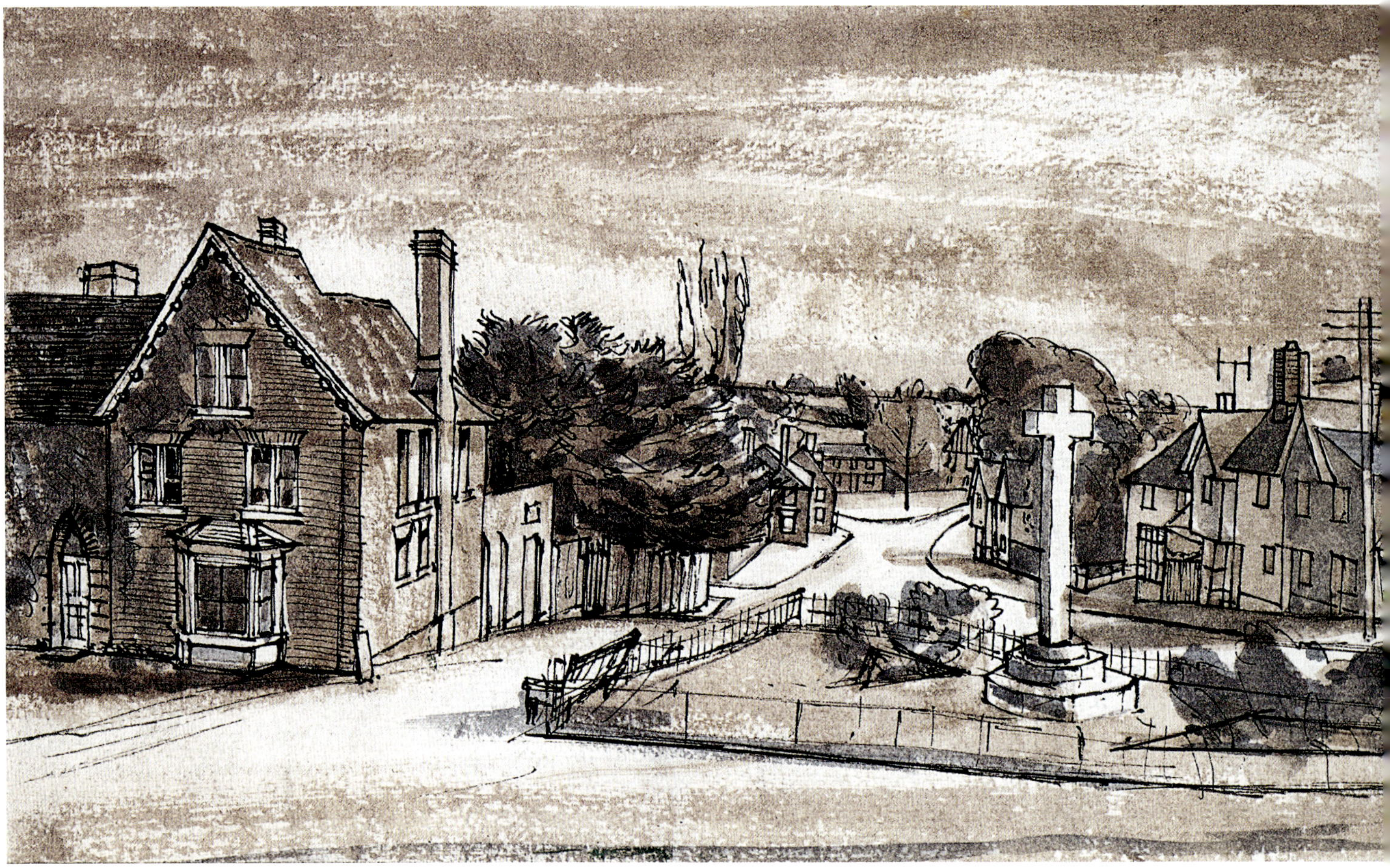

John Aldridge: *Panorama of Great Bardfield*, 1951, pen and ink and watercolour, 180 x 600 mm (Fry Art Gallery).

Central School of Art and Design, and Colchester School of Art where he was befriended by John Nash. The art schools had expanded tremendously after the war and such teaching posts were to be had in plenty.

Finally, at the age of 45, he discovered the Rhondda: 'I got a fantastic shock. I realised that here I could find the material that would perhaps make me a painter at last' and indeed it did for the next forty years. This was his 'Valley of Vision', though it could not be more different from Palmer's at Shoreham. From this time on he was only an Essex painter in the sense that he lived in the county, working in the midst of its lush greenery to depict grey industrial Wales. As an atheist and ex-communist Chapman was more in tune with the realism of Euston Road, earlier Sickert, or Josef Herman than he was with the war-time Neo-Romanticism, or the post-war pastoralism of the other village artists. He first rented, then bought for £100, a cottage in Rhondda (ruined of course), where several of the Bardfield artist families visited him and the Rothensteins bought another cottage nearby. Then in 1955 he sold Vine Cottage in Great Bardfield and moved to Crown House, the old saddler's on the High Street, where he lived and worked up his Welsh sketches into etchings or paintings (he built a studio for each activity) until he left first for Norfolk, and then permanently for Wales in 1964. His mission was to

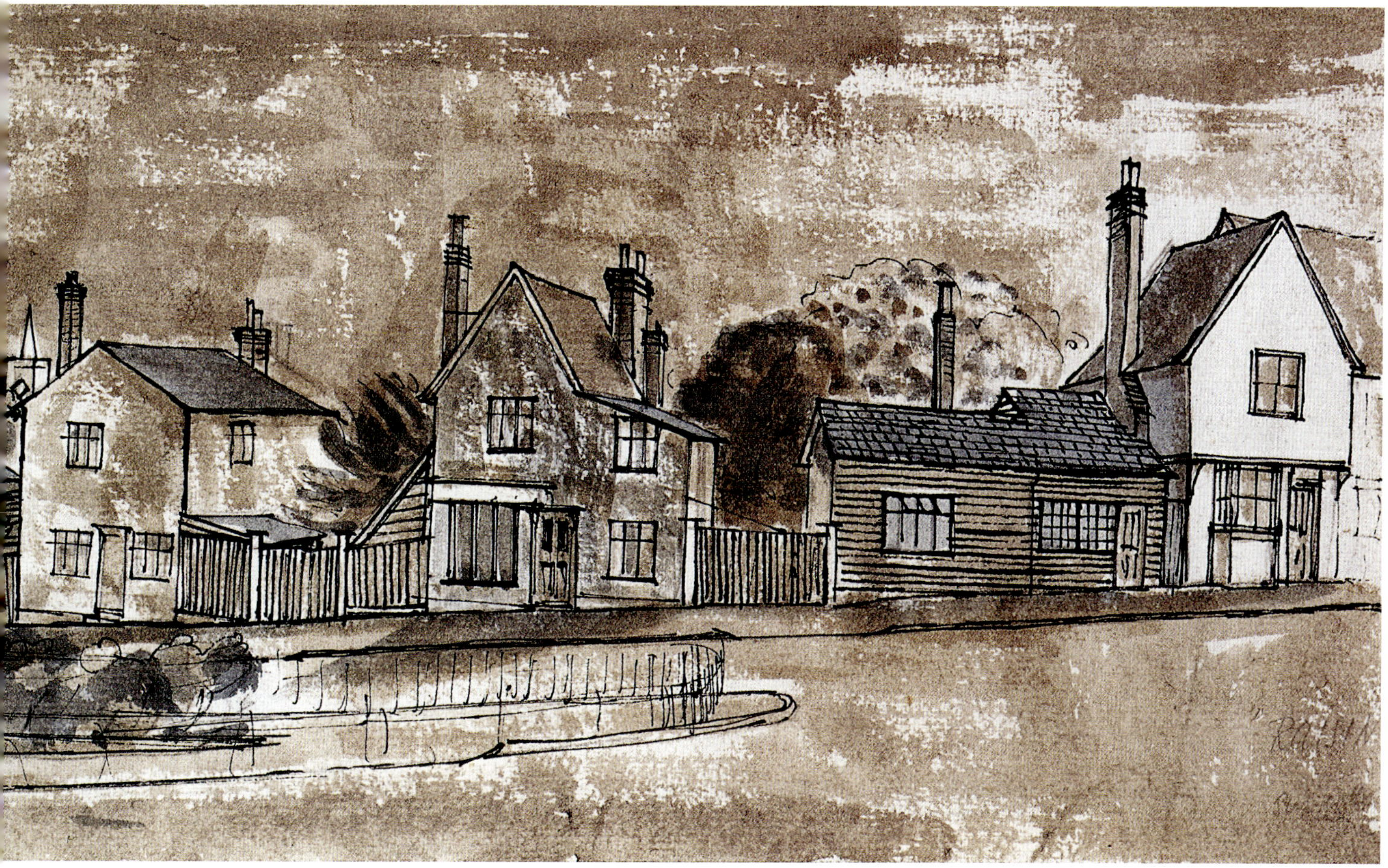

'paint a sort of visual novel of the mining valley concentrating entirely on the life that is going on there and describing everything the people are doing'. His *Rhondda Suite* etchings of 1960 are a world away from Ravilious' *High Street* and Bawden's *Life in an English Village*.

In the years that followed, Chapman's kind of tough working-class subject matter fell out of fashion as Pop Art and Abstraction took over the galleries and he stopped painting for eleven years, only getting his confidence back around 1984 when he took up his Rhondda themes once more, though by now the mining community he had painted was changed beyond recall and his earlier works of pit heads, regimented terrace houses, car-free streets and pit heaps had become historical records. Great Bardfield had changed too, of course, but not in such a dramatic way, for apart from a few more cars and television aerials, it still looked like an idyllic village.

One change was that the population of artists in the village had suddenly increased. They were attracted by the cheap housing and improved transport links to London where most of them taught and exhibited. It was also pleasant to live in a community of like-minded people who talked your kind of 'shop'. At the centre of it all was Edward Bawden, still socially inept but undoubtedly the doyen. Two incomers who were Bawden admirers were his

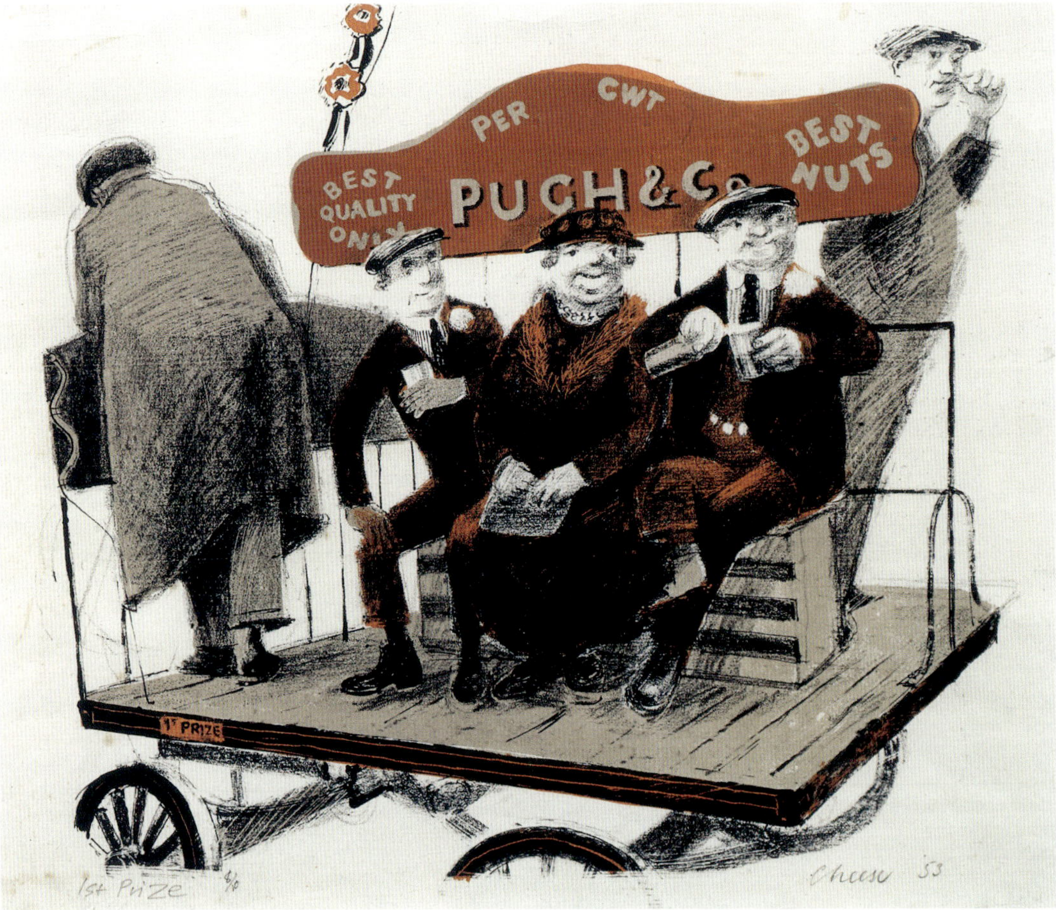

Bernard Cheese, *First Prize*, 1953, lithograph, 325 x 377 mm (Fry Art Gallery).

former students at the RCA in the late 1940s, Bernard Cheese (b.1925) and his wife Sheila Robinson (1925-1987). They moved to Bardfield End Green near Thaxted in 1953 and Bernard rented the Bardfield fish and chip shop as a studio. Cheese was a gifted watercolourist and printmaker with a quirky sense of humour rather like Bawden's own, who had also worked on the Festival South Bank site making a kaleidoscope for the Shot Tower, which was subsequently demolished like so much else. At this time he taught with Hoyle at St Martin's School of Art in London but later Bawden recommended him to Horton at Ruskin College as 'a most skilful lithographer, a good artist as well as a skilled technician'. Sheila was an illustrator, perhaps best known now for her *Sons and Lovers* (New York, Limited Editions Club, 1975), a printmaker who used cardboard cuts rather than lino or wood to achieve the most delicate effects, and a watercolourist very much in the style of Bawden. She was also a poster artist for London Transport, a designer of stamps and responsible for the Schweppes advertisements. Once settled in, both Cheeses took the Essex countryside as subject matter for their paintings.

Sheila had helped Bawden with his Festival mural and she continued to help him, often printing his illustrations on the ancient Albion Press he had bought for £10 just after the war ended, or on the RCA lithography presses. One such task was in 1952 when she printed his *Take The Broom*, a story he had written for his children during the war about

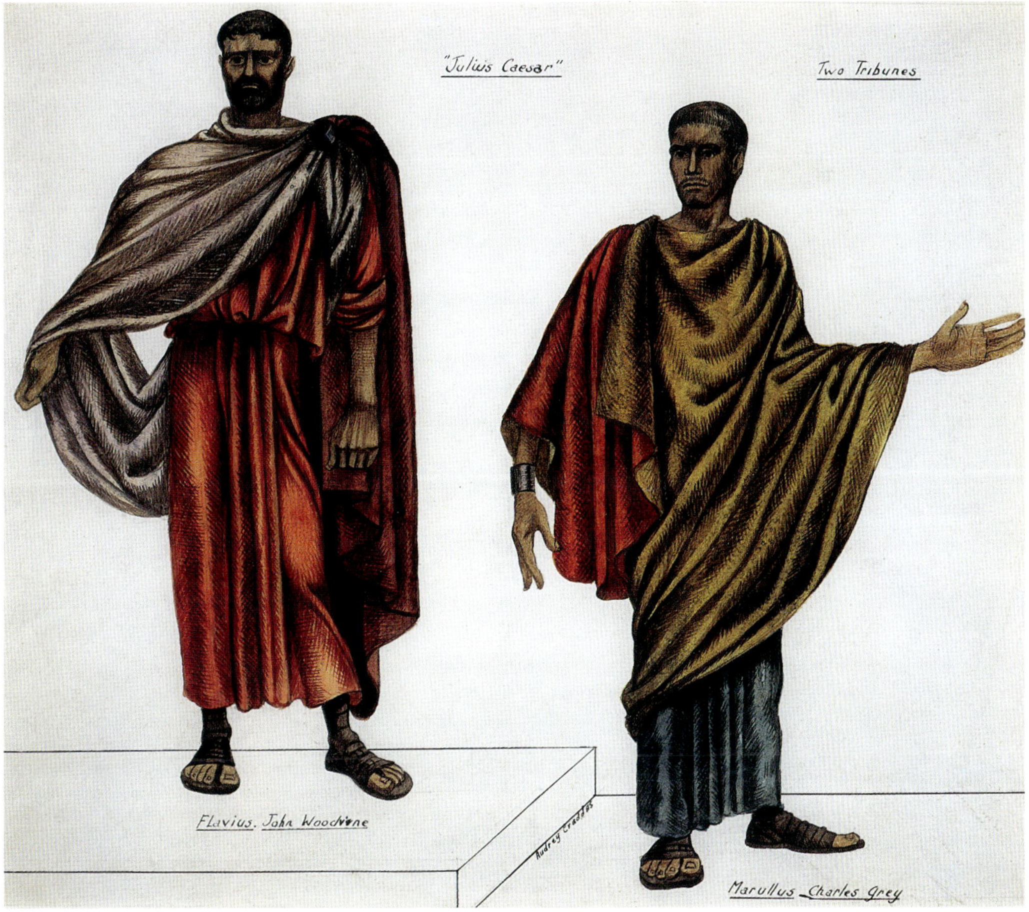

Audrey Cruddas, *Julius Caesar, Two Tribunes*, 1962, watercolour, 350 x 390 mm (Fry Art Gallery).

an ant family. He wrote to Sheila giving her total freedom to choose the colours and also the following observation: 'I watched an ant die a perfectly natural death one day this summer. Suddenly it staggered, rolled over and twitched a little and then lay still. It was all over in a minute yet the body became covered in dust – yet, as you know, ants don't normally pick up any.' Underneath he was still the inquisitive 'brat with a microscope' he had been at seven.

The Cheeses had two children and one of them, Chloë, would eventually achieve fame as a print-maker herself, not surprisingly since she wandered in and out of her parents' studios and Bawden's and grew up thinking printing was the most natural activity there was. Unfortunately the Cheeses' marriage did not last but the Bawdens and most of the village took Sheila's side in this and welcomed her subsequent move into Cage Cottage near the centre of Great Bardfield, next to the old lock-up. Her children first attended the village primary school, and later went on to the Friends' School at Saffron Walden.

Directly joining on to Brick House is Walton House, formerly the police station and into this moved Audrey Cruddas (1912-1979) in 1950. She and Bawden established a bantering friendship from the start. Cruddas was a South African who had come to England to study at the Royal Academy School and went on to work in the Women's Land Army during the war until she was invalided out. She then took up stage and costume design and was soon employed by The Old Vic, Covent Garden,

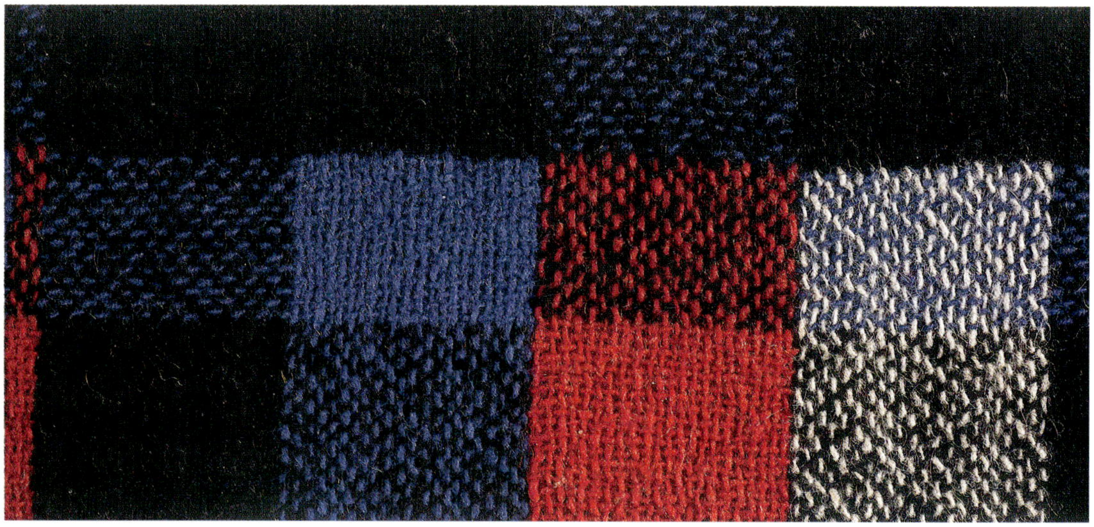

Marianne Straub, textile design, 11 x 20 cm (Fry Art Gallery).

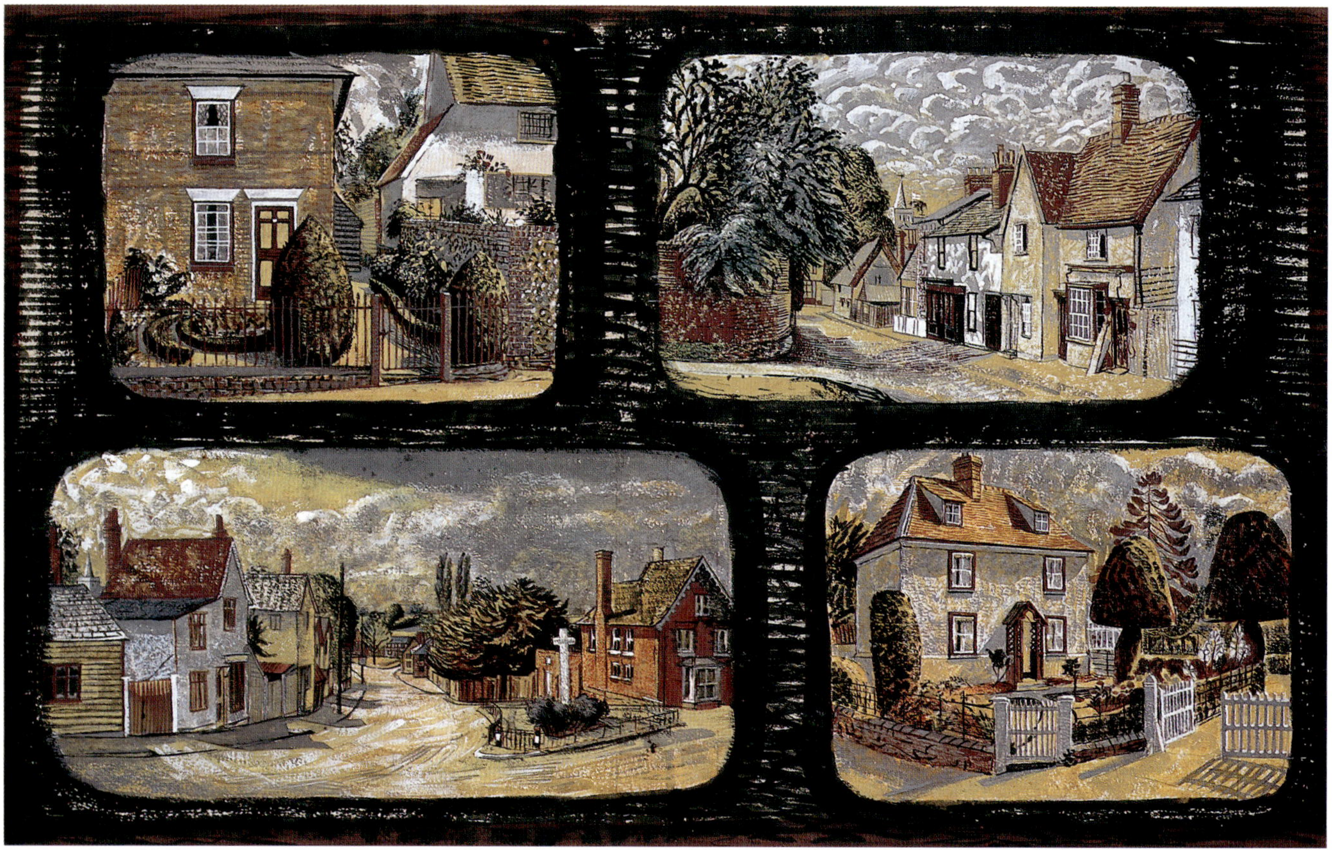

John Aldridge: Great Bardfield scenes, pen and ink and watercolour, *c.*1955, 440 x 700 mm (Fry Art Gallery).

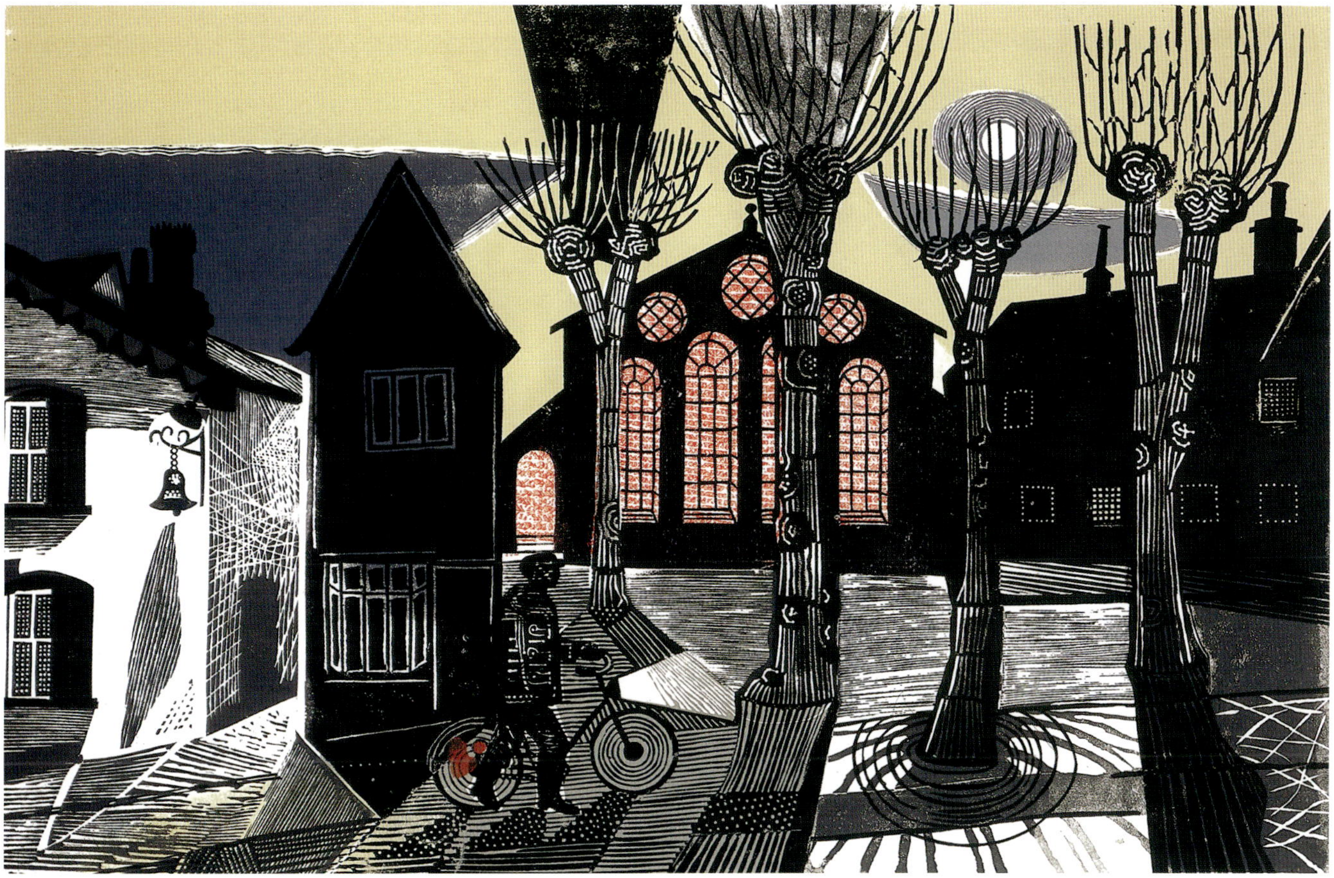

Town Hall Yard (Great Bardfield), 1956, linocut, 405 x 612 mm
(Trustees of Cecil Higgins Art Gallery, Bedford).

The Royal Shakespeare Company, York Mystery Plays and numerous west-end theatres. As a competent water-colourist she exhibited regularly in the London galleries. She and her partner, Mary Chesildine also opened the village tea shop.

Another creative woman who arrived soon after was the weaver and textile designer Marianne Straub (1909-1994) who had connections across the whole art and craft community. A childhood illness had left her lame, but she had a forceful personality and was soon involved with the community's artistic and social affairs. She had learned weaving as a child in Switzerland but came to England to study it professionally at college before working as a designer in the Welsh woollen mills during the 1930s and later for the company Helios in Manchester. In 1950 she began designing for Warner and Sons in Braintree, where at a later time Bawden's daughter Joanna worked for her. Bawden himself tipped off Straub that Trinity Cottage, opposite Brick House and next to the Rothensteins, was for sale and she settled there in 1953, bringing a huge loom with her. It was an incongruous abode for a designer with an international clientele but she was frequently away from the village on her travels abroad. Like so many of her neighbours she had RCA connections, teaching part-time there, and she was a friend of Douglas Percy Bliss, being an external examiner for his Glasgow College of Art. The potters Lucie Rie and Hans Coper were close acquaintances and she soon found common ground with

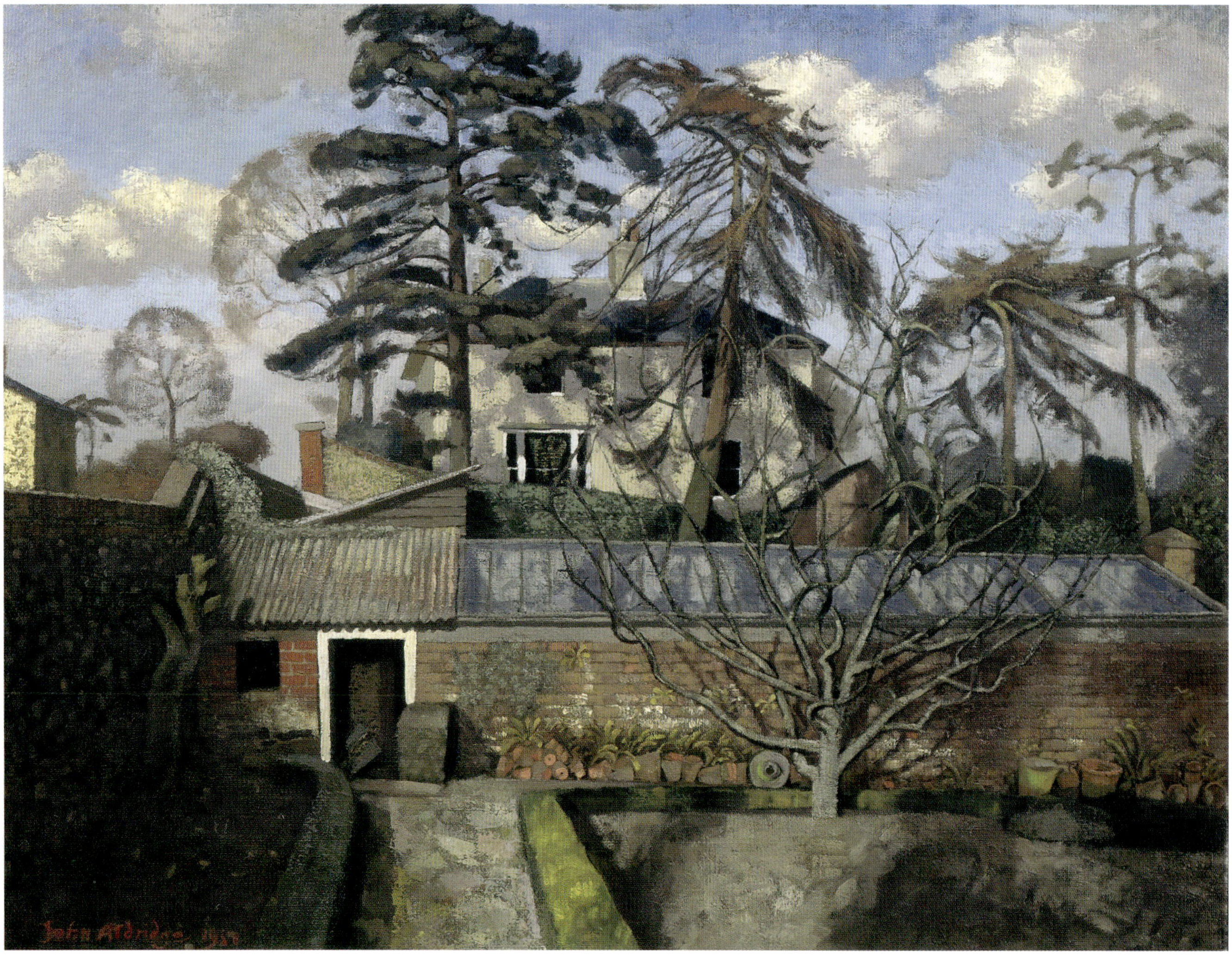

John Aldridge, *February Afternoon, Place House Garden, Great Bardfield*, 1958, oil, 765 x 920 mm (Fry Art Gallery).

Sheila Robinson, the Bawdens, Chapmans, and Walter Hoyle for whose cottage she made the curtains.

The next painter to settle in the village had a modest talent but a big personality. Stanley Clifford-Smith (1906-1968) had begun to read medicine, had spent the war in the RNVR, and then switched to freelance designing before he rented Buck House, a sprawling Victorian pile on the High Street with his wife, the designer Joan Glass. Later he moved across the road to The Old Bakery, two doors away from the Rothensteins. There he settled down to teach himself to become a professional painter, growing a beard and affecting a more bohemian manner than those artists who arrived before him. He took inspiration from Rouault and painted with a palette knife, using oils mixed with plaster or sand to create moonscapes or overly sweet madonna and child figures, the landscape around him having no input to his imagery. Smith had energy and it was probably he who suggested that the village artists combine and follow up the open day of the 1951 Festival with another to show their wares.

The first of these Bardfield open-house exhibitions took place July 8th to 17th 1955, houses and studios being open from 11 a.m. to 7 p.m. Maps were printed for motorists, and buses hired to collect London and Cambridge visitors from the station at Bishop's Stortford. Aldridge, Bawden, Rothenstein, Smith, Straub and Cruddas opened their doors and since Hoyle lived a little outside the village his work was hung in Brick House, while Chapman showed his in the Rothensteins' house. David Low, the famous political cartoonist had bought Sergeant Bendlowe's Cottage in Brook Street and he showed some of his *Modern Rake's Progress* drawings in Smith's house. Further textiles and prints were displayed at nearby Park Hall, home of the Crittall family where tea in the grounds was available. Ariel Crittall (b.1914) was herself a painter who studied in Munich and at St Martin's and the Slade and, co-incidentally, her husband's family firm made metal windows and had once owned the ironmongery shop in Braintree where Bawden's father was manager.

The artists made available to visitors a signed communal statement: 'The various personalities are too obviously different to suggest a common viewpoint and, beyond an active liking for Bardfield no body of shared convictions is in question.'

The artists put away their valuables, hung their works all round their houses and sat back to see what would

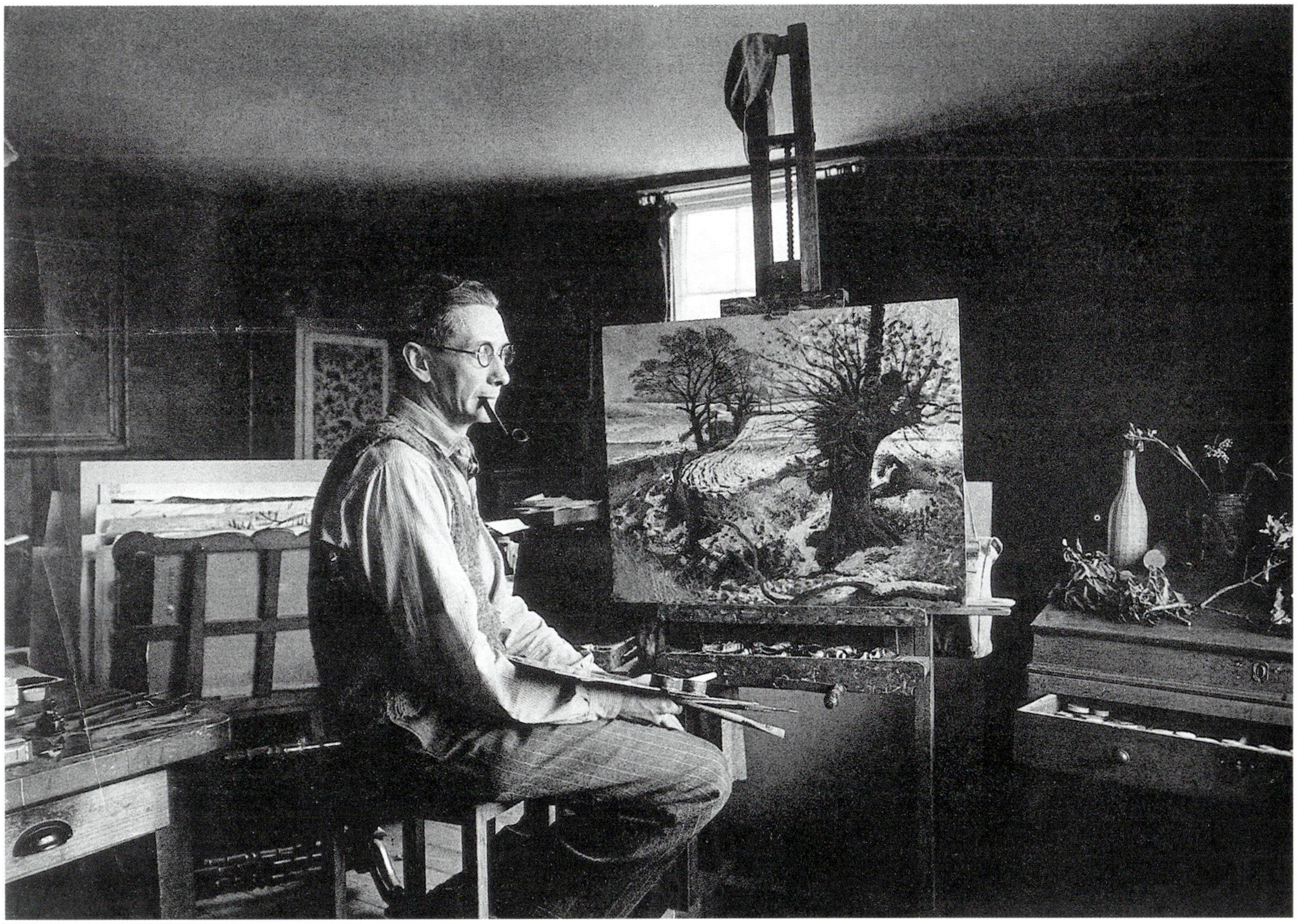

John Aldridge in his studio, *c.*1960 (Fry Art Gallery).

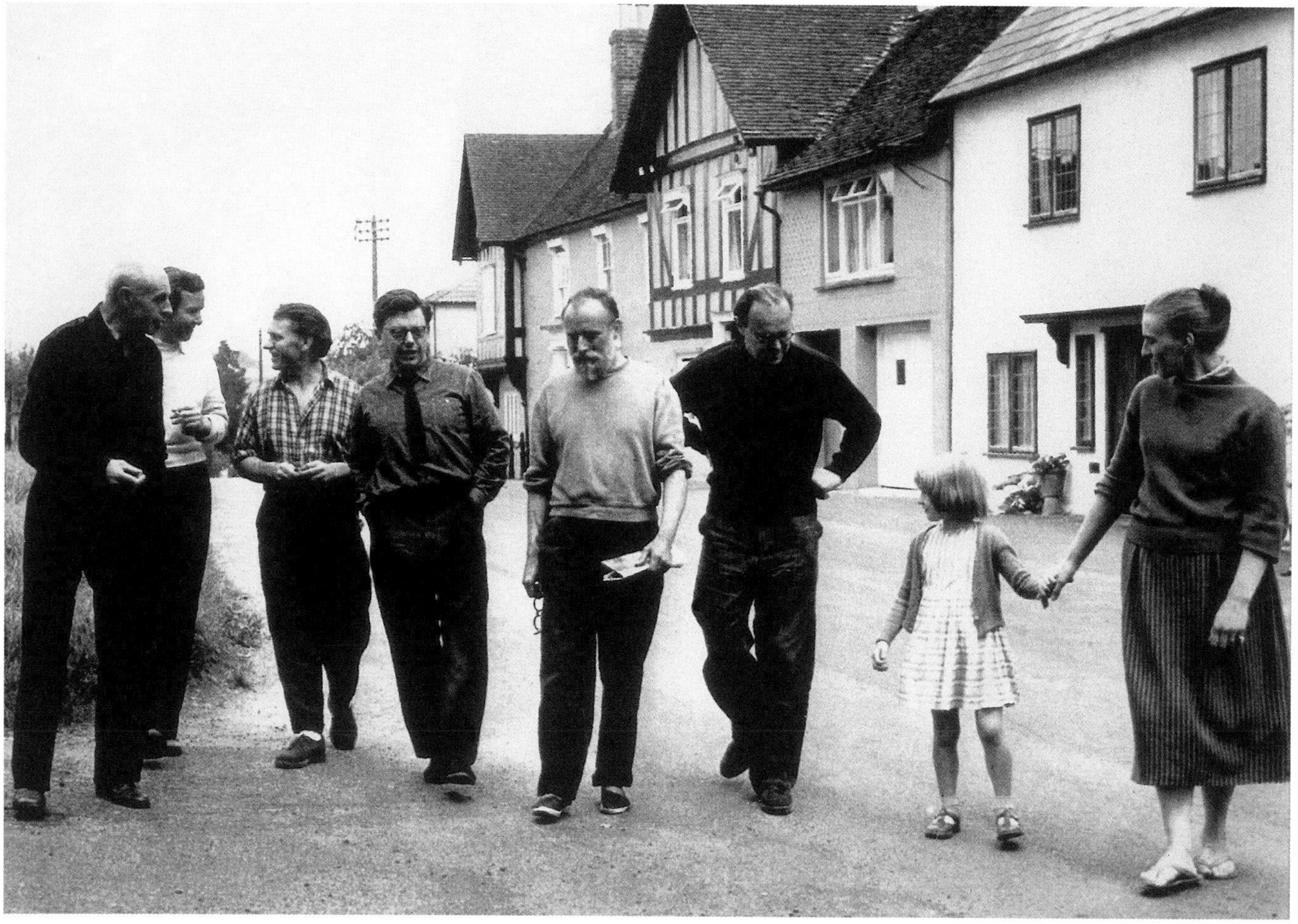

Bawden (left) walks in Great Bardfield with fellow artists Walter Hoyle, George Chapman, Laurence Scarfe (art editor of *The Saturday Book*, visiting for the day), Stanley Clifford-Smith, Michael Rothenstein, and Chloë Cheese with her mother Sheila Robinson, 1956 (Fry Art Gallery).

happen. To their astonishment they were overwhelmed by ten thousand visitors in the nine days. The locals came again for another pry round, but this time so did some of the national press. The *Daily Telegraph* reporter ignored the art but was agog at the interior decoration in this 'remote and possibly unheard of place'. She found all the old brown beams and panels had been painted white, walls had giant patterned wallpapers, cupboards were painted and not hidden, strong colours were everywhere; there was a pink checked ceiling, blue garden doors, a yellow stair carpet with blue balustrade and Straub's thatched cottage walls were almond green!

Other visitors spotted that, with the exception of Aldridge who confined himself to oil painting and gardening, the artists were not ivory-tower dwellers but put their many talents at the service of the wider community; they designed fabrics, furniture, posters, wallpapers, decorated ceramics, and made various kinds of prints which were the cheapest form of original art. Rothenstein, for example, was currently at work on a

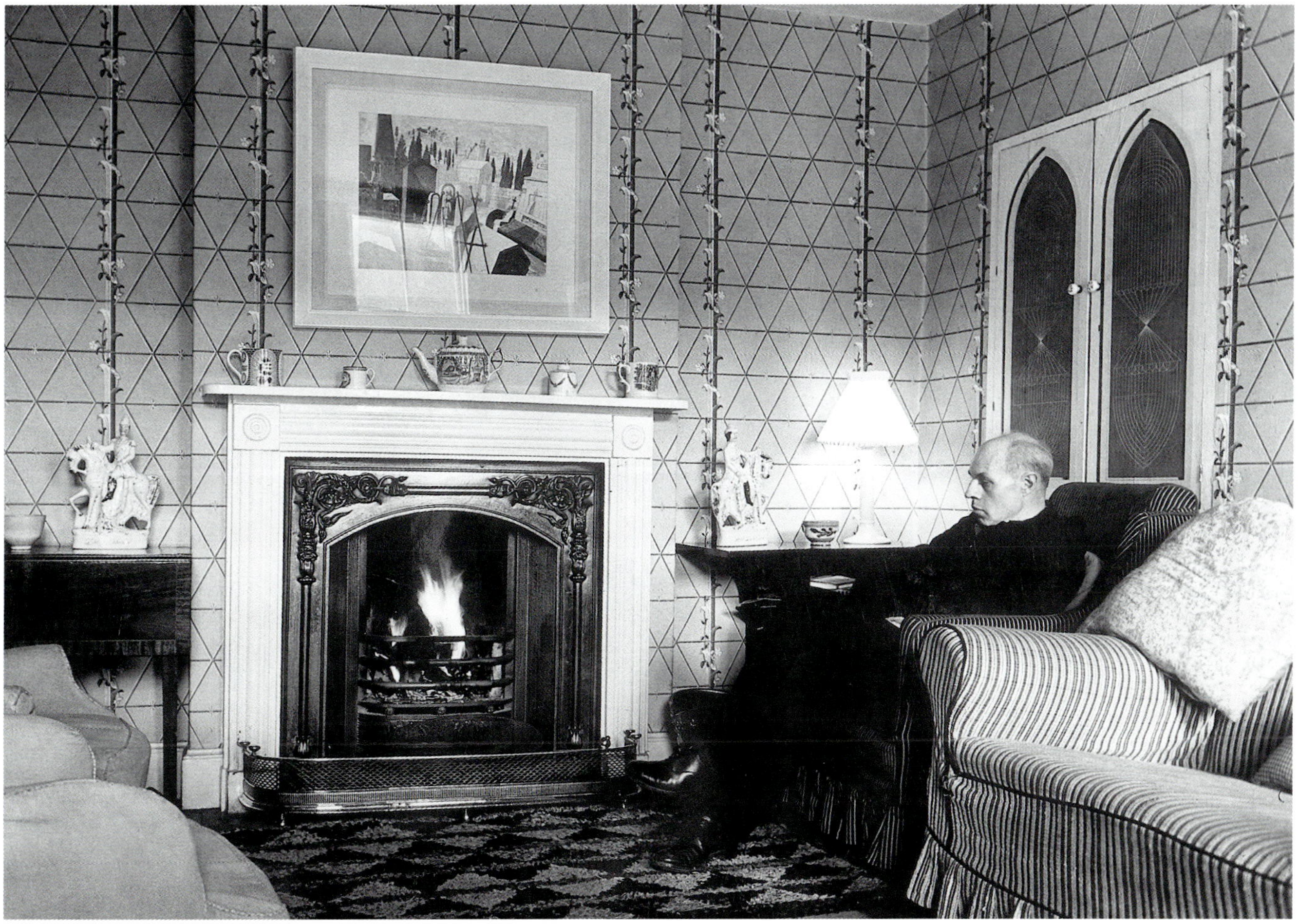

Bawden sitting in the living room at Brick House, *c.*1960: the room is papered with his *Periwinkle* wallpaper, and one of his Sicilian paintings hangs above the fireplace. The cupboard had been painted by him in about 1948, and the rug was made by Lucie Aldridge; a pot made by Lucie Rie is on the left hand side of the table by the fireplace and material by Marianne Straub covers the sofa. (Trustees of Cecil Higgins Art Gallery, Bedford).

sixty-foot long mural in a school using laminated prints on paper.

The exhibition was a financial success, and there were no agents' or gallery fees to pay. There was a further bonus for Walter Hoyle: he met his future wife, Denise Colombo (b.1935). She was the French au pair to one of Rothenstein's lady friends in London, visiting the village at his invitation and whilst she was viewing Hoyle's works in Brick House the two came together and by 1957 were married. Denise had studied painting and pottery at the Grande Chaumiere in Paris, though like the other wives she seemed to neglect her talents somewhat once she moved to Great Bardfield. Hoyle gave up his spartan bachelor cottage and the couple moved into Rosemary Cottage in Great Saling, three miles down the road, where they stayed until 1974. He commuted to teach at the Central and St Martin's Schools of Art until 1964 and then he moved to Cambridge School of Art for the rest of his career.

Open days were held again in 1957 and 1958 when

Bawden claimed 9,000 visitors tramped through Brick House in just one hot day. Charlotte was furious because they brought tar in on their shoes and ruined her carpets. In 1958 work worth £5,000 was sold. In addition to the previous exhibitors there were Sheila Robinson (Bernard Cheese had already left), and Peter White who showed his paintings of Jamaica in Rothenstein's house. White had trained at Wimbledon and the Stained Glass Department at the RCA but was employed by Rothenstein as a printing assistant, and when work was slack there he crossed the road to help Bawden. Chapman advised White: 'Don't stand any nonsense from Edward. Tease him.' White soon detected a growing rivalry between Bawden and Rothenstein. Another exhibitor, a guest artist from outside the village, was Laurence Scarfe (1914-1993) yet another RCA graduate who had worked alongside Bawden on the Festival site and on murals for liners.

Douglas Percy Bliss must have been one of the visitors because he reported in *The Scotsman* that Bawden 'had painted Essex churches, quarries and farms. All of them have a bold integrity. There is not a heart-throb of subtlety in them. Stone by stone, brick by brick they stand in their stark innocence.' (21st July 1958). *Tatler* called Great Bardfield 'The Montmartre Village' and the *Daily Herald* reporter, disappointed to find no trace of wild parties, drunkenness and tax-evasion, solicited the locals' opinions. 'I'm not saying anything against them, but they're not local people', said the postman; the butcher's wife thought her own house 'just as artistic as any of theirs', while a shopkeeper admitted grudgingly: 'At least they pay their bills regular.' 'We like Mr Aldridge's paintings and Mr Bawden's. We can understand them' said the landlord of the White Hart pub, Albert Clapson, 'but, lor, I'll tell you about Mr Rothenstein. He wanted to paint my chickens one day. So he did. And I looked at it. And I didn't say nothing, but I thought: "If them's my prize layers, I'm a Buff Orpington".' (9th July 1958).

Michael Rothenstein, an articulate, sophisticated, Jewish urbanite puzzled the villagers most of all, especially after he told reporters 'I hate country life as such' and that he was only there to escape the distractions of London. He was indignant that one of them had asked his wife Duffy, ' "Don't you get fed up with having your husband lounge around all day?" Lounge around indeed! I often work fourteen hours a day.'

After the 1957 show the artists sent their collected works on tour to eight venues around the country, as far apart as Northern Ireland, Gateshead and Eastbourne. In May 1959 the same village artists (Aldridge, Bawden, Chapman, Cruddas, Hoyle, Rothenstein, Robinson and Smith) called themselves The Great Bardfield Artists' Association and sent an exhibition to The Royal West of England Academy in Bristol. Rothenstein wrote in the catalogue: 'Arriving in the village from time to time, with no particular ideas held in common, there is an active antipathy among the painters that anything like a Great Bardfield School should be in question, as a glance round the walls will attest.'

By this time Rothenstein saw himself as more 'advanced' than the others, a player in an international arena rather than in a rural backwater. In 1957 he had briefly visited Atelier 17, the Paris studio of Stanley William Hayter (1901-1988), the most innovative printmaker in Europe, and returned an inspired man worshipping new gods. 'He [Hayter] ran such a remarkable operation! . . . it was all happening against the great backdrop of what Picasso was doing, and what Braque and Matisse were doing – to me it was an absolute revelation. He opened a doorway to a large and well-horizoned place of glittering vitality. For me it came at exactly the right moment and enabled me to turn my back from the constraints of in-turned provincial life . . . .' [4]

Initially Bawden had encouraged Rothenstein to make linocuts because they were cheaper than paintings and so more easily sold, but soon Rothenstein was printing from any surface which would take ink, often from metal, plastic, fabric, or weathered wood rescued from rubbish tips. On one occasion, to Bawden's scorn, he had a friend drive his Rolls Royce over a print to add pressure and texture. All this took place directly opposite and below Bawden's attic studio in Brick House and one suspects he

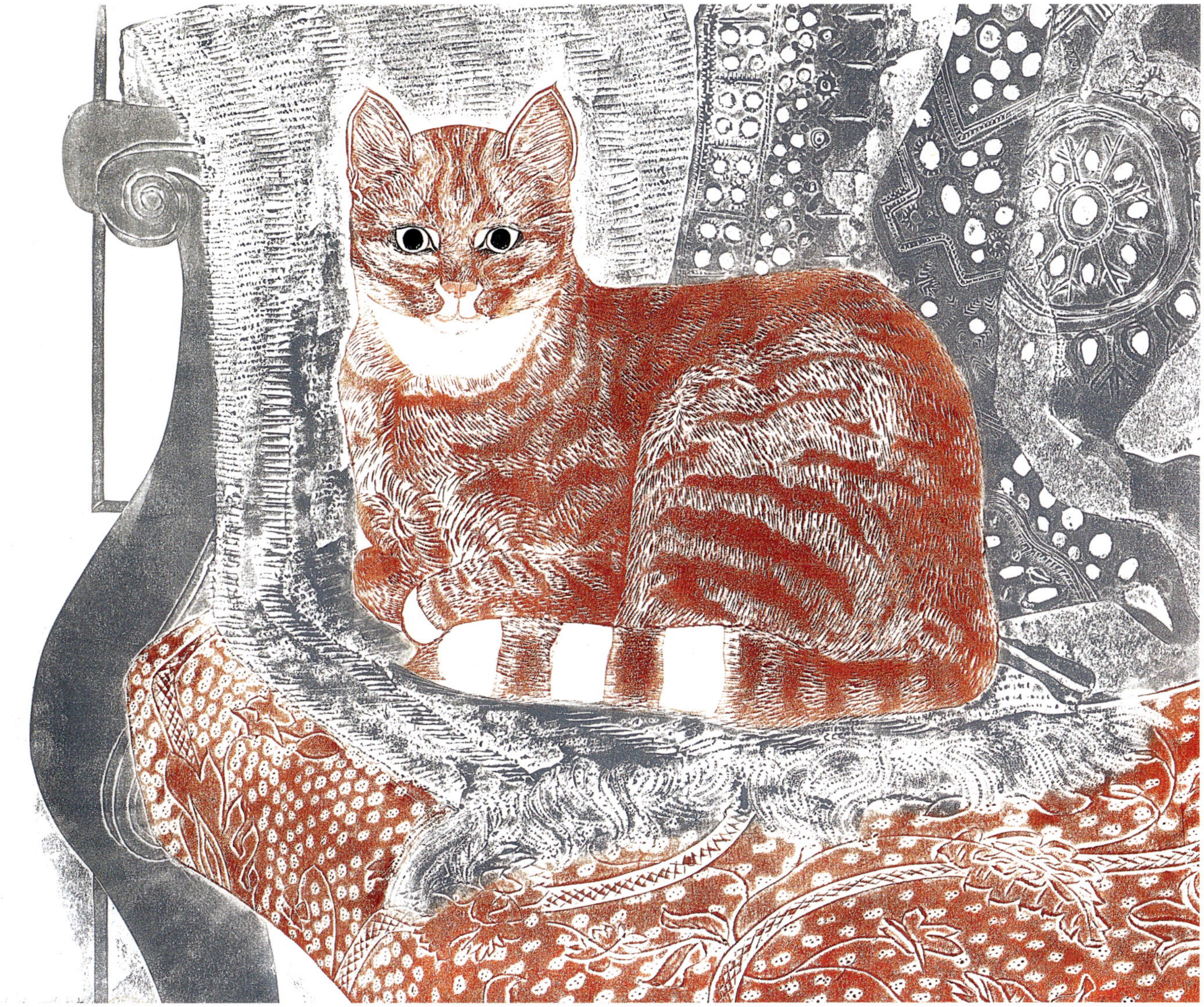

Sheila Robinson, *Cat on Chair*, 1971, cardboard cut, 460 x 490 mm (Fry Art Gallery).

was irritated by it, especially when Rothenstein began to win prizes in 1954 and 1956 for his linocuts, and then went on to write books about how to make prints. Rothenstein had offered to swap one of his father's drawings for a lino print and then exchange one of his own experimental prints for one of Bawden's and Bawden had turned down both offers, a terrible rebuff to a proud and sensitive man. The two men were beginning to get on each other's nerves. Rothenstein's disclaimer about there being no School of Great Bardfield could be seen, therefore, as an attempt to disassociate himself from the older and more famous Bawden who seemed to be peopling the village with his admirers.

Despite Rothenstein's claim the question remains: can we still talk about a School of Great Bardfield artists? Certainly there was never a manifesto, and if there were any common beliefs they were held tacitly rather than forged in open discussion, but perhaps a few generalisations are possible. Central to the majority of the Bardfield artists' concerns was the depiction of the English rural landscape – a statement which immediately excludes Straub, Cruddas, Smith, and the Welsh-fixated George Chapman, formidable painter though he was. The rest saw themselves as within a native landscape tradition stretching from the 18th and through the 19th century to Paul Nash, but they were technically innovative and sought to say new things about old subjects, extending the tradition rather than remaining complacently inside it. They were committed to depicting nature in a well-drawn, figurative, but not slavishly realistic, manner. Rothenstein had begun in this mode but later deliberately drew away and followed other paths which led him towards abstraction, as did Rowntree in his later years.

John Aldridge was a fine academic landscape painter mainly in oils which seemed to set him slightly aside from his neighbours whose most characteristic works are in watercolour or print media. Watercolours are, of necessity, small scale but they can be painted outdoors in front of the motif and this seems to have been common practice around the village. A tendency to combine subdued colours, dryish brushwork, firm design and defining line can be detected in the works of Bawden, Cheese, Robinson and Hoyle. That we should find common elements in the outputs of these four is perhaps not surprising, since we have one influential teacher and three of his students. They also shared a William Morris and RCA-fostered belief in being able to tackle any medium and in deliberately blurring the distinction between design work and fine art, or indeed between art and life. Working to commission was not seen as demeaning, but as a challenge to provide something well crafted and useful. This group were neither naïve nor political, they were modern but not stridently so, and serious but not solemn. They made no pretensions to being a rival centre to St Ives, where under the leadership of Nicholson and Hepworth artists continued the pre-war experimentation with abstraction. Carel Weight's comment on Bawden: 'I know of no other artist so uninfluenced by other artists or by current art fashion whose work sits so comfortably in the modern scene', could also apply to this group round him.

From the 1950s to the 1970s British art was buffeted by many whirlwind fashions – in no particular order: Pop Art, Op Art, Social Realism, Kinetic Art, Conceptual Art, Minimalism, Land Art, Body Art, Process Art, Kinetic Art, Cybernetic Art, Assemblage, Neo-Dada, Super-Realism, Language Art, Video Art, Neo-Expressionism and Post Modernism, and sweeping in from the Atlantic, a cyclone of Abstract Expressionism, all of them hostile to oil, watercolour, lithographic or linocut depictions of Essex churches, village gardens or London monuments. Donald Judd spoke for many in these decades when he pronounced: 'if someone calls it art it's art'.

All the Great Bardfield artists commuted to teach in London art colleges, all talked to students eager to embrace the latest trends, all attended exhibitions and read the journals so they were well aware of this turmoil. Their decision to continue with the figurative depiction of the natural world was a conscious one, and for them a right one. The obvious refuge for the Great Bardfield painters until the storm blew over was the Royal

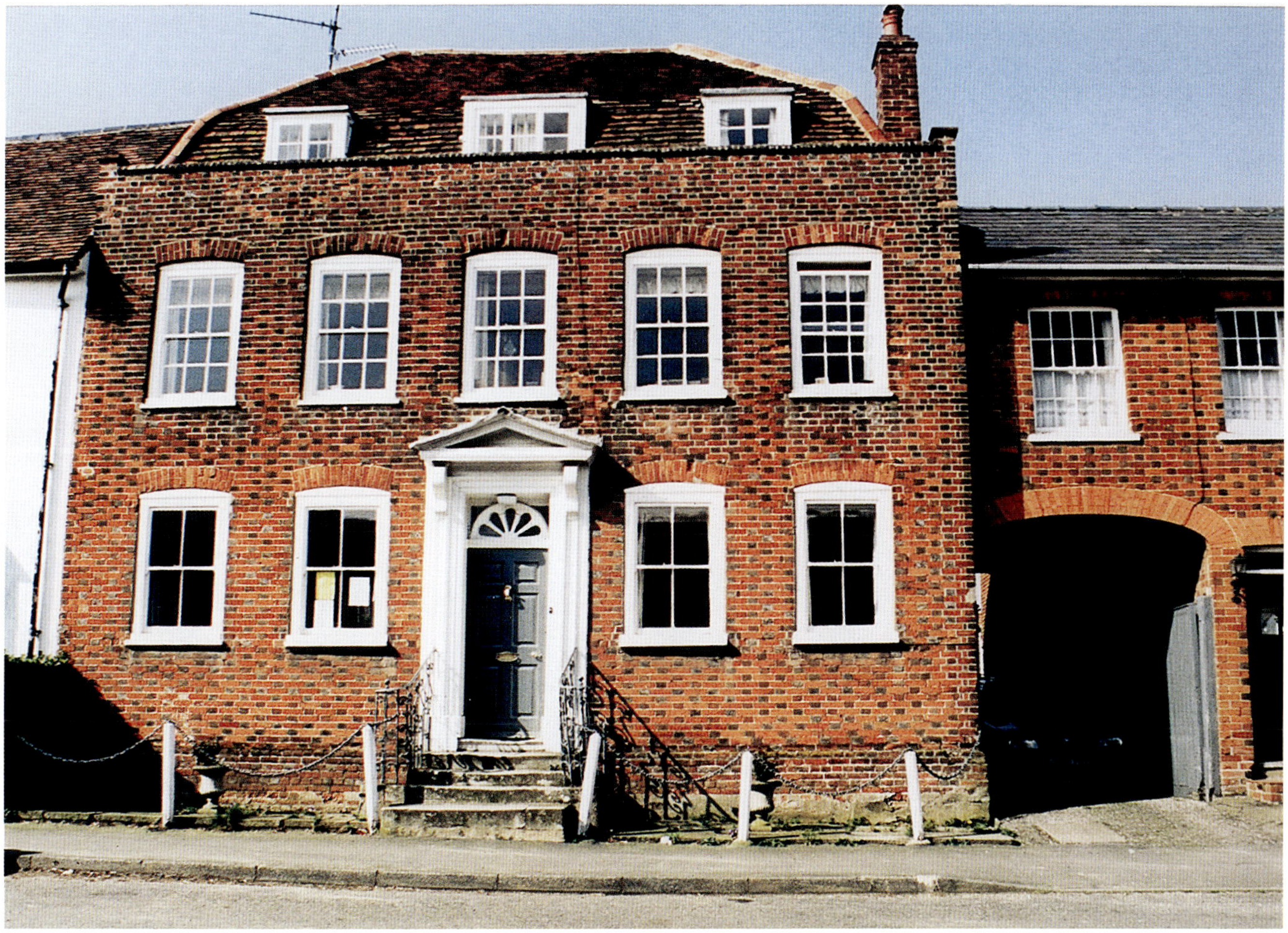

Brick House, Great Bardfield, probably 1960-70.

Academy, especially after the reign of the rabidly anti-modernist President, Sir Alfred Munnings, came to an end in 1949. Every artist in the village submitted works to the annual Summer Exhibition, though only Bawden and Aldridge were asked to become full Academicians, both in 1956, Bawden grumbling that it 'was like being put on the shelf'. He exhibited there every year from 1948 until the end of his life. Even Rothenstein for all his radical pretensions and his later admiration for abstract American art showed there from 1932 onwards and later became an ARA, then elected full RA in 1984. The effect of their entry was to help shake the Academy out of its complacency and to force it to admit modernism within its walls.

1. Hoyle, W., *To Sicily with Edward Bawden*, Introduction by Olive Cook, Previous Parrot Press, 1998.
2. Quoted in Howes, J., *Edward Bawden: A Retrospective Survey*, Combined Arts, 1988, p.59.
3. Hoyle, W., ibid, p.40.
4. Rothenstein, M., 'Private View', *Cambridge Print Editions*, No. 3, Spring 1984.

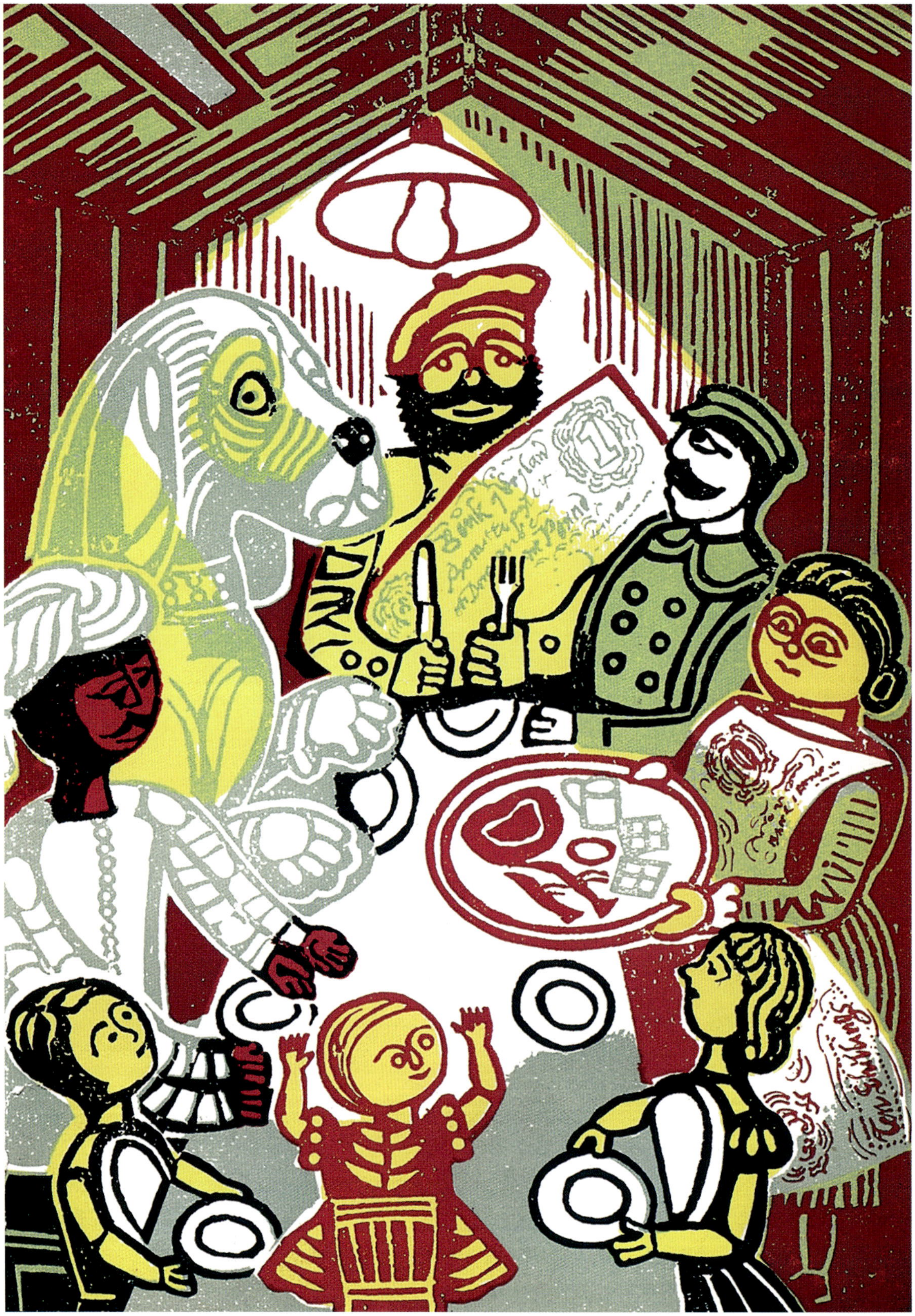

11. THINGS FALL APART

In 1956 Bawden illustrated a banal little fantasy by the poet Louis MacNiece called *The Sixpence that Rolled Away* (Faber and Faber), the author making the mistake of writing down to his child readers whilst Bawden's six four-colour linocuts and five black and white drawings made no such concessions. Bawden always claimed he disliked children but his son Richard recalled 'Edward was quite childish himself and liked jokes about bottoms, and spiders, and creepy-crawlies etc. Edward took a great delight in illustrating his letters to us and his friends with humorous scribbles, cats and cocktail parties etc. He felt freer doing this sort of thing particularly if there was a cruel streak . . . his own childhood, being an only child, might have been more intense and inward.'[1]

When he was away at the war Richard and Joanna had received six tiny books (10 x 13 cm) from him whose main characters were a flea, an ant, a beetle, a worm, rooks and a woman who goes to live with Eskimos. However, in *Right Away Driver* a train passenger is named Mr Draw de Nedwab, and two children called Annajo and Chardri peep over his seat. When these were published together as *Hold Fast By Your Teeth* (Routledge and Kegan Paul, 1963) even the blurb writer had to admit they were 'amusing and heartless'. Bawden evidently felt freer in expressing his affection for his two children in drawings and letters than he did in person where he shunned physical contact and withdrew into his studio to work, or absented himself on painting expeditions, often taking Charlotte with him as driver.

By the time this compendium volume appeared the two young Bawdens were established in their careers and had children of their own, Richard going on from his public school to Chelsea and St Martin's Art Schools before, inevitably, ending at the RCA in the Department of Engraving and Etching. He was taught lithography by Bernard Cheese, and engraving by Edward Ardizzone amongst others, but not by his father. From there on his achievements closely matched his father's – posters for London Underground, murals, book illustrations, a mosaic, designs for glass, linocuts, cast-iron garden furniture, watercolours and editions of prints for Curwen and Editions Alecto. After his first marriage broke up Richard married a potter, Hattie. Bawden wrote to Bliss and confessed 'Richard is a far nicer chap than his old dad as Charlotte often said'. Joanna too was art trained, having attended the Ruskin School of Art at Oxford where she was taught by Percy Horton before moving on to the RCA to study textiles, to teach at the Central School, and then to open a wool shop in Camden Town. When three grandchildren appeared and came to visit, garish plastic toys were scattered over Brick House's exquisitely tasteful rooms because, as Bawden explained to John Norris Wood, 'Charlotte, like all grand-mothers, sucks up to the grandchildren'.

When he had the time Bawden still managed to get out and about to paint watercolours (he shared an exhibition with Carel Weight at Zwemmer in 1954, and at the same gallery in 1963 had a one-man show of pictures he had

Opposite: Linocut illustration for *The Sixpence that Rolled Away*, 1956; 21 x 15 cm.

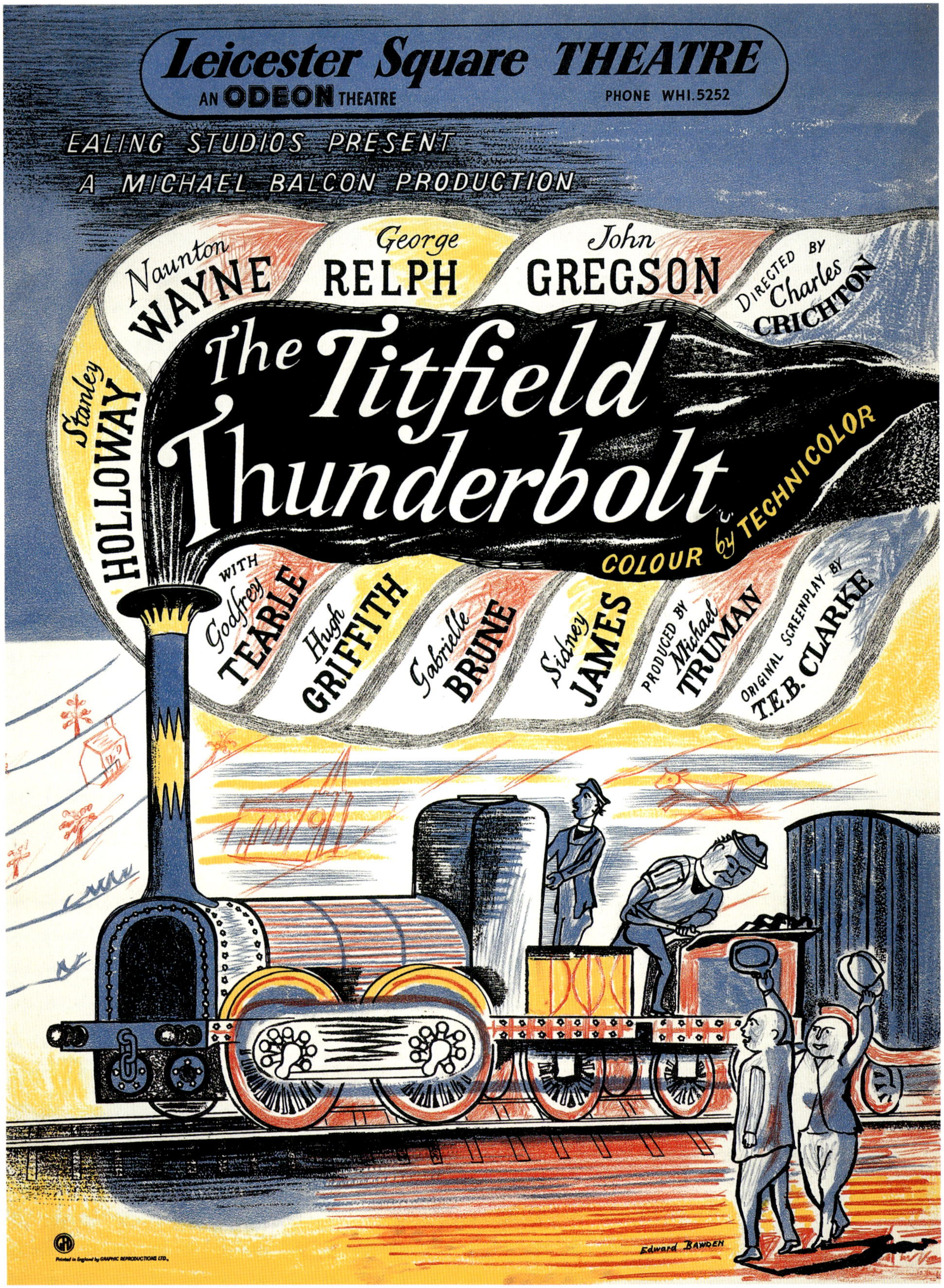
Leicester Square THEATRE
AN ODEON THEATRE
PHONE WHI.5252
EALING STUDIOS PRESENT
A MICHAEL BALCON PRODUCTION
Stanley HOLLOWAY
Naunton WAYNE
George RELPH
John GREGSON
DIRECTED BY Charles CRICHTON
The Titfield Thunderbolt
COLOUR by TECHNICOLOR
WITH Godfrey TEARLE
Hugh GRIFFITH
Gabrielle BRUNE
Sidney JAMES
PRODUCED BY Michael TRUMAN
ORIGINAL SCREENPLAY BY T.E.B. CLARKE
Printed in England by GRAPHIC REPRODUCTIONS LTD.
Edward BAWDEN

made during a tour of Ireland with Charlotte as his chauffeuse), but during the sixties his talents seemed to be pulled in all directions. His 'innocent eye' style and brand of humour was now out of fashion with advertisers who preferred trendier, and cheaper, photographic images. He admitted it was a young man's game and needed a fresh mind. Instead he designed Christmas cards, beer mats, bottle labels, a tin tray, trade brochures, book jackets, wallpaper, a poster for the film *The Titfield Thunderbolt*, menu cards, decimal coins (unused), Fortnum and Mason catalogues, playing cards, a coat of arms for Lloyds, a painted piano for Harrods and the Bilston cast-iron garden seat of 1956 – his only venture into three dimensions. He had once commented: 'I've no sense of form. I could never have been a sculptor. I'm a pattern maker.' He professed to be allergic to sculpture.

He was still an illustrator to be reckoned with and in 1968 was involved in decorating the first two volumes of *The Old Testament* published by Oxford University Press. Gross, Ardizzone, Weight, Burra, Hockney and Sheila Robinson were also employed. Bawden drew upon his Middle Eastern experiences and produced small pen and ink images which modestly served the text and again demonstrated how well he could orchestrate crowd scenes. Ten years later he supplied forty-eight small drawings for *The World's Greatest Story: The Epic of the Jewish People in Biblical Times* (Weidenfeld and Nicolson, 1978), but his quirky humour keeps bubbling through so that, for example, Jezebel seems to be falling to her death because her huge bosom has toppled her over the battlements. His illustrations to *The Song of Songs* demonstrate how temperamentally unsuited he was to depicting the sensual or erotic: compare his plump dolls in a pumpkin patch to Eric Gill's fervent wood-engravings of the same subject.

Bawden continued to teach, but art education was in turmoil throughout the 1950s and 1960s and nobody at the RCA could ignore the new ideas being chewed over in both the Senior and Junior Common Rooms. Art education changed its aims and structure under the impact of Professor William Coldstream's two Reports of 1960 and 1970, and the content was shaken up by Richard Hamilton and Victor Pasmore working out an abstract foundation course called 'Developing Process' in Professor Kenneth Rowntree's Department of Fine Art at Newcastle upon Tyne, before Hamilton moved on to the RCA in 1957. In the years around 1960 such students as Blake, Bratby, Tilson, Auerbach, Kossof, Caulfield, Kitaj, Jones, Phillips, Berg, Boshier and Hockney (the last much admired by Bawden) became stars before they left the RCA, matching that 'outbreak of talent' Paul Nash had identified in the early 1920s – though none of them were painting landscapes.

Immediately after the war, exhibitions of Picasso and Matisse at the Victoria and Albert Museum had swept aside the Gothic gloom of Neo-Romanticism and announced that the continent was open for business again, but Bawden was temperamentally at odds with Matisse's dazzling hedonism and indifferent to Picasso's attempt to make propaganda for the Communists. Nearer home the so-called Kitchen Sink School of Bratby, Greaves, Middleditch, Coker and Jack Smith (all RCA students) portrayed Sheffield housing estates, squalid interiors, downtrodden wives and drowned chickens; their deliberate lack of taste seemed to chime in with the iconoclasm of the 'Angry Young Men' creating contemporary dramas and novels. Other RCA students were exploring the opposite extreme in Pop Art, employing all the razzle-dazzle of American consumerism and taking as a slogan 'the democratisation of culture'. At the Institute for Contemporary Art (ICA) others began to come to terms with American culture instead of resisting or despising it as most British artists had done hitherto. Also from America came the biggest threat of all: Abstract Expressionism, first revealed at the Tate Gallery in 1956.

Opposite: Poster design for *The Titfield Thunderbolt*, 1952, 57 x 42 cm, printed by Graphic Reproductions Ltd.

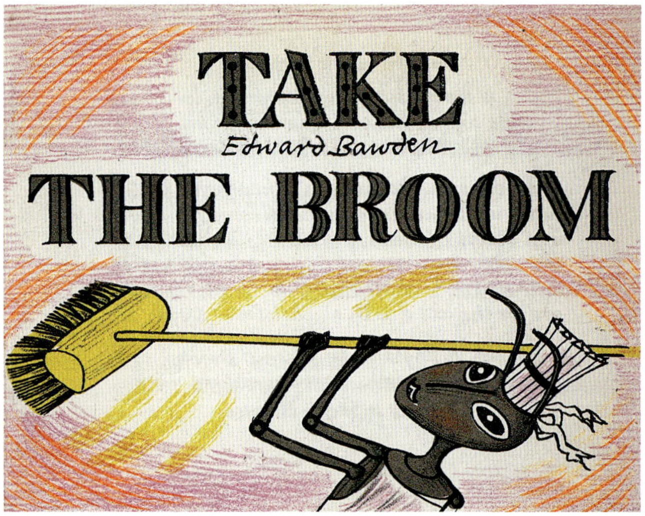
TAKE
Edward Bawden
THE BROOM

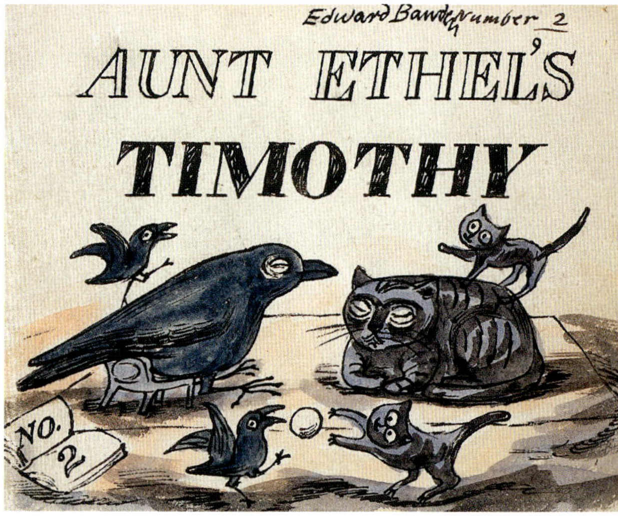
AUNT ETHEL'S
TIMOTHY
NO. 2

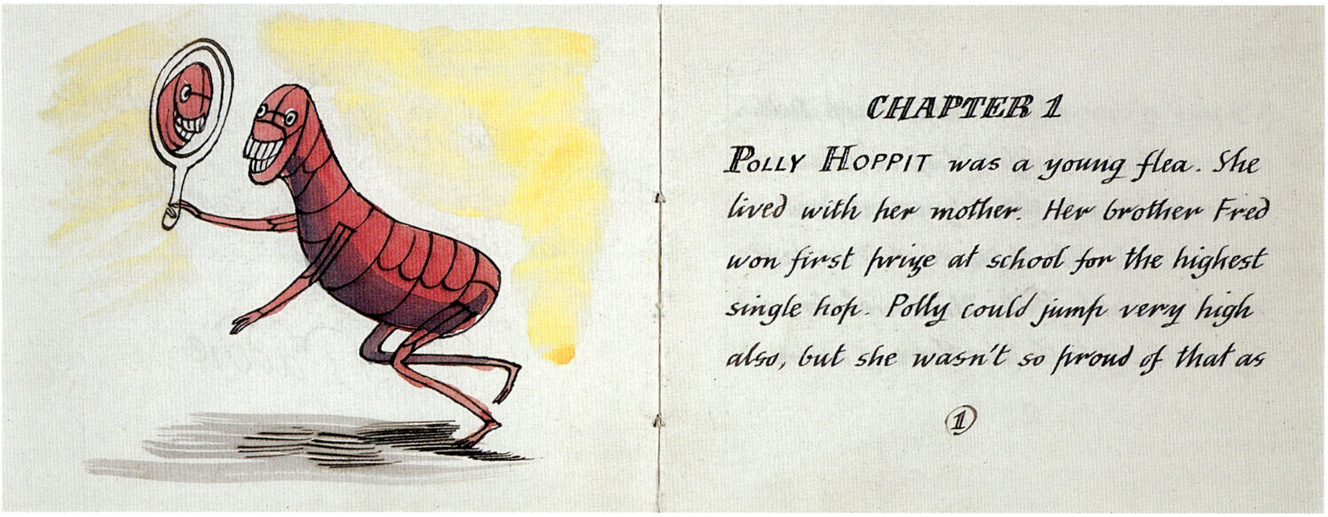
CHAPTER 1
POLLY HOPPIT was a young flea. She lived with her mother. Her brother Fred won first prize at school for the highest single hop. Polly could jump very high also, but she wasn't so proud of that as
1

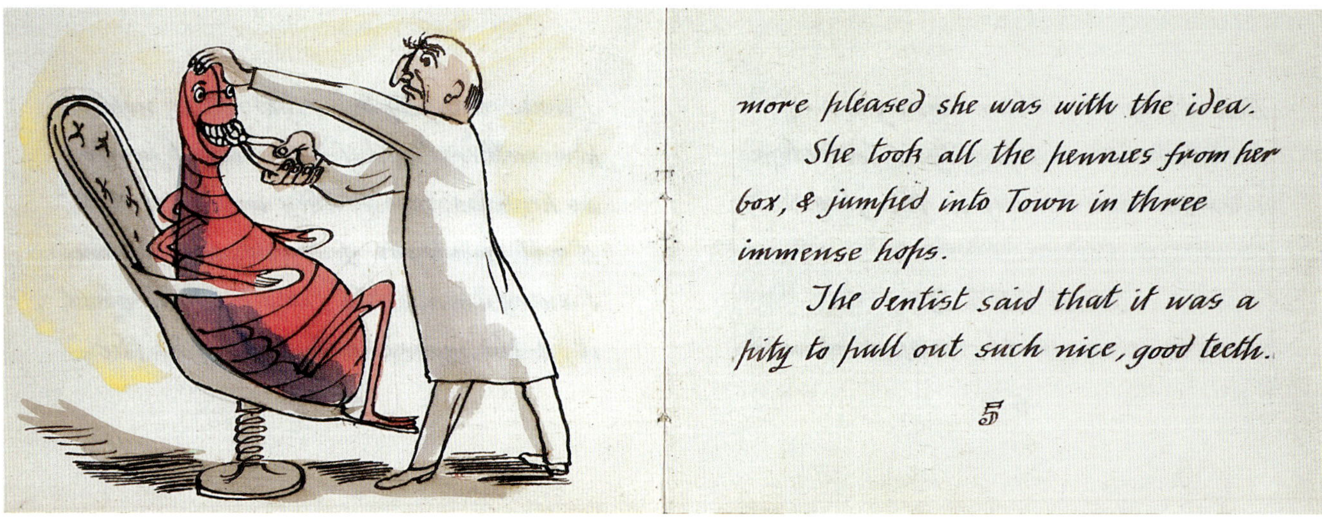
more pleased she was with the idea.
She took all the pennies from her box, & jumped into Town in three immense hops.
The dentist said that it was a pity to pull out such nice, good teeth.
5

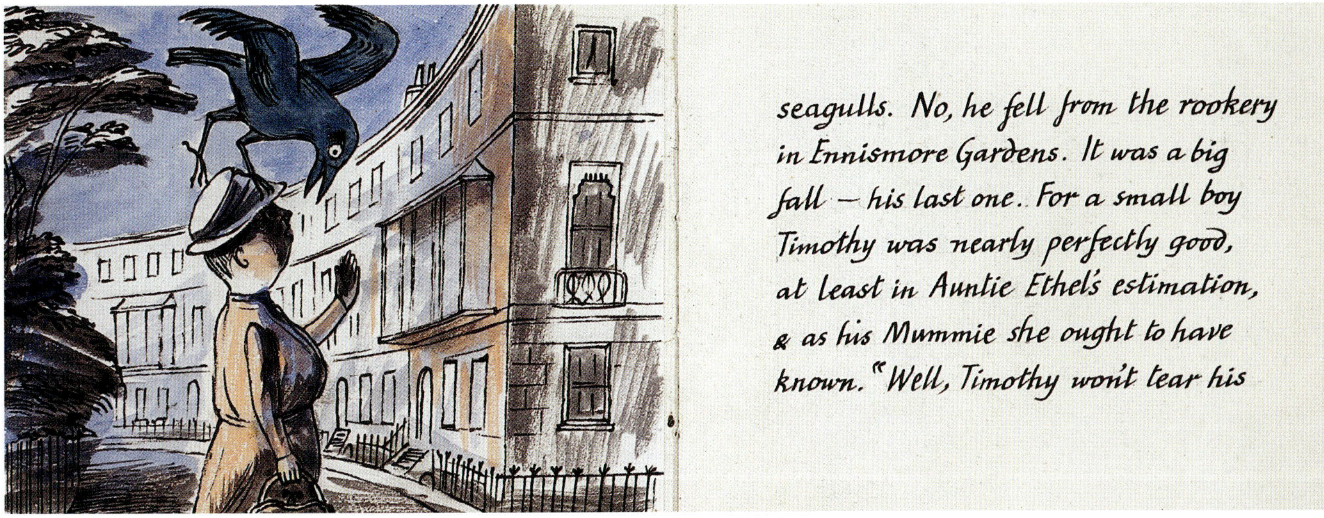

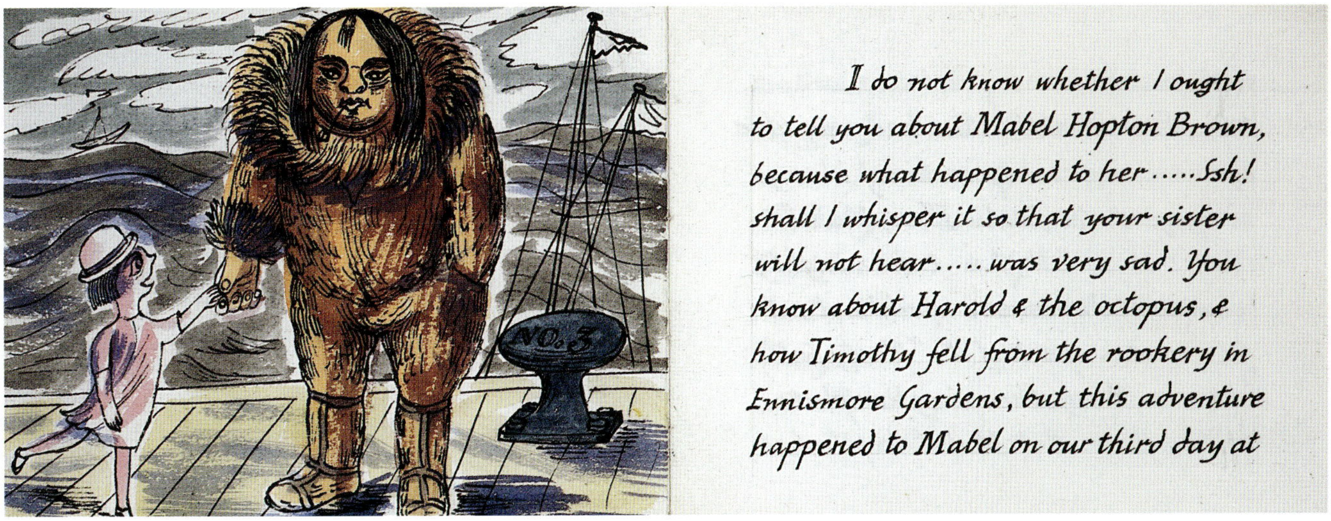

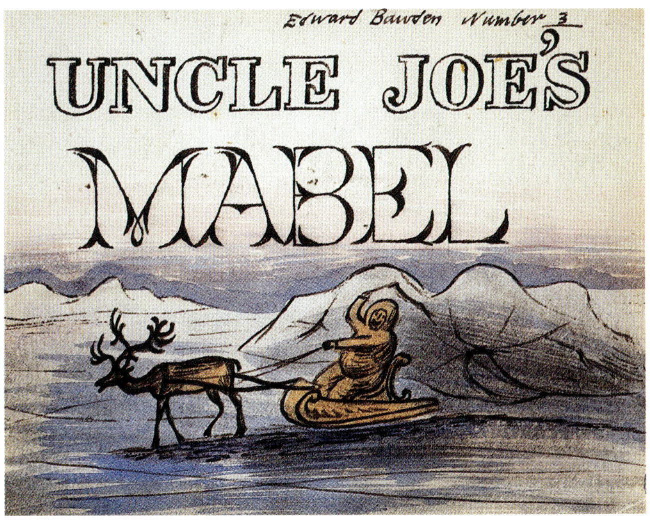

Pages from the little booklets devised by Bawden for his children while away during the war, later gathered together for *Hold Fast By Your Teeth*, each page 10 x 13 cm.

This jettisoned subjects altogether and researched the matter of paint itself and the artist's gesture in applying it, often on huge canvases. Bawden's only response was to say you could cycle up and down an exhibition of abstracts and afterwards not be able to recall a thing.

Others took it more personally: George Chapman stopped painting for eleven years and John Minton, Bawden's colleague at the RCA and left-over Neo-Romantic committed suicide in 1957, in part because abstraction was making his vision of the world redundant. Bawden was deeply upset at this waste of talent and began to make bitter jokes at his own expense: 'I died fifty years ago', 'I really belong to the Thirties', and of one of his works, 'a typical Victorian job'.

He was no colourist, dripper, realist, Pop artist nor abstractionist, but then neither were the majority of the public. When in 1958 Morley College asked for a replacement mural for their cafeteria, they wanted him to provide something figurative, traditional and accessible.

This time Bawden chose to illustrate episodes from *The Canterbury Tales*, namely stories by the Knight, Squire, Prioress, Pardoner, Nun's Priest and Wife of Bath, so avoiding the bawdier ones. In his large studio at the back of Brick House he painted wooden panels with emulsion paint and then installed them at both ends of the long refectory, the side walls being occupied by windows and serving counters. The Tales' narrators ride stiffly along between two fences at the lower level and their characters act out the stories above them in an airless world of tilted up perspective, where cabbages can be bigger than a knight astride his rocking horse and people only appear in full face or profile. Perspective is always a problem with a picture surface wider than the spectator can see without turning his head but Bawden has made a virtue of this by reverting to pre-Renaissance ways of organising the picture space.

Douglas Percy Bliss described the figures well: 'To those of us who remember their predecessors of the original building how different the new characters look. In the pre-war decoration the characters, marionette-like, had not walked or even stalked. They had danced or pirouetted. They were airborn and insubstantial. But Bawden's new characters are flat and heraldic, somewhat like playing-card figures. They are no longer droll and

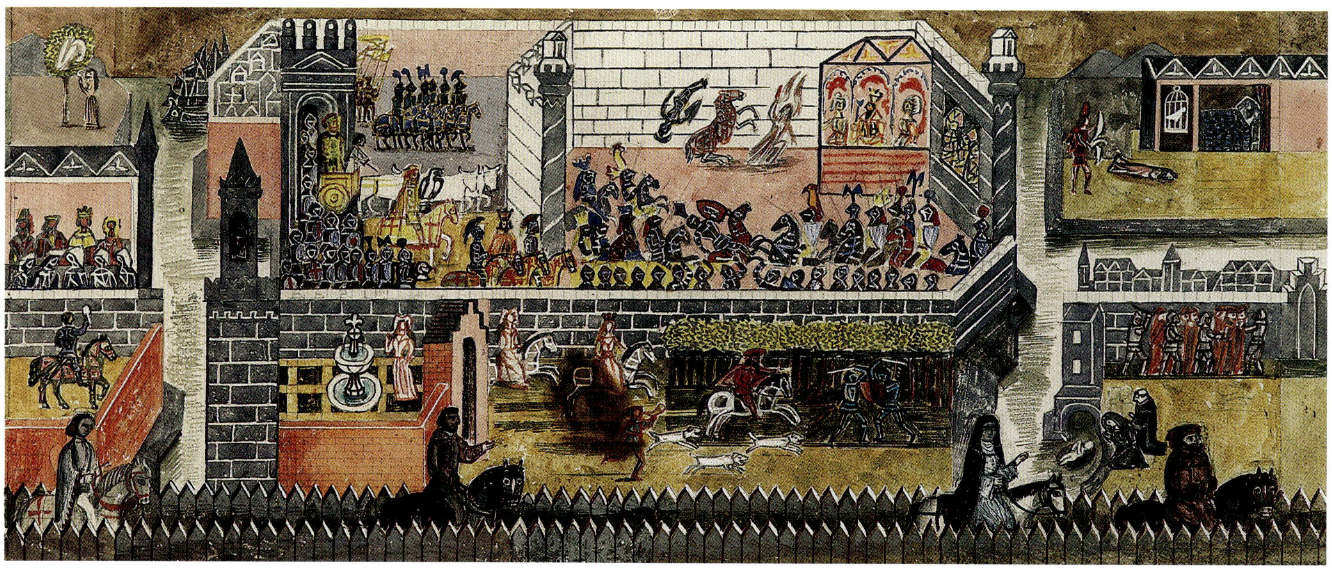

Design for *Canterbury Tales*, the new mural at Morley College, 1958, and (opposite) a contemporary photograph of the finished work (Trustees of Cecil Higgins Art Gallery, Bedford).

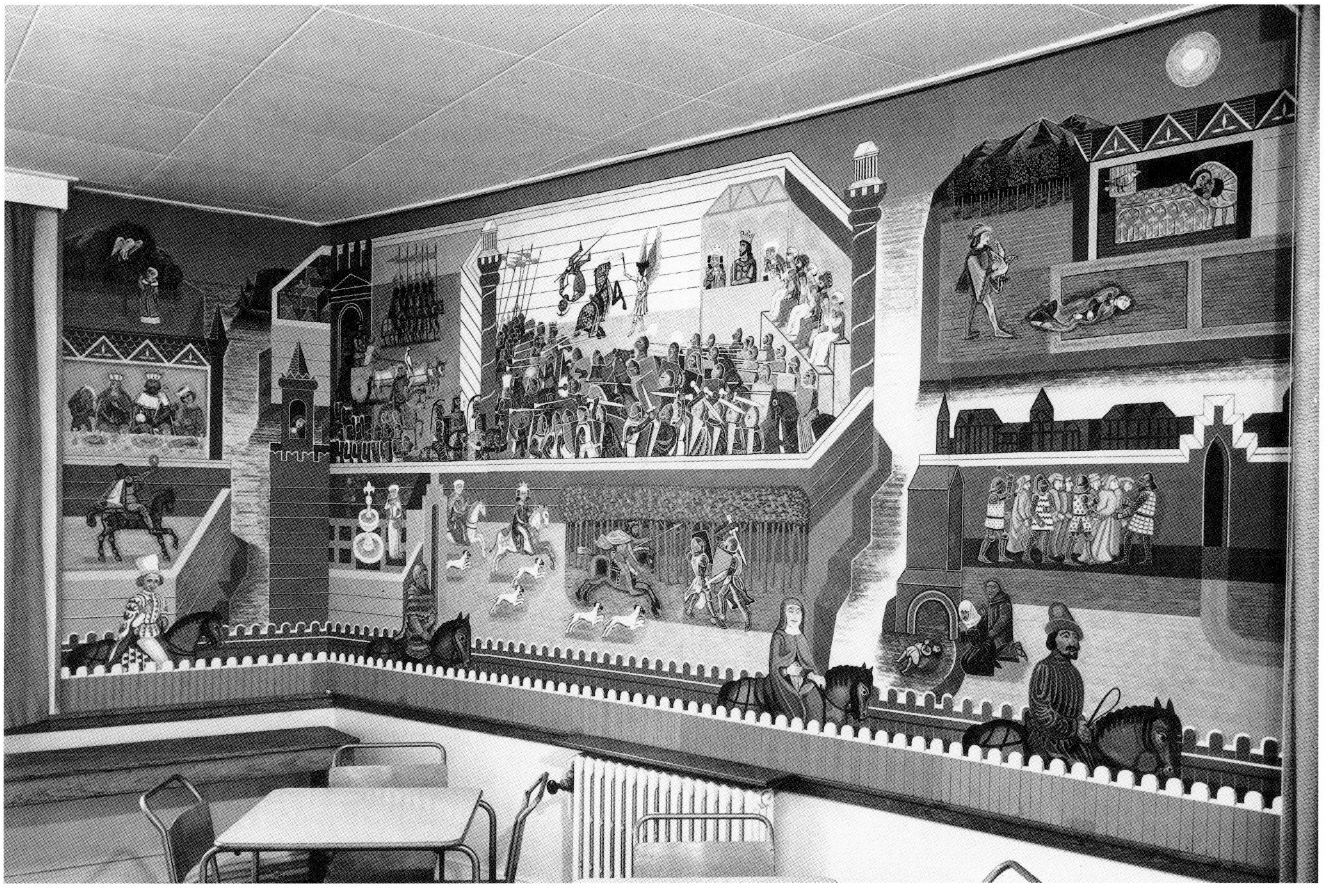

lyrical. They are grotesque and comical and even fierce with their round eyes staring at us. They are flat like the figures in Gothic tapestries who wear beautiful clothes in a horror-vacui of vegetation, except that his figures move in a more barren world.' [2]

There are macabre touches, as one might expect by now from Bawden, and one wonders what the present-day students think of the whole thing as they eat their chips – especially of the Pardoner's parable of drunkenness and death in one dark corner.

Bawden revisited his mural twenty years later and found it 'in a shocking condition . . . the lower area is covered in tea and coffee stains and the white has gone a nasty gingery colour . . . it's a bit discouraging.' The Principal produced a fragment of painted plaster from a cupboard, the only surviving piece of the 1928 mural and said that it was the only bit of work that they had by Ravilious. Bawden looked at it closely and said, 'I'm afraid it's probably by me. The Boy would have done it better.'

Other mural commissions came in this period, the largest of them sixty-four feet long and thirteen and a half feet high, for the restaurant of the British Petroleum Company in the City of London. To research this he and Charlotte were sent in 1966 on an all-expenses trip to Isfahan and Mashad to study Saracenic architecture. The result is a serene, intricately-patterned frieze of domes, minarets, doorways and distant mountains. Three assistants and many rolls of masking tape were necessary to get the flat clean-edged shapes he required. This mural has since been transferred to the Chelsea and Westminster hospital.

Another project for which assistance was necessary, this

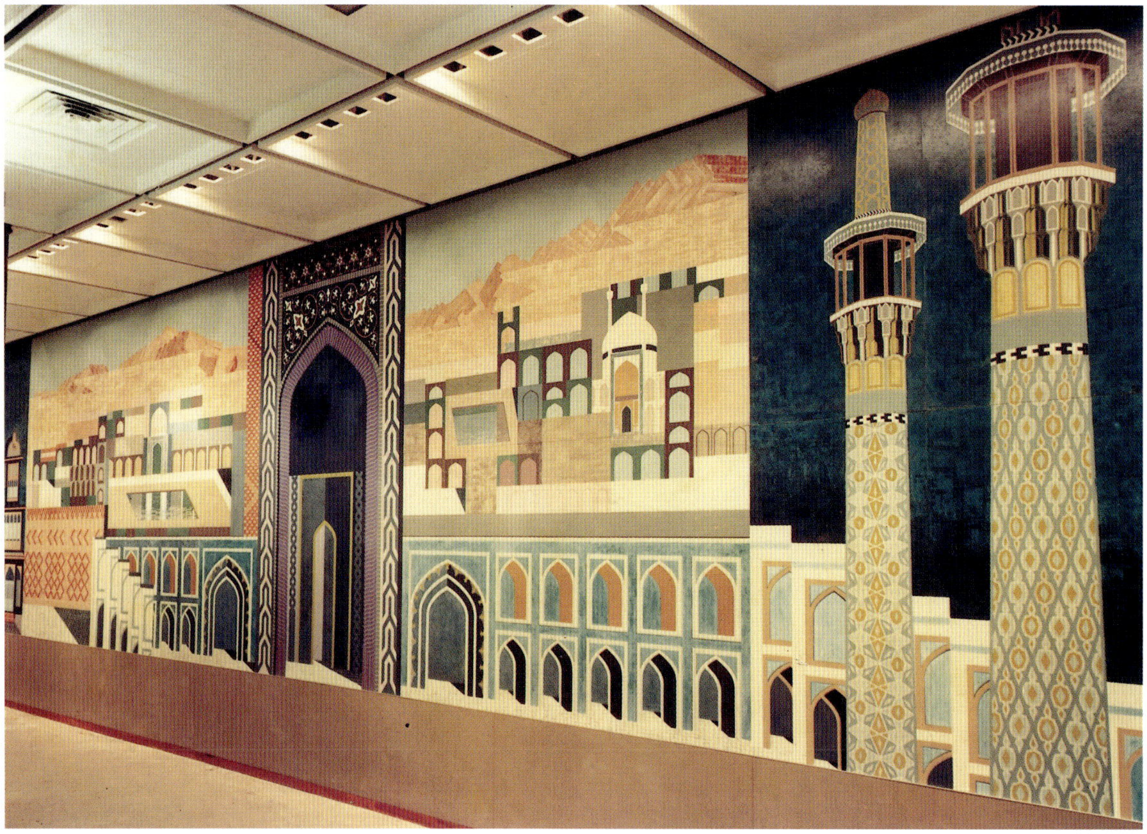

Part of Bawden's mural on the theme of Saracenic Architecture, made for British Petroleum, and (below) the artist at work on the mural at Brick House.

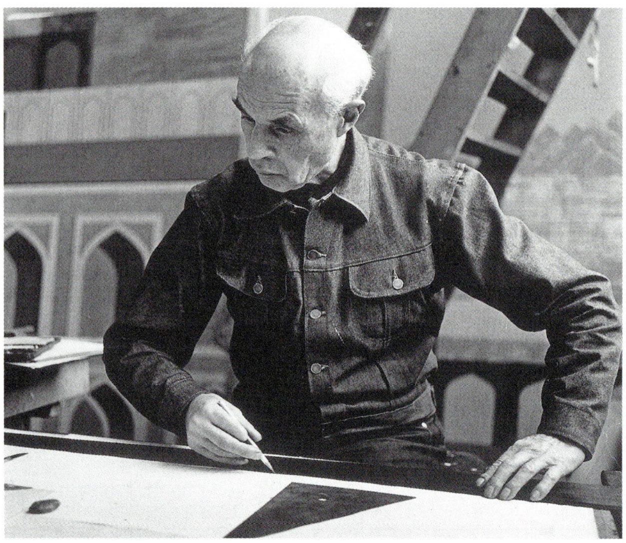

time with his old friend Walter Hoyle, was in making a giant Royal Coat of Arms for the Brussels exhibition of 1958. His interest in all things heraldic was also exploited in the linocuts for *The Queen's Beasts* (1953), issued to celebrate the new Queen's coronation. *The Observer* newspaper also asked him for a linocut of the royal lion and unicorn for its masthead in 1962. In each of these he was working within very traditional restraints but still managed to make the images look fresh and contemporary.

Several other murals for industry and Academe were completed in these years: an abstract one for the Physics Block of Hull University, another for the Microbiology Department at Queen's Belfast, one on glass-blowing subjects for Pilkington's and another for Associated Electrical Industries, all worthy rather than remarkable. For Carr's Lane Congregational Chapel in Birmingham he largely abandoned paint and used 20,000 nails, saying his ironmonger father would have been proud of him. He hammered the nails into two large circular boards and an oval one to provide tactile interest and shadow in depicting the chapel and listing all its pastors since 1748. It was a witty handling of an otherwise drably routine assignment.

None of the above murals are readily available to the public, but his final one for Blackwell's bookshop in Broad Street Oxford is. He was asked to show Oxford's greatest men on five joined panels over a stairwell. The worthies are grouped historically from medieval to Victorian times against appropriate Oxford buildings, but there is nothing reverential about his treatment of either. Some characters float above the rooftops alongside winged horses and a monkey parson riding an eagle, whilst at ground level the Roundheads and Cavaliers are mastiffs and King Charles spaniels; Lewis Carroll photographs the White Rabbit and the Scapegoat paints Holman Hunt. Many things remain inexplicable in spite of the key Bawden provided –

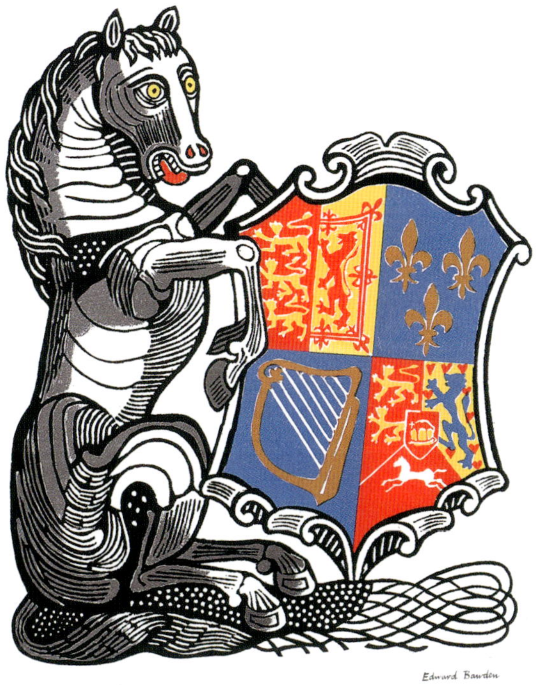

Linocut of the White Horse of Hanover from *The Queen's Beasts*, 1954, 240 x 195 mm (Fry Art Gallery).

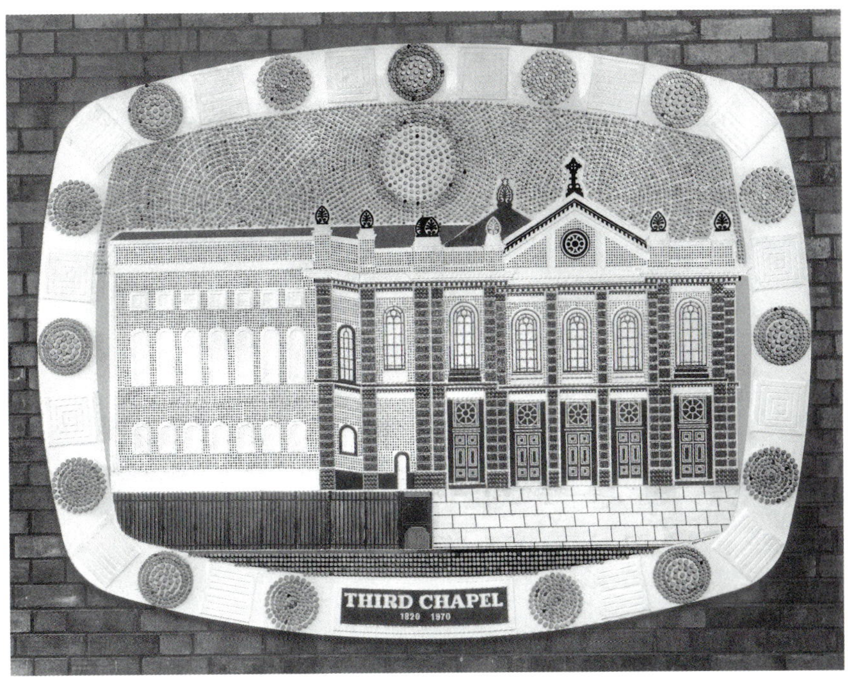

Detail of the mural at Carr's Lane Congregational Chapel, Birmingham, 1971, in which Bawden used 20,000 nails.

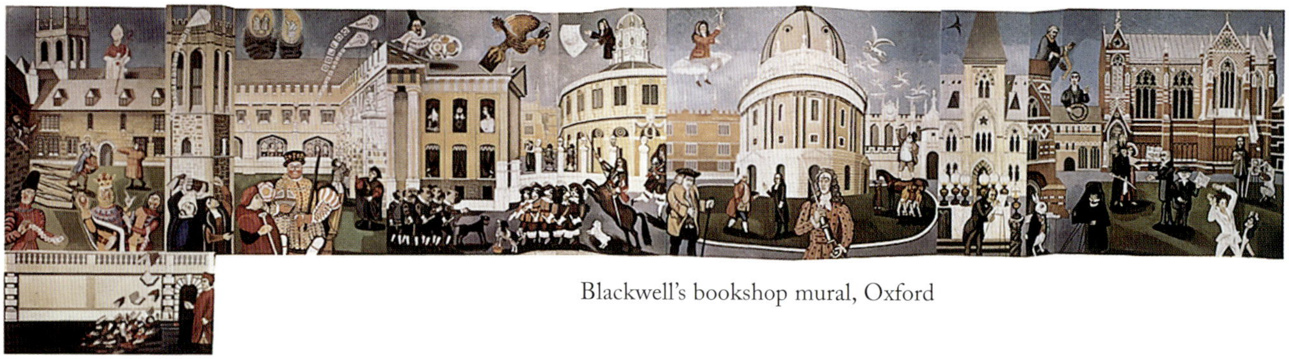

Blackwell's bookshop mural, Oxford

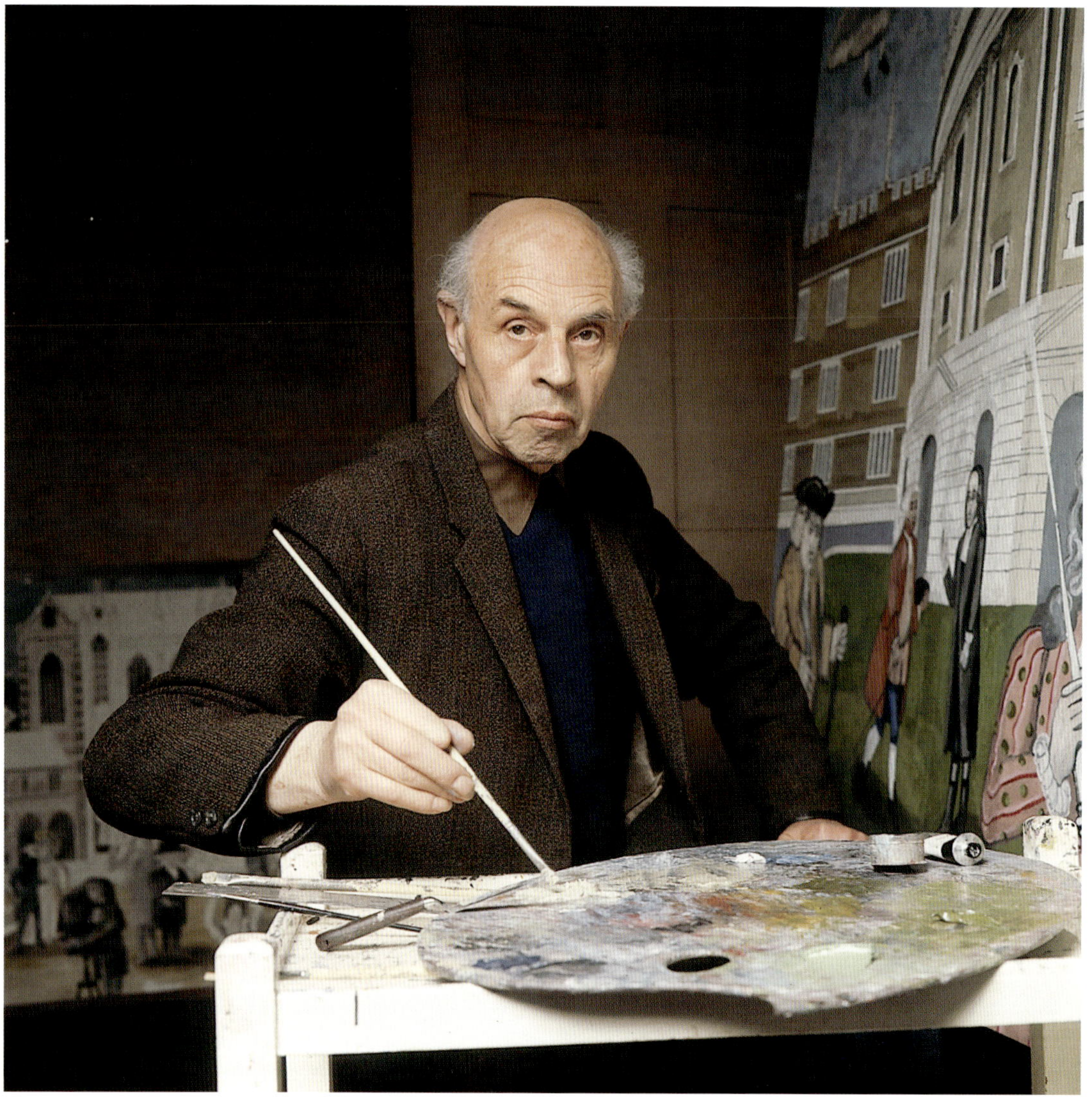

Bawden at work on the mural for Blackwell's Bookshop in Oxford, photographed by Stephen Moreton-Prichard in early 1973 (The Warden & Fellows of Merton College, Oxford).

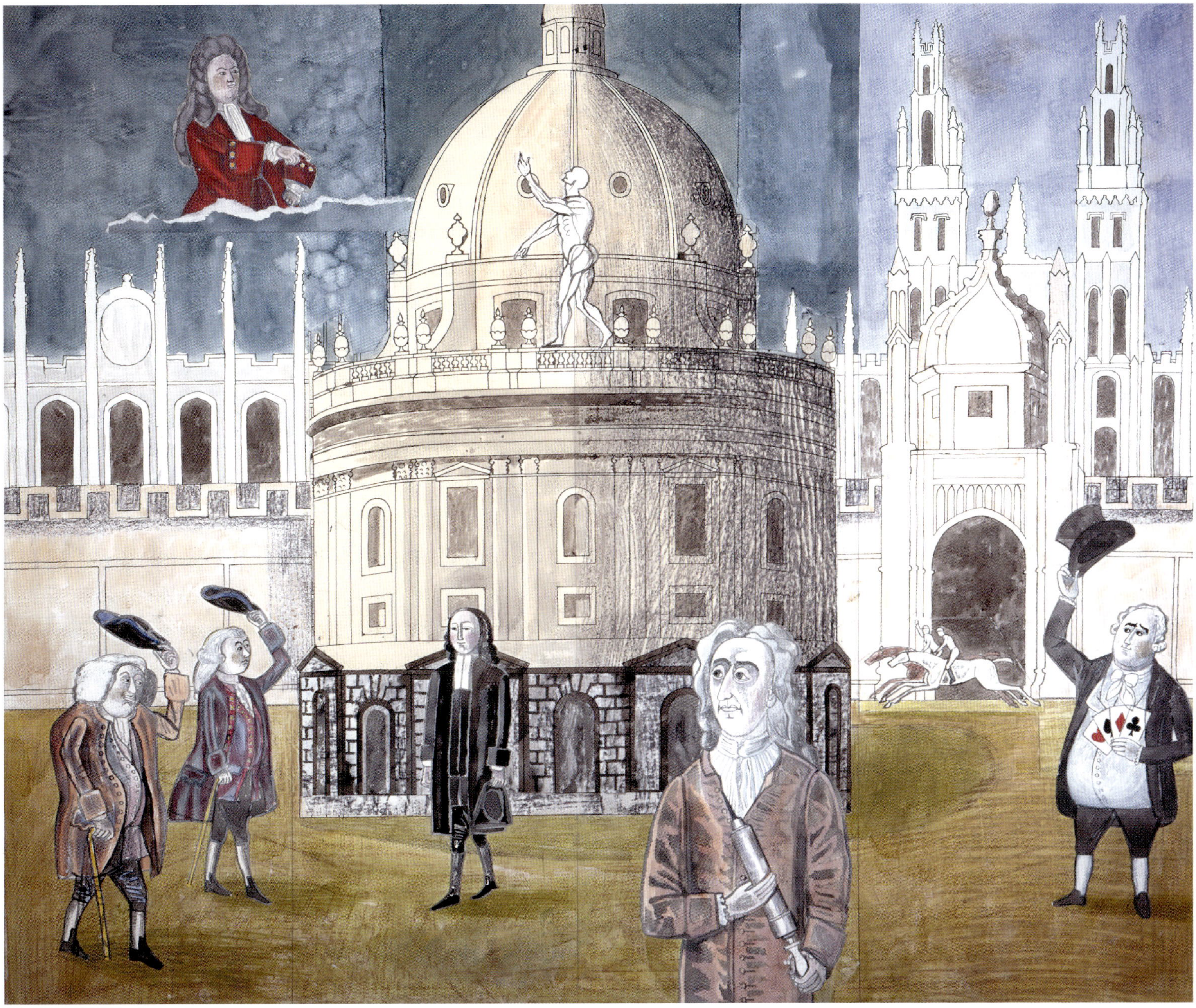

(This page and overleaf) Cartoons for panels of the mural design for Blackwell's Bookshop, Broad Street, Oxford (The Warden & Fellows of Merton College, Oxford). Above: Dr Johnson and James Boswell greet John Wesley; John Locke in the foreground; to the right is Charles James Fox (standing on a horse, with three jockeys in the finished mural); the central building is All Souls and Radcliffe Camera; Dr John Radcliffe points down from the sky.

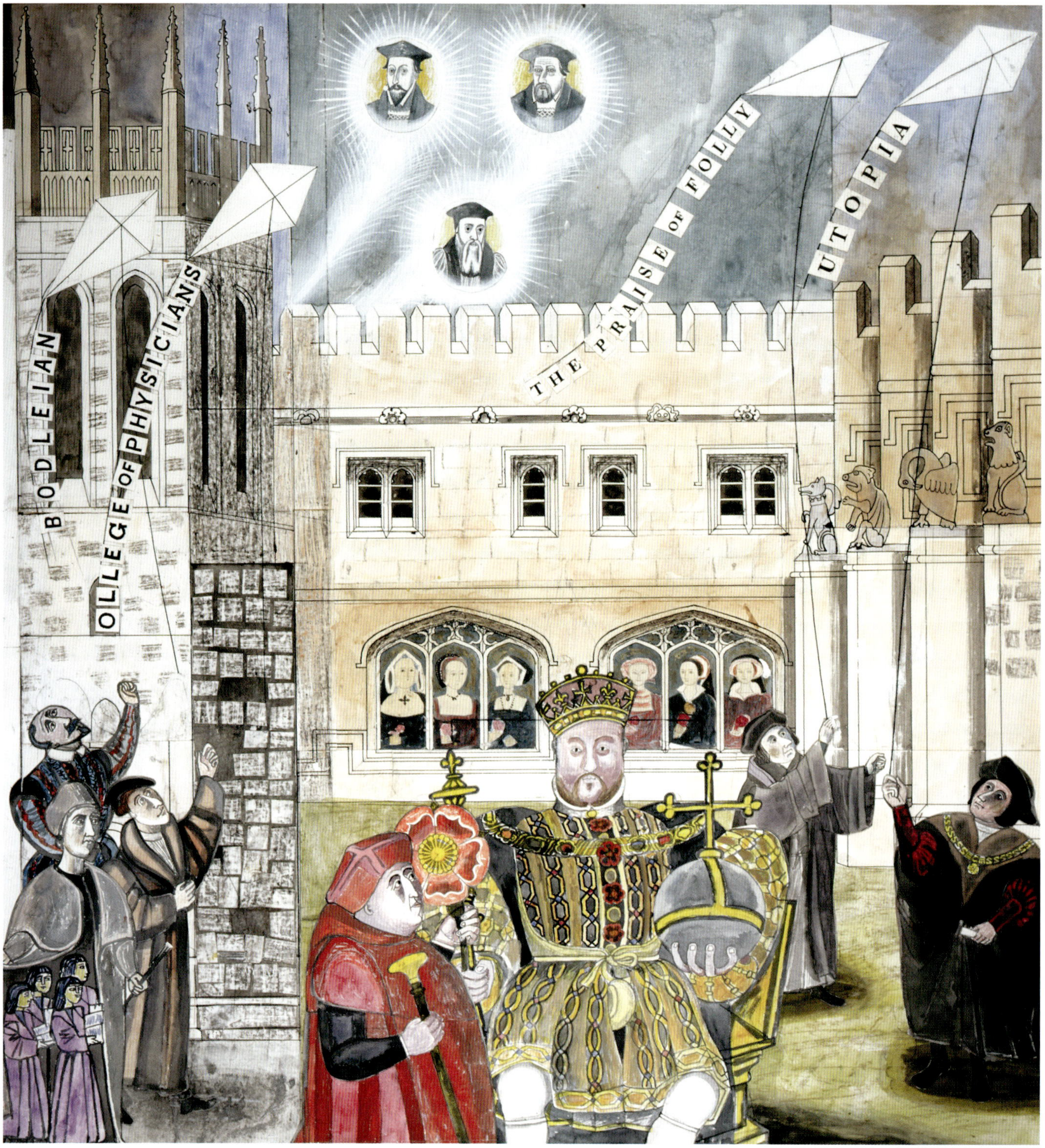
BODLEIAN
OLLEGE OF PHYSICIANS
THE PRAISE OF FOLLY
UTOPIA

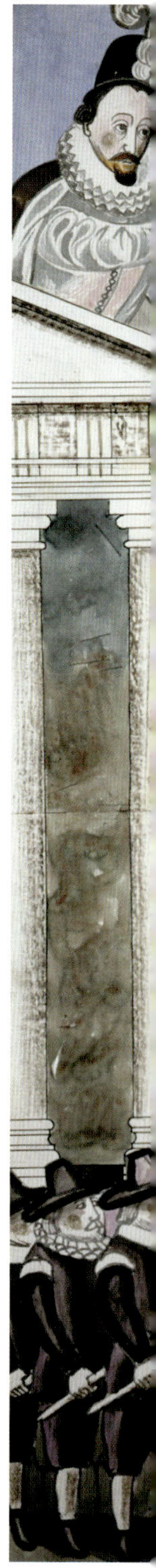

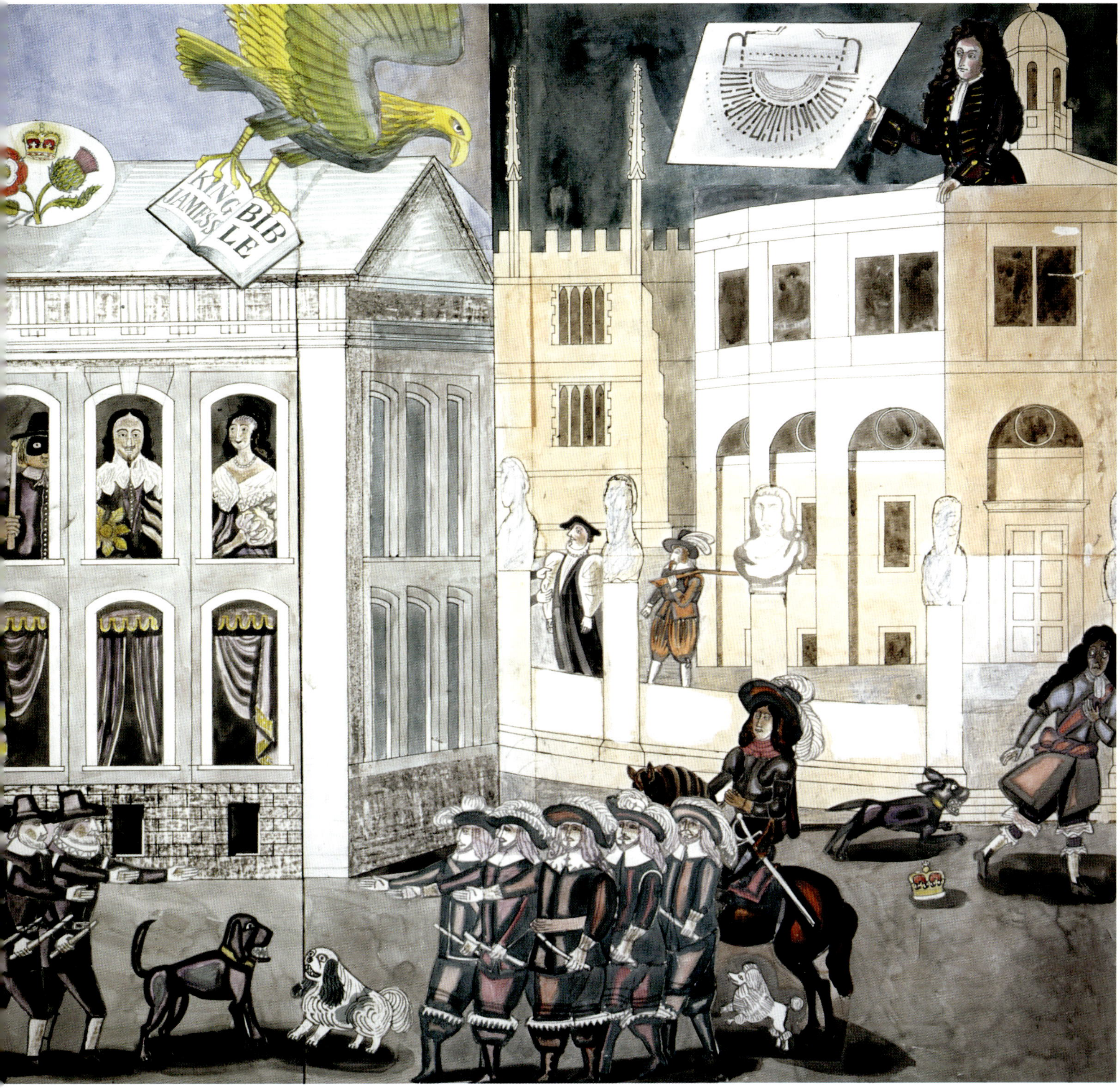
KING JAMES
BIB LE

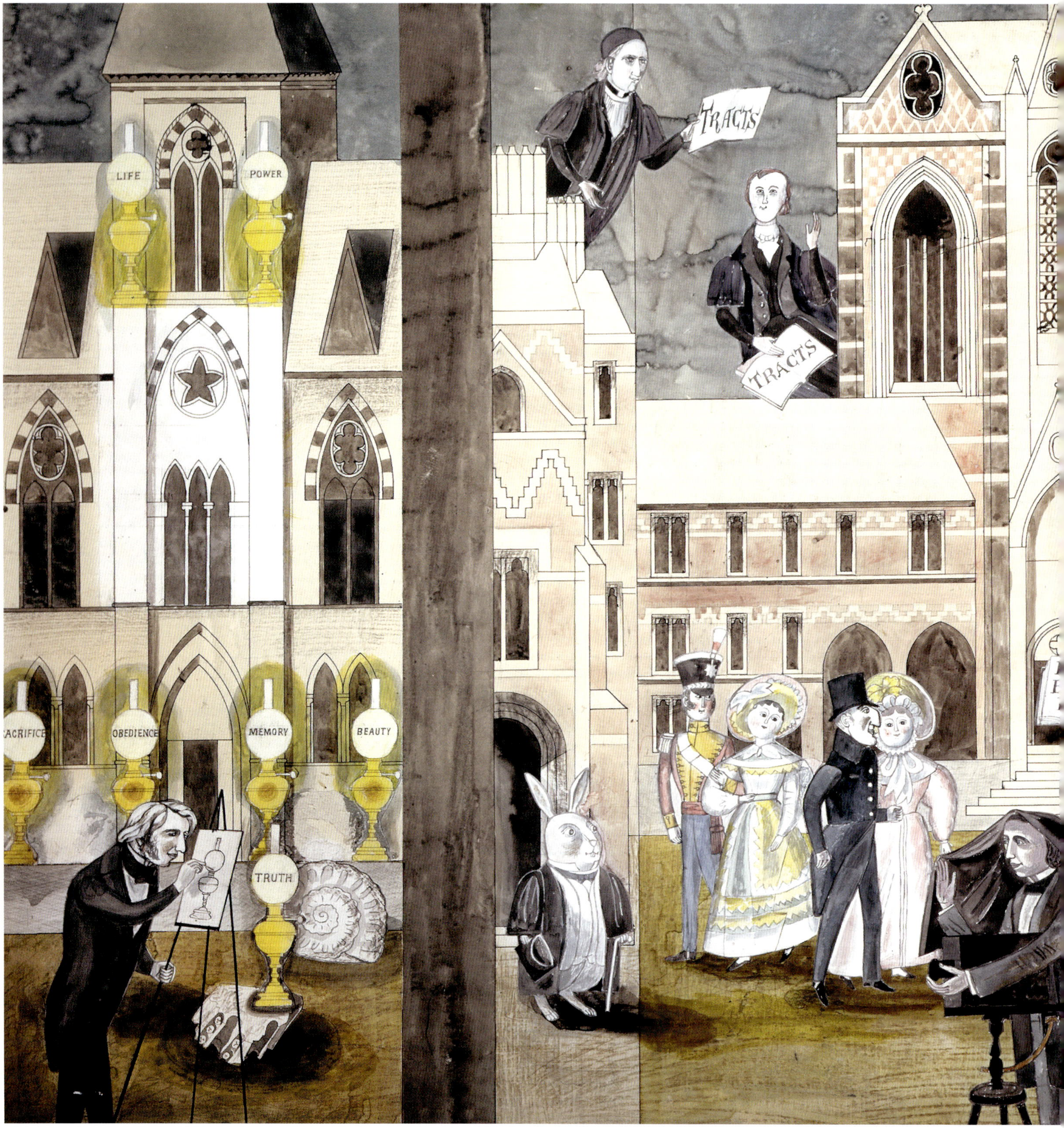
LIFE
POWER
OBEDIENCE
MEMORY
BEAUTY
TRUTH
TRACTS
TRACTS

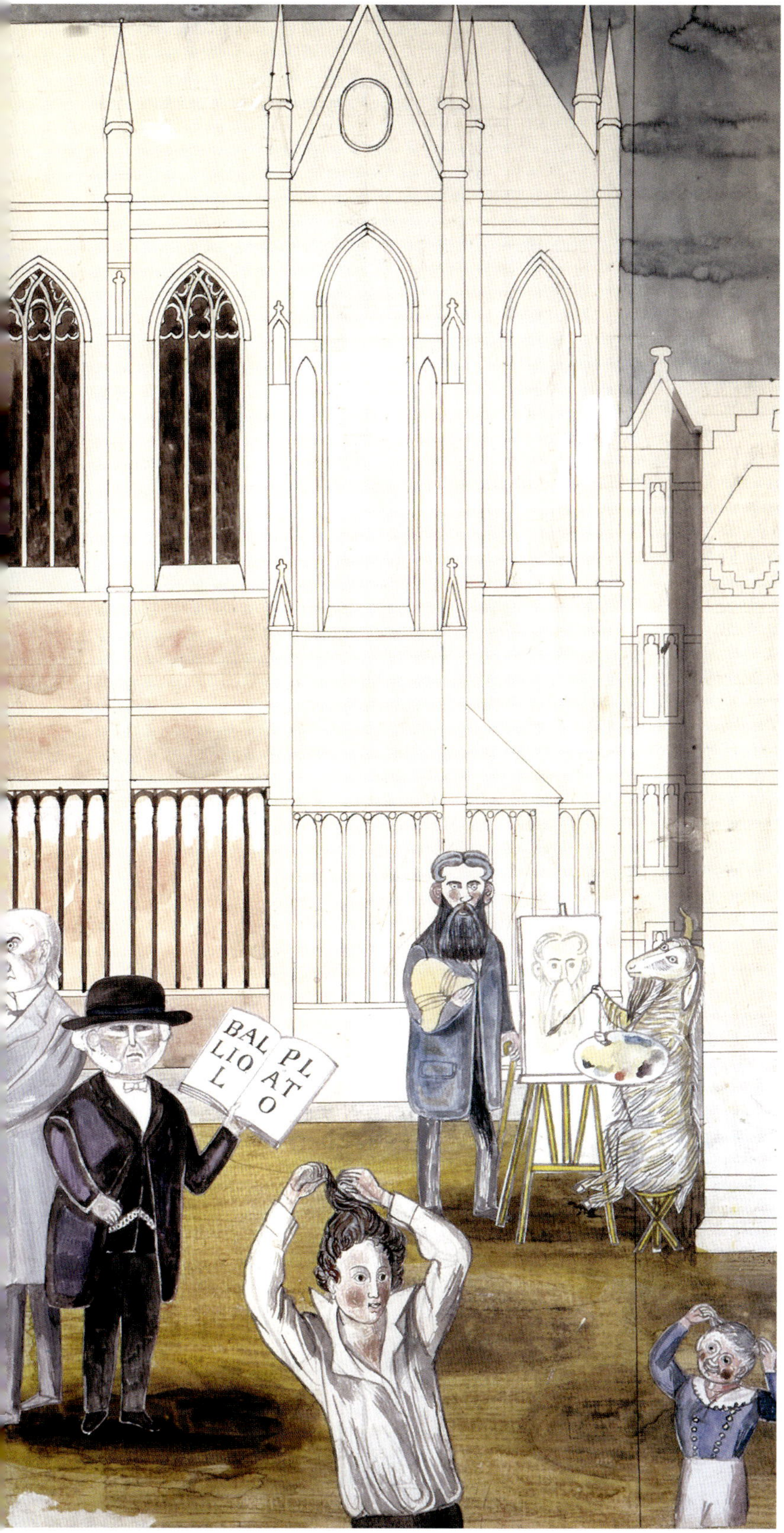

(Previous page 202) From left, Roundheads and Cavaliers face each other, with Boye (Prince Rupert's poodle killed at Marston Moor) underneath Prince Rupert on his horse; leaving to the right is James II; looking out from the windows are Charles I, flanked by his executioner and Henrietta Maria; on the pediment, left, James I holds the emblem of the Union of England and Scotland; the eagle holds King James' Bible (guided on the finished panel by a monkey parson); on the roof, right, Sir Christopher Wren holds a plan of the Theatre of Marcellus; behind the statues Archbishop Laud goes off to the Tower under guard.

(Previous page 203) From left, Thomas Linacre flies a kite for the College of Physicians, and Sir Thomas Bodley flies one inscribed Bodleian, with John Colet. King Henry is attended by Cardinal Wolsey, his six wives looking out from the windows; Erasmus and Sir Thomas More; in the sky are portraits of Ridley, Latimer and Cranmer.

(This page) Cartoon for part of the mural design, at Blackwell's Bookshop, Broad Street, Oxford (The Warden & Fellows of Merton College, Oxford). To the left is John Ruskin with his easel and the Seven Lamps of Architecture; on the rooftops are Dr Pusey and John Keble with their Tracts; the White Rabbit is photographed by Lewis Carroll while beyond them the Duke of Wellington walks with Harriet Wilson; Gladstone stands with Dr Jowett; Holman Hunt is portrayed by the Scapegoat, and at bottom right are Shelley and Leigh Hunt's son. (Key by courtesy of Blackwell's Bookshop).

why, for example has the Wife of Bath brought her four dead husbands here in their coffins? And why is John Locke holding a very large enema? Bawden explained his general strategy to John Rothenstein: 'Figures appear in the sky because to a designer it sometimes seems necessary to spread spots of interest, tapestry fashion, more or less evenly over the whole surface of the mural. The surface, unlike that of most murals, is not flat against the wall but projects and recedes slightly, by a few inches only, to create a division that is not too obvious between the different historical periods: medieval, tudor, 17th c. & Victorian.'[3] Despite its somewhat unattractive paint surface and rather dated look this is perhaps Bawden's

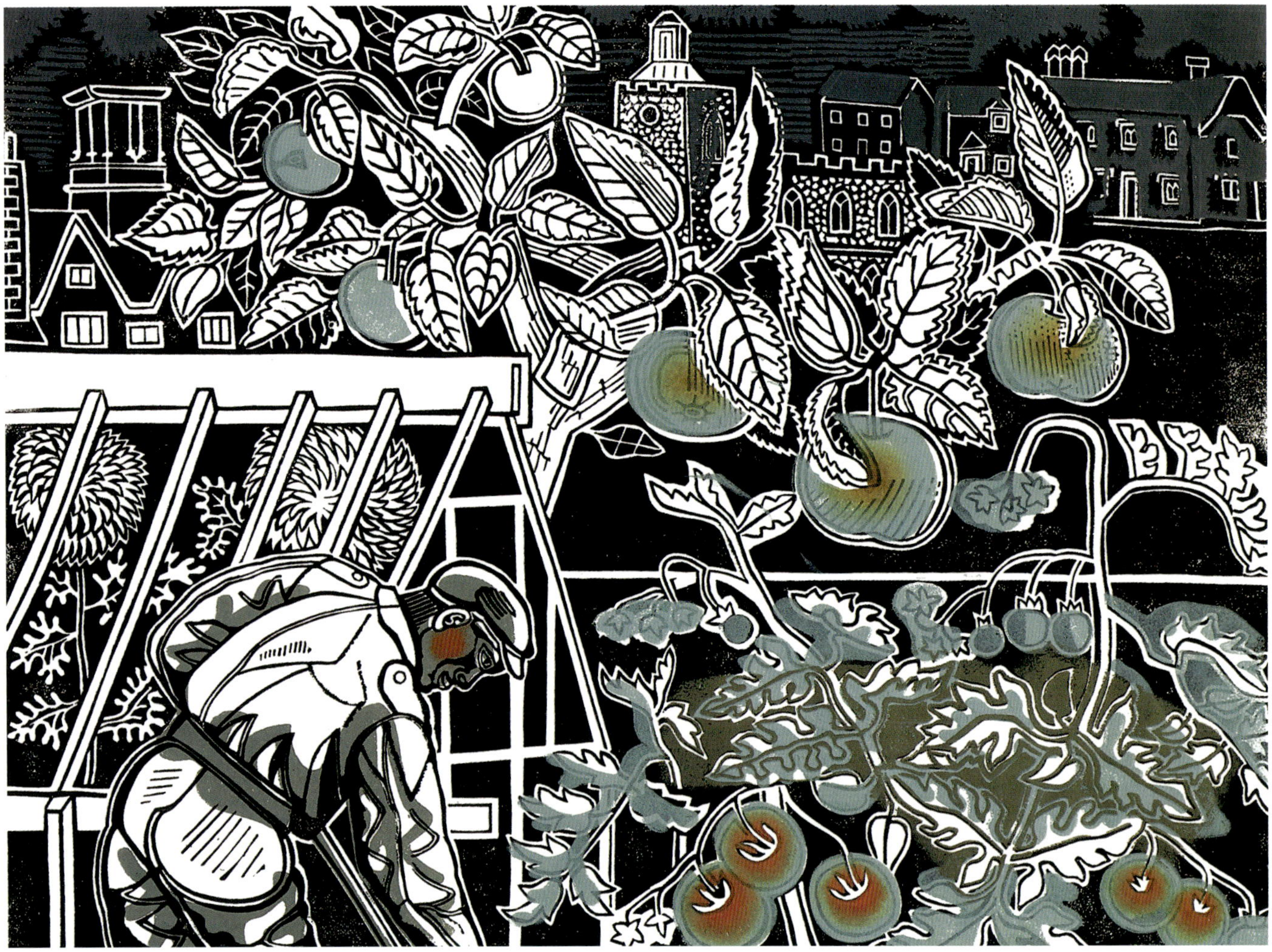

Autumn, 1950, linocut, 381 x 504 mm (Fine Art Society).

best and most light-hearted mural, irreverent, weird, decorative, full of ideas and fun.

In spite of the attractions of the Blackwell work Bawden's final reputation will not rest upon these large public works. Too many have been lost or remain hidden and others are merely workmanlike responses to corporate demands – decorative backgrounds to more important activities such as making money.

The market for linocut or lithographed book illustrations waned after the war as camera-based photolithography took over, but there was a compensatory demand for original prints to hang on walls. Oliver Simon died in 1956 but his son Timothy and the expert printer Stanley Jones set up a separate Curwen Studio near Tottenham Court Road to make fine editions, Bawden responding by taking linocutting to yet further extremes of ingenuity and expressiveness. There was an ambitious series in 1953-1959 of Brighton showing the pier and pavilion and, by breaking the image down into sections and building them up again using a fresh piece of lino for each colour, he could make some of these extremely large – over five feet wide in some cases. The need for simplification of form, flatness of colour, strong linear framework and lack of modelling all seemed to play to his

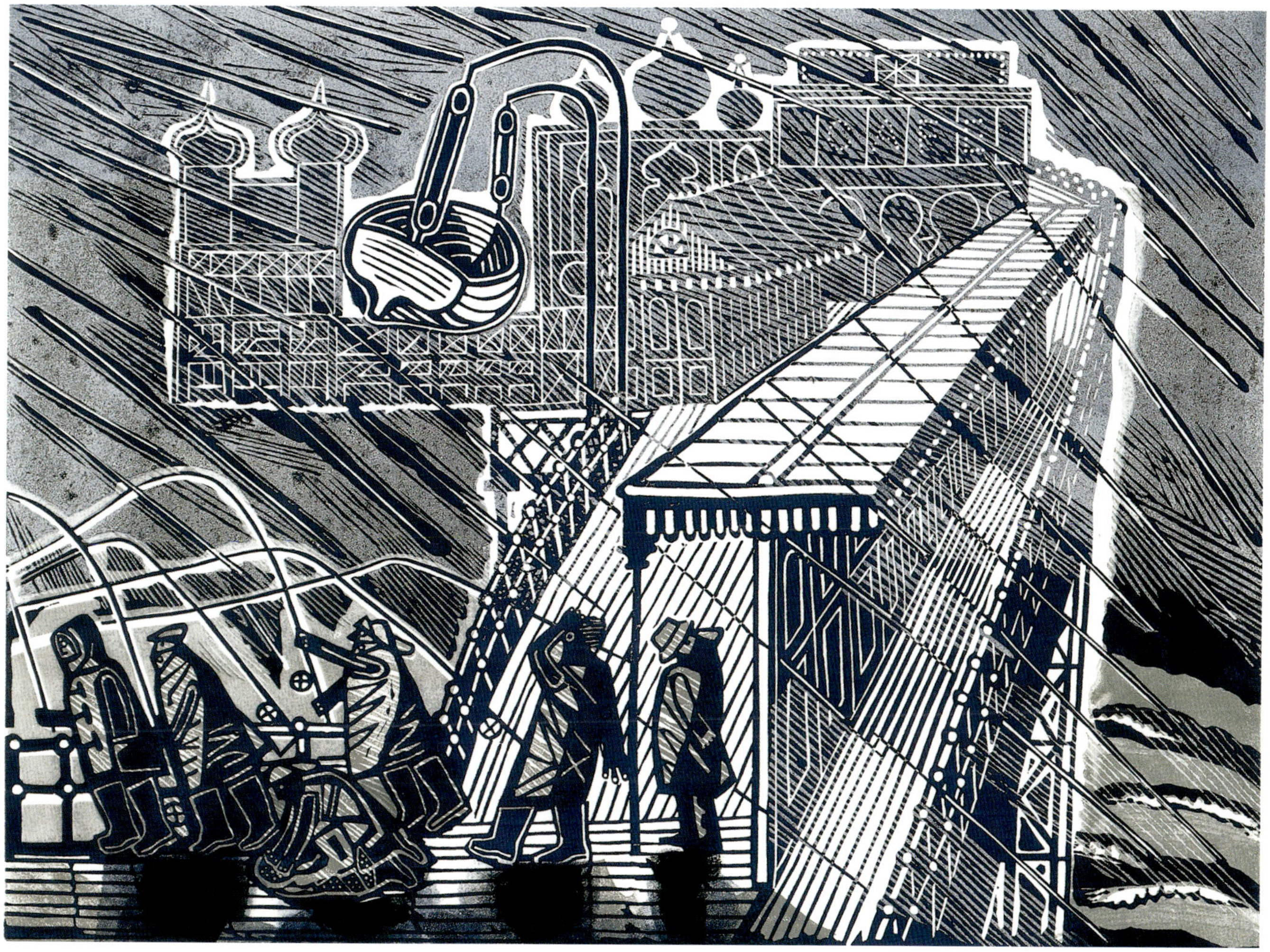

Snowstorm at Brighton, 1956, linocut, 461 x 611 mm (Fine Art Society).

natural inclinations. Yet, in one depicting a snowstorm on the sea front, he demonstrates that this seemingly homely medium is capable of the most subtle colouring and delicate effects. His images of Liverpool Street and Braintree stations were also large and complex cuts which demonstrate there was little he could not now achieve. The editor of the magazine *Motif* (Number 9, Summer 1962) sent Bawden to Portugal with a brief to make adventurous linocut illustrations of his trip, which he did by abandoning perspective, applying colour in an almost arbitrary way and by using one simple element, e.g. a car, again and again to build up more complex compositions. These clearly demonstrate that wit can be expressed visually as well as verbally.

His previous contact with the Portuguese had been to provide more conventional pen and ink drawings (with swipes of an inked roller for texture) to *English as She is Spoke* by Pedro Carolino (1960, for the RCA's own Lion and Unicorn Press). This was a limited edition book (see page 13) which fully exploited the possibilities of an 1869 text-book's hilarious mistranslations between the two languages.

Bawden was now at his peak as a printmaker as he worked on some local Essex linocuts (*The Nag's Head Braintree; Ives*

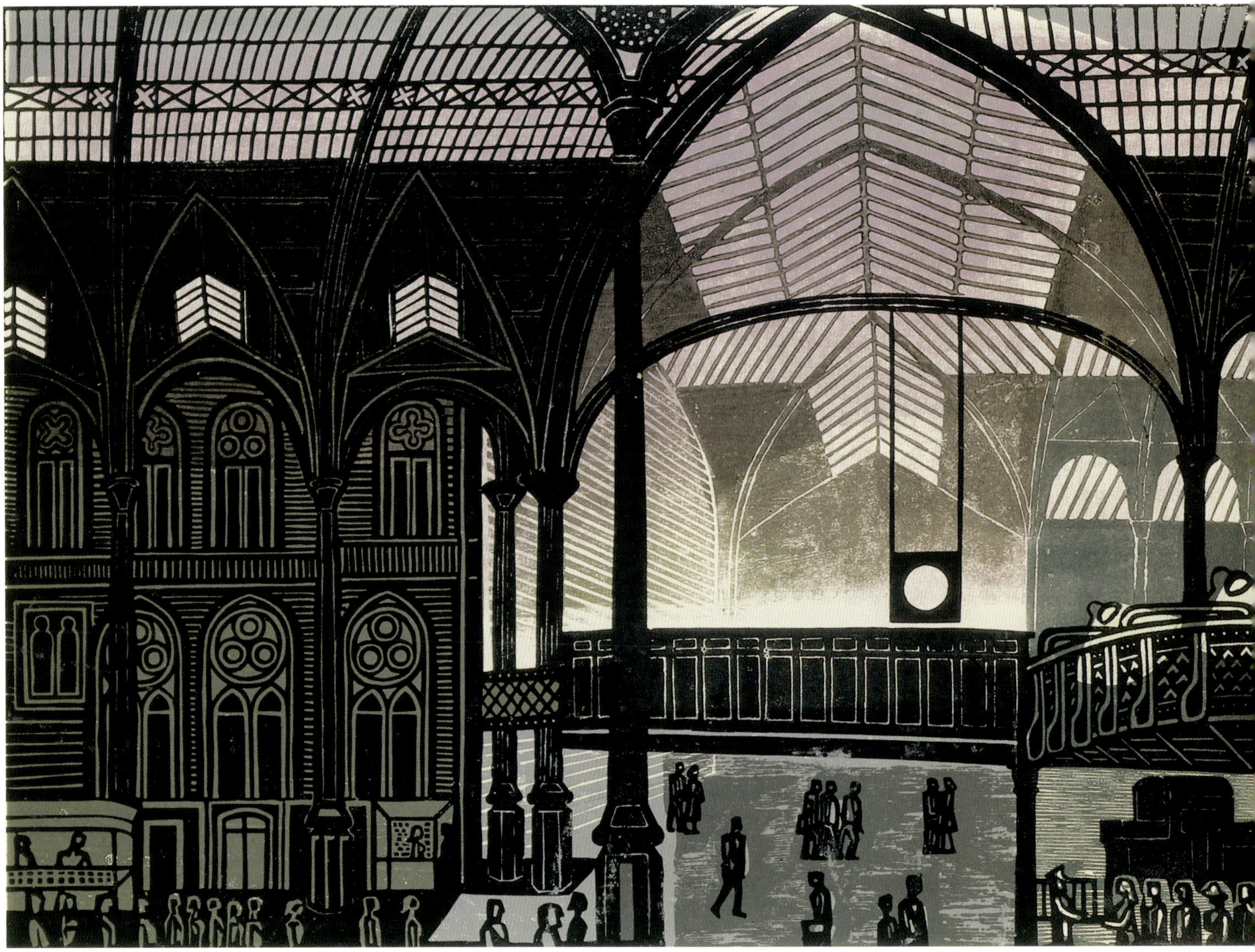

Liverpool Street Station, 1960, linocut, 530 x 1455 mm (Fine Art Society).

Farm, Great Bardfield; Blue Tractor, Saffron Walden; Lindsell Church) before switching to making autolithographs of London scenes in *The Coal Exchange*, *The Stock Exchange*, *Lloyds* (its rows of desks depicted entirely in greys) and his old student favourites *The Pagoda* and *The Palm House* at Kew Gardens. In 1966 came a superbly varied series of linocuts of *Nine London Monuments*, followed by *Six London Markets* in 1967 for which Bawden rose early and cadged a lift into the still-sleeping city with the Bardfield butcher. Then, for Curwen, he did nine linocut illustrations for *Aesop's Fables* (1970), the watercolour drafts for which have survived and show how little his ideas changed once they had been clarified on paper. He is at his most inventive here – he seems to find lions, eagles, foxes, crabs, peacocks, and hares so much easier to manipulate and make expressive than humans.

These linocuts of Bawden's maturity are unsurpassed by any other exponent of the medium. They both simplify a

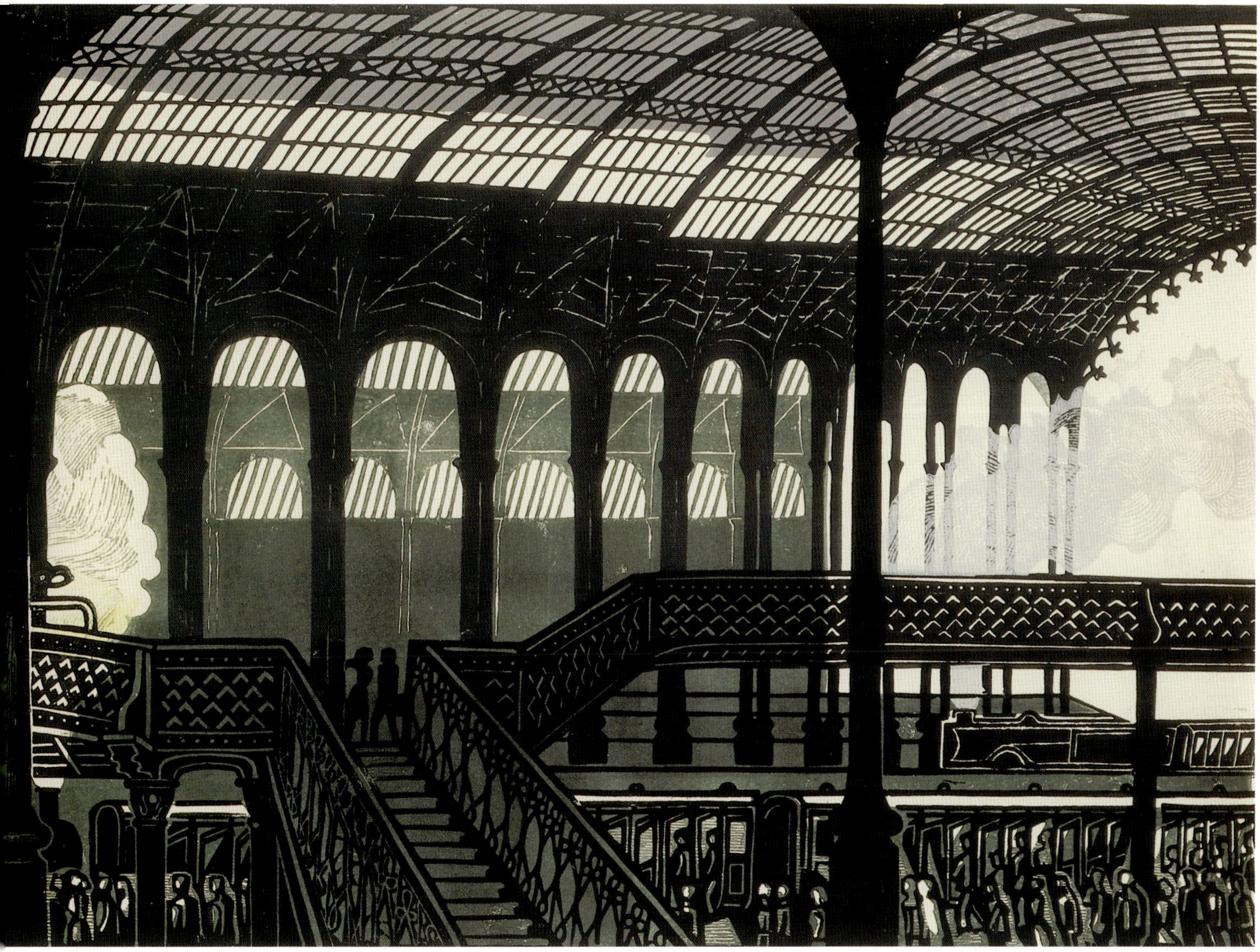

subject to its essentials yet make it complex again by the sheer ingenuity with which he manipulates a supposedly intractable material. Inks are reduced so that transparent layers can be over-printed to make a new colour or to allow the initial one to gleam through, all of which demands the most precise alignment before the whole image is pulled together by the final printing of the outlines. Each image is recognisably in Bawden's style, yet there are no repeated effects or mannerisms – look, for example, at how many ways he finds to portray the sky, or grass, or flowing water. Bliss concluded: 'He may well be remembered, despite all his other accomplishments, as Master of the linocut.'

Bawden undertook other work in this period up to 1970, not all of it equally successful. For example, *Tales from the Greeks and Trojans* (1951) offers an uneasy compromise between stiff archaic Greek figures acting out their dramas in more realistic landscapes for which the

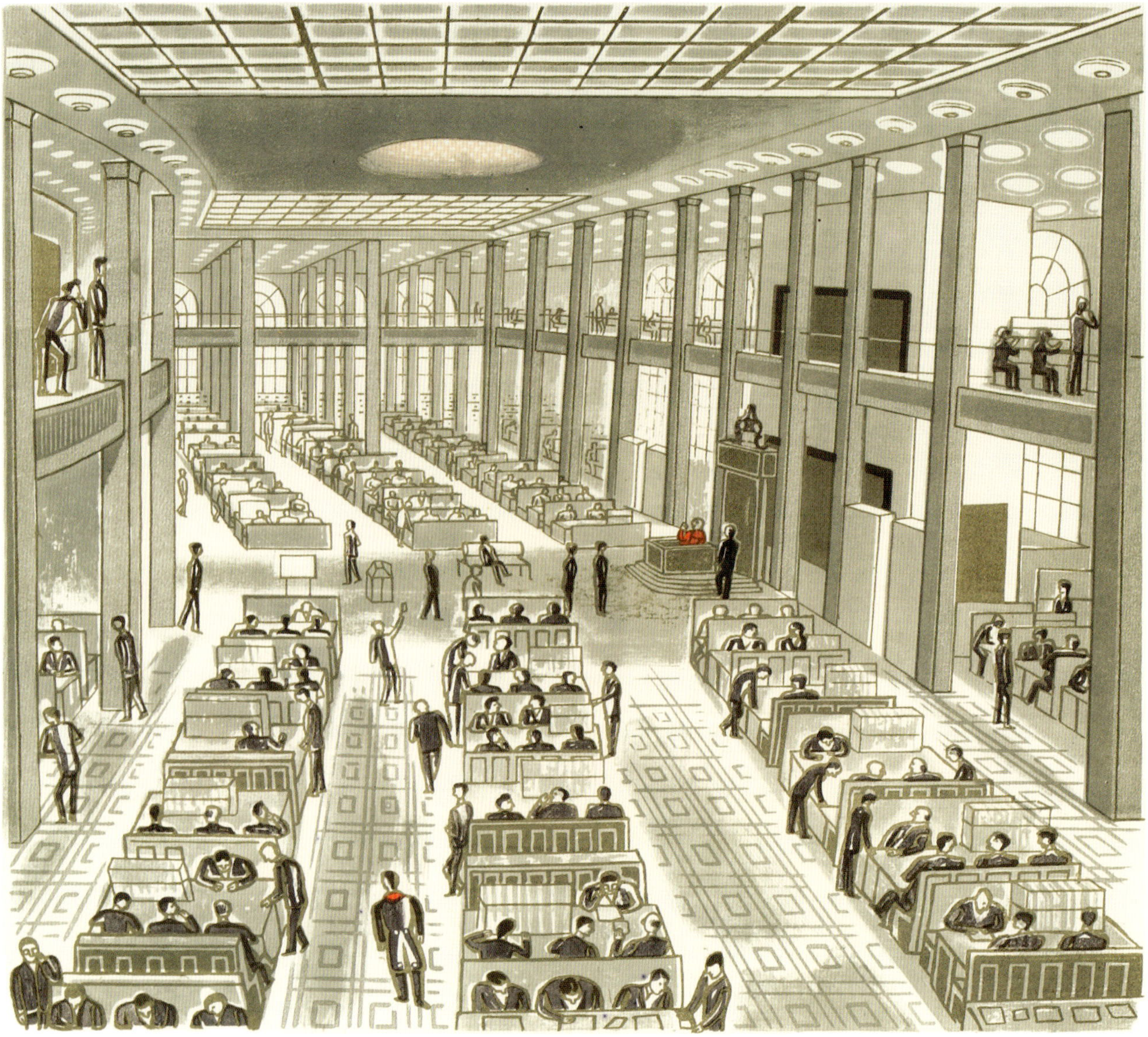

Lloyds, 1963, autolithograph, 410 x 451 mm (Trustees of Cecil Higgins Art Gallery, Bedford).

(Opposite top): *The Tower of London*, linocut, 1966, 510 x 665mm.
(Opposite bottom): *Leadenhall Market*,
colour lithograph from linocut, 1967, 458 x 614 mm.

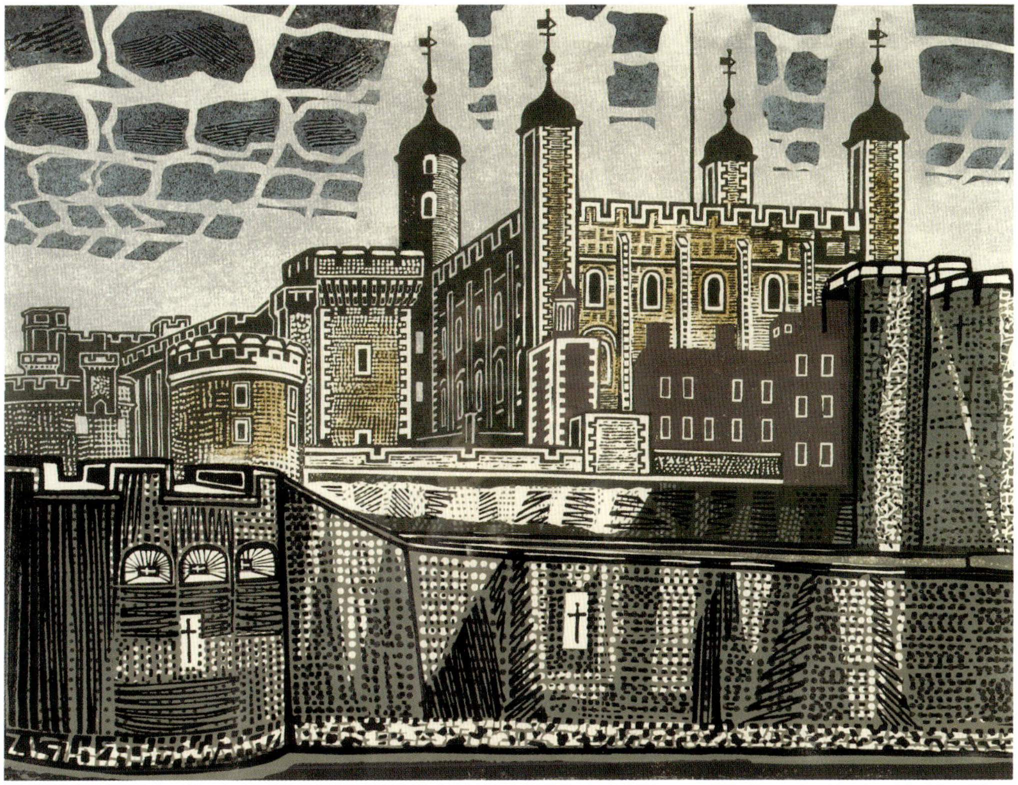

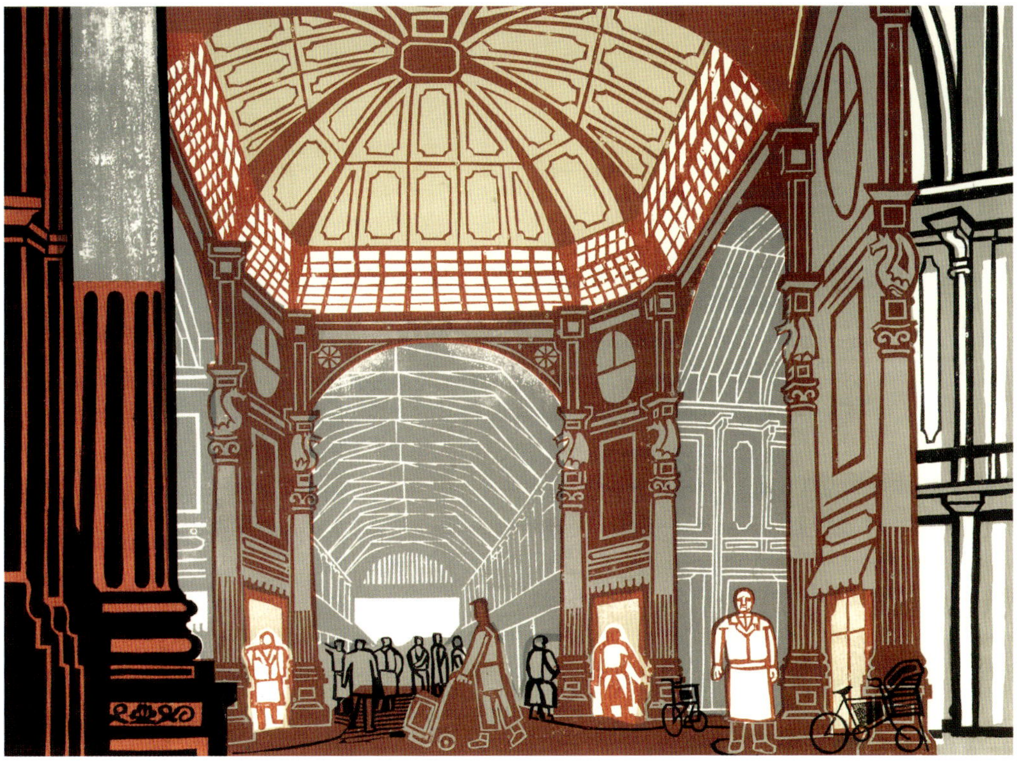

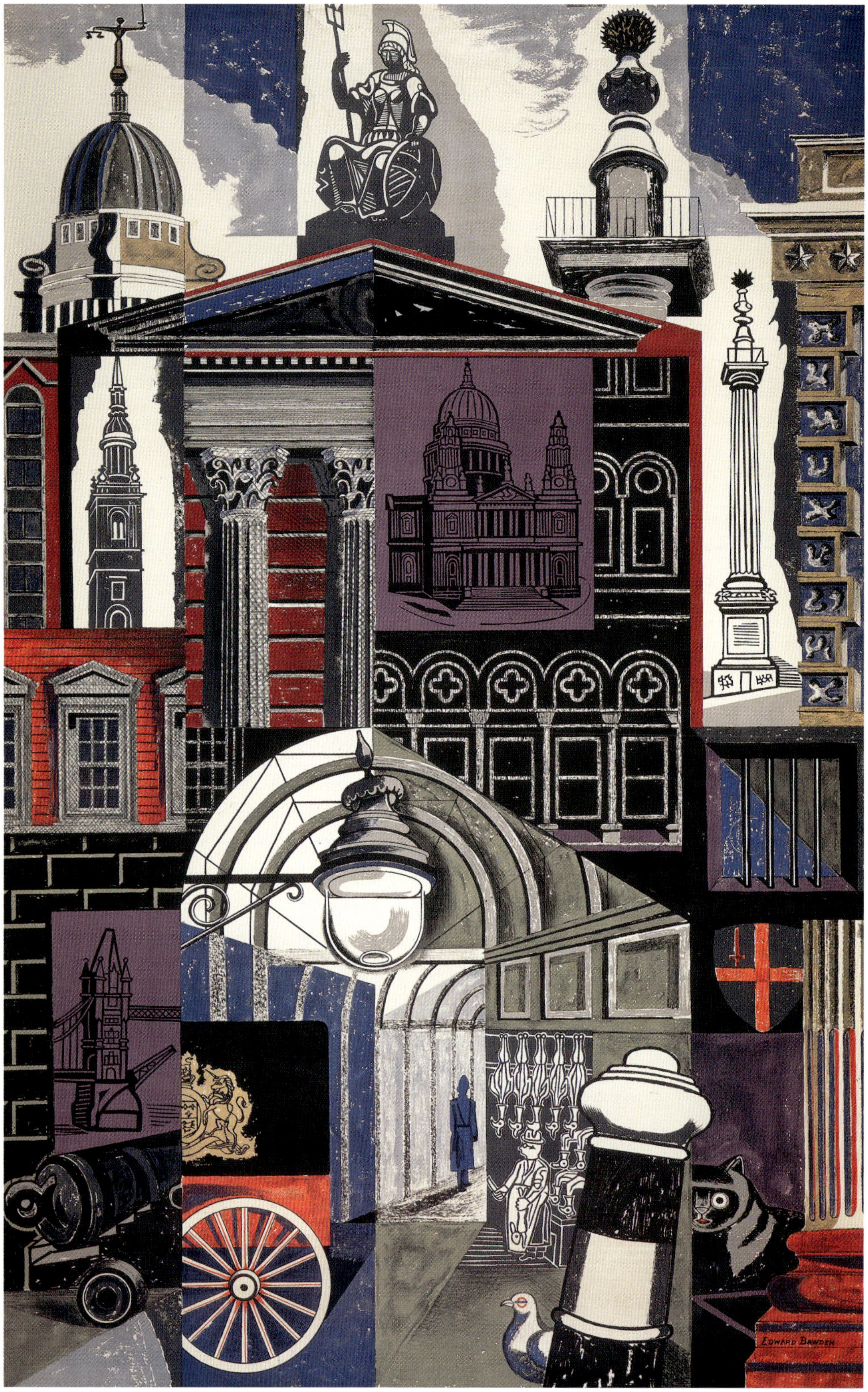

The City, poster design for London Passenger Transport Board, 1952, printed at the Curwen Press, 1014 x 634 mm.

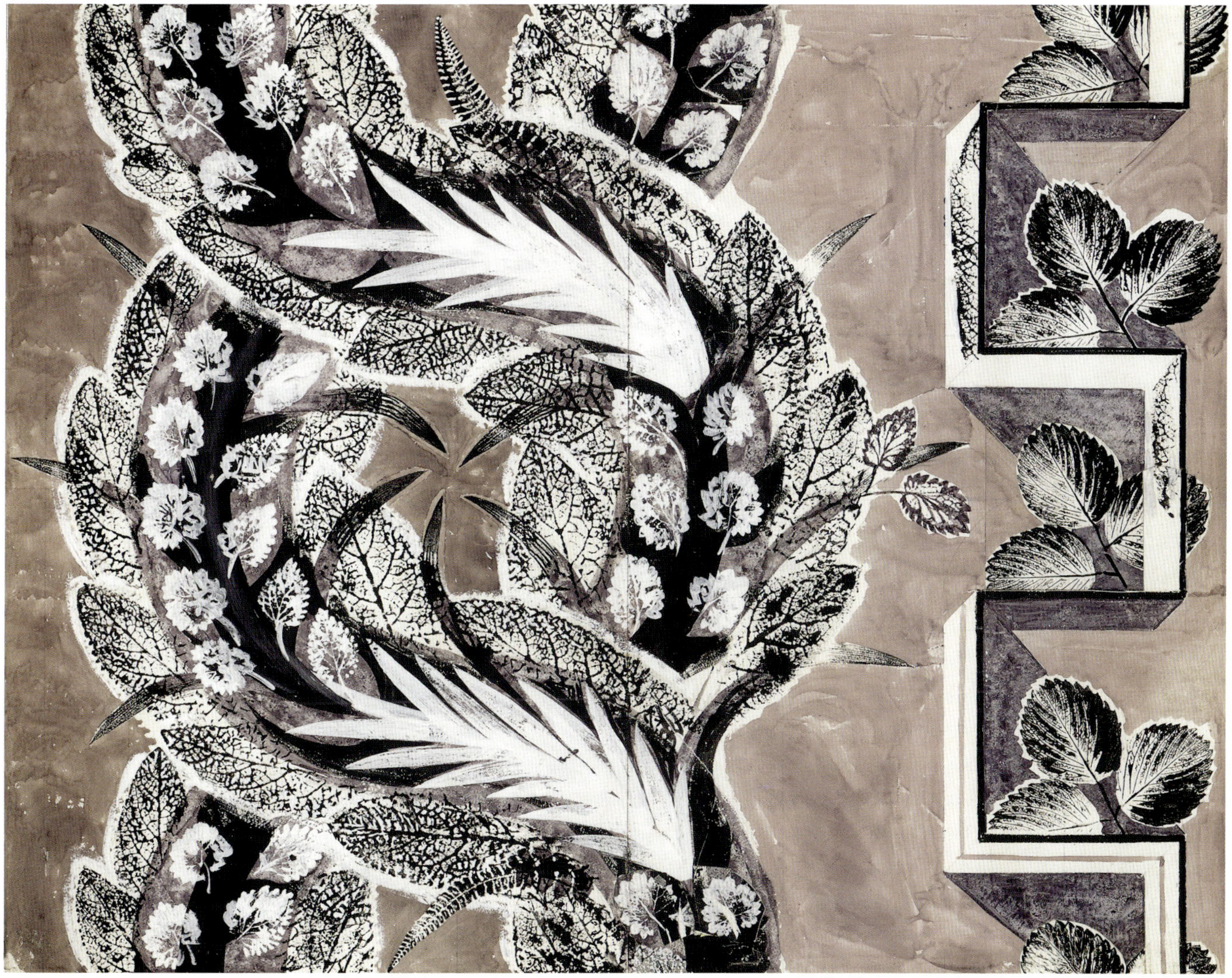

Fabric design in gouache with collage, *c.*1955, 60 x 76 cm (Fine Art Society).

ancient Greeks could offer no models. *The Historical Ballads of Denmark* (1958) when pitted against Bliss' *Border Ballads* seems to me the less impressive. And the colour separations for the eight double-spreads for Gustave Flaubert's *Salâmmbo* (1960, Limited Editions Club, New York) are lurid in the extreme and look as if they have been filled in with felt pens.

On the other hand, certain commissions made his creative juices flow. Bawden said: 'Reading is my hobby and I love books with good illustrations. An illustrator is limited of course by the sort of books he can or cannot illustrate. For me Jane Austen is untouchable but *The Histories of Herodotus* is absolutely my cup of tea.' And so it proved to be when he made one hundred action-packed line drawings for the two volumes of *The Histories of Herodotus of Helicarnassus*, published by the Heritage Press, New York, in 1958. Predictably *Gulliver's Travels* in both the 1948 and 1965 editions for the Folio Society was right up his street too, the author's view of mankind's absurdities coinciding neatly with his own. For these lithographs he invented a plumper, more sympathetic formula for the human figure than we have seen previously, though his naked and hairy female Yahoo is deliberately repellent. He tackled other heavy-weight classics for the Folio Society: *Vathek* (1958), *Utopia* (1972) and *Rasselas* (1975), each being fantastic, full of ideas and involving settings distant in time and place. Bliss had illustrated *Rasselas* as early as 1926 and Bawden wrote to him to assure him he 'had done it without a crib because I have lost my Bliss'. The Folio Society were good patrons providing a challenging, well-printed text in each case and giving him a free hand with the lithographs and colour combinations.

With all this experience under his belt Bawden, in 1967, at the age of sixty-four, felt he could approach the Fine

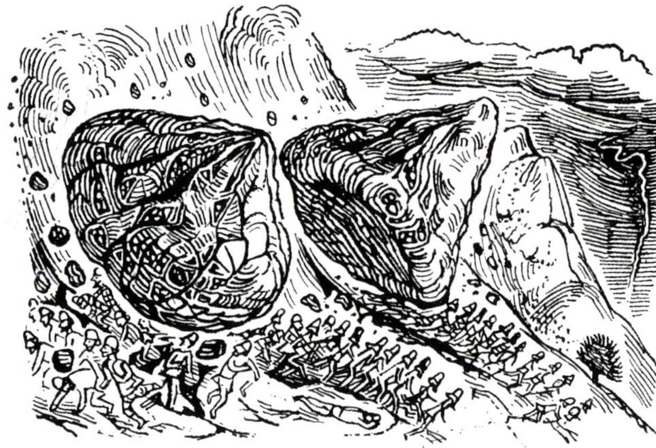

Illustration by Bawden from *The Histories of Herodotus of Helicarnassus*, 1958, actual size (Manchester Metropolitan University Library).

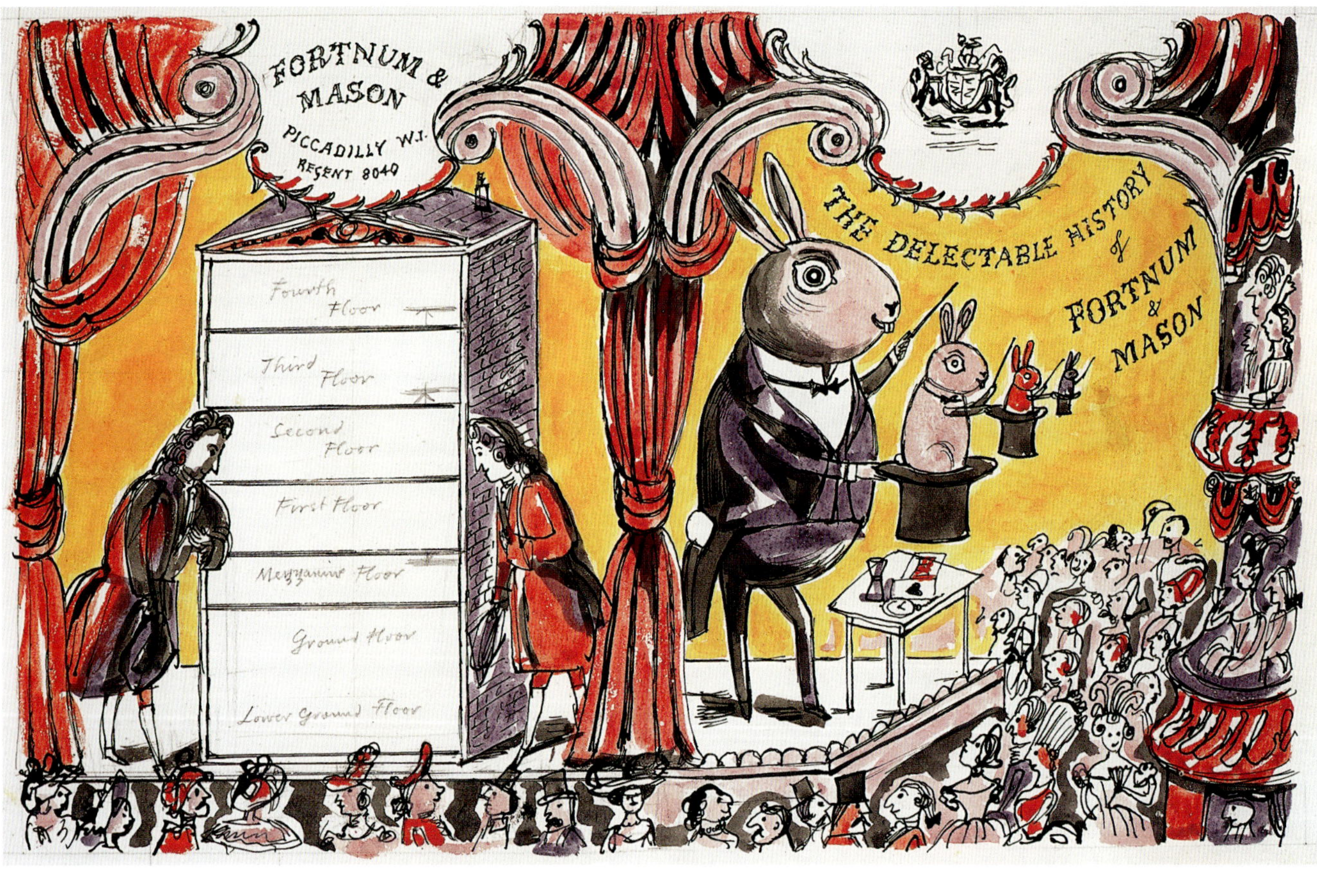

Design for Fortnum & Mason from Bawden's scrapbook (27 x 40 cm), 1957.
Right: tapestry on a farming theme, 1958, woven by Edinburgh Tapestry Company, 180 x 135 cm (Victoria & Albert Museum). Note the tail-less turkey.

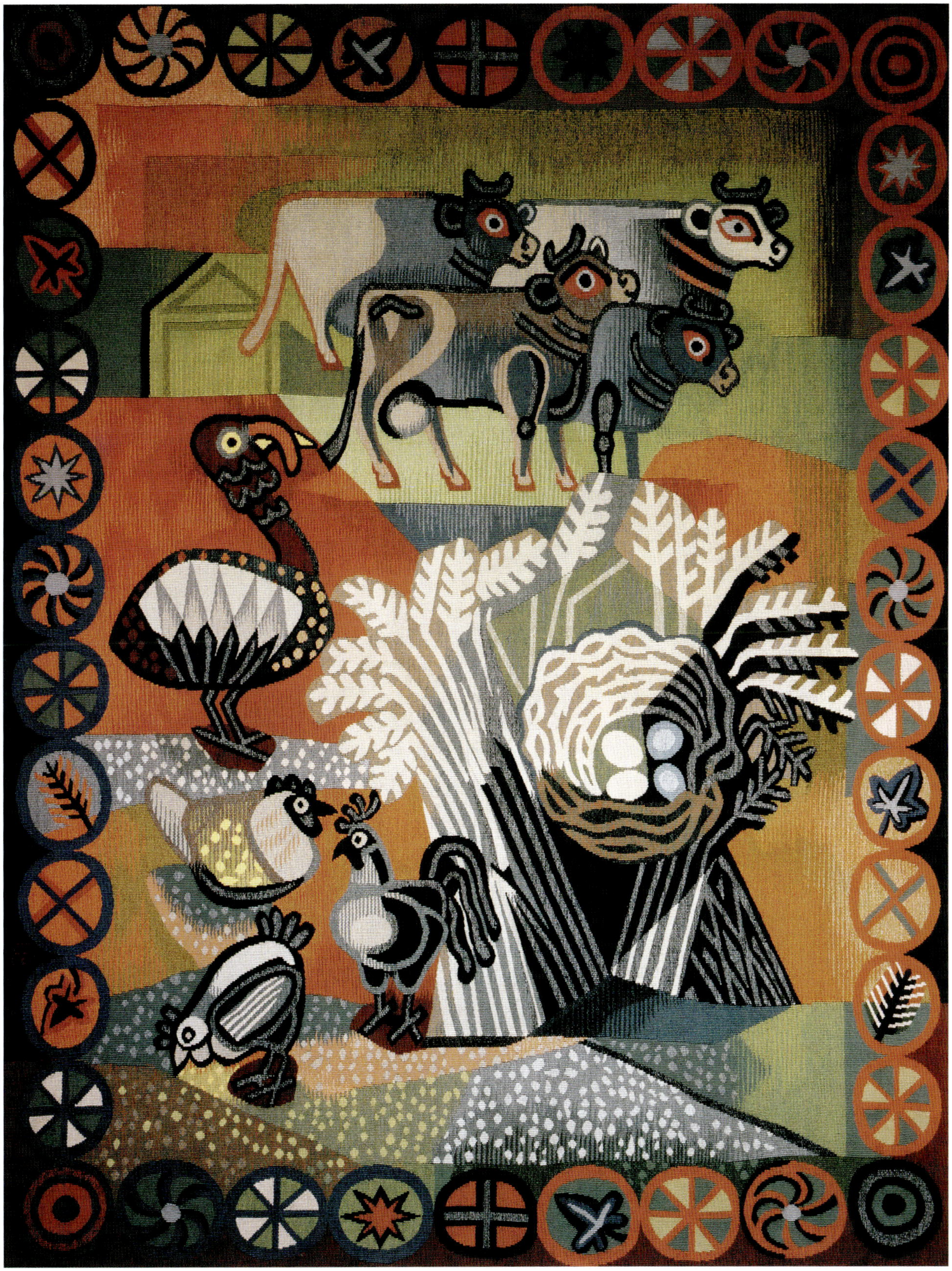

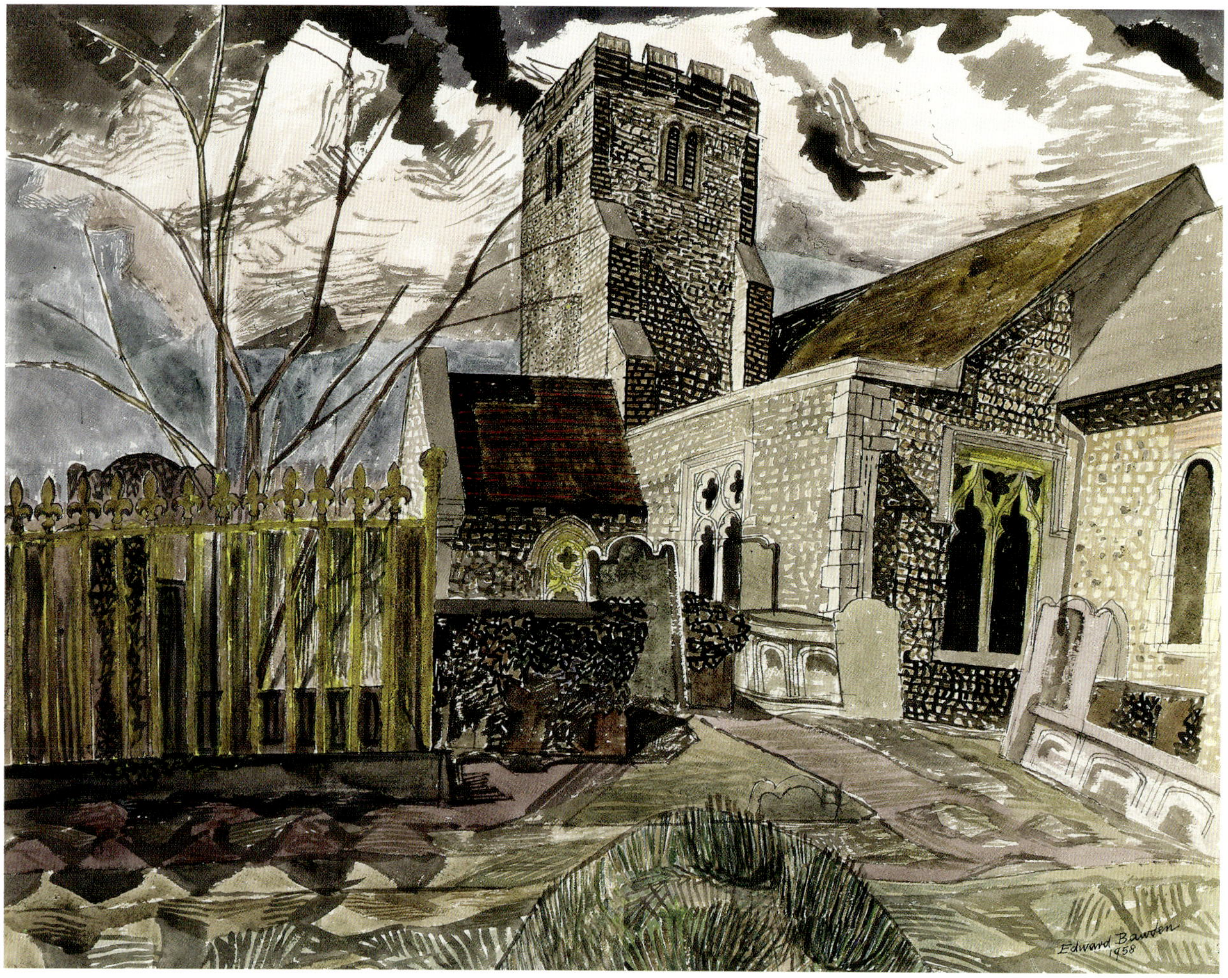

Lindsell Church, Essex, No. 6, 1958, watercolour, 463 x 578 mm (Fine Art Society).

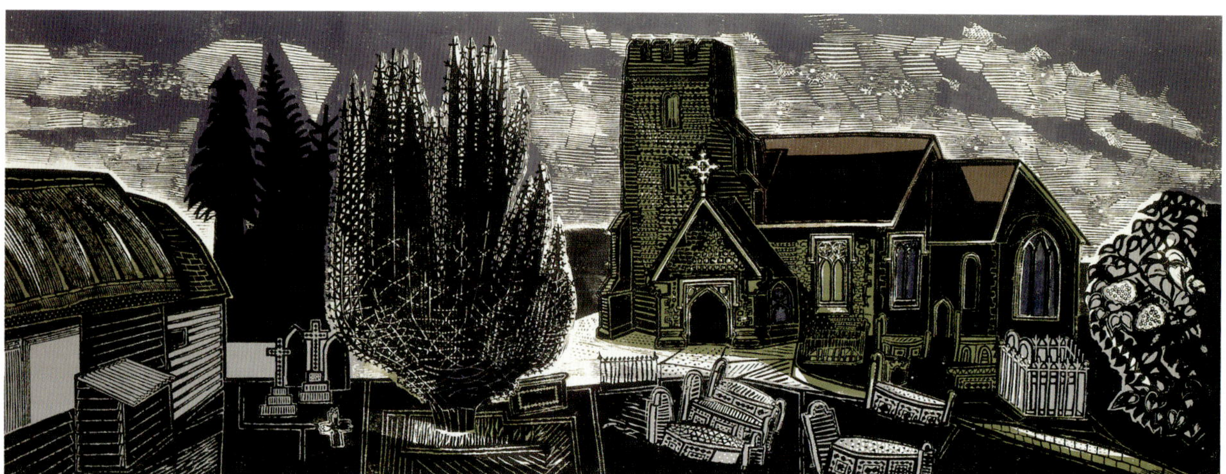

Lindsell Church, 1963, linocut, 616 x 1540 mm (Fine Art Society).

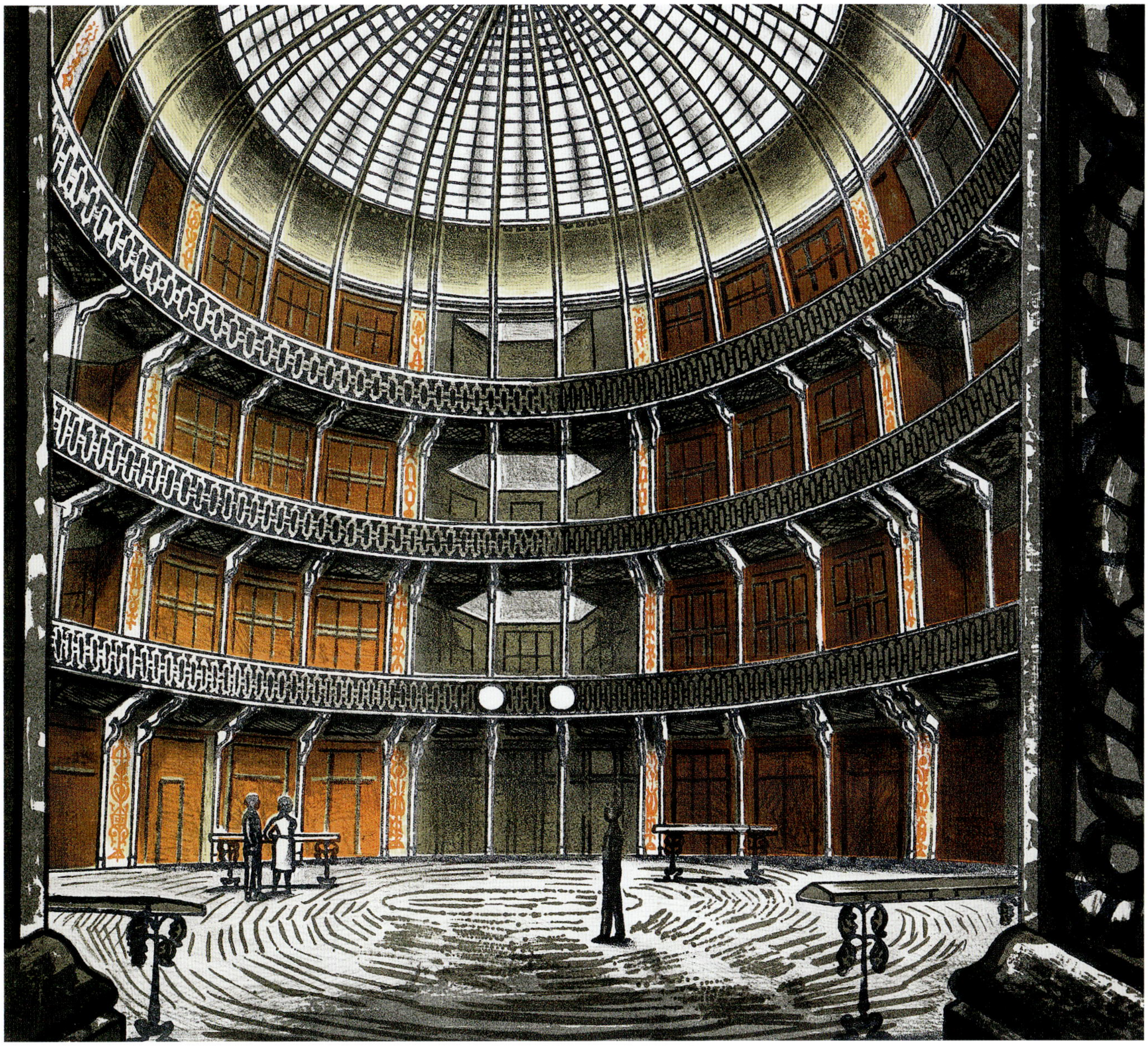

The Coal Exchange, 1963, autolithograph, 413 x 459 mm.

Art Society gallery in New Bond Street with a few samples. Peyton Skipwith, one of the directors and henceforth his friend and advocate recalls he entered 'more diffidently than most students carrying a portfolio, which he wondered if we might care to look at'. He was accepted of course and immediately given the first of many exhibitions, but it was clear that for all his success and years in teaching there was still a shy man in there who would prefer not to be noticed and left to get on with things, alone, back at the studio.

However, he could not lock himself in the studio all the time and even he must have noticed that the village beneath his attic window was changing. Not all the changes were to his liking. The population was creeping

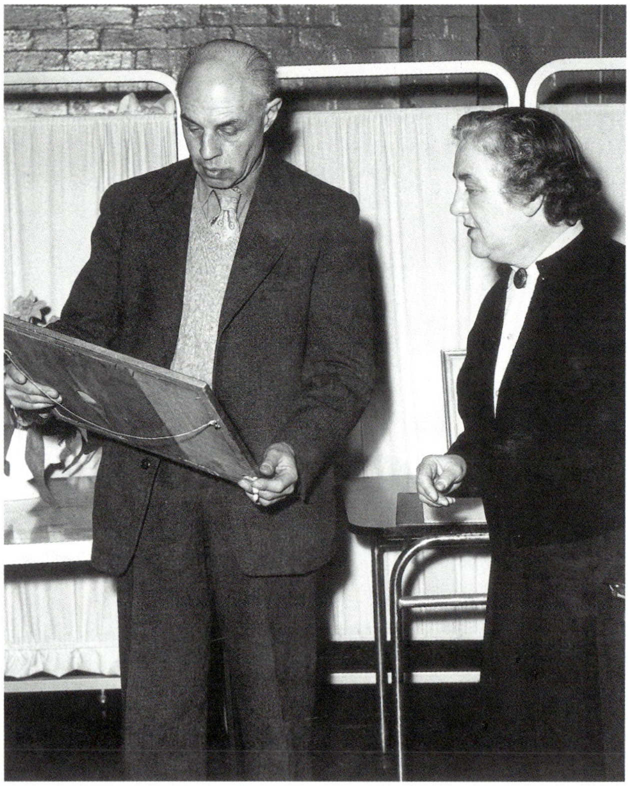

'Mr and Mrs Bawden judging paintings at the Weathersfield American Airbase', USAF photograph *c.*1960 (Trustees of Cecil Higgins Art Gallery, Bedford).

towards one thousand and cars were now commonplace, doors had to be locked at night and bicycles secured. The milk was no longer delivered in a pony and trap, lawns were not cut by scythes and most of those establishments and craftsmen he had drawn in 1949 for *Life in an English Village* had long vanished.

Worse still, the artistic community had begun to fragment in ways the puritanical Bawden strongly deplored. Bawden and Michael Rothenstein had finally become estranged over a printing technique for wallpaper that Rothenstein had sought to patent, but Bawden, perhaps not knowing this, set it as an exercise for his students. Lawsuits were threatened and relationships severed. In 1958 Rothenstein divorced Duffy and took a second wife, Samantha; they moved out of the village to a house named Columbia (after his printing press) in nearby Stisted where he built a new and bigger print studio and began to write his books on printmaking. Duffy took the children out of the Friends' Junior School at Saffron Walden, went to live in London and a year later married Eric Ayers, to whom she was introduced by Walter Hoyle. He was a friend of George Chapman and a former student of Bawden's at the RCA. Ayers was also a Director of Editions Alecto who printed some of Bawden's lithographs in the 1960s.

Bernard Cheese had left his wife when she was expecting her second child and with a new wife also moved to Stisted, becoming a close neighbour of Rothenstein's. The Bawdens gave Sheila practical support and he helped her get a full-time teaching job at the RCA (where she taught her own daughter Chloë). Worst of all, his oldest friend in the village, John Aldridge, separated from Lucie in 1960 and divorced her in 1970 when he

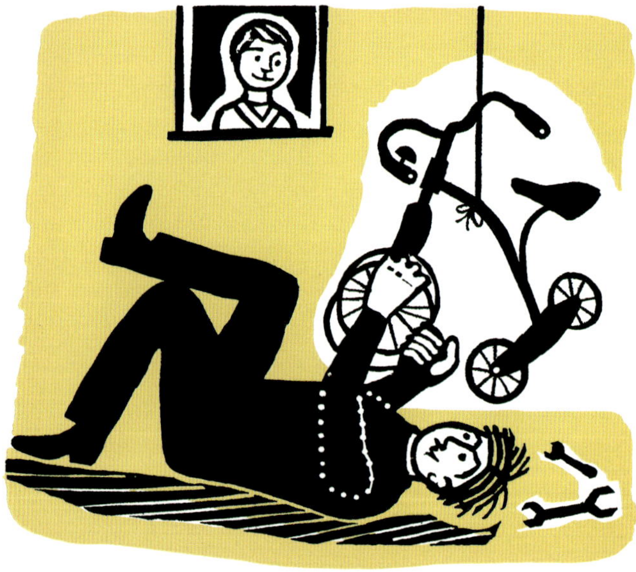

Linocut illustration from *Dunlopera*, 1961; 'It was with the home-made tyres, fitted on to his son's tricycle (with materials bought from a chemist's shop) that John Boyd Dunlop started the whole huge business in 1888'; actual size (Manchester Metropolitan University Library).

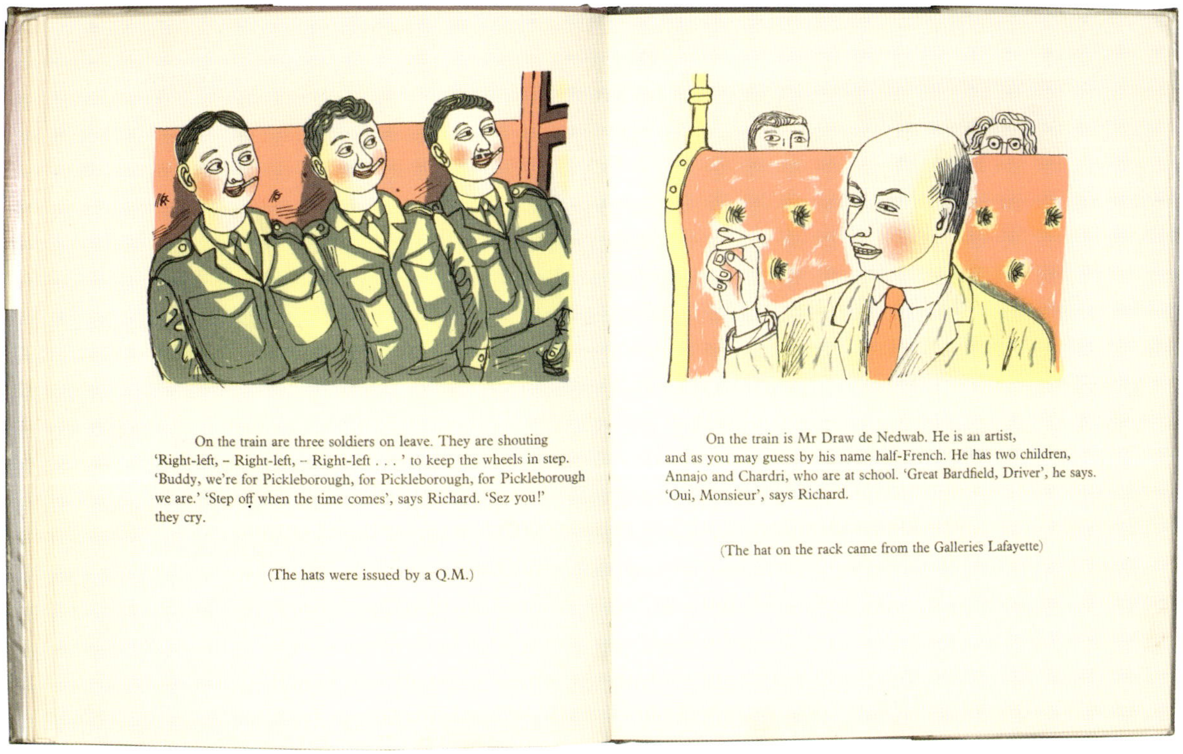

On the train are three soldiers on leave. They are shouting 'Right-left, – Right-left, – Right-left . . . ' to keep the wheels in step. 'Buddy, we're for Pickleborough, for Pickleborough, for Pickleborough we are.' 'Step off when the time comes', says Richard. 'Sez you!' they cry.

(The hats were issued by a Q.M.)

On the train is Mr Draw de Nedwab. He is an artist, and as you may guess by his name half-French. He has two children, Annajo and Chardri, who are at school. 'Great Bardfield, Driver', he says. 'Oui, Monsieur', says Richard.

(The hat on the rack came from the Galleries Lafayette)

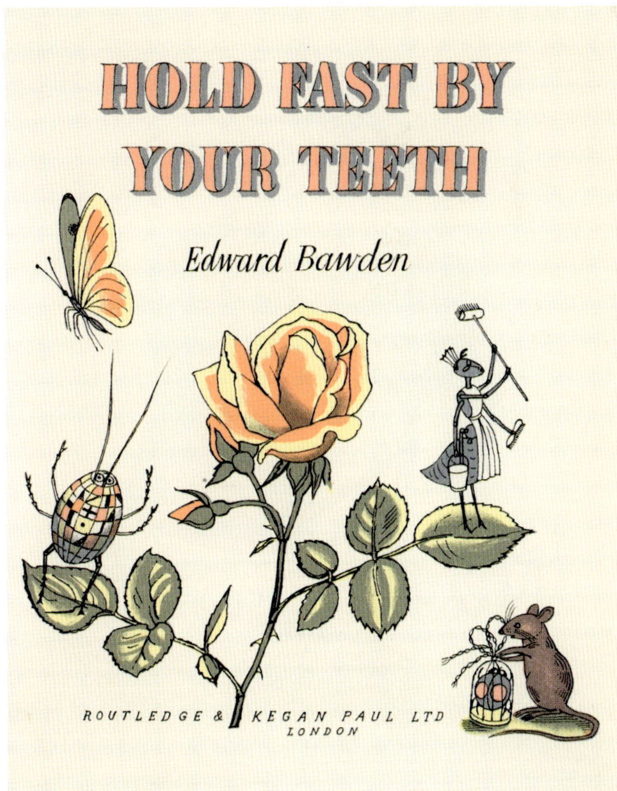

HOLD FAST BY YOUR TEETH

Edward Bawden

ROUTLEDGE & KEGAN PAUL LTD
LONDON

Bawden's 1963 caricature of himself as Mr Draw de Nedwab, and his children Joanna (Annajo) and Richard (Chardri), in *Hold Fast By Your Teeth*, with its title page (Manchester Metropolitan University Library).

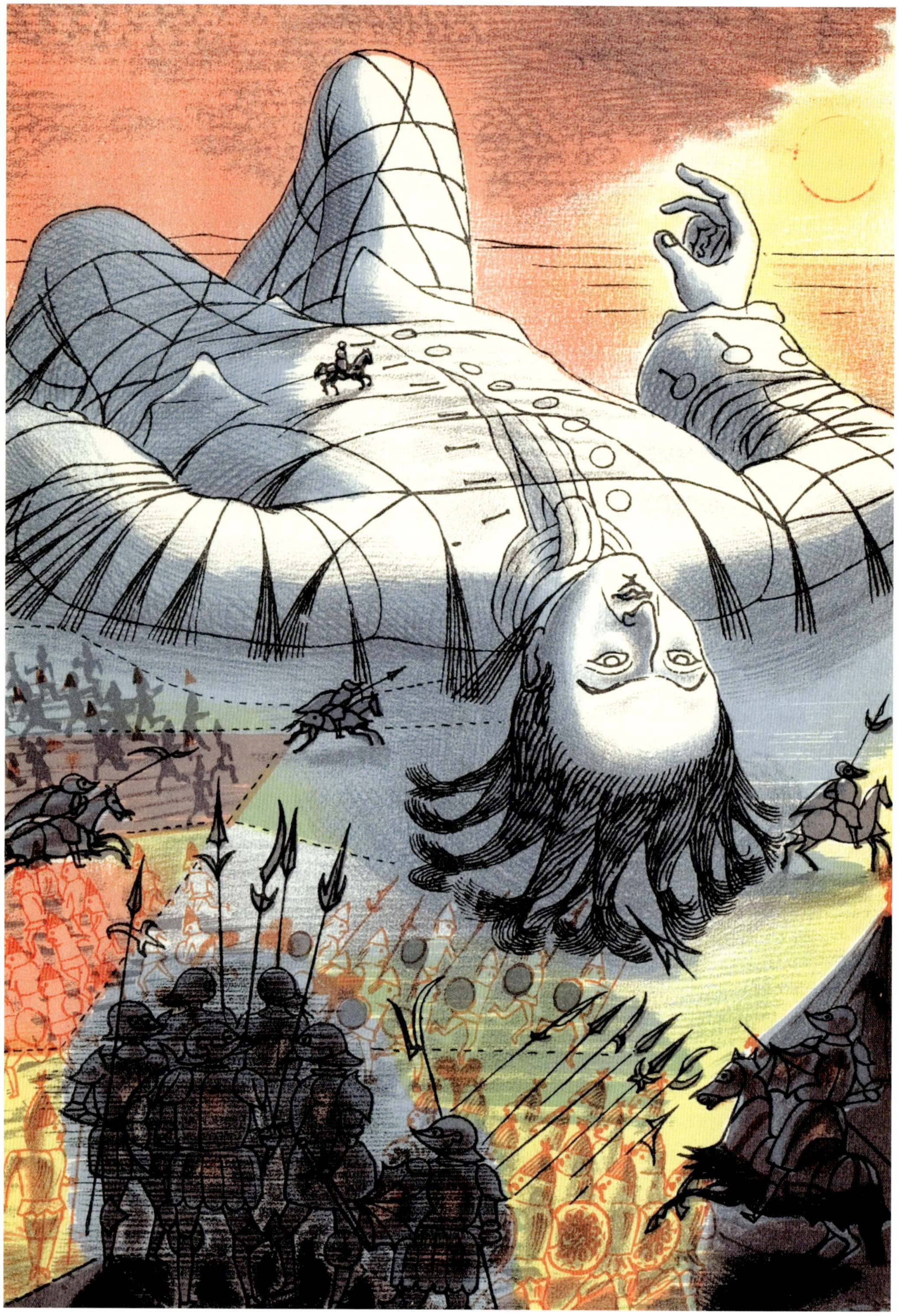

Illustration from *Gulliver's Travels*, 1965,
(Manchester Metropolitan University Library).

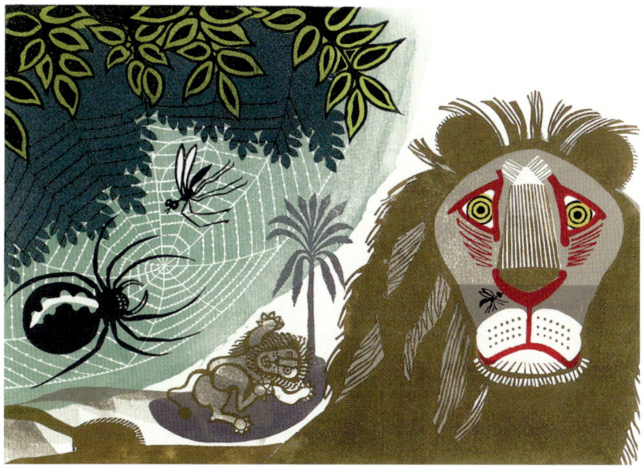

The Gnat & the Lion, 1970, linocut from the *Aesop's Fables* series, 405 x 558 mm (Fine Art Society).

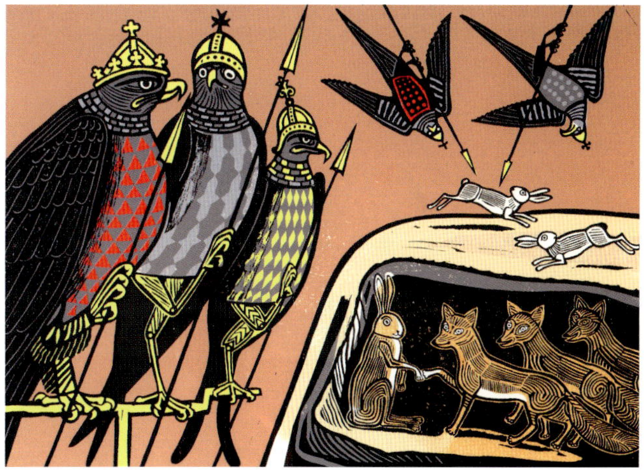

Hares, Foxes & Eagles, 1970, linocut from the *Aesop's Fables* series, 403 x 561 mm (Fine Art Society).

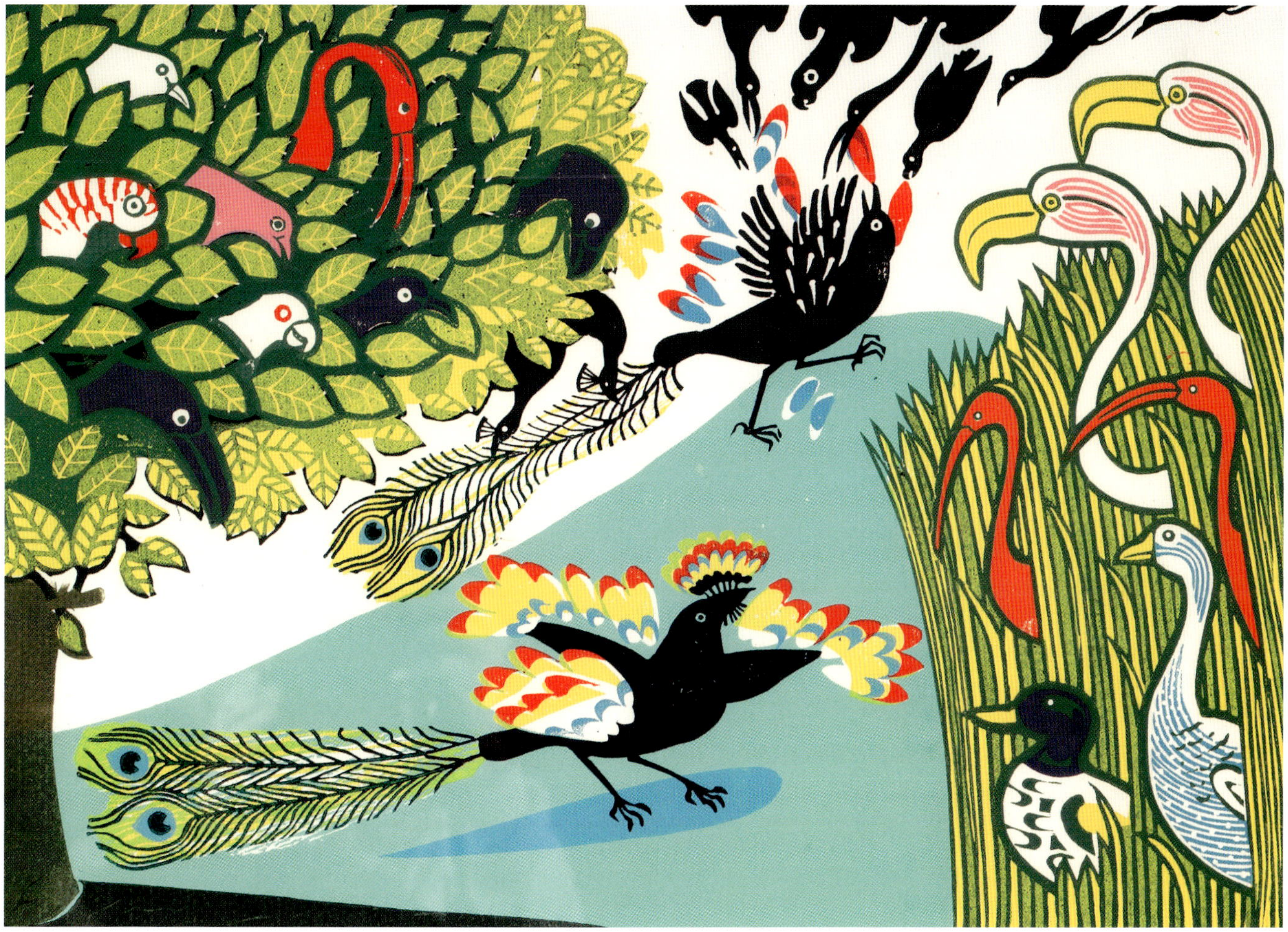

Daw in Borrowed Feathers, 1970, linocut from the *Aesop's Fables* series, 405 x 558 mm (Fine Art Society).

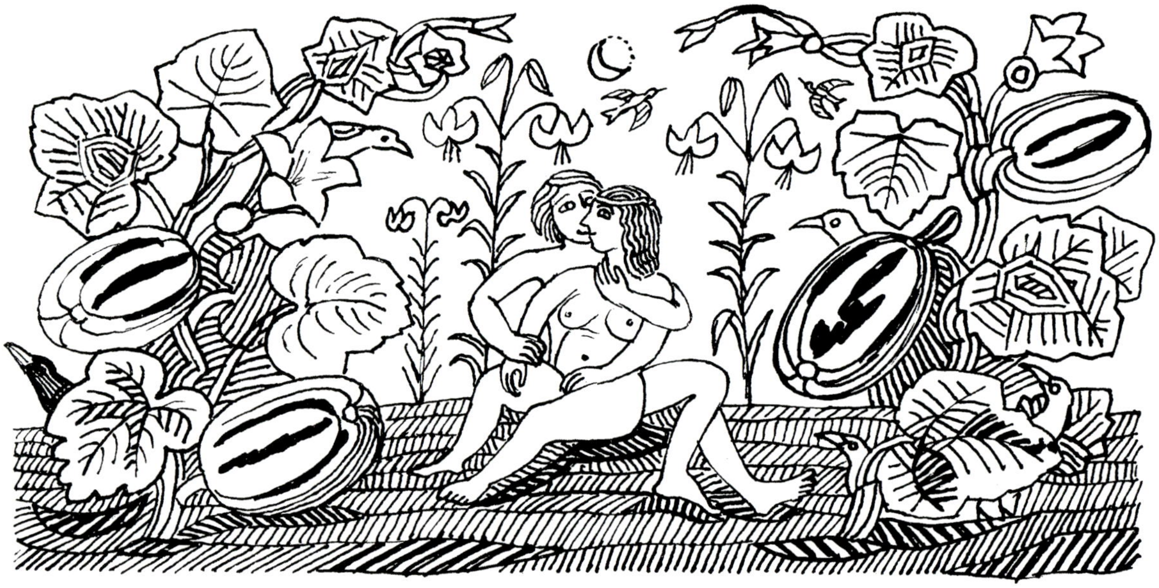

Illustration from *The World's Greatest Story: the Epic of the Jewish People in Biblical Times*, 1978 (Fry Art Gallery).
(Opposite) Original drawing for *The History of Rasselas, Prince of Abyssinia*, 1975; actual size as shown (Fine Art Society).

married his long-time companion Margareta Anna Maria Cameron (née Bajardi), known as Gretl, who was the widow of the poet Norman Cameron. In all these divorce cases Bawden and Charlotte took the side of the wives. Bawden never spoke to Aldridge again and rebuked his son Richard for having supper at The Place House, while John Norris Wood had to turn off the engine of his motor bike before he reached the village street so Bawden couldn't hear him paying Aldridge a visit. At the turn of the century Bawden's father had sacked any employee in the ironmongery firm who had committed adultery, and Bawden was no less unforgiving. Eric Ravilious' affairs were the only exceptions he made.

Others began to leave for different reasons. The Chapmans left for Wales in 1960, the Hoyles moved to Great Saling and then to the south coast, Audrey Cruddas to Diss, Sheila Robinson to Saffron Walden, and Marianne Straub to Cambridge before moving back to Switzerland.

Then Charlotte began to slow down with heart problems. She resigned from being a magistrate, and had to give up her Chairmanship of the British Women's Institute and her many external examinerships. As she could no longer drive she arranged for the two of them to move to a house in Park Lane in the centre of Saffron Walden where most things were within walking distance, but before this could happen she died. In 1970 Bawden had suddenly lost his home, two studios and Charlotte, his greatest support. He was aged sixty-seven and increasingly isolated by his deafness. Things looked grim.

1. 'Children's Books', *Line*, No. 2, APU, Department of Arts and Design, Cambridge, 2002.
2. Bliss, D. P., *Edward Bawden*, Pendomer Press, 1979, p.151.
3. Rothenstein, J., *Modern English Painters, Volume 2: 'Nash to Bawden'*, Macdonald and Co., 1984, p.307.
4. Bliss, D. P., ibid, p.165.

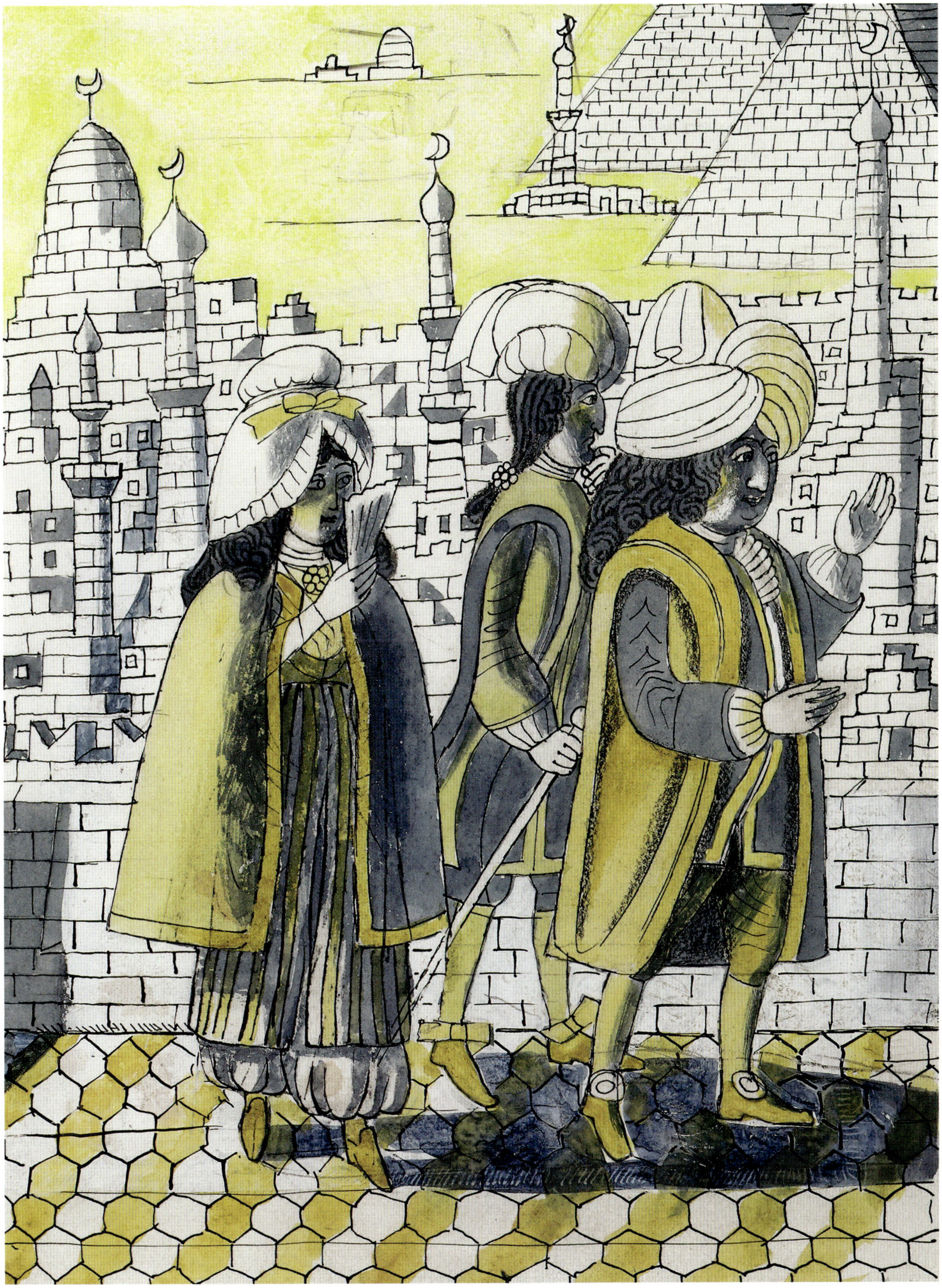

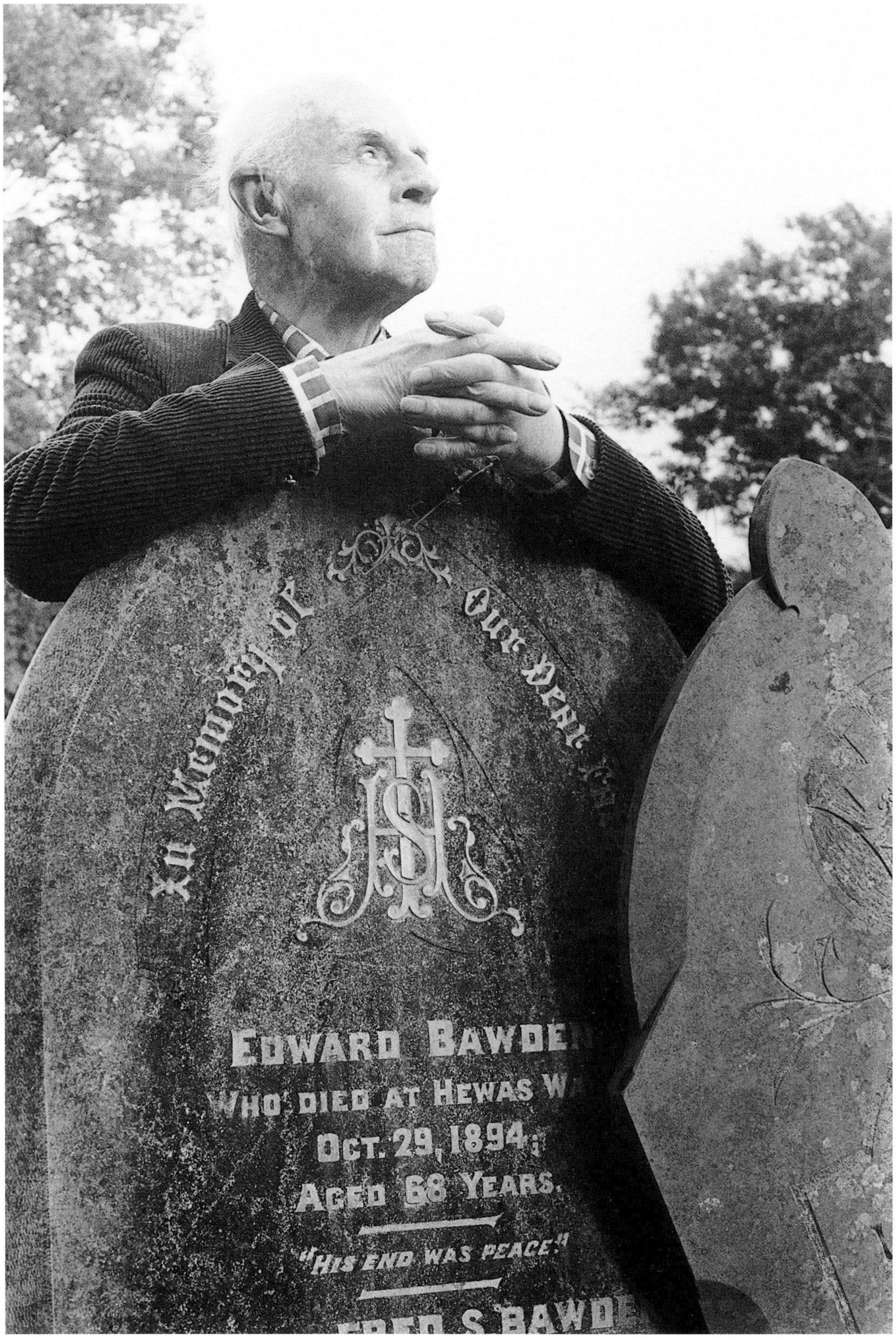

Bawden leaning on a Cornish gravestone in St Ewe churchyard, 1982, though it does not belong to one of his ancestors (©Christopher Brown).

12. THE LAST YEARS

Bawden moved into number 2 Park Lane, Saffron Walden, in 1970. It was next to the Co-op car park whose bustle and animation he quite enjoyed and he was not bothered by the noise because he could not hear it. The house at number 1 had a macabre history he would have appreciated: it was once owned by a baker who allegedly put his murder victims into pies and was eventually hanged on Market Hill.[1] Park Lane had had many other names down the centuries and after his death it would be redeveloped and have another one: Edward Bawden Court.

He made it feel like home by papering the walls with his own designs – the *Dove and Church* on the staircase, Mermaid in the bathroom and *Sand Dune* in the bedroom. Most of his valuable library of illustrated and historical books was sold to leave more room in his specially-built studio on the top floor, though he quickly came to regret this and began to buy them back again. The studio was twenty feet by twelve and had a trap door in the floor so he could get mural panels in. There was a garden front and back, though nowhere near as big as the one at Brick House. It was snug and convenient but, typically, he called it 'a horrid little house'. There was no point in buying a television he couldn't listen to and he relied on his daily *Guardian* for news of the wider world.

Bawden knew Saffron Walden well from his school days onwards and found a ready-made artistic community there to welcome him: Paul Beck, John Bolam, Anthony Deigan, Olga Lehmann, Olga Marshall and David Myerscough-Jones, all had solid national reputations in their various specialisms. Later there came the Church Street Gallery which would commission and enthusiastically show Bawden's work as well as that of Aldridge, Hoyle, Sheila Robinson and Bliss. Bawden said of Saffron Walden: 'A fine town, but then good architecture always attracts interesting residents', and he was right.

With Charlotte gone he might have resigned himself to a lonely isolation but in many ways he became more expansive, emerging from his shell and finding he liked company after all, especially that of women. He had a jolly housekeeper, Betty Missing, and Sheila Robinson had moved to the town two years earlier to be near her children at the Friends' School; now she repaid the Bawdens' kindnesses to her by keeping an eye on Edward. She drove him around, and in 1973 she and Marianne Straub took him on holiday to Turkey, from where he smuggled cactus plants home in his sponge bag. Sheila helped him to print on his Albion Press and offered her criticism of his work, which he respected and acted upon, and in return he cooked her an evening meal on the days when she returned from teaching at the RCA. She is reputed to be the only person to whom he was never rude, and her daughter Chloë speculates that Bawden would willingly have married Sheila if only she had agreed. Several other ladies also claim they were proposed to, but how seriously we cannot tell. Marianne Straub visited most weekends and the Hoyles came over from Cambridge.

One devoted Saffron Walden friend to whom he was frequently very rude was Olive Cook (1912-2002), a Cambridge graduate in Modern Languages and a former staff member at the National Gallery. She earned her living as a writer on art history, architecture and guide books but she longed to be a painter. In this she had been

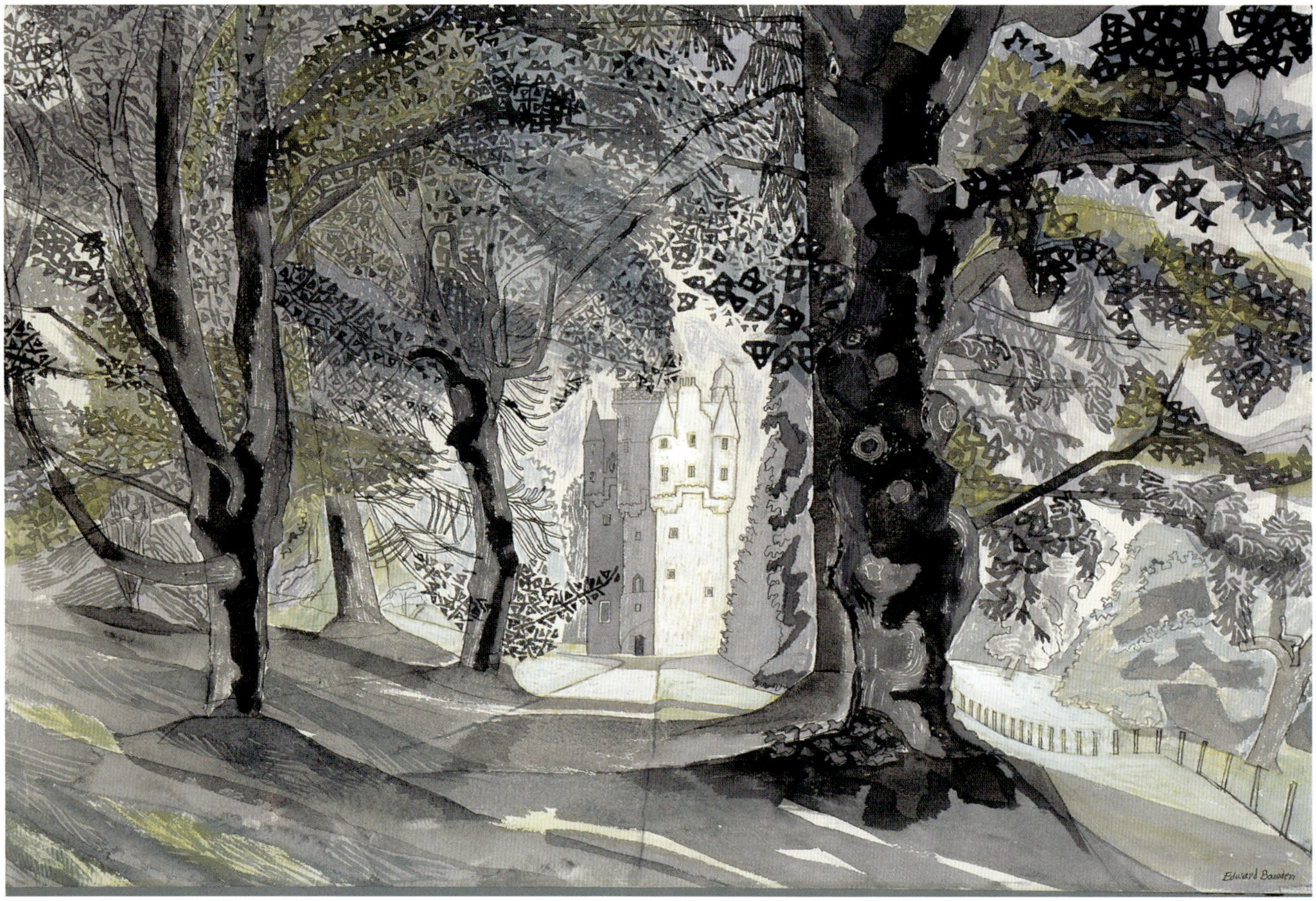

Craigievar Castle 3, 1972, watercolour, 495 x 749 mm (Harlow Council Collection).
(Opposite) *Audley End Park III*, 1974, watercolour, 740 x 535 mm.

encouraged by Cedric Morris, Tom Hennell, William Rothenstein and Bawden himself. Her husband, Edwin Smith (1912-1971) also had painting ambitions but was more famous as a photographer who had published forty books, most of them about English country houses and gardens, many with texts by his wife. Another new friend, a Greek lady who lived in Saffron Walden, persuaded Bawden to go away to Greece with her, but on their return he never spoke to her again and cut her dead in the street. His teenaged granddaughter Louise, daughter of Richard, also came to live with him for long periods and though there were inevitably inter-generational differences of opinion, they established a close bantering relationship. One wonders if Bawden remembered writing to Gwyneth Lloyd Thomas in 1939 about Ravilious' fear of losing his talent as he aged: 'Eric in his middle twenties spoke of the early thirties as the difficult time and now in his middle thirties he casts an eye upon fifty as the turning point in a painter's life. So it may be: but I would not like to undertake the appalling burden of experience borne at eighty and ninety, when wise beyond one's dreams and expectations, the sketching apparatus and a frail old body

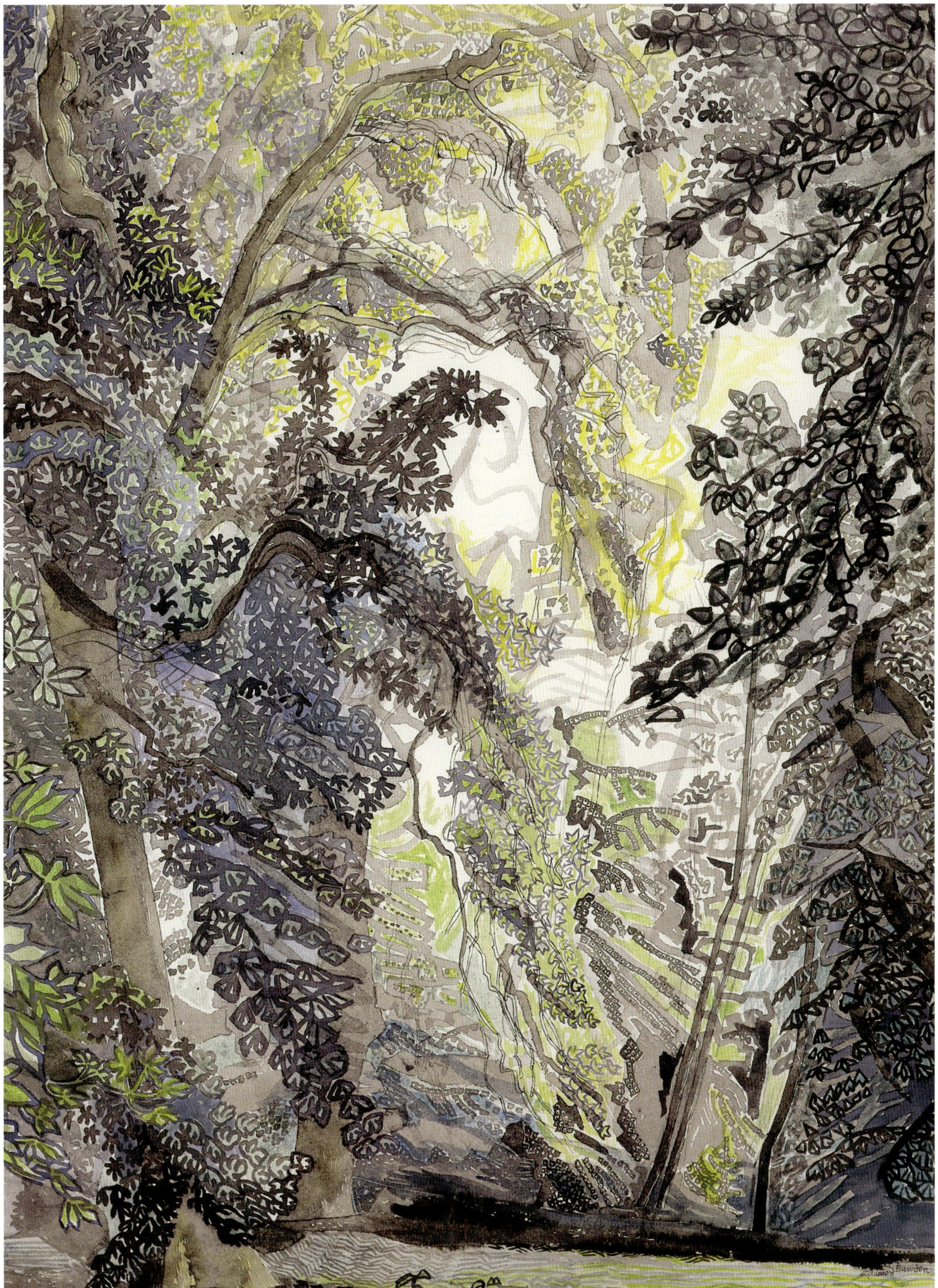

is wheeled out into the garden by a grand-daughter in blond curls and a little spotted pinny.'[2]

Further afield Muriel Rose, an authority on hand-made patterns and a friend of his and Charlotte's from before the war, lived in London where until he was seventy-five, Bawden still kept up his part-time connections with the RCA. So if he had to attend an evening function there, or at the Royal Academy, he would write to her asking for a bed, decorating his teasing letters with pictures of himself as a tom, and she as a queen cat tying his bow tie.

Bawden soon had his leg pulled about these female 'Muses' all dancing attendance. He told an interviewer: 'As soon as you become a widower you find that your circle of women friends is greatly increased! I didn't realise that. When my wife died, I thought, well, that's the end of me too. That was ten years ago and I still manage to survive. It's very refreshing knowing so many women, they're so civilised. And I suppose my own occupations are to a great extent feminine. I like cooking moderately and I'm sure I could turn my attention to embroidery.'[3]

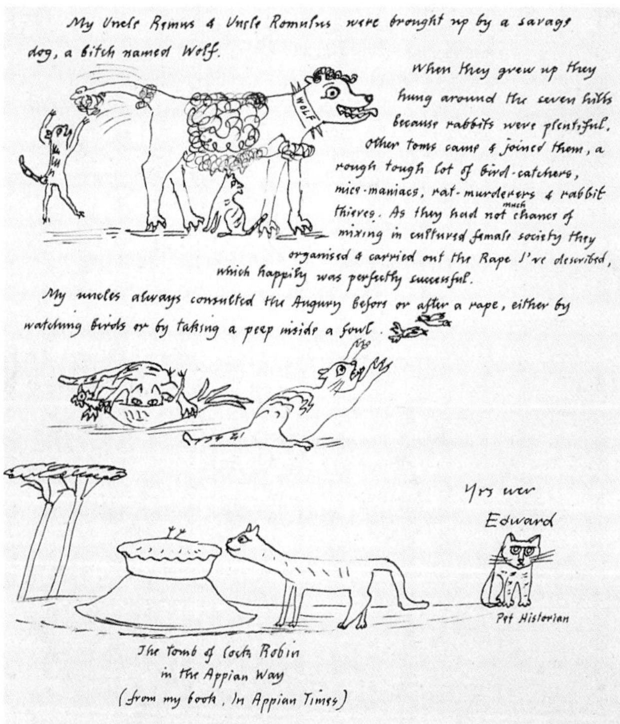
My Uncle Remus & Uncle Romulus were brought up by a savage dog, a bitch named Wolf.

When they grew up they hung around the seven hills because rabbits were plentiful. Other toms came & joined them, a rough tough lot of bird-catchers, mice-maniacs, rat-murderers & rabbit thieves. As they had not much chance of mixing in cultured female society they organised & carried out the Rape I've described, which happily was perfectly successful.

My uncles always consulted the Augury before or after a rape, either by watching birds or by taking a peep inside a fowl.

Yrs ever

Edward

Pet Historian

The tomb of Cock Robin in the Appian Way (from my book, In Appian Times)

One of Bawden's feline letters to Muriel Rose.

Then a group of nineteen women came into his life when he was asked to provide a tapestry design for the Cecil Higgins Art Gallery in Bedford. He rejected all their suggestions for modern subjects and chose Bunyan's *Pilgrim's Progress*. For this he designed a large grid (59 x 93 inches) of eighty squares, twenty of which show Bunyan behind prison bars thinking of a golden heaven. The others are based on a snakes and ladders board where a red thread leads the eye from one square to another as Pilgrim travels his arduous path. The ladies of the Needlework section of the Bedford Music and Art Club worked on his designs from 1977 to 1979. The finished work has the mixture of seeming folksyness and sophistication with touches of sly wit that one has come to expect in Bawden's public works.

Another late large-scale piece was the wall-map of the British Empire as it was in 1947, which he made for the 'Style of Empire' exhibition at the Miami Dade Community College, USA, in 1985. The commission came through Peyton Skipwith of the Fine Art Society. Bawden was assisted in this by Joanna's son, Tommy, and Stanley Jones made a Curwen lithograph of it afterwards.

Around the time of his move to Saffron Walden, Douglas Percy Bliss came back into Bawden's life. They had exchanged visits through the years, Bawden calling at their Derbyshire cottage and sometimes upsetting Phyllis by being critical of the garden. He also wrote to her, 'sometimes I wish I had a garden like yours, queerly overgrown and full of hidden Satanic sculpture, with Baptists singing in the bushes and birds in the trees'. (30th June 1974). The two men swapped frequent letters about old times and their ailments (for example Bawden wrote after a hernia operation, 'I came home six weeks ago sewn up coarsely like an old sock and deprived of pubic hair'). Bliss had retired in 1964 to paint landscapes and cultivate his Windley garden after a distinguished career as Director of Glasgow School of Art, but for all his achievements as a writer, administrator and con-

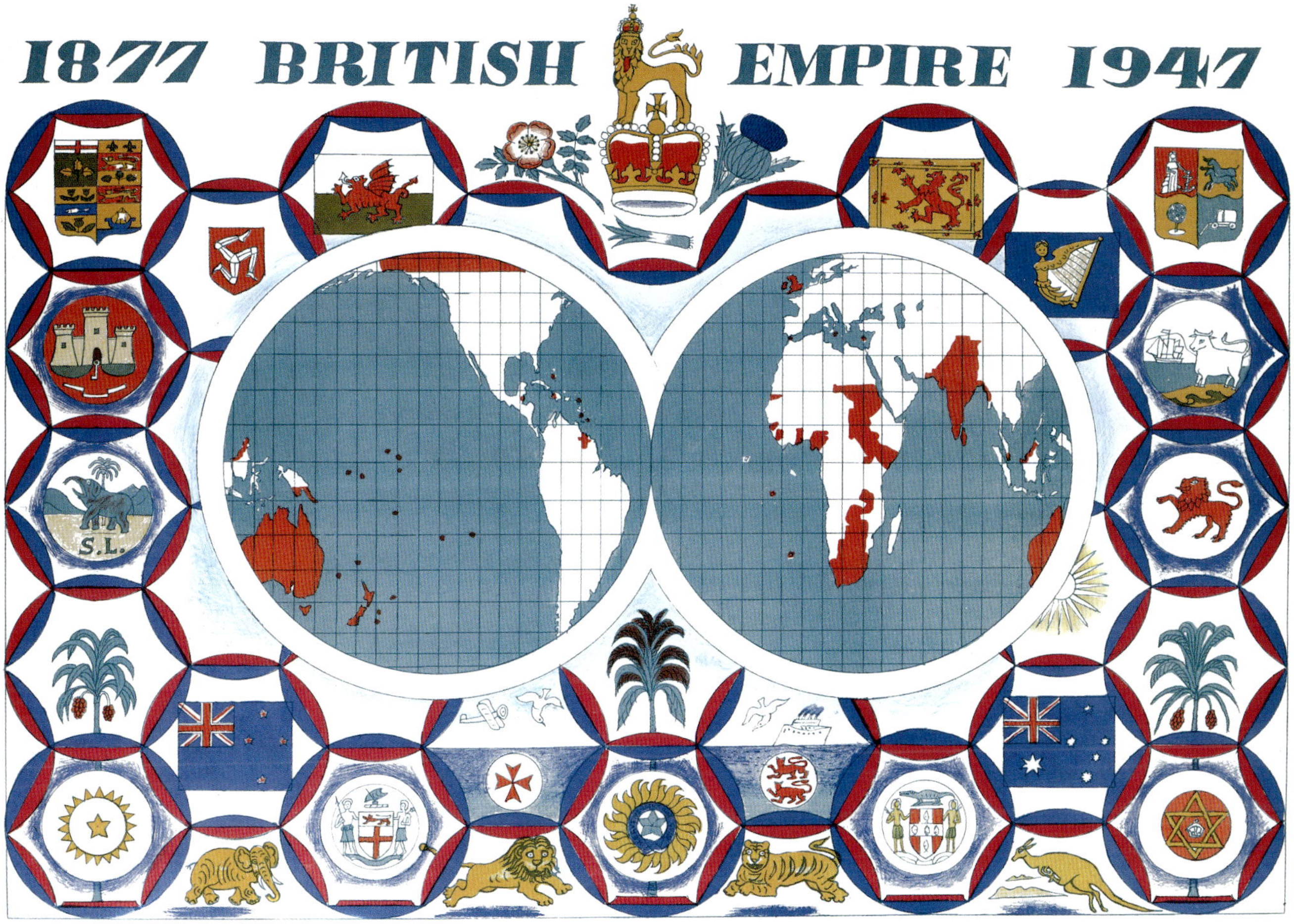

British Empire Map, 1985, colour lithograph drawn on plastic, 490 x 710 mm.

servationist he must have felt he never matched Bawden as an artist. He wrote to ask: 'Is anybody doing a book about you? I expect so. If not I wouldn't mind having a go myself. After all you have been the biggest single influence on my life.' (Undated).

In 1978 Bliss was commissioned to write such a book by the Pendomer Press, whose only previous book had been on John Nash. It appeared a year later when Bliss was seventy-nine and Bawden seventy-six and there can never have been a more affectionate, bantering book written by one elderly artist about another. Sheila Robinson drove Bawden to Windley where Bliss presented him with a finished copy bound in a reproduction of one of Bawden's wallpapers. Bawden retired to his bedroom to read it and the only reservation he had next morning was about its penultimate paragraph which reads:

> Bawden has never played games. He listens to no music, he views no television. He turns a deaf ear to politics and economics. He is a little deaf, nowadays, but he likes the conversation of *persone di cultura*. He reads greatly and diversely and is an extravagant collector of books. They are mostly about art and are of the lavishly illustrated kind. He is also a lover and purchaser of gardening books and travel books. When last I stayed with him he pressed upon me for night reading Mary Kingsley's account of her journeyings with the savages of equatorial Africa and some other heroic spinster's account

> of her agonising existence among Australian cannibals. He himself was deep in *What Katy did at School.*

Bawden thought Bliss had not been sufficiently attentive to Katy who was a fine creature, and the book about her a profound and moving one.

They continued to correspond about their various exhibitions and Bawden told Bliss about the current state of the RCA. The Diploma illustrators' show was 'Quite dazzling . . . . I must say the experience made me feel very small, I realised I hadn't lived or done anything'. He ate with the students and one had the cheek to suggest 'I might apply for re-admission as a student next year'. (22nd June 1981). On the other hand, 'the College has become a technological institute concerned with analysis and research, with "cost centres" and "profit centres" and the tool of the trade, the computer'. (November 1981). In retrospect his own student days seemed privileged, especially 'when I was an uneducated cub and could learn a lot from you. The Barbarian from the North was a dynamic chap'.

In the same year that Bliss' memoir appeared, 1979, another old friend Ruari McLean, typographer, book designer and editor of *Motif* magazine reproduced a

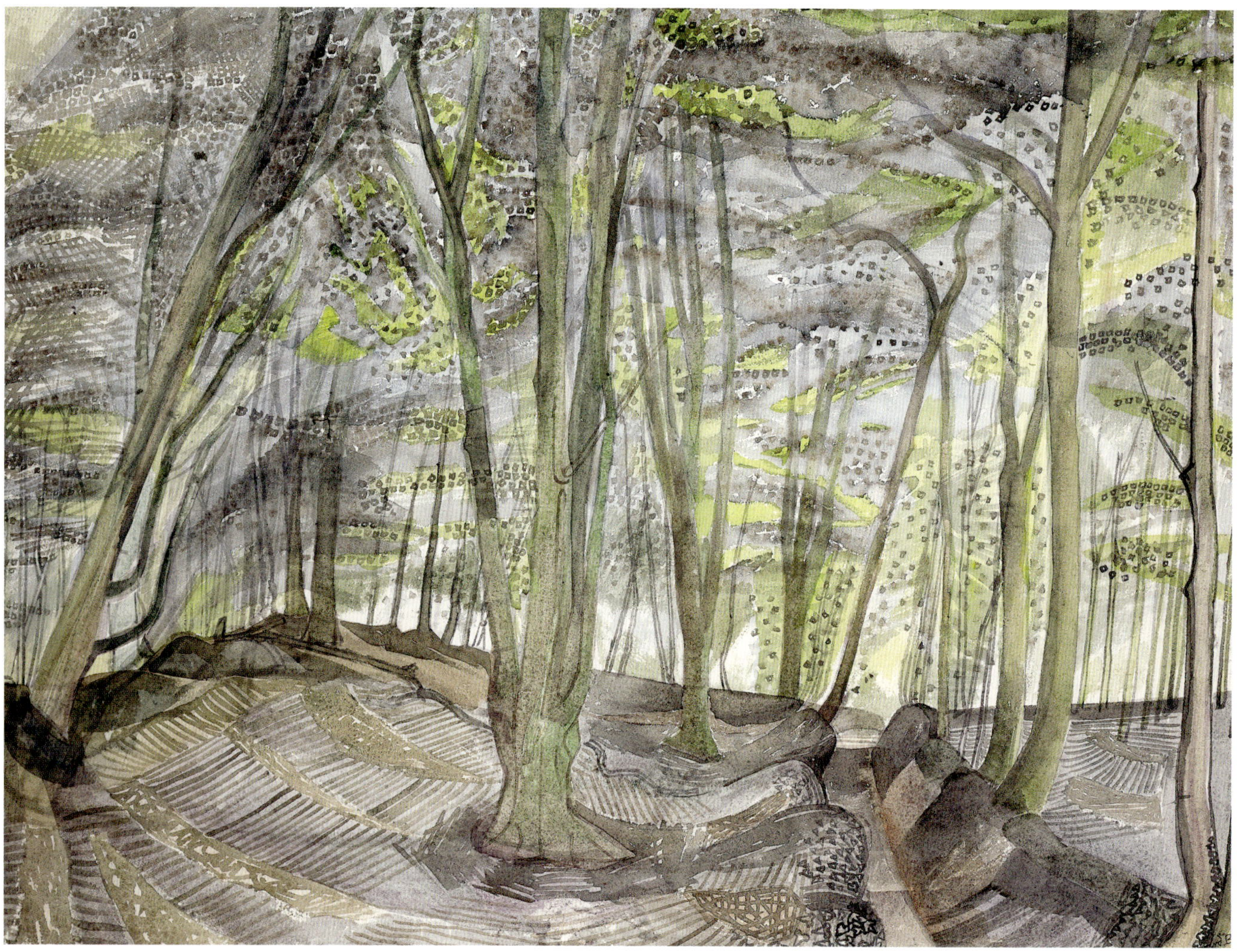

Broomfield, Somerset, 1976, watercolour, 540 x 750 mm.

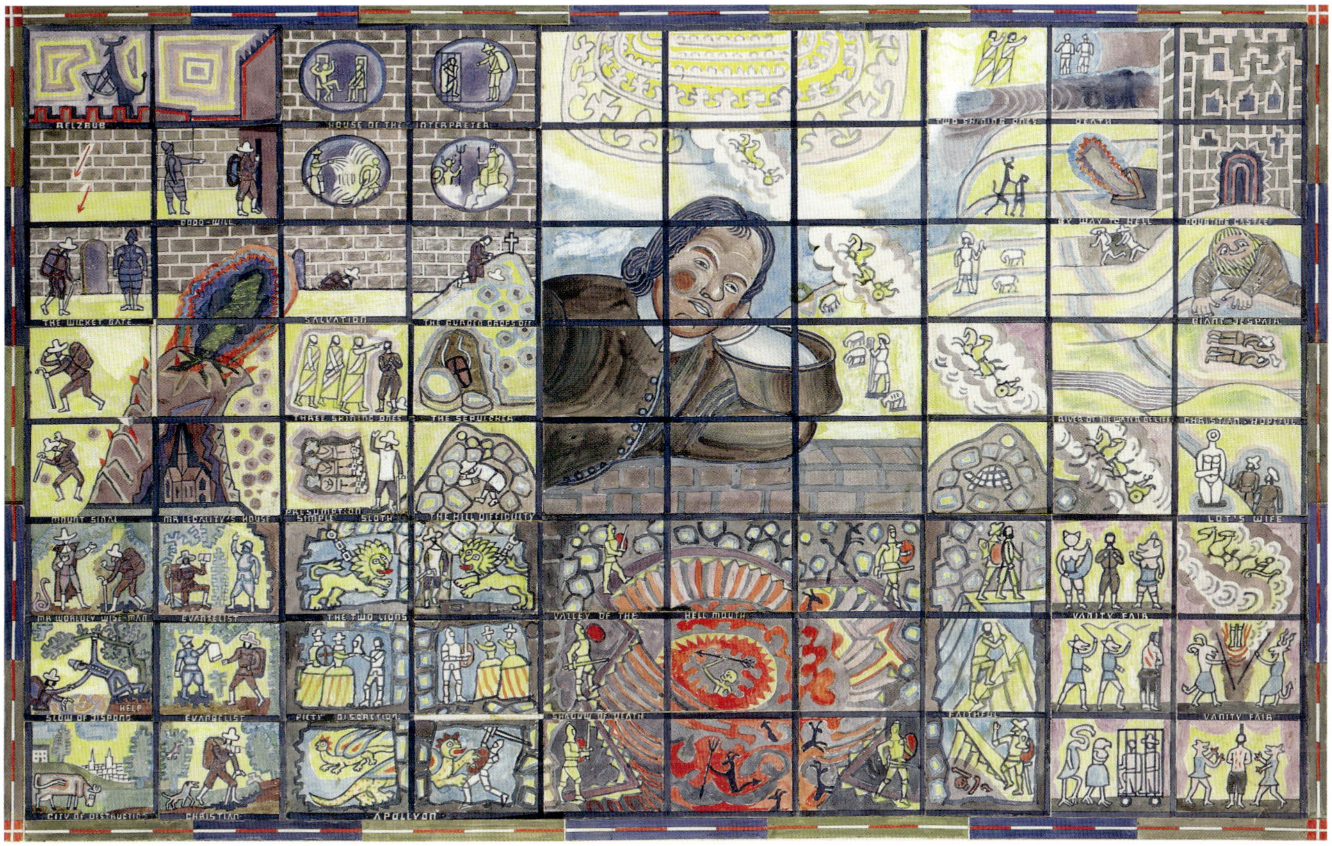

Cartoon for *Bunyan's Dream*, the tapestry commissioned by the Trustees of the Cecil Higgins Art Gallery, Bedford, 1977, 565 x 892 mm (Fine Art Society).

selection of Bawden's black and white linocuts, each printed full-size (*A Book of Cuts*, Scolar Press) and Bawden wrote a note for it explaining his method of working.

Bliss had always been the scholarly one in the Bawden group and in 1964 had received an Honorary Doctorate from Manchester College of Art. Ten years later Bawden was given a Doctorate by Essex University and his old friend John Nash wrote in 1974, just to remind him he wasn't the only one in the honours stakes: 'The robes I assure you are very becoming and the Tudor-style hat quite something. From John Nash CBE, RA, DU Essex, to Edward Bawden CBE, RA, DU Essex. We advance pari passu!'

More attention came Bawden's way when he had a walk-on part in Freda Constable's book *The England of Eric Ravilious* (Scolar Press, 1982) which he found conscientious, but thought Bliss would have done it better. When Helen Binyon's book about her former lover, titled *Eric Ravilious: A Memoir* (Lutterworth Press, 1983) was published four years after her death he thoroughly approved (he had read it in manuscript and given assistance). Bawden told her modestly 'that though he had got so much from Eric artistically Eric hadn't got anything from him'. Both books helped remind the public of Bawden's and Ravilious' joint achievements before the war and informed them of how the three friends had set out from Redcliffe Road to conquer the art world. Sadly, the third member, Bliss, after two retrospective exhibitions of his work in 1981 and 1983, had a heart attack and died in March 1984. Bawden wrote to his widow Phyllis to

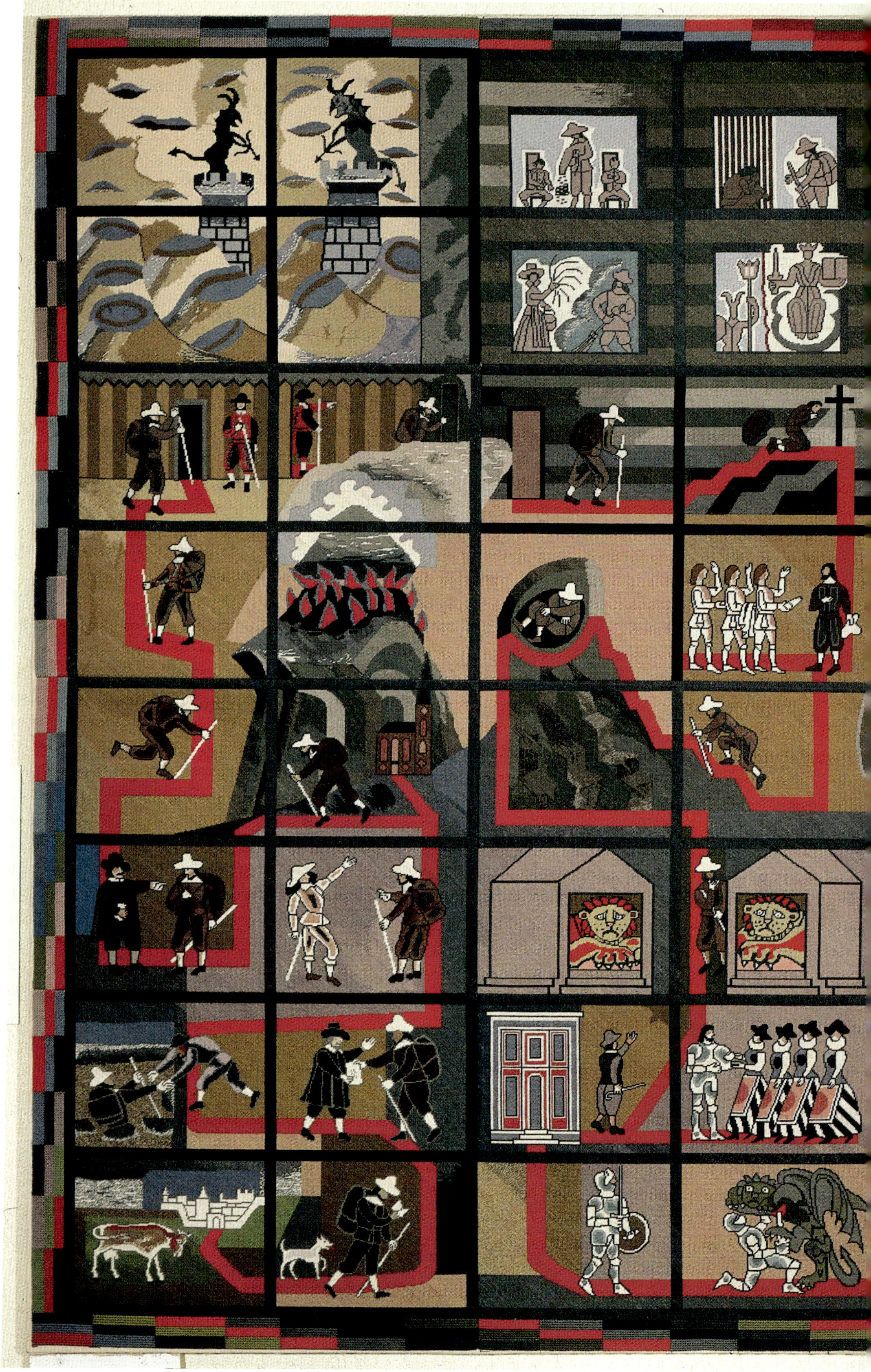

Bunyan's Dream, from *The Pilgrim's Progress*, tapestry; commissioned by the Trustees of the Cecil Higgins Art Gallery, Bedford, 1977, and worked by local needlewomen to celebrate the tercentenary of *The Pilgrim's Progress*, and the Queen's Silver Jubilee. (Trustees of Cecil Higgins Art Gallery, Bedford).

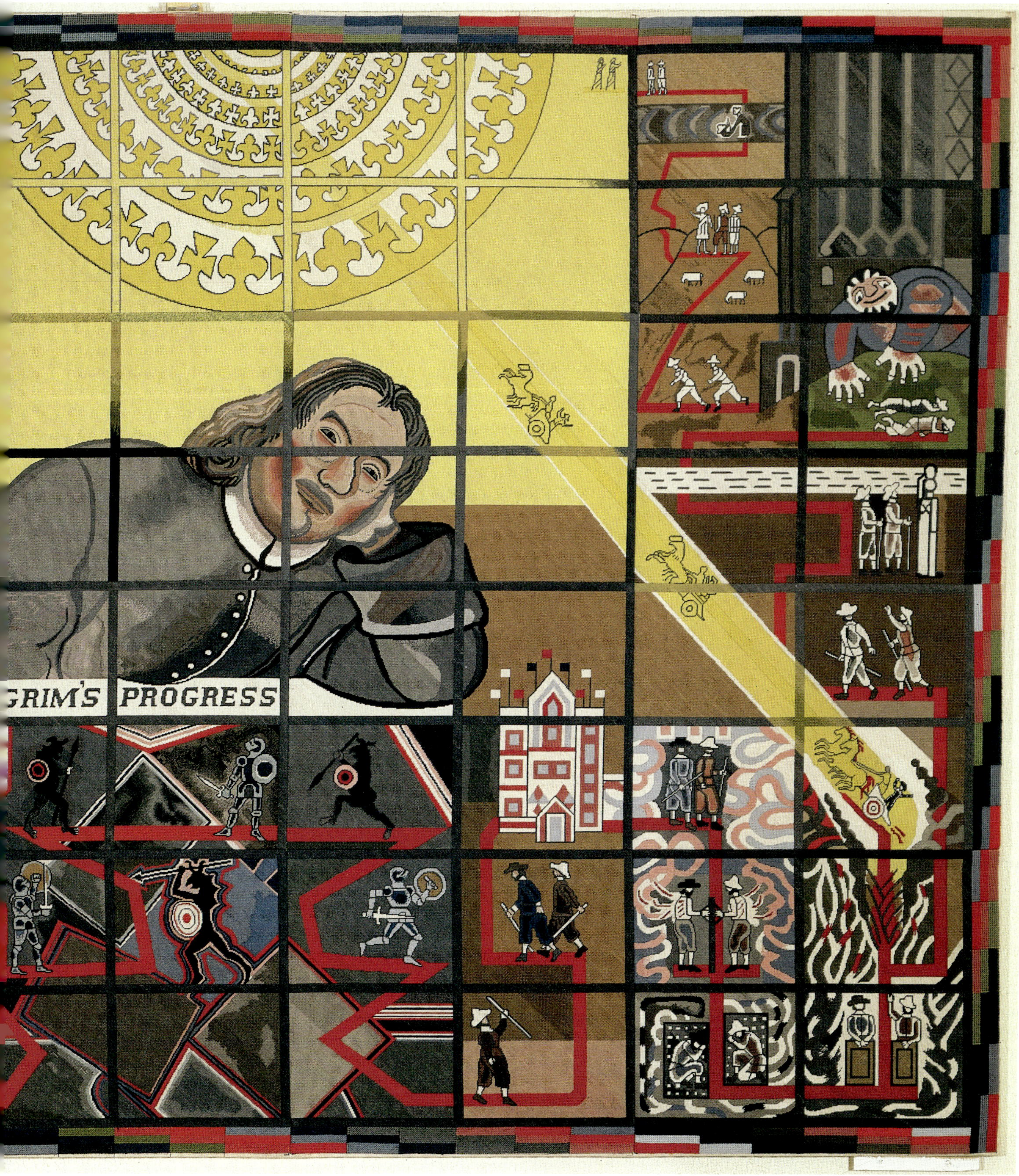
GRIM'S PROGRESS

console her and to invite her to come and stay with him in Saffron Walden, which she did. Phyllis lived on, even though she became blind and could no longer paint, until she died in 1995 in her ninety-sixth year.

What Phyllis' daughter Prudence wrote about her would seem fair comment on the art of both her parents: 'My mother had no desire for novelty or exaggeration, nor, being a thoroughly well-adjusted domestic person, did she have any subjective vision to impose; she was never interested in jumping onto any modern theoretical "bandwagon". Her art consisted of an honest direct response to things seen, and she was happy to produce in people the pleasure of recognising what she represented.' [4]

Bawden was still at work on book illustration, though the publication of *Lady Filmy Fern* in 1980 (Hamish Hamilton) involved him in only providing a few new watercolour and line drawings to supplement those which he had placed down the well in the garden of Brick House forty odd years before. For this strange volume he received the Francis Williams Prize for Book Illustration, but typically he looked a gift horse in the mouth and grumbled: 'It's always reserved for a geriatric practitioner'.

For the black, brown and yellow lithographs of *The Discovery and Conquest of Peru* (Folio Society, 1981) he invented yet another seemingly archaic style to convey the terrible events. Then his next big venture was Sir Thomas Malory's *Chronicles of King Arthur* (1982), a book he'd first read as a boy. He commented ironically that he'd recently

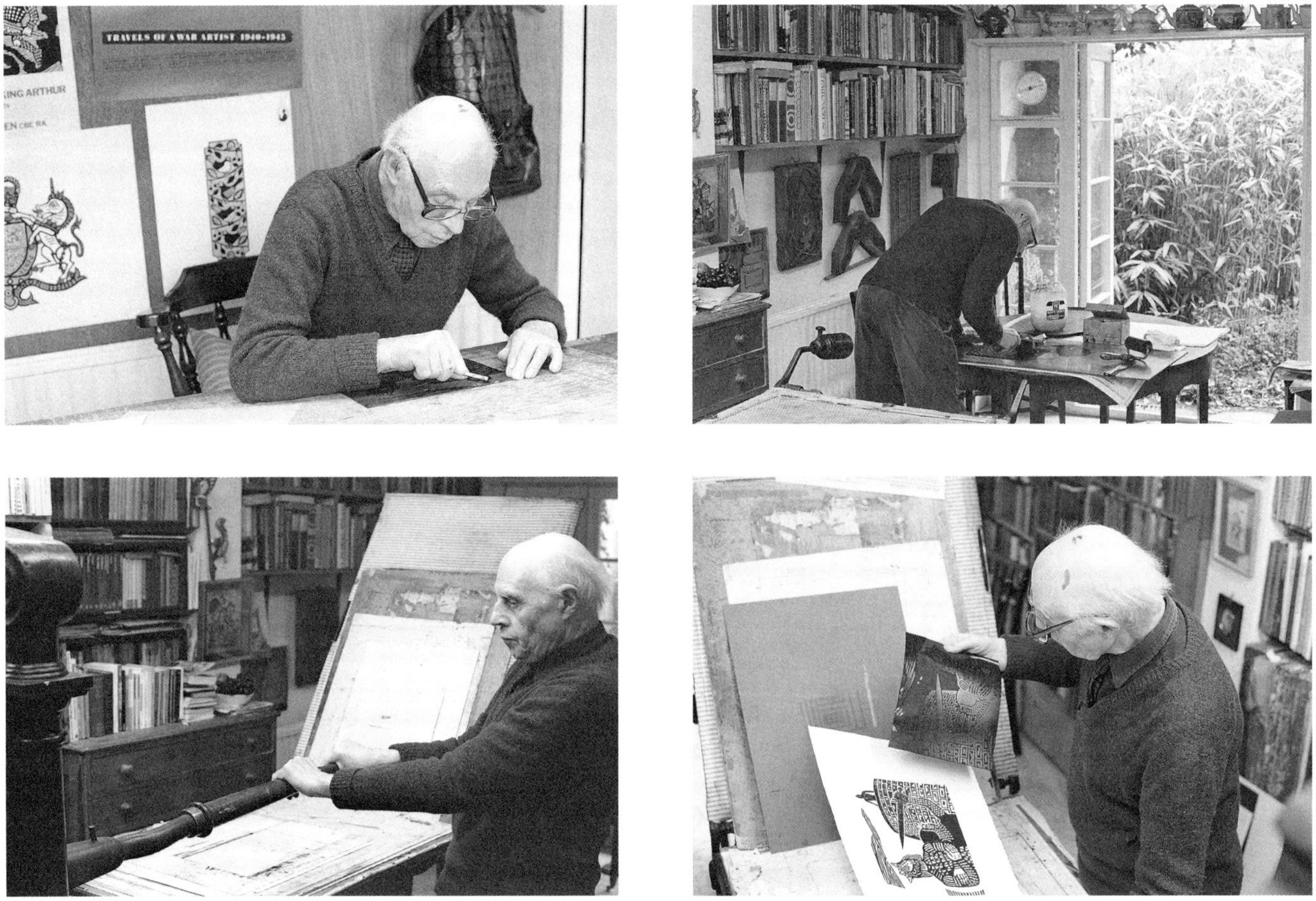

Photographs of Bawden printing the linocuts from *Chronicles of King Arthur* ©Christopher Brown.

Twelve of the seventy-one linocuts for *Chronicles of King Arthur*, 1982, each approximately 206 x 268 mm (illustrations reduced to 76 x 102 mm). (Richard Bawden.)

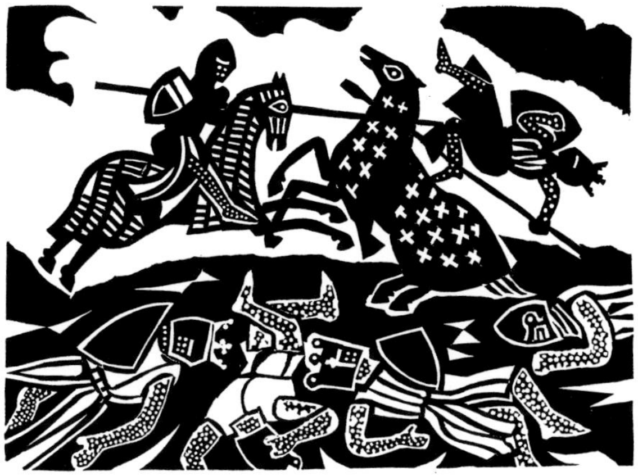

'Sir Kay smote him so hard that the stroke clove the helm & head to the earth.'

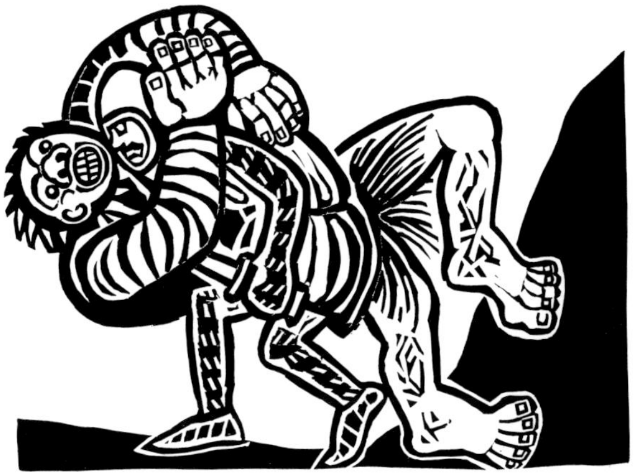

'Sir Arthur swipes his genitals asunder, then the glutton cast away the club & caught the king in his arms.'

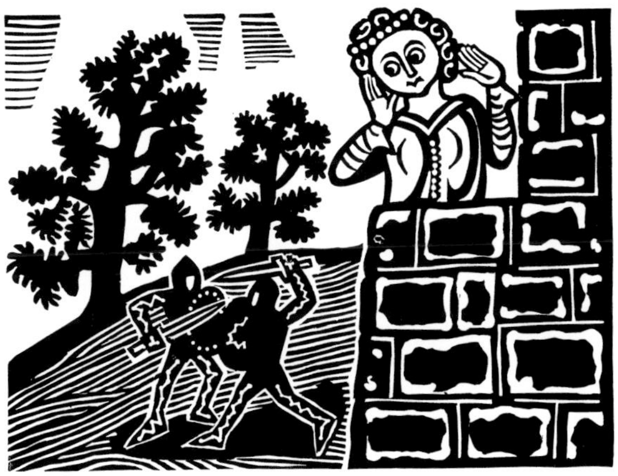

'La Beale Isode swooned & said "Alas that one I loved & yet do, & the other I love not, that they should fight."'

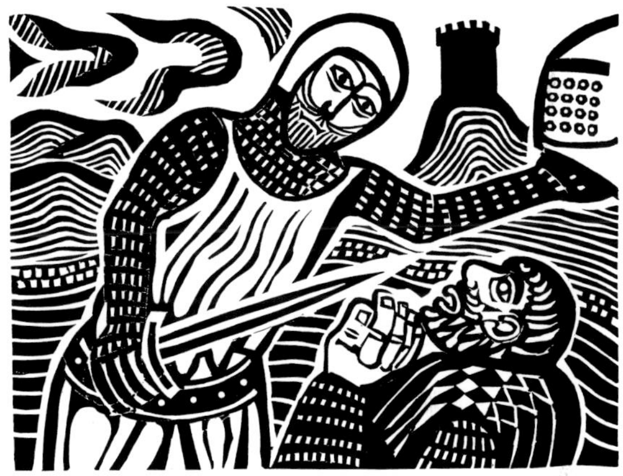

'When sir Brian saw that he should be slain he yielded him to sir Lancelot.'

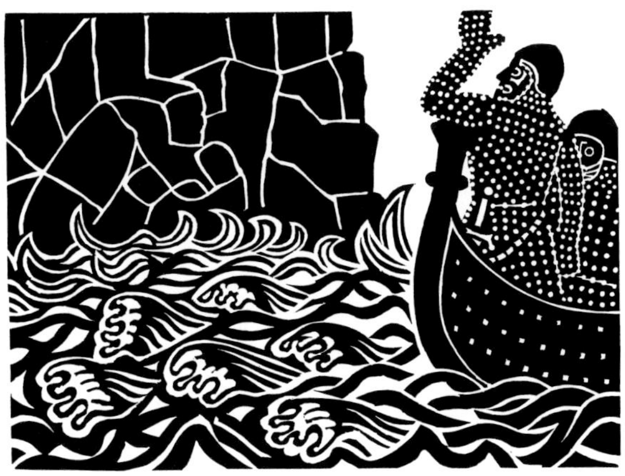

'And forthwith sir Tristram & sir Dinadin took the sea.'

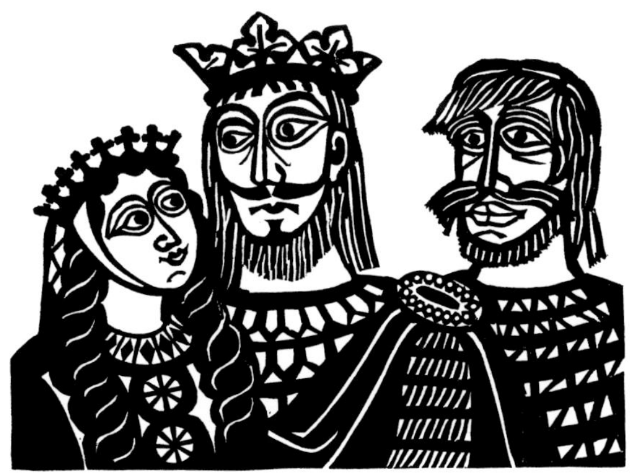

'"With right good will", said king Arthur, "for sir Galahalt shall have you in governance."'

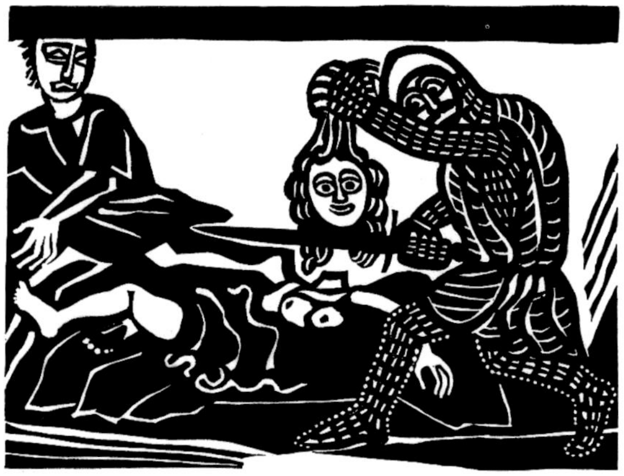

'"Alas, why have you slain your mother that bore you?"'

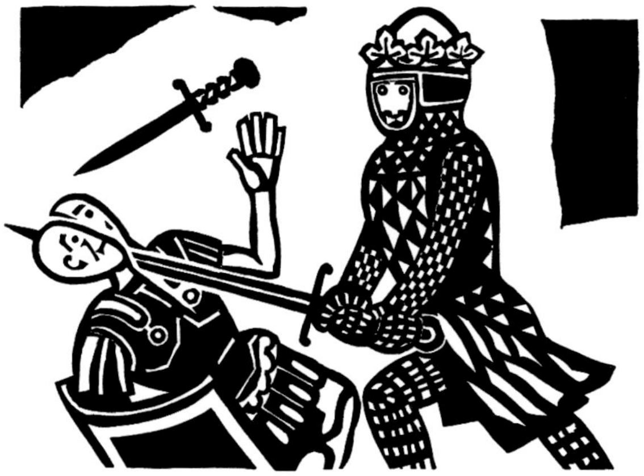

'Sir Arthur was wroth & gave him another buffet so that from the crest of his helm unto the paps it went down.'

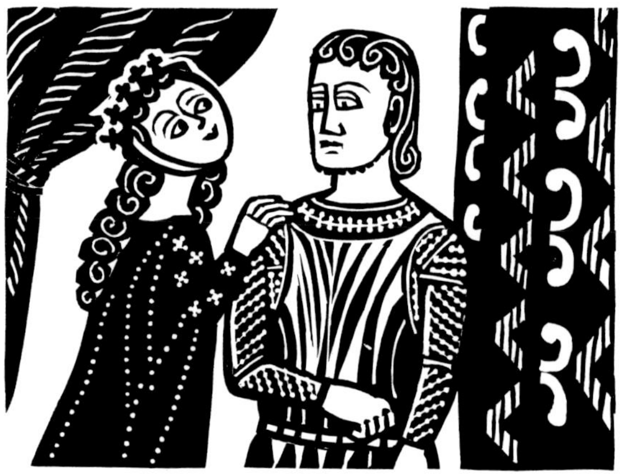

'"And son unto Sir Lancelot," she said. As to that he said neither yea or nay.'

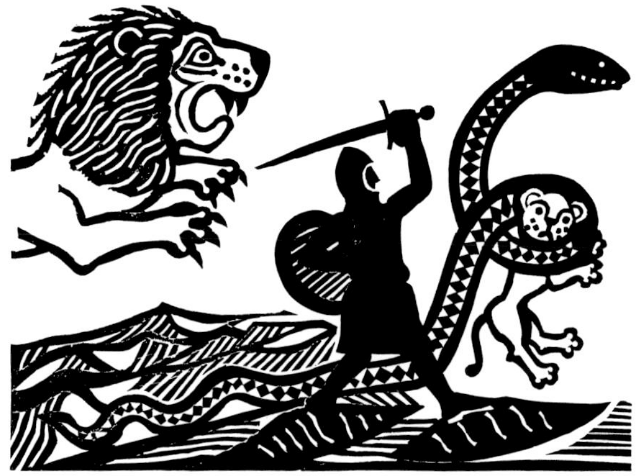

'So with that came a great lion crying & roaring after the serpent.'

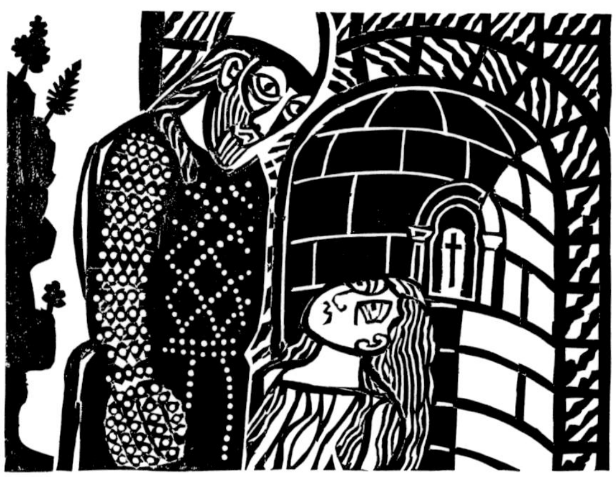

'"Ah, Lancelot", said she, "as long as you were knight of earthly knighthood you were the most marvellous man of the world."'

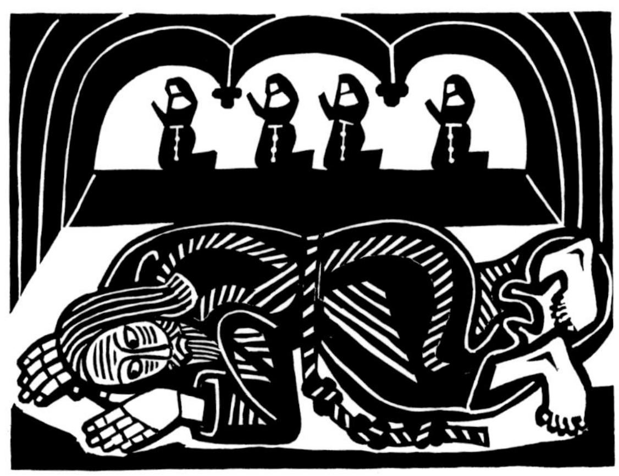

'Ever was sir Lancelot lying grovelling on the tomb of king Arthur & queen Guinevere.'

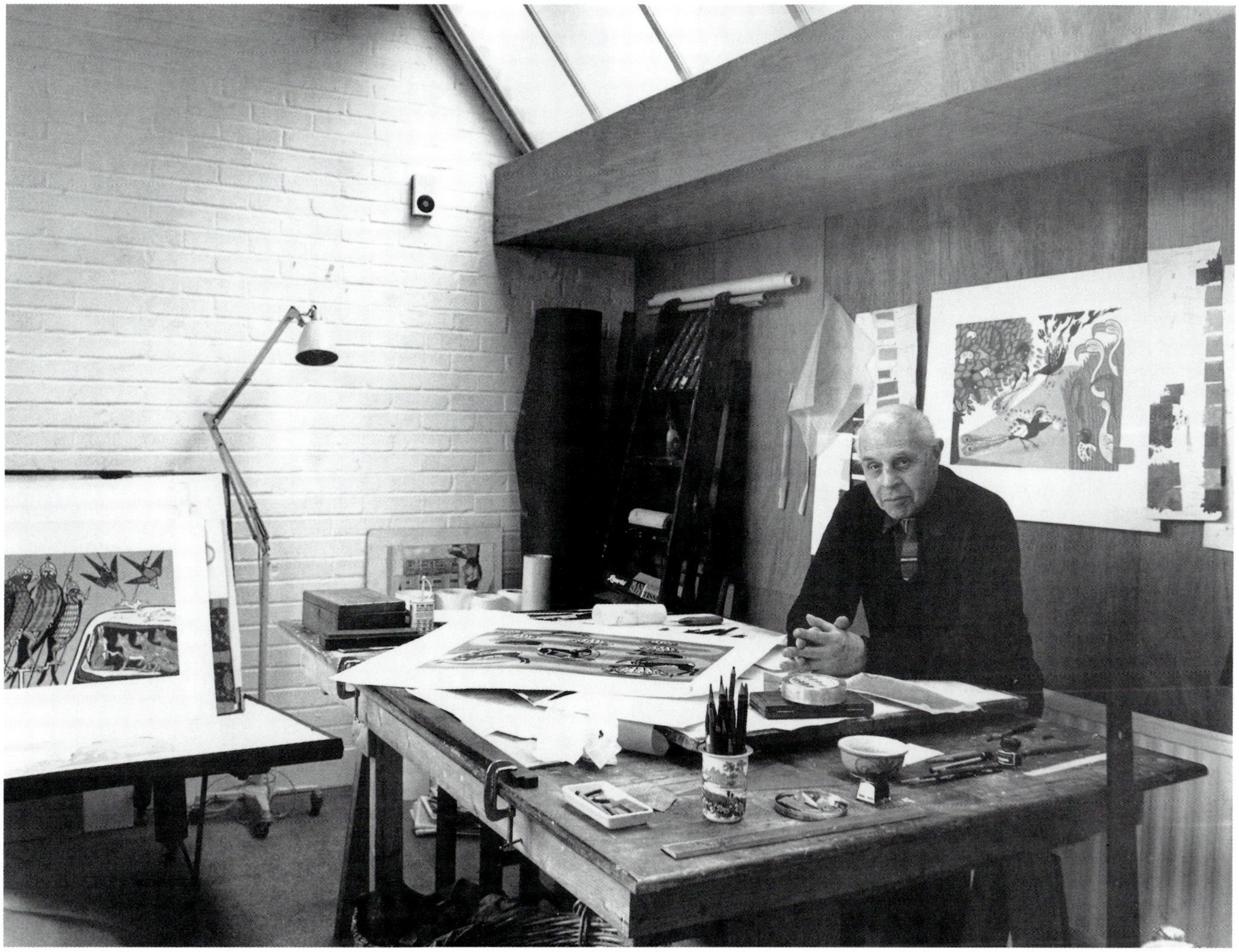

Bawden in his studio at Saffron Walden, 1978,
(Fine Art Society; copyright Jorge Lewinski Archive, Chatsworth).

re-read it and thought it incredibly boring, but when he received the Folio Society commission it suddenly became 'thrilling!' He picked out all the bloody bits and indulged his warped humour to the full, depicting Sir Gaheris hacking off his mother's head and Arthur slicing Lucius 'from the crest of his helm unto the bare paps' – 'It's just like real life!' Bawden chortled. He confessed to an interviewer: 'All my life I've been fascinated in a horrible sort of way, by people being hung, tortured, burnt at the stake, the beastly side of life is very very present. I think I'm an escapist.'[5] His grandson Tommy confirms this and remembers how Bawden kept books on murder, crime, horror stories and the occult on open display in the hope they would shock his female visitors.

He found the task of illustrating these three volumes 'so immensely interesting and so exciting that I accepted the task of cutting seventy lino blocks', each eight inches by ten inches, which were then reduced to around three inches by four and scattered through the 902 pages of the three-volume book. He chose to work this way because 'pen drawings would have been too thin. With a pen line you can do something witty. With a thick lino line you can hardly be witty, you could be comic, sardonic if you like. Sardonic humour is what seems to suit *Morte d' Arthur*.' His humour, he apologised, was 'endemic – I just can't help it'. He obviously enjoyed the ludicrous episodes of knights hacking each other's limbs off, but the images don't sicken the reader because the necessary simplification of black and white lino and the child-like style keep the events at an emotional arm's length, but in this he is working against the grain of the text as much as with it. What he could not do in this medium is convey true pathos, sexual passion, male nobility or female allure.

He made linocuts of more modern-dress protagonists when he came to illustrate *The Hound of the Baskervilles* (1987). He'd told the Folio Society when he was eighty-two: 'I've always wanted to do *The Hound of the Baskervilles*: You'd better catch me before I pop off', and so they did. He bought a deer-stalker hat and went off to tramp Bodmin Moor as part of his research. He smuggled in his own visual comments on the text in the form of a cat chasing a mouse, a spider entrapping a fly, owls, bats and so on. Again, the illustrations are more droll than dreadful. Shrewdly he chose linocuts for this popular book because he could run off ten sets and singles of his own on the Albion press and sell them privately: 'I hope to make a little money, not very much – perhaps a thousand pounds. I suppose I am as rapacious as any other artist, but not very greedy. I don't think I would do a job simply because there was a lot of money involved.'

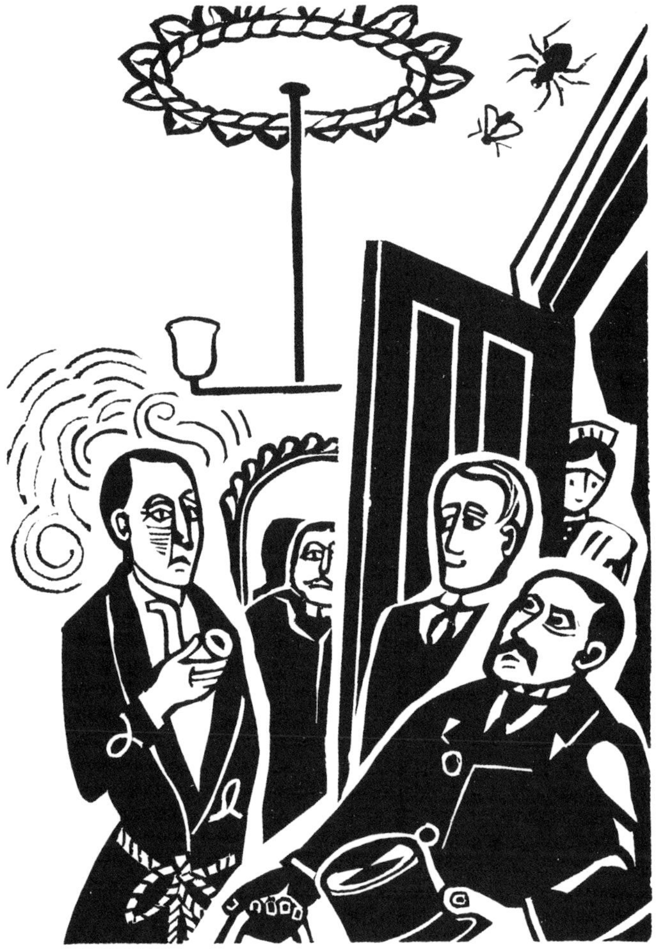

Illustration from *The Hound of the Baskervilles*, 1987, linocut, 457 x 310 mm (illustration reduced to 152 x 104 mm) (Manchester Metropolitan University Library).

Bawden's work was much admired by another specialist in the humorously-sinister genre, the famous American illustrator Edward Gorey. Gorey told his biographer in 1996: 'Actually the person I most wish I could draw like is someone you've probably never heard of named Edward Bawden, who's probably dead by now. He's an English artist who did both fine art and illustration. For instance, he used to do catalogues for Fortnum and Mason, and he illustrated a two volume edition of Herodotus. He does little black and white illustrations. He works in colour sometimes, but mostly sort of black and white. He's got a black and white technique I'd kill for.' [6]

By now Bawden was becoming a Grand Old Man of British art. The galleries were full of conceptual art and installations made by artists who found words hard to handle, and the journalists gladly turned to this cranky old grouch in Essex who was always good for a quotation and who seemed to enjoy teasing and shocking his questioners, especially if they were young women. In November 1983 Anglia TV showed a film of him in his natural habitat and he told Bliss that even though his front tooth dropped out the night before and had to be fixed in haste, 'I enjoyed being filmed and evidently gave satisfaction because my fee was doubled'.

Stories of his eccentricities grew. One interviewer is supposed to have turned up at his door and introduced herself as being sent from the magazine *Modern Painters*. 'There aren't any in Essex', he said and shut the door. Another apocryphal story tells of him stolidly eating his way through a charity dinner given by the Tarmac company, for whom he had done some publicity material. The PR man bellowing into his ear a list of all the firm's philanthropic activities was ignored until he asked, in a sudden silence, if Bawden could think of any more appropriate charities the Tarmac company should support. 'Road victims', came the terse reply. Peyton Skipwith is convinced that Bawden was one of the few people to enjoy being deaf – he certainly could use it as a weapon against anyone encroaching too near, or asking questions he was not willing to answer.

The interviewers found him 'gently malicious', or blunt, cynical and apt to turn the questions back on them. The cheeky schoolboy who gave his teachers such a hard time seems to have made a reappearance. He avoided all talk of aesthetic theory ('theology might be more interesting'), revelled in his reputation for eccentricity, and in general thought modern society was going to the dogs ('The world since the Thirties seems more and more strange and idiotic'). A typical description of the Saffron Sage might be: 'He is a pared down figure with a nubbly nut-brown bald head. His eyes are black and penetrating. His mouth is pursed perpetually in an expression of wry deprecation (self as well as general). He delivers frequent gags with a Buster Keaton impassivity. He made a wonderful pantomime of not wanting to be photographed.'[7] Another thought him more like a marmoset, bright-eyed and bushy-tailed and commented on how he smoked very daintily, the cigarette being held on a pin.

Women interviewers got a particularly rough ride. If Bawden had ever heard of 'political correctness' he certainly ignored it. He read the Women's page in his *Guardian* and wondered whatever the Women's Lib movement could have left to demand from men: 'I think perhaps what you want is for people like myself to be confined to the house, looking after children, and cooking and cleaning. I would be quite content to cook and do needlework but not to look after children. Children are wet, smelly and unpredictable. I do admire your sex enormously; heavens what you go through in childbirth! I was staying in a pub in Norfolk once, sketching and just before lunch the landlady took me outside to see a pig giving birth. We saw all the little piglets coming out and it put me off my lunch COMPLETELY!'[8] He said his mother had always been dominated by his father, but that was because she wore corsets which restricted her in every way. 'Now dress is free and easy like relationships, which is excellent. There's no formality. In half an hour I would be calling you Maureen, but it's such a dreadful Christian name – I simply can't tell you! Women's Christian names are not pleasant. Mary's a splendid name and I don't dislike my own. My own children are called Richard and Joanna. I did toy with Tarvia which was a name I saw written on a tar barrel.'

To demonstrate how he was still curious about the world he told another woman journalist: 'If you got run over outside by a great lorry I'd rush out to see what it was like and get there before the firemen. I'd like to see if you'd be flat as a pancake or not.' This echoes two earlier episodes recounted by John Norris Wood. Bawden and a guest were relaxing in the garden of Brick House when the man almost choked on a live wasp that had been floating in his cider. Bawden had seen it but, he explained, had given no warning because he wanted to see what would happen. On another occasion a house in the village burned down and Charlotte took in the distraught couple. On his return from teaching in London Bawden said to them: 'What a shame I missed it! It must have been an absolutely splendid sight', and was surprised when the lady left in tears.

He evidently enjoyed all the attention and began to polish his aphorisms: 'the secret of drawing is a sharp pencil and don't take it off the paper.' 'I like to have an inward laugh at what I'm doing.' 'Temperament is for amateurs.' 'The feet should be used for vintage, be it cuts or wine.' 'I'm a humble man: you have to be with clients.' 'An artist should be able to go up and down the scales.' 'I prefer to draw with a pen. To stand out in the middle of the street. The line is sharper. There's more risk. It's more exciting.' 'Get rid of your work and seek the next problem.' 'If you take it [work] seriously, it's one's essential self.' 'Obviously if you're working slowly your mind is not at full pressure. You've got to run, then you don't fall down.' 'Every man feels threatened by his son.' And cryptically: 'One can have too much of Japan.'

Interviewers always commented on how neat his house and studio were, but after more than sixty years of relentless creativity he was having storage problems. In 1981 he decided to give a large part of his oeuvre ('the Bawden remains') to the Cecil Higgins Museum in Bedford, there then being no suitable alternative in his native Essex, and as a Trustee of the Tate Gallery he knew that any gift to that institution would only end in a vault and never see daylight again. In 1988 a Retrospective Survey of this Bedford material by Justin Howes was published and it remains crucial for any future research into Bawden's work. The Museum gave him an 86th birthday party in the gallery, complete with blazing cake and brass band, but he was so deaf by then he heard none of it, nor the laudatory speeches.

In some ways he came to regret his generosity to Bedford when the Fry Public Art Gallery was restored and reopened in Saffron Walden in 1987, a short stroll from his house. This had been a mid-nineteenth century purpose-built public gallery, but now under the directorship of Nigel and Iris Weaver its sole purpose is to collect, exhibit and publish the artists of north-west Essex, those of Great Bardfield and Saffron Walden in particular. Before her death in 2002 Olive Cook, who seemed to know everyone of consequence in the art world, acted as their unofficial chronicler. Bawden became a patron and made a handsome donation towards its collection and upkeep. He had an exhibition of his book illustrations in April-September 1988 and his work is permanently on show alongside all the artists we have mentioned in this book.

As he entered his eighties Bawden could no longer get around the local landscape to paint, though he still travelled when friends drove him. He liked to take a painting break in Cornwall each year, always staying at the same Rose Cottage in St Ewe. In 1980 he went with Richard, the pair of them painting the same scenery, Bawden rebuffing a man who came up and said 'Good morning' with a curt, 'I don't think so'. Then for three years he had as companion a former student of Sheila Robinson's, Christopher Brown, whom he enjoyed embarrassing over restaurant meals with his talk of motions and syrup of figs, or by asking loudly, 'Chris, why do these common people have so many children?' His stentorian comment on a restaurant owner who was a dilettante artist was: 'Amateurs shouldn't be allowed, after all I don't go to an amateur dentist.'[9] He had also found a gravestone in St Ewe churchyard which read: 'Edward Bawden, died 29th October 1894, Aged 68 years: His End Was Peace', and had Brown photograph him leaning on it. He told Brown he was descended from the Cornish 'Sir Bawdewyn or Sir Bawdy for short, mentioned in Malory'.

Brown was interested to observe that Bawden did several pencil sketches of the location before he settled into the best viewpoint. He propped himself against a wall so he couldn't be overlooked and made a bold pencil drawing on heavy paper which did not need stretching. He then drew with the brush, having little patience with the 'washy' tradition of watercolour. There was a morning and an afternoon picture on the go and it usually took two days to finish them, plus a few pencil or pen lines back in the studio to pull them together. Brown was also invited back to Saffron Walden to use the Albion Press for his own linocuts – 'but beware; I am intolerant of rivals', he was warned. Chattering was also forbidden.

These landscapes of Bawden's late maturity have come an astonishing distance from those early tentative ones he made sitting beside Ravilious in the garden of Brick

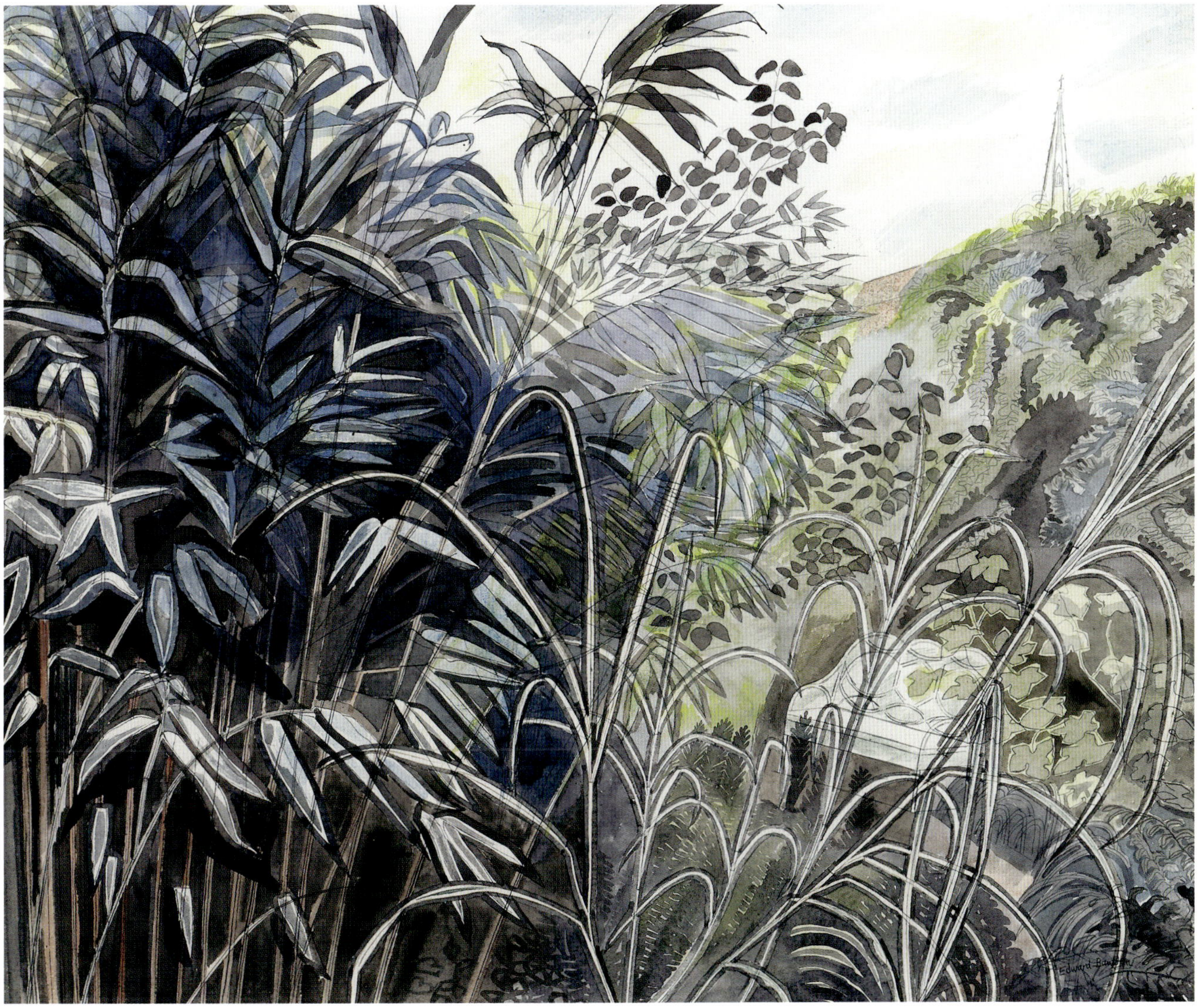

Bamboos and Garden Seat, 1979, watercolour, 525 x 620 mm; a view from Bawden's studio window at Saffron Walden; his Bilston garden seat and the spire of Saffron Walden Church can be seen (Fine Art Society).

House. Now he works big and bold; taking liberties with his compositions so that a tree trunk splits the picture down the middle; the whole foreground is a mass of blossom; we glimpse things through spiky leaves or railings; or he sits close in to a building so its perspective soars away from him. Sometimes he sets himself to paint in variations of just one colour (he is no longer afraid of green), at others to draw every flint on a church exterior or to put a square outline round every leaf in a wood. These are the playful but highly effective strategies of a man in total control of his medium.

In 1985 he revisited Egypt with his grandson Tom and Joanna's partner Brooke (Tirzah Ravilious' nephew). He gleefully stirred up some mischief amongst the ladies of the tour party and relished the attention he gained by being constipated when the rest of them had just the opposite problem. Bowel movements were one of his favourite topics, especially in public places. 'The

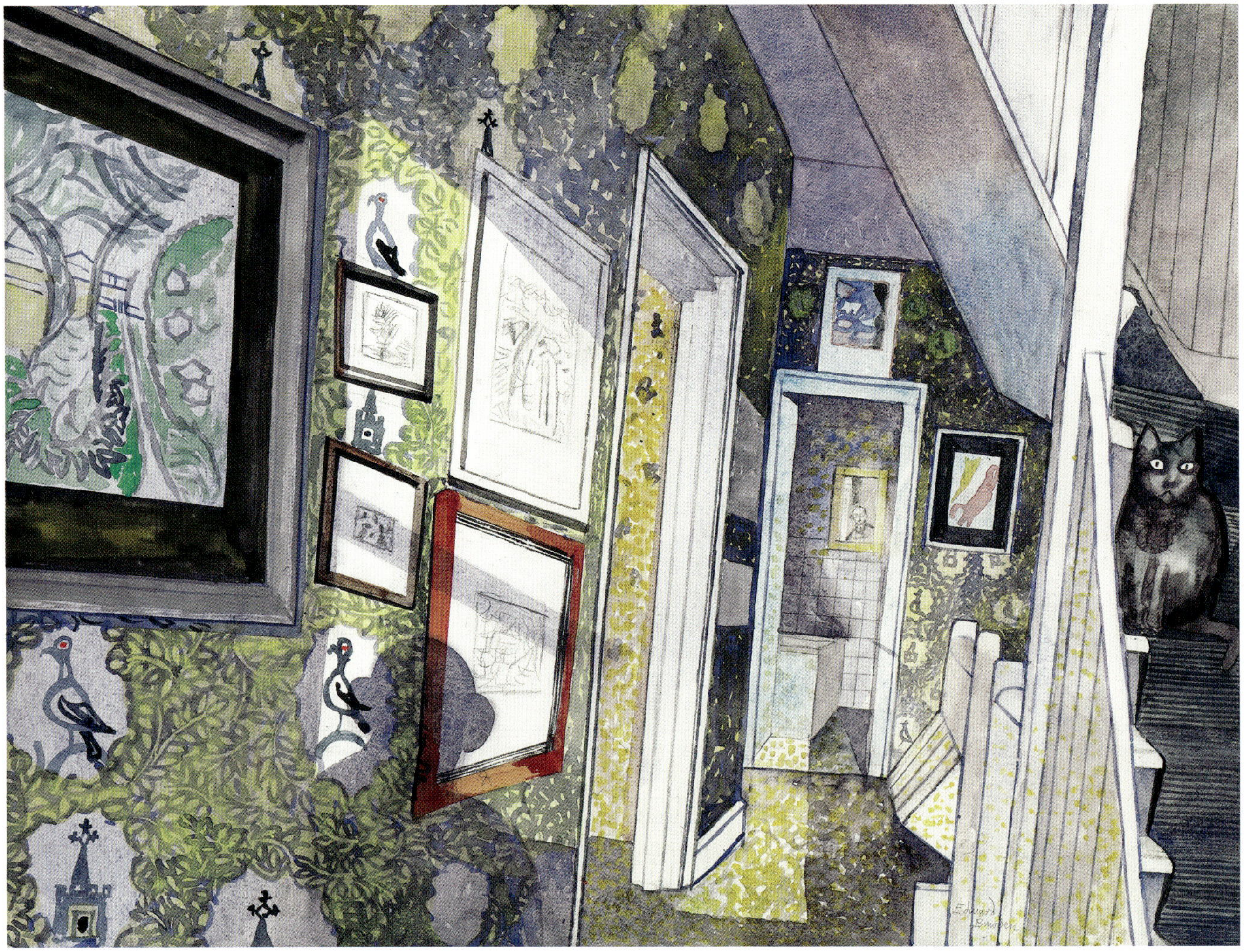

Cat Among Pigeons, 1986, watercolour, 490 x 640 mm.

[Egyptian] men wore long white shirts', he reported, 'it was very nice indeed to see them cycling'. He carried tiny sketch books and used them to make several imaginative watercolours on his return.

For most of the year he was more house-bound than he had ever been and this forced him into new subject areas. In 1986 he began a series of watercolours which depicted his own rooms, his studio, his plants, his glowing oriental carpets, his gas fire, his cat Emma Nelson, and, eventually, this most private of men made his own face the subject of his art. Emma Nelson was a stray (originally thought to be male, hence her two names), but she soon became his constant companion and model. At first he left a space in the painting into which he would fit her, but soon found it easier to paint the cat first and arrange the room around her. He told an interviewer from *House and Garden:*

> No cat will suffer being lifted up and dropped into an empty space intended for her to occupy; that procedure led inevitably to Emma, tail up, walking away at once, so I had to wait patiently until Emma had enjoyed a good meal of Coley and was ready to choose her daily

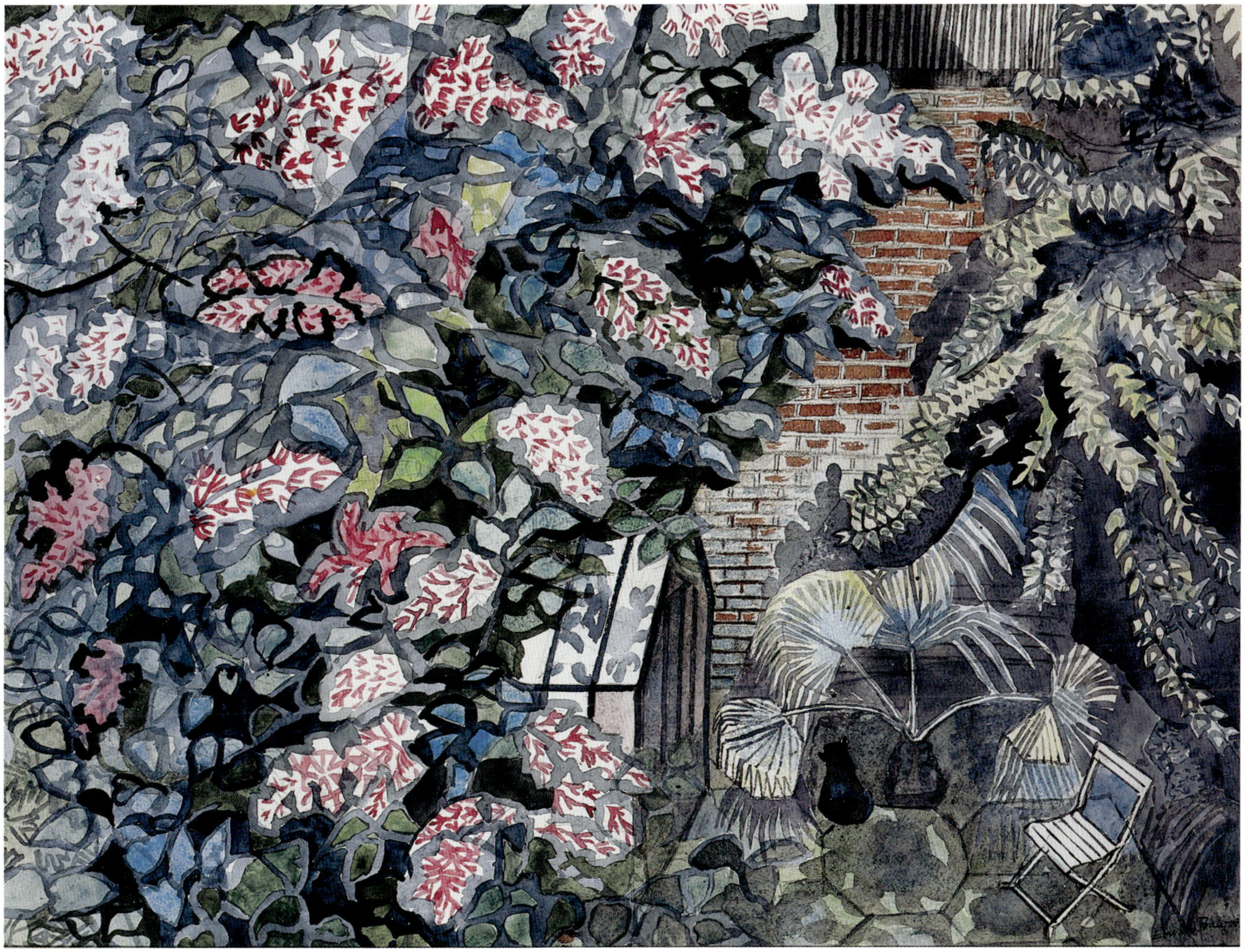

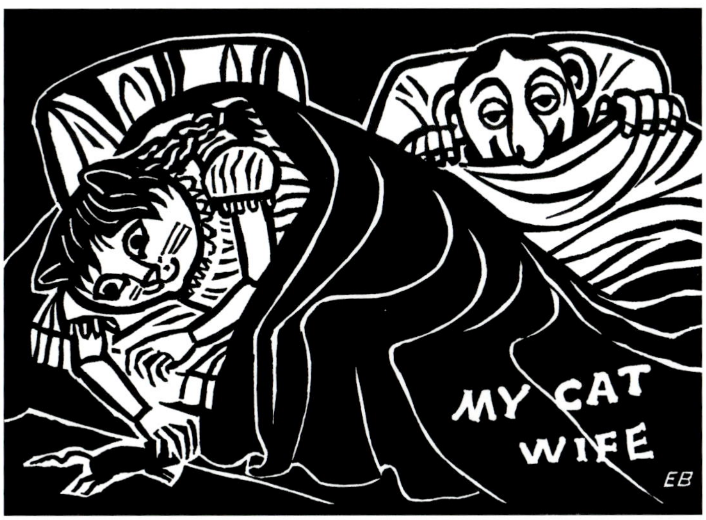

Cat and Greenhouse, 1986, watercolour, 485 x 635 mm.

My Cat Wife, or *A Midnight Snack*, *c.*1983, linocut, 210 x 297 mm.

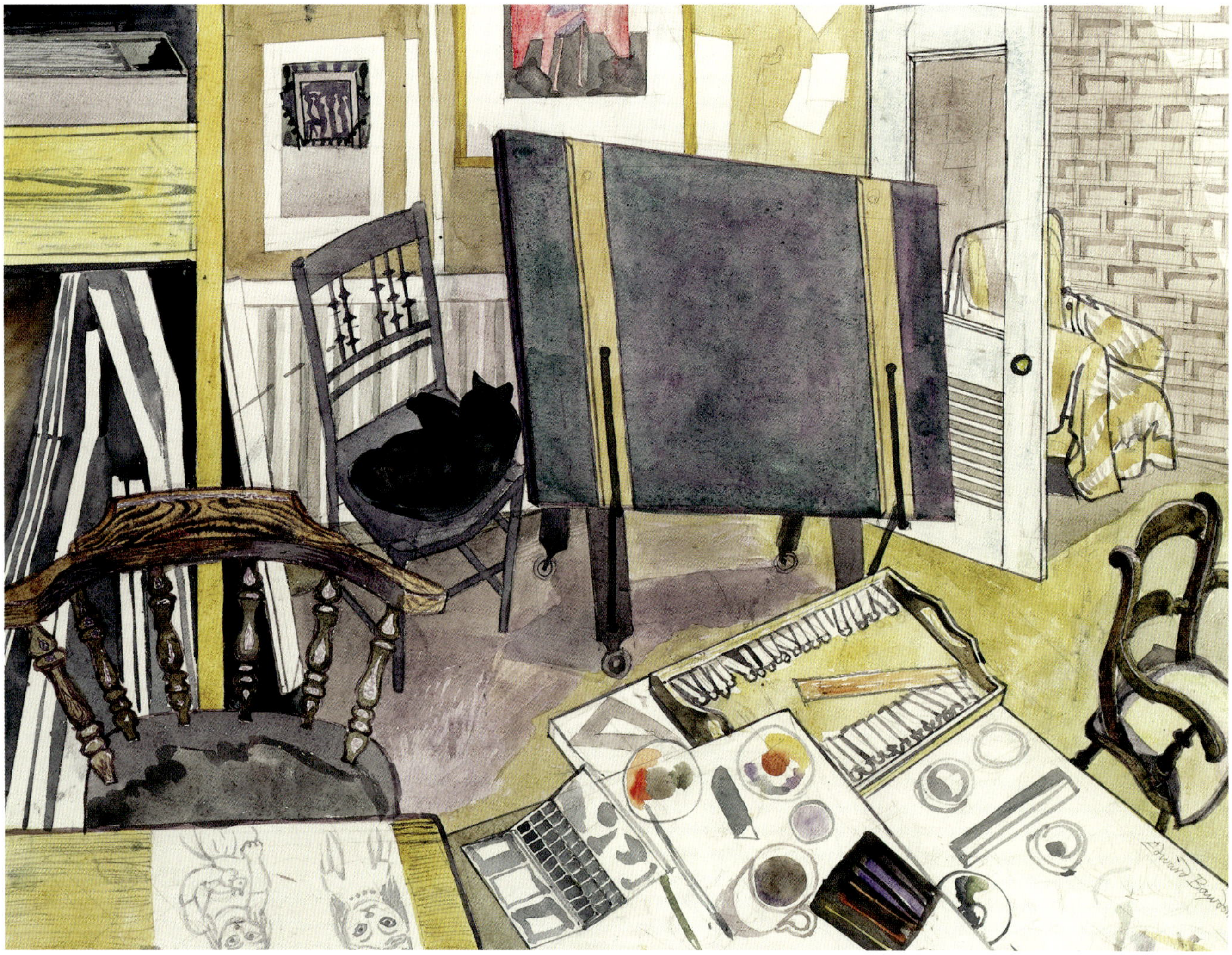

Cat on a Chair, 1987, watercolour, 480 x 620 mm.

> sleeping place, wherever it might be. I would then spring into action with brush and colour, choosing almost by hazard or chance the place on a sheet of white paper which ultimately might turn out to be the cornerstone of the design. These paintings are, therefore, the joint creations of cat and artist, of Emma and Edward.[10]

Eventually his own shadow creeps into the pictures, then his profile in a mirror and finally his grumpy full-face peering over his drawing board, still defying anyone to take any liberties with him. There is no self-pity or sentimentality, just a wry recording of the effects of old age. The National Portrait Gallery acquired this last painting.

These late pictures are in no way inferior to earlier ones. They are perhaps even richer in colour (all those Persian carpets on the floor and flowers on the tables) and his hand is as steady as it has ever been in depicting the detail of pattern and texture. He takes liberties with appearances ('I generally paint in front of the motif even if it is not as I see it . . . . I don't wish perspective to be my master'),

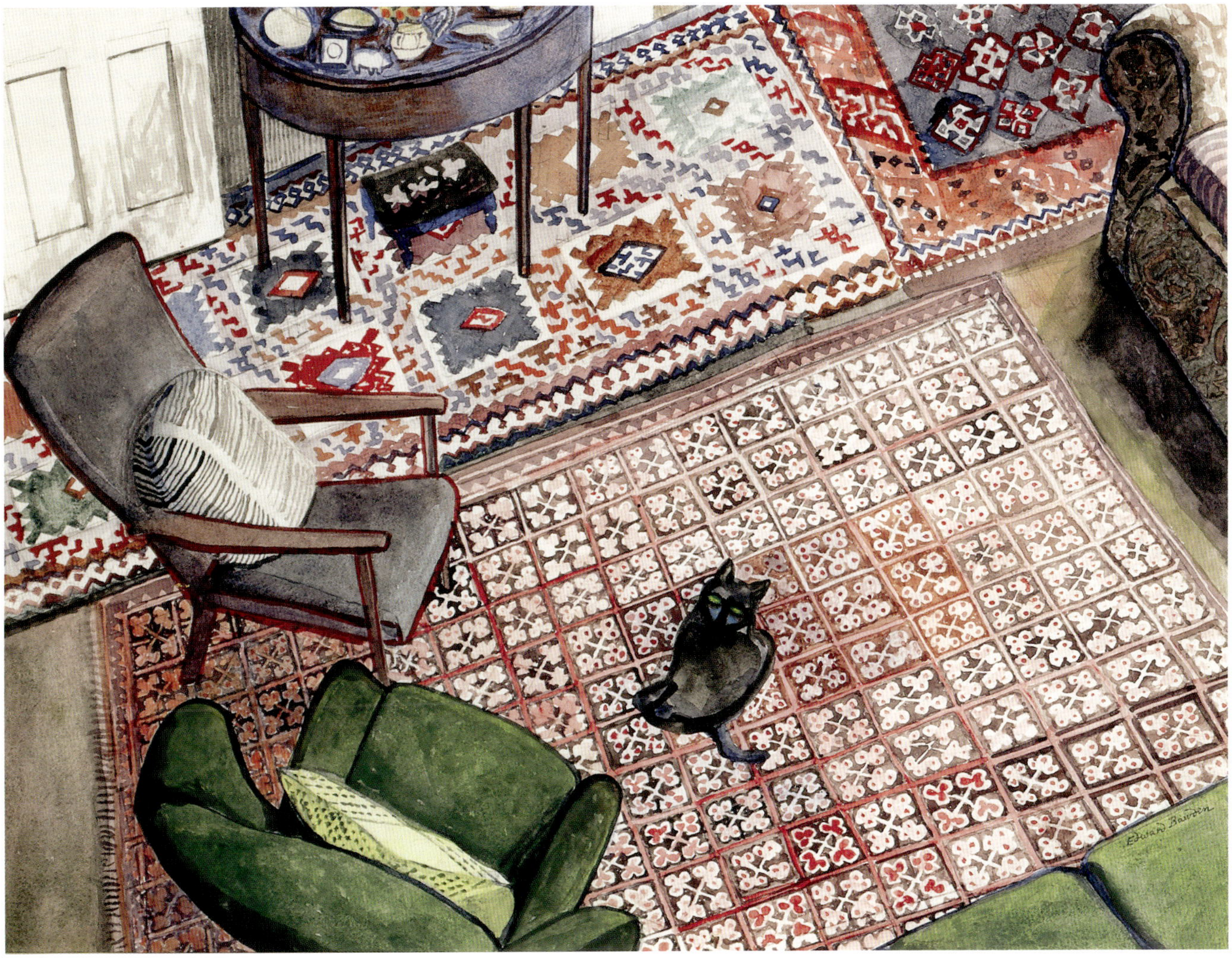

Cat on a Carpet, 1987, watercolour, 480 x 620 mm (Fine Art Society).

tipping up floors, cat baskets, tables or a tray of paints at will to satisfy the composition. At his most stylised Bawden had always remained close to nature and, conversely, even at his most explicit, as here, the abstract design underpins every image.

He acquired a nude wax lay figure for fifty pence from Oxfam and she features in some of his late studio views, as bizarre a presence as any dummy by de Chirico. He continued to decorate his home for Christmas as Charlotte had done at Brick House and again arrived at an effect which can only be described as surreal, as Peyton Skipwith describes it: 'The studio, setting for the party, came in for special attention. The wall behind the gas-fire leaped into flames from floor to ceiling, and in the depths of the fire skulls were consigned to perpetual torment. It was typical Bawdenesque perversity to celebrate the season of peace and goodwill with a scene reminiscent of medieval doom. The contrast of snow outside, the neatly ordered studio, the domesticity of the cats with the wayward patterning and warmth of the simulated flames appealed to him; the juxtaposition of the trappings of a comfortable and secure old age with the reminder of the

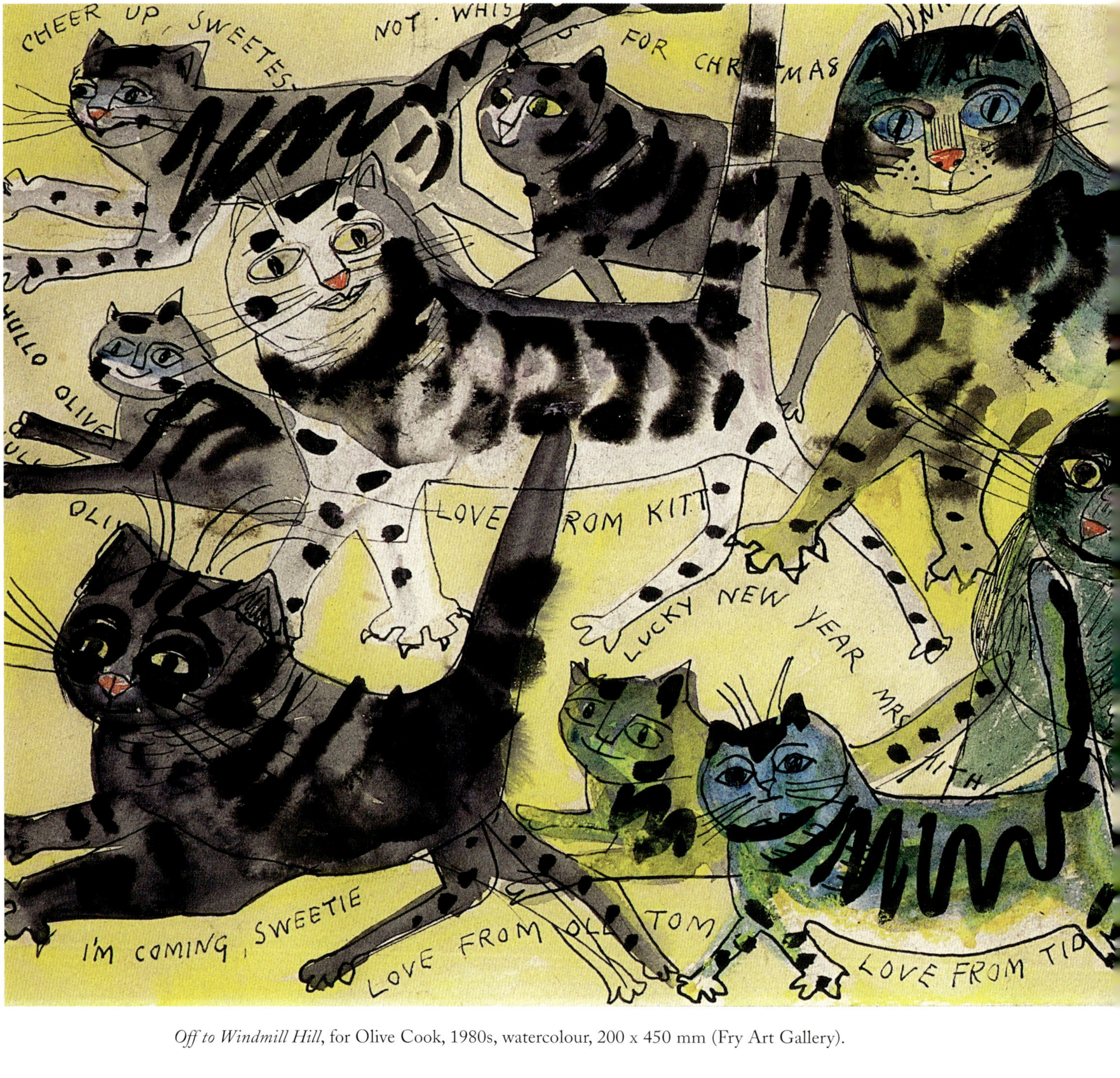

Off to Windmill Hill, for Olive Cook, 1980s, watercolour, 200 x 450 mm (Fry Art Gallery).

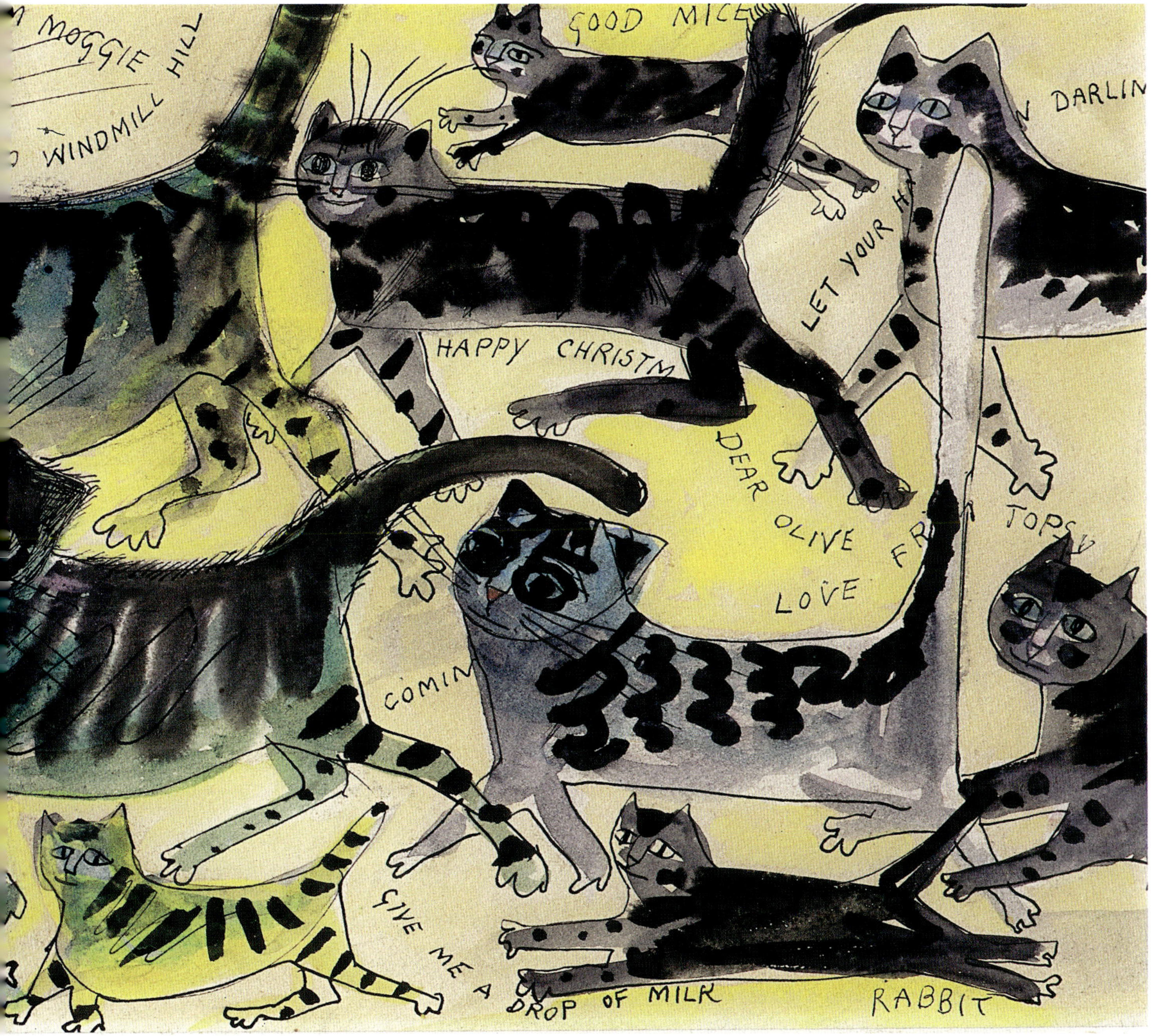
MOGGIE
WINDMILL HILL
GOOD MICE
DARLIN
LET YOUR H
HAPPY CHRISTM
DEAR OLIVE
LOVE
TOPS
COMIN
GIVE ME A DROP OF MILK
RABBIT

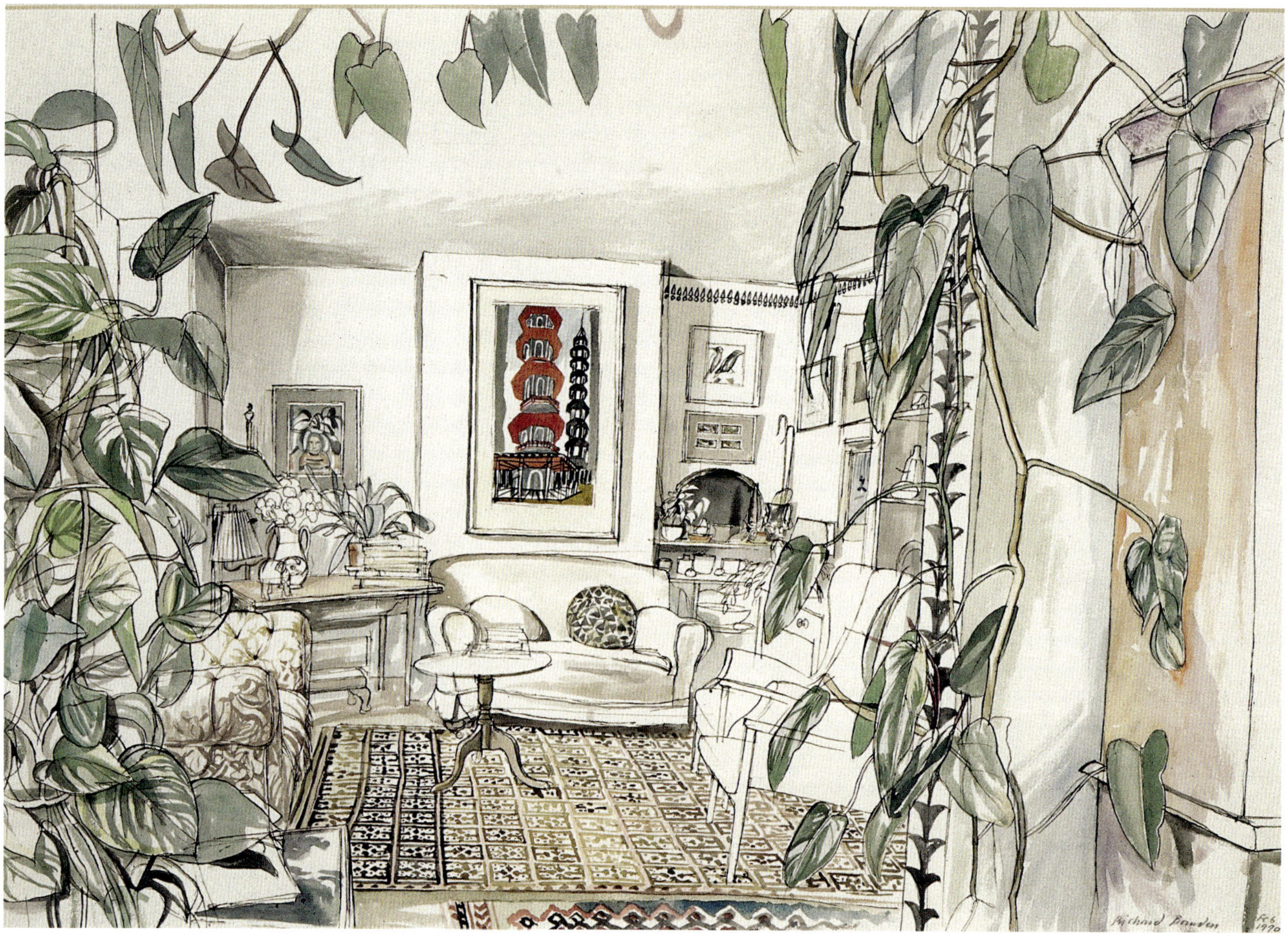

Richard Bawden, *Sitting Room at 2 Park Lane, Saffron Walden*, February 1990, watercolour, 430 x 585 mm (Richard Bawden).

Calvinistic doctrine of the threat of eternal hell-fire and damnation in which he had been raised was too good to resist.' [11] Bawden was so pleased with the effect that he made a painting of it.

He told one interviewer, with one of his characteristic chuckles that 'the world like myself is facing oblivion'. He faced it with some dignity. By the last year of his life in 1989 Bawden was about the only survivor of that golden year at the RCA in 1922. Aldridge, the one artist to stay in Great Bardfield for the rest of his life had died a few months after his wife Gretl, in 1983, still unforgiven and unreconciled to Bawden. The Victoria and Albert Museum came to photograph every room of Aldridge's house and Kew Gardens took away some of his exotic plants. Ardizzone, Freedman, Coldstream, Gross and John Nash, his friends from the war years were all dead, but in 1989 Ruari McLean brought out a collection of Bawden's war letters which must have brought their memories back to him (*Edward Bawden: War Artist*, Scolar Press, 1989).

The worst blow of all was when Sheila Robinson died of a brain tumour in 1988. Bawden seemed to shrink without her and soon suffered a series of minor strokes. In the last two months of his life an exhibition of Bawden's work was mounted at the Fine Art Society, and another called 'The Art of Design' was mounted, not at the Royal Academy, but fittingly at the Victoria and Albert Museum where he had begun to learn his craft all those years ago. By then he was in Addenbrooke's Hospital, Cambridge, following a stroke and could go to neither of them, though he read the reviews. He returned home but after a morning spent doing a linocut he died on 21st November 1989 aged 86.

Open by his bedside was William Hazlitt's 1823 essay *On the Old Age of Artists*, in which the author portrays several octogenarian RAs and concludes: '. . . from these striking examples, the Diploma of Royal Academician seems to be a grant of a longer lease of life, amongst its other advantages'. Hazlitt asks, 'Why should such persons ever die? It seems hard upon them and us! Care fixes no sting in their hearts, and their persons "present no mark to the foeman". Death in them seizes upon living shadows. They scarce consume vital air: their gross functions are long at an end – they live but to paint, to talk, or think.'

When his own father, Ted, had died in January 1952, Bawden, with his love of the morbid, had made two careful drawings of him in his coffin, with eyes closed and jaw tied up to prevent it from dropping. Richard now came and did the same for his father, making a drawing and a beautiful watercolour. Richard hopes someone will in turn do the same for him.

At his Memorial Service in St James, Piccadilly, the President of the Royal Academy, Sir Hugh Casson, observed that Bawden had been variously described as enigmatic, solitary, shy, fastidious, frugal, austere, irreverent and that 'he clanked with descriptive adjectives like some bemedalled Russian general'. Bawden's own favourites amongst these were 'Methodist' and 'curmudgeonly'.

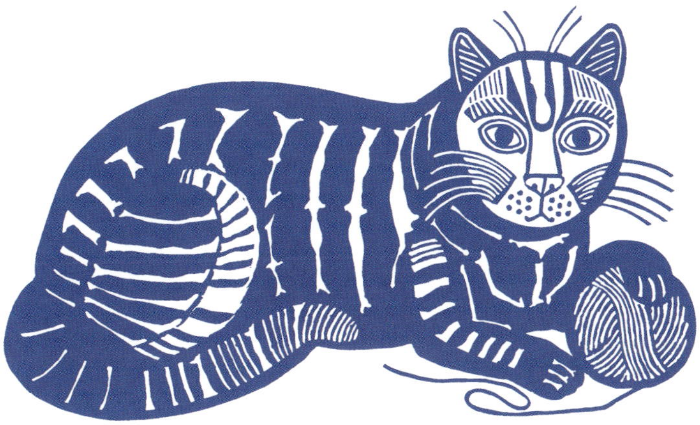

Cat with ball of wool, 23 x 35 cm, linocut (Fry Art Gallery).

1. 'Was there a Demon baker in the Lane?' *Saffron Walden Weekly News*, 22nd November 1990.
2. Quoted in *Ravilious at War*, edited by Anne Ullmann, Fleece Press, 2002, p.137.
3. *Sunday Telegraph Magazine*, October 1979, p.78.
4. Bliss, P., *Phyllis Dodd 1899-1995*, Newport Museum exhibition catalogue, October-December 1995.
5. Anglia Television, *Edward Bawden*, film broadcast November 1983.
6. Ross, C., and Wilkin, K., *The World of Edward Gorey*, Abrahams, 1996, p.18.
7. *Sunday Telegraph Magazine*, October 1979, p.78.
8. 'The Maureen Cleave Interview', *Evening Standard*, 3rd October 1980.
9. Brown, C., *Tribute to Edward Bawden*, The Fine Art Society catalogue, July 1992, p.9.
10. *House and Garden*, December 1987.
11. Skipwith, P., 'Edward Bawden,' obituary in *Modern Painters*, Vol. 3, No. 1, Spring 1990, p.112.

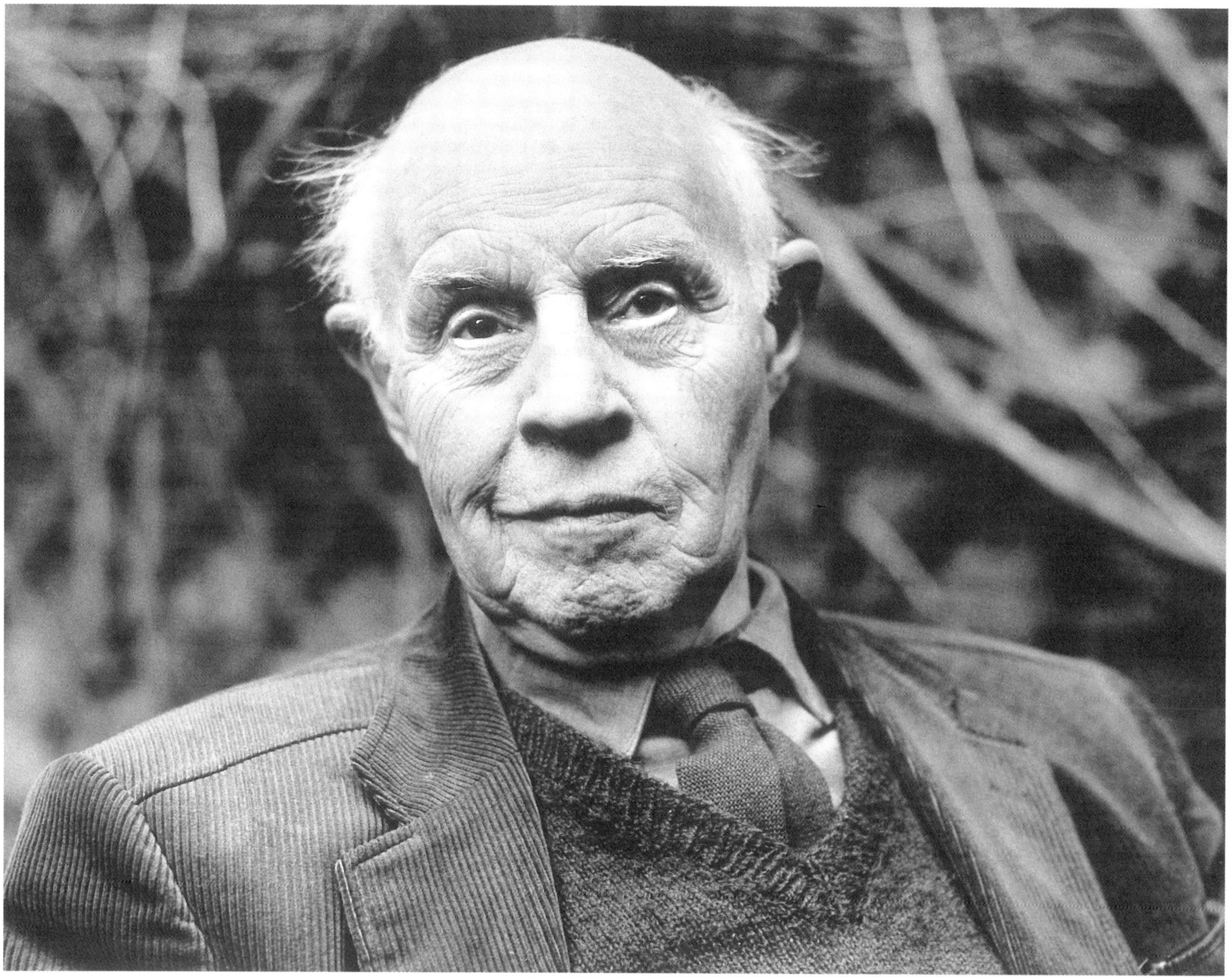

Bawden in his garden, Saffron Walden, mid 1980s.

(Overleaf) Christmas card designed by Edward Bawden for the publisher Faber and Faber (1952).

CONCLUSION

In spring 1987, two years before Bawden's death, the Royal Academy mounted an exhibition entitled 'British Art in the Twentieth Century', subtitled 'The Modern Movement'. Bawden's work did not appear in it, nor that of Ravilious, Michael Rothenstein or any other of the Great Bardfield artists. This was on the grounds that they were too 'British' and not 'Modern' enough. Now it is true that Bawden lived for most of his life along a sixteen mile line stretching from Braintree to Saffron Walden via Great Bardfield, but then Cezanne spent his working life in Aix and Constable found his delight in 'all that lies on the banks of the Stour,' with nobody accusing either of provincialism. Obviously it is not his address which makes an artist parochial, but his attitude. This narrow corridor in north-west Essex inspired some of Bawden's finest work, but then so did the landscapes of the Western Desert, Egypt, Sudan, Ethiopia, Libya, Persia and Saudi Arabia, and so did an Ethiopian Emperor, Kurdish levies, Assyrian officers, Emirs, Basutos and Italian partisans who sat for their portraits. Who, too, has made more adventurous prints of London's markets, churches, bridges, Tower, Kew, Stock Exchange and many another site? Any charge of narrowness, if it refers to Bawden's subject matter, is clearly absurd.

What then of his Modernist stylistic credentials? There had been an earlier attempt to give an over-view of modern British art in *Private View* (Nelson, 1965) by three men who knew it well: Bryan Robertson, John Russell and Lord Snowdon. In this book Bawden is given a short paragraph acknowledging that he has had no truck with 'The System' with its international dealers, accountants, publicists, agents, television promotions and its arbitrary show-business definitions of what constitutes 'Art'.

> . . . there are people who opt out. Edward Bawden, for instance, is a topographical watercolourist of the top class, and some of his illustrated books – his Herodotus, for instance – are marvels of wit and concentration. Bawden has never cared to run with the pack, but you can see from his late watercolours that he has looked at abstract painting and taken from it what was useful to his purpose. [12]

Bawden was indeed too much of an individualist to enlist in any School. By temperament he could never be an unbuttoned Expressionist; he was too interested in line to be an Impressionist, and his intense curiosity about people, plants and places meant he could not abandon appearances to become an Abstractionist. Yet his work could have appeared in no other century than the twentieth. That playfulness with space and perspective was sanctioned by Cubism; the patches of vivid colour which cross the boundaries of forms have precedents in Leger and Dufy, whilst his visual puns have clear parallels in Surrealism, the only modern movement to tolerate humour in art. The checks and balances built into his every composition also show him thinking in abstract terms. We must conclude that he quietly assimilated what he needed from Modernism for his own ends, rather than committing himself to any of its factional campaigns.

Other factors have prevented Bawden's entry into the highest pantheon of British art. His own genuine modesty about his work has too often been accepted at face value

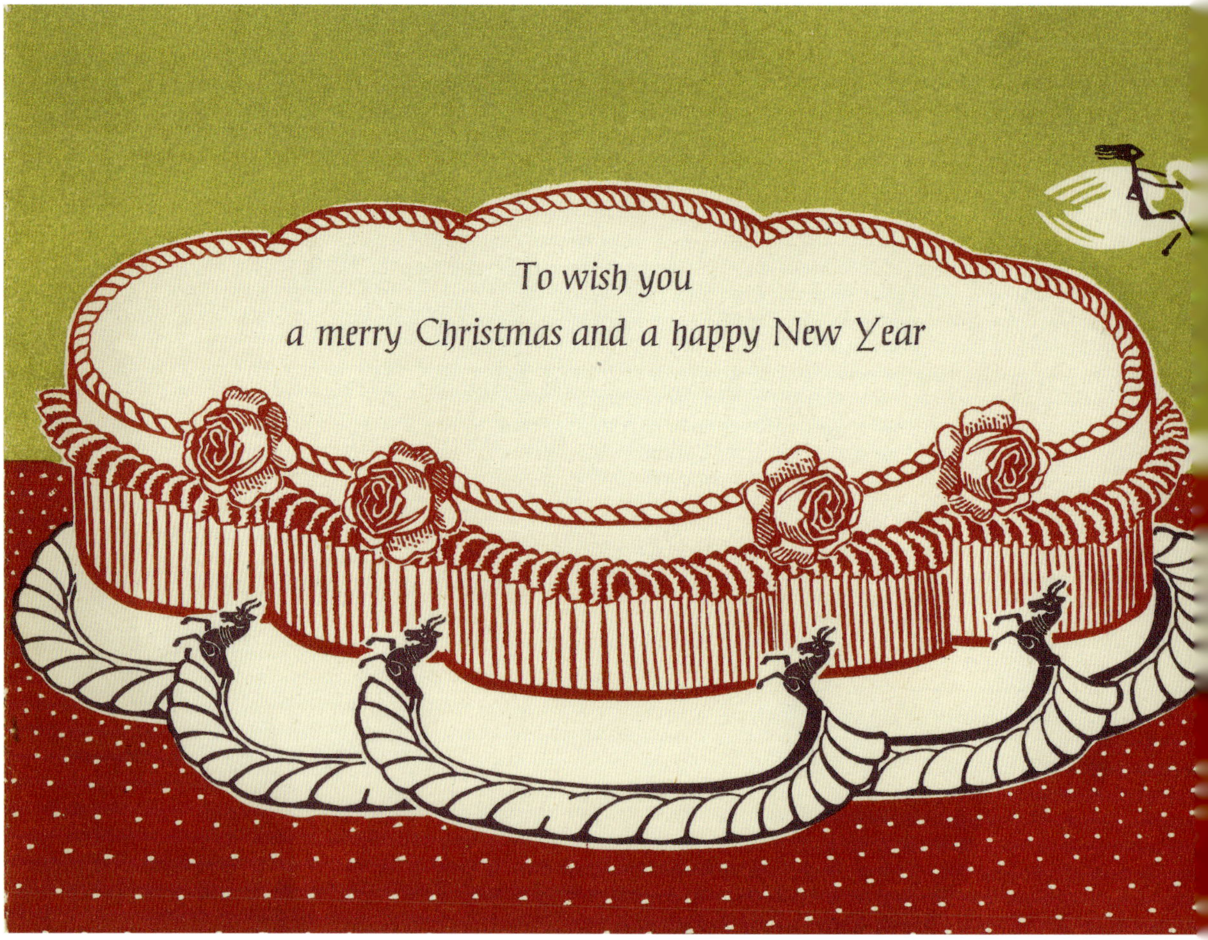
To wish you
a merry Christmas and a happy New Year

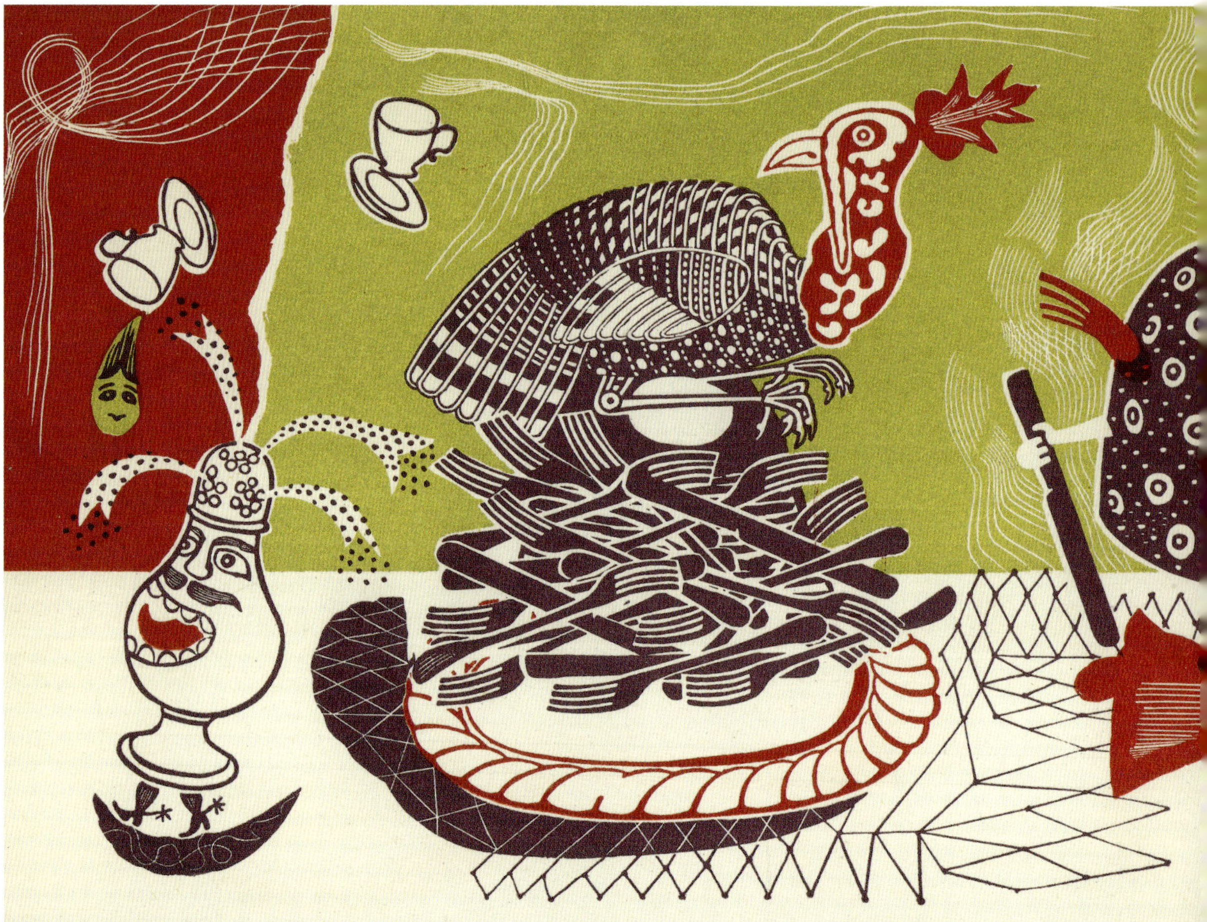

This Christmas card is designed

by Edward Bawden for Faber and Faber

24 Russell Square, London

1952

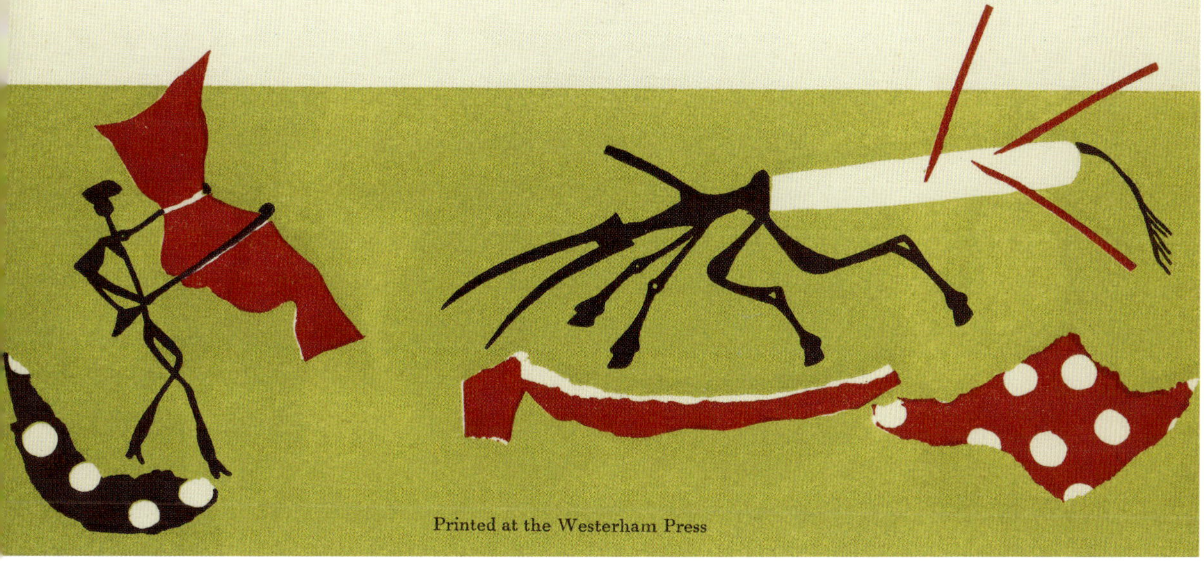

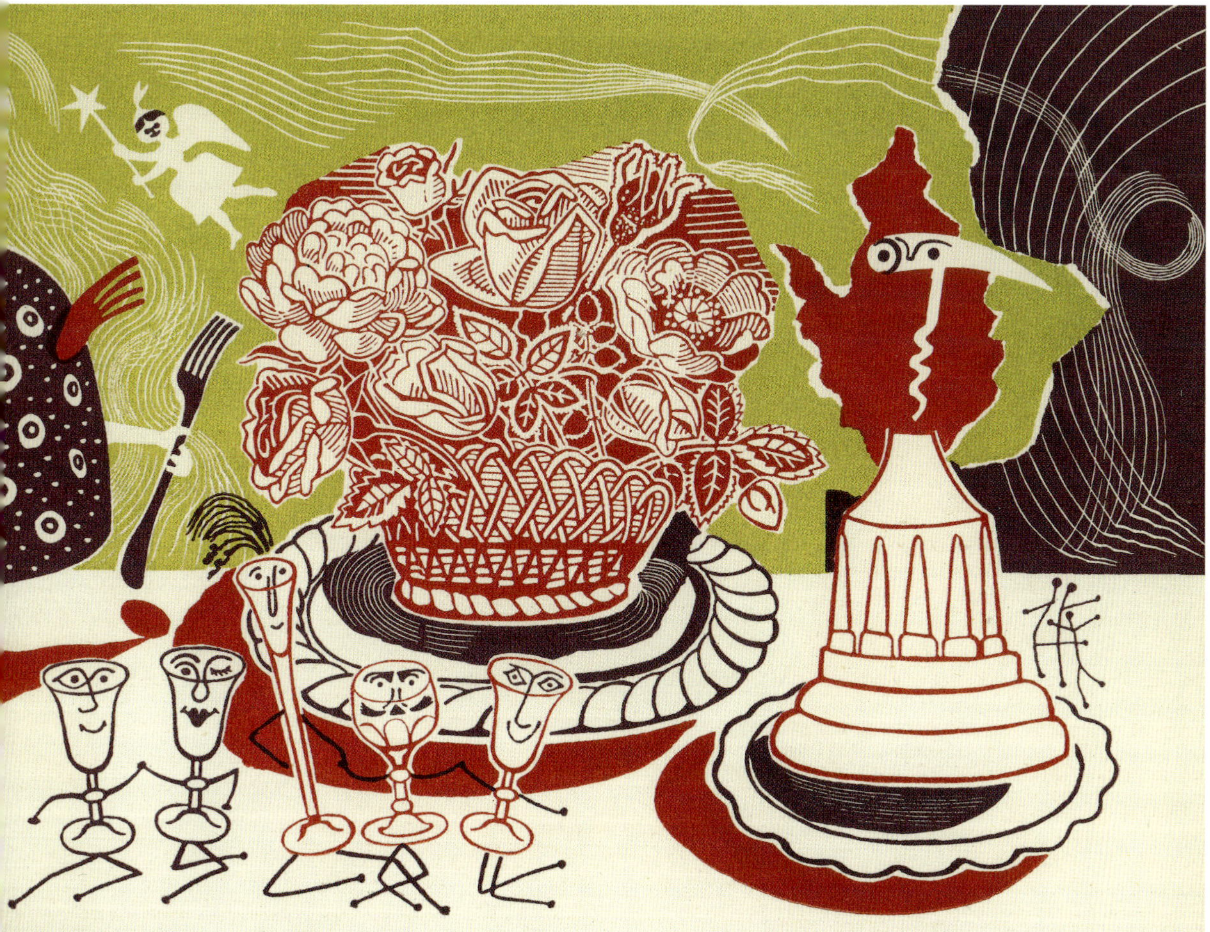

and his constant striving for clarity and directness have left critics with little to write about or interpret. Then he worked in pen and ink, watercolour, lithography and lino-cuts, all media with very little historical prestige, though each needs a high level of skill to handle. How could serious art be made out of a cheap bathroom floor covering? Bawden spread himself very thinly, working across an enormous range of advertising, book illustration, war art, murals, printmaking, landscape painting and ephemera. Many of these works are now lost or available only in photographs, or in out-of-print books, and others, because they were once topical and tied to a specific commission now look dated. Connoisseurs tend to admire the specialist rather than the all-rounder, but Bawden inveighed all his life against the critics' and dealers' division between 'Fine' and 'Applied' art. 'I behaved like an amateur in an age of professionals', he lamented, but nothing he did was amateurish. Each 'problem', whether making a beer-mat or painting a sixty-foot mural, was tackled with dexterity and taken to a stylish finish – both critically unfashionable qualities by the time he died.

In a review of Bawden's final exhibition which appeared in *The Times* its writer concludes: 'Perhaps because this is an English manner of going about art, we suppose that lightness of effect is incompatible with essential seriousness. If Bawden were French, now, we would have more notion of how to appreciate his unique combination of intelligence and fun, true emotion and light lyric grace. Bawden remains unclassifiable, and therefore impossible to estimate. Which is probably just the way he wants it.'[13]

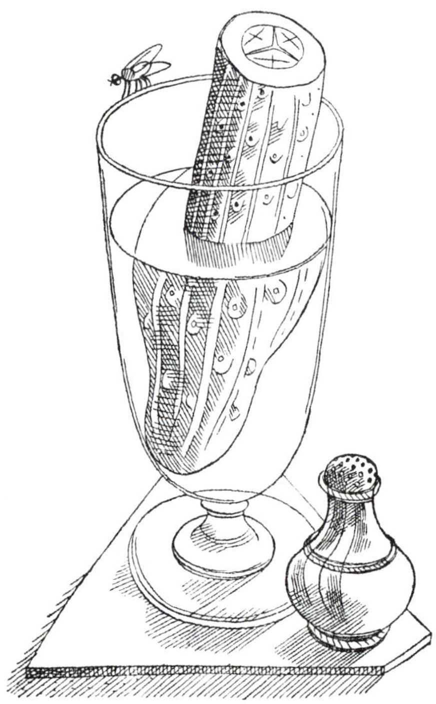

Tailpiece from the *Good Food* books.

12. Robertson, B., Russell, J., Snowdon, Lord, *Private View: The Lively World of British Art, Nelson and Son*, 1965, p.183.

13. Taylor, J. R., 'As if through the Eyes of a Child', *The Times*, 9th September, 1989.

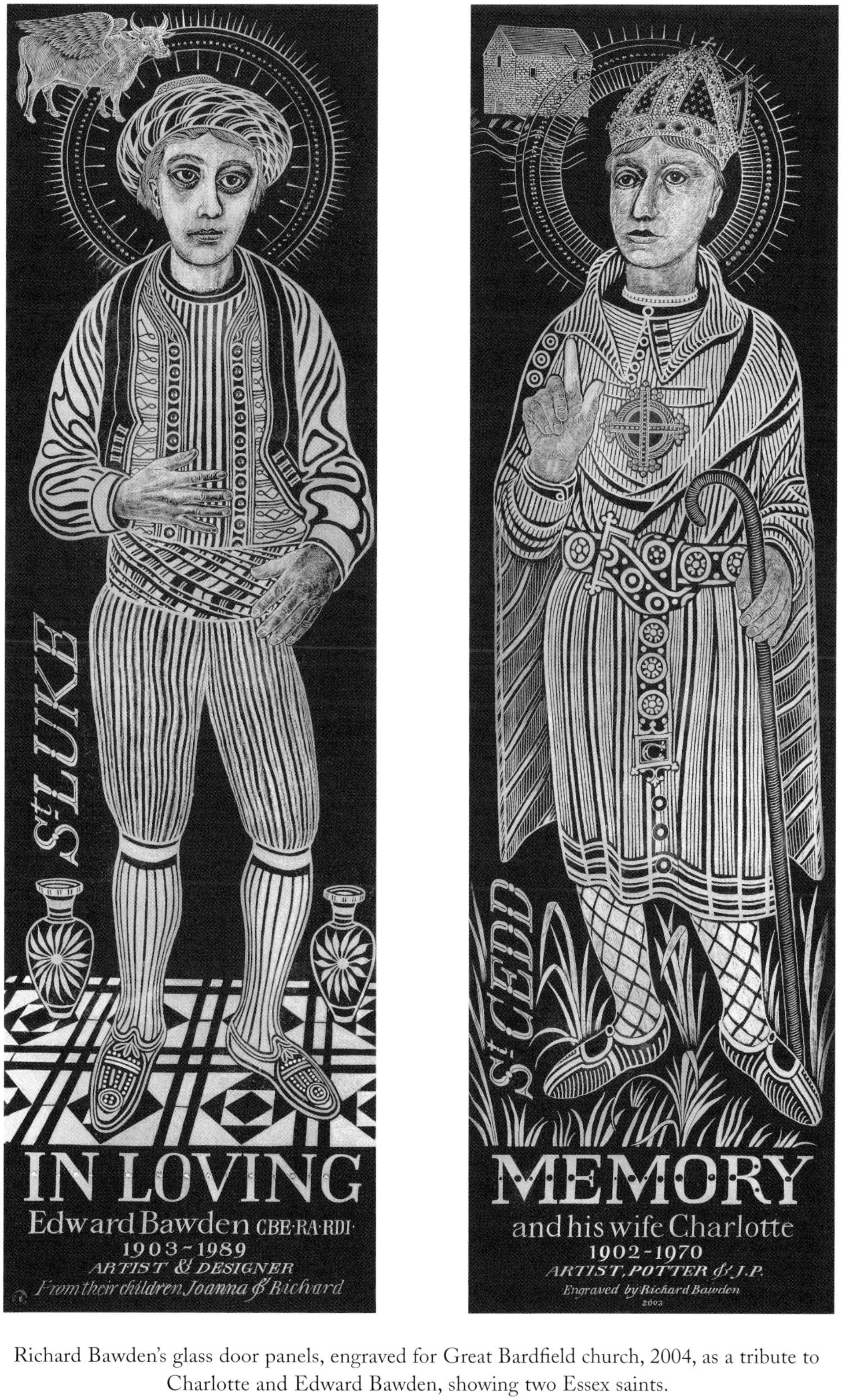

Richard Bawden's glass door panels, engraved for Great Bardfield church, 2004, as a tribute to Charlotte and Edward Bawden, showing two Essex saints.

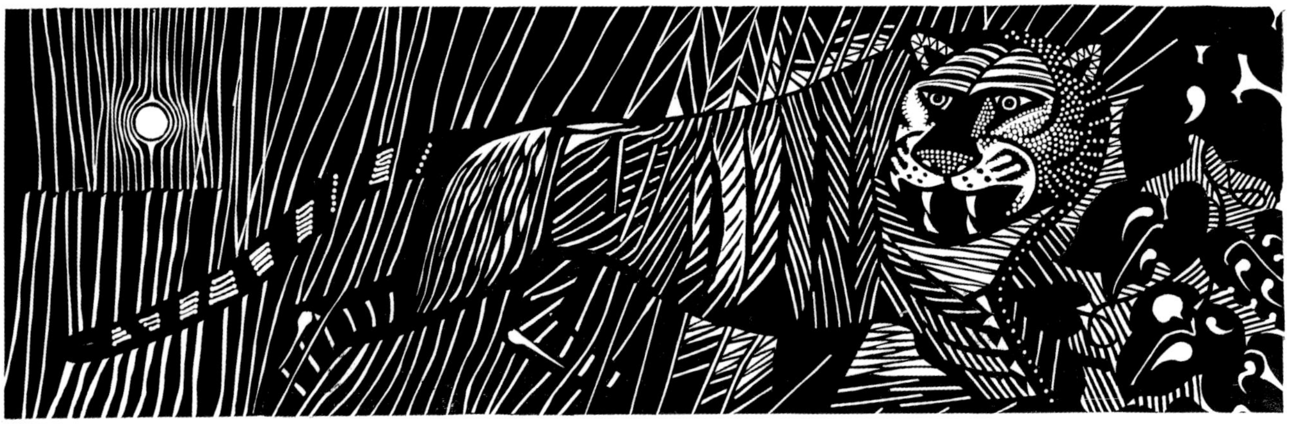

AFTERWORD

In my room at work, I have two big, colourful Bawden linocuts. One is 'Our Family', a giant stylised black and yellow frog with some tiny little tadpoles below it. The other, a more sophisticated piece of work, is one of the *Aesop's Fables* series, 'Hare & Tortoise', a brilliantly playful serpentining story in five cunning colours, in which the hare frolics, gyrates, flashes about, curls itself up, bounds on wide-eyed, and the serious blue tortoise keeps plodding along to the end, where it turns and faces its competitor. 'What about that, then?' it seems to say. Whenever I catch their eye, looking up from a difficult piece of writing or a dull stretch of marking or in the middle of a meeting with an anxious student, they lighten my heart. I like their stylishness, their light, bold outlines, and their joviality.

I love living with Bawden's work and like everyone who admires him (and there seem to be more and more of us now). I feel as if he was my own private discovery. It is not like having a Bonnard or a Picasso, something fabulously noticeable, on your walls; it is more like having a jug or a rug or an embroidered cushion of such striking originality and charm that people stop in mid-use to look closer and to ask about it. Bawden's attractiveness to me comes from this domesticity, accessibility and usefulness, often combined, when you look closer, with something disconcerting, odd, even alarming.

He was an artist who did not draw a line between art and craft, high and low, public and private – which partly accounts for his curiously muted reputation. Though, as this book vividly demonstrates, he could be grumpy and old-fashioned, he was the opposite of elitist. My friend the actress Diana Quick tells me that when she was touring with the radical, agitprop Red Ladder Theatre Company in the early 1970s, Bawden opened his doors to

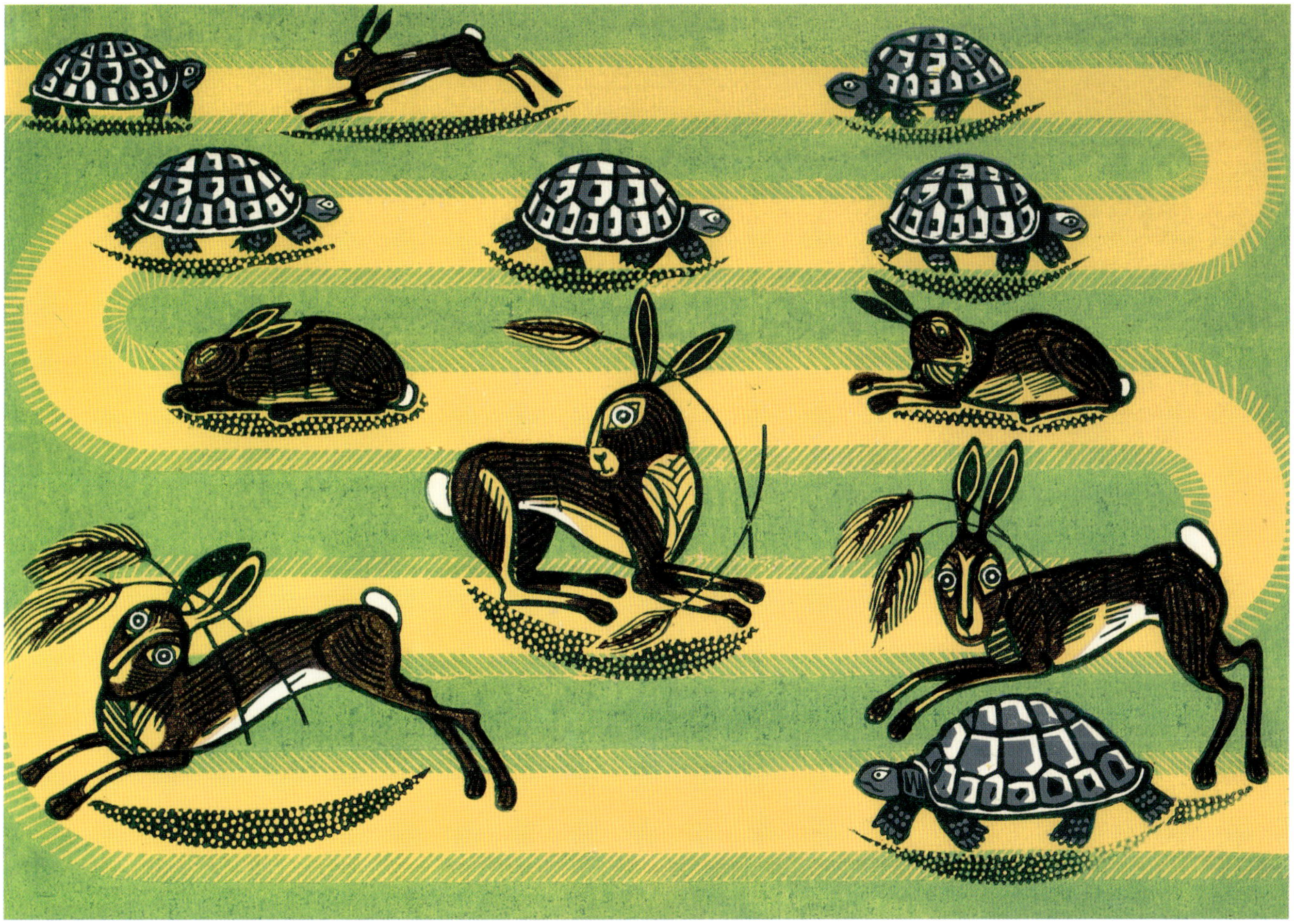

Aesop's Fables: *Hare & Tortoise*, 1970, colour linocut, 407 x 560mm.

(Right) Watercolour of the above print, original 405 x 558mm.
(Both Trustees of Cecil Higgins Art Gallery, Bedford).

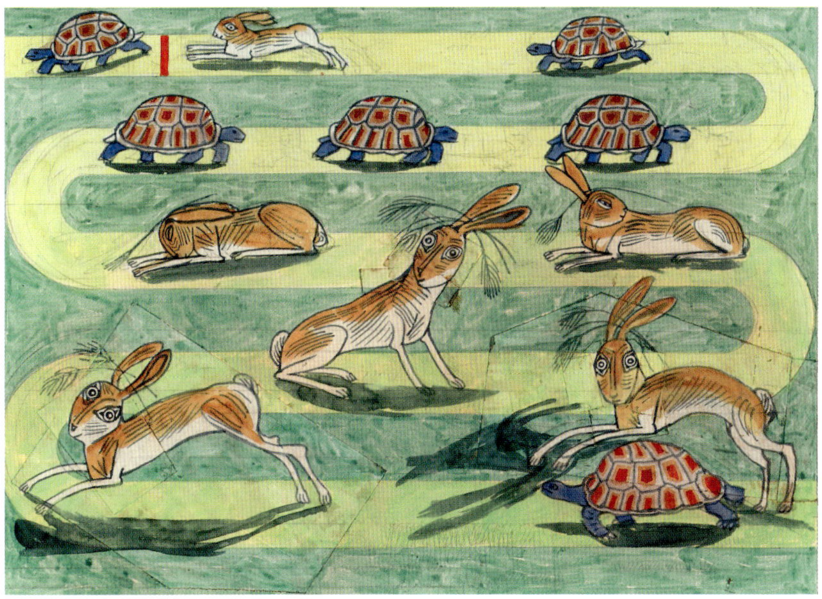

(Opposite) "Tyger! Tyger!", 1974, linocut for William Blake's *Song's of Experience*, 202 x 631mm.

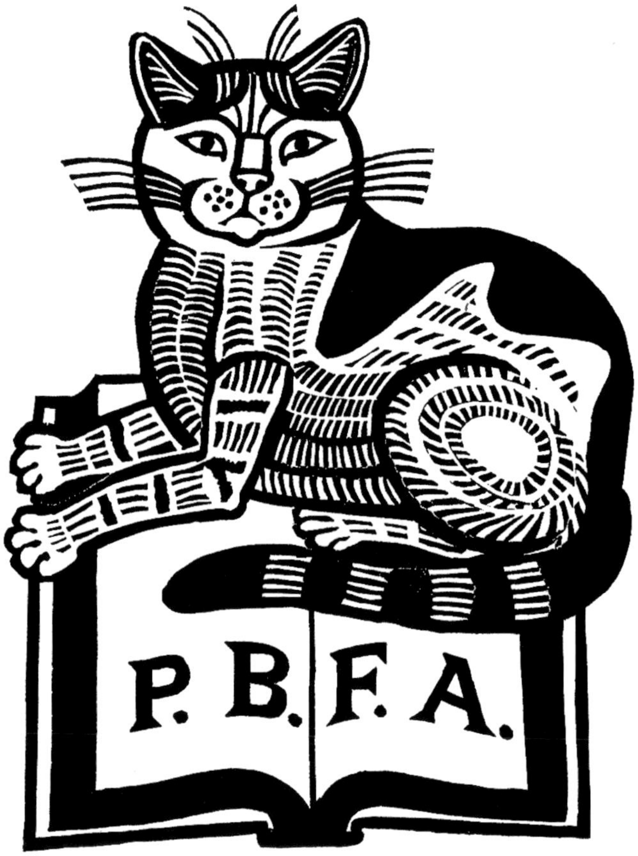

Logo for Provincial Booksellers Fairs Association, 1983, linocut, 331 x 245mm (Fry Art Gallery).

them and came to their feminist show. That fits with an artist who worked in media (like lino) that were not thought 'artistic', who was so interested in technology, jobs, industry, hobbies, urban as well as rural life, who was so pragmatic, workmanlike and adaptable. I have, for instance, his illustrated Fortnum catalogue of cocktails, 'Everything for cocktail parties' (a present from Julian Barnes, who keeps an eye out for Bawdeniana for me); his vigorously illustrated book about the Dunlop rubber company and three of his wallpapers designs. I often go across the road in Oxford to look at the wildly inventive, brightly coloured historical mural which is still on the ground floor wall of Blackwell's Bookshop. He was adventurous and bold as well as eclectic. It would be easy to caricature him as a parochial, eccentric Little Englander, but (after Edward Lear) he was one of the most eloquent British artists of the Middle East.

I first found out about Bawden in the late 1970s, when I was working at York University, and Ken Spelman's splendid bookshop had a Bawden exhibition. That is when I realised that the jaunty black-and-white cat used on posters for Booksellers' Fairs was his. I bought, then, the Bawden I most cherish, the black-and-white linocut 'Tyger!, Tyger!' (which Douglas Percy Bliss used as the chapter-headings for his book on Bawden). It is a startlingly powerful exercise in stripes and bars and lines; all the energy and force of Blake's creature in its dark jungle leaps out at you. I could not afford any of the watercolours that were on show then, a great regret to me now that his prices have shot up.

Since then I have acquired the mysterious, delicate line engraving 'Lane in Moonlight', his pen and watercolour sketch for the fishmonger in the Ambrose Heath *Good Food* book, and, most recently, the tiny, surreal, enchanting engraving 'Reverie' with its big cat sleeping and dreaming of birds in trees. I have some of the illustrated books, the pretty, elegant flower lithograph 'Columbine and Campion', and, mixed in with my Bawdens, a very few, haunting, Gwen Raverat woodcuts, Tirzah Ravilious's funny a crocodile of schoolgirls, and one magical Italian scene, a woodcut by Ravilious. It is not a big collection – I am not a collector, just an enthusiast – but everything in it gives me intense satisfaction, from the scales on the fish and the crosshatching in the moonlit lane, to the elegant 1920s figures having fun in the 'Riviera' wallpaper. When I look at my Bawdens, it seems to me that everything is in motion, every detail is fine, nothing is sentimental or heavy-handed, everything is cool and light and intelligent. And everything makes me smile.

Hermione Lee
Oxford 2007

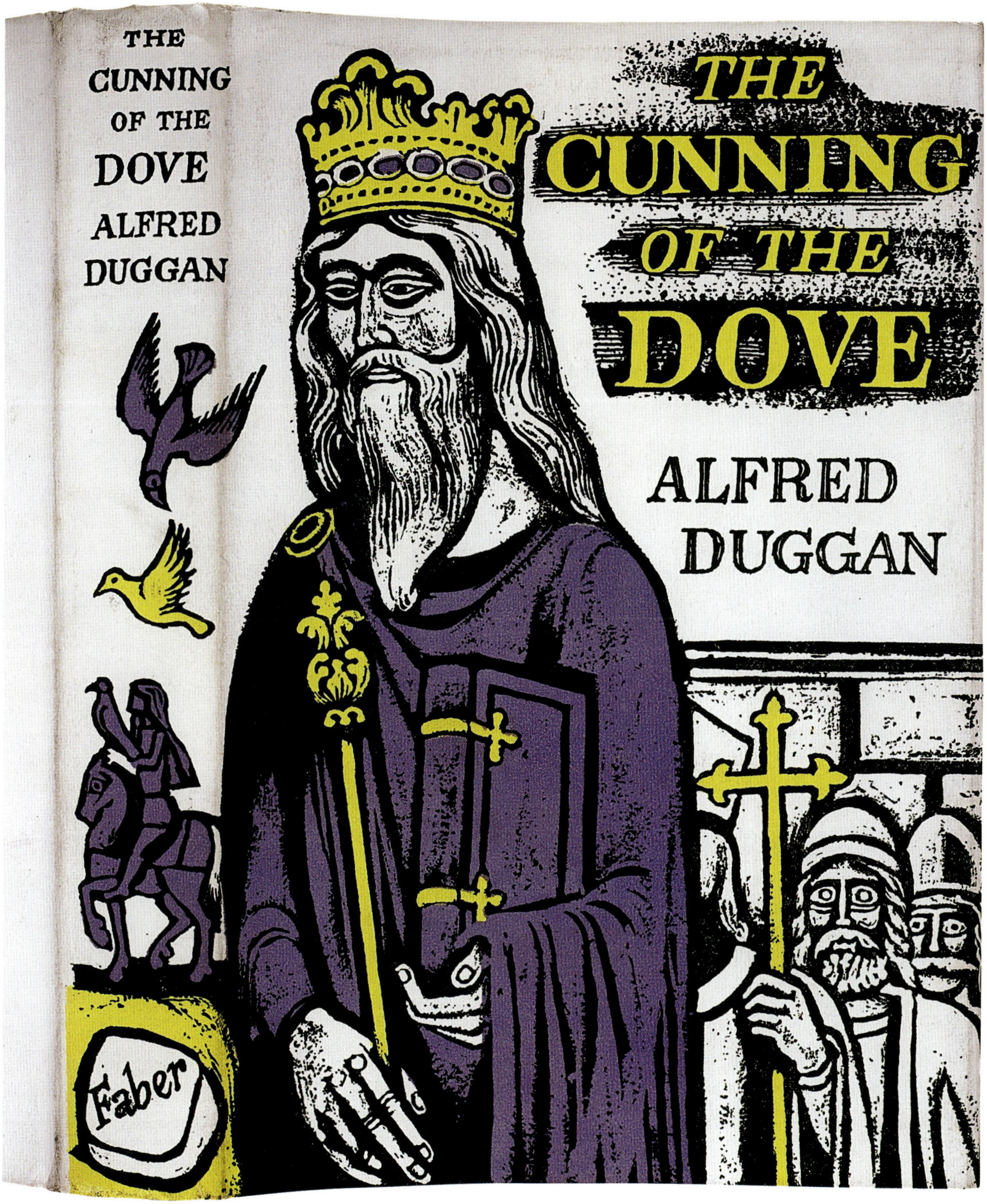

*The Cunning of the Dov*e, 1960, dustjacket design
(Manchester Metropolitan University Library).

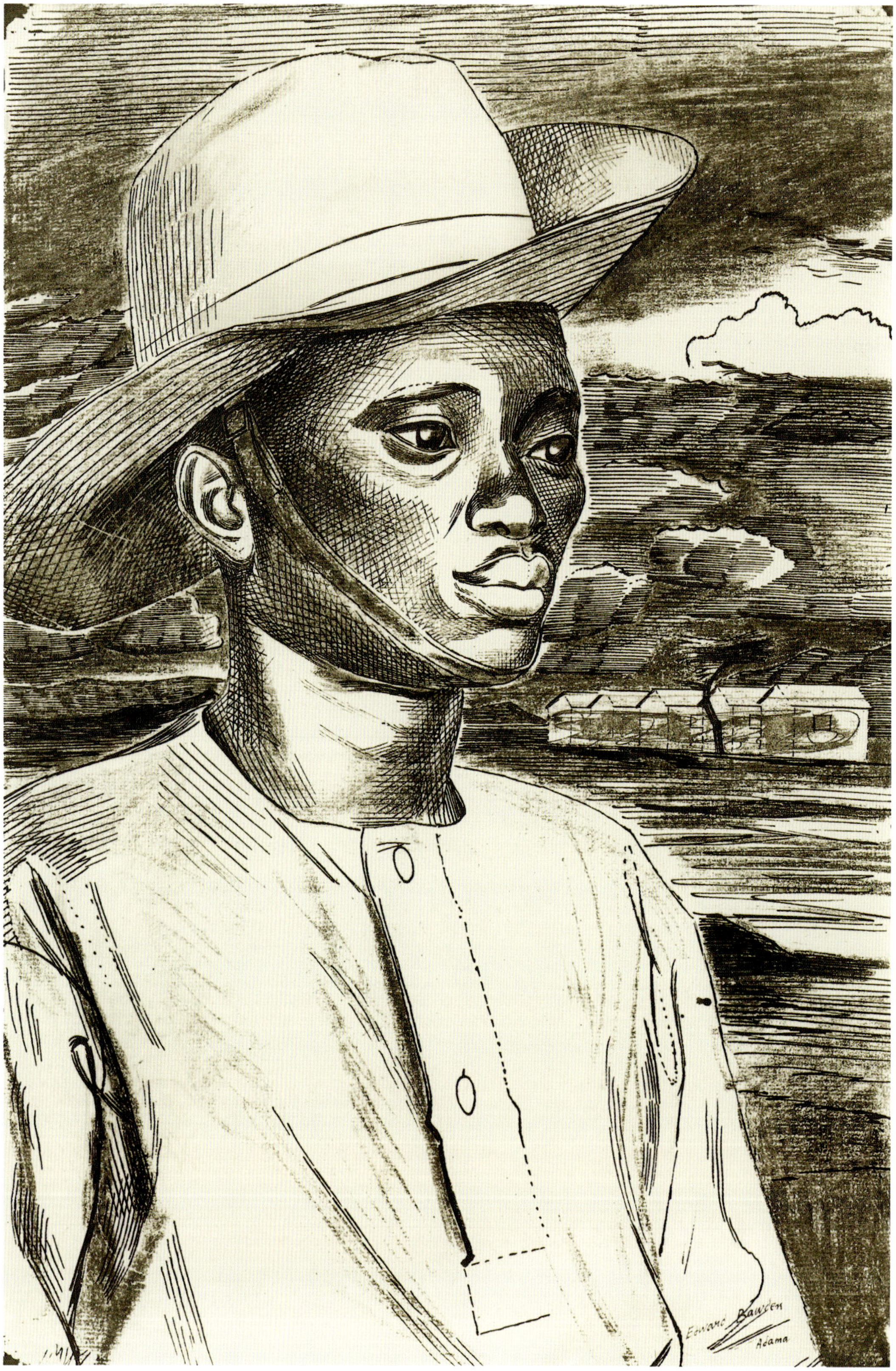

Adama, pen and ink, *c.*1942 (present location unknown).

NOTE ON THE REFERENCES

Bawden gave many magazine and newspaper interviews, especially later in his life, and I have drawn on these extensively. Rather than acknowledge the source of every sentence quoted I have listed the main articles below:

Brown, C., 'Best Illustrator: Edward Bawden', *Designer*, October 1982.

Carrington, N., 'Edward Bawden', *Graphis Magazine*, Vol. 3, No. 17, 1947, pp.30-43.

Cleave, M., 'An Artist from the Bottom Up', *The Evening Standard*, 3rd October 1980, p.17.

Hillier, B., 'Bawden Comes of Age', *The Sunday Telegraph Magazine*, October 1979.

Maurice, C., 'Profile: Edward Bawden', Royal Society of Painter-Etchers and Engravers, catalogue, August-September 1984 (reprinted in *Royal Academy Magazine*, No. 2, March 1984).

Skipwith, P., 'Vision and Versatility', *Royal Academy Magazine*, No. 22, Spring 1989, p.38.

Spalding, F., 'Edward Bawden', *Arts Review*, 26th September 1980, p.417.

Taylor, J. R., 'Buoyant Survivor', *Art and Antiques Weekly*, 20th October 1979, p.26.

Usherwood, N., 'An Eminent Octogenarian', *The Artist*, May 1987, pp.23-26.

Whitbread, M., and Hughes, K., catalogue to 'Edward Bawden: The Art of Design', exhibition at the Herbert Read Gallery, Canterbury College, Kent, October 1988.

Three recent books of interest to Bawden enthusiasts are:

Edward Bawden: Editioned Prints, Jeremy Greenwood, The Wood Lea Press (2005).

Away We Go! Advertising London's Transport: Edward Bawden and Eric Ravilious, essays by Oliver Green and Alan Powers, The Mainstone Press (2006).

Edward Bawden and Eric Ravilious DESIGN, Brian Webb and Peyton Skipwith, Antique Collectors' Club in association with the Fry Art Gallery (2005).

INDEX

Page numbers in **bold** refer to illustrations.

Index

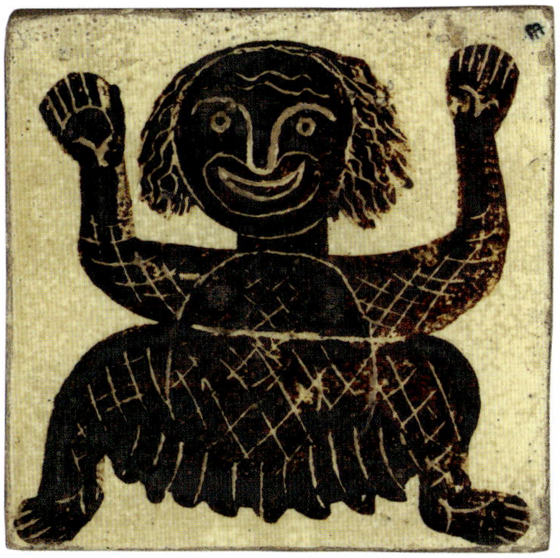

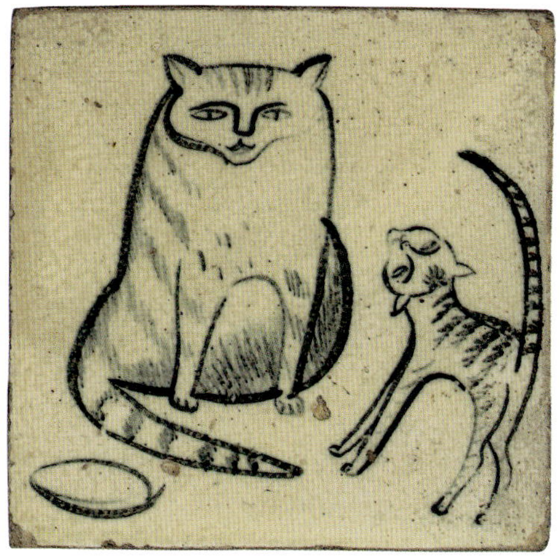

Two tiles designed by Bawden whilst courting Charlotte Epton who studied with Bernard Leach at the St Ives pottery between 1927-1930. Both backstamped with Leach Pottery mark.

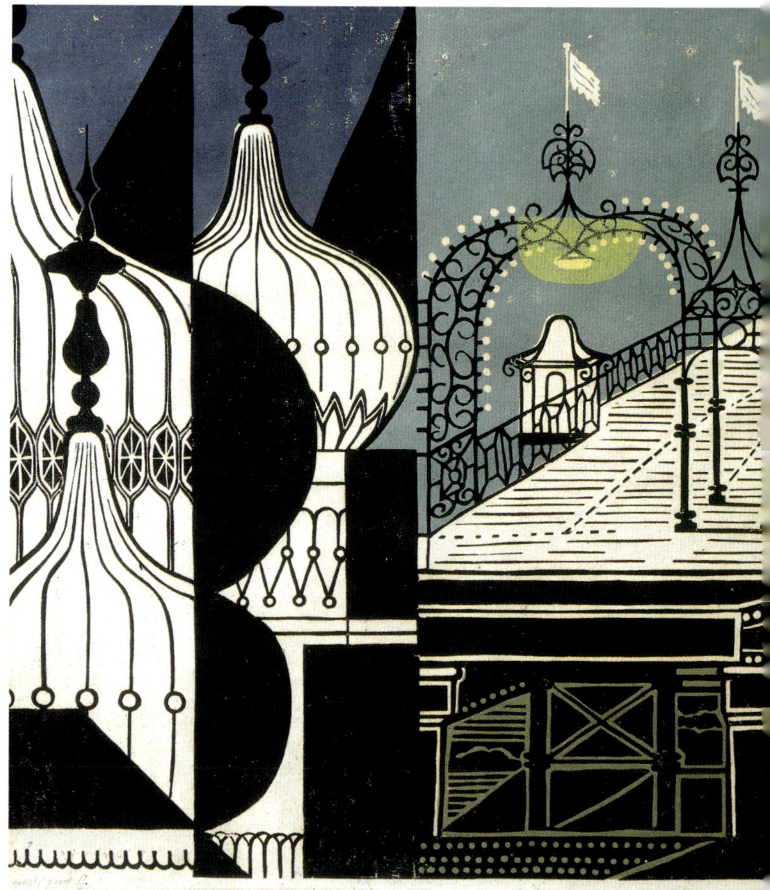

Index

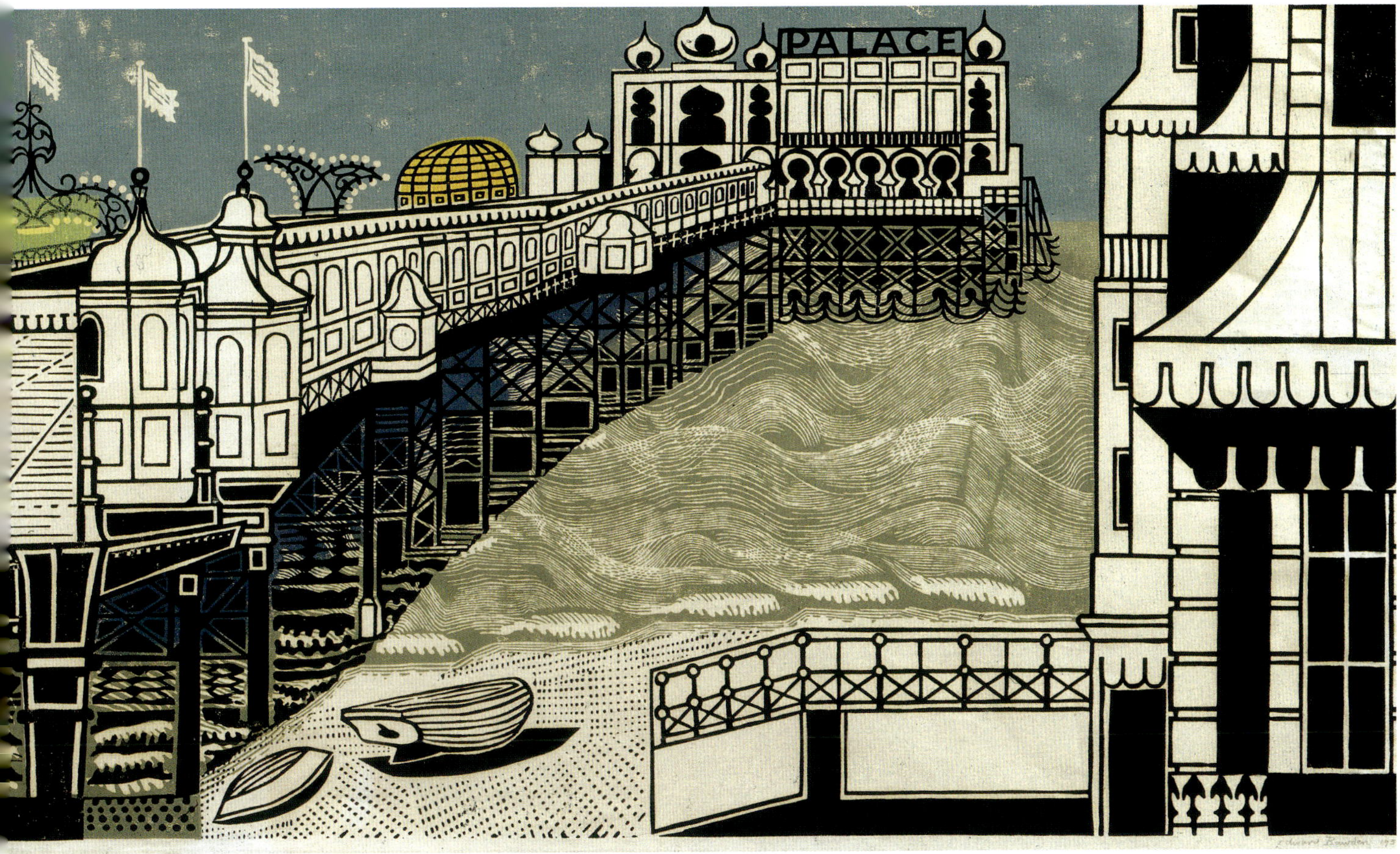

Brighton Pier, second edition, 1977, linocut, 530 x 1445 mm.

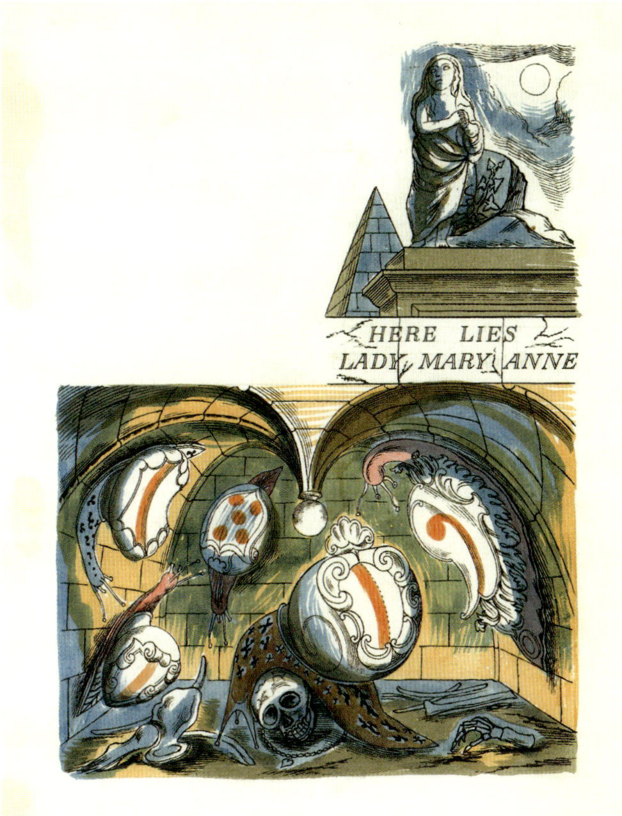

Illustration from *A Handbook of Printing Types* by John Lewis, published by W.S. Cowell in 1947.

REFERENCES TO EDWARD BAWDEN'S WORK

Page numbers in **bold** refer to illustrations.

Index

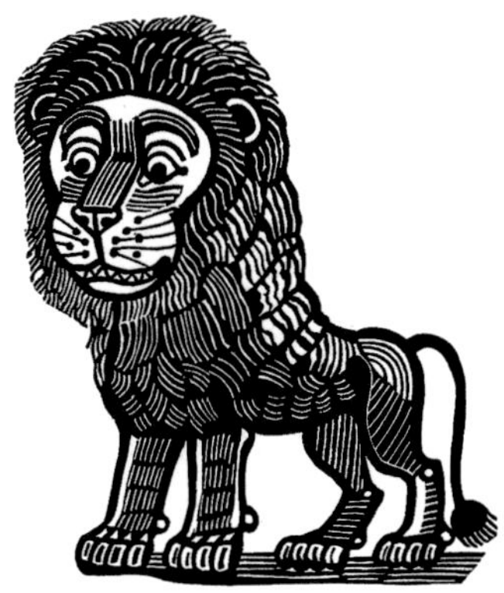

THE FRY ART GALLERY

Castle Street, Saffron Walden, Essex CB10 1BD

This book had its genesis in the Fry Art Gallery, Castle Street, Saffron Walden, whose collection inspired the author at an early stage. The curators opened up their archives, made many useful introductions and provided illustrations both of Bawden's work and those of other artists living in Great Bardfield. The Fry is run by volunteers to professional standards who combined in 1985 to restore a disused Victorian gallery in order to create and display what is now known as the North West Essex Collection. Edward Bawden gave enthusiastic support to this project. The collection also contains works by artists beyond the immediate Bawden circle, such as Michael Ayrton, Isabel Lambert, Robert Colquhoun and Robert McBryde, but all of them at some stage lived and worked in Essex during the last century, contributing thereby to an artistic legacy which has yet to be fully assessed. The Gallery is open part of each week from Easter to October. For further information or to join the Fry Art Gallery Society please telephone 01799 513779 or visit www.frygallery.org

Malcolm Yorke

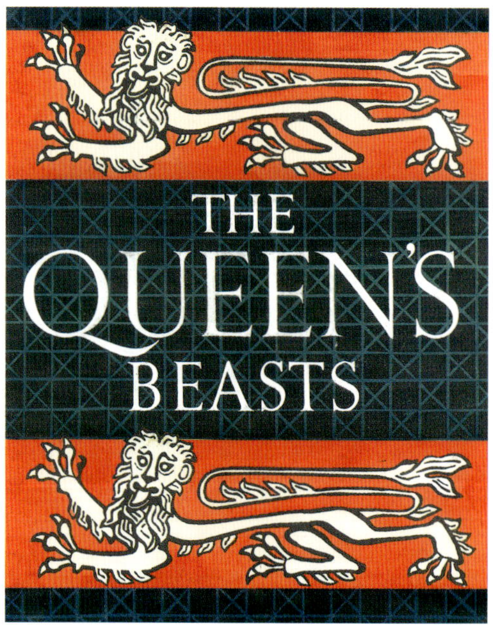

Unpublished cover for
The Queen's Beasts, 1953.

ACKNOWLEDGMENTS

This book was a pleasure to write both because I enjoyed my encounters with Edward Bawden's work and wit and because the research brought me into contact with so many generous and interesting people.

The first version of this book, which was voted Book of the Year in the 2006 British Book Design and Production Awards, was published in a limited edition by Simon Lawrence, the brains and hands behind the Fleece Press and Simon shares my gratitude to the following people who originally helped us.

Richard and Joanna Bawden and their respective partners, Hattie and Brooke, gave us access to their archives and family treasures, as did Prudence and Rosalind Bliss, the daughters of Percy Douglas Bliss and Phyllis Dodd. The Ravilious works reproduced are copyright of the Estate of Eric Ravilious and were used with the permission of Anne Ullmann, his daughter. Nigel and Iris Weaver of the Fry Art Gallery and Peyton Skipwith formerly of the Fine Art Society and responsible for the Estate of Edward Bawden were consistently and practically supportive and we had crucial assistance from the following: Duffy Ayers, Christopher Brown, Bernard Cheese, Chloe Cheese, Peter Cott, Ariel Crittal, Robert Jones, Michael MacLeod, Louise Marr, John Meek, Patricia and Robin Pickard, John Rogers, Diana and Adam Rowntree, Tom Russell, Laurence Sach, the late Peter Tregathen-Jenkins, Brian Webb, Peter White, Christopher Whittick, Claudia Wolfers and John Norris Wood. The staff at East Sussex Public Record Office, Tate Britain, Cambridge University Library, Harlow Council's Frederick Gibberd Collection, Cecil Higgins Art Gallery, the Royal College of Art, the Victoria and Albert Museum, Chelmsford Art Gallery and Scarborough Art Gallery all took time and trouble on our behalf. We are similarly in debt to Manchester Metropolitan University Library for opening up its archives and Book Design collection. The Imperial War Museum was as accommodating as ever and the University of Northumbria Department of Historical and Critical Studies gave us technical support. Photographs were taken by Douglas Atfield, Stephen Curtis and Tony Richards. Jeremy Greenwood has generously allowed us to reproduce some of the plates from his own fine book, *Edward Bawden: Editioned Prints*, in this new edition.

David Gentleman and Hermione Lee have added their personal reminiscences of Bawden which enrich the reader's understanding of the man and his work.

I thank Mark Eastment for commissioning this edition and finally wish to express my gratitude to my wife Mavis for her research, editing, proof reading and brow mopping.

Malcolm Yorke 2007

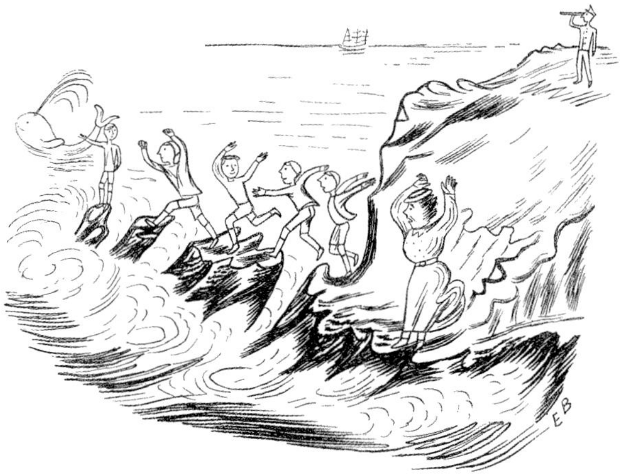

LAND'S END

First published in a limited edition by
Simon Lawrence at his Fleece Press 2005
This revised and expanded edition
first published by the Antique Collectors' Club 2007

Reprinted 2010

ISBN: 978-1-85149-542-9

British Library Cataloguing-in-Publication Data
A catalogue record for this book is available from the British Library

Mixed Sources
Product group from well-managed forests, controlled sources and recycled wood or fiber
FSC
www.fsc.org Cert no. SGS-COC-003548
© 1996 Forest Stewardship Council

Printed in China
for the Antique Collectors' Club Ltd., Woodbridge, Suffolk, England

---

Endpapers: (Front) *Brighton Pier*, second edition, 1977, linocut.
(Back) *Cat Among Pigeons*, 1986, watercolour.

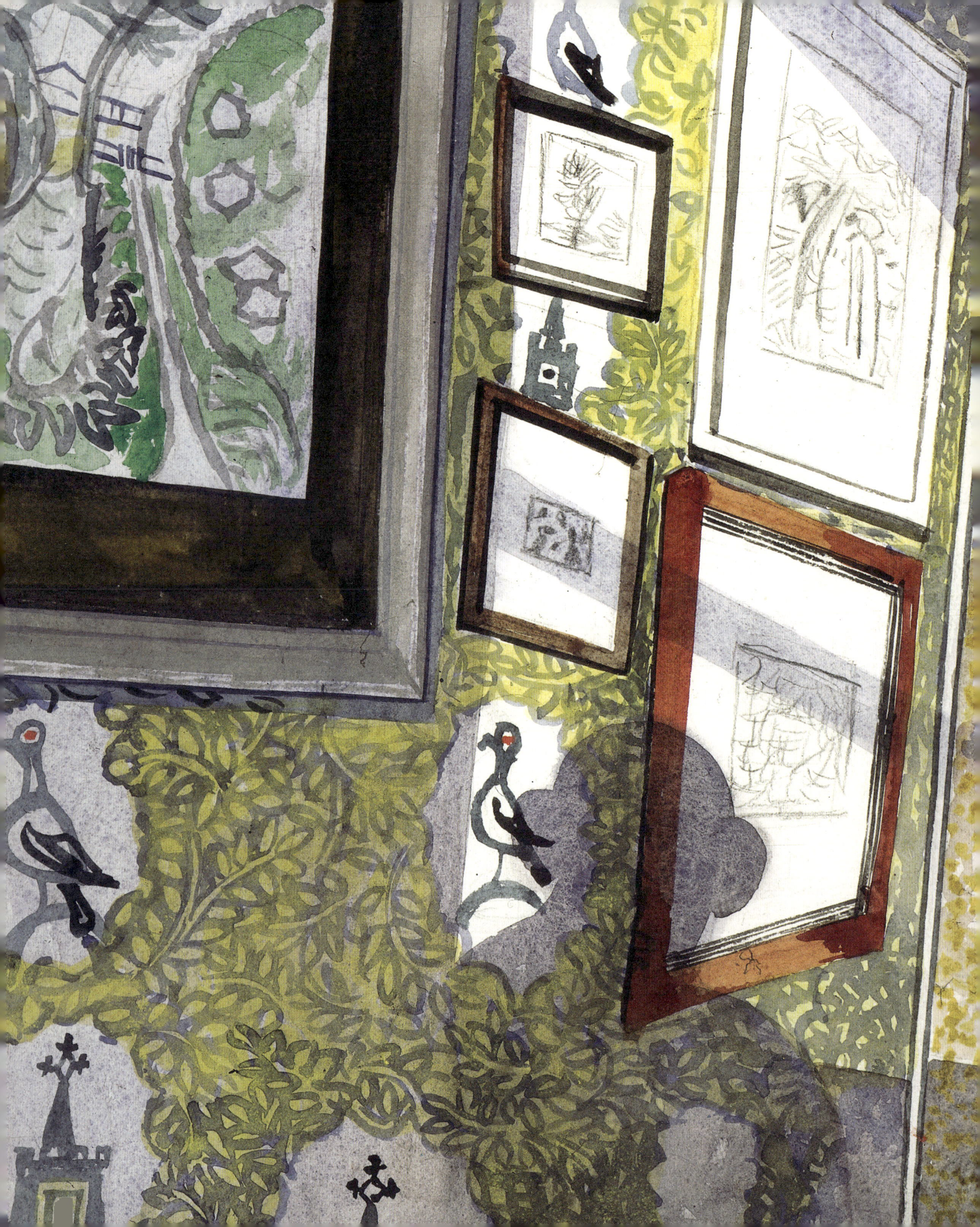